BOONE AND CROCKETT CLUB'S

26th Big Game Awards
2004-2006

▼ ▼ ▼ ▼ ▼ ▼

Boone and Crockett Club's 26th Big Game Awards, 2004-2006
Edited by Eldon L. "Buck" Buckner, Jack Reneau, and Ryan Hatfield

ISSN: 1939-4527
ISBN: 978-0-940864-57-3
Published September 2007

Published in the United States of America
by the
Boone and Crockett Club
250 Station Drive
Missoula, Montana 59801
Phone (406) 542-1888
Fax (406) 542-0784
Toll-Free (888) 840-4868 (book or merchandise orders only)
www.booneandcrockettclub.com

BOONE AND CROCKETT CLUB'S

26th Big Game Awards
2004-2006

▼ ▼ ▼ ▼ ▼ ▼ ▼

**A Book of the Boone and Crockett Club
Containing Tabulations of Outstanding North American
Big Game Trophies Accepted During the
26th Awards Entry Period of 2004-2006**

**Edited by
Eldon L. "Buck" Buckner
Jack Reneau
Ryan Hatfield**

2007

Boone and Crockett Club

Missoula, Montana

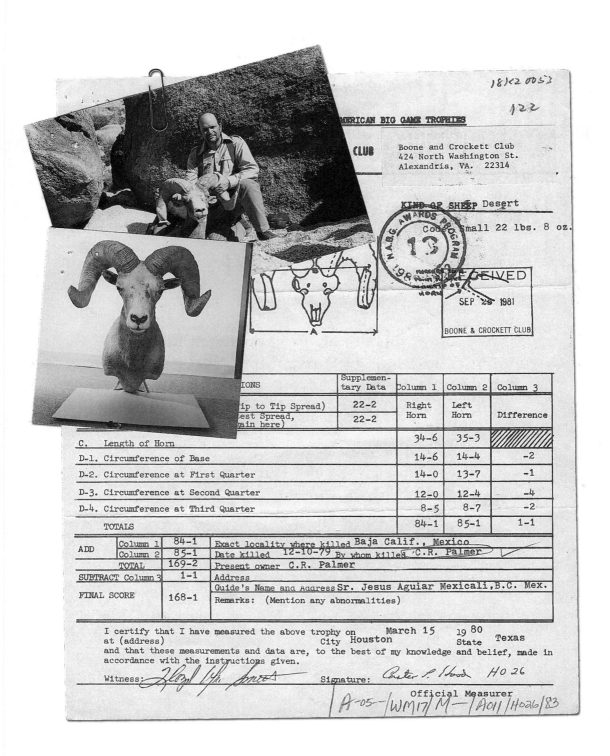

18K2 0053

122

AMERICAN BIG GAME TROPHIES

CLUB

Boone and Crockett Club
424 North Washington St.
Alexandria, VA. 22314

KIND OF SHEEP Desert

Code Small 22 lbs. 8 oz.

N.A.B.G. AWARDS PROGRAM
13

RECEIVED
SEP 25 1981
BOONE & CROCKETT CLUB

...IONS	Supplemen-tary Data	Column 1	Column 2	Column 3
(...ip to Tip Spread)	22-2	Right Horn	Left Horn	Difference
(...est Spread, ...ain here)	22-2			
C. Length of Horn		34-6	35-3	////////
D-1. Circumference of Base		14-6	14-4	-2
D-2. Circumference at First Quarter		14-0	13-7	-1
D-3. Circumference at Second Quarter		12-0	12-4	-4
D-4. Circumference at Third Quarter		8-5	8-7	-2
TOTALS		84-1	85-1	1-1

ADD	Column 1	84-1	Exact locality where killed Baja Calif., Mexico
	Column 2	85-1	Date killed 12-10-79 By whom killed C.R. Palmer
	TOTAL	169-2	Present owner C.R. Palmer
SUBTRACT Column 3		1-1	Address
FINAL SCORE		168-1	Guide's Name and Address Sr. Jesus Aguiar Mexicali,B.C. Mex.
			Remarks: (Mention any abnormalities)

I certify that I have measured the above trophy on March 15 19 80
at (address)   City Houston   State Texas
and that these measurements and data are, to the best of my knowledge and belief, made in
accordance with the instructions given.

Witness: _____   Signature: Chester P. Wood   HO 26

Official Measurer

A-05--/WM17/ M--/A011/H026/83

FOREWORD

▼ ▼ ▼ ▼ ▼ ▼ ▼ ▼ ▼

C. ROBERT PALMER
President of the Boone and Crockett Club

The Boone and Crockett Club is entering its 120th year since being founded by a small group of big game hunter-conservationists. The story is well known—by 1887, several North American big-game species faced threats to their survival. The total loss of certain species was a serious possibility. The massive herds of bison were but a memory. The populations of pronghorn, bighorn sheep, elk, and mule deer were in steep declines.

The causes were clear. Most big-game animals were considered food for a growing population that was migrating west. And, they also considered wolves, bears, and cougars to be competitors for the food. There were no hunting regulations, no closed seasons, no bag limits, and the young and the female animals were easier to hunt — and tasted better than the old males.

Along came the Boone and Crockett Club with a vision. The Club's founders intervened. Change was rapid. Soon the concept of hunting for trophy male big-game animals gained favor. Seasons, bag limits, and protection of the young and females were a part of the "wise use" of our natural resources.

Big-game populations began to recover. By 1932, the Club was ready to recognize those hunter-conservationists with the publication of a book in conjunction with the National Collection of Heads and Horns at the Bronx Zoo in New York. The hunters and the trophies were listed to demonstrate that the efforts to halt the decline of North America's big game were important. Entry in the book was open to all hunters who met certain guidelines for quality trophies taken under conditions of Fair Chase.

Today, with the 26th Big Game Awards book, we can see the benefits of the vision of wise use and the conservation of our natural resources. Nearly 4,700 trophies entered during the last three years have met or exceeded the requirements for entry, and three entries are new World's Records.

> TO TAKE A TROPHY THAT QUALIFIES FOR ENTRY IN THE RECORDS BOOK IS A GREAT ACHIEVEMENT — IT IS RECOGNITION BY ONE'S PEERS THAT "YOU HAVE ARRIVED!" I REMEMBER HOW ELATED I WAS—28 YEARS AGO—WHEN MY DESERT SHEEP "MADE THE BOOK."
>
> YET I WOULD CAUTION, WE MUST NOT LET THE RECORDS BOOK BECOME OUR HOLY GRAIL. THERE IS A MUCH GREATER REWARD FOR HAVING SHARED A SUCCESSFUL HUNTING EXPERIENCE WITH FRIENDS AND FAMILY.

To take a trophy that qualifies for entry in the records book is a great achievement — it is recognition by one's peers that "you have arrived!" I remember how elated I was—28 years ago—when my desert sheep "made the book."

Yet I would caution, we must not let the records book become our Holy Grail. There is a much greater reward for having shared a successful hunting experience with friends and family. To me, nothing has been more satisfying than organizing and accompanying our children and grandchildren on outdoor adventures while camping, fishing, and hunting.

Each of the adventures was composed of three parts — the planning, the event, and the memories. The last was the most enjoyable and long lasting, even if the first two were not exactly perfect.

Enjoy the 26th Big Game Awards book. I am certain in three years there will be another book also filled with great memories.

In the meanwhile, I hope you will find time to read two other items. First, Jack O'Connor's grand spoof of trophy hunting, "How K.R. Bolz Won the Famous Krautbauer Trophy" in his book *The Best of Jack O'Connor*. This chapter was originally penned by O'Connor under the name Bill Ryan and was published as an article in the 1968 edition of *Gun Digest*. And the second book to consider is Ortega y Gasset's *Meditations on Hunting*. ▲

Bob Palmer has been a member for 25 years and currently is president of the Boone and Crockett Club. He started hunting at age five with a Daisy BB gun. Bob graduated from Southern Methodist University-BSME 1957 and MSEA in 1966. In 2006, Bob retired after 53 years, 32 of which he was chairman and CEO of Rowan Companies Inc., an international drilling contractor.

Bob and his wife Rebecca have been married 53 years. They have two children and six grandchildren. They live in Houston and spend an inadequate amount of time on their ranch in South Texas.

RECORDS OF NORTH AMERICAN BIG GAME COMMITTEE

Eldon L. "Buck" Buckner, Chair
Baker City, Oregon

Gilbert T. Adams
Beaumont, Texas

James F. Arnold
Austin, Texas

Mark O. Bara
Hemingway, South Carolina

Lee M. Bass
Fort Worth, Texas

Jack E. Beal
Fort Lauderdale, Florida

George A. Bettas
Stevensville, Montana

Tommy L. Caruthers
Denton, Texas

Craig A. Cook
Anchorage, Alaska

John O. Cook III
North Bend, Washington

Ernie Davis
Cotulla, Texas

H. Hudson DeCray
Bishop, California

Richard T. Hale
Ottawa, Kansas

Robert H. Hanson
Wapiti, Wyoming

Vernon D. Holleman
Temple, Texas

Frederick J. King
Gallatin, Montana

William C. MacCarty III
South Boston, Virginia

Butch Marita
High Bridge, Wisconsin

Earl E. Morgenroth
Missoula, Montana

Jack S. Parker
Carefree, Arizona

Marie Pavlik
Fort Lauderdale, Florida

John D. Pearson
Sheldon, South Carolina

James M. Peek
Moscow, Idaho

Arthur C. Popham Jr.
Village, Kansas

John P. Poston
Helena, Montana

Richard D. Reeve
Anchorage, Alaska

Jack Reneau
Missoula, Montana

Glenn A. St Charles
Seattle, Washington

Mark B. Steffen
Hutchinson, Kansas

Wayne C. van Zwoll
Bridgeport, Washington

Paul D. Webster
Wayzata, Minnesota

TABLE OF CONTENTS

Award Winning Trophy Stories Continued...

Award Winning Trophy Stories Continued...

Tabulations of Trophies Accepted in the 26th Awards Program 383

Photograph courtesy of Frederick J. King

The 26th Awards Program Judges Panel is pictured above at Cabela's Fort Worth store. Standing, Left to Right: Ryan B. Hatfield, Missoula, MT (Asst. Dir. of Big Game Records); Patrick H. McKenzie, Regina, SK; Mark B. Steffen, Hutchinson, KS; Jack Reneau, Missoula, MT (Dir. of Big Game Records); Robert H. Hanson, Wapiti, WY (Chair, 26th Awards Judges Panel); Larry R. Carey, Spokane, WA; Eldon L. "Buck" Buckner, Baker City, OR (Chair, Big Game Records Committee); Frederick J. King, Gallatin Gateway, MT; Glenn W. Abbott, Portland, OR; Mark O. Bara, Hemingway, SC; L. Victor Clark, Verdi, NV; and Ralph C. Stayner, Nutrioso, AZ. Kneeling, Left to Right: Ken Witt, Arlington, TX; Richard C. Berreth, Prince George, BC; Larry C. Lack, Thompson Falls, MT; and Warren D. St. Germaine, Yellowknife, NWT.

26TH NORTH AMERICAN BIG GAME AWARDS

PANEL OF JUDGES
Fort Worth, Texas
2007

Chairman
Robert H. Hanson
Wapiti, WY

Glenn W. Abbott
Portland, OR

Patrick H. McKenzie
Regina, SK

Richard C. Berreth
Prince George, BC

Ralph C. Stayner
Nutrioso, AZ

Larry R. Carey
Spokane, WA

Mark B. Steffen
Hutchinson, KS

L. Victor Clark
Verdi, NV

Warren D. St. Germaine
Yellowknife, NT

Larry C. Lack
Thompson Falls, MT

Ken Witt
Arlington, TX

CONSULTANTS

Mark O. Bara
Hemingway, SC

Frederick J. King
Gallatin Gateway, MT

Eldon L. "Buck" Buckner
Baker City, OR

Paul D. Webster
Wayzata, MN

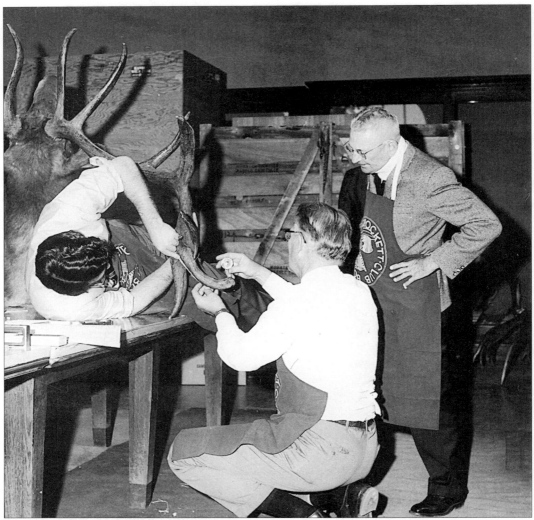

Chairman Frank Cook, on the table, and two other members of the 14th Awards Judges Panel measure one of the four elk that were sent in to have their scores verified. The 14th Awards Judges Panel convened at the Carnegie Museum in Pittsburgh, Pennsylvania, in 1971, to measure 89 select trophies. Today's Judges Panels operate nearly the same as they did over three decades ago, with pairs of Official Measurers teaming up to verify the scores of the invited trophies. Members of the 14th Awards Judges Panel included: Frank Cook (Chairman), Anchorage, AK; George T. Church, Jr., Ligonier, PA; B.A. Fashingbauer, St. Paul, MN; Arnold O. Haugen, Ames, IA; Ovar Uggen, Calgary, AB; Philip L. Wright, Missoula, MT; Donald S. Hopkins (Panel Consultant), Spokane, WA; and Elmer M. Rusten (Panel Consultant), Wayzata, MN.

INTRODUCTION

▼ ▼ ▼ ▼ ▼ ▼ ▼ ▼ ▼

Mark B. Steffen
Chairman, Boone and Crockett Club Publications Committee

The pinnacle of fair chase hunting was once again recognized by our austere organization, the Boone and Crockett Club. The 26th Awards, covering trophy submissions from 2004-2006, delineates the continued success of the North American model of wildlife management. Simply distilled, this model supports and promotes the public ownership of our wildlife coupled to the wise, scientific management of our habitats. The data and stories chronicled within this volume clearly support the ongoing, even escalating, success of our conservation efforts.

The Boone and Crockett Club scoring system has its roots in a three-man committee that included Theodore Roosevelt. Formed in 1902, this group was charged with evaluating specimens of our quickly fading wildlife herds. This was but one of the fronts on which Boone and Crockett Club fought. Through the following decades, Club members ardently strove to make advances for conservation through regulation, politics, and habitat protection. As a result, our scoring system now is an account of the flourishing wildlife populations of North America. Similarly, Boone and Crockett Club functions today as it did in its infancy. Focusing on conservation, education, and big-game records keeping, Boone and Crockett Club remains committed to serving the hunter-conservationist.

26TH AWARDS JUDGES PANEL

Robert H. Hanson, Chair — Wapiti, WY
Glenn W. Abbott — Portland, OR
Richard C. Berreth — Prince George, BC
Larry R. Carey — Spokane, WA
L. Victor Clark — Verdi, NV
Larry C. Lack — Thompson Falls, MT
Patrick H. McKenzie — Regina, SK
Ralph C. Stayner — Nutrioso, AZ
Mark B. Steffen — Hutchinson, KS
Warren D. St. Germaine — Yellowknife, NT
Ken Witt — Arlington, TX

CONSULTANTS

Mark O. Bara — Hemingway, SC
Eldon L. "Buck" Buckner — Baker City, OR
Frederick J. King — Gallatin Gateway, MT
Paul D. Webster — Wayzata, MN

At the conclusion of the triennial period (January 1, 2004, to December 31, 2006), invitations were sent to the fortunate hunter-owners whom the good Lord blessed with possessing the highest scoring animals in each Boone and Crockett category. The Records Committee, headed by chairman Eldon L. "Buck" Buckner and Director of Big Game Records Jack Reneau, drew from the Club's pool of trained Official Measurers to serve on the

Judge's Panel. These individuals have proven themselves highly proficient in applying our complex scoring system through many years of service to the Club as Official Measurers. Additionally, integrity and commitment to the promotion of ethical hunting under the stringent rules of fair-chase hunting is a prerequisite to selection. The Boone and Crockett Club, since its inception, has been a champion of the promotion and definition of "Fair Chase" hunting. This precept remains a major focus for the Records Committee and Club. There are few honors among the hunter-conservationist community as lofty as the invitation to serve on a B&C Judges Panel. Those selected as Judges for the 26th Big Game Awards are listed on the previous page.

In late April 2007, more than 90 trophies and the Judges Panel came together in Fort Worth, Texas. The panel devoted an entire week to verifying trophy scores. Two teams of two measurers each scored each animal to ensure precision. The complexity of many of the trophies prompted intense discussions as well as great debates. The measurers relied upon the Official Measurer's manual and committee elders to resolve differences. Friendships were forged for life as the group worked seamlessly through the week to honor this exceptional collection of North America's finest big-game specimens.

The panelists spent evenings at the round table exchanging information, opinions, and concerns regarding hunting in its current state. A common topic involved the degradation of the quality of the hunt, towards the concept of a rapid harvest as all-important. As time accelerates, we seem to be losing touch with the timeless pleasures of our natural environment. We have the "baby boomers," the "X generation," and now, unfortunately, the "easier is better" hunting generation. Armed with technological gadgets designed to simplify the take of the quarry, we rush to the hunt, frequently bragging of how quickly and at what great distances we were able to bring it to a conclusion. Is there a risk to this? Absolutely!

Ultimately, the future of hunting will depend on our ability to portray to the populace our sincere concern for the animals and their habitat first and our role in their management second. Technology in hunting, as in other sectors, is running at an unfettered pace. We need to take a step back and reanalyze our reasons for being out among the animals. Aldo Leopold in *A Sand County Almanac* and in other writings can help one grasp the concept of serving a role, versus being the "center" of the great outdoors. There are very few Boone and Crockett animals, but an unlimited number of Boone and Crockett hunts. Neither comes easy or without honing the skills necessary to harvest them.

The time is drawing near for all of us interested in the future of hunting (hunters, wildlife professionals, outfitters, and manufacturers) to address the current ethical dilemmas. The outcome of these deliberations has the opportunity to guide individuals, state commissions, and federal agencies. The result is the safe navigation of the acceptance of sport hunting through primarily urban waters. Boone and Crockett Club will be a leader.

Through the decades, B&C has worked to define many aspects of the "Fair Chase" hunt and incorporate those qualities into requirements for entry of a hunter-taken trophy into the Records Book. Revised as recently as June 30, 2006, our Entry Affidavit reads:

For the purpose of entry into the Boone and Crockett Club's® records, North American big game harvested by the use of the following methods or under the following conditions are ineligible:

    I. Spotting or herding game from the air, followed by landing in its vicinity for the purpose of pursuit and shooting;

    II. Herding or chasing with the aid of any motorized equipment;

    III. Use of electronic communication devices to guide hunters to game, artificial lighting, electronic light intensifying devices (night vision optics), sights with built-in electronic range-finding capabilities, thermal imaging equipment, electronic game calls or cameras/timers/motion tracking devices that transmit images and other information to the hunter;

    IV. Confined by artificial barriers, including escape-proof fenced enclosures;

    V. Transplanted for the purpose of commercial shooting;

    VI. By the use of traps or pharmaceuticals;

    VII. While swimming, helpless in deep snow, or helpless in any other natural or artificial medium;

    VIII. On another hunter's license;

    IX. Not in full compliance with the game laws or regulations of the federal government or of any state, province, territory, or tribal council on reservations or tribal lands;

Please answer the following questions only if the entry is for a cougar, jaguar, or bear:

Were dogs used in conjunction with the pursuit and harvest of this animal? ☐ Yes ☐ No

If the answer to the above question is yes, answer the following statements:

    1. I was present on the hunt at the times the dogs were released to pursue this animal. True or False

    2. If electronic collars were attached to any of the dogs, receivers were not used to harvest this animal. True or False

To the best of my knowledge the answers to the above statements are true. If the answer to either #1 or #2 above is false, please explain on a separate sheet.

     I certify that the trophy scored on this chart was not taken in violation of the conditions listed above. In signing this statement, I understand that if the information provided on this entry is found to be misrepresented or fraudulent in any respect, it will not be accepted into the Awards Program and 1) all of my prior entries are subject to deletion from future editions of Records of North American Big Game 2) future entries may not be accepted.

     FAIR CHASE, as defined by the Boone and Crockett Club®, is the ethical, sportsmanlike and lawful pursuit and taking of any free-ranging wild, native North American big game animal in a manner that does not give the hunter an improper advantage over such game animals.

     The Boone and Crockett Club® may exclude the entry of any animal that it deems to have been taken in an unethical manner or under conditions deemed inappropriate by the Club.

Our stance is to honor the animal. The rigors of our Entry Affidavit ensure that this code of honor is shared by the hunter as well.

Boone and Crockett Club, along these same lines, has outlined the tenets of Hunter Ethics:

> *Fundamental to all hunting is the concept of conservation of natural resources. Hunting in today's world involves the regulated harvest of individual animals in a manner that conserves, protects, and perpetuates the hunted population. The hunter engages in a one-to-one relationship with the quarry and his or her hunting should be guided by a hierarchy of ethics related to hunting, which includes the following tenets:*
> 1. *Obey all applicable laws and regulations.*
> 2. *Respect the customs of the locale where the hunting occurs.*
> 3. *Exercise a personal code of behavior that reflects favorably on your abilities and sensibilities as a hunter.*
> 4. *Attain and maintain the skills necessary to make the kill as certain and quick as possible.*
> 5. *Behave in a way that will bring no dishonor to either the hunter, the hunted, or the environment.*
> 6. *Recognize that these tenets are intended to enhance the hunter's experience of the relationship between predator and prey, which is one of the most fundamental relationships of humans and their environment.*

In response to the public and media's need and demand for leadership from the Boone and Crockett Club in regards to the changing face of hunting, we have compiled a series of position statements. These statements provide an ethical basis, not just for the Club, but for hunter-conservationists across the continent.

Trophies and Trophy Hunting

What constitutes a trophy is a matter of personal choice and experience. B&C has long supported selective hunting for mature animals that have already genetically contributed to overall herd health. Selective hunting also supports conservation and game management efforts when a balanced age structure within a given big game population is an objective of State wildlife managers. While not every animal taken will qualify for B&C records, any animal taken legally and fairly can be a trophy.

Technological Advances

B&C is in support of technological advances in hunting equipment and techniques as long as these tools do not undermine a positive public image of hunting and diminish the skills necessary to be a fair and responsible hunter, or set a bad example for young hunters.

Records Books

B&C believes that records books represent the history of successful conservation and game management policies that have been supported by hunter-conservationists for more than a century. As such, records books celebrate these programs by recognizing the big game animals taken as a result of science-based game management and successful sportsmen and sportswomen.

Contests

B&C does not support programs, contests, or competitions that directly place a bounty on game animals by awarding cash or expensive prizes for the taking of wildlife.

Scoring Live Game

B&C is concerned about the growing practice in the use of its copyrighted scoring system to score live game animals that have been tranquilized or constrained for the purpose of establishing the commercial value of an animal or to determine the winner of a contest.

Trophy Restitutions

B&C does support the use of all or any part of its copyrighted scoring system by State wildlife officials to determine and assess fines for illegally taken game.

THE TIME IS DRAWING NEAR FOR ALL OF US INTERESTED IN THE FUTURE OF HUNTING (HUNTERS, WILDLIFE PROFESSIONALS, OUTFITTERS, AND MANUFACTURERS) TO ADDRESS THE CURRENT ETHICAL DILEMMAS. THE OUTCOME OF THESE DELIBERATIONS HAS THE OPPORTUNITY TO GUIDE INDIVIDUALS, STATE COMMISSIONS, AND FEDERAL AGENCIES. THE RESULT IS THE SAFE NAVIGATION OF THE ACCEPTANCE OF SPORT HUNTING THROUGH PRIMARILY URBAN WATERS.

Trophy Fees

B&C does not endorse the use of its copyrighted scoring system to determine a trophy fee for animals harvested by hunters.

B&C Trophy

An animal is not a B&C trophy and therefore should not be considered or identified as such until such trophy has been entered, verified, and accepted by the B&C Records Department.

Fair Chase

The Boone and Crockett Club defines Fair Chase as the ethical, sportsmanlike, and lawful pursuit and taking of any free-ranging wild, native North American big

Vice President of the Club's Big Game Records Division, Eldon L. "Buck" Buckner (center), works with 26th Awards Judges Panel members Glenn W. Abbott (right) and L. Victor Clark (left) as they verify the measurement of the new World's Record tule elk, which scores 379 points. Much has changed in the world of hunting over the last several decades, but the Boone and Crockett Club's Judges Panels continue to diligently measure the top North American big game trophies using the time-tested techniques developed by their predecessors.

game animal in a manner that does not give the hunter an improper advantage over such animals.

Canned Shoots
The Boone and Crockett Club condemns the pursuit and killing of any big game animal kept in or released from captivity to be killed in an artificial or bogus "hunting" situation where the game lacks the equivalent chance to escape afforded free-ranging animals, virtually assuring the shooter a certain or unrealistically favorable chance of a kill.

Genetic Manipulation of Game Animals
The Boone and Crockett Club condemns artificial and unnatural enhancement of a big game species' genetic characteristics. Unacceptable practices for genetic enhancement include, but are not limited to, artificial insemination, controlled or unnatural breeding programs, cloning, and translocation of breeding stock for canned shooting purposes.

The "Fair Chase" hunts chronicled within span all parts of North America. A myriad of hunting techniques were employed to harvest these magnificent creatures. The common denominator is each hunt and hunter fulfilled the stringent requirements of the Boone and Crockett Club to honor their harvest. In doing so, they brought honor to themselves as well. During the 26th Awards Entry Period we recognized nearly 4,700 new Boone and Crockett animals, including three new World's Records. For those of us dedicated to the pursuit of "Fair Chase," truly the good ol' days are now! ▲

Mark Steffen has spent many years moving through the ranks of the Boone and Crockett Club membership. First as an Associate member, advancing to Lifetime Associate membership shortly after inception of that program. Mark became an Official Measurer in 1995 and a Regular Member in 2002. He currently serves as Chairman of the Publications Committee and Big Game Profiles Committee.

Mark is a proud alumni of Northwestern Oklahoma State University and the University of Oklahoma School of Medicine. Certified by the American Board of Anesthesiology, Dr. Steffen's practice focuses on Interventional Pain Management serving the central Kansas region.

BOONE AND CROCKETT CLUB'S

26th Big Game Awards
2004-2006

▼ ▼ ▼ ▼ ▼ ▼ ▼

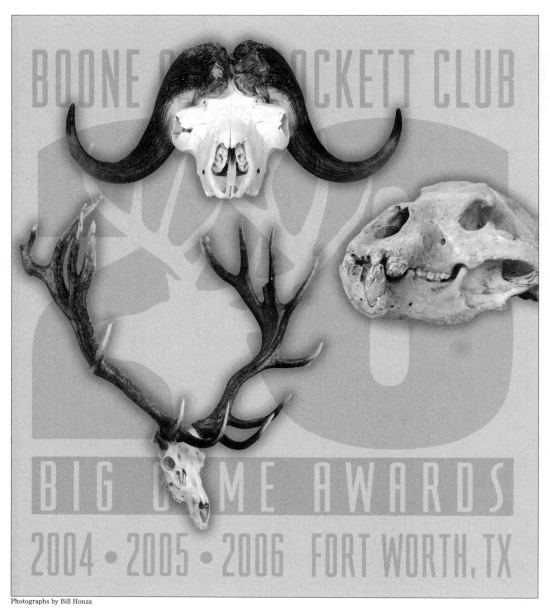

Photographs by Bill Honza

Three new World's Records were declared at the 26th Big Game Awards Judges Panel. Clockwise from the top: Jim Shockey's musk ox scoring 129 points (tie); Gordon Scott's grizzly bear scoring 27-13/16 points; and Jeff and Julie Lopeteguy's tule elk scoring 379 points.

REVIEW OF THE 26TH AWARDS PROGRAM

▼ ▼ ▼ ▼ ▼ ▼ ▼ ▼ ▼

ELDON L. "BUCK" BUCKNER
Vice President of Records and
Records of North American Big Game Committee, Chair

AND

JACK RENEAU
Director, Big Game Records

Boone and Crockett Club's 26th Big Game Awards Program closed on December 31, 2006, with the greatest number of entries ever accepted in a three-year entry period. Some 4,615 trophies were accepted in 35 of the 38 categories of big game recognized by the Club, representing a 16% increase over the 25th Awards Program three years ago. No entries were received in the polar bear, Atlantic walrus, or jaguar categories. Hunting opportunities for both polar bear and Atlantic walrus are limited; the latter being especially problematic as legally taken Atlantic walrus cannot be imported into the United States. Jaguar are protected by the Endangered Species Act and cannot be hunted in North America.

The Boone and Crockett Club's 26th Awards Program and related activities were held in Fort Worth, Texas, from April 21 through June 23, 2007. The scores of 91 invited trophies, representing 31 categories recognized by the Club, were certified by the 26th Awards Program Judges Panel and authorized to receive the coveted Boone and Crockett Club medallions and/or plaques. The trophies were on display at Cabela's Fort Worth, Texas store for seven weeks where thousands of people had the unique opportunity to view this spectacular collection of animals. The Awards were presented on the evening of June 23rd at the 26th Awards Banquet, which was held at the Doral Tesoro Hotel and Golf Club in Fort Worth.

Three new World's Records were announced for tule elk, grizzly bear, and musk ox (tie). Following is a brief discussion and summary of all the trophies that were honored and recognized in Fort Worth. As can be seen, hunters are continuing to take many trophies that rank in the All-time top ten or at the top for their state or province. Many are new state or provincial records. Whether we realize it or not, we may be living "the good old days."

BEARS AND COUGAR
BLACK BEAR
Andrew Seman's black bear, which he took in one of those nearly impenetrable laurel thickets in Fayette Co., Pennsylvania, in 2005, scores 23-3/16 points, tying it for third place

in the All-time records book. Since the first and second place bears are listed as picked up, Seman's bear is tied for the largest black bear ever taken by a hunter.

GRIZZLY BEAR
Needless to say, the highlight of the grizzly bear category is Gordon Scott's new World's Record (27-13/16) that shattered the old World's Record by 11/16th of an inch. Scott picked it up while on a black bear hunt on Lone Mountain, Alaska, in 1976.

ALASKA BROWN BEAR
The Alaska brown bear category, which was topped by Scott Weisenburger's First Place Award winner, scoring 29-7/16 points, made a fantastic showing at the 26th Awards Program. Weisenburger took his bear on the Meshik River, Alaska, in 2004. All three of the remaining Alaska brown bear skulls in Fort Worth equaled or exceeded the First Place Award winners (29-3/16 points; three-way tie) received at the 25th Awards Program three years ago.

COUGAR
Joseph Gore's cougar, which scores 16-2/16 points, ranks third in the All-time records book. Gore took this incredible tom (that he says tipped the scales at 225-1/2 pounds) without the aid of hounds near Sundance Lake, Alberta, during the 2005 hunting season.

ELK
AMERICAN ELK
Utah and Arizona are two of the top trophy elk producing states at this time, and both were well represented in Fort Worth by very impressive typical bulls. Doug Degelbeck's bull, which scored 412-7/8 points and received the First Place Award, was taken in Utah County, Utah, in 2006. This bull is the Utah state record as we go to press with this book. Dan J. Agnew's typical Gila County, Arizona, bull, which was harvested during the 2003 hunting season, is that state's new number four bull at 410-5/8 points. In the non-typical American elk category, Peter J. Orazi, Jr.'s, bull, taken in 1977 in Latah County, Idaho, is the new non-typical Idaho state record. It scores 433-1/8 points, and at 70-3/8 inches, has the widest spread of any elk ever entered in the Club's records books. Ted Wehking's bull, taken in Nye County, Nevada, in 2005, scored an impressive 415-6/8 points and is Nevada's new number two in the non-typical category. It will be interesting to see what trophies will show up in these two categories at the 27th Awards Program in 2010.

ROOSEVELT'S ELK
The Roosevelt's elk category was well represented with a bull taken by James V. Stewart near the Gold River, British Columbia, in 2003. At a score or 371-2/8 points, it took the First Place Award in its category.

TULE ELK

The 26th Awards Program Judges Panel certified Jeff and Julie Lopeteguy's trophy bull as the new World's Record tule elk. This magnificent bull, which scores 379 points, was found dead on their ranch in Glenn County, California, in 2005. The cause of death could not be determined by California Department of Fish and Game personnel. Considering that tule elk were on the verge of extinction in 1886, these animals have come a long way since hunting seasons were reestablished in 1989.

DEER

MULE DEER

Both the number one typical and the number one non-typical mule deer, which received First Place Awards in Fort Worth, were taken by women. In the typical category, Myra S. Smith's buck, which scored 210-2/8 points, is the largest ever taken by a woman. She found her B&C buck while hunting with her husband in Sonora, Mexico, in 2006. Catherine E. Keene took her non-typical trophy, scoring 285-4/8 points, during the 2004 season in Fremont County, Wyoming. Cathy was given an incredible second chance at this deer, and made the most of it. It is one of the largest non-typicals ever taken by a woman.

COLUMBIA BLACKTAIL DEER

Two older trophies, tying for 9th place in the typical Columbia blacktail deer All-time rankings, were recognized with First Place Awards. Both trophies score 170-6/8 points. Frank G. Merz's buck was taken in 1979 in Siskiyou Co., California, and Larry Naught took his buck in Clatsop County, Oregon, in 1955. After Larry passed away, the antlers continued to hang on the wall of his home until his son, Allan Naught, had them scored at the Pacific Northwest Sportsman's Show in Portland, Oregon, in 2005. Merz's buck ranks number two in California; Naught's is tied for 5th place in Oregon. Peter Morish's buck, scoring 185-1/8 points, received the First Place Award in the non-typical category. Morish took his buck, the third largest ever recorded for California, in 2005 in the rugged, brush-covered country of the Trinity Alps in northern California.

SITKA BLACKTAIL DEER

Sitka blacktail deer hunters James A. Sharpe and Davey W. Brown were 12 and 14 years old, respectively, when they accomplished something that most big game hunters will never accomplish in a lifetime; they both took trophy bucks that make Boone and Crockett Club's records book and received Place Awards in Fort Worth for their accomplishments. In 2004, Sharpe took his once-in-a-lifetime buck, scoring 120-1/8 points, on Prince of Wales Island, Alaska, and received the Second Place Award. Brown took his Fourth Place Award winner, which scores 117-6/8 points, the same year on Etolin Island, Alaska.

WHITETAIL DEER

A record number of 1,606 whitetails (1,006 typicals; 600 non-typicals) were accepted during

When the Judges Panel finished scoring these two incredible bucks, both scored an unbelievable 295-3/8 points. The odds of two bucks, built so differently, scoring exactly the same must be astronomical. Schmucker's buck (right) has a typical 7x6 frame that scores 219-1/8 inches and 22 abnormal points that total 76-2/8 inches. Dexter's rack (left) has a 5x5 typical frame that only scores 164-6/8 inches, but there are 37 abnormal points totaling 130-5/8 inches that make up for the lack of a large typical frame.

2004-2006 in the 26th Awards Program. The top typical in Fort Worth was Bradley S. Jerman's Warren County, Ohio, buck taken in 2004 with a crossbow. The shed antlers of this animal from the previous year were found by another person a short distance from where Jerman harvested this buck. At 201-1/8 points, Jerman's buck is Ohio's new state record typical by 2-6/8 points, outranking a 198-3/8 buck also present at Fort Worth taken by Timothy E. Reed in Muskingum County.

Ohio and Illinois were both extremely well represented in the non-typical category at the 26th Awards Program. Jonathan R. Schmucker's buck, commonly referred to as "the Amish Buck," was taken in Adams County, Ohio, during the 2006 season with a crossbow. Scott R. Dexter took his in McDonough Co., Illinois, two years earlier with a .50-caliber muzzleloader. When the Judges Panel finished scoring these two incredible bucks, both scored an unbelievable 295-3/8 points. The odds of two bucks, built so differently, scoring exactly the same must be astronomical. Schmucker's buck has a typical 7x6 frame that scores 219-1/8 inches and 22 abnormal points that total 76-2/8 inches. Dexter's rack has a 5x5 typical frame that only scores 164-6/8 inches, but there are 37 abnormal points totaling 130-5/8 inches that make up for the lack of a large typical frame. These two bucks tie for sixth place in the All-time records book. If you overlook the top two non-typicals in this category, which were both found dead, Schmucker's and Dexter's bucks tie for fourth place as the two best whitetails ever recorded by B&C for a modern-day hunter.

COUES' WHITETAIL DEER
The First Place Award-winning typical Coues' deer was a 4x4 taken by Terry C. Hickson in 2005 in Sonora, Mexico. At 122-4/8, Hickson's buck is a perfect example of why Boone and Crockett Club's scoring system was devised to recognize symmetry in its final score. With only 1-5/8" of deductions, this buck is one of the most symmetrical deer ever entered in the Club's Awards Programs.

MOOSE
ALASKA-YUKON MOOSE
While there were no new World's Records moose in Fort Worth, all three categories were represented by respectable bulls. The fourth largest Alaska-Yukon moose ever taken received the First Place Award. It was taken by Austrian hunter Franz Kohlroser along the Kvichak River, Alaska, in 2005. It scored 254-5/8 points.

CANADA MOOSE
British Columbia is noted for producing big Canada moose, and Frank A. Hanks' bull lives up to this reputation. Hanks received the First Place Award in this category with a bull he took on Kawdy Mountain in 2004 that scored 227-6/8 points. It is the fifth largest Canada moose from that province, and ranks seventh in the all-time listing.

SHIRAS MOOSE
Chad Hammons filled his Idaho Shiras moose tag in 2005 with a 187-1/8 bull from Shoshone

Photographs by Bill Honza

Four impressive Rocky Mountain goats were on display at the 26th Big Game Awards exhibit. Clockwise from the top left: Edward E. Toribio's billy scoring 54-4/8 points; Craig L. Rippen's goat scoring 54-2/8 points; Robert E. Reedy, Jr.'s, Rocky Mountain goat scoring 52 points; and Daryl K. Schultz's billy scoring 53-4/8 points.

County that is the fifth largest recorded for the state. Mark Babiar's Shiras bull, which was also taken in 2005, is Washington State's new number one moose. It was taken in Stevens County.

CARIBOU

Five woodland caribou were invited to Fort Worth, and all of them showed up, contributing to one of the most spectacular caribou displays at any Awards Program. At 384-2/8 points, James H. Holt's bull, which he took near Sam's Pond, Newfoundland, in 2005, is the new number four for this category and the best woodland stag taken in the last 39 years. Woody Groves' Quebec-Labrador caribou, scoring 424-2/8 points, is the best specimen of its kind taken since 1993. Groves took his trophy near Clearwater Lake, Quebec, in 2005. Interestingly, none of the five barren ground caribou invited to Fort Worth were sent in by their owners. Entries in this category have declined dramatically from a record number of 147 in the 22nd Awards Program 12 years ago, to only 19 in the 26th Awards Program. The reasons for this decline are unclear, but it will be interesting to watch what happens to this category in the coming years.

HORNED BIG GAME

ROCKY MOUNTAIN GOAT

Apparently, Edward E. Toribio not only knows a great goat when he sees one, but he also knows where to find them. His billy, taken on Revillagigedo Island, Alaska, received the First Place Award. Three years earlier, he guided Ross Groben to another Alaskan billy, scoring 54-6/8 points, that received the First Place Award at the 25th Awards Program. Craig L. Rippen received the Second Place Award for a billy that he took in Duchesne County, Utah, in 2006 scoring 54-2/8 points. It is a new Utah state record, as well as the largest goat ever taken in the lower 48 states.

MUSK OX

Hunters continue to harvest incredible trophies in the musk ox category. Noted Canadian outdoor writer Jim Shockey took first place honors with a battle-scared bull, scoring 129 points, that tied the current World's Record set three years ago. Shockey felt that this old bull, which he took near the Coppermine River, Nunavut, in 2006, probably wouldn't have survived another season.

BIGHORN SHEEP

Montana continues to dominate the bighorn sheep category with 84 of 144 specimens entered in the 26th Awards Program from ten states and two Canadian provinces. Robert E. Seelye's ram, taken in 2004 in Montana's Missouri Breaks, is Pope and Young Club's new World's Record. It scores 199 points and received the First Place Award.

DESERT SHEEP

There were larger desert sheep at Fort Worth than any of the previous 25 Awards Programs. All four were over 182 inches. The First Place Award winner, taken by Russell A. Young in Hidalgo County, New Mexico, is the largest desert ram ever taken by a hunter in that state, and scored 188-2/8 points. Terry J. Frick's ram, which received the Third Place Award, was taken in Brewster County, Texas, in 2005 and is the new state record. It scores an incredible 183-5/8 points and is one of only six desert sheep entered in the Club's records books from Texas since that state opened its first sheep season in 1988. The efforts of the Texas Bighorn Society to restore desert sheep to their native habitat are paying big dividends.

DALL'S SHEEP

Cody A. Miller received the First Place Award for his Dall's sheep scoring 178-4/8 points that he took in 2005 in the Mackenzie Mountains. It is the new provincial record for Northwest Territories.

STONE'S SHEEP

Only ten Stone's sheep were entered and accepted in the 26th Awards Program, yet Jelindo A. Tiberti II managed to connect with the largest ram taken in this category since 1998 while hunting near Hook Lake, British Columbia, in 2005. The Judges Panel certified the score of Tiberti's sheep at 179-5/8 points, and gave it the First Place Award. A ram of this stature is a once-in-a-life-time trophy for Jelindo, as well as a once-in-a-generation trophy for the hunting community.

The 26th Awards Program was a success, as well as a memorial to the conservation efforts initiated by the Boone and Crockett Club in 1887 and carried on by today's sportsmen. Today's hunters are reaping the rewards of the efforts of those hunter-conservationists who came before us as evidenced by this records book. While new and different challenges face today's sportsmen and will affect future chances to harvest trophies like those featured in this book, we believe that Theodore Roosevelt, George Bird Grinnell, and their contemporaries would look on today's hunting opportunities with pride and consider their efforts a resounding success. ▲

Eldon L. "Buck" Buckner is the current Vice President of Big Game Records and Chairman of the Boone and Crockett Club's Records of North American Big Game Committee. First appointed an Official Measurer in 1968 while serving as a U.S. Forest Service range conservationist in Arizona, Buck has served as Judges Panel Chairman, Consultant, and Judge for Boone and Crockett Club Awards Programs since 1989.

Jack Reneau is a certified wildlife biologist who has been Director of Big Game Records for the Boone and Crockett Club since 1983. He was responsible for the day-to-day paperwork of the Boone and Crockett Club's records-keeping activities from 1976 to 1979 as an information specialist for the Hunter Services Division of the National Rifle Association (NRA) when NRA and Boone and Crockett Club cosponsored the B&C Awards Program. Jack earned a B.S. in Wildlife Management from Colorado State University and a M.S. in Wildlife Management from Eastern Kentucky University. Jack has also worked for the Colorado Division of Wildlife, Kentucky Department of Fish and Wildlife Resources, as well as the Pike-San Isabel, Daniel Boone, and Six-Rivers National Forests.

AWARD-WINNING TROPHY STORIES

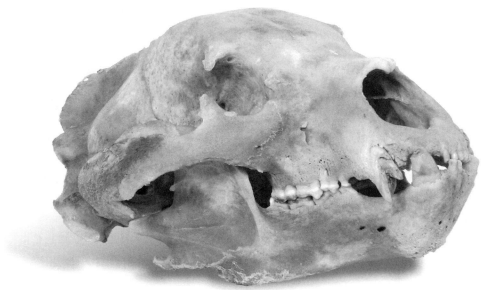

Photograph by Bill Honza

TROPHY STATS
▼ ▼ ▼ ▼ ▼

Category
Black Bear

Score
23 ³/₁₆

Skull Length
14 ⁹/₁₆

Skull Width
8 ¹⁰/₁₆

Location
Fayette Co., Pennsylvania – 2005

Hunter
Andrew Seman, Jr.

BLACK BEAR
First Award – 23³/₁₆

▼ ▼ ▼ ▼ ▼ ▼ ▼ ▼ ▼

ANDREW SEMAN, JR.

By Brian J. Seman (Andrew's brother)

As we gazed at the enormous bear that lay there before us, we couldn't help but think about how everything had fallen into place to make this truly a day and a bear to remember. Never did we imagine, though, that the bear my brother AJ had just taken would turn out to be a tie for the largest hunter-taken black bear in Boone and Crockett Club's records book.

A Bear to Remember

Though luck certainly played a big part in our success that day, we are far from novice hunters. My brother Andrew Seman, Jr. (or AJ, as most call him), and James, David, and I have combined for more than a century of hunting seasons among us, and most of them were in this area of Fayette County, Pennsylvania. In fact, several of us have taken bucks within a hundred yards of where AJ encountered his trophy bear. We have also taken dozens of big game animals through the years in Pennsylvania, West Virginia, Idaho, and Colorado.

As for Pennsylvania bear hunting, we usually hunt in the traditional bear counties of Lycoming and Tioga, and in the Allegheny National Forest, and while we did hunt hard and find plenty of bear sign, those trips were as much preseason deer scouting expeditions than anything else. In recent years, though, we've heard of many good bears being taken here in Fayette County, and we even tracked and trailed bears through the dense laurel thickets and over the steep rocky slopes that we consider our hunting grounds, but never had any of us ever raised a gun on a bear.

We have hunted State Game Land (SGL) 51 for many reasons. Our knowledge, experience, and love of this area have grown through the years and extended through several genera-

Photograph by Jack Reneau

Andrew Seman, Jr., accepting his plaque and medal from Buck Buckner, Vice President and Chairman of the Big Game Records Committee.

tions in our family. There is a special feeling to hunt where previous generations walked, hunted, and grew up. In fact, our grandparents grew up in log cabins very near where this great bear lived and died. This area also has a rich American history, with Fort Necessity and Jumonville, and the early centers of iron and coal.

Many have asked if we knew the bear was in the area and if we were hunting it specifically. In reality, we had no idea it was there. The only indication was in seeing a huge bear several years ago while mountain biking in the area, and that may have been this bear. We decided to hunt SGL 51 because of the tracks and other sign we found there the year before.

WE HAVE HUNTED STATE GAME LAND (SGL) 51 FOR MANY REASONS. OUR KNOWLEDGE, EXPERIENCE, AND LOVE OF THIS AREA HAVE GROWN THROUGH THE YEARS AND EXTENDED THROUGH SEVERAL GENERATIONS IN OUR FAMILY. THERE IS A SPECIAL FEELING TO HUNT WHERE PREVIOUS GENERATIONS WALKED, HUNTED, AND GREW UP. IN FACT, OUR GRANDPARENTS GREW UP IN LOG CABINS VERY NEAR WHERE THIS GREAT BEAR LIVED AND DIED.

Plus, we have a hunting camp nearby. Recently built on a stone barn foundation, our rustic camp (with no running water or electricity) is an ideal escape from the modern world, and a reminder of how life was here not that long ago.

Opening day was uneventful. AJ and Jim posted for the first day. I had come in from Colorado the day before, and was not planning on hunting bears but after purchasing my regular hunting license, I just couldn't resist picking up a bear license, too. Finding a nonresident bear tag locally turned out to be difficult, but contacting the Game Commission's regional office I learned I could buy one over the Internet.

Thankful for the advances in licensing technology (and for what turned out to be one of the best returns on $36 I'll ever have), I met up with AJ and Jim in the afternoon. Later that evening, after a meal cooked on the wood stove and a few songs strummed on a guitar or two, we planned the next day's hunt.

Jim, slowed down by a recent hip operation, would post in various places throughout the day based on where AJ and I would be hunting. Through the years, with sometimes just a few of us hunting, we developed a method of mini-drives or "coordinated stalking." An alternating walk-and-stop technique, it's worked well for us, especially with small groups, providing all those involved know the area and are familiar with one another. Timing and maintaining the agreed-upon course is key.

With Jim posted, AJ and I began stalking thickets and other areas in a coordinated manner; stalking and stopping every 50 to 100 yards, separated, at times, by up to 200 yards. Every stalk seemed to be working perfectly as far as the timing, wind, and other factors were concerned, and we did see very fresh sign of where a small bear had been foraging. We also heard a flock of turkeys.

After covering three or four miles, and seeing several other hunters, we returned to camp for a late lunch. After some warm soup, we met up with Jim and discussed our options. Initially, we decided to head off in different directions. That changed, however, as we kept reminding ourselves that every year we had found fresh bear sign nearby along some of the old clearcut trails that ultimately wound through very thick laurel patches and rock ledges of the game lands. Because Jim was already planning on posting in the area, AJ and I decided to continue our stalk-and-stop technique in a large circle around his location.

BLACK BEAR
First Award – 23 ³/₁₆
▼ ▼ ▼ ▼ ▼
ANDREW SEMAN, JR.

It was thick and tough to cover, especially without snow to aid visibility and quiet the movement. Neither of us really expected to get a shot but felt Jim had a good chance if we jumped anything. AJ and I mapped out how we would work the area, and where we could visually check each other's progress and realign as necessary. A clearing divided the area we were hunting, and Jim was posted nearby watching the clearing. After crossing the open area we planned on moving very slowly because at that point game would likely be pushed away from Jim.

After AJ and I visually checked each other's position in the clearing, AJ was to move in first and stop. Then I would move in and, alternately, we would work through the area. This area had been clearcut in our youth; the giant oaks that shaded the slopes were but a distant memory. Some areas were so thick we couldn't see even 20 feet, but we also figured game would be naturally funneled or concentrated into this area.

After waiting several minutes for AJ to move into position, I started into the thickest part of the old clearcut. After a short distance, I heard a faint snap. Almost immediately after, a shot followed, then another. At first I thought Jim had shot, but moments later I heard AJ indicate he had shot a bear. The shots had come from his .280 Sako.

I was no more than a hundred yards from him but could see no more than a few feet. As I worked toward him, I went about 20 feet before coming across the bear's bedding site. Then, when I saw where AJ had stopped, I realized that a few feet variation in any direction for either of us, and we would have never seen the bear.

The time was 3 p.m. as we gathered around AJ's trophy. We seemed to just keep saying, "Wow, that's a big bear!"

Being the first bear any of us had harvested, we figured it was just our inexperience that made the bear seem so impressive. After several attempts to move him, we guessed he was at least 400 or 500 pounds. The head was so massive it was difficult to lift it off the ground. We took several pictures and discussed what to do next.

After several unsuccessful attempts to move him, we lashed him to a pole to position him for field-dressing. Thankfully, several young hunters stopped by to lend a hand. After moving him to a nearby logging road, Jim arrived and we tied the pole to the back of his quad and pulled the bear to the clearing. After the problems we had moving him just to that

Photograph courtesy of Andrew Seman, Jr.

Andrew Seman, Jr., with his award-winning black bear taken in Fayette County, Pennsylvania, during the 2005 season. Seman's bear, which scores 23-3/16, ties for the largest hunter-taken black bear ever and received a First Place Award at the 26th Big Game Awards Program in Fort Worth, Texas.

point, we knew we didn't have enough manpower to get the bear up the last steep hill. With fresh snow starting to fall, we felt AJ's four-wheel-drive truck was not likely to make it. And, even if we had the truck there, we would never be able to lift the bear into the bed. Then we remembered the four-wheel-drive John Deere tractor with the front-end loader AJ had just purchased. After a brief discussion, it was agreed to be our only option.

Returning with the tractor, we were able to slide the bucket under the bear, lift it, drive it to the truck, and then transfer it into the truck bed. Though it was not easy, we had the bear out of the woods within six hours after it was taken.

After calling friends and family, some with more experience with bears than us, it soon became apparent that this was an exceptionally large bear. The taxidermist later supplied the following dimensions: the bear standing would have been 92 inches tall; from nose to tip of its tail, 83 inches; neck, 32 inches; girth, 70 inches. At the Game Commission's southwest regional office in Ligonier, we learned that bear had an estimated live weight of 733 pounds, which turned out to be the heaviest bear taken in during the 2005 season and the eighth heaviest ever recorded! We learned later that the bear was approximately 15 years old.

One of the officers at the check station asked how we got the bear. He mentioned that as bears become older and experienced, they're less likely to bolt from a drive, but like a mature buck, stay in heavy cover. As we reflected on

BLACK BEAR
First Award – 23 ³/₁₆
▼ ▼ ▼ ▼ ▼
ANDREW SEMAN, JR.

what the officer said, it further confirmed how fortunate it was that all the circumstances came together.

The bear moved with hardly a sound and headed crosswind away from me, then turned with the wind, apparently in an attempt to circle back around and bed down again in the thicket once I passed. This sneak, circle, and bed technique may have helped this bear survive for so many years. It was only one small sound from a broken twig that alerted AJ to the bear's presence.

Going back to the site the following day allowed us to reconstruct what happened. I attempted to walk the path the bear took while AJ determined where he had shot from — he even found his spent shell casings. It was so thick that the only shooting lanes were no more than several inches wide. AJ eventually found that the first shot hit and passed through a small tree. How he hit the bear on the second shot in such cover is amazing.

After the mandatory 60-day drying time, the skull was measured at the Game Commission's southwest regional office by B&C Official Measurer Michael J. Hardison, and witnessed by PA Game Commission Representatives and family. It was officially listed as having a length of 14-9/16 and a width of 8-10/16 for a total of 23-3/16 and will stand as the new state record black bear taken by a hunter.

AJ always mentioned that if he ever got a bear he would have a rug made from it. AJ's wife Susie and others instead convinced AJ that a bear this big and important should be preserved as a life-sized mount. Interestingly, the taxidermist AJ selected, Mike LaRosa, from Acme, took a bear in Fayette County in 1996 that had been the county's largest at 488 pounds and a score of 20-8/16.

AJ's father-in-law, Joe Habina, who took AJ on his first elk hunt to a favorite place in Idaho, has often been heard to say, "I'd rather be lucky than good." On that first hunt, on the first day, the first elk AJ saw was a large 6x7 bull that he took with one shot. The first bear he ever shot at turned out to be not just a new state record but one that tied for first among all black bears ever taken by a hunter. We could all use that kind of luck. ▲

Photograph by Bill Honza

TROPHY STATS

▼ ▼ ▼ ▼ ▼

Category
Black Bear

Score
22 $^{15}/_{16}$

Skull Length
13 $^{14}/_{16}$

Skull Width
9 $^{1}/_{16}$

Location
Monroe Co., Pennsylvania – 2004

Hunter
Jeremy Kresge

BLACK BEAR
Second Award – 22 15/16

▼ ▼ ▼ ▼ ▼ ▼ ▼ ▼ ▼

JEREMY KRESGE

On November 23, 2004, Jeremy Kresge and some hunting companions headed out into the Pennsylvania woods for a bear hunt. Little did they know the history they were about to make, on a hunt that would end with two of the 20 biggest bears taken in their state's history.

Jeremy, along with step-dad William Graver, Matthew Berger, Daniel Graver, Sean Daly, and Sean Patrick, got into their positions well before first light. Jeremy and William were on stand while the others began a big push.

15 Minutes

Jeremy patiently waited in his stand, watching an occasional whitetail doe, listening to surrounding sounds, and letting his thoughts wander. He had been there since first light, and it was now 4 p.m.

The daylong silence was finally broken when he heard a shot. It sounded like it came from his step-dad's stand. He would later find out that William had taken a gigantic bear. It would take its place among the best in the state, with an eye-popping score of 22-1/16 points!

Jeremy continued to scan the edges from his vantage point. They had been hunting a burned-over area, so parts of it were short and scrubby. Spots the fire had missed still had the dense laurel thickets remaining.

About 15 minutes after hearing those distant shots, Jeremy heard something headed his way. It continued to build up volume until it sounded like a Mack truck. Limbs were breaking and brush was rustling as the sound came closer. He peered in the direction of the sound until he saw its maker — a giant black bear, and it was headed toward him!

Jeremy knew instantly this was everything he had hoped for. He shouldered his .30-06 and fired one shot as the bruin moved within 30 yards of his stand. Soon, all was quiet.

In that moment, he had filled his bear tag and carved his name into history. This bear would soon officially become the third-largest black bear in state history, and the sixth-largest black bear ever recorded by B&C. In a 15-minute span, Jeremy and his father-in-law, William Graver, had taken two of the top 20 bears ever recorded in their state. It's a feat not likely to ever be duplicated. ▲

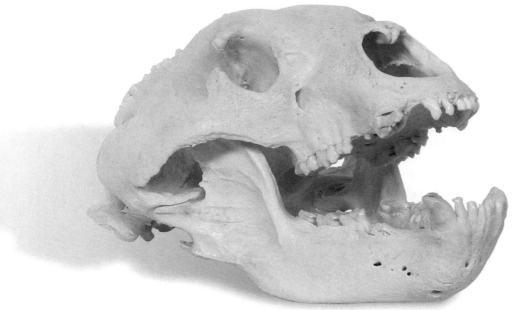

Photograph by Bill Honza

TROPHY STATS

▼ ▼ ▼ ▼ ▼

Category
Black Bear

Score
22 $^{11}/_{16}$

Skull Length
14 $^{3}/_{16}$

Skull Width
8 $^{8}/_{16}$

Location
Chippewa Co., Wisconsin – 2003

Hunter
Duane Helland

BLACK BEAR
Third Award (Tie) – 22¹¹/16

▼ ▼ ▼ ▼ ▼ ▼ ▼ ▼ ▼

DUANE HELLAND

The 2003 bear season turned out to be a very special one for me. When I received my 2003 bear permit, I immediately started to bait. Here in Wisconsin, you are allowed to put out 10 gallons of bait per day at each bait station. As the summer wore on, the sign of bears coming to the bait began to get heavier. Trails were forming, and the bait and ground were licked clean every night.

On two nights in particular there were two bears feeding in the clover. On the first night, I thought it must be a sow and cub. A couple of nights later, though, my dad Delbert and I got a closer look at the bigger bear as we were going out to bait. The same two bears were in the field. As we went along the field, they moved into the woods. When we got to the spot where they went in, to our surprise, there he stood only 15 yards inside the woods. He just stood there looking at us with beady little eyes. We could tell that he was a nice bear; he had a huge head and stood bow-legged, with his belly hanging way down.

After that night, all I could think of was getting a shot at that bear. Finally, opening day arrived. That day at work was the longest one ever. I planned on sitting near the bait site that evening. When I got home, my dad and two brothers, Dale and Delbert Jr., were waiting there. In the past, we had videotaped other hunts of ours in the same trees, so this year would be no different.

We got in the stand, and at about 4 p.m., a bear showed up. It wasn't the big one, but it was a shooter. He probably weighed about 250 pounds. As he got closer, I decided to shoot him. In this area, if you don't shoot a bear on opening weekend, you just might not get one. The bears seem to get wise after the first couple of days.

As the 250-pounder got closer, I had to turn a little bit to get a good shot. As I tried to move, he saw me and backed right out of there. I never got a shot.

It was about 20 minutes later when my brother saw a bear coming from the east. As it

Photograph by Jack Reneau

Duane Helland accepting his plaque and medal from Buck Buckner, Vice President and Chairman of the Big Game Records Committee.

came into the opening, we knew it was the big one we had seen during the summer. This bear walked right into the bait, turned, and sat down. He was facing away from me at 12 yards.

I pulled my bow back, took aim, and let the arrow fly. It hit right where I wanted — a perfect heart shot! He took off like a bullet, ran into a tree, got up again, went about 30 yards, and fell over.

When we walked over to the bear, we estimated him to weigh 400 pounds and be about 15 to 20 years old. His head was grey, and his teeth were rotted to almost nothing. There was very little hair on his hindquarters.

When we got him out of the woods and hung him up, he was eight feet from the top of his head to the bottom of his feet. He weighed out at 426 pounds and was 21 years old. My bear skull ranked number one in the state for a bow kill in Wisconsin.

I received the First Award trophy plaque for black bear at the 2003-2004 Pope and Young Club Convention in Springfield, Missouri. I also received the Big Game Award from the Wisconsin Buck and Bear Club. This black bear, which I also entered in Boone and Crockett Club's 26th North American Big Game Awards Program, was accepted as an entry on August 18, 2004. ▲

B&C Photo Archives

Three of four trophy owners for black bear were in attendance at the 26th Big Game Awards Program held in Fort Worth, Texas, in June 2007. They are pictured above during press day with their award-winning skulls – from left to right: Joseph T. Brandl (Third Place Award – tie), Andrew Seman, Jr. (First Place Award), and Duane Helland (Third Place Award – tie).

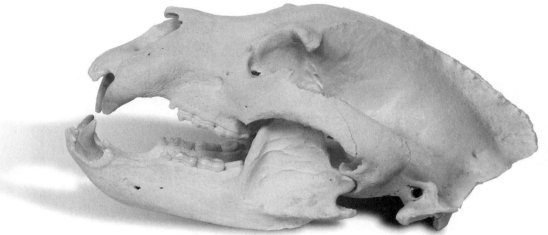

Photograph by Bill Honza

TROPHY STATS
▼ ▼ ▼ ▼ ▼

Category
Black Bear

Score
22 $^{11}/_{16}$

Skull Length
13 $^{15}/_{16}$

Skull Width
8 $^{12}/_{16}$

Location
Price Co., Wisconsin – 2006

Hunter
Joseph T. Brandl

BLACK BEAR
Third Award (Tie) – 22 ¹¹/16

▼ ▼ ▼ ▼ ▼ ▼ ▼ ▼ ▼

JOSEPH T. BRANDL

It was Sunday evening on September 17, 2006. After much anticipation, I had finally arrived at our hunting camp in Park Falls, Wisconsin, ready to go hunting the next morning. There I met up with my father, Tom Brandl, who had been there since the previous Wednesday. We talked for a while about the hunts they had been on in his time there and then decided to go to bed early.

The next day, Tom was up at 4 a.m. to go bait. He soon found out that a big bear had

The Race Is On

been there. Once he knew that, there was no reason to bait anymore. He rushed back to the A-frame cabin we were staying in and woke me up. "The big one has been there; we have to get ready to go."

We got the dogs loaded up, and then went to Donney Seigler's cabin and talked it over. At about 6 a.m., we all went to the bait site and let the dogs go before daybreak. They instantly set out at a good pace.

In the meantime, my brother Judd Brandl had arrived. We jumped on the four-wheeler and rode down the trail about a half mile and stopped. It seemed the dogs were barking steady. A few minutes later, the dogs came out of the woods and onto the trail. This time they weren't even barking.

Judd, Jim, and I decided to walk the dogs back in the woods and see if the bear had made a sudden turn. Just like that, the dogs were off and running.

Once they got moving again, Judd and I drove ahead on the four-wheeler for about a half mile. We stopped to listen and decided we were fairly close to the dogs. It sounded like the dogs were treeing the bear or may have stopped him on the ground.

I was leading, with Judd right behind. We were getting close when we realized the bear was not in a tree. We both spotted the bear at

Photograph by Jack Reneau

Joseph T. Brandl accepting his plaque and medal from Buck Buckner, Vice President and Chairman of the Big Game Records Committee.

Joseph T. Brandl with his award-winning black bear taken in Price County, Wisconsin, during the 2006 season. Brandl's bear, which scores 22-11/16, is tied for the second largest taken in Wisconsin and tied for a Third Place Award at the 26th Big Game Awards Program in Fort Worth, Texas.

the same time. I pulled my .308 to my shoulder as my brother yelled, "Shoot!"

I thought I had made a good shot, but I had missed completely! Now the race was on. We headed back to the truck. Just as we got there, the bear broke out onto the road, turned around, and went right back into the woods. Once again, we stopped the dogs and led them in the right direction.

At this point, I grabbed my gun and went in the woods following the dogs, knowing that wherever the dogs were is where the bear was going to be. When I first went back into the woods, I thought I was going to be very close. From that point on, every minute that went by the farther the bear and the dogs were from us.

A few hundred yards into the woods, I met up with John Treml and Mike Rydzewski. We continued on, following the dogs farther into the woods. We went another half mile when we stopped on the edge of the marsh. We looked and listened, and knew that we were a long way from the action. We also knew that dogs were not coming back in our direction.

We didn't want to go through the marsh, but that was our only option to track this bear. We committed to the chase and continued on, jumping over and crawling under trees. We then heard a loud yelp from one of the dogs. That definitely made us move faster! We later found out that it was my dad's dog, Boone, and that he had broken a rib, likely from the bear swatting him into a tree.

When we finally caught up to the dogs, we found Jeff Mader and my brother Judd already there. They were watching the bear for some time and were waiting for me.

BLACK BEAR
Third Award (Tie) – 22 $^{11}/_{16}$
▼ ▼ ▼ ▼ ▼
JOSEPH T. BRANDL

I knew what I had to do, but I was out of breath from running through the marsh. I continued to look all around for the bear. I came around a tree and saw that the dogs had him surrounded. I pulled up and shot but missed. I also missed a second shot. He didn't go far, as I think he was getting tired from running from the dogs. I walked closer to the marsh and there he was again. I pulled up for a third time, and thankfully the last shot connected at about 30 feet. He jumped between two fallen trees, ran a short distance, and landed next to a huge pine tree.

I ran up with my gun to my shoulder, but didn't need to shoot again. As I approached, I noticed that I had grazed his hide on his left side on the first shot.

It took some time for the group to get into the woods where we were. There were five of us there when I shot the bear — Judd Brandl, Mike Rydzewski, Jeff Mader, John Treml, and me. When we actually started dragging the bear out of the woods there were about 15 people! That was a good thing, considering we had 428 pounds of bear to carry. ▲

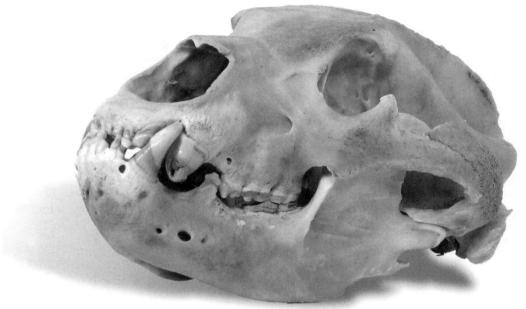

Photograph by Bill Honza

TROPHY STATS
▼ ▼ ▼ ▼ ▼

Category
Grizzly bear

Score
26 $^{13}/_{16}$

Skull Length
16 $^{5}/_{16}$

Skull Width
10 $^{8}/_{16}$

Location
Otter Creek, Alaska – 2001

Hunter
James C. Blanchard

GRIZZLY BEAR
First Award – 26¹³/₁₆

▼ ▼ ▼ ▼ ▼ ▼ ▼ ▼ ▼

James C. Blanchard

It was early March 2001 when I received an email from friend and outfitter Jerry Austin about an unexpected cancellation he had for a spring grizzly hunt. His operation, Austin's Alaskan Hunting Adventures, which I came to know while on several prior hunts out of St. Michael, has had great hunter success on grizzly bears, with many trophy-class animals to his credit. As the saying goes, this was an opportunity I couldn't refuse.

A Bear from Above

Within several days, I had made the necessary arrangements to arrive in St. Michael on April 17 for my third attempt for an elusive griz. While on the plane to Anchorage, I had plenty of time to reflect on past hunts and what this adventure could possibly bring. With the soothing hum of the jet engines and vivid memories of eating berries on a tundra-covered hillside while glassing for bears, there was a thought that I could not get out of my mind.

This day, ironically, marked the one-year anniversary of my wife's passing. With more than 21 days logged to date for grizzly with no success, I had a comforting premonition that my luck was about to change.

St. Michael is a small, native Eskimo community nestled along the shores of Norton Sound in the Bering Sea. As my plane touched down from the short flight from Unalakleet, I could see Jerry and his son Tony awaiting my arrival. After a warm greeting and a few hugs on the airstrip, it was off to the range to check my gun and unpack from what seemed like a never-ending journey from Chicago. Sleep wasn't a problem that night.

The plan was to get up early and leave St. Michael on snow machines to look for a specific bear Jerry had seen several times the previous fall. John Long, who had arrived in camp several days before me, would be the primary hunter. Jerry, Tony, guides John (J.D.) Richardson and

Photograph by Jack Reneau

James C. Blanchard accepting his plaque and medal from Buck Buckner, Vice President and Chairman of the Big Game Records Committee.

Glen (Shears) Shipton, native tracker Mathew Andrews, and I would complete the group.

By early afternoon the next day, we had found a set of fresh tracks; Jerry was convinced this was the big boar we were looking for. Because John had a limited time schedule, Jerry asked that I refrain from shooting if the bear happened to pass within range. I agreed and Jerry quickly headed off with John to follow the tracks.

While waiting with Glen and Tony, it wasn't long before we caught a glimpse of a grizzly moving 300 yards above us through the alder thickets. In what seemed like seconds, the bear suddenly popped out within 50 yards and stood broadside gazing at us, as if he knew I wouldn't shoot. Soon, the bear ambled off in the direction that John and Jerry had taken. In the blink of an eye, an opportunity of a lifetime on a large grizzly had come and gone.

As I stared at where the bear had stood just moments ago, my thoughts of bewilderment were soon interrupted by the report of John's rifle. Several shots later, we could hear the faint shouts of excitement — John had harvested a beautiful 9-foot blonde grizzly. After some high-fives and pictures, Jerry pulled me aside and thanked me for honoring his request. "Just wait, my friend; we'll find you an even bigger bear."

ADRENALIN FELT LIKE IT WAS POURING OUT OF MY SKIN. THE COMBINATION OF THE THICK ALDERS AND DEEP SNOW CREATED AN EERILY QUIET SURROUNDING. I COULD HEAR AND FEEL MY HEARTBEAT. THIS SILENCE WAS SHATTERED AS THE BEAR PAUSED TO ASSESS ITS DANGER. WITH EAR-PIERCING GROWLS, MOUTH FOAMING, AND TEETH SNAPPING, THE BEAR SLOWLY SWUNG AND ROLLED HIS ENORMOUS HEAD SIDE TO SIDE. THE PROBLEM WAS HIS HEAD WAS SO LARGE IT COVERED A MAJORITY OF HIS CHEST.

"Bigger bear; yeah, right," I thought as I went to sleep that night. Sure, I was very happy for John because he truly was one of the nicest people I've ever had the pleasure to share a hunting camp with. Selfishly, though, I knew that my grizzly jinx could have been over. This time, however, it just wasn't meant to be.

The next day was spent back in St. Michael as we prepped John's bear hide and reorganized for our next journey. As with all great bear guides, Jerry had a definite intuition on the area he wanted to hunt next. I was now the only hunter in camp, and the minutes were passing like hours.

Saturday's early-morning departure was marked with frigid cold, yet bright sunshine. As we raced across the ice-covered bay to shorten our ride to Klikitarik, the snow machines left a trail of swirling snow that glistened against the backdrop of the burning sun. Seals were sunning on the ice while various sea birds soared overhead. This barren and unforgiving land was alive and well.

The ride to Klikitarik was uneventful. We would travel a stretch and pull aside to glass for fresh tracks, only to find the landscape void of any sign that the big boars were coming out of hibernation. Once back on land, it seemed like there was a covey of ptarmigan in every opening and snowshoe hares in every thicket we passed. When the day was done, we had covered nearly 100 miles through some of the most beautiful tundra country I had ever seen.

GRIZZLY BEAR
First Award – 26 $^{13}/_{16}$
▼ ▼ ▼ ▼ ▼
JAMES C. BLANCHARD

We spent the night at a modest outpost camp near Klikitarik that Jerry keeps stocked with supplies for his hunting clients and emergencies. After a hot meal and a few hands of cards, it was off to sleep. The snowmobile ride was very strenuous, as much of the tundra at sea level had only scattered patches of snow. At times I thought it would have been easier to stay atop a bucking bronco, as snow machines and bumpy, frozen tundra don't go together very well.

Sunday, as we ate a quick breakfast, the enthusiasm in camp was noticeably high. The guides were confident that more bears would be out with each day that passed. Today we would again cover miles and miles of rough country, but our luck was about to change.

As we picked our way through the various creek drainages, each ridgetop would open up to an expansive series of new drainages on the other side. On one particular peak, we finally glassed the unmistakable tracks of a bear on a distant hillside. After a closer look, Tony soon spotted a big grizzly moving in our direction. Unfortunately, it turned out to be a mature sow with two cubs in tow. The bears worked their way into the creek bottom and up the hillside we were glassing from. To avoid a confrontation, we quickly backed off the ridge and worked our way to an adjacent drainage, Otter Creek.

It wasn't long before J.D. motioned to me that he had spotted another bear. By the expression on his face, it was obvious that whatever he was glassing surely had his attention. I quickly made it to his vantage point, but I only caught a flash of a dark object heading into a large alder thicket. In hindsight, it's probably a good thing I didn't get a good look at this bear.

After discussing possible strategies on how to best approach this animal, we decided to first snowshoe down to a set of tracks we could see below us and check them for size. Since the snow was over five feet deep in spots, walking without snowshoes would have been impossible. Glen, who had the longest legs, made it to the tracks first as the rest of the group anxiously awaited his assessment. Looking at J.D., he calmly said, "Good bear."

However, as I glanced away from Glen to say something to Jerry, I caught Glen out of the corner of my eye with his arms stretched wide, implying to J.D. that it was a "huge" bear instead. For good reason, he probably didn't want to put any extra pressure or fear in me for the inevitable stalk that awaited us.

Jerry, Tony, and Mathew stayed put as Glen, J.D., and I worked our way around the alders. After making a circle around the thicket, it became obvious the bear was still inside and in no hurry to leave his sanctuary.

Photograph courtesy of James C. Blanchard

James C. Blanchard is pictured above with his grizzly bear scoring 26-13/16 points. The award-winning bear was taken near Otter Creek, Alaska, in 2001.

With less than two hours of good daylight left and a major snowstorm fast approaching, Jerry offered a now-or-never plan that would at least give us a chance at harvesting this incredible animal. "Against my better judgment, I want the three of you to work your way back around to the high side of the alders. When you find a clean entry point, I want you to stay at arm's length and carefully, slowly ease in to see if you can spot where the bear is lying up. If the visibility is too low or something, or anything doesn't feel right, I want you to back out immediately. Mathew will stay here while Tony and I cover your back trail. Don't do anything stupid and get my hunter hurt."

With that said, we were off and running like three kids chasing down the ice cream truck. We found a clearing at the top of the thicket, and slowly eased in for a closer look. Visibility was nearly 80 yards, so we felt comfortable moving in a little deeper. Several steps later I spotted what appeared to be the torso of a massive bear, with its legs obviously buried in the deep snow. I whispered to J.D., "That's him, isn't it?"

"Yes, it is," he calmly replied.

"What do we do now?"

"Just wait," he said.

"With our scent blowing directly at him, he'll probably get up and run the opposite way, don't you think?" I inquired.

J.D. and Glen knew better. When that bear was good and ready, he would get up and investigate the three foreign objects that were pestering him for the last few hours. This was his territory, and I now know that we weren't welcome.

GRIZZLY BEAR
First Award – 26 13/16
▼ ▼ ▼ ▼ ▼
JAMES C. BLANCHARD

Glen mused, "When that bear gets up and sprints our way, don't turn and run. He'll stop before he reaches us to assess what we are, at which time you need to find an opening and place a good shot."

"Don't worry, Glen, I'm not running anywhere."

With that said, the bear promptly stood up and looked directly at us. Within seconds, the huge boar was in a full charge directly at our position. Even through the deep snow, the bear plowed his way effortlessly to us in mere seconds and closed the distance to 20 feet. I have never seen an animal cover ground as quickly as this irritated bear did that afternoon.

There is nothing on this earth that can duplicate the feeling of being charged by an angry grizzly. Adrenalin felt like it was pouring out of my skin. The combination of the thick alders and deep snow created an eerily quiet surrounding. I could hear and feel my heartbeat. This silence was shattered as the bear paused to assess its danger. With ear-piercing growls, mouth foaming, and teeth snapping, the bear slowly swung and rolled his enormous head side to side. The problem was his head was so large it covered a majority of his chest.

Finally, the bear moved his head far enough to one side to expose the center of his chest and front shoulder. Without hesitation, I fired my Winchester Model 70, .375 H&H, rolling the bear onto his back. The bear quickly regained his composure and started to angle away from us. My second shot hit true behind the left shoulder, knocking the bear down again in the deep snow. Still moving, I fired a final and fatal shot into the massive grizzly just below the hump.

After thousands of travel miles and endless hours of hiking, riding, glassing, and stalking, my dream of a trophy grizzly had finally come true. As I stood over my bear in absolute awe of its sheer size and beauty, I realized that all things happen for a reason.

I also realized that on this particular trip, I was hunting with my angel…. ▲

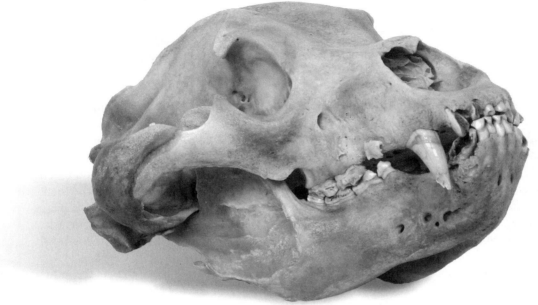

Photograph by Bill Honza

TROPHY STATS
▼ ▼ ▼ ▼ ▼

Category
Grizzly Bear

Score
26 $^5/_{16}$

Skull Length
16 $^2/_{16}$

Skull Width
10 $^3/_{16}$

Location
Klikitarik Bay, Alaska – 2004

Hunter
Dennis H. Dunn

GRIZZLY BEAR
Second Award – 26⁵/₁₆

▼ ▼ ▼ ▼ ▼ ▼ ▼ ▼ ▼

Dennis H. Dunn

As the monster bruin broke into a dead run right down the beach trail I was kneeling on, I knew instantly I was about to have a very close encounter. Having to think on your knees in front of a charging grizzly has a way of accelerating your thought processes. Indeed, things had happened so fast, I barely had time to nock an arrow and come to full draw. Because he was running so hard, his head was up, fully exposing his huge chest. I suspected one of two things was most likely to occur in the 4 a.m. half-light of the Alaskan spring night. Either he would not see the obstacle in his path and would run right over the top of me, or else he would see me at the last second and veer to the side.

If, in fact, he was going to run right over me, the decision I had to make was whether to bury the arrow in his chest at 20 yards or wait until he was a mere eight or ten feet away. It occurred to me that if he felt the sting of the arrow too soon, he might have time to put on the brakes and come to a stop just as he reached me. That might not be what I wanted.

On the other hand, if I waited to release the arrow until he was almost on top of me, it would probably take him 10 yards to slow down and reverse direction so he could come back and hold me accountable. If things happened that way, I'd at least have time to get my pepper spray out of its belt holster and defend myself.

Instead, only 7 yards away, the boar realized there was an obstacle in his path and veered to the side. As he whizzed by me at 12 feet, I swung with him and let the arrow fly. I saw the red-and-yellow fletching flash against his rib cage, and my instant impression was that I had made a perfect double-lung shot! However, I was in a hurry to nock another arrow in case the bear did put on the brakes, and while trying to do so in my crouching position I lost my balance, toppling over backwards. As the bear disappeared around a corner, I never got another look at him, but I felt certain he'd be dead soon.

In no time at all, my guide (who had been watching in horror from the top of the bluffs about 70 yards away) was at my side, hyperventilating and offering hearty congratulations. He hadn't seen where the arrow struck the bear, but he had heard the arrow hit the animal. High fives were exchanged, and a premature celebration was underway!

This all happened in May 2003 along the Bering seacoast of Norton Sound, south of Unalakleet. Eric Umphenour of Hunt Alaska (based in Fairbanks) was guiding me on a hunt during the annual herring-spawn that occurs along several miles of the coast's rocky beaches in late May, when the winter ice breaks up. The grizzlies, shortly after emerging from hibernation, come down from the mountains, cross the open tundra, and feed on the dead herring that get washed up into the cracks between the rocks during the spawn.

The "beaches" there are almost entirely composed of really big rocks, so they offer lots of ambush possibilities. Almost everywhere along that coastline are bluffs rising 40 to 50 feet above the high-water mark. At this time of year, so far north, the sun only dips slightly below the horizon for a few hours, and the bears are almost entirely nocturnal. We discovered quickly that we needed to be sleeping during the day and hunting at night.

When the winds were calm enough, the best method of hunting was to parallel the shoreline in a small boat with a quiet motor, some 700 to 800 yards offshore, and cruise slowly along — glassing as we went.

Halfway through the hunt, around 2:30 a.m., we spotted what looked to be a very large bear. He was visible against the yellow tundra coming down from the hills and, as soon as he hit the coast and turned south, we proceeded to get about a mile in front of him before going ashore. Once on the beach, I verified that the breeze was in my face, and I suggested to Eric that he get on top of the bluff and head north, more-or-less abreast of me. I figured his higher elevation would allow him to spot the bear before I could from the lower trail. This soon proved to be a mistake, because I had forgotten about the nightly offshore crosswind that was blowing from inland out over the water.

NOW DON'T ASK ME WHY THIS 8-FOOT GRIZZLY HAD CHOSEN THIS PRECISE MOMENT TO STOP, TURN, AND ADMIRE THE VIEW OUT OVER THE OCEAN, BUT AT THE SOUND OF MY GUIDE'S WARNING, THE BIG BOY STOOD UP ON HIS HIND LEGS, PEERED DOWN AT ME OVER THE TOP OF THE ROCK, AND REVEALED HIS HEAD, NECK, AND THE UPPER THIRD OF HIS CHEST.

We had progressed perhaps a half mile when I suddenly saw the bear approaching about 90 yards ahead. He was walking slowly down the very same path I was on. As I knelt with no cover nearby, I looked at Eric and realized he couldn't see the bear from his position some 70 yards away, and maybe 20 yards forward of me. I looked back at the bear just in time to see him sniffing the air and picking up my guide's scent. With that, he broke into a trot. Two seconds later, upon seeing Eric's profile against the sky, he accelerated to a dead run. Before I even had time to realize this boar was the biggest one I'd ever seen, the "moment of truth" was upon me.

I'd made my shot, and Eric and I had made "celebration footage" on our two video cameras. We then set out to follow the blood-trail.

But just 20 yards to the south of us, we found my arrow lying on the ground almost intact! The few tiny specks of blood on the shaft extended only a few inches above the broadhead. Obviously, the deep penetration I thought I'd gotten was a figment of my imagination!

More mysterious was the fact that the only parts of the arrow missing were the broadhead's three blades and the first inch of the ferrule that once held them in place. The latter looked as if someone had cut it cleanly in half with a hacksaw!

Aside from a few miniscule red spots, which we laboriously traced for maybe 100 yards, the blood trail was virtually nonexistent. It was painfully obvious the 9-foot-plus grizzly had escaped.

GRIZZLY BEAR
Second Award – 26 $^5/_{16}$

▼ ▼ ▼ ▼ ▼

DENNIS H. DUNN

Back in camp a few hours later, we hashed and rehashed all the evidence, and what follows is the only plausible explanation we could come up with:

As the bear charged past me at full tilt, his front legs were hyper-extending, forward-and-back, forward-and-back. I had put the 645-grain arrow right where I wanted to, yet just as it arrived at the ribcage the big knucklebone on the point of the elbow interposed itself and absorbed all the energy of the shot from my 70-pound Martin Cougar 2000. Then, as the bear continued his mad dash for the top of the bluff, he passed close by a large rock, and the protruding arrow broke at mid-ferrule — flush with the surface of the heavy bone in which it was embedded. Sometimes you just don't see what you think you see.

If a bear is walking, the point of the elbow never gets high enough, nor far enough back, to block broadside access to the lungs. At a full run, it did!

Three nights later, I found myself in an ambush situation similar to the first close encounter. From the boat, around 1 a.m., we spotted a good-sized boar traveling north along the "low road." Again, we managed to get ashore well ahead of him, and I chose for my ambush location a seven-foot-tall boulder situated just eight yards off his path, toward the water's edge. The offshore breeze could not give away our presence, and the north side of the big rock rose up almost vertically from the contiguous, three-foot-high rock I decided to sit on. I knew by the time the traveling bruin came into view he'd already be fully broadside to me.

Eric, wearing a camo headnet and gloves, hunkered down amongst the dark rocks a couple yards closer to the water so he could see better. The plan was that, when it came time to draw, he would tap me on the foot with the tip of his rifle barrel. Finally, the bear appeared, meandering down the beach trail in our direction, and I made ready. When I finally felt the silent contact with my boot, I drew back the three-blade Savora broadhead I've used with total confidence for 25 years and found myself thinking, "This is going to be a slam-dunk!"

But, after being anchored at full draw for several seconds, I wondered where the bear was. Suddenly, my right eye picked up a flicker of motion above and nearly behind me. As my eyes focused on a pair of ear tips visible just over the top of the tall rock, I heard Eric whisper, "He's up above you!"

Now don't ask me why this 8-foot grizzly had chosen this precise moment to stop, turn, and admire the view out over the ocean, but at the sound of my guide's warning, the big boy stood up on his hind legs, peered down at me over the top of the rock, and revealed his head, neck, and the upper third of his chest.

Since I was already at full draw, I only had to swing my bow-arm over and up, refine my aim, and let fly. Because he was facing me directly no more than seven or eight feet away, I

Dennis H. Dunn is pictured above with his award-winning grizzly bear scoring 26-5/16 inches. The bear, which was taken with a bow, was declared Pope and Young Club's new World's Record.

knew any dead-center shot was going to be quickly lethal.

Yet when the arrow flew, the sparks also flew, and my shaft sailed right over the animal's shoulder without even touching him! Instantly, he was down on all fours, running back the way he had come. What I had not taken into account, of course, was that the nock of my arrow, being anchored under my cheekbone a good two inches below my eye, was going to push the arrow on a slightly different path from the one my vision was tracing to the point of impact. The broadhead had just barely clipped the lip of the rock it needed to clear!

Frustrated beyond words, but more determined than ever, I vowed to return the following year.

On May 18, 2004, Eric and I, during our third night of hunting, located another big bear a couple miles to the south of us. He was coming our way, right along the edge of the water, scavenging for herring. We hurried on foot to meet him, not knowing how long he might remain in the open, but feeling certain he was too big and blocky to be a sow. After we had covered about a mile, he had closed to within 400 yards of us, and I realized I needed to choose a good ambush spot quickly.

My choice was a five-foot-high boulder right on the water's edge. When he finally stepped onto the big flat rock right next to the one I was hiding behind, I came to full draw. I had to wait about ten seconds until he gave me the broadside opportunity I was looking for. I knew the breeze was in my favor, and I was counting on the weak early-morning light to combine with his relatively poor eyesight to prevent him from picking up the motion of the top limb of my bow as I drew back.

GRIZZLY BEAR
Second Award – 26 $^5/_{16}$
▼ ▼ ▼ ▼ ▼
DENNIS H. DUNN

He seemed unaware of my presence a mere eight yards away.

At the moment I released the arrow, I was standing in a foot of sea-water, with the waves lapping around my calves. The Easton Aluminum Super Slam shaft sailed through both lungs and landed 25 yards beyond him among the rocks.

Four hours later, when it was finally light enough to distinguish stains of red on the dark stones of the beach, we began trailing and quickly found him about 175 yards away, lying on his back in a willow creek bottom. Perseverance and determination had paid off.

My griz, with few teeth left in his mouth, turned out to be the new World's Record with a bow! Three of his four canines were completely missing, long since broken off at the gum line and rotted away. His hide carried at least five healed scars from old bullet wounds, and the Alaska Fish & Game tooth-study report aged him at an amazing 28 years!

Even though the hide only squared a little over eight feet, the monster's skull turned out to be immense, which is all that matters for the record books. On October 4, 2004, my bear was accepted into the Boone and Crockett Club Records Porgram with a score of 26-5/16, at the time tying it for 28th place in the All-time records. It is currently tied for 32nd place.

On February 24, 2005, the skull was officially panel-measured by the Pope and Young Club at 26-3/16, making it P&Y's new World's Record.

Because I'd been unwilling to settle for a female without cubs, this bear, which finally completed the North American Super Slam for me, did not fall to my arrow until my seventh hunt for the species over the span of three years, eight months. I spent a total of 77 days in the field while my wife and mother worried themselves to death back at home! Don't let anyone tell you that hunting is not a family sport! ▲

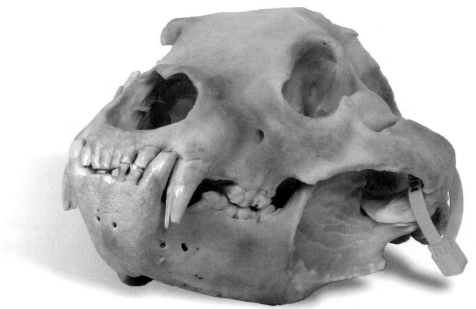

Photograph by Bill Honza

TROPHY STATS

▼ ▼ ▼ ▼ ▼

Category
Grizzly Bear

Score
26 $^4/_{16}$

Skull Length
16 $^4/_{16}$

Skull Width
10

Location
Radio Creek, Alaska – 2003

Hunter
Matthew J. Williams

GRIZZLY BEAR
Third Award – 26⁴/₁₆

▼ ▼ ▼ ▼ ▼ ▼ ▼ ▼ ▼

MATTHEW J. WILLIAMS

Matthew Williams traveled across most of the North American continent on his quest to take a trophy grizzly and to experience the wilds of Alaska. A Piper Cub delivered him to his hunt destination on Radio Creek, a tributary of the Yukon River.

After a raft trip, and two days after arriving, he found himself just about as close as he would ever like to be to a giant grizzly — eight yards! The bear was sleeping next to a moose gutpile, the bear's dinner and upcoming breakfast.

It was about 12 p.m. on September 18, 2003, when the .300 Remington Ultra-Mag. barked. Matt's many nights of anticipation leading up to the hunt had been replaced with an incredible trophy before him, one that would earn him a Third Place Award at B&C's 26th Big Game Awards Banquet. ▲

New World's Record

Photograph by Bill Honza

TROPHY STATS
▼ ▼ ▼ ▼ ▼

Category
Grizzly Bear

Score
27 $^{13}/_{16}$

Skull Length
17 $^{4}/_{16}$

Skull Width
10 $^{9}/_{16}$

Location
Lone Mt., Alaska – 1976

Hunter
Picked Up

Owner
Gordon E. Scott

GRIZZLY BEAR
Certificate of Merit – 27¹³/₁₆

▼ ▼ ▼ ▼ ▼ ▼ ▼ ▼ ▼

OWNER – GORDON E. SCOTT

A friend and I flew to the McGrath area in Alaska in April 1974 in a Piper Super Cub and hunted grizzly bear for more than three weeks. During our scouting we encountered scores of grizzly bears. We had covered a large area and settled on a couple of locations where large boar grizzlies were present. We concentrated our efforts at these places and were able to take two large grizzlies. One of these bears is listed in the current B&C records as being taken by Curtis C. Classen, McGrath, AK, 1974, and scoring 25-2/16. The other was taken by me, but never entered in the records.

As you see, this area produces big grizzlies. I went back in the spring of 1976 to hunt black bear. While on an extended hike out in the tundra bogs, I stumbled across the bones of an animal partially frozen in the moss and overflow ice. After a closer inspection, it turned out to be a grizzly bear.

I brought out the skull and a few assorted vertebrae. The skull was smelly but I knew it was big and worth the effort. It had meat and hide still somewhat present on the back part, and some of the teeth were missing.

I cleaned it up somewhat, and judged it to be a nice mature brown bear. From that point on, I stored it in my attic for many, many years.

A few years ago, I was remodeling the attic and came across the skull again and decided to score it. Much to my surprise, it was larger than I thought. After some research, I found that it was considered a grizzly for scoring purposes, according to B&C's boundary description. I had it officially measured and was amazed to learn that this was, in fact, the largest grizzly ever recorded. It was quite a find. ▲

Photograph by Bill Honza

TROPHY STATS

▼ ▼ ▼ ▼ ▼

Category
Alaska Brown Bear

Score
29 $^7/_{16}$

Skull Length
18 $^4/_{16}$

Skull Width
11 $^3/_{16}$

Location
Meshik River, Alaska – 2004

Hunter
Scott Weisenburger

ALASKA BROWN BEAR
First Award – 29⁷/₁₆

▼ ▼ ▼ ▼ ▼ ▼ ▼ ▼ ▼

SCOTT WEISENBURGER

In January 2004 I met Joe Klutch of Katmai Guide Service at the SCI Show in Reno. Before I knew it, I was signed up and on my way to Alaska for a brown bear hunt.

I flew from Phoenix to Seattle and on to Anchorage the first day, and on the following day flew from Anchorage to King Salmon. Joe and one of his guides met me at the airport, after which we did a little bit of final shopping and off we went to the other side of the airport where Joe kept his Cessna 185.

His pilot, Dale, flew me and a plane loaded full of gear about an hour and ten minutes farther out the Alaskan Peninsula to base camp on an old abandoned runway used during World War II. Here I met up with several other hunters that were all getting ready for opening day of spring bear season. The cook shack and dining room was a metal building that had been pulled in on a sled 60 years ago to accommodate the workers who were building this and many other runways strung along the Alaskan Peninsula. Although it was cold and windy outside, it was cozy warm inside.

Somehow, Joe had talked a former chef from a five-star restaurant to come out to this desolate place; therefore, the food was top notch. By the end of the day, all of the hunters had arrived. Over dinner, Joe began pairing up hunters, guides, and spike camps. His pilot would fly each group out to their spike camp in a Husky with big tundra tires.

After he had gone all the way around the table, he came back to me and said that I would be with a guide named Lance Kronberger, but he didn't mention what camp we were going to. After a little bit, I asked Lance where we were headed. He asked me if I was up for an adventure. With a little bit of trepidation, I asked what he had in mind. He said he knew a great place to go but we would have to backpack. I couldn't say no, so our plan was set.

The next day, I picked through all of my gear for just the essentials and loaded my rifle

Photograph courtesy of Scott Weisenburger

Scott Weisenburger and his guide Lance were dropped off at their spike camp in a Husky equipped with big tundra tires.

and pack in the Husky for another 40-minute flight to another abandoned runway where we would begin our adventure. We had about six miles to go from the valley floor along the base of the mountains. We had hip waders on and occasionally would sink almost to the top of them as we slipped into the marshy muskeg. The further we got back into where Lance wanted to go, the more bear tracks we began to see. I was becoming really excited.

We finally got to where we were going to camp but we had to cross a stream that was deeper than the last time Lance had been here. The stream was really moving, and the water was just inches from filling up my waders. I wasn't very excited about beginning my hunt with all wet gear, but luckily we made it across without mishap.

We set up our tent and made dinner. Spring had arrived in this area and the mosquitoes were so thick that we had to walk fast with our food to keep from being attacked. Even while walking, we had a cloud of mosquitoes swarming around us all the time. We finished eating, cleaned things up, and crawled into our little backpack tent to get ready for tomorrow — opening day!

> **MY FLASHLIGHT HAD DIED AT THE END OF THE SKINNING PROCESS AND SOMEHOW MY HEADLAMP HAD BEEN LEFT AT BASE CAMP WHEN I WAS LIGHTENING MY LOAD. I FOLLOWED LANCE PRETTY CLOSE TO AVOID SINKING IN TO MY WAIST ON THE WAY BACK. WITH THE SMELL OF BLOOD ALL OVER ME, EVERY TIME I HEARD A TWIG SNAP, MY HEAD TURNED EXPECTING SOMETHING TO COME OUT OF THE DARKNESS LOOKING FOR AN EASY DINNER.**

The next morning we were up and on our way. Lance led me several miles up and over two ridges. We finally climbed on top of a knob were we could watch 270 degrees. Lance said this would be our spot for several days watching for bears traversing the mountains. We would watch for them in the snow on the ridges to the left and right and on the ridge that our knob was part of. He said to look for their tracks that he called "zippers" and follow them from each end to find a small spot. We would then get our scopes out and determine if the bear would be worth stalking and if we felt we could get to it.

We saw about half a dozen bears that first day, but all were either not the size that we were looking for, or they were headed in a direction so that we would never be able to get to them. You could tell how powerful they were as they climbed straight up, over and back down the other side of these rugged mountains. They didn't miss a beat no matter what the terrain. With the beginning of the long days of summer, it was late when we began back to camp to start all over again tomorrow.

The next day we were back in the same spot on our knob glassing and glassing. Lance had told me to be prepared that bear hunting was 98% boredom and 2% sheer adrenalin rush. By the end of this day, I was beginning to understand what he was saying. Even though we were still seeing bears, I was starting to get tired of sitting in the same spot. Lance said that we would try our spot one more day and then maybe think about moving to a different knob.

ALASKA BROWN BEAR
First Award – 29 7/16
▼ ▼ ▼ ▼ ▼
SCOTT WEISENBURGER

Day three was to be a day to remember. After a couple of hours on our knob, Lance spotted a bear that he thought we should watch for a while. It came over the ridge to our left and began strolling down the mountain to the valley floor. Once it reached the valley floor, it appeared to be a nice-sized bear. Lance thought that this might be the bear for us.

Amazingly, it turned and began across the valley toward us. When it got to our side of the valley, it began up our ridge in the cut that our knob was next to. The intensity was growing. About halfway up the ridge, Lance unfortunately said this was not the bear that we were looking for. If it had been closer to the last day of the hunt, maybe, but not on the third day. I have to admit I was a little disappointed. This bear kept coming right toward us. It was almost as if it smelled us.

When it got to about 75 yards, out popped a little bear cub from the bushes. This little bear must have been there all day. The big bear began chasing this little bear. They got to about 60 yards and then the little bear took off down the ridge to the valley floor. We never really saw them come out on the valley floor. I was looking over my shoulder for hours after that, wondering what happened to that big bear.

After a while, we went back to glassing for bears. From my spot, I could see different ground than what Lance could see. At about 5 p.m., I saw a dark spot in the snow on the second knob along our ridge. I watched it for a long time and it finally moved a little. Sure enough it was a bear.

I called over to Lance to take a look and he thought that it might be a nice one. It was too far away to see very well and, because of its location on that knob, there was no way to get any closer. We were going to have to wait and see which way it went down that knob. We figured it was unlikely that it would come toward us on the ridge and if it went to the left or away from us, we would never be able to catch up with it. We would have to hope that it went down the ridge to the right.

We watched this bear for hours. It never looked up or cared about its surroundings. It just lay in its little patch of snow and occasionally rolled from side to side. At about 10 p.m., it got up and began to walk down the knob out of sight to the left. We thought that we were done, but a couple of minutes later it popped out of the brush on the right. The bear had gone down to the left and circled around the knob just below the top and come out on the side we needed.

Lance and I couldn't believe it! We packed up our gear and raced down the ridge toward the valley floor. It was more like a controlled slide because the terrain was so steep. About halfway to the bottom, we saw the bear come out on a rock outcropping and survey the valley floor. We only got a brief look, but he looked big. We estimated where we thought he would enter the valley floor and continued our slide to the floor.

Scott Weisenburger was hunting near Alaska's Meshik River in 2004 when he took this award-winning Alaska brown bear. The bear, which squared 10'8", has a final score of 29-7/16.

When we got to the bottom, we began making our way up the valley floor along the side of the ridge toward the spot we had identified. We came around a little protrusion in the ridge and there was a perfect bump in the valley that would make a great rest and keep us above the grass. We got everything ready and waited.

Lance said to let the bear come out in the opening about 25 yards or more so that he could get a good look and confirm that this was the bear for us. He said that if it was the bear, Lance wanted me to shoot until it dropped. Lance said if the bear turned in our direction, I had better shoot fast, or he was going to send some lead over as well. We were too far out in the middle of nowhere to have issues.

A couple minutes later he came out of the brush and Lance started checking him out. I had him in the sights of my .375 H&H Magnum that my father had given me for this hunt. When Lance said shoot, the lead started flying. Within minutes, I had my first bear — and a big brown bear at that! We walked toward him but stopped about 10 yards short until we knew he was done. We could tell that he was a giant! What an unbelievable day! Lance guessed he was more than 9 and maybe 10 feet!

We took a bunch of pictures and then began the daunting task of skinning a huge bear. It took us until about 3:30 a.m. to finish. I packed all of Lance's optics and gear in my bag along with the skull and then we stuffed the hide in Lance's pack. It was so heavy that we couldn't pick it up to get it on his back. We set it on a high spot and got Lance sitting on the ground in the pack. It took both of us to get him up off the ground.

ALASKA BROWN BEAR
First Award – 29⁷/₁₆

▼ ▼ ▼ ▼ ▼

SCOTT WEISENBURGER

Finally, we were headed back to camp with our trophy. My flashlight had died at the end of the skinning process and somehow my headlamp had been left at base camp when I was lightening my load. I followed Lance pretty close to avoid sinking in to my waist on the way back. With the smell of blood all over me, every time I heard a twig snap, my head turned expecting something to come out of the darkness looking for an easy dinner.

We went about two miles towards camp when Lance said he couldn't go any further. We still had a pretty large hill to go up and the other side was straight down. Even if I got it up the hill, going down the other side in the brush at night wasn't going to be any fun. We decided to leave it on a gravel bar along the stream in the middle of the valley and come back in the morning. Hopefully then we could get it over the ridge, or possibly find or make a landing strip long enough that Dale could fly in and get it. I hated leaving it behind but Lance didn't think anything would mess with it. This guy was clearly the king of the hill. He figured it would be left alone until the other animals knew it was dead. I reluctantly agreed, and we went back to camp for a little rest and a quick bite to eat.

First thing in the morning, we were back at it. We decided that we could make the gravel bar just long enough for the plane. Lance called him and directed him in on the radio that he carried, and we waited for his arrival. He made two passes over the strip to see if it was long enough and finally gave it a try. To give himself all that he could, he actually skimmed the water when he landed. We repositioned the plane, loaded him up, and off he went back to base camp. He would be back to get us that afternoon at our original drop point. We again had some work in front of us.

When we arrived at our pickup point and Dale flew in to get us, the first thing that he asked was if we had any idea how large the bear was? We knew that it was large but we had lost our tape measure somewhere along the way. Lance guessed that it would square 10 feet and that the skull would score 28 inches. Dale wouldn't tell us the actual size. He just grinned. He was going to make us wait.

He ferried us both back to base camp. I went first, and when I arrived some other hunters were out looking at three bear hides spread out on the ground. They said that mine was the largest and I couldn't believe it! When Lance got back, we laid a tape across the hide. We didn't even bother to pull it tight. It was an unbelievable 10'8"! I had never put any thought into the size of a bear hide, but a 10'8" bear has almost 40% more surface area then a 9' bear. We did the best we could to measure the skull but the calipers they had weren't large enough. We estimated it at 29 inches!

After the mandatory drying period, a B&C Official Measurer in Phoenix scored it at 29-7/16 inches — just amazing! Thanks Joe and Lance for the hunt of a lifetime! ▲

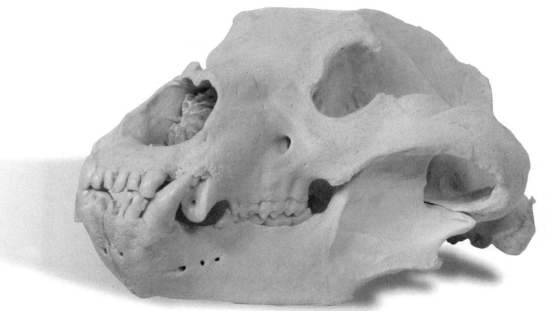

Photograph by Bill Honza

TROPHY STATS

▼ ▼ ▼ ▼ ▼

Category
Alaska Brown Bear

Score
29 5/16

Skull Length
17 13/16

Skull Width
11 8/16

Location
Bear Lake, Alaska – 2006

Hunter
James H. Doyle

ALASKA BROWN BEAR
Second Award – 29⁵/₁₆

▼ ▼ ▼ ▼ ▼ ▼ ▼ ▼ ▼

JAMES H. DOYLE

Jim Doyle boarded the Cessna 185 in Kenai, destined for his third Alaska brown bear hunt. It may have been his third hunt, but the excitement and anticipation never seemed to dim. The hum of the engine made it easy to let his mind drift toward hunts he had taken and hunts he still had before him. It was a four-hour flight, but with nice weather it quickly turned into a fantastic sight-seeing trip and chance to reflect.

11 Tough Hours

The next day he met his guide, Mike Shepard. They quickly sorted gear that they would be taking to spike camp, boarded another small aircraft, and then flew into camp.

After getting settled in, they took a quick hike on a nearby knoll to see what might be roaming about. They watched several bears until almost dark, then returned for an early supper.

The next morning, they grabbed their rifles and packboards and headed toward that same knoll. Jim had high hopes and expectations and had given strict orders to his guide that he should not be allowed to take any bear that would square less than 10 feet.

They walked up the valley for a closer look at their surroundings. At one point, they stopped for a breather. Mike pointed up to the top of a mountain and said, "Do you see that big rock up there?"

Jim looked for a moment, said he saw the rock, and then heard Mike say, "That rock moved!"

Mike didn't bother to ask if they should go and look at it; he simply said, "Let's go get that bear."

At times, their stalk forced them to break through snow up to their waists, but they were eventually able to get within 75 yards of their quarry. He was lying in the brush and had no

Photograph by Jack Reneau

James H. Doyle accepting his plaque and medal from Buck Buckner, Vice President and Chairman of the Big Game Records Committee.

Photograph courtesy of James H. Doyle

clue the two hunters were anywhere in the area. Two shots from Jim's .338, and his prize was down.

As they approached, Jim's fatigue and emotion came rushing to the surface. He couldn't even manage to lift the giant head of his trophy. It had been 11 tough hours from the time they had left camp until the bear was down. Jim's giant Alaska brown bear squared 11'3". ▲

James H. Doyle with his award-winning Alaska brown bear taken near Bear Lake, Alaska, during the 2006 season. Doyle's bear, which scores 29-5/16, received a Second Place Award at the 26th Big Game Awards Program Banquet in Fort Worth, Texas.

Moments in Measuring

Photograph Courtesy of Frederick J. King

A special measuring box was used by members of the 26th Awards Judges Panel, Larry Carey (left) and Warren St. Germaine (right), to get precise length measurements of skulls. The correct line of measurement for skull length is a straight line from the sagittal crest region at the rear of the skull to the frontal portion of the teeth. This line must be parallel to the surface on which the skull is resting. This means that the front of the skull may have to be elevated, as shown above, to achieve the proper measurement line.

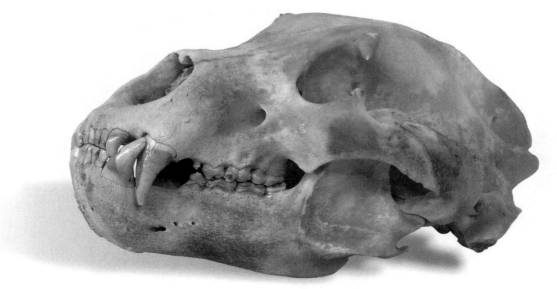

Photograph by Bill Honza

TROPHY STATS

▼ ▼ ▼ ▼ ▼

Category
Alaska Brown Bear

Score
29 $^3/_{16}$

Skull Length
18 $^2/_{16}$

Skull Width
11 $^1/_{16}$

Location
Lake Iliamna, Alaska – 2004

Hunter
Jack G. Brittingham

ALASKA BROWN BEAR
Third Award (Tie) – 29³/₁₆
▼ ▼ ▼ ▼ ▼ ▼ ▼ ▼ ▼

JACK G. BRITTINGHAM

The origin of this hunting story goes back more than two years to a previous trip I made to Alaska in search of a giant brown bear. On that trip, I hunted with my good friend Fred Sims on the south side of Iliamna Lake, where we spent more than a week chasing these impressive animals with archery equipment. During the course of the hunt, we saw five bears: a sow with one two-year-old cub, two respectable boars that would square in the high 8-foot or low 9-foot range, and one huge bear whose hide would easily exceed 10 feet square.

A Bear for the Ages

Having taken a great bear with Fred seven years ago, a trophy that squared 9 feet 5 inches, I was not interested in anything under an honest 10-footer. In Alaska, if you kill a bear, you may not hunt again for four years, so you want to be certain the bear you kill is worth the long wait. The bear Fred and I happened upon was just such a bear. We were able to watch him as he fed on the edge of a swamp splitting time between the swamp, and a large patch of alders where he would sometimes retreat and lay up. As these animals have an incredible sense of both smell and hearing, we wanted our conditions to be perfect before we attempted an approach. Unfortunately, the spring conditions two years ago were wonderful for camping, but they couldn't have been worse for sneaking within bow range of such a wary animal. Over the course of seven days, we saw the huge bear three times, and on the last day of my hunt, I decided to make an attempt to sneak in on him as he napped in the middle of the swamp.

As I came out of the timber on the edge of the swamp, I was able to range the bear at 220 yards, easy rifle range, but with my archery equipment, the hunt was just beginning. More than two hours later, after an agonizingly slow stalk through the 10-inch-deep water and foot-long dry grass protruding out of the marsh, I found myself 57 yards from the biggest brown bear I had ever seen!

But that is where things started to go badly for me. Up to that point, I had been able to keep the light breeze in my favor, and I had been able to keep a group of low, red-leafed bushes between me and the bear. Now, at 57 yards, I was out of cover. There was nothing between me and the bear except the dry marsh grass. The light breeze was not nearly strong enough to cover a crawling approach, so my only choice was to nock an arrow and sit in the water of the marsh, hoping that when the bear got up from his nap, he would offer a shot.

As the sun continued to descend toward the western sky and the breeze continued to dissipate until it was beginning to shift back and forth, the worst possible thing happened — a light breeze touched the back of my neck! I knew then it would only be a matter of seconds before the bear of my dreams would be aware of my presence. As I slowly counted down the seconds I thought it would take for the bear to react, his response was almost perfectly on cue. He didn't jump up and bolt out of the marshy meadow as I had suspected. Instead, he first lifted his huge nose to sniff the tainted air, then rose to his feet, and began to angle away from the danger he had detected.

I came to full draw, even though the bear was 60 yards away. If he turned broadside, I would have taken the shot because the conditions for such a shot were perfect. I was calm. The winds were calm. I knew the exact distance, and the animal I would be shooting at weighed more than 1,000 pounds and had a kill zone the size of a large pumpkin. All the days, weeks really, of practicing with my bow at distances to 130 yards had prepared me well for just this occasion. However, the bear did not cooperate. He kept angling away. The late-afternoon sun was shining through his long coat, which gave him a glowing appearance as he drifted out of sight.

The whole time, Fred was right next to me with his .338 Winchester Magnum. I could have easily reached over and grabbed the rifle to make what would have been a simple 75-yard shot at the largest bear I had ever seen, but the thought never crossed my mind. I was more than satisfied with the way the hunt had gone. To be able to hunt hard for seven days and end the hunt by spending more than three hours within 60 yards of such a magnificent beast was rewarding enough. We were able to capture the entire experience on video, and I have relived the hunt many times over the last two years.

> STILL INTENT UPON LOCATING HIS ATTACKER, HE CAME UP ON HIS HIND LEGS AND SCANNED THE AREA. HE REMINDED ME OF GODZILLA IN THE OLD BLACK-AND-WHITE MOVIE, SWATTING DOWN HELICOPTERS AS THEY FLEW BY!

As we made our way back to camp, I could not get the big bear out of my mind. I knew I would return, in hopes of getting another try at him or one just like him.

On May 10, 2004, with a very busy work schedule that would only allow another seven-day hunt, I returned to Alaska for another try. I felt that even a short bear hunt (most bear hunts are 10 to 14 days) was better than no hunt at all. Upon my arrival, the weather was once again less than ideal for hunting, with mild temperatures and almost no wind. We made our way to camp and got set up to see what we could locate in the area.

On the first morning, Erin Ames (Fred's assistant guide), Bill Sims (Fred's dad), my cameraman for the hunt, and I climbed a small hill to glass for bears. The first animal we saw was a black wolf moving across the hills to the east. Later in the morning, Erin spotted the first bears of the trip; a sow with two two-year-old cubs moved along the timber's edge almost a mile away. Even though they were too far to video, we enjoyed watching the cubs tussle and play as they romped along in the warm morning sun. The hunt was off to a good start.

On the next day, we spotted a large bear to the west of our location moving along the edge of the swamp. We took off immediately for the mile-long hike to see if we could catch him before he got back in the timber or alders. After a very fast approach, which brought us rapidly to within a quarter mile of where we had seen the bear, we were unable to locate him, and Fred thought it unwise to move any closer

ALASKA BROWN BEAR
Third Award (Tie) – 29³/₁₆

▼ ▼ ▼ ▼ ▼

JACK G. BRITTINGHAM

because our scent would surely spook him. We returned to our hill for more glassing, which proved uneventful for the balance of the day.

On the following day, we were up early with plans to hike several miles to the south. This would take us into country that we had yet to explore. By 9 a.m., we were on top of a hill overlooking a large swamp that ran parallel to the large, tree-lined creek that flowed down the center of the valley. The winds had picked up as a low-pressure system moved into that part of Alaska. I was thrilled with the change in the weather, though I knew it might mean much colder weather and even rain. We moved off the top of the hill and crawled in behind some alders to break the wind. We spent the morning and early afternoon hours glassing, eating lunch, and wishing for a sighting of a big bear.

Early in the afternoon, our wishes came true! A huge brown bear appeared down the hill and moved out into the marsh. With no delay, we were off the hill and making our way through the alders to intercept the bear. Almost an hour later, we found ourselves breaking out into the edge of the marsh. We moved along slowly, using the timber as cover, stopping periodically to glass ahead for some sign of the bear. We repeated this technique over the next several hundred yards, careful to keep moving into the wind in the direction the bear had been moving when last seen.

Suddenly, out of nowhere, the monstrous animal appeared in the marsh about 250 yards ahead! It happened so fast we were unsure if he had stepped out of the brush along the edge of the creek or whether he had simply stood up from a nap in the tall grass. We watched as he made his way across the marsh toward the timber's edge, all the while angling slightly away from us and into the wind. It was the perfect setup; he was unaware of our presence. We had the timber for cover, and he was not looking back as he worked his way across. As I watched his huge body moving along, I wondered if this may actually be the same bear from two years before. With a tail-end as big as a Volkswagen, I thought it unlikely that there would be two bears of such size in the same location.

We were able to close the distance to less than 140 yards as the bear edged close to the timber. Just as it looked as if he would disappear into the timber, he did something that would prove to be a fatal mistake. The giant beast had found a location suitable for his afternoon nap! Down he went like an oversized dog, first on his stomach, and then over on his back. Obviously the dominant bear in the area, he had very little to fear. Occasionally, he would raise his huge head and look around for any sign of danger, but it was a half-hearted effort.

Erin, Bill, and I wasted no time lining up the small dead spruce trees between us and the bear and began carefully making our way to within bow range. As we did so, the animal's

Photograph courtesy of Jack G. Brittingham

Jack G. Brittingham is pictured above with his bow-kill Alaska brown bear, which has been certified as a new World's Record Pope and Young Club trophy. The bear scores 29-3/16 inches.

immense size became more apparent. Now within 70 yards, I stopped long enough to set up my Sony video camera and tripod and train it on the bear before making my final stalk. I had already picked out the last dead spruce I could crawl to and zoomed in the lens so I would just barely be visible in the corner of the frame. Then, crouching over as low as we could, Erin and I began our final advance while Bill found a spot from which to video.

As we moved in, my biggest concern was that the bear might suddenly get up and move away just before we could get a shot. Not wanting to rush the stalk and make a mistake, I forced myself to slowly move forward toward the small dead spruce. Once there, I loosened my quiver and removed it from the bow, so that a gust of wind would not catch the fletchings on my arrows just as the shot went off, causing a bad hit. Next, I pulled out my Grizzly 50 AE, a very powerful pistol that suddenly looked inadequate, and laid it on the grass next to the quiver. After nocking an arrow, I ranged the bear at 34 yards. I was thrilled to have moved into position without being detected.

The wind was strong and right in my face. Knowing this could take some time, I tried to focus my attention completely on the bear so I would be ready in case he got up unexpectedly. As we waited, the huge beast rolled over on his back. I almost decided to take the shot at his vitals, but his massive forearm was too close to the area I wanted the arrow to penetrate. Switching positions, the bear then rolled onto his side with his back facing us. Once again, I evaluated the shot opportunity and quickly eliminated it because the chance of hitting only one lung was too great.

More time passed, and the huge animal rolled onto his stomach with his forelegs stretched out in front of him, exposing the heart and lung area completely. No shot opportunity could have been better! Almost immediately, I was coming to full draw with my 84-pound Bowtech Tech 29. As my arrow slid silently up the Trophy Ridge arrow rest, I glanced at the tiny Wasp Boss Bullet, fixed three-blade broadhead. With only a one-inch cutting diameter, I was aware my hit would need to be perfect. I settled my thumb into the back of my neck and allowed my eye to center itself in the peep sight. As I found my 30- and 40-yard pins, I used them to bracket the location behind the bear's shoulder where I wanted the arrow to go. I took extra care to make

ALASKA BROWN BEAR
Third Award (Tie) – 29³/₁₆
▼ ▼ ▼ ▼ ▼
JACK G. BRITTINGHAM

sure my shot would be perfect. I had no desire to have to follow this beast into the alders after a bad hit.

When everything looked just right, I carefully released the arrow and sent it on its way. It was a shot that I could tell would fly true the instant it left my bowstring! It struck the bear in the intended location just behind his left shoulder. He was on his feet in a flash. I was amazed at how fast he moved. He spun around looking for his assailant. Not seeing anything behind him, he was immediately back facing the other direction. The arrow had buried up to the fletchings in the bear's side.

Still intent upon locating his attacker, he came up on his hind legs and scanned the area. He reminded me of Godzilla in the old black-and-white movie, swatting down helicopters as they flew by! In just seconds, you could see the bear was feeling the effects of the razor-sharp blades that had severed the arteries above his heart. As his blood pressure began to rapidly drop, he sat down briefly on his haunches. He then got up and walked slowly into the edge of the timber where he went down and quickly expired. All of the events described above took place in less than two minutes, but it was an adrenaline-packed two minutes!

After he was down and motionless, we retreated for about fifteen minutes of "insurance time" before we approached the bear. On our way in, Erin and I spread apart about six yards distant to make sure that if we did get charged, we wouldn't both get bowled over. Our precautions proved to be unnecessary as the giant bruin was clearly down for good. What a magnificent beast he was!

After taking lots of photos, we began the tedious job of skinning the bear and preparing him for transport back to camp. This is a job of incredible difficulty with such a large hide. Erin, the youngest and strongest of our group, accomplished most of this task. Bill and I assisted by carrying the bear's skull, camera gear, and other essentials. After an extremely long, exciting, and arduous day, we made our way back to our camp very tired but extremely happy!

His size was unbelievable. His hide was in perfect condition. His teeth showed great wear, indicating a bear in excess of twenty years. His claws were white and very long, and his head was immense! My original guess was that he would have at least a 28-inch skull measurement, but it turned out I wasn't close. As he was sealed by Alaska Department of Fish and Game, he was measured at a green score of 29-5/16. At the 2005 Awards Banquet in Springfield, Missouri, the Pope and Young Club certified this magnificent animal as the new bowhunting World's Record, with a final score of 29-3/16. In June 2007, it tied for the Third Place Award at Boone and Crockett Club's 26th Big Game Awards Banquet in Fort Worth, Texas. Truly a bear for the ages. ▲

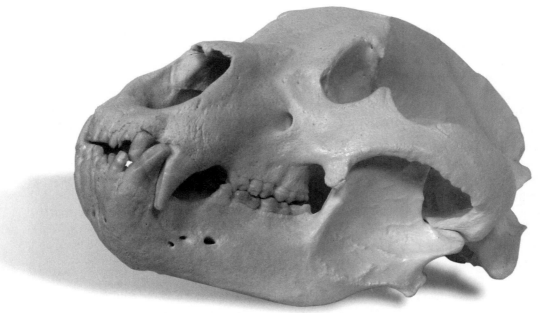

Photograph by Bill Honza

TROPHY STATS

▼ ▼ ▼ ▼ ▼

Category
Alaska Brown Bear

Score
29 $^3/_{16}$

Skull Length
17 $^8/_{16}$

Skull Width
11 $^{11}/_{16}$

Location
Buskin Lake, Alaska – 2004

Hunter
Gary Darrah

ALASKA BROWN BEAR
Third Award (Tie) – 29 3/16
▼ ▼ ▼ ▼ ▼ ▼ ▼ ▼ ▼

GARY DARRAH

Gary Darrah's search for a big Kodiak Island Alaska brown bear began more than ten years ago. During this stretch, he had passed up many good bears. He was determined to wait for just the right one or take none at all.

On the morning of November 17, 2004, Gary and his friend Dan Clark were out at first light near Buskin Lake. They were after a specific bear that they had been tracking the day before. It had snowed during the night, allowing for some excellent tracking opportunities — too good, in fact. They soon cut the tracks of two additional bears, and had to spend a fair

Photograph courtesy of Gary Darrah

Gary Darrah is pictured above with his Alaska brown bear scoring 29-3/16 points. The award-winning bear was taken near Buskin Lake, Alaska, in 2004. The bear squared out at 10' 2" and had a perfect dark brown hide with no rub spots.

Photograph by Jack Reneau

Gary Darrah accepting his plaque and medal from Buck Buckner, Vice President and Chairman of the Big Game Records Committee.

amount of time deciphering the information on the ground. They finally got back on the largest track, which took them through some thick alders.

Tracking an Alaska brown bear in thick cover can be tricky. After two hours of penetrating the alder, they heard the bear walking through the brush 50 yards ahead! They kept on and were just coming out of a small creek when Gary looked up and saw the bear only 20 feet from him!

At that point, everything became a blur to Gary. He whispered, "There he is."

A few minor expletives were whispered while Gary was trying to find a good shot; he had only the head at that point. The bear started to move, offering Gary an opening. He fired his .338 and struck the bear in the chest. The enraged bruin started spinning and slapping at the sting, literally spraying the hunters with snow. Gary sent another round behind the shoulder, which sent the bear down the hill at full speed. It drifted out of sight before coming to rest 150 yards away.

They waited for more than half an hour before moving in. The bear was finished, and so they set to work on getting their huge prize out of the bush. Two days later, silhouetted by moonlight, they finished the grueling packout. They used a kid's sled, which became so heavy that they had to rig harnesses and pull it out like a dogsled.

Gary Darrah's decade of patience had paid off. His bear squared out at 10' 2" and had a perfect dark brown hide with no rub spots. At 29-3/16 B&C, it was also one of the largest bears accepted into the Club's 26th Awards Program. ▲

B&C Photo Archives

The trophy owners recognized at the 26th Big Game Awards Program traveled from all over North America to attend. During the reception leading up to the awards presentation, trophy owners and guests have time to meet and swap stories about their hunting adventures. Pictured above are three hunters whose trophies received awards: James H. Doyle – Alaska brown bear, center; Daryl K. Schultz – Rocky Mountain goat, to his right; and Gary Darrah – Alaska brown bear, far right. They are joined by Schultz's father Ken, far left, and his brother Chris.

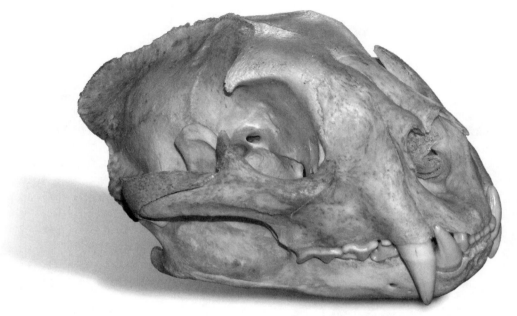

Photograph courtesy of Joseph Gore, Jr.

TROPHY STATS

▼ ▼ ▼ ▼ ▼

Category
Cougar

Score
16 $^2/_{16}$

Skull Length
9 $^8/_{16}$

Skull Width
6 $^{10}/_{16}$

Location
Sundance Lake, Alberta – 2005

Hunter
Joseph Gore, Jr.

COUGAR
First Award – 16²/₁₆
▼ ▼ ▼ ▼ ▼ ▼ ▼ ▼ ▼

JOSEPH GORE, JR.

Hunting, fishing, and a love of the outdoors have been in my blood ever since I was a boy. I spend most of my year preparing for the coming hunting season, right down to the last detail, including loading my own ammunition. My rifle of choice is chambered for the .270 Winchester, which the late Jack O'Connor — and I — happen to believe is the best cartridge ever made.

Usually my good friend and hunting partner Joe Smith (yes, that's his real name) joins me and my wife Debbie for a rigorous two weeks of hunting in the foothills of the Rocky Mountains near Hinton, Alberta. We usually head up around my birthday on the weekend near November 11. This year was no exception; however, it would be the first trip for my 13-year-old son, Zeb. He had been practicing all year with his compound bow, and both he and I felt that if opportunity knocked, he would be ready.

Photograph courtesy of Joseph Gore, Jr.

Joseph Gore, Jr. is pictured above with his award-winning cougar scoring 16-2/16 points. The tom was taken near Alberta's Sundance Lake in 2005. Joseph and his son Zeb had returned to their regular deer hunting area with a tag after seeing an overwhelming amount of cougar sign.

The season proved to be very successful; no one went home empty handed. This particular excursion also proved to be unsettling. I have spent the last 20 years or so hunting this area, but throughout this trip I had spotted cougar tracks, and while in my tree stand, I saw two cougars. For the remainder of the trip, we kept on alert and reviewed the precautions we would take for the duration of our stay. On my way home, I couldn't help but be intrigued by this ghost of the forest.

With a lull in my work load, I suggested to my son that we come back up and try our luck at cougar hunting. We packed up the camper Wednesday night and headed out early Thursday morning. We made one stop on the way for a few extra supplies and to purchase my good luck cougar tag that we thought we'd never use.

We arrived at our camp about 2 p.m. and were greeted by a 6-inch blanket of snow, making both the spruce and pine trees beautifully hypnotizing. It was like a Norman Rockwell painting. We set up camp, put out the generator and started up the heater. We headed out the door to see how much snow was on the cut line that headed into the lake near camp.

After walking about 300 yards, we crested the top of the hill from camp and stopped to take in the view. The cut line we were standing on ran north/south and was approximately 150 yards wide, accommodating a gas pipeline that was buried under it years before.

I had just leaned my .270 against a tree when we were startled by a deer bolting out from the bush. It looked like it was running for its life about 175 yards away down the hill on the same side as us. A few seconds later a second deer followed in full dash. It was like watching Mutual of Omaha's *Wild Kingdom* when the largest cougar I have ever seen appeared right on the heels of the second deer! The cougar pounced on the back of the deer, knocking it briefly to the ground before the deer bounced back up to make an escape.

I instinctively shouldered my rifle. Just before the cougar made the other side of the cut line I had him clearly in my sights. All I remember after that was the bang and then seeing the giant stumble and run for the forest. I remember hearing my son say, "You got him Dad. You got him!"

With my heart pounding I was trying to take in the entire situation when my son said, "Let's go get him."

I said, "Did you see the size of that thing? Let's go back to camp and get our winter gear, the quads, your gun, and change my underwear!"

We changed our clothes and set off to collect the tools we'd need to recover the cat.

Following the tracks from where the cougar knocked down the deer, it was easy to see where the cougar tumbled when my shot found home. To my shock, there was no blood and no hair to be found. Now the seriousness of our situation struck me. I was now tracking the largest cougar I had ever seen alive with my 13-year-old son, and the cat was wounded!

I told Zeb to wait while I went to look, but he would have no part of that. I could see arguing with him was fruitless, so we agreed we would go in back to back, guns at the ready, slow and steady. We followed the tracks for what seemed like eternity, looking under and up every tree.

After about 50 yards, I spotted what looked like the hind end of the cougar up ahead under a tree. I told my son to train his rifle on the cougar, telling him to "Aim small, miss small."

COUGAR
First Award – 16²/₁₆
▼ ▼ ▼ ▼ ▼
JOSEPH GORE, JR.

I took five steps on an angle, pointed my rifle at the cat, and followed the tracks toward where it fell. I looked through the scope every two or three steps to see if it was still breathing. I would have shot it again without hesitation. With one hand, I gave the cat a poke with my rifle barrel as I would a dead whitetail. To my relief, it was dead.

I told my son to safety and shoulder his rifle and to come up here immediately. I then leaned over, grabbed the rear paw and tried to pull the cat out, to no avail. When my son got there, I told him to grab a paw. To our surprise, we could barely move him. Setting our rifles against a tree, we got a serious grip and pulled the cat out. That's when the enormity of the cat's size began to hit us.

It was going to be dark soon. We took pictures and figured out how we were going to load the cat. The only way to lift it was like lifting an unconscious man, so, grabbing it from behind under the shoulders, I locked my arms and lifted him up. When I straightened my legs, the cat's giant head pressed against mine — cheek to cheek — and I dropped it like a hot rock!

My son asked, "Are you okay, Dad?"

"Just let me get my head around this for a second."

After a second attempt, we loaded the cat onto the quad and applied our good luck tag. We went inside for coffee and tried the cell phone. No service; no surprise. Reviewing the regulations, we noted that you must call in ASAP after harvesting a cat. This is so they can monitor the hunt to ensure the cats aren't over-harvested. So we had to head in.

Once we made the road, I made several phone calls. I called my wife, Fish & Wildlife, and my hunting partner to inform him we were coming home.

I had a long time to reflect about what had just happened — driving home in a snowstorm took me nine hours!

During the trip, I recalled the words of my late father. He used to tell me, "Go to bed boy; there is no such thing as monsters."

All I could think now was, "What else was Dad wrong about?"

The next day I woke early, called Fish & Wildlife, and told them I had a cat to bring in for verification. When I brought it in, they were amazed. They told me to get it weighed because it might be a record. I was astonished when it weighed in at 225-1/2 lbs., and that it probably lost weight being frozen overnight. We were also shocked to learn that it was 96-3/4 inches from nose to tail.

When I brought it to Bob Wilson, my taxidermist who is familiar with African lions, he told me it was the size of a lioness and must be one of the biggest cougars on record. It wasn't until a few months later, after the drying time was over, that we found out just how big it really is. ▲

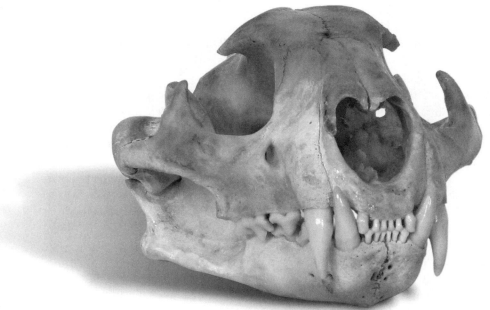

Photograph by Bill Honza

TROPHY STATS

▼ ▼ ▼ ▼ ▼

Category
Cougar

Score
15 $^6/_{16}$

Skull Length
9

Skull Width
6 $^6/_{16}$

Location
Archuleta Co., Colorado – 2004

Hunter
Dick Ray

COUGAR
Second Award (Tie) – 15⁶/₁₆

▼ ▼ ▼ ▼ ▼ ▼ ▼ ▼ ▼

DICK RAY

He glared at us with golden green eyes that danced with contempt. He had no use for those of us beneath his tree, and we knew it. He was huge by any standard, but I had no need, no wish, no desire to take his life. The day had begun with only the hope of finding a lion track that the hounds could trail, and perhaps, catch and release.

The day prior, an outfitter friend, Mark Davies, of Grand Junction, Colorado, had arrived at our place near Pagosa Springs, Colorado. Mark had wanted to take a pair of our hounds that might replace a couple of dogs

A Big Lion, Like Gold, Is Where You Find It

in his pack of lion dogs. Well, a little snow was predicted to fall that night, so my son Mike and I encouraged Mark to stay over and hunt with us the next day. More than half the time, predicted snow fails to materialize, but when we looked out at 4 a.m., sure enough, about one and a half inches had fallen.

It was February 25th, and that late in winter, such a small amount of snow usually melts by 9 or 10 a.m. But if you can find a track early, sometimes you can get a lion treed before the track and scent vanishes.

We left with high hopes, invigorated by the cold, crisp, clear morning and knowing that we had as good a chance as anyone to find a lion track that day. We knew that some of the numerous other hunters in the area were sure to be out and about as well. The quota for this area was almost full, with only one lion left to be harvested. With so many hunters out, that would almost surely happen,closing the season by sundown.

Mike and I chose to try Devil Mountain because we had seen sign of a big lion there about ten days earlier. Mike made his way up a drainage, while I went up another a few miles west. I found the track of a female lion right away and released my three dogs on it. The snow was already melting, for the steep slopes were composed of black shale that held warmth from the day before. The dogs were able to trail up and onto a ridge for nearly a mile before the sun took the track and its scent away from them. They weren't going to make any progress and didn't, as I climbed up to them. Catching and leashing them, I headed back.

I went to see if I could find Mike, knowing that our trailing conditions and time were passing fast. Mike had come back down his mountain, and we got together. He had a story. He had found a big lion's track up higher, where there was a little more snow. If we hurried, and were lucky, the dogs might still be able to work it.

It took us about an hour to get up to the track. That which had been a big, beautiful

Dick Ray, right, and his son, Mike, are pictured above with Dick's award-winning cougar. The tom was taken in Archuleta County, Colorado, in February of 2004.

fresh track at daylight was now a pathetic half-melted, barely recognizable line threading under old-growth Ponderosa pines.

Mark took a long look and said, "It's big, but most hunters would say that it's too melted out to work."

I said, "Mark, we would agree, but let's see what the hounds say."

We released all six dogs, and they took the track onward. And on they went, over a ridge and out of hearing. Now you always hope that a lion has a fresh kill just over the next ridge and that the dogs will tree him not far from the kill. It happens sometimes, but not that day. As we climbed and crested the ridge, we could again hear them in the distance, trailing; then, out of hearing again. A few steep, slick shale slopes more, and then we could hear the dogs bark treed.

As we walked up to the tree, he appeared the same as every lion I had ever seen — splendid, noble, and a word that is overused but should be reserved for the truly special — awesome. We gazed up at him, and he glared back. Both Mark and Mike urged me to take the lion. I had never killed a lion in Colorado, and had never planned to. In 1985, Mike and I treed a lion in New Mexico, which I took with my Bear take-down bow. I had wanted to take that lion. It scored 15-8/16 and was the New Mexico state record for 11 years. I didn't need another lion.

COUGAR
Second Award (Tie) – 15 6/16
▼ ▼ ▼ ▼ ▼
DICK RAY

Mike and I have enjoyed our years of work guiding lion hunters. The first Boone and Crockett lion that I ever saw was the one Father Anderson Bakewell, a Catholic priest, took with me in 1978. Mike's first lion was a Boone and Crockett that he took alone in 1982, just out of high school. How could I justify taking another lion of this class?

Suddenly, it became very personal to me. To be sure, the novice may kill without question, having not done it before — he has not experienced the pondering and twinge of remorse that accompanies the still, lifeless form that the act of killing produces. Why we kill is a mystery, outranked only by the mystery of death itself.

Once again, Mike said, "You may as well take him. If the quota doesn't fill today, someone else will kill him on the next snow. Besides, at your age, this might be the last really huge lion that you ever see."

"True," I thought. "I don't have a gun," I said.

Mike handed me his .44 from his backpack. I questioned my conscience and wondered if it would be enough to immortalize this creature with humble respect and a life-size mount? And then, at the shot, he fell from the tree, dead.

As I looked at his splendid form, I wondered, "What stories could this lion have told?" He was about seven years old. Being an obligate carnivore, he had to kill to survive, and at a rate of about a deer or an elk a week, he would have made several hundred kills.

We packed out his hide and his meat in our backpacks and led the dogs back across the canyons and down the mountain. As we walked, I remembered Ray Bailey's Boone and Crockett lion taken with us in 1986. It wore a collar that had been placed on it five years earlier west of Grand Junction, Colorado. We took the lion about 300 miles south of there in northern New Mexico. It made me wonder, who is this lion? Where did he come from? Has anyone ever laid eyes on him before? Does he have a brother out there? And then I thought, a lion is what we would all like to be — a true free spirit. He goes where he wants, kills when he's hungry, and doesn't pay taxes.

My last thought before I came to peace with myself was that I hoped that he had left many sons behind, for all living things will die, and be replaced by their own kind. It is the nature of things. ▲

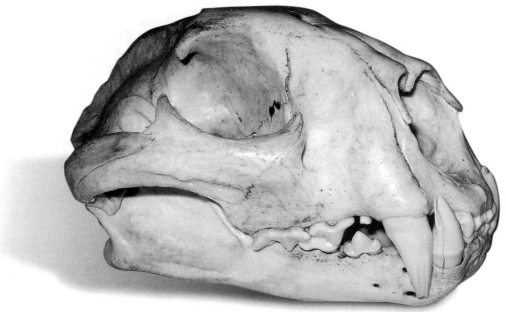

TROPHY STATS

▼ ▼ ▼ ▼ ▼

Category
Cougar

Score
15 $^6/_{16}$

Skull Length
9 $^1/_{16}$

Skull Width
6 $^5/_{16}$

Location
Jackfish Lake, Alberta – 2003

Hunter
Darryl L. Kublik

Darryl L. Kublik accepting his plaque and medal from Buck Buckner, Vice President and Chairman of the Big Game Records Committee.

COUGAR
Second Award (Tie) – 15⁶/₁₆
▼ ▼ ▼ ▼ ▼ ▼ ▼ ▼

DARRYL L. KUBLIK

For years I had heard about cougar hunting and had spoken to a lot of hunters about it at Alberta Bowhunters Association banquets. I was unsure if I wanted to take a cougar with dogs, but after talking to numerous hunters and houndsmen, I learned of their passion for the hunt, the animal, the chase, and the time spent with the dogs. I decided from all my previous discussions that I would book a trip with Ted Hansen, who used dogs to hunt cougars.

What an Adventure!

I was driving from Edmonton to Vermilion in early January 2003 for an annual Vermilion River Archers Bunny Hunt when I received a call from Ted. He told me that he had been hunting with a client for a few days, but that the client had to return home that night. Ted asked if I could meet him the next day so we could start hunting.

I replied, "I'll be there."

For three days we hunted, with no luck other than one cougar we treed but lost. Due to the warm temperatures and lack of snow, we decided to end the hunt and hope for new snow. I learned a lot in those three days about tracks, cougar scent posts, feeding the dogs, running the dogs, getting to know the dogs, and the terrain and travel corridors of the cougars. It was all amazing.

About a week later, we tried again. There had been a little snow during the past week, so we were hoping for good things. We drove about 150 kilometers of roads and found a couple of small cougar tracks. We found one track we knew was fresh, so we took the quads and blocked in the track. The dogs were released, and we could tell from the baying that followed that they were in hot pursuit.

At one point, we were on a cut line and could hear the dogs baying and coming directly

Photograph courtesy of Darryl L. Kublik

After talking with numerous houndsmen, Darryl L. Kublik learned of their passion for hunting cougars with dogs and decided to book a hunt of his own.

Darryl L. Kublik is pictured above with his award-winning cougar scoring 15-6/16 points. Kublik was hunting near Jackfish Lake in Alberta when he took this tom during the 2003 season. He placed a perfect shot with his bow to bring down the cougar.

toward us. We thought the cat might actually come out on top of us. As it was, the cougar crossed the cut line 200 yards below us, and we never saw him.

We followed the dogs again and they soon had the cat treed. After all of our efforts, we could now see the tom about 50 feet up a large spruce tree.

We tied the dogs up and I was now trying to figure out how I could make the best possible shot. There was a hole through the branches about the size of a pie plate into the chest area. I told Ted that I was not comfortable with shooting through a hole that size. I was used to shooting at antelope and mule deer on the open prairies. Ted advised that the only other option was to push the cougar higher up the tree, but that didn't seem to be much of an option. Instead, I took my time, carefully aimed, and shot the cougar through the chest. The cougar took two lunges up the tree and let go. The arrow did its job, and the cougar was dead before it came to rest on the ground.

Once the cougar was on the ground, the dogs were heavily rewarded. I was amazed at the sight of the big tom; he weighed 180 pounds and was nearly eight feet from the nose to the tip of the tail.

We met up with some friends that night and shared the story and skinned and prepared the hide. I also took the cougar meat, and we gave some to the local Fish and Game Association wild game dinner organizers.

The whole hunt, camaraderie, learning about the dogs, and the scenery

COUGAR
Second Award (Tie) – 15⁶/₁₆
▼ ▼ ▼ ▼ ▼
DARRYL L. KUBLIK

were something I will never forget. I had a very good friend and hunting partner of mine, Ryk Visscher, officially score the cougar skull. Ryk told me that my cougar would be the sixth-largest cougar shot with a bow in Alberta. Soon after that I called Ted Hansen, and told him Ryk had measured the skull. I asked Ted if a score of 15 B&C is big for a cougar, and he said not only is it huge but that it would be a Boone and Crockett trophy. Ted asked if my skull scored 15.

"No. It's 15-6/16!" Ted was ecstatic.

Before this hunt began, I just wanted to hunt a cougar and have a nice representative mount. When I received the Alberta Bowhunters Association's Gold Award for Cougar, I was honored. Now, due to the size of this cougar, the story keeps going.

In 2005, I attended the Pope and Young Club's 24th Biennium Convention and Awards Banquet in Springfield, Missouri. I received the bronze plaque for my cougar. In 2007, I was honored by the Boone and Crockett Club in Fort Worth, Texas. There I received the Second Award (tie) at the Club's 26th Awards Program and Banquet. It's all been quite a thrill. ▲

Photograph by Bill Honza

TROPHY STATS

▼ ▼ ▼ ▼ ▼

Category
American Elk – Typical Antlers

Score
412 $^7/_8$

Length of Main Beam
Right: 54 $^7/_8$ Left: 54 $^4/_8$

**Circumference Between
First and Second Points**
Right: 9 $^7/_8$ Left: 10 $^4/_8$

Number of Points
Right: 6   Left: 6

Inside Spread
53 $^5/_8$

Location
Utah Co., Utah – 2006

Hunter
Doug Degelbeck

AMERICAN ELK
TYPICAL ANTLERS
First Award – 412 ⁷/₈

▼ ▼ ▼ ▼ ▼ ▼ ▼ ▼ ▼

DOUG DEGELBECK

My story began in the summer of 2006 when my wife, two boys, and I stopped by the Mule Deer Foundation banquet held in Midway, Utah. I had heard that they were auctioning off a muzzleloader Wasatch bull elk tag, and it piqued my interest. I purchased a dinner-for-four package, which included $100 worth of raffle tickets. Call me lucky, but I walked out with three guns, a bow, and the coveted Wasatch tag!

I was stoked about the upcoming hunt and couldn't wait to start scouting. I have to give credit to my wife and family because I dragged them up to the mountains every weekend we could manage from July to the week before the hunt to see if I could find the bull I wanted. Each week we went, I would video 10 to 15 bulls and go home and try to score them from the video.

The Degelbeck Elk Experience

The muzzleloader hunt was to open after the rifle hunt, and my dad, brothers, and sons wanted to be up there to see what was going on in my area. Opening morning of the rifle hunt seemed to be slow for those with permits, but we still saw 15 mature bulls and very few hunters, which made me all the more excited.

My dad and two brothers, Mike and Greg, wanted to be there to support me and help if I were to get one. The day before the opening, we set out with food, supplies and hopes for the big bull. I was planning on hunting the entire season, if necessary. On the other hand, I wanted to get a big one quickly because my wife was expecting our third son any day.

Opening morning came and my older brother Mike and I headed up a ridge where we had seen a lot of big bulls. We were able to get right where we wanted to be as the sun broke over the mountain.

Photograph by Jack Reneau

Doug Degelbeck accepting his plaque and medal from Buck Buckner, Vice President and Chairman of the Big Game Records Committee.

Photograph courtesy of Doug Degelbeck

Doug Degelbeck and his son Easton are pictured above with Degelbeck's typical American elk scoring 412-7/8 points. The award-winning bull was taken in Utah County, Utah, in 2006. The bull, which was taken with a muzzleloader, is the new Utah state record.

At first light, we had a five-point bull within shooting distance. I passed it up because I knew there were bigger bulls in the area. We then spotted a big six-point bull with his harem of cows in the head of a canyon. We took off hiking but never saw this herd again, or anything else for that matter.

We hiked out in the dark, getting back to our trailer about 9 p.m. In the meantime, my dad had gone home to take care of his mink ranch and returned with my other son Easton, who is six. He was promised he could come the second day to hunt. My brothers went home because they had to work.

I was very discouraged. We watched a couple of hunting videos in the trailer that night and commented on how they made it look so easy. We talked about our strategy for the next day and decided my dad, Easton, and I would try a new area.

The next morning we hopped in the truck to go around the backside of the spot we had hunted the day before. From the road we spotted a nice 6x6 with ten cows and two or three smaller bulls. We knew we needed to get closer. We started driving up a small side road to

BOONE AND CROCKETT CLUB'S

get closer, but it soon dead-ended. We decided to hike across several ravines to get to the elk.

AMERICAN ELK TYPICAL ANTLERS
First Award – 412 7/8
▼ ▼ ▼ ▼ ▼
DOUG DEGELBECK

At this point, we split up. My dad went high, and Easton and I went low and moved slowly toward the elk. We had gone a short distance when several bulls started bugling back and forth. The brush was thick, and we were having a hard time staying quiet as we moved. Easton was full of quirky smiles as the elk bugled back and forth. We kept moving slowly toward the bugling when I heard a branch break on the hillside above me. I knew my dad was in the area, so Easton and I stopped to see what was breaking the branches.

All of the sudden, I saw this huge rack coming through the quaking aspen, and I told Easton not to move or even breathe loudly. The monster bull came running down the hill about 220 yards from us and then stopped to look back up the hill. I thought perhaps my dad had scared it down.

His pause gave me five seconds to take the freehand shot, which connected perfectly on this majestic animal. After the smoke cleared and I reloaded, I looked and the bull was gone. We had just stepped forward when the bull turned and came back down the hill. I could see from his reaction that I had hit him well. Within seconds, he put his head down and was on the ground. My boy and I gave each other big hugs.

Easton said, "Nice shot, Dad!" He was my good luck that day.

We sat down for a minute to regain our composure and then tromped through the brush to this amazing animal. I could not believe how big he was. I yelled out for my dad to come see. As he approached us and saw the huge rack on this six-point bull, the look on his face said it all. He gave me a big hug and said, "Good job! That's a monster, bud. What now?"

It was all the two of us could do to turn the elk over so we could field dress the bull. We then headed down to get some help. I knew he was a big one. I also knew my wife would be happy that I was done in only two days!

I had no idea the attention this bull would receive. A good friend of our family, John Gray, came over to score him for me. As he told me what he thought, I could not believe that I had killed an animal of that size. After the official 60-day drying period, the actual score was 412-7/8, which is the new World's Record muzzleloader typical American elk.

In retrospect, I know I was just in the right place at the right time. ▲

Photograph by Bill Honza

TROPHY STATS
▼ ▼ ▼ ▼ ▼

Category
American Elk – Typical Antlers

Score
410 $^5/_8$

Length of Main Beam
Right: 63 $^1/_8$ Left: 66 $^3/_8$

**Circumference Between
First and Second Points**
Right: 8 $^3/_8$ Left: 8 $^2/_8$

Number of Points
Right: 6   Left: 6

Inside Spread
39 $^7/_8$

Location
Gila Co., Arizona – 2003

Hunter
Dan J. Agnew

AMERICAN ELK
TYPICAL ANTLERS
Second Award – 410⁵/₈

▼ ▼ ▼ ▼ ▼ ▼ ▼ ▼ ▼

DAN J. AGNEW

I had spent nine days walking up and down the steep hills of the San Carlos Indian Reservation at an altitude of 6,000 feet, all in the mid-September heat of south-central Arizona. In that time, I had lifted my binoculars a hundred times and had seen dozens of great bulls, but not the one I was looking for.

I was completely exhausted, and decided to take the next day off and make the three-hour drive to Phoenix and spend a day visiting my daughter. This day off turned out to be fortuitous.

Photograph courtesy of Dan J. Agnew

Dan J. Agnew is pictured above with his typical American elk scoring 410-5/8 points. The award-winning bull was taken in Gila County, Arizona. At 66-3/8 inches, this tremendous bull has the distinction of having the longest main beam of any elk in the Boone and Crockett Club's records books.

Photograph by Jack Reneau

Dan J. Agnew accepting his plaque and medal from Buck Buckner, Vice President and Chairman of the Big Game Records Committee.

On my day off, my guide, Homer Stevens, decided to investigate and try a "new" area in the reservation's Dry Lake Unit that we had not hunted since my arrival. Homer took his brother, Tim, who also had a tribal-member tag, with him that morning and found him a great 8x7 that Tim took with a bow. When I arrived back in camp that night, Homer said, "We saw lots of cows, and I think we've got a great shot at finding a big bull tomorrow."

The 4 a.m. alarm came early, but I was reinvigorated and eager to get back to hunting. At around 7:30 a.m., we heard the low growl and grunt of a bull that sounded like he was worth checking out. He had cows with him, and it was obvious he was on the move. We had to keep moving because Homer wanted to get in front of the bull and intercept him before the elk headed into the dense cover of a known bedding area.

Heavy with sweat and out of breath because of the race we'd run to get in front of the bull, we froze as we saw the bull and several cows come out of the brush and cross a road only 35 yards in front of us. What a monster 6x6; his main beams were incredible!

I passed on a shot because we were getting good video footage of the bull. Back at camp, the video said it all. Homer said, "Those are the longest main beams on any elk I've ever seen."

The next couple of days we pressed hard in that same area looking for the bull again. We followed bugle after bugle, and I was beginning to fear that he had disappeared.

On the third morning after our surprise encounter, at around 7:30 a.m., we heard the distinct sound of crashing antlers in a park-like area that had been thinned for timber management purposes. We knew some big bulls were going at it, and we were close. As I lay prone on the ground, I suddenly had the bull in my view. There he was in all his magnificence, having just successfully fended off two smaller bulls intent on stealing his harem of cows.

I extended the bi-pods on my .30-.378 Weatherby, took a deep breath, and watched as the bull trotted into full view chasing a stray cow that had wandered too far away. I squeezed the trigger, and my 180-grain Nosler found its mark behind the bull's right front shoulder. What a great 6x6 bull he is. With a left main beam of 66-3/8 inches, he has the distinction of having the longest main beam of any elk in the B&C record book. ▲

B&C Photo Archives

Dan J. Agnew, left, and Lynn Stinson, second from left, both had American elk that received awards at the 26th Big Game Awards Banquet. Agnew's typical American elk, scoring 410-5/8 points, received a Second Place Award, and Stinson's bull, scoring 417-1/8 points, also received a Second Place Award in the non-typical category. The two men are joined by Kirk Kelso, a B&C Lifetime Associate and Official Measurer, and Homer Stevens, far right, who guided Agnew to his trophy elk.

Photograph by Bill Honza

TROPHY STATS

▼ ▼ ▼ ▼ ▼

Category
American Elk –
Non-Typical Antlers

Score
433 $^{1}/_{8}$

Length of Main Beam
Right: 50 $^{4}/_{8}$ Left: 51 $^{1}/_{8}$

Circumference Between First and Second Points
Right: 7 Left: 7 $^{2}/_{8}$

Number of Points
Right: 11 Left: 12

Inside Spread
44 $^{5}/_{8}$

Location
Latah Co., Idaho – 1977

Hunter
Peter J. Orazi, Jr.

Photograph courtesy of Peter J. Orazi, Jr.

In this 30-year-old field photo, Peter J. Orazi, Jr. poses with what would later be determined to be the widest elk (70-3/8 inches) ever recorded by Boone and Crockett Club.

AMERICAN ELK NON-TYPICAL ANTLERS
First Award – 433 ¹/₈

▼ ▼ ▼ ▼ ▼ ▼ ▼ ▼ ▼

PETER J. ORAZI, JR.

Finding places to hunt near the Moscow area of northern Idaho can be challenging. This region, known as the "Palouse," consists largely of vast seas of wheat, lentils, and other crops. Tucked in between large agricultural expanses lay isolated and scattered timber patches and draws, and mostly privately owned ground. Unless a hunter is able to take a major trek to the national forest lands to the north or east, hunting opportunities at the local level can be at a premium.

Peter J. Orazi, Jr., woke up a bit late on a fall morning in 1977 during the general elk season. He had a spot just east of Moscow near the Troy area he wanted to try, and it wasn't too far to drive, so despite a bit of a late start, he headed east on Highway 8. He turned onto a graveled county road, eventually pulling up not too far from a good timbered draw. The hunt didn't exactly have the makings of something historic, but any elk was a good elk for Peter.

He had been in this spot just a few days previous and had seen what he thought was an elk in this same draw, but couldn't make out a properly identifiable target. That's why the elk liked it here, of course — nice and thick, and easy to hide in and escape.

Peter stepped into the cold morning air and was welcomed by a fresh blanket of snow; he hoped it might make for some good tracking. He started toward the draw on a typical windy day on the Palouse. It was a weekday, and a guy could be doing a lot worse things than chasing elk, he thought to himself. He made his way into the second growth timber and hoped for something big and brown to cross his path.

He was about ten minutes removed from the friendly confines of the cab of his vehicle when he saw something he could hardly make himself believe. Bedded ahead of him, only 75 yards away, was the biggest elk he had ever seen. The bull was chewing his cud, half in a trance, with glazed-over eyes.

The bull's vitals were covered by the brush, but the bull's huge head remained free of distraction or cover. Not one to question the circumstance or wait for a situation to deteriorate, Peter shouldered his .30-06 and aimed right between the eyes of the dozing bull. The simple twitch of a finger was all that it took. The bull never heard the shot, nor gained his feet. A few obligatory kicks and it was all over.

With one squeeze of the trigger, Peter J. Orazi, Jr. had just made history. His 1977 Latah County bull would become the largest non-typical elk ever taken in the state of Idaho. At 70-3/8 inches wide, it is also the widest elk ever recorded by Boone and Crockett Club. ▲

Story courtesy of "Idaho's Greatest Elk" by Ryan Hatfield.

TROPHY STATS

▼ ▼ ▼ ▼ ▼

Category
American Elk –
Non-Typical Antlers

Score
417 $^{1}/_{8}$

Length of Main Beam
Right: 47 $^{3}/_{8}$ Left: 47 $^{6}/_{8}$

Circumference Between First and Second Points
Right: 10 $^{6}/_{8}$ Left: 11

Number of Points
Right: 6   Left: 8

Inside Spread
40

Location
Apache Co., Arizona – 2004

Hunter
Lynn H. Stinson

Photograph by Jack Reneau

Lynn H. Stinson accepting his plaque and medal from Buck Buckner, Vice President and Chairman of the Big Game Records Committee.

AMERICAN ELK NON-TYPICAL ANTLERS
Second Award – 417 ¹/₈

▼ ▼ ▼ ▼ ▼ ▼ ▼ ▼ ▼

LYNN H. STINSON

Few places in North America have a better reputation of producing giant bull elk than the famed San Carlos Apache Reservation in Arizona. This was a fact not lost on Lynn Stinson. Lynn made the necessary arrangements and was soon booked for a September 2004 hunt.

Lynn was guided on the hunt by Homer Stevens. They were hunting the Dry Lake area of the reservation, an area with a long history of producing giant bulls.

At 4:10 p.m. on September 5, six days after his arrival, Lynn wasn't disappointed by the view in front of him. It was a giant of a bull, somewhat narrow, but with mass and point lengths that were phenomenal.

Lynn finalized the decision to take this incredible trophy by shattering the afternoon silence with a shot from his .300 Weatherby. At 200 yards, it was plenty enough to get the job done.

Lynn's incredible 6x8 non-typical has some of the longest tine lengths imaginable on an elk. His G-4s stretch the tape to 27-3/8 (right) and 25-4/8 (left). Perhaps even more impressive are the G-5s, which at 23-1/8 and 23-6/8, respectively, are among the longest ever recorded. ▲

Photograph courtesy of Lynn H. Stinson

Lynn H. Stinson is pictured above with his non-typical American elk, which scores 417-1/8 points. The bull's G-5s are among the longest ever recorded.

Photograph by Bill Honza

TROPHY STATS

▼ ▼ ▼ ▼ ▼

Category
American Elk – Non-Typical Antlers

Score
415 $^6/_8$

Length of Main Beam
Right: 57 $^3/_8$ Left: 58 $^1/_8$

**Circumference Between
First and Second Points**
Right: 7 $^5/_8$ Left: 7 $^5/_8$

Number of Points
Right: 7   Left: 7

Inside Spread
46

Location
Nye Co., Nevada – 2005

Hunter
Ted L. Wehking

AMERICAN ELK
NON-TYPICAL ANTLERS
Third Award – 415 6/8

▼ ▼ ▼ ▼ ▼ ▼ ▼ ▼ ▼

TED L. WEHKING

We named this bull Lucky Number Seven for a variety of reasons. First, he was a 7x7 non-typical. Second, I had been applying for an elk tag in Nevada for 27 years. Also, I was hunting with my 7mm Magnum, and I ultimately shot him at 277 yards.

I was fortunate to have my two boys join me for the first four days of the hunt. Doug would be on the spotting scope, and David would handle the rangefinder. I made the decision to hunt for Lucky Number Seven while the boys were with me, settling for another bull on the last three days of the hunt if necessary.

Having a general knowledge of the wilderness area we would be hunting and knowing the value of the coveted tag I had drawn, I planned to use the services of an outfitter. Upon the advice of friends who had hunted with him, I booked my hunt with Jim Stahl, owner of Mustang Outfitters.

Friday morning we met Jim and his sub-guides and the two other hunters at the trailhead of Barley Creek in the Monitor Range of central Nevada. After a scenic three-hour horseback ride into our wilderness tent camp, we quickly stowed our gear. We spent the afternoon before the season opener glassing the area from a nearby mountain for rutting bulls and their harems. It was the last week of September 2005, and the rut was in full swing.

After a short time glassing, my guide, Tanner Allen, spotted (at over a mile away) and pointed out to me a large six-point bull with a non-typical point on either side of his massive antlers. He recognized the bull from the previous year when another hunter was indecisive, and the bull seized the opportunity to depart the area. We immediately began making plans to put a hunt on for this particular bull.

Opening morning we hiked southwest

Photograph by Jack Reneau

Ted L. Wehking accepting his plaque and medal from Buck Buckner, Vice President and Chairman of the Big Game Records Committee.

Photograph courtesy of Ted L. Wehking

Ted L. Wehking and his sons with Wehking's award-winning non-typical American elk. The bull, which scores 415-6/8 points, was taken in Nye Co., Nevada.

out of camp just as it was starting to get light. Within 20 minutes we were hearing bugling bulls. We continued to head toward the general area of where we had spotted the big seven-point Friday afternoon. While still in the morning shadows of Table Mountain, we could identify elk several hundred yards to the west of us. As we tried to close the distance for positive identification, they also spotted us. We quickly jogged to a higher vantage point, only to see four bulls and several cows trailing down the next ridge approximately 300 yards away.

I set up as quickly as I could for a shot. My guide and Doug, using their 10-power binoculars, identified one of the bulls as Lucky Number Seven and excitedly shouted at me to shoot. In the poor morning light, looking through my rifle scope, I could see running bulls and cows between scattered mahogany on the next ridge. Under the circumstances, I decided not to chance this difficult shot. As the elk disappeared over the ridge, we were pleased we had located the bull we were after and were hopeful our paths would soon cross again. We covered a lot of ground the remainder of the day looking for the big non-typical, but had no luck finding him, returning to camp well after dark.

On Saturday and Sunday mornings, both of the other hunters in camp had connected on very respectable six-points in the 340 to 350 point range. We were seeing bulls every day; however, many of them had broken points.

Monday morning, as we were glassing from a high rocky point, we watched another outfitter and hunter drop into the drainage to the north of us. Shortly after, he filled his tag. Moments later, approximately 20 cows and two bulls in the 350-class came running within 50 yards of where we were sitting.

After searching high and low for two and half days in the general area we had seen the big non-typical bull, we again heard the familiar sound of bugling bulls. This was the third day of our hunt and we were on horseback to expand our search. As we moved from one vantage point to another to glass, my guide spotted a bull at a distance. We quickly reined in and tied off the horses and climbed up a nearby ridge to take a better look. The bull he had spotted was a five-pointer on the southern edge of a mahogany draw to the east of us. Shortly thereafter we located a six-pointer and a spike in the trees on the ridge above the same draw. While these bulls strutted and bugled, we kept hearing another bugle coming from the draw.

AMERICAN ELK
NON-TYPICAL
ANTLERS
Third Award – 415 6/8

▼ ▼ ▼ ▼ ▼

TED L. WEHKING

My guide asked if I wanted to wait the bull out or bust him out. With a very strong wind blowing in our face, I asked him to make his way around and upwind of the draw. Our hope was to push out and identify the bugling bull in the draw that we could hear but not see. Tanner was gone almost 30 minutes when the six-pointer from the top of the ridge came busting out to our right at approximately 400 yards. Doug quickly picked him up in the spotting scope and reported that the third and fourth points on his left side were broken.

A minute or so later, about 20 cows (that we had not seen) came out of the draw on a dead run, followed shortly thereafter by another ten cows and Lucky Number Seven. Doug immediately had the spotting scope on him and said, "Dad, that's him! He's huge; no broken points. Shoot him!"

When the bull slowed from a full run to a trot, David had the rangefinder on him and said, "He's 277 yards. Shoot him! Shoot him!"

Within a second, the 160-grain Nosler Partition took out both of his lungs. The bull stopped in its tracks momentarily and then started to slowly quarter away from me. One more shot and he was down.

My guide heard the unmistakable hits and was running back, jumping three-foot sagebrush in stride to join in on the celebration. As we approached the downed bull, there was total silence; then the air erupted with hollering. We were all amazed at the size of the trophy that lay before us; he was bigger than any of us had estimated.

As an added surprise, the bull had barbed-wire wrapped around the base of his antlers. He had apparently taken out a section of fence. We unwound and removed the barbed-wire and paced it off and it measured 32 feet in length.

Following high fives and a lot of pictures, the four of us had the bull caped, skinned, quartered, and hanging in game bags in short order. Then it was back to camp to continue the celebration.

The next day we broke camp and, with the help of packhorses, gathered up the meat and antlers and headed down to the trailhead. What an enjoyable ride it was going down the mountain looking at the antlers straddling the backside of the packhorse. I relived the hunt over and over again.

It meant the world to me to have my two boys on the hunt, and taking a bull of this caliber was definitely the highlight of my hunting career. ▲

Note: This bull took first place in the Nevada Wildlife Record Book *annual competition for 2005 and also became the new number two All-time non-typical bull elk taken in the state of Nevada.*

Photograph by Bill Honza

TROPHY STATS
▼ ▼ ▼ ▼ ▼

Category
Roosevelt's Elk

Score
371 $^2/_8$

Length of Main Beam
Right: 49 $^5/_8$ Left: 50 $^4/_8$

Circumference Between First and Second Points
Right: 8 $^7/_8$ Left: 9 $^7/_8$

Number of Points
Right: 9   Left: 8

Inside Spread
35 $^1/_8$

Location
Gold River, British Columbia – 2003

Hunter
James V. Stewart

Photograph by Jack Reneau

James V. Stewart accepting his plaque and medal from Buck Buckner, Vice President and Chairman of the Big Game Records Committee.

ROOSEVELT'S ELK
First Award – 371²/₈

▼ ▼ ▼ ▼ ▼ ▼ ▼ ▼ ▼

JAMES V. STEWART

I enjoy life very much, and participate in many activities; however, I am passionate when it comes to water, coffee, salmon, and elk. My passions have many things in common but in particular to elk, I love the way they look, sound, feel, smell, behave, and especially the way they taste. I love to be in the places where they are found. I spend the better part of September, October, and November hunting American elk in Washington, Montana, Idaho, or New Mexico, depending on the luck of the draws.

My preference is to hunt on my own, unguided, setting up a camp along with my horses, with or without friends. I have hunted with guides and appreciate their hard work but, to me, when doing so it becomes their hunt, their timing, their rhythm, their focus.

It was unusual for me to sign up for a guided Roosevelt's elk hunt on Vancouver Island with Dave Fyfe of North Island Guide Outfitters in 2003. I met and became acquainted with Dave's elk hunts while being guided by him on a spring steelhead fishing trip. His professional operation, the spectacular surroundings, and abundance of game gave me no choice but to fill a cancellation vacancy for the upcoming October 10 elk season opener near Gold River.

My wife, Luz Marina, and I drove up to Campbell River from our home in a blinding rainstorm two days prior to the hunt. The rain never let up! I could not believe it was possible to get close enough to shoot an elk in rubber raingear, but going without it was out of the question. I could understand, with all the rain, how the trees got so big and the brush at ground level got so thick and impassable. I could not imagine ever seeing an elk in this thickness.

The key to this hunt is the personal guide and the incredible number of days he/they spend in preseason scouting. Clearcuts are a blessing on this hunt. Terrain is so steep and thick with vegetation and giant downfall that not even the elk venture far from the edge of these clearings; in themselves, they are still nearly impassable.

The elk on Vancouver Island are essentially not hunted. There are 200 resident permits issued plus seven non-resident permits, of which Dave Fyfe is allotted four. It is not like folks go to their favorite spot and hunt year after year. Dave spreads his hunters out over 400,000 acres, so the only issue with other hunters is that someone out for the first time stumbles into your pre-scouted hunt. The odds of this are good. Luckily, there seems to be an etiquette that if you find a vehicle parked on a logging road that leads to a clearcut you continue on to another spot.

My guide, Morris Trace, had spotted two nice bulls the evening before the opener that he judged to score 320 and 330, respectively. The smaller of the two he dubbed, "the can opener," because it had distinctive 3- to 4-inch tines coming off the top of each browtine.

Photograph courtesy of James V. Stewart

James V. Stewart (center) and his wife Luz Marina are pictured above with his Roosevelt's elk scoring 371-2/8 points. The bull was taken near Gold River, British Columbia, during the 2003 season and received a First Place Award at the Boone and Crockett Club's 26th Big Game Awards Program.

The next morning, Morris and I got out of bed at 2 a.m. This is a popular spot and these are the nicest elk I have seen all year. Sure enough, about 4 a.m. another hunter came along, having seen the same bulls. He was disappointed by our presence but gave way to our claim.

Dave took my wife, who I rely on for spotting elk, up an adjacent road to keep an eye on the clearcut from above. They were maybe halfway up when they stopped to stretch and fill their coffee cups. My wife stood up and there he was, 20 yards below — "the can opener." My wife is the type of person that no matter where she looks she will be looking at an elk. I knew I should have stuck closer to her.

Meanwhile, Morris and I had been scoping out our spot all morning without much action. We had just returned to the truck when Dave and the Missus pulled up with their news. The bull had ambled down our way so we decided to back off until later.

Morris and I were walking back to our spot at about 3 p.m. when all of the sudden there he was, bedded with about a dozen cows, out maybe 275 yards. I instinctively focused on the bull. Morris put his pack down on the road to use as a shooting rest. All we had to do now was wait until he stood up.

This bull, with heavy long main beams, was the bigger of the two bulls spotted earlier – not "the can opener." Without going into detail, I can tell you the bull did not die that day.

Morris, in his dedicated effort to please me asked, "How do you like him?"

In that moment of indecision, that moment of loss in focus, the bull stood up and presented the shot. Then, in the same instant, intermingled with the cows and walked away.

ROOSEVELT'S ELK
First Award – 371 2/8
▼ ▼ ▼ ▼ ▼
James V. Stewart

My greatest fear on this trophy hunt and I think the biggest challenge to shooting a trophy elk is not to shoot a small one. My experience hunting elk in the Rocky Mountains on public land would lead me to judge any Roosevelt's bull to be big. In addition to locating the game in very inhospitable terrain, the guide's judgment as to the trophy quality is essential.

We hunted that clearcut early and late for the next three days in pouring rain. I had to wonder if the rifle, a Browning BAR in .300 Winchester Magnum, would really function in spite of being cleaned, dried, and oiled nightly. Morris had the good idea on day three to move up the bank, giving us a better view with better wind but necessitating a longer shot in the event that one was offered. In so doing, we were able to put up a sort of roof to provide a little protection from the rain. We also had a huge cedar stump to use as a blind as well as for a stable rest. Sitting in the rain day after day is not the type of hunting I like. I am a September bugle guy or a November track them to their bed type.

Suddenly, there it was late on day four. We heard a definite bugle, followed by 15 minutes of painful silence. First, the lead cow appeared; then, one by one, 11 more cows; finally, an immense set of antlers bobbing up the trail supported by 1,100 pounds of elk. In my scope I saw the can openers. Morris whispered, "When you have the chance, shoot that bull!"

No questions asked. We waited for what seemed like forever, as the lead cow was nervous. The herd opened up and there stood the bull, broadside at 257 yards. I fired. What was that sound? It sounded kind of like a squishy underwater sort of cough, just enough to alert the cows, who began to move off. Two more shots showed no apparent reaction. The bull moved about ten yards closer and turned straight at us. BOOM! Down he went. We discovered later that we had been shooting through some unnoticed dead fir branches. When the elk stepped closer he presented the clear shot, coming under the branches.

This animal was truly beautiful. Dave did a field measurement as we field-dressed and caped the bull. "You're not going to believe this — 398 gross is what I get."

This bull was born to score. He was judged on the hoof at 320, the smaller of the two! They were both very symmetrical, which is why we think the predicted score on the hoof was so low. I saw the other bull as well. He was heavier, wider, and had longer main beams, but were his tines as long? This one has a 24-1/8-inch G-4, for example. I had to find out, so I booked for 2004. I still don't know the answer.

We admired the bull. He was a 9x8 with long tines, can-opener eyeguards, and had a palmated crown. We gave thanks, and I honor this great great elk by hanging it for public admiration at the Stock Farm Club in Hamilton, Montana. In closing, it does have a flaw, though. It only had one ivory! Now what can you do with one ivory? ▲

Photograph by Bill Honza

TROPHY STATS
▼ ▼ ▼ ▼ ▼

Category
Roosevelt's Elk

Score
344 $^{1}/_{8}$

Length of Main Beam
Right: 53 $^{4}/_{8}$ Left: 53 $^{6}/_{8}$

Circumference Between First and Second Points
Right: 9 $^{5}/_{8}$ Left: 9 $^{5}/_{8}$

Number of Points
Right: 6   Left: 7

Inside Spread
40 $^{2}/_{8}$

Location
Clallam Co., Washington – 2005

Hunter
William R. Treese

ROOSEVELT'S ELK
Second Award – 344¹/₈

▼ ▼ ▼ ▼ ▼ ▼ ▼ ▼ ▼

WILLIAM R. TREESE

Living in the upper Elwha River valley, located 15 miles west of Port Angeles, Washington, in the foothills of the Olympic Mountains, I am lucky enough be in an area where the Roosevelt's elk migrate to during the fall and winter months. Unlike some other areas on the Olympic Peninsula, we enjoy the elk living amongst us during these months. In the ten years since I had moved here from Pennsylvania, I had been lucky enough to tag only one smaller brush-racked bull. I'll be the first to admit that I am not a very adept hunter.

Once in a while, some cows will stay behind in the valley to calve while the rest of the herd goes wherever they go in the late spring. The summer of 2005 was obviously one of these situations, as I saw three or four cows with a couple of calves in early summer.

One morning in mid-August, I was on my way to work when I saw the cows and calves feeding underneath the power lines coming up my driveway. As I drove up on them, one of the elk picked up its head, and in the early morning fog I could tell that this was no cow. Slowing down to a crawl as I got to within a couple hundred feet of them, standing there looking at me was without a doubt the biggest bull I had ever seen!

When I got up next to them, the cows spooked and bolted into the timber, with him right behind them. Around four that afternoon, I saw him and the cows grazing in one of the fields, which was pretty discouraging and not very good for me. If I was seeing him in the open in the middle of the day, others surely would, too, and word would get out about this monster. The biggest downside for me was that hunting him with a rifle meant that he would have to make it through early archery and muzzleloader seasons. With two and a half months until rifle season, the last thing I needed was for him to be feeding in the fields in the middle of the afternoon.

Over the next few weeks and into the beginning of early archery, I had the elk where-

Photograph by Jack Reneau

William R. Treese accepting his plaque and medal from Buck Buckner, Vice President and Chairman of the Big Game Records Committee.

William R. Treese (left) is pictured with Dave Schultz and Treese's award-winning Roosevelt's elk scoring 344-1/8 points.

abouts locked down pretty good. When they weren't feeding in my field, they would be in a large patch of timber that adjoined my property. I felt pretty good about this because my field cannot be seen from the main road.

As I had suspected, though, I was not the only prospective hunter to have noticed this bull. Toward the end of archery season, a friend of mine who lived nearby stopped in to see if I had heard of or seen this monster bull that had been around. He was a very proficient hunter who has taken a lot of elk with his bow. I told him I had seen the bull once or twice. He said he had seen the bull with some cows feeding in a field along the road in mid-August but had not seen them in any of the fields along the road since then. This bull, he said, was the largest bull he had seen in his many years of hunting these animals. I then mentioned to him that they had been in my field that morning. He asked if he could take his bow and walk down through a swamp bottom, which is located down below me. I told him to go ahead. I then remember thinking to myself that had to be one of the stupidest things I had ever done. About 30 minutes after he left, the small group of elk came charging out of the brush and through the field at a full sprint. They were gone.

From that point until the beginning of rifle season, a month and a half later, they didn't show themselves in my field or any of the fields they would feed in if they were nearby. They either moved entirely out of the area or down into the river bottom. The river bottom would be a plausible location, with plenty of area and feed to sustain a small group of elk for that time period, although I had my doubts because that's a long time for them not to show themselves in any of the fields up above the bottom. If this was where they went it could be awfully difficult to find a small group of elk as there is a lot of land into which they could be settled down. Even though there is an old grade that runs up through the bottom, there are areas of dense, thick, swampy underbrush, as well as large areas of maple and alder, mixed with stands of evergreens.

Although I had purchased an elk tag for the opening day of rifle season (November 5, 2005), I decided against going out as I figured the elk had probably long moved out of the area. Early that afternoon, my father-in-law, who had not purchased a tag, stopped by and talked me into walking up through the bottom with him. We figured if we walked up the grade and there were any elk down there we might see some sort of sign along the grade. Walking the entire length of the bottom, we were unable to see any discernible sign of any elk having been in that area.

ROOSEVELT'S ELK
Second Award – 344¹/₈

▼ ▼ ▼ ▼ ▼

William R. Treese

After getting back to the house, I told my father-in-law that the next morning I would go into the bottom and spend the day crashing the brush to see if maybe I could find some elk. After walking through the bottom, it seemed like a futile task, but maybe I'd get lucky.

The next morning I woke up around 7 a.m. to my father-in-law calling to see if I had left yet. I had overslept! It was already light out and I had planned on being on the trail at daybreak. I seem to have a bad habit of sleeping in during hunting season. I figured I had already overslept so I had couple of cups of coffee before I took what I figured to be my walk of futility through the river bottom.

I reached the trailhead around 8 a.m. and thought I would walk the grade and then hunt the timber and brush back along the edge of the river. It was unusually dry for this time of year, which made it difficult to be quiet. I walked the grade down into the bottom at a normal pace. Once I got down into the bottom, there were a lot of fallen leaves and brush in the trail. I had to take my time if I wanted to be quiet. For every step I took, I would stop and listen for 10 to 15 seconds.

I started off walking through a small stand of timber and then through a large area of thick underbrush. As I left the brush, I came into an area where I had some thick vine maple mixed in with some fir and cedar. Another 100 to 150 feet and I would be in solid timber, which would allow me to see for more than 25 feet off the trail.

As I came up around the corner, there was an elk feeding on the edge of the trail not 25 yards in front of me. His rear end was facing me and he was feeding with his head down. It became obvious that this was the same bull that I had been watching a couple of months earlier. My heart was pounding and I froze. I don't know how long I stood there dumbfounded, but I finally came to my senses and got down behind some vine maple that had fallen down across the trail. If he had been facing me I am sure that he would have been gone.

I rested my rifle on the vine maple but still did not have a good shot. I was looking straight on at his backside and did not want to shoot him there. I had to wait for him to pick up his head or turn broadside to me. My heart was pounding a mile a minute and time seemed to come to a standstill. Finally, he lifted and started to turn his head. At that point I fired one shot, aiming directly behind his ear. He immediately dropped in his tracks. I could hear some elk crashing through the dense brush I had just walked past after the echo from the gun blast cleared.

The way I see it is there wasn't much skill in the killing of this animal, but there sure as heck was a lot of luck. If he had been facing me when I came around the corner, he'd have been gone. If one of the other elk had stepped out of the brush I had just walked by, they would have spooked and there's a good chance I would have never seen him. This is definitely one of those occasions where I have no problems saying I'd rather be lucky than good. ▲

Photograph by Bill Honza

TROPHY STATS

▼　▼　▼　▼　▼

Category
Tule Elk

Score
341 $^4/_8$

Length of Main Beam
Right: 45 $^7/_8$　Left: 46

Circumference Between First and Second Points
Right: 8 $^2/_8$　Left: 8 $^3/_8$

Number of Points
Right: 9　Left: 9

Inside Spread
43 $^7/_8$

Location
Colusa Co., California – 2004

Hunter
Val O. Olenski

TULE ELK
First Award – 341⁴/₈

▼ ▼ ▼ ▼ ▼ ▼ ▼ ▼ ▼

VAL O. OLENSKI

It was the last week in April 2004. Justin Sites, a friend of mine, was applying fertilizer in a rice field for the company I work for. I was checking on his progress and the conversation turned toward hunting. He asked me if I was applying for an elk hunt. I told him yes, as I pointed south. I told him that I had two preference points for the hunt. His response was "No," then he pointed due west. "You should put in for that hunt."

I asked him why, and he replied that there was a brand new hunt this year over that way. I asked, "Why would I want that hunt?"

"The world record bull lives there."

"How in the heck do you know that?"

"They've been eating my dad's hay for the past four years."

I told Justin I didn't know where to hunt in that area and that I have never been to Stonyford before. He assured me that I would be hunting with a game warden. I made sure and let Justin know I would need his expertise while hunting these elk, if I was lucky enough to draw.

I started telling my small group of hunting buddies about this new elk hunt and the chance to harvest a world record bull. I couldn't draw any interest from them at all, as they figured this hunt was too good to be true.

At the end of June, the California draw results came out. I drew my usual deer tag, but the next day my wife told me I had received another letter from the Department of Fish and Game. I was excited because I thought I drew a California sheep tag. I opened the letter and the opening statement said, "Congratulations. You have drawn the East Park Reservoir elk tag."

I was so excited. My wife thought my reaction was that of winning the lottery. I told her I had drawn one of only two bull elk tags. I showed Justin Sites the letter and told him we would be going to hunt for the world-record bull elk, "Longtine."

Photograph by Jack Reneau

Val O. Olenski accepting his plaque and medal from Buck Buckner, Vice President and Chairman of the Big Game Records Committee.

The next thing to do was call the local game warden, Brett Gomes, and have him enlighten me about this elk herd. When I met Brett a few days later, he told me how lucky I was to have drawn this tag. Brett mentioned that there were several large bulls in the herd. Brett also informed me that the herd was broken up and spread all over Stonyford. These elk would start moving to Catholic Point, which is the hunt area by mid- to late-August. Brett invited me to go scout this area once the elk moved in.

During my prescouting trips to Stonyford, I saw at least eight bulls that would easily make the records book. One bull in particular, I truly feel could be a world record. Pat Callahan and I guessed his score at around 380 B&C. Finding him on my four-day hunt and harvesting him might be a completely different matter.

On September 19, we packed our camping gear and supplies. We headed off to East Park Reservoir to set up camp. I didn't want to miss one minute of my four-day hunt. Daryl Dirks, Michael Dirks, Vern Hart, Ken Olenski, and I arrived at East Park Reservoir and set up camp.

Brett Gomes met me at 3 p.m. that afternoon for my orientation at Catholic Point as a hunt requirement. Brett showed me all areas that I could hunt and also gave me the rules that pertain to the hunt. When we were finishing the orientation, we pulled up on a knoll and started glassing. We sat down under some oak trees and saw a bull lying sound asleep. His cows were bedded below him. Not much was moving due to the late afternoon heat.

Brett asked me if I had my cow call and I told him yes. I had just purchased a cow call and thought it would be one of those calls that looks good, but usually ends up in the garbage at the end of the season. I told Brett it had two tones, "Hey big boy I am over here" and "I'm in the mood for love." After gaining his composure, he asked if I was ready, and we gave three calls. The hillside came alive with several bulls that started bugling. Two were up fighting; the napping bull woke up and was gathering his cows. Brett had a big smile on his face when he turned and looked at me. He said, "I think the call is working."

Brett took me over to Mary Quiberg's house. Mary was a treasure to meet and talk to. I asked for permission to hunt elk on her property, and she agreed. She showed me the property lines and told me where she thought would be the best place to harvest a bull.

Late that evening, I brought the gang over to Mary's. We found the travel route the elk were using. They bedded up in the oak trees during the day and came down to Mary's fields in the evening. They ate most of the night and returned to their bedding area in the morning. We only saw one bull, a 5x6.

If you hunt on state-owned property, the use of a muzzleloader is required. You can use a regular centerfire rifle on privately owned land that you have permission to hunt on.

Finally, 5 a.m. arrived. As I left the tent, the gang wished me well. As I pulled into Mary's driveway, my designated partner, Justin Sites, called. He said he was running late and that I should go on without him. He planned to catch up later.

I grabbed my Remington .300 Ultra Mag. and a handful of handloads. I arrived at my predetermined spot and watched the sun rise. Just before shooting hours, three wild pigs passed within100 yards of me. Then I noticed a big body with antlers coming up from below.

The bull stopped about 150 yards from me and started feeding. There was something wrong with his right antler. Finally he turned and looked in my direction and I noticed he had broken off his antler just above his G-4. I had no idea what an important part he would play in my success when I passed on him.

TULE ELK
First Award – 341 4/8

▼ ▼ ▼ ▼ ▼

VAL O. OLENSKI

As the morning passed, I saw some great bulls on Mary's neighbor's place. At about 9 a.m., I left my spot and met Brett and Justin at Mary's barn. Justin asked if I was thinking about shooting one of those "dinks." I told him if they were closer and on Mary's property I might have considered it. Justin said, "You have permission to hunt over there, because Leroy Walkup had told me that you could hunt his property if you wanted to."

Brett asked, "Did you see the bull that walked up into the trees behind you?"

"No."

They told me that was the biggest bull they had ever seen. I thought to myself, Longtine must be around. Just then Pat Callahan drove up and asked how I was doing. After hearing the story about the big bull, he asked me if I wanted to go up into the trees and call him out into the open. Pat rents the property next to Mary's and he told me there was a stock pond near the trees where the bull was headed.

After a 20-minute walk, we arrived at the pond and Pat tried his cow call. It is a reed call, and we didn't have much success. I could see small antlers moving through the trees, but they wouldn't respond to the call. Pat suggested we build a ground blind and set up there for the evening hunt. I told Pat that I would meet him at 5 p.m. and I headed back to camp.

On my way, I stopped at the General Store in Stonyford to purchase a flyswatter. The bees were terrible at camp. Unfortunately they had sold the last one, so the young lady handed me the one they use in the store. This is typical of the people who live in Stonyford, California.

At 5 p.m., we met Pat at the gate. I think he was a little overwhelmed with the five of us. I told him not to worry, they are all buck hunters and they all know what to do. Pat said, "Okay; let's do it."

On the way through the pasture, we started seeing elk coming down to Mary's field. Pat said, "This is a good sign. It could be our lucky day."

Everyone spread out in some kind of cover. Pat and I sat in the blind that we had made that morning. We were about 75 yards from the fence line. On one side, there were a lot of trees with a few small openings; the other side was fairly open.

It was pretty quiet around us when Pat asked if I had brought my cow call. We gave three calls and some bulls immediately responsed. A nice 7x7 came up and started looking at us. Then a 5x6 came up and joined the 7x7. I think if Pat had called one more time those bulls would have been in our laps! All of a sudden a bugle started with a very low growl and graduated into a high-pitched squeal. I told Daryl, who was sitting a few feet away, "That's him."

Val O. Olenski is pictured above with his award-winning tule elk taken in Colusa Co., California.

As we listened, I could hear the cows starting to talk and I could see the ivory tips of some big antlers moving through the trees. I caught movement out of the corner of my eye; it was my brother trying to get my attention. He kept waving for me to come down to where he was. I slowly worked my way down to where he was and he said, "There he is."

The elk were only 50 feet from the fence that separates "No Man's Land" from Mary's. The first thing I noticed, besides the fact that he was a huge bull, was the hanger on his G-3 on the left antler. I was also looking at the four to five points after the G-4! All of his other points carried good length on both sides except for the last two points on the end of his main beam.

Now there were only two elk left. All of the other elk had hopped the fence and headed down to Mary's field. The last two elk were my big bull and a cow. She walked up to the fence and tried to hop over but was unsuccessful. She moved down the fence line and tried again with the same result. It was painfully obvious her hindquarter was injured and she couldn't jump.

Now the waiting game started. I became tired of holding my rifle on him, so I picked up my binoculars and watched. The end of shooting time was approaching, and I was wondering if we were going to make it in time. I kept asking my brother what time it was; he kept telling me we were fine. I started to worry that I wasn't going to get an opportunity at this beautiful bull.

Suddenly, I looked down and saw my old buddy "Broken Horn." He was coming up from Mary's side to challenge my big bull that my brother and I nicknamed "Flyswatter."

He wanted Flyswatter's cow. Broken Horn stopped at the fence, and here came Flyswatter answering the call. All I could do was watch and hope he would not break off any points. They got into a pretty good battle, but just as quick as it started, it ended. Broken Horn backed off and headed toward the pasture.

Now the cow decided to try crossing the fence again. I don't know if the bull fight broke the top strand of the wire or just pushed it down but the cow finally made it across the fence. I can't describe the feeling I had when Flyswatter laid his antlers back and cleared the fence. The cow walked out about fifty yards and stood with Flyswatter in tow.

I aimed for his vitals. I was lying in a prone position, with an oak tree base as a rest. Just squeeze the trigger, I told myself. In the recoil, I did not hear the bullet hit. I asked my brother, "Did I hit him?"

"No, but where did all of the dirt come from?"

I must have hit a squirrel mound in front of us, so I moved up about six inches on the tree. The bull had not moved. Again, I aimed. As I squeezed the trigger and the gun went off, I heard the sound of the bullet hitting my bull. I looked out and there he lay.

Everyone was immediately up and yelling, with high fives and a lot of big smiles. As we got closer to the bull, his antlers started to look better and better. The first thing I noticed was the hanger on his G-3. I could not believe the mass. Unofficially, I counted 10 points on each side. What a bull!

It was starting to get dark when a caravan of vehicles came into the field. Justin Sites was the first one to greet us, telling us he had the whole thing on his digital camera. Mary was next to arrive. She said she thought that cow would never cross the fence! The nice thing about having this many people is getting help to get the bull from the ground to the bed of the pickup.

After all of the pictures and the congratulations, we left the field and headed for Pat's house. It was quite a gathering, with 20 to 25 people showing up at Pat's house to admire my bull. I really appreciate Pat and his wife accommodating all of these people with no notice. Everybody was eager to help in any way possible. We caped the shoulders, neck, and head, making sure we left plenty of hide for the taxidermist. Brett showed up and congratulated me and validated my tag. I got to bed at about 1 a.m. and had another sleepless night. We packed up the next morning and headed for home.

If anyone is roaming around northern California in the fall, go to Stonyford and admire these magnificent animals. Stop in at the General Store, purchase a cold drink, and take a look at my bull on the wall. I think he is worth the drive and yes, the flyswatter is hanging next to him.

I personally would like to thank the Bureau of Reclamation, the Department of Fish and Game, Mary Quiberg of the Moody Ranch, Pat and Em Callahan, Justin Sites, the Dermodys, and my family.

Most important, I want to thank all of the people of Stonyford for the help and kindness they gave me. I still have never seen the bull I went after, Longtine. This gives me the excuse to return to Stonyford and look for him, this time to shoot him with a camera, not a rifle. ▲

Photograph by Bill Honza

TROPHY STATS

▼ ▼ ▼ ▼ ▼

Category
Tule Elk

Score
331

Length of Main Beam
Right: 42 $^2/_8$ Left: 41

Circumference Between First and Second Points
Right: 9   Left: 9 $^4/_8$

Number of Points
Right: 8   Left: 9

Inside Spread
36 $^7/_8$

Location
Colusa Co., California – 2005

Hunter
Todd A. Robillard

TULE ELK
Second Award – 331
▼ ▼ ▼ ▼ ▼ ▼ ▼ ▼ ▼

TODD A. ROBILLARD

Today's hunting in the western U.S. involves the need to understand the application process for special hunting permits. These special permits can often create some incredible opportunities for those fortunate enough to obtain one. Such was the case with Todd Robillard, who overcame odds of 259:1 in drawing a tule elk permit for central California.

With tag in hand, Todd had no intentions of doing anything less than his best in fulfilling this special opportunity. Along with a couple of friends and a guide, he began scouting

Photograph courtesy of Todd A. Robillard

Todd A. Robillard, right, and his friend Matt Albertson, are pictured above with Todd's award-winning tule elk. The bull was taken in Colusa County, California, during the 2005 season and has a final score of 331 points.

Photograph by Jack Reneau

Todd A. Robillard accepting his plaque and medal from Buck Buckner, Vice President and Chairman of the Big Game Records Committee.

the area. He saw plenty of elk, but none that Todd felt were good enough to fill a premium tag. That was about to change.

The night before the opener, a member of Todd's group videotaped a bull that left them all speechless. Most of them had the same thought — tule elk aren't supposed to get that big! With those visions fresh in his mind, Todd was unable to sleep for most of the night.

The next morning, the group headed out into typical tule elk habitat; it was dry, open, and grassy, with groves of oak dotting the rolling hills. Only one thing was different today — the overwhelming anticipation.

They found the bull and his harem at 9:30 a.m. Todd squeezed the trigger on his .45-caliber muzzleloader, and the bull hunched up. Todd scrambled to reload, eventually taking a second shot that found the mark and quickly ended the bull's reign.

The rut was in full swing, and no sooner than the big bull hit the ground, two six-points ran over to smell him. Sensing his demise, they began fighting right there for the right to take over his harem.

Todd says the intensity of the whole experience was overwhelming. He is very humble and grateful for the chance to experience something so special, and appreciative of all the help given to him during his quest. ▲

All of the elk that were part of the 26th Big Game Awards Program, 12 in all, were grouped in a display together at Cabela's Fort Worth, Texas, store. Above, Todd A. Robillard stands by his award-winning tule elk scoring 331 points.

Photograph by Bill Honza

TROPHY STATS

▼ ▼ ▼ ▼ ▼

Category
Tule Elk

Score
325 $^1/_8$

Length of Main Beam
Right: 44 $^6/_8$ Left: 47 $^4/_8$

**Circumference Between
First and Second Points**
Right: 9 $^7/_8$ Left: 9 $^1/_8$

Number of Points
Right: 10   Left: 7

Inside Spread
46 $^1/_8$

Location
Solano Co., California – 2006

Hunter
Reed Mellor

TULE ELK
Third Award – 325 ⅛
▼ ▼ ▼ ▼ ▼ ▼ ▼ ▼ ▼
REED MELLOR

Written by Reed Mellor's son Jade

I love to go hunting. A lot of the time my dad gets to go hunting, but I have to stay in school. My dad told me one day that he had found a hunt in August and that we could all go as a family and not have to worry about homework and missing school. I wanted to know what, where, and when. He said that we

A Family Affair

were going tule elk hunting in California in August. It was only February, and I was already looking forward to fall.

Finally, it was time to head to California. One of my dad's best friends, Doyle Moss, left a day before we did. It took a long time to get to California. My mom and dad took turns driving and my brother Gabe and I read books and listened to my mom read books.

As we left Reno, we were stopped at a stoplight and a car ran into the back of our truck. I wondered if this would affect the hunt. My dad said that she was just a young girl, and the bumper was barely scraped. I was happy we did not have to wait very long for that.

We stopped to see one of my aunts in Sacramento. They bought us lunch and gave me and Gabe a present. It was Thursday about noon when we finally arrived and settled into the motel. The motel had a pool, and I love to swim. I chose to go spotting that night, so swimming would have to wait.

Spotting tule elk the first night was awesome. It was almost like duck hunting. The elk like to stay in the thick marsh and are very hard to see. We saw a lot of elk, including two good bulls. We named them Number 1 and Number 2. The hunt was to start on Saturday, and we had one more day to look. Friday we did not see any of the elk that we wanted to hunt, but we saw a lot of other elk.

Friday night the Rocky Mountain Elk Foundation held a dinner at camp for about 50 people. Gabe and I helped serve the dinner, and we played with a lot of the other children that were there. I could not believe how much fun I was having.

I really enjoyed meeting all of the people, and we met the other hunter who was there. They had found our Number 1 bull that day and they were determined to go after him. I couldn't believe that they found him that day, and we did not.

Finally, it was the morning of the hunt. We saw elk and more elk, but not the one that we wanted. I was nervous that the other hunter would find the elk, but I never heard any shots. We hunted everywhere. We glassed, and we glassed, and we glassed. At noon, everyone headed in for lunch except for my dad and his friend Doyle. They kept hunting, but I had to get something to eat. We took lunch back out to them, and we kept hunting. Later in the afternoon, my mom and Gabe headed back to camp for a nap. I decided to stay with my dad. It was about 2 p.m. when we spotted the bull. We started to get closer, but the wind was blowing right at him. He took off running, and I thought we would never see him again. I thought we blew it.

MY MOM AND GABE SHOWED UP FOR THE PICTURES. IT WAS SO NEAT TO HAVE THE WHOLE FAMILY THERE FOR THE CELEBRATION. I DON'T KNOW MUCH ABOUT SCORING BUT EVERYONE SAID THAT THIS TULE ELK IS BIG. HE ENDED UP SCORING 325-1/8 POINTS. THE MINIMUM SCORE FOR A TULE ELK TO MAKE THE RECORDS BOOK IS 270. SO, I GUESS THEY WERE RIGHT; HE WAS BIG.

We headed to the area where he had headed and set up to glass. We caught a glimpse of the bull that he was running with, but not the big one. We sat in one spot the rest of the day and glassed. I was so tired I could hardly keep my eyes open. It was about one hour until dark and I fell asleep.

The next thing I remember was my dad opening the truck door and telling me, "Come on; we just killed the big bull."

I guess after I fell asleep the big bull emerged on the far side of the area that we were glassing. Doyle and my dad ran about half a mile to get in position just before dark. I guess it is lucky that I was asleep, because I don't think we all could have made it around there. The game warden that was watching the whole event said that we shot the bull with six minutes of legal shooting time left in the day.

My mom and Gabe showed up for the pictures. It was so neat to have the whole family there for the celebration. I don't know much about scoring but everyone said that this tule elk is big. He ended up scoring 325-1/8 points. The minimum score for a tule elk to make the records book is 270.

So, I guess they were right; he was big. ▲

Award-Winning Moments

B&C Photo Archives

Val O. Olenski points out some of the unique characteristics of his tule elk to his fellow attendees at the Trophy Display Fiesta held at Cabela's during the 26th Big Game Awards Program. Olenski's tule elk, which scores 341-4/8 points, received a First Place Award.

Photograph by Bill Honza

TROPHY STATS

▼ ▼ ▼ ▼ ▼

Category
Tule Elk

Score
312 $^2/_8$

Length of Main Beam
Right: 45   Left: 43 $^1/_8$

**Circumference Between
First and Second Points**
Right: 7 $^2/_8$ Left: 7 $^2/_8$

Number of Points
Right: 7   Left: 11

Inside Spread
48

Location
Monterey Co., California – 2005

Hunter
Kevin S. Small

TULE ELK
Honorable Mention – 312²/₈

▼ ▼ ▼ ▼ ▼ ▼ ▼ ▼ ▼

KEVIN S. SMALL

The La Panza tule elk hunt was the first limited draw tag I have drawn in my home state of California; therefore, I immediately began doing my homework. I quickly realized that this would be a challenging area to hunt, with the largest concentration of elk on the Chimineas Ranch, surrounded by private landholdings.

Prior to the hunt, the Fish and Game Department had a mandatory orientation meeting at the Corrizo Plains National Monument. Two lucky hunters were drawn to hunt the Chimineas Ranch, which is now owned by the State. As luck would have it, I was not one of the two. Now I really needed to do some research and scouting.

Due to recent boundary changes, the hunt was located in both Monterey and San Louis Obispo Counties. The terrain varies from gently rolling grasslands to steep brushy hills. Being familiar with the ranches in Monterey County, I contacted a friend, Clint White, who is currently involved with Private Land Management (PLM) and hunts the tule elk region. We contacted four ranches that Clint thought might have a few elk, and started scouting. After little success, we finally contacted the Cross Country Ranch, owned by August Harden. August guides deer and pig hunters throughout the year and said if we wanted to take a look, he would be glad to show us around.

We met August one afternoon and proceeded up a canyon behind his house. We parked the truck and walked up a grass ridge abundant with oak trees. It wasn't long before we spotted a herd with six bulls. One particular bull stood out, a 6x6 without any broken tines. The other bulls were either young or had broken points. I observed, over the course of the hunt, that many of the bulls had a lot of broken tines. After looking over this one particular bull through the spotting scope, August told us that he had seen better bulls earlier in the year; however, he didn't know where they were located this time of year, due to the fact he never had the opportunity to hunt them. Now I was getting really excited, as

Photograph by Jack Reneau

Kevin S. Small accepting his plaque from Buck Buckner, Vice President and Chairman of the Big Game Records Committee.

Photograph courtesy of Kevin S. Small

Kevin S. Small is pictured above with his tule elk scoring 312-2/8 points. The bull was taken in Monterey County, California, during the 2005 season.

we just passed up a six-pointer that scored in the 270s. I hadn't even seen an elk close to this size while scouting on any of the other ranches prior to season.

I made arrangements with August to pay a day fee in order to hunt the remainder of the season. He was just as excited to hunt as we were. It was a week before Thanksgiving and my family and I were staying at the beach house. Over the next few days, we checked out some pretty good bulls; however, the issue of broken tines was prevalent. One particular bull stood out, but he had a broken G-4 almost to the base. I have never seen a bull this heavy. He had nine-inch bases and carried the weight all the way up. It was great to see a bull with this type of genetics.

One morning we decided to look at some dry-farmed property across the highway. All we saw were a lot of wild pigs. I kept thinking that it was too open for elk to lie up in the middle of the day. I kept looking across the road, back into the canyons and the grassy oak ridges. I spotted an elk lying under an oak tree about 1,500 yards away. It really caught my attention, so I hiked back to the truck and was setting up a spotting scope when August and Clint showed up.

I hadn't seen very many tule elk since the state started a hunting project in 1979 with a three-year pilot program. In 1983, the California legislature voted to make it a long-term program. Tags are limited, so not many of us fellow hunters know how to properly score a tule elk. We couldn't count all of the points from this distance, but he had crowns on both sides. When Clint looked through the scope, he said, "That's what we are looking for."

There was only one problem; my potential trophy was lying on private property, belonging to the neighbor, who was not pro hunting. The piece of land couldn't have been more than a few hundred acres. I thought to myself that

TULE ELK
Honorable Mention – 312 $^2/_8$

▼ ▼ ▼ ▼ ▼

KEVIN S. SMALL

we just need to be persistent. I have always believed things will payoff if you are persistent.

The next morning we were up at 4 a.m. to discuss our strategy for the day. We determined that he was feeding down into some pasture during the night, so we put a plan in place to cut him off before he went over the fence. As we hiked up to position ourselves, we spotted a bull already on the other side of the fence, but it wasn't him. In an instant, our view of one bull turned to six. There he was, 300 yards away heading up to his bedding area; he was already on the other side of the fence. We still had the afternoon, but they were not traveling in the daylight; therefore, our luck ended for the day. It was Thanksgiving Day and we all agreed that it was a day for family, so we cancelled the hunt for the day.

Returning to the challenge on Friday, we were back on track, attempting to outmaneuver the wind and six sets of eyes traveling to their sanctuary. This time they took a different route. There was no way to get within 1,000 yards without one of them seeing us. Again, they had given us the slip.

By Saturday, we were running out of time. As I was driving to the ranch, thoughts of strategic approaches crossed my mind. How could we use the wind to our advantage? I came up with a plan to follow the bulls with the wind in our face, just to see if we could get close enough before they went over the fence.

We spotted them on a ridge and let them go. August decided this might turn into a sprint, so he decided to stay behind. Clint and I were off and running. We finally got within 400 yards of two bulls, but not our choice bull. After glassing the ridge, Clint said, "I just caught a glimpse of the crown of a bull going over the skyline. I believe it was our bull."

We needed to circle around the mountain and get in front or they were going to beat us to the fence. Even though the wind was swirling, we went for it. With a mad sprint down the hill, then up the draw, we belly crawled to the top of the ridge and up to one lone oak tree. It's hard to hide two people behind an oak tree with elk less than 100 yards in front of you and the wind swirling in every direction. Clint was lying on his belly, while I straddled his back.

We could see five elk but he was not among them. I was thinking that this can't be happening. Three of the bulls were feeding away from us and two were right in front of us, but our choice bull had disappeared. Suddenly, out of the corner of my eye, I saw something move. It was the crown points of a bull walking up the fence line. It was him! He hadn't jumped yet.

I motioned to Clint to cover his ears. He was right there and all I could see was antler. A hundred yards away and it seemed like an eternity until he made a few more steps to give me the opportune shot with my .300 Ultra Mag. I anchored him. With no ground shrinkage, he was actually more of a trophy than we had estimated. ▲

New World's Record

Photograph by Bill Honza

TROPHY STATS
▼ ▼ ▼ ▼ ▼

Category
Tule Elk

Score
379

Length of Main Beam
Right: 47 2/8   Left: 51

**Circumference Between
First and Second Points**
Right: 9 4/8   Left: 8 7/8

Number of Points
Right: 8   Left: 8

Inside Spread
39 3/8

Location
Glenn Co., California – 2005

Hunter
Picked Up

Owner
J. & J. Lopeteguy

TULE ELK
Certificate of Merit – 379

▼ ▼ ▼ ▼ ▼ ▼ ▼ ▼ ▼

OWNERS – JEFF & JULIE LOPETEGUY

We live on a ranch in the Mendocino National Forest between the small communities of Elk Creek and Stonyford in northern California. This portion of the ranch has been in the family since 1964 when Julie's parents Don (a former San Francisco Forty-Niner) and Nan Garlin purchased their cattle ranch.

There is a good population of tule elk that frequent this area of California. The bull elk from the herd roam and graze through the mountains and ranges near and around our home, many times stopping within a few yards

Elk Creek Elks

of our back door. For years now, we have enjoyed watching these "giant fellas" rest, graze, and roam freely on our property.

In October 2005, one of the larger bulls was discovered dead near our home. The California Department of Fish & Game took the bull to their facilities in an attempt to determine why he had died. No determination could be made, and in October 2006, the remains of the elk were returned to us. We were told by the Fish & Game officer that this bull was approximately six to seven years old, and that it was possibly the second largest ever recorded.

We were thrilled at the prospect that one of our local "boys" could be of record size. Jeff coached football at Elk Creek High School for nine seasons. With only around 25 to 40 students (boys and girls), Elk Creek High School is one of the smallest schools in our state to compete in football. We thought how wonderful it might be to have a record-size elk displayed in our gym, the home of the Elk Creek Elks.

We learned later that it was not the second-largest tule elk ever recorded. It was, in fact, the new World's Record! ▲

Photograph by Bill Honza

TROPHY STATS

▼ ▼ ▼ ▼ ▼

Category
Mule Deer – Typical Antlers

Score
210 $^2/_8$

Length of Main Beam
Right: 26 $^7/_8$ Left: 27 $^2/_8$

Circumference Between Burr and First Point
Right: 5 $^1/_8$ Left: 5

Number of Points
Right: 5   Left: 5

Inside Spread
28 $^6/_8$

Location
Sonora, Mexico – 2006

Hunter
Myra S. Smith

BOONE AND CROCKETT CLUB'S

MULE DEER
TYPICAL ANTLERS
First Award – 210 $^2/_8$

▼ ▼ ▼ ▼ ▼ ▼ ▼ ▼ ▼

MYRA S. SMITH

This hunt actually started over two years ago. One evening in the summer of 2004 after I had put our boys to bed, my husband Greg and I were watching the Outdoor Channel. They were hunting mule deer in Sonora, Mexico. Near the end of the show, the ranch "accommodations" were highlighted. They had a pool, game room, and they described how the cooks made homemade tortillas. I laughed and told my husband (who goes hunting in Canada every year), "You always want me to go on a hunting trip with you. Well, I'll go to Rancho Grande."

Myra's Monster Muley

Before I knew it, we were booked. We flew to Hermosillo, Mexico, in January 2005 for a six-day hunt. We were both fortunate enough to harvest nice mule deer. On the second day Greg took a 5x7 that scored 199; the pressure was on! That same afternoon I dropped my mule deer in his tracks. He was a 4x4 with a kicker (I love kickers) and had an outside spread of 29 inches and grossed 179. After such a great hunt, we signed up for 2006.

In 2006, we returned to Rancho Grande in hopes of getting something 190 or better and 30 inches wide! Upon arrival, Jesus Fimbres welcomed us to his home again, and we settled in for our hunt.

I had my same guide as the previous year, Roberto Nunez. He knew I wanted something better than last time. We saw lots of does and several bucks the first three days. Roberto pointed out a few he thought were shooters, but not in my mind! Also on the third day, Greg took a nice 5x5 that measured 178 gross. Did I mention I'm very competitive?

On the fourth day, we saw lots of does and a few smaller bucks, but no shooters. Two days

Photograph by Jack Reneau

Myra S. Smith accepting her plaque and medal from Buck Buckner, Vice President and Chairman of the Big Game Records Committee.

Myra S. Smith stole the show at camp with this award-winning typical mule deer scoring 210-2/8 points. Pictured above is the group that helped her; back row from left – Roberto, Roberto Nunez (her guide), and Greg Smith (her husband); front row from left – Fernando Flores, Myra, Sergio, and Carlos.

left, and the clock is ticking!

On the fifth of six days, Greg hunted Coues' deer, and Roberto and I were back at it. We were glassing as the sun came up. We soon spotted a buck that had great potential, but we were too far away to determine his size. We positioned ourselves, hoping to see him. It is amazing how desert mule deer blend in. We finally spotted him 300 yards away in the trees. He was extremely wide and tall. He had good back forks. All this time my guide was telling me to shoot him. I had to see the front forks before I would squeeze the trigger. He didn't stand very long and took off running. I never saw his front forks.

When Greg returned that evening, I told him the story. I noticed he was not overly concerned, as he usually is with my hunting woes. He seemed particularly excited but I didn't know why — he had not taken a Coues' deer. He finally got me off to the side and started telling me about a buck he and his guide, Fernando Flores, had seen. He was so animated he could barely speak and what he did say can't be printed. Greg and Fernando had guessed his spread at around 40 inches. He said he was tall, wide, and had deep front and back forks.

What more could a girl want!

After a conference with Jesus, Roberto and Fernando, we put together a plan to hunt this deer. I usually fall asleep when my head hits the pillow. This night, however, I lay there with my heart pounding while Greg slept. Buck fever was getting the best of me.

MULE DEER
TYPICAL ANTLERS
First Award – 210 ²/₈
▼ ▼ ▼ ▼ ▼

MYRA S. SMITH

It was now the last day of the hunt, and we moved in right after sunup. It was also the coldest morning so far. I was shaking, but was it from the cold or nerves? As we entered the area, nothing was moving.

We finally began seeing bucks with does moving around. We glassed from several points — still no big buck. It was also warming up quickly. By now I was beginning to wonder if we would see him. It was also in the back of my mind that time was running out on my last day.

At 9:40 a.m., Roberto saw a doe. Then, suddenly, I saw a huge buck take two jumps and duck into the thick brush. I told Roberto, *"Muy grande!"*

I didn't know if it was the one spotted by Greg and Fernando, but it was a shooter — the one for me! No more looking through binoculars. I was ready.

The buck had gone into a low, thick area. He either had to travel the length of the low area or up the other side. We eased so very slowly looking for him. I spotted him under a tree, in the shade, and looking straight at us! I didn't say a word; I simply put my crosshairs on his neck and squeezed the trigger. Roberto said, "High."

I already had another shell in the chamber. I put the crosshairs back in the same place and squeezed again. Roberto yelled, "He's down."

The buck went straight down, but I already had another shell in the chamber ready. It wasn't necessary, though, as he was down for good. Roberto ranged him at 267 yards. It happened so quickly, I never had time to be nervous. Afterward, though, I was shaking like a leaf. My knees were weak.

With his color, the shade, and the terrain, we could barely see him until we were 30 yards away. I have heard about ground shrinkage, but I swear this buck was getting larger as we approached him. I had tagged the "Big One."

We all met back at the ranch house. Roberto said Greg seemed more excited than I was. I was speechless, which is really unusual.

My buck weighed 255 pounds — the heaviest ever taken at Rancho Grande. His final score was 210-2/8, the largest typical mule deer ever taken in Mexico. He is also be the largest typical ever taken by a woman. His outside spread is 38-2/8 inches and inside spread is 28-6/8 inches. What a buck!

Needless to say, I enjoyed the rest of the afternoon. Greg went back out and got his first Coues' deer, a giant that scored 108 even with a four-inch G-2 broken off. Greg and his buck didn't get the attention they deserved, because his wife had stolen the show. ▲

Photograph by Bill Honza

TROPHY STATS

▼ ▼ ▼ ▼ ▼

Category
Mule Deer – Non-Typical Antlers

Score
285 $^4/_8$

Length of Main Beam
Right: 26 $^2/_8$ Left: 27 $^6/_8$

**Circumference Between
Burr and First Point**
Right: 4 $^7/_8$ Left: 4 $^6/_8$

Number of Points
Right: 17   Left: 16

Inside Spread
27 $^2/_8$

Location
Fremont Co., Wyoming – 2004

Hunter
Catherine E. Keene

MULE DEER
NON-TYPICAL ANTLERS
First Award – 285 4/8

▼ ▼ ▼ ▼ ▼ ▼ ▼ ▼ ▼

CATHERINE E. KEENE

I was exposed to hunting as a little girl. I can remember being carried on my mom's shoulders as my parents walked up a hill to get a deer my dad had just shot. I began carrying a gun and shooting my own game soon after I met my husband of 23 years, who has become my own personal guide and hunting partner. I look forward every year to hunting season as a way to get out and relieve the stress of my job as a CEO of a healthcare organization serving my Native American people. I am a member of the Eastern Shoshone Tribe living the majority of my life on the Wind River Indian Reservation.

Second Chance Buck

For years I have always wanted to take a nice mule deer. The last decade I have been fortunate enough to have harvested three bighorn sheep, two moose, several whitetail deer, mule deer, elk, and numerous pronghorn. I was successful in drawing two late-season trophy deer tags over the prior three years, but never really saw the caliber of buck I was looking for.

Because my husband Gary is a taxidermist, and he and I own a taxidermy and Native American Arts retail store on the Wind River Indian Reservation, he is often told stories of a "big one" being seen somewhere. So with information of a large buck filed away in our minds, I put my name in for a late season tag and, if unsuccessful, my name would go into the drawing for an "any deer" tag. I was hopeful to draw one or the other, but when the list came out from the Tribal Game and Fish, my name was not there. I had given up hopes that this year would be the year and had resigned myself to the fact that I would not be hunting the reservation for deer. I later found out that through a computer error,

Photograph by Jack Reneau

Catherine E. Keene accepting her plaque and medal from Buck Buckner, Vice President and Chairman of the Big Game Records Committee.

my name was omitted from the draw. I was given a second chance and ended up with the last "any deer" tag for the Owl Creek Mountain deer area.

Gary and I decided to follow up on one of these rumors and see what the season opener might bring. We had decided to make it a family outing, so we loaded up our six-year-old daughter, Kali, still in her pajamas, and headed out for the three-hour drive to the area we had heard of a large mule deer being seen the year before. It was an area we had hunted a few times on a previous trophy tag.

The morning was overcast and cold with a misty rain falling. We began spotting the hillsides at sunrise and from our years of hunting for bighorn sheep, we began picking the hillsides apart. We began seeing mule deer right away. We spotted five mule deer bucks and pretty soon the deer began to make themselves known on the hillsides. This was an awesome sight to see. I had never seen this many mule deer in an area before. One of the bucks was a borderline shooter but, since this was opening day, I had time to look around. We began to move around and scan other parts of the mountain when I noticed movement in my binoculars about a mile away. I could tell there were several deer, but that was about it. I was sitting on the hillside with my daughter when Gary decided to pull out the spotting scope to take a better look. Gary came back with his hands in the air indicating one of the deer out there was huge.

THE DEER HAD NO IDEA THEY WERE RUNNING IN OUR DIRECTION SINCE THEY WERE ALL EITHER FEEDING OR LYING IN THEIR BEDS WHEN THE GUN BARKED. HE WAS NOT ALONE, EITHER; THERE WERE NINE BUCKS IN ALL RUNNING TOWARDS US. THEY HAD NO IDEA WHERE WE WERE, BUT SHOULD HAVE FOR THE RUCKUS GOING ON AROUND ME. I COULDN'T SETTLE DOWN.

We planned our stalk and prepared our daughter for the mile-plus walk. We had a difficult canyon to tackle and hoped the wind would stay in our favor. We took it slow and easy, resting often with our daughter. We finally reached the top of the last steep grade; our daughter was tired, but knew we still had a couple hundred yards to go to get a better view of how far the deer actually were. Kali was comfortably bundled up in our coats, sitting next to a boulder while my husband and I crept forward on our hands and knees.

I was now over 400 yards away and couldn't get closer without exposing myself. I found a comfortable place to rest and told Gary, "I can make this shot."

The previous year I had dropped my bighorn sheep at 415 yards, so I felt I could do it again. Gary kept saying, "It's just like shooting at a target. Don't look at his antlers; it's just a target."

I could easily pick out this huge buck in my scope and was waiting for him to stand up. Just then we heard something behind us and turned around to see our daughter walking straight up in full view of the deer. We got her to drop down and luckily she was undetected. After that shake up I refocused my attention on the buck. He stood up, and I pulled the trigger. A "thwop" sound followed and both Gary and I said, "Got him."

It was at this point that the buck turned and we got our first view of his amazing spread. Neither of us could believe the sight. I started to stand up when Gary said, "You better get another bullet in the chamber 'cause he's coming right at us."

MULE DEER
NON-TYPICAL ANTLERS
First Award – 285 4/8

▼ ▼ ▼ ▼ ▼

CATHERINE E. KEENE

I think that's when buck fever set in. I'd pull up my gun and see black, couldn't hold the gun steady, had butterflies and who knows what else in my stomach.

Gary kept saying, "Wait 'til he stops and shoot again."

He continued to close the gap between us, which was now at 250 yards. The deer had no idea they were running in our direction since they were all either feeding or lying in their beds when the gun barked. He was not alone, either; there were nine bucks in all running towards us. They had no idea where we were, but should have for the ruckus going on around me. I couldn't settle down. All my previous experience meant little at this point; I truly had been shaken. The huge buck stopped, and I shot over him, then I tried to lead him, and shot in front of him. He was now going straight away and I fired for my fourth miss.

Gary and I sat on the top of the ridge, now joined by our daughter. Gary said that buck was probably 40 inches wide and the biggest buck he had ever seen. He told me he was going to need "mental therapy" knowing that I had just missed the buck of a lifetime. I laughed, but he quickly responded, "I'm serious; I'm really messed up."

I probably didn't get to appreciate the size of him, since I had such a hard time getting him in my sights again. Gary went to check for blood sign, while I proceeded to slowly follow in the direction the big buck went. The terrain was such that tracks and blood sign were difficult to follow. I topped the next ridge with no clue as to where he could have gone. Gary couldn't recover any blood sign, so I accepted I must have missed on that first shot. The weather was getting worse and had started to drizzle more now. We decided to get out and not push this deer anymore, and, hopefully, let the area settle down.

The rest of the day, all we could think about was the opportunity I had just missed. We actually talked ourselves into thinking maybe I didn't miss on that first shot. We both dreamed about it. Gary kept telling me he was serious about needing therapy, so we decided we would head out every chance we got to look for some sign that I may have shot him. We got up early the next morning and headed out, knowing we were expecting family at anytime. We spotted throughout the morning and talked of plans to come out at every opportunity we could arrange. Gary's entire family was expected to be here on a planned family outing to hunt pronghorn, and Gary and I were to be their guides.

It was a good thing Grandpa understood, being that they just traveled 1,700 miles to see us. With Grandpa and Grandma left behind to baby-sit on the morning of the third day, Gary and I headed out again. We began spotting deer right away. We were almost ready to

Photograph courtesy of Catherine E. Keene

Catherine E. Keene got a second chance on this outstanding non-typical mule deer. The buck, which scores 285-4/8 points, received a First Place Award at the 26th Big Game Awards Program in Fort Worth, Texas. Keene was hunting in Fremont County, Wyoming, in the fall of 2004.

move on when Gary spotted a few bucks heading into a draw. These were part of the group from two days before. This group was about a half-mile away from where I had shot on the first day. The wind was not in our favor, so we came up with a plan to come around the back side. This would be the opposite approach from the first day. The countryside was not what we expected; the stalk ended up being over three miles. It was also very hard to pinpoint which draw the deer had headed into. The terrain looked much different coming in from the opposite direction. We knew that as we got closer, we could pinpoint more accurately where we saw the bucks.

We started the drive around, noting a road on the map that might get us within a few miles, we saw a large group of elk grazing on the hillside behind us. As we started our trek, we spotted a group of bighorn sheep grazing, and several groups of pronghorn where the bucks were busy trying to keep their does together. As we were stalking, several pronghorn bucks were curious enough to get closer to us. We had to stop and wait for them to realize we were something they should stay away from.

We were nearing the draw we believed the deer were in when two pronghorn bucks chased a doe which wandered away from the herd. The larger buck, likely a record-book buck, came within 38 yards of us. At the time, we thought the pronghorn would blow our stalk; instead they likely helped us get closer.

MULE DEER
NON-TYPICAL ANTLERS
First Award – 285 4/8

▼ ▼ ▼ ▼ ▼

CATHERINE E. KEENE

When we topped the draw, we began to doubt that this was the draw, since we could not see any sign of deer. The pronghorn bucks began chasing each other and the doe up and down and around the draw. Then the deer just started to appear. Gary saw a small two-point buck grazing in the opposite end of the draw and said, "We're in the right draw."

At that moment, I began to see deer lying all over the hillside. We thought we were exposed, but we think they were actually paying attention to all the pronghorn activity instead of us. Then Gary said, "There he is; you get another chance!"

I slowly pulled up the Remington .300 Ultra Mag., pulled down the bipods, and got in position. I waited briefly for the deer to turn. Gary said, "261 yards."

The deer was facing me with his body almost broadside, and I pulled the trigger. He bounded twice into the bottom of the draw and didn't come out. I was ready with another bullet in the chamber; he was not going to get away this time.

What an amazing sight it was. Nine bucks ran directly across the ridge from us and stood around waiting for their leader, who never came out from the bottom. We sat there and watched the other nine bucks as they began to lie back down in their beds, obviously feeling it was safe, as if the big buck was lying down. We watched this magnificent sight until Gary went back to retrieve his backpack. They finally noticed us and began to line out over the ridge and out of sight.

The most amazing sight was when we walked down to the bottom of the draw and saw this beautiful deer lying there. Gary congratulated me and gave me a hug. He then pulled out the camera and remembered we forgot to buy more film. There were three shots left so we made the best of them. That's when I truly began to appreciate what I had just done.

I think I saved myself some money in the long run for not having to pay for therapy for Gary. As Gary left me with the deer to see if he could get our vehicle closer, he said, "If you see that pronghorn buck again, shoot him; it would be awesome to get two record-book animals in one day."

I asked Gary what he thought it might score, and he thought in the 240 to 250 range. He later told me he was being really conservative. His final score ended up being 285-4/8. This deer is massive, with 33 points (17x16), and has one of the most beautiful profiles of any non-typical I have ever seen, whether in pictures, magazines, or videos.

The 2004 hunting season turned into the best season we ever could have hoped for. Gary's family filled four out of five pronghorn tags, and Gary got his second chance as well on a late season mule deer. Gary bagged a 31-inch, 6x6, missing four shots on the first day; he also got his second chance on his third day. ▲

Photograph by Bill Honza

TROPHY STATS

▼ ▼ ▼ ▼ ▼

Category
Mule Deer – Non-Typical Antlers

Score
272 $^1/_8$

Length of Main Beam
Right: 24 $^3/_8$ Left: 26 $^2/_8$

Circumference Between Burr and First Point
Right: 5 $^7/_8$ Left: 6

Number of Points
Right: 14   Left: 10

Inside Spread
25 $^3/_8$

Location
Mohave Co., Arizona – 2004

Hunter
Thomas D. Friedkin

BOONE AND CROCKETT CLUB'S

MULE DEER
NON-TYPICAL ANTLERS
Second Award – 272 ¹/₈
▼ ▼ ▼ ▼ ▼ ▼ ▼ ▼ ▼

THOMAS D. FRIEDKIN

Thomas D. "Dan" Friedkin entered the famous "Arizona strip" in early September 2004 with hopes of finding a mule deer of a lifetime. This was not his first trip into the famed backcountry that borders Utah; he had hunted this region before and knew of its potential to grow trophy mule deer.

After several days of arduous treks up and down steep hills and mountains, he had gotten a few glimpses of a mule deer that was breathtaking. On September 4, he watched the giant bed down for a mid-morning siesta, and began his long stalk toward the napping animal.

He got within rifle range relatively quickly, but that would be the easy part. The buck was now surrounded by smaller satellite bucks and a few does that would not allow Dan to change his position for a better shot. The large muley was still napping behind some scrub brush that made a clean shot impossible, and the presence of the other animals all casually grazing around made moving impractical. So he waited for the buck to move.

Time crawled by for what seemed like hours. Finally, Dan saw antlers moving; then, suddenly, the buck stood up. Dan saw that there was a very small window of opportunity for taking a shot, due to the brush on either side of the buck. He quickly positioned the huge muley in his crosshairs at 114 yards and squeezed the trigger of his .300 Winchester Magnum. The buck bounded once and disappeared.

Dan approached the area cautiously and found his mule deer. As high as his expectations were, the deer on the ground easily surpassed them. He could hardly believe what lay there before him. There was no doubt that Dan was fortunate enough to harvest the mule deer of a lifetime... possibly several lifetimes. This deer, scoring 272-1/8 points, is the eighth-largest non-typical mule deer ever recorded from Arizona, and the largest in 35 years. ▲

Photograph courtesy of Thomas D. Friedkin

Thomas D. Friedkin with his award-winning mule deer.

Photograph by Bill Honza

TROPHY STATS

▼ ▼ ▼ ▼ ▼

Category
Columbia Blacktail Deer –
Typical Antlers

Score
170 $^6/_8$

Length of Main Beam
Right: 24 $^2/_8$ Left: 23 $^7/_8$

**Circumference Between
Burr and First Point**
Right: 4 $^1/_8$ Left: 4 $^3/_8$

Number of Points
Right: 5   Left: 5

Inside Spread
21

Location
Siskiyou Co., California – 1979

Hunter
Frank G. Merz

COLUMBIA BLACKTAIL DEER TYPICAL ANTLERS
First Award (Tie) – 170 6/8

▼ ▼ ▼ ▼ ▼ ▼ ▼ ▼ ▼

FRANK G. MERZ

My eye caught some movement below me as a buck that was bedded on the steep sidehill tried to run through the brush-choked draw. I didn't get a good look at the rack, but I knew it had antlers as I brought up the .300 Weatherby and fired.

In the '60s and '70s, I was cattle ranching near Gazelle in northern California. Eric Peters, a local friend, called and said to grab some horses and a couple of mules to go deer hunting. I went to the barn and loaded two mules and three horses into the stock trailer. I was to meet Eric and his buddy outside of Etna at the Pacific Crest Trailhead leading into the Marble Mountains, a wilderness area.

After riding the trail for about two hours, we found a flat area to make our camp. The tent went up, and the horses and pack animals were tended to and fed. A good warm dinner soon followed, and we turned in early.

The next morning, Eric and his buddy hunted up toward the peaks one way, and I worked north below the trail we came in on. The deep, steep canyons broke away, and there were small meadows and water near the top. This is where I started seeing tracks, and I felt the deer were still high. A deer trail working its way along a sidehill and leading up to a saddle showed some promising tracks.

As I made my way to the saddle, all I could hear was a gentle wind through the trees. Standing on the trail in the saddle, my glasses revealed no hidden monsters on the other side of the canyon. It was cold, so I rested a little while I glassed.

Shortly after 10 a.m., I pushed on along the sidehill. After going about 200 yards, an animal bedded below the trail started moving out in the brush and trees. There was a flash of antler as the gray form was noisily going through the brush. The Weatherby sounded off and the deer got the full force at about 75 yards and crumpled.

Slowly, I made my way down the steep slope to where the buck lay. He was a nice 4x4. I dressed him out, and then decision time came. I felt that my wandering had taken me about 500 to 600 feet below the elevation of camp; the valley floor was possibly 1,500 feet below. I decided it would be easier to take him down than up. The canyon started to ease out as I dragged the deer to the canyon floor below, far easier than trying to drag it 500 feet up and then to camp. I left the deer next to Mill Creek where it entered the valley.

When I started the hike up the hill to the camp, it began to rain lightly. Three and a half hours later, my legs wearily carried me into camp, and the rain had turned to snow.

Eric had some luck — there was a nice 4x3 hanging in the tree near camp. The stock had been tended to and a warm dinner hit the spot. We called it a day. The snow kept falling all night.

The next morning all the trees and hills were covered in white as the early storm raged on. It was tricky and slippery just getting around camp, much less going down a steep trail. We elected to stay put. Later that afternoon, we saw patches of blue sky and the snow began to melt. The next day, we would get out of the snowy high country.

At first light, we threw the camp together, put Eric's deer on a pack animal, and left the frozen peaks. Satan, my horse, threw a shoe on the way in and had stone bruises on his front hoof, so I had to lead him back to the trailhead. The tired mounts gladly got into the stock trailer because they knew they were going home.

> **WHEN WE CAME OFF THE MOUNTAIN AND HIT THE VALLEY FLOOR, ERIC AND I GRABBED A MULE AND TWO MOUNTS AND RODE AROUND THE HILL TO WHERE I DEPOSITED MY BUCK. WE LOADED HIM AND HEADED HOME. ONCE AT THE RANCH, I PUT MY BUCK IN MY COOL BOX TO AGE AND HUNG THE ANTLERS IN THE TACK ROOM. THAT WAS 1979.**

When we came off the mountain and hit the valley floor, Eric and I grabbed a mule and two mounts and rode around the hill to where I deposited my buck. We loaded him and headed home. Once at the ranch, I put my buck in my cool box to age and hung the antlers in the tack room. That was 1979.

I was planning to get out of the cattle business and retire to Sonoma. The first of the ranches was sold in 1978. I retained the home ranch and rockhouse with 50 acres until 2004. At that time, I brought down to Sonoma the last of my personal possessions, including the horse tack and deer rack.

Bob Silva, an old friend, came to the house one evening and saw the rack and asked where it came from. I told him that it came from the Marble Mountains years ago when I had the cattle ranches. I'd hunted Wyoming and all over for mule deer, and this was smaller than any mule deer, and so didn't mount it. Bob said he had a friend who would want to see it.

We ended up getting it measured, only to find out that it was one of the biggest Columbia blacktails ever taken. ▲

Award-Winning Moments

As the official host of Boone and Crockett Club's 26th Big Game Awards Program, Cabela's played a major role in its overall success, including making room in their Fort Worth, Texas, store for six weeks to house the trophy display and host other events. Accepting their special recognition plaque from B&C's Keith Balfourd is Stephanie Perry, the store's marketing and communications manager.

Photograph by Bill Honza

TROPHY STATS

▼ ▼ ▼ ▼ ▼

Category
Columbia Blacktail Deer –
Typical Antlers

Score
170 $^6/_8$

Length of Main Beam
Right: 24 $^2/_8$ Left: 24 $^3/_8$

**Circumference Between
Burr and First Point**
Right: 5 $^1/_8$ Left: 5 $^2/_8$

Number of Points
Right: 5   Left: 4

Inside Spread
20 $^7/_8$

Location
Clatsop Co., Oregon – 1955

Hunter
Larry Naught

Owner
Allan Naught

COLUMBIA BLACKTAIL DEER TYPICAL ANTLERS
First Award (Tie) – 170 ⁶/₈

▼ ▼ ▼ ▼ ▼ ▼ ▼ ▼ ▼

HUNTER – LARRY NAUGHT   OWNER – ALLAN NAUGHT

Larry Naught was hunting an area known locally as the Tillamook Burn in October of 1955. It was near Saddle Mountain, a place Larry often enjoyed spending his hunting days.

The exact circumstances of how hunter and deer came together were lost when Larry died, but the deer's trophy antlers have been a constant fixture in the Naught home. They also serve as a reminder of Naught's best days in the mountains.

Over 50 years later, Larry's son, Allan, decided that the antlers should get the recognition they deserved. He had them measured in the spring of 2006, only to find that his dad's set of antlers he so dearly prized would have a legacy all its own. Larry's deer not only made B&C's records book, but is one of the largest sets of antlers ever recorded for Columbia blacktail deer. Allan takes pride in knowing that it was his dad who took this great deer and that the rack still resides in the same house that Larry lived in all those years ago. ▲

Photograph by Jack Reneau

Allan Naught accepting his plaque and medal from Buck Buckner, Vice President and Chairman of the Big Game Records Committee.

Photograph by Bill Honza

TROPHY STATS

▼ ▼ ▼ ▼ ▼

Category
Columbia Blacktail Deer –
Non-Typical Antlers

Score
185 $^1/_8$

Length of Main Beam
Right: 23 $^5/_8$ Left: 24 $^5/_8$

**Circumference Between
Burr and First Point**
Right: 3 $^7/_8$ Left: 4

Number of Points
Right: 8   Left: 8

Inside Spread
16 $^1/_8$

Location
Trinity Co., California – 2005

Hunter
J. Peter Morish

COLUMBIA BLACKTAIL DEER NON-TYPICAL ANTLERS
First Award – 185 ¹/₈

▼ ▼ ▼ ▼ ▼ ▼ ▼ ▼ ▼

J. PETER MORISH

The views are breathtaking, the air is clean, and the hunting is exceptional. For 27 hunting seasons, I have experienced all that the Trinity Alps had to offer. For anyone who desires to hunt public land and wants a memorable hunting experience, the Trinity Alps may be their dream area; it has been for me.

I have taken many deer in the Trinity Alps, both small and big. As the years passed, I became more selective on the size of deer I wanted to harvest. I found that passing up a legal buck was just as

Trinity Dream Come True

rewarding as taking a deer. When I got to the point of passing up a decent four-point buck to try for a larger one, then I knew that my perspective on hunting had changed. Most hunters in the United States don't associate good hunting with California, especially trophy deer hunting; however, I do.

The name Alps speaks for itself. Though the height of the Trinity Alps does not come near to the elevations found elsewhere, the steepness and ruggedness of the back country rivals the most well known of tough hunting areas. Add to this the thick underbrush and you have a challenge for even the most seasoned hunter. The blacktail is certainly not as well known, or even hunted as much as the mule deer or the whitetail deer. However, it is every bit as much of a challenge and worthy adversary as any other species of deer. For many, the blacktail is one of the most difficult deer to hunt. To find a nice buck is a difficult and oftentimes daunting and consuming task. A trophy buck can require a lifetime of hunting. If you are able to hunt hard and choose to do so, then a trophy can be found in the coastal mountains of northern California.

Photograph by Jack Reneau

J. Peter Morish accepting his plaque and medal from Buck Buckner, Vice President and Chairman of the Big Game Records Committee.

As I have done for 26 prior seasons, I headed for my favorite hunting grounds in mid-September of the 2005 season. I often choose to not hunt the first weekend because of heightened opening-day hunting pressure. After the opening weekend, the number of hunters in the backcountry drops significantly. Usually, the only hunters you see, if any, are those like yourself who have also hunted the area for years.

On this particular weekend, I planned on going with a hunting buddy but, at the last moment, he cancelled. Hunting in the wilderness is certainly not something I would recommend someone doing on his or her own. However, being that I had been planning this hunt since the end of the prior season, I decided to go anyway.

> IT TOOK A COUPLE OF MINUTES TO COMPOSE MYSELF AND REALIZE WHAT HAD JUST HAPPENED. I KNEW I HAD JUST HARVESTED A DEER AND HE WAS HUGE, POSSIBLY THE LARGEST DEER I HAD YET TAKEN. IT WAS STILL VERY EARLY, SO I DECIDED TO SIT ON THE ROCK OUTCROPPING AND RELISH THE MOMENT. I SAT ON THAT ROCK FOR AN HOUR WATCHING THE SUNRISE AND TAKING IN THE BEAUTY THAT WAS REVEALED BEFORE ME. THE MORNING COLORS SEEMED BRIGHTER AND THE VIEW EVEN MORE MAJESTIC. I THOUGHT THEN THAT I PROBABLY HAD SHOT THE DEER OF A LIFETIME.

The first leg of my hunting trip was to drive to the trailhead. I arrived early on a Friday morning. It was mid-September, which is often just an extension of summer. This day was clear, with temperatures in the low 90s. Though this area is known for hunters who horse pack into the wilderness area of the Trinity Alps, I had chosen to backpack. I did this because I have been able to do so physically and because I just didn't want those who would pack me in to know just how well I did hunting. It takes about seven hours of hard hiking to reach my camp. It is only about four or five miles, but the terrain is either up or down.

By the time I arrived at camp, I was extremely tired and sore. I was reminded of earlier hunts when it was difficult but not so consuming, and I wondered how much longer I would be able to do this kind of hunting. But, I was here now, and tomorrow would begin another hunting season.

First, I needed to set up camp. When backpacking, you learn to pack in only the essentials. If you do get a deer, then you will be packing out both the deer and all your gear. This can be a very heavy pack if you do not wisely choose what you bring. If I did get a trophy deer, I would bone it out, cut off the antlers, and skin out the cape. One of the positives of hunting blacktail deer when backpacking is its size. It is smaller than mule deer or whitetail, so packing out the meat isn't too bad.

My camp was relatively simple. Over the years, I had cut out a level pad in a timber stand on the side of a mountain. This time of year the weather is often very nice, so a tent is not needed. I lie out under the trees and peer through the tops to watch the stars. This is when I think about what tomorrow may hold and where I would hunt. The air was still, and the skies were clear. Not the best conditions for hunting, but I was in the backcountry of the Trinity Alps and anything was possible.

COLUMBIA BLACKTAIL DEER NON-TYPICAL ANTLERS
First Award – 185 1/8

▼ ▼ ▼ ▼ ▼

J. Peter Morish

The hunting area is so steep, rugged, and dense with brush that you just don't do any walking or stalking for deer. The area I wanted to hunt overlooks two ravines and a sidehill. It usually takes me about 30 minutes in the dark to find the rock outcropping where I would sit for the next three or so hours. From this place I would setup and spot for any deer that might be around.

I awoke well before dawn. I took my pack, which has an external frame. It comes in handy should I need to pack out a buck. I left for one of my favorite hunting sites.

I hiked out of the timber from camp and into a manzanita patch on the south side of the mountain. I snaked my way through brush and finally reached my rock. It was still dark and I had made little noise. I had made this trek from camp many times, and I can do it in the dark with the help of a small flashlight, which I keep pointed on the path in front of me and toward the ground. I didn't want to alert the deer or other hunters that may be across the canyon. As I quietly set up on the rock, I began to see the faint light of the sunrise to the east. I could see the outline of part of the Alps. It was very quiet and still.

I use a lightweight eight power pair of binoculars and find that binoculars are the most important item in harvesting the deer other than my firearm. I began this morning by slowly working my binoculars across the hillside just adjacent and below me. With the binoculars, I continued to follow two ravines below the rock I was sitting on. I began to glass a second time, starting with an area directly across from me. I looked intently into an opening in the brush patch. The rays of sun were beginning to show over the mountains, but it was still relatively dark in the lower parts of the canyon.

I saw something across from me that looked out of place, but I couldn't see if it was a deer or just a shadow. I looked away and began to look lower on the hillside. It was still quiet and I hadn't heard or seen anything. I looked back at that spot adjacent to me and felt that something just wasn't right. I again looked intently, but I wasn't convinced that there was anything there. It was less than 100 yards away and I figured that I should be able to see a deer if it was there.

I looked downhill and then felt I needed to look back to that partial opening again. As I studied the area with my binoculars and as the light was getting better, I thought I saw what looked like a fork to a set of antlers. I just wasn't sure because there was so much brush in the area and things were not clear. As I was straining to see what was in the brush, I saw the entire top of the brush patch move slightly! I realized immediately that I had spotted a buck, and the brush that moved was the deer's rack! I couldn't tell how many points it had but, as it moved, the rack looked to be the extensions of the brush patch that it was standing in front of!

I had seen and shot many big blacktails but rarely had my heart begun to race at the sight of a deer. This was certainly the exception, and my heart was pumping fast. It was now getting light enough that I could make out the outline of the deer's body. The deer was facing uphill and the front half of the body was behind a brush patch. Only his antlers from the middle of the ears up were visible above the brush. In the opening of the brush I could see from the middle of the deer's body to its back end. I immediately thought that all the buck had to do was take one step forward and he would be safe. From where he was standing, there was a steady and thick patch of brush running up the mountainside. If I was to get this deer, I was going to need some luck.

My gun was already positioned on the rock on top of my pack. I quietly slid down onto my stomach and positioned the gun toward the deer. I located the deer in my scope, which I later determined to be 65 yards away, and to my surprise it was still standing in the same position. I could see him from midway back and felt this was going to be my only chance. Because of the size and number of points to the antlers, I was going to have to give it a try. I decided I had a pretty good chance of getting this buck if he would just stay still for another few seconds. If I could get a spine shot midway on the deer, it would be fatal. Being that the deer was as close as he was, I decided to take the shot. I lined up on the deer, held steady and shot!

Through the scope, I saw the buck flinch and take a step backward. As I pulled away from the scope, I looked up to see the buck take another backward step and fall to the ground. He fell partially in the open in the brush, but only enough to see part of the body. He was down on his side and wasn't getting up.

It took a couple of minutes to compose myself and realize what had just happened. I knew I had just harvested a deer, and he was huge, possibly the largest deer I had yet taken. It was still very early, so I decided to sit on the rock outcropping and relish the moment. I sat on that rock for an hour watching the sunrise and taking in the beauty that was revealed before me. The morning colors seemed brighter and the view even more majestic. I thought then that I probably had shot the deer of a lifetime. It had taken 27 years for my dream of a trophy to come true, but it happened, and it occurred in the most beautiful area I have been fortunate enough to hunt — the Trinity Alps. ▲

B&C Photo Archives

J. Peter Morish stands next to his award-winning non-typical Columbia blacktail on display at Cabela's Fort Worth store. Morish's buck has a final score of 185-1/8 points and received a First Place Award at the 26th Big Game Awards Program.

Photograph by Bill Honza

TROPHY STATS

▼ ▼ ▼ ▼ ▼

Category
Columbia Blacktail Deer –
Non-Typical Antlers

Score
168 ³/₈

Length of Main Beam
Right: 22 ²/₈   Left: 22 ⁵/₈

**Circumference Between
Burr and First Point**
Right: 4 ²/₈   Left: 4

Number of Points
Right: 9   Left: 11

Inside Spread
18 ³/₈

Location
Trinity Co., California – 2004

Hunter
Tim A. Nickols

COLUMBIA BLACKTAIL DEER NON-TYPICAL ANTLERS
Second Award – 168 ³/₈

▼ ▼ ▼ ▼ ▼ ▼ ▼ ▼ ▼

TIM A. NICKOLS

I started up the hill about an hour before daylight. It was 32 degrees, very unusual for opening weekend in northwestern California. It rained most of the night, with a clear and cold forecast — better than perfect hunting conditions! I was very excited about the day in front of me. Today was Sunday, September 19th, 2004, in Trinity County, California, an area known for producing trophy blacktails.

Saturday, the opener, went well. We saw five good bucks. My son Adam shot a nice forked horn, so he wasn't hunting with me today. My adrenaline was going strong, making the one-hour uphill hike easy.

At first light, I was looking at an open ridge with some scattered pine trees. Within minutes, I noticed some deer on the ridge about 120 yards away. There were three mature does prancing around and acting unusual. They chased each other over the ridgeline then back into sight. I was watching the does when a massive buck with his head down crested the ridge and chased one of the does back over the ridge out of my view. My heart rate increased several times. This buck was unbelievably huge! The doe appeared again with the monster buck right behind her. His head was down; he was acting like a full-rut whitetail on a hunting video. They were about to go over the ridge. I only had a neck shot on the moving buck and felt I needed to take it.

Shooting freehand, I fired my semi-automatic Browning 7mm Magnum. I didn't hear my bullet hit, and all the deer disappeared over the ridge.

I felt nauseous, knowing I just missed the buck of a lifetime. I ran over to where the deer were. No blood. No buck! My head was spinning with too many thoughts. Why did I shoot? Why

Photograph by Jack Reneau

Tim A. Nickols accepting his plaque and medal from Buck Buckner, Vice President and Chairman of the Big Game Records Committee.

Tim A. Nickols is pictured above with his award-winning non-typical Columbia blacktail deer. The buck was taken in California's Trinity County during the 2004 season. The buck, which received a Second Place Award, has a final score of 168-3/8 points.

didn't I take my time? Why didn't I take a rest? How did I miss? I'm an excellent shot. That numbing effect of failure was mentally crushing me!

I prayed "Dear God, please let me have another chance."

The back of the ridge, in the direction the deer went, dove steeply into a heavily timbered canyon. The other side of the canyon rose up even steeper, with dense timber, then white thorn, rock, and buckbrush near the top. Just below the ridgeline was an opening about 75 yards wide, with a narrow chute leading up to it. I guessed it to be about 300 yards away. A heavily used deer trail ran across the rock opening toward the ridgeline.

I scanned the hillside. Wanting to see the buck so badly, I prayed again. My prayers were answered. One, two, and then three does came up the steep chute. They followed the trail across the opening, and went out of sight. I got an extreme rush of adrenaline. Miraculously, the buck appeared in the bottom of the chute, taking the same path as the does.

I threw my rifle up and tried to steady the crosshairs of my Leupold 3x9 scope on the buck's shoulder. Not a chance. There was no way I could make the shot freehand. My crosshairs were moving like a leaf in the wind. I wasn't going to miss again! I dropped to my butt and rested my elbows on the insides of each knee. Thinking 300 yards, I held high on the buck's shoulder and squeezed the trigger. Boom! Thwop. I heard the bullet hit. The buck lunged up the hill and bolted away into the brush. Now there was total silence except for my heart pounding in my chest. I knew I had hit him, and gave thanks for an answered prayer.

COLUMBIA BLACKTAIL DEER NON-TYPICAL ANTLERS
Second Award – 168 3/8
▼ ▼ ▼ ▼ ▼

TIM A. NICKOLS

About 15 minutes later, I made it up the steep hill to where I hit the buck. I found a little blood spattered on the rocks and a piece of flesh and blood about the size of my thumbnail. I was concerned not seeing any more blood in the direction the buck went, and the fact that most all the bucks I shoot drop. I followed the path of disturbed shale rock to the edge of the brush. No blood, and no buck!

I contacted my lifelong friend and hunting buddy Vince Elliot. I told him I shot a monster buck and could use some help tracking it. We ranged the shot at 292 yards. I clued Vince in with the details as we both scanned for blood up to the edge of the brush. There was a small crawl hole I figured the buck must have entered. I looked hard at the leaves for blood. No blood.

Vince said, "There's your buck down there!"

I looked down the hill below the deer trail we were on and saw the back legs of the buck sticking out of the brush. Looking so hard for blood, I didn't see where the buck fell and slid down the rock. He was piled upside down, so we couldn't see his antlers. I pulled his head up and was in disbelief at the size of his rack — huge mass, width, tine length, and points going everywhere. He was by far the most impressive blacktail I have ever had my hands on. I was overcome with joy. I thanked God for the harvest of this incredible buck.

Vince and I sat there in awe for the next several minutes, counting points and taking some measurements. We managed to drag the buck downhill to an old skid road, where Vince was able to get his quad. We loaded the buck and rode down the mountain to a good spot and took several pictures. I was still amazed that I had been the one to take this world-class blacktail.

Those of us who hunt blacktails know how rare it is to see a giant buck during daylight in rifle season, let alone kill one. I know if it were not for the unseasonably cold weather I could not have killed this buck. Except for huge private land ranches, you just don't see giant blacktails.

It was truly the hunt and buck of a lifetime. I owe a special thanks to my friend Vince for finding time to scout our hunting areas. I am forever grateful to my awesome wife Annette and our children, Stesha, Adam, Savanna, Paige, and Courtney. We all enjoy hunting and all other outdoor activities. Thank you, Dad, for teaching me to hunt. You know the hunting tradition continues. ▲

Photograph by Bill Honza

TROPHY STATS

▼ ▼ ▼ ▼ ▼

Category
Sitka Blacktail Deer – Typical Antlers

Score
120 $^7/_8$

Length of Main Beam
Right: 17 $^3/_8$ Left: 17 $^4/_8$

Circumference Between Burr and First Point
Right: 4   Left: 4 $^1/_8$

Number of Points
Right: 5   Left: 5

Inside Spread
14 $^7/_8$

Location
Wrangell Island, Alaska – 2006

Hunter
Dave L. Brown

SITKA BLACKTAIL DEER TYPICAL ANTLERS
First Award – 120 7/8

▼ ▼ ▼ ▼ ▼ ▼ ▼ ▼ ▼

DAVE L. BROWN

August 1st marks the annual deer-season opener in Alaska. At this time of year, the bucks are up high in the alpine getting fat on deer cabbage. Normally, we would go on a three- or four-day alpine camp-out hunt. But because my son and I had drawn Dall's sheep tags for a special unit in the interior part of the state, all of our backpacking gear was packed and ready for this special 10-day sheep hunt. I didn't want to get it all wet, so I figured we would just day hunt near town.

With rainy and foggy weather, the first and second days of the season were a bust. I didn't even leave the house. In the meantime, a friend of mine had gone out and taken a pair of bucks. Now I really felt bad for staying in bed and staying dry.

The third-day forecast was a little better, so I decided to try a day hunt in an alpine area near where I live. The plan was to hike up high, hunt hard, and get back down by evening. I didn't have high hopes because I tried the same area the year before and hadn't seen much. The bugs had been really bad that year, and the deer seemed to be lower on the mountain than usual.

After three hours of brush busting, I completed my soaking-wet hike (every blueberry bush leaf had a big drop of water resting on it). There's just no way to stay dry; if you wear raingear you sweat badly, and if you don't, you soak up the water off the vegetation. So I just wore a cotton t-shirt and let it get soaked on the way up, then changed into polypropylene clothing once I reached alpine.

The fog was thick, and I was using my GPS to find my way. At about 9 a.m., I was sitting on an open alpine ridge about 3,000 feet above sea level. The fog was still hanging on the ridgetops.

I started stillhunting, even though I could only see 50 yards or so. After half a mile, I

I CONTINUED ALONG THE RIDGE, WITH FOG ROLLING IN AND OUT. I STOPPED TO EAT A SNACK AND COULD SEE A DOZEN OR SO COMMERCIAL SALMON GILL-NETTERS FISHING IN THE BAY A MILE AWAY. MY SON WAS CREWING WITH ONE OF MY FRIENDS ON ONE OF THE BOATS. I ALMOST FELT SORRY FOR THEM HAVING TO WORK WHEN THERE WERE DEER TO BE HUNTED!

spotted a two-point buck and a doe. They appeared in the fog like ghosts. I watched them for a minute as they fed on deer cabbage. They then faded back into the fog.

I continued along the ridge, with fog rolling in and out. I stopped to eat a snack and could see a dozen or so commercial salmon gill-netters fishing in the bay a mile away. My son was crewing with one of my friends on one of the boats. I almost felt sorry for them having to work when there were deer to be hunted!

I hiked a little further and the fog soon burned off, exposing the entire ridge. I began to glass the area in its entirety. The deer are really reddish this time of year and are relatively easy to spot. After a bit, I saw a couple of deer shapes on a green knob about 100 yards away. I moved a few feet and could see one of the deer had a nice rack. I moved forward quickly to get a rest, took aim at his brisket (he was looking head on at me), and squeezed the trigger.

At the shot, the buck slid down the steep slope and clear out of sight. I made my way over and found him in a heap at the bottom of the draw. It's been my experience that most of the time they get smaller as you get closer, but not this one. He was bigger than I thought, with long and symmetrical points.

As I boned out the buck and put the meat in game bags, I realized how lucky I was. I was fortunate to hunt such a magnificent buck in such great country, and to live in such a great land. ▲

B&C Photo Archives

The Dallas Safari Club, their staff, and volunteers provided invaluable assistance in helping with the events leading up to the 26th Big Game Awards in Fort Worth, Texas, especially the trophy display within the Cabela's store. Accepting this special recognition plaque from B&C's Keith Balfourd is Dallas Safari Club President Bill Swisher (center) and their Executive Director and B&C Professional Member, Gray Thornton.

Photograph by Bill Honza

TROPHY STATS

▼ ▼ ▼ ▼ ▼

Category
Sitka Blacktail Deer – Typical Antlers

Score
120 $1/8$

Length of Main Beam
Right: 18 $2/8$ Left: 17 $3/8$

Circumference Between Burr and First Point
Right: 3 $6/8$ Left: 3 $6/8$

Number of Points
Right: 5   Left: 5

Inside Spread
15 $3/8$

Location
Prince Of Wales Island, Alaska – 2004

Hunter
James A. Sharpe

SITKA BLACKTAIL DEER TYPICAL ANTLERS
Second Award – 120 $\frac{1}{8}$

▼ ▼ ▼ ▼ ▼ ▼ ▼ ▼ ▼

JAMES A. SHARPE

I woke up on November 17, 2004, not expecting anything unusual. I was 12 years old and getting ready for another day at school. I got up, showered, and headed out the door.

About 20 miles of the way through our 30-mile drive into Klawock, we encountered a car almost coming to a complete stop. We slowed down a little, but we were running late.

School-Day Buck

It was then I noticed the reason why the car was stopping. A buck that I thought at the time was a 3-pointer ran out from in front of the car. I was ready, because up here it's not uncommon to see a buck or two on the island's road system. Hunting mainly for meat, I always have my rifle in the car. A lot of people do that on Prince of Wales Island.

I hopped out of the car about the same time the buck started to trot off. After getting a good look at him, I was really starting to want him. I headed off in hot pursuit into the brush. After I got into the brush, I checked my surroundings but didn't see him. Just as I was going to head back, I saw his antlers about 70 yards away. I waited a little while until he lifted his head. He finally lifted up just enough for me to get a great neck shot, and I got him with my .270. ▲

Photograph by Jack Reneau

James A. Sharpe accepting his plaque and medal from Buck Buckner, Vice President and Chairman of the Big Game Records Committee.

Photograph by Bill Honza

TROPHY STATS

▼ ▼ ▼ ▼ ▼

Category
Sitka Blacktail Deer – Typical Antlers

Score
118 $^2/_8$

Length of Main Beam
Right: 17 $^2/_8$ Left: 17$^6/_8$

Circumference Between Burr and First Point
Right: 4 $^6/_8$ Left: 4 $^4/_8$

Number of Points
Right: 5   Left: 5

Inside Spread
14 $^4/_8$

Location
Prince Of Wales Island, Alaska – 2003

Hunter
Tim Koentopp

BOONE AND CROCKETT CLUB'S

SITKA BLACKTAIL DEER
TYPICAL ANTLERS
Third Award – 118 $^2/_8$

▼ ▼ ▼ ▼ ▼ ▼ ▼ ▼ ▼

TIM KOENTOPP

Steve Merritt has spent decades chasing Sitka blacktails, and he takes a lot of pride in his hunting. He and Tim Koentopp decided to go for a deer hunt together on November 1, 2003, and headed out to one of Steve's hunting spots on Staney Creek on Prince of Wales Island. It was a nice, sunny day, perfect for chasing deer.

They hiked in about two miles to get into a likely deer spot. Hiking two miles on Prince of Wales Island might as well be ten in most places. The thick, old-growth rainforest, heavy brush, and occasional muskeg patch can make a hunter expend quite a bit of energy getting around.

They set up in a likely spot, with Steve about 100 feet in front of Tim. Steve began to do a fawn-type bleat, hoping to attract a rutting buck. He had been at it about three minutes when Tim could see it was working. A nice buck was headed their direction without much hesitation. Steve couldn't see the buck, however, so Tim said, "Steve, get down."

Steve did, and Tim unloaded on the buck with his .30-06 at 40 yards. The shot counted, and the buck was soon securely anchored to the ground. As they approached, Steve started "freaking out" as Tim would describe later. Steve had been chasing these deer for a long time, but had never seen one as big as this one before. Tim, who was used to seeing mule deer in Colorado before making the move to Alaska, didn't realize what he had accomplished.

Tim received the Third Place Award in 2007 for his typical Sitka blacktail at B&C's 26th Big Game Awards Banquet in Fort Worth, Texas. ▲

Photograph by Bill Honza

TROPHY STATS

▼ ▼ ▼ ▼ ▼

Category
Sitka Blacktail Deer – Typical Antlers

Score
117 $^6/_8$

Length of Main Beam
Right: 19 $^1/_8$ Left: 19 $^3/_8$

Circumference Between Burr and First Point
Right: 4   Left: 4 $^1/_8$

Number of Points
Right: 5   Left: 5

Inside Spread
16 $^2/_8$

Location
Etolin Island, Alaska – 2004

Hunter
Davey W. Brown

SITKA BLACKTAIL DEER TYPICAL ANTLERS
Fourth Award – 117 $^6/_8$

▼ ▼ ▼ ▼ ▼ ▼ ▼ ▼ ▼

DAVEY W. BROWN

Our hunting trip began on August 1, 2004, with a two-hour boat ride from our home to the south end of Etolin Island. My dad had been hunting this area for years, but this was my first time. As we neared our destination, there were thousands of pink salmon jumping in the bay where we were going to anchor the boat.

We loaded our internal frame packs with enough food and camping gear for three days and proceeded up the mountain, headed for the alpine. There was an abundance of devil's club (with nasty thorns) and blowdown for the first couple of hours of the hike. It took us

Photograph courtesy of Davey W. Brown

Davey W. Brown and his father, Dave Brown, who received the First Award for typical Sitka blacktail in this book, made camp at 3,200 feet after a five-hour hike from sea level.

Davey W. Brown with his award-winning Sitka blacktail. The buck has a final score of 117-6/8 points and received a Fourth Place Award at the 26th Big Game Awards Program.

five hours to hike from saltwater to our camp at 3,200 feet. We set up our small tent and stove, got our sleeping pads and sleeping bags out, and made camp. We had freeze-dried dinners and made Kool-Aid snowcones from a snowbank, then glassed the area for deer before we turned in for the night.

The next morning we got up around 4 a.m. It gets light early that time of year. We had some oatmeal, grabbed some lunch stuff, and then headed out. We hiked about a half mile before stopping to glass. My dad called this place "Rod's Spot," because his friend used to glass from there and always spotted deer. We immediately spotted a large group of elk feeding in the alpine (elk were transplanted to the area a few years ago). Five or six of them were big bulls. There were also a couple of small bucks feeding less than 50 yards from the elk.

We tried to work our way closer to the deer, but the elk winded us and off they went. This caused the deer to bolt as well, so we kept walking down the rocky slope.

We had stopped to take a break when we glassed a big buck lying down about 500 yards downhill. After dropping our packs, we figured out a game plan to stalk him. We got up to within 150 yards and peeked over a small rise. He was still there! He looked like a nice 4x4, not counting the eyeguards.

I rested my .30-06 on my pack and set up for a shot. Just then, the buck got nervous and stood up. His body language looked like he was going to take off, so I aimed behind the shoulder and squeezed the trigger. The buck managed barely 20 yards before he was down. My dad said, "Nice shot! That buck is bigger than anything I've ever taken."

On our way to the buck, we had to cross a steep rockslide. My dad slipped and managed to put a pretty good gash on his head, but we were so excited it didn't even slow us down. When we got to the deer, we were both overjoyed! We admired his handsome rack for a while, took some pictures, and then cut up the deer to fit in our packs.

When we got back to camp, I put the meat on the snow to cool. The next day we woke up to rain and fog, loaded everything up, and headed home. It was a great trip, and one that I'll never forget! ▲

B&C Photo Archives

The first product ever to bear the name Boone and Crockett was a Leupold riflescope. Because of this and their commitment to conservation and fair chase, the Club will always have a special relationship with America's Optics Authority. Accepting Leupold's 26th Big Game Awards sponsorship recognition plaque from B&C's Keith Balfourd (left) is Tim Gauthier, videographer and producer of the Club's television series, *Leupold Big Game Profiles.*

Photograph by Bill Honza

TROPHY STATS

▼ ▼ ▼ ▼ ▼

Category
Sitka Blacktail Deer –
Typical Antlers

Score
122 $^{1}/_{8}$

Length of Main Beam
Right: 18 $^{1}/_{8}$ Left: 19 $^{2}/_{8}$

**Circumference Between
Burr and First Point**
Right: 3 $^{6}/_{8}$ Left: 3 $^{6}/_{8}$

Number of Points
Right: 5   Left: 5

Inside Spread
15 $^{1}/_{8}$

Location
Prince Of Wales Island, Alaska – 2004

Hunter
Picked Up

Owner
James F. Baichtal

SITKA BLACKTAIL DEER TYPICAL ANTLERS
Certificate of Merit – 122 ¹/₈

▼ ▼ ▼ ▼ ▼ ▼ ▼ ▼ ▼

OWNER – JAMES F. BAICHTAL

No one will ever know the exact circumstances behind the demise of this great Sitka blacktail, or how it came to rest in the karst feature where it was found. That knowledge perished at the moment this buck was entombed in his unexpected makeshift grave.

Southeast Alaska contains vast areas of pure limestone. With the rainfall, weather, and climate of Southeast Alaska, extensive cave systems have formed into most of the limestone outcrops. As the forest geologist for the Tongass National Forest, I get to explore many of these karst areas and the caves and vertical pits within them. On June 17, 2004, two others and I were exploring one of these areas late in the evening after work. We discovered a 40-foot-deep vertical pit at the contact between marble and phyllite in the alpine of an unnamed ridge. We then discovered a small hole blowing air down-slope from the pit. The hole was connected to the pit.

I crawled in and was able to work my way to the bottom of the pit. I then began photo-graphing the pit's interior and opening. As my eyes adjusted to the darkness, I noticed two buck skulls on the floor of the cavern, positioned as if they had once been locked together. It seems that these two bucks had fought in the alpine and fell into the pit still locked together; they must have died from either the fall or from starvation. The freshness of the bones on the pit floor suggested that they were only there for one or two seasons, most likely locked in the snow, which filled the shaft for most of the year.

Something had made its way into the pit since the bucks had died, as it was apparent some of the bones had been broken for marrow. Both bucks' antlers had now shrunk to the point that they could be easily separated. I retrieved both skulls from the pit. The largest of these scored 122-1/8. I believe an animal as grand as this should be honored. ▲

Photograph by Jack Reneau

James F. Baichtal accepting his plaque from Buck Buckner, Vice President and Chairman of the Big Game Records Committee.

Photograph by Bill Honza

TROPHY STATS

▼ ▼ ▼ ▼ ▼

Category
  Sitka Blacktail Deer –
  Non-Typical Antlers

Score
  124 $^2/_8$

Length of Main Beam
  Right: 18 $^3/_8$ Left: 16 $^6/_8$

**Circumference Between
  Burr and First Point**
  Right: 3 $^6/_8$ Left: 3 $^6/_8$

Number of Points
  Right: 6   Left: 7

Inside Spread
  15 $^4/_8$

Location
  Prince Of Wales Island, Alaska – 2005

Hunter
  William C. Musser

SITKA BLACKTAIL DEER NON-TYPICAL ANTLERS
First Award – 124 $^2/_8$

▼ ▼ ▼ ▼ ▼ ▼ ▼ ▼ ▼

WILLIAM C. MUSSER

I was getting ready to go trapping on Kuiu Island in southeast Alaska. I needed to get to my trapping teepee on Prince of Wales Island to get some of my gear for the trip farther north. I had my 14-year-old son, Sunny, and my 22-year-old son, Duke, with me. The teepee, which is two stories with a sleeping loft, is about a half-hour hike in and sits back in the trees on the edge of a secret lake, with some pretty meadows just before the lake.

My cousin Ralph and I had previously found a hidden game trail that connected a logging road with the lake. My two sons and I had just entered the first part of the trail, when I spotted some really large deer tracks. I stopped and pointed them out to the boys. I had seen a huge 10-pointer in there the week before, and I thought that's what I was tracking. I told them that I'd like to get one more buck (the limit is four per season) before winter since I would be gone trapping for more than a month.

The trail goes through some really beautiful old-growth timber. We stopped just back from the meadows and took a few minutes to catch our breath. It was misting a little, and there was some morning fog hanging over the valley. The trail crossed back and forth over a small creek that helps feed the lake. I was jumping across for the fourth time when I saw something in mid-jump. As I straightened up on the other side, Sunny landed beside me and whispered, "Big buck!"

I focused on the shape in the waist-high grass. All I could see was antlers, head, and neck. I was packing my .243 Smith & Wesson stainless rifle. He was looking right at us. I tried for a neck shot but nothing happened. He was only 40 yards away, but he just stood there, so I put the crosshairs in the center of his chest and shot again. That time he sat down on his haunches; I had hit him in the spine. This told me instantly that my gun was not shooting true. A little bit of buck fever was starting to take over as well. I shot one more time at his neck, and shot two points off of his left antler. I actually saw one go flying. I then went up close and finished him.

All three of us stood there looking down at the biggest rack we had ever seen taken in our area. That's when buck fever got us all. We looked around, but could not find the two pieces of antler. Later, my wife Vanette and I walked back in to get more trapping supplies, and I showed her the spot of the kill. The wolves had been there and had matted the grass down flat. I couldn't believe it when I spotted the largest piece of antler just lying there. It was the only thing the wolves had left. ▲

Photograph by Bill Honza

TROPHY STATS

▼ ▼ ▼ ▼ ▼

Category
Whitetail Deer – Typical Antlers

Score
201 $^1/_8$

Length of Main Beam
Right: 29 $^6/_8$ Left: 29

Circumference Between Burr and First Point
Right: 5   Left: 5

Number of Points
Right: 6   Left: 5

Inside Spread
24 $^1/_8$

Location
Warren Co., Ohio – 2004

Hunter
Bradley S. Jerman

WHITETAIL DEER
TYPICAL ANTLERS
First Award – 201 ¹/₈

▼ ▼ ▼ ▼ ▼ ▼ ▼ ▼ ▼

BRADLEY S. JERMAN

The first time I saw the buck was at last light the night before taking him. I'd taken my video camera with me for the afternoon hunt to film some does and a small buck I'd seen that morning. The view was poor because they were 150 yards away in some trees, and it was getting dark quickly. Noise to my right made me turn the camera just in time to see the monster emerge from a thicket about 125 yards away. I did my best to keep my hands steady as I captured 45 seconds of video before he angled away and disappeared into the darkness.

Even though I could no longer see him or the other deer, I knew they were less than 200 yards away, and there was only some light timber and a few thickets between us. It was at this point that my brain stopped working. I believe it short-circuited due to overload. I called my wife on my cell phone and told her I planned to spend the night in my stand. I thought this would be the best way to keep from alerting the deer to my presence. I was in a comfortable tripod on private property and thought I could make it.

Surprisingly, she didn't offer any protest. She knows I'm a nut when it comes to hunting, so she simply accepted the call as standard strangeness. She wished me well after mentioning that I was missing one of my favorite Mexican dinners.

Reality set in a few hours later. I was dressed for an afternoon hunt and missing several layers of clothes that would've made the stay possible. I just couldn't take the cold. So, with my crossbow perched on the shooting rail of the tripod, I removed the bolt and placed it on the platform and slowly descended the ladder. I wanted to stay as unhampered as I could, knowing I would be back well before light.

I crawled from the thicket where my stand was, staying on my knees for another 100 yards

Photograph by Jack Reneau

Bradley S. Jerman accepting his plaque and medal from Buck Buckner, Vice President and Chairman of the Big Game Records Committee.

Photograph courtesy of Bradley S. Jerman

Bradley S. Jerman with his award-winning whitetail deer taken in Warren County, Ohio, in 2004. The buck scores 201-1/8 points and received the First Place Award.

across a mowed field opposite of where the deer were. With the camera tucked in my jacket, the exit seemed to go well.

Once home, I headed straight for the TV to play the tape. My wife, surprised to see me, quickly gathered my three children. We watched the video in amazement. The video was dark, but his antlers were bright white. He was magnificent.

I began preparing for the next day's hunt. I laid out some extra layers and covered my camo with scent-free spray. I readied a daypack in preparation for an all-day hunt if needed, remembering to include some heat packs, which I was so desperately missing earlier that evening.

After tinkering with everything, I lay down and tried to get some rest, but my mind was still buzzing. I found myself nervously looking at the clock every few minutes. I was not going to sleep, even though I tried for a couple more hours.

At 2 a.m., I decided that if I was going to be that wide awake, I might as well be in my stand. I raided the fruit bowl and headed for the shower. At that time, I had no idea how important being scent free was going to be.

By 3 a.m. I was back at the edge of the field and decided that I should crawl back in. It took me 45 minutes to cross the 100 yards back to the thicket. While still on my knees, I hung a scent bomb on a limb just behind my stand.

I was proud to have gotten there without making a sound, but that arrogance was quickly dashed. As I stood, a briar that had latched on to one of my pant legs made a loud popping sound that tore through the silence. Just then, a deer that I believe was the monster buck blew loudly and took off. In a panic, I blew back and followed with a few short grunts. The deer stopped after three bounds and was quiet.

It was very dark. I was in full camo, and the deer was on the other side of the thicket; I don't think he could see me. I heard the deer move away slowly, so I slid up the ladder and sat down dejected.

I put my pack down and started praying for all I was worth. Hunters know that when a deer blows at you, it is usually the kiss of death. My spirits were lifted, though, when about 20 minutes later the deer snort/wheezed at me from some distance away. I believe that having the deer blow actually helped me be bolder; I felt there was nothing to lose. So I tried to mimic what I had just heard as loudly as I could.

All was quiet for an hour, then I heard crunching leaves from the direction I had seen the buck the night before. Afraid that he might lose interest, I used a can doe-bleat call and added a few tending grunts. I did this two more times before daylight whenever I heard noise from that area. It was a miracle that he didn't respond any of those times and bust me before shooting light.

WHITETAIL DEER TYPICAL ANTLERS
First Award – 201 1/8

▼ ▼ ▼ ▼ ▼

BRADLEY S. JERMAN

As the first glimmers of daybreak arrived, I was able to make out a couple of does browsing near my stand. Shortly after, as if they were glow-in-the-dark, a huge set of white antlers appeared. I could tell immediately that this was the same deer I'd seen the night before. I then tried to ignore the antlers and began focusing on the task at hand.

Now within range, he was moving between the does, causing them to jump away. I readied for the shot as he once again made a doe jump. This time she lunged right at my stand and continued to walk right up one of my shooting lanes. To my surprise, he followed her until they were both right underneath me. I remained frozen!

He was only a foot from one of the legs when he pointed his nose up and sniffed at the estrous scent I had put out. Letting the doe walk, he huffed at the scent and moved into the thicket without offering me a shot. With a couple of head-bobs, he disappeared completely into the brush and stopped just out of sight.

This gave me a chance to breathe again. I scanned all sides of the thicket as I waited. It was almost 15 minutes before a doe appeared in the closest shooting lane to the thicket. This caused him to respond by lowering his head and pushing through the thicket, bending several small trees over as he muscled his way out.

The buck was angling away sharply when he began to give chase. As soon as there was a shot I took it, hitting him just behind the ribs on the right side. The bolt from my crossbow went through the diaphragm, right lung, and the arteries above the heart. He picked up speed as he hooked left behind the thicket, but I could see his head drop. When that happened, he snagged on some ground vines, flipped over and was not able to get back up. His last breath was less than 10 seconds later.

I remember telling one of my friends that day that I had just killed a "Booner." I had no idea that I had just taken what would become the 11th-largest typical whitetail ever recorded by Boone and Crockett. He was also the largest typical entered in B&C's 26th Awards Program, as well as the new Ohio State Record. I feel blessed beyond measure, and am having a great time with the deer. ▲

Photograph courtesy of the Pope and Young Club

TROPHY STATS

▼ ▼ ▼ ▼ ▼

Category
Whitetail Deer – Typical Antlers

Score
198 $^3/_8$

Length of Main Beam
Right: 26 $^7/_8$ Left: 26

Circumference Between Burr and First Point
Right: 4 $^7/_8$ Left: 4 $^7/_8$

Number of Points
Right: 7   Left: 7

Inside Spread
19 $^4/_8$

Location
Muskingum Co., Ohio – 2004

Hunter
Timothy E. Reed

WHITETAIL DEER TYPICAL ANTLERS
Second Award – 198 $^3/_8$

▼ ▼ ▼ ▼ ▼ ▼ ▼ ▼ ▼

TIMOTHY E. REED

With archery season already underway a month, my hunting buddy John Hank and I headed for Muskingum County in southeastern Ohio. We arrived at the home of some very special friends of ours, Randy and Trudye Bonar, where we set up our camper for a week of bowhunting.

We spent most of Saturday setting up stands. We waited to hunt until Sunday, which came and went with only small bucks and does moving through the area.

Monday found me back in my stand with a couple does feeding here and there, and then moving off. It's hard to let a nice doe pass by, but you don't want to shoot one that's possibly leading a nice buck around, either.

As we were sitting around the supper table talking, Randy told John and me that he had been seeing a lot more buck movement. Randy owns and runs oil wells, so he gets around to different areas daily. With this in mind, I decided to hunt my most productive stand the next couple of days.

With the stand already set, I slipped into the woods and up the tree before daylight. As I set up my stand a couple of days ago, I had noticed a couple of big deer tracks in the area. Maybe, if I'm lucky, I'll get to see one of these guys.

Some does and small bucks passed by my stand for the morning hunt. I climbed down and headed back to camp for dinner and to see how John did. The evening hunt produced one forkhorn and four does in a four-hour span.

I HAD JUST TURNED TO RETRIEVE MY BOW ROPE HANGING FROM MY SEAT WHEN I CAUGHT MOVEMENT BEHIND ME. EVEN WITH JUST A QUICK GLANCE, I KNEW HE WAS A SHOOTER. AT 30 YARDS OUT AND AT A STEADY PACE, HE WAS CLOSING THE DISTANCE FAST. I REACHED FOR MY BOW AND REMEMBERED THE QUIVER WAS ON THE BOW AND NO ARROW WAS ON THE STRING.

As I woke up on Wednesday, November 10, 2004, and got ready for the morning hunt, I realized the week was already half over. Time always goes by too fast when you're hunting.

I arrived at my stand before daylight and decided to put out a scent pad dipped in doe-in-heat. I put it 15 yards out and 10 yards behind my tree.

I climbed into my stand and settled in for a morning that could not be matched by any other in my 28 years of bowhunting. As it started to get daylight, it wasn't long before I had

Photograph courtesy of Timothy E. Reed

Timothy E. Reed took this award-winning buck with his bow during the 2004 season in Ohio. The buck scores 198-3/8 points and received a Second Place Award.

my first visitor, a young doe and a small 4-pointer 20 yards behind her. Half an hour passed when I spotted a couple of legs coming toward me through the brush — a buck 30 yards out and headed toward me. As I held my bow in hand, he got to 15 yards before he got a nose full of doe-in-heat. He then bolted back about five yards and looked around. I was thinking maybe I should have left this stuff in the bottle when he turned and walked right under my stand.

As he passed by, I could see he was a nice 9-pointer with crab claws at the end of the main beams. In another year, he would be a good buck. But it is still early in this county and, at this time of year, you never know what is going to walk by your stand.

At 8:15 a.m., I spotted another deer — a young 6-pointer 30 yards away. At 10:50, I hadn't seen any more deer so I decided to climb down and get some lunch. I pulled the arrow from the string, placed it back into the quiver, popped the quiver back on my bow, and hung the bow back on its hook.

I had just turned to retrieve my bow rope hanging from my seat when I caught movement behind me. Even with just a quick glance, I knew he was a shooter. At 30 yards out and at a steady pace, he was closing the distance fast. I reached for my bow and remembered the quiver was on the bow and no arrow was on the string. My main focus now had to be to get an arrow nocked, and to forget about taking the quiver off.

As I pulled an arrow from the quiver, I peeked to see where he was at — ten yards behind me with his nose pressed up against the pad dipped in doe-in-heat. Boy, was I glad I put that stuff out! It was just the extra time I needed to get an arrow nocked. I peeked a second time. He was now 20 yards from the tree broadside to me. It was then or never. If he went ten more yards, I would have had no shot because of brush and limbs.

I drew, settled the pin on his shoulder, and let it fly. He bolted about ten yards and stopped. Then he walked off and disappeared. As I searched the ground with my binoculars, I spotted my arrow sticking in the ground and covered with blood. I decided to climb down and check out the arrow, sneak out of there, and give him a couple of hours.

When I got back to camp, John greeted me. After an hour, we decided that since it was a public hunting area, we had better go find my buck. Once back at the stand, we picked up the blood trail. One hundred yards later, it didn't look good. Just as I started to get worried, it picked back up again. After 150 yards more, we came up over a small ridge, and there he was, with 14 points towering over his head. What a sight at 50 yards! It's a sight I will never forget. ▲

Photograph by Frederick J. King

26th Awards Judges Panel members Rick C. Berreth, left, and Mark B. Steffen (Chairman of Boone and Crockett Club's Publications Committee) collaborate on the difficult task of identifying points on Scott R. Dexter's non-typical whitetail. The award-winning buck, which has a final score of 295-3/8 points, has 47 scorable points.

Photograph by Bill Honza

TROPHY STATS

▼ ▼ ▼ ▼ ▼

Category
Whitetail Deer – Non-Typical Antlers

Score
295 $^3/_8$

Length of Main Beam
Right: 21 $^6/_8$ Left: 24 $^5/_8$

Circumference Between Burr and First Point
Right: 6 $^5/_8$ Left: 6 $^6/_8$

Number of Points
Right: 25   Left: 22

Inside Spread
18 $^4/_8$

Location
McDonough Co., Illinois – 2004

Hunter
Scott R. Dexter

WHITETAIL DEER
NON-TYPICAL ANTLERS
First Award (Tie) – 295 ³/₈

▼ ▼ ▼ ▼ ▼ ▼ ▼ ▼ ▼

SCOTT R. DEXTER

It was November 21, 2004, the last day of the first shotgun weekend in Illinois. As the alarm chimed loudly, I reluctantly got up, turned it off, and sat down in my rocker. Recalling the two previous days' activities, I decided to lie back down and not worry about beating the sun out to the timber of our 160-acre family farm just outside of Macomb, Illinois.

Dave, Joe, Paul, and I had all filled our antlerless deer tags on Friday and Saturday. Paul and Dave had family obligations on Sunday, and Joe was called into work, so I would have the woods all to myself. A late, relaxed start this morning was well deserved. The weather had been foggy and rainy the first two days of the season, but the sun was now trying to poke through.

I finally left the back door about 10 a.m. and headed for the food plot that I had planted in early September. This plot is on top of a ridge, and deer tend to drift off the north side and bed down on the adjacent south-facing slope. That's where I started my Sunday hunt.

As I slowly cruised the north edge of the food plot, I stopped, sat, and glassed for half an hour at a time, waiting for some movement before moving on to the next point on the ridge. I watched a young buck run a hot doe around, hoping maybe a mature buck would come in and try to romance the doe away from her young suitor.

About 12:30 p.m., I was getting chilled after sitting in the shade for two and a half hours and decided to head to the south side of the food plot and sit in the sun. I found the perfect tree to sit under, halfway up the hillside that looks over the creek bottom. I kicked the leaves away from where my feet would settle in, got comfortable, and waited for the action to start.

It's amazing how warming the sun is, even when the temperature is 35°F. Fighting to stay awake, I kept turning my head because squirrels made a relentless rustling on the hillside around me.

At 1:30 p.m., I made a mental note that if

Photograph by Jack Reneau

Scott R. Dexter accepting his plaque and medal from Buck Buckner, Vice President and Chairman of the Big Game Records Committee.

Photograph courtesy of Scott R. Dexter

Scott R. Dexter is pictured above with his award-winning whitetail buck scoring 295-3/8.

I didn't see a mature buck by 2:30 p.m., I would slowly make my way up to the hayfield and wait for the parade of does that come out to feed before the end of shooting hours.

At 1:45, the squirrels caught my attention again. As I scanned the perimeter, about 150 yards out I saw movement that was bigger than a squirrel. At that distance, I could see it was a deer heading my way. If it stayed on the trail, it would pass right below me at about 20 yards. At about 125 yards, I could tell that it was a buck and still coming my way. At 100 yards, I could tell it was a really good buck. At 80 yards, I could see the double drop points and palmated main beams.

I soon lost all ability to think coherently. Is this the same buck a nearby landowner told me about three years ago? I could not believe this magnificent animal was still heading my way. He had a routine of walking a few yards, stopping to sniff the air and looking around. I watched him make a scrape and continue my way.

I suddenly felt a cold breeze on the back of my neck. I quickly scanned the trail ahead of him, looking for an opening in the brush for a good clean shot before he entered my scent trail. I found an opening and brought my new Traditions muzzleloader up to my shoulder to look through the scope, but couldn't see anything. I realized I wasn't breathing and had gone temporarily blind. I had not had buck fever this bad since my first deer kill 25 years earlier, and that was a doe.

I finally regained control of my emotions and talked myself into breathing again. I blinked my eyes and regained my sight. I looked through the scope again, got the picture I wanted, and waited for him to move into the only good shooting lane I had.

He kept up his routine, stopping and checking the breeze. My nerves were nearly shot. I took the safety off; he kept on coming. As if on cue, he stopped right in my shooting lane and began checking the wind. He was 60 yards away when I pulled the trigger.

My luck with muzzleloaders and big bucks had not been very good in the past, usually due to operator error — oil in the barrel, damaged primers, something. Hopefully this new muzzleloader would not fail me. It was my first inline muzzleloader. I had always used sidelock models before.

My last thought before I pulled the trigger was, "I hope this gun goes off."

The unmistakable explosion and cloud of smoke from the end of the barrel proved that the gun worked, but had I hit the deer? Was my aim true? The cloud of smoke was so thick that I couldn't tell if I had hit my target. I heard him run and stumble as he cleared the smoke cloud. He then collapsed about 20 yards below me on the hill.

I jumped to my feet only to find my legs were as limp as licorice whips. Watching the deer and trying to reload was just about impossible. Multi-tasking with that much adrenalin running through me was not working. It took me five minutes to reload, even though I was using speed loaders.

Finally loaded, I reached into my front pocket and removed an Indian arrowhead I had found while putting up stands in September, just up the hill in my food plot from where I was now standing. I had been carrying it all fall while bow hunting, hoping this relic would bring me luck.

The old monarch had not moved since he hit the ground. I approached with extreme caution. The last thing I needed right now was to take a running shot through the thick brush just below the big buck's present resting place.

Poking him with the muzzle of my firearm, he did not flinch. Once again I gave thanks to the Almighty, my grandfather who got me started hunting when I was 10, my parents, and the maker of the arrowhead I had found.

I took the arrowhead from my pocket, placed it on the deer's shoulder, and thanked my hunting brother from the past for bringing this magnificent buck to me.

As I looked at this trophy, I was intrigued by his one-of-a-kind rack. My first thoughts were, "I'll probably win the ugly buck of the year award."

At this point, I realized that I did not bring my camera, my hunting knife, or a cell phone to call the house. Needing some critical supplies, I reluctantly left the buck and headed for the house. It was about 400 yards away, and I was confident there wasn't anyone else in the timber that might come across my deer and try to claim it.

Back at the house, I grabbed my knife and checked the camera. The battery was dead. I called my dad and asked if he had a throw-away camera, if his digital camera worked, and if he wanted to help me with my deer.

"Did you get one?"

"Yeah, a pretty nice one with a messed-up rack. It'll look really cool on the wall."

"Sure. Where is it?"

"Down by the creek."

"How are we going to get it out of there?"

Knowing Dad is 76 years old and doesn't need to be dragging deer out of the woods if there are other options, I said, "I'll get the tractor, and we can put it in the bucket."

As we approached the downed monster, Dad's first comment was, "You're right; he is ugly."

After photos (I realized later that I did not take nearly enough) and field dressing, we loaded the deer and started the long trip back to the truck, through the timber, across the creek to the old campsite and out. We put the deer in the back of the truck and headed to the house. When we got there, Mom came out. We took some more photos, and then headed off to the check station.

I hunt every year with the same goal. Use my antlerless tag first then look for a mature buck. If I don't see a mature buck, shoot another doe. ▲

Photograph by Bill Honza

TROPHY STATS

▼ ▼ ▼ ▼ ▼

Category
Whitetail Deer – Non-Typical Antlers

Score
295 $^3/_8$

Length of Main Beam
Right: 30 $^2/_8$ Left: 29

Circumference Between Burr and First Point
Right: 5 $^4/_8$ Left: 5 $^7/_8$

Number of Points
Right: 18   Left: 17

Inside Spread
25 $^1/_8$

Location
Adams Co., Ohio – 2006

Hunter
Jonathan R. Schmucker

WHITETAIL DEER
NON-TYPICAL ANTLERS
First Award (Tie) – 295 ³/₈

▼ ▼ ▼ ▼ ▼ ▼ ▼ ▼ ▼

JONATHAN R. SCHMUCKER

The Amish buck had a home, and John Schmucker knew his address. Having observed the old buck for the past three years, the buck had grown in both size and notoriety. Knowledge of the buck was a little kept secret within the small Amish community on Wheat Ridge in Adams County, Ohio. Only a few hunters outside the Amish community knew of the buck's existence, and they weren't talking either. It became the secret of Wheat Ridge, spoken only within the hushed gatherings of a few local Amish deer hunters who had personally seen the old buck and its magnificent rack.

The Amish Buck of Adams County

Dave Raber, who is also Amish and a neighbor to Schmucker, said even though the buck was well known within the community, he was confident if the buck survived hunting seasons it would find safety during the off season within the farmland of the Amish community.

"We knew where the deer was staying, and it was surrounded by Amish farms," said Raber, "We knew no one within the Amish community would poach him and the buck would be protected."

Adams County lies in the southwestern river hills of Ohio, at the west edge of the Appalachian Plateau. It is largely a rural county with white oaks and red cedar mix forest, small fields of corn and soybeans, and an abundance of thick,wooded hillsides, old farms, and weedy fields that deer utilize for cover. Adams County was one of only three counties open in Ohio during the state's first deer season in 1956.

The first time Schmucker had seen the buck was in August of 2004. It was standing in a 22-acre hayfield not far from his home. John had observed the deer only three times during that late August–early September time frame. "Same Hayfield," said Schmucker.

In 2005, John again saw the buck two evenings in a row in the same hayfield as the previous year. "We never saw the deer during the summer, just in late August or early September standing in the same hayfield," he said, "and then never saw him again the rest of the year."

During 2006, Schmucker observed the big buck on numerous occasions. "This year I saw him in May, and the hayfield is now a bean field, and he was just starting to get his rack," said Schmucker. "I didn't see him again until early July, and then I didn't see him until the rack was pretty much done growing the last of July. During August and September I saw him almost every night come out into the same bean field and feed. I would climb up on the barn roof in the evenings and watch for him."

"Out of a week, I probably saw him five times," said Schmucker. "He never came out of the same corner; maybe one night the buck would come out at one end, then the next night the deer came out at the other end. There was a corn field with woods on both sides. I figured he stayed in there. Sometimes the buck came out of the woods; sometimes he came out of the corn."

John would usually observe the buck during the summer evenings. "Usually just before dark. Sometimes he would come out 7 to 7:30 p.m., and a lot of times you could only see him for 15 to 20 minutes before it was too dark."

"Not everybody saw the deer; only four of us saw him in 2006," said John, "There was another Amish hunter who had seen him that was after him, but he hadn't started hunting yet."

ONLY A FEW HUNTERS OUTSIDE THE AMISH COMMUNITY KNEW OF THE BUCK'S EXISTENCE, AND THEY WEREN'T TALKING EITHER. IT BECAME THE SECRET OF WHEAT RIDGE, SPOKEN ONLY WITHIN THE HUSHED GATHERINGS OF A FEW LOCAL AMISH DEER HUNTERS WHO HAD PERSONALLY SEEN THE OLD BUCK AND ITS MAGNIFICENT RACK.

John was the first one to see the deer in 2004, and then a neighbor saw the buck cross a road that same year while riding in a truck. By 2006, and after several sightings, word of the Amish buck spread around the community and drew the attention of several local deer hunters. He knew of three Amish hunters and three other non-Amish hunters that were after the buck. "Everybody who hunted knew something was in the wind," John said.

"You would see the deer during late summer but the buck always disappeared come fall. He would hunker down somewhere or go nocturnal. I saw where the buck left plenty of big rubs and scrapes during the 2005 hunting season, so I knew he was there. Where I saw the deer during the summer was the same place I would see his sign during the fall."

Other than observing the buck at a distance, Schmucker never intruded on the corn or bean field during the summer of 2006. "I just stayed out of there; I didn't go into the woods until opening day that evening."

Rain on that opening Saturday morning, September 30, of Ohio's bow season had canceled out work for the day. "I was working my horse until noon," said Schmucker. "It was the first time we had him hooked to a buggy."

Around noon, Schmucker was finished with the horse and prepared to go hunting that evening. "It was probably about 3 to 3:30 p.m. when I got everything ready to go hunting and it took about 20 minutes to get back there," said Schmucker.

"I kind of knew the area I wanted to be in, but I had to wait to get back there to find a tree I wanted to climb." Schmucker had carried his climbing stand and his second-hand crossbow to the edge of the bean field in a fence row near where he had observed the buck so many times that summer.

WHITETAIL DEER NON-TYPICAL ANTLERS
First Award (Tie) – 295 ³/₈

▼ ▼ ▼ ▼ ▼

JONATHAN R. SCHMUCKER

"I spent a few minutes locating a tree," John said, "and I quickly picked the best available tree and went about 18 feet up. There was one branch I had to clear from the shooting lane. I hoisted my equipment up and sat down; I was ready to go by 4:30 p.m. I then sprayed myself with scent eliminator because I was sweating a little bit after the climb."

John said, "Around 5 o'clock, I saw two small bucks, a 6-pointer and a small 8-pointer. They were about 100 yards away, and came into the bean field. It was windy, cloudy, overcast, and sprinkling rain."

About a half hour later, a 3-pointer came into the bean field. "During the summer, I would watch this small 3-pointer come out first, and then the big one would follow about five minutes later," said Schmucker. "When I saw the 3-pointer come out, I knew the big one was close by."

"The small buck came out of the corn field into the woods and then jumped the fence into the bean field about 5:30 p.m. to feed," said Schmucker. "After the small buck came out, the big one followed about five minutes later. He came through the corn and jumped the fence right into the bean field."

According to Schmucker, about 70 yards separated the big buck from the 6- and 8-pointer already feeding in the field. "Then the big buck picked up his head, checked the wind, and started feeding. After a while the 6- and 8-pointer started to feed closer to the bigger buck."

"When the 8-pointer got close, the big buck stretched out his neck looking at him, and the other one came up to smell him," said Schmucker. "That's when the big one made a threatening lunge at the 8-pointer and started chasing both small bucks and that's when they started heading my way."

"After a while, the 8-pointer came to within five to ten yards; actually, he went right behind me," said Schmucker. "The 6-pointer was still out 30 to 40 yards, the small 3-pointer was about 30 yards, and the big one was right there with them, maybe ten yards behind."

John knew things were about to go his way. "I knew things were going to work out. I moved around a little bit because I knew where my opening was and to get ready to take the shot."

The three deer left in the bean field calmly walked and fed toward John, with the big one feeding and watching the 8-pointer still standing behind John's stand. "The big one came toward the 8-pointer. I figured he was going to chase him the way he was acting. He was feeding, watching the 8-pointer, and slowly coming my way."

The buck walked into the shooting lane Schmucker had cleared. "I wasn't nervous,"

Jonathan R. Schmucker's outstanding non-typical whitetail deer tied for the First Place Award at the 26th Big Game Awards Program held in Fort Worth, Texas. The buck has a final score of 295-3/8 points and was taken in Adams County, Ohio, in 2006.

said Schmucker. "When he first came out I was a little bit nervous but, after watching him for a half hour, things eased off a little bit. Some people say they'd rather shoot a quick shot than watch him so long; I think I'd rather see him for a while and then shoot."

The buck got into the opening at the edge of the bean field and John leveled the cross-hairs on the deer. "It didn't take me long to take the shot."

The deer twisted and bolted to John's left and then took out across the bean field. The remaining smaller bucks ran for a short distance along the fencerow and then stopped. A tree blocked John's view of the buck he had just shot, but he could see the other bucks looking toward the big one as it ran across the field.

"The smaller bucks started stomping their feet and snorted. I heard a crash out in the bean field, and they took off," said Schmucker. "It looked like a good shot."

After five minutes, John got out of his stand and walked over to where the deer had been standing when he shot. "I found the bolt about two feet beyond where the buck was standing."

After Schmucker found his bolt, which confirmed he had made a good hit, he gathered up his equipment and tree stand and returned home. "I called my brother-in-law, Gary Miller, and he came over, and my neighbor and his boy came over to help me, too," said Schmucker. "Then we walked back to where I made the shot and started to follow the blood trail. About 80 yards from where I shot him, he was piled up."

Word spread fast throughout the tightly-knit Amish community that the big buck had been taken. "For three days solid, I had a lot of people over here; actually, I still can't believe I killed it," said Schmucker.

WHITETAIL DEER NON-TYPICAL ANTLERS
First Award (Tie) – 295 3/8
▼ ▼ ▼ ▼ ▼
Jonathan R. Schmucker

Schmucker called a neighbor to help take the deer to a checking station in Peebles, as is required by Ohio law. When John returned from the check station, a large crowd of people had gathered. "I could barely get in the driveway. As soon as we got in and lifted the deer out of the truck, everybody was right there taking pictures and admiring the deer. It was about 11:30 p.m. before I could finally skin the deer out."

For three days, people of all sorts came from Adams County and neighboring counties to see the massive buck that John Schmucker had taken. The phones were ringing off the hook as well.

It hasn't quite sunk into John Schmucker that he has taken a buck so large that it will rank as one of the top whitetails of All-time. "Every time I see him I think is this actually the one that was walking around back there," said Schmucker. "Like some of the neighbors said, you go past in the evening and look back there and imagine can still see the buck. It's just now sinking in that I really did get the big one." ▲

Courtesy of Tom Cross and North American Whitetail *magazine.*

Photograph by Bill Honza

TROPHY STATS

▼ ▼ ▼ ▼ ▼

Category
Whitetail Deer – Non-Typical Antlers

Score
267 $^{1}/_{8}$

Length of Main Beam
Right: 25 $^{7}/_{8}$ Left: 27 $^{4}/_{8}$

Circumference Between Burr and First Point
Right: 6 $^{4}/_{8}$ Left: 7

Number of Points
Right: 16   Left: 21

Inside Spread
18 $^{2}/_{8}$

Location
Mason Co., Illinois – 2003

Hunter
David H. Jones

WHITETAIL DEER
NON-TYPICAL ANTLERS
Second Award – 267 ⅛

▼ ▼ ▼ ▼ ▼ ▼ ▼ ▼ ▼

DAVID H. JONES

Early November 2001 was extremely hot during the rut. I was out hunting one day, and at 1 p.m. I saw a giant whitetail buck on the heels of a doe. They were just walking, not running, and he had his nose right up her tail. They walked to within 80 yards of me and started to move away. I had my antlers hanging beside me, so I reached over, quietly grabbed them, and rattled. Both deer stopped and looked my direction and then moved on. I was kicking myself for not having a bleat call with me.

Though I didn't get a real good look at him, I could see he had quite a number of points and a unique look I couldn't forget! Even then, I didn't think him to be a spectacular deer — just a really nice deer. I had already taken a mature 7-pointer before this, then a 12-pointer shortly after. I never saw the deer again in 2001.

The following summer, I purchased a trail cam and placed it about 50 yards beyond where I saw the buck the previous fall. By early fall, I was busy with work and never found the time to check the camera. With it getting close to hunting season and not wanting to disturb the area, I just left it in there. We had gotten behind with chisel plowing, so I spent most of my vacation from my factory job in the tractor. Finally, by mid-November, we were caught up. I had only been hunting a few times up to this point.

Early in the morning, with a northeast wind, I sat in my new stand. I had put it up that summer, not far from where I saw the buck the year before. Most deer I see there come from the east, so the wind was right. There is a spot to the east of me about 100 yards where the timber juts out into the pasture a little with an easy way for deer to cross a small ditch that runs along the timber and pasture border.

Right at first light, I heard deer back in that spot. Then I heard a buck tearing up the brush with his antlers. The first thing I thought was "Mass"! Just by the sound, I could tell it was a heavy-racked deer! Shortly after, I could see a doe coming toward me, with a buck in hot pursuit. It appeared the buck was pushing her in the direction he wanted her to go.

The buck was now in plain sight. He stopped about 25 yards. I drew my bow but could not see my sight pin! I let up and could see the buck still standing there, so I drew again. Same problem! I rolled the string with my fingers a bit and could see most of my sight but not the pin tip. I used this as a guide and decided to shoot. That was a move I instantly regretted. The buck ran back about 50 yards and stood. He then walked around and off toward what I figured to be his bedding area.

After things settled down, I climbed down to get my arrow. I also decided to grab the camera I had set up, which wasn't far from my stand. My girlfriend took the film to get developed, brought them home, and said there were some good pictures of a buck she thought I'd like. There were three photos of the monster I had just missed a couple days before.

As the season went on, I never saw him again. I did, however, see a number of bucks with broken tines; I wonder why? As it turned out, it had been the worst deer season I'd had in years. Even so, I still enjoyed it very much:

On March 8, 2003, I was surprised on my birthday with a cake that had the trail cam photo of my big buck on it. My girlfriend Lisa knew I was fascinated by this deer. It made me hope more than ever for another chance at him.

Also in 2003, after nearly 20 years of shooting a bow with fingers, I switched to a release aid. This was hard for me, but having debated this the last few years I finally decided to change. I must admit I just never liked them. So, I switched my bow over to a prong rest, had the draw shortened, had a string loop installed, put in a low-light peep with fiber-optic sights, and purchased a release. I felt like a sinner!

But I convinced myself to stay the course. After awhile, I was really enjoying my new style of shooting. From late winter on, I practiced as much as my little free time would allow. By the end of summer, I felt confident. With a couple of worn out targets, I was sure I could hunt with my release.

Throughout the year, the picture of the big buck was posted on our refrigerator. I can't begin to guess the number of times I paused to look at it, many times taking it down, sitting at the table, and looking him over.

In November 2003, taking vacation time from the factory, I planned on working through Wednesday on the farm and then hunting hard the next four days. Deer sign on previous trips had revealed some good buck activity, and I felt confident the opportunity to take a nice buck this week was definitely there.

The weather was quite warm at the beginning of the week. On Tuesday night, however, a cold front moved in! On Wednesday, November 5, the temperature really dropped. It was a dark and gloomy day, and I knew the bucks would be fired up!

It's about a 20-minute drive to the farm. Driving down the road with the rut on my mind and seeing some deer out in a field, I just couldn't take it anymore. About halfway there, I decided to turn back and prepare to go hunting.

The stand I went to was on top of a hill at the edge of some woods bordering a pasture. From this stand, I have a good view of the oak ridge this buck often traveled when leaving his bedding area. It is the same ridge where I had missed him the previous year.

I put this stand up in 2002, but it didn't offer the view I wanted, so I moved it about 50 yards. Around 3:30 p.m., I saw a few does and fawns milling around on the oak ridge. Then, a group of young turkeys came across the pasture and went into the oaks. For the longest time they fought. They were really starting to irritate me; they finally quit and walked off up the ridge a ways. All was now quiet but the wind.

Shortly after, I saw a small buck dart out of the lower end of the ridge about 200 yards or so to the northeast. He went up the hill and into another small woodlot. I already had my rattlin' antlers at the ready but could tell he was too small. I thought to myself that he sure seemed to be in a hurry. About that time, another deer darted into sight. I thought this deer to be a nice 6-pointer I had passed on earlier in the season. Again I thought to myself that, boy, he was in a rush!

WHITETAIL DEER NON-TYPICAL ANTLERS
Second Award – 267 1/8
▼ ▼ ▼ ▼ ▼
DAVID H. JONES

Then, here came the big boy darting out the end of the ridge! It was time to bang some bone! With the buck halfway up the hill, I hit the antlers together hard. One good hard hit and a quick rattle. The buck stopped and glared my way. He stood there for about 30 seconds and then took off toward the woodlot where the other two bucks had gone. As he disappeared into the woods I banged the antlers again, this time even harder, as hard as I could. I slammed the antlers so hard at one point that I lost my balance and slipped to the edge of my seat! I then turned, hung up the antlers, grabbed my bow, and stood up.

The wind had been blowing mostly from the north, and the small woodlot was to the east. I thought if he was going to come, he would do so by circling around to the south of me, which would put him downwind of my location. I kept watch for nearly 10 minutes but nothing ever happened. At that point, I figured he must have chased the other two bucks out of the county.

I turned to hang my bow on the hanger, turned my head back toward the open pasture in front of me, and — uhoh! There he stood in a low spot about 100 yards away, glaring my way! I thought I was busted. He just stood out there, and then he started walking my way! As he was walking, I reached around for my bow, which was on the opposite side of the tree. I just couldn't believe he was coming from the open and upwind side of me.

When he was within 70 yards, those darned turkeys started fighting again and he locked up. He just stood there glaring toward the ruckus. I thought again it was going to be all over. He was acting a little spooked now. Then, once he realized what the noise was, he started coming again.

As he got close to the woods, he didn't immediately step in. Brush and debris lay right in front of my stand, which forced him to circle out around my tree. As he walked 25 yards out in front of me, and with his vision blocked by a large limb, I drew my bow. He stopped but there were limbs blocking his vitals. He just stood there looking intently for the fighting bucks he had heard earlier. Then a few more steps and the same thing again; no shot! All this time I had been holding back my bowstring. I was now beginning to get a little uncomfortable. Then he moved again, stepping into the woods.

Most often in this situation I have mouth grunted or whistled to stop a walking deer for a shot, but something told me I shouldn't try that with this buck. I decided I would shoot him on the walk. There is a dirt mound on this trail just inside the woods. Just as I was lining

David H. Jones is pictured above with his award-winning non-typical whitetail deer. The buck, which scores 267-1/8 points, was taken in Mason County, Illinois, in 2003.

up my 20-yard pin, he stepped up on the mound and stopped, glaring down into the woods. It was almost as if he was saying, "Here I am; take me if you can!"

That's when I let the arrow fly. The buck spun and ran after the shot, sprinting across the open pasture and into the oak ridge, without a doubt headed back to the safety of his bedding area. As he was angling up the ridge and just getting out of sight, I thought I saw him stagger and his tail flutter. I felt confident he was down but, not wanting to take a chance, I sat in my stand for 20 minutes. I then climbed down and went over to inspect my arrow, which was stuck in the ground. It was covered with blood.

I backed out and went to my truck to call for help. I finally got in touch with my friend, who said he would be out to help. Soon, he was there, and we were off to look for the buck. By now it was dark. We went into the woods where I thought he had gone and searched for blood. We went out 75 yards but found nothing. We came back and started looking a little higher on the ridge. We found a good blood trail and followed.

We didn't have to look far. I looked up the ridge in the glowing lantern light and couldn't believe my eyes. There he lay! That rack looked so monstrous. After a handshake and congrats from Dan, I grabbed hold of the rack and smiled from ear to ear! What a moment! I think it took me three or four times to count all the points; I kept losing track.

On March 8, 2004, I was surprised with another cake. Only this time it was no trail cam picture, but a picture of the mounted trophy! ▲

Award-Winning Moments

B&C Photo Archives

B&C Official Measurer and Lifetime Associate, Ira D. McArthur, left, and his wife Jennifer are joined by Eldon L. "Buck" Buckner at the 26th Awards Trophy Display Reception held at Cabela's in Fort Worth, Texas. McArthur is one of 1,093 B&C Official Measurers located across North America who volunteer their time to Boone and Crockett Club by scoring North American big game trophies.

Photograph by Bill Honza

TROPHY STATS

▼ ▼ ▼ ▼ ▼

Category
Whitetail Deer – Non-Typical Antlers

Score
256 ³/₈

Length of Main Beam
Right: 25 ⁵/₈   Left: 25 ⁷/₈

Circumference Between Burr and First Point
Right: 6 ¹/₈   Left: 6 ²/₈

Number of Points
Right: 12   Left: 10

Inside Spread
20 ⁵/₈

Location
Marshall Co., Illinois – 2004

Hunter
Steve Wallis

WHITETAIL DEER
NON-TYPICAL ANTLERS
Third Award – 256 ³/₈

▼ ▼ ▼ ▼ ▼ ▼ ▼ ▼ ▼

STEVE WALLIS

Deer hunting has long been an important tradition for my family and friends. It's been a way of life for us for more than 30 years. Deer season for me started in 1990, and I haven't missed a single shotgun season in 16 years. Prior to the 2004 season, my largest buck was a 125-inch 10-pointer taken in 1994. But like most avid Illinois hunters, I've often dreamed of shooting a true Prairie State monster. Little did I know that on November 20, 2004, ten years after taking the 10-pointer, I would make that dream a reality by harvesting a world-class Illinois giant that would dwarf anything our hunting party had ever seen before.

As always, anticipation for our hunting party was high just before opening day of the 2004 shotgun season. The Marshall County farm where my father Dan Wallis, my brother Glen Hasenheyer, my cousin Tim Leifheit, some friends, and I have hunted for many years is typical of northern Illinois farmland. Our property is mostly open cropland with small scattered patches of rolling woods containing excellent cover. The farm has produced a number of good bucks for various members and friends of my family over the years.

Friday, November 19th, started out like most opening days for the Wallis clan. A hot breakfast at 4:30 a.m. was accompanied by the usual talk of giant racks and holding out for a monster buck. By 5:45 a.m., I was sitting securely in my favorite stand overlooking a winter wheat field. The temperature was in the mid-30s. The forecast called for light winds and up to an inch of rain throughout the day.

At 7 a.m., I watched as five does worked past my stand into the nearby woods, where they would probably bed for the day. The remainder of the morning was uneventful, despite the fact that bucks had been seen chasing does all week long in the area and the rut was in full swing. Late

Photograph by Jack Reneau

Steve Wallis accepting his plaque and medal from Buck Buckner, Vice President and Chairman of the Big Game Records Committee.

that afternoon, several more deer came out to feed in the wheat field in front of my stand. First, a doe with her button-buck fawn appeared. Shortly after that, a young basket-racked, 10-pointer made his way out into the open. Another young buck missing half his rack joined the 10-pointer. The half-racked buck chased the doe for several minutes as I sat and watched. Later, at dinner, everyone compared notes and talked about the various deer sightings made that day. No one in the group had fired a single shot all day long — not quite the opening day everyone had expected.

Saturday started out much the same. After a hot breakfast, I was in my stand well before the morning's first light. The forecast called for warmer temperatures and winds out of the southwest with scattered rain. The morning hunt was tough — not a single deer came past my stand.

DOING MY BEST NOT TO LOOK AT THE BUCK'S MASSIVE RACK, I TRIED TO LINE UP THE IRON SIGHTS OF MY WINCHESTER PUMP ON THE BUCK'S VITALS. THE CHERISHED OLD SHOTGUN HAD BEEN GIVEN TO ME BY MY DAD, AND IT HELD A LOT OF FAMILY HISTORY. MY MOTHER HAD BOUGHT THE GUN FOR MY DAD SOME 32 YEARS EARLIER.

Despite the lack of activity around my stand, my brother Glen managed to score on a trophy 8-pointer that he rattled in. Glen's buck had been a main-framed 5x5, but both brow tines were broken off. I decided to take a break and give my brother a hand dragging his trophy out of the woods. Later, I remembered what Glen had told me.

"This year is going to be your year to shoot a big buck," Glen had said prophetically. "You're due for a big one."

After taking some field photos and shooting some video footage of Glen's buck, I headed back to my stand for the afternoon hunt. My spirits were immediately lifted as I watched a highracked 8-pointer chase a doe through some nearby woods. The buck never offered me a shot. Instead, it managed to stay just out of range. I tried rattling and grunting to get the buck's attention, but it was plain to see this buck had no intention of leaving the doe he was shadowing. A short while later I saw six does making their way toward my position. Having both an antlerless tag and an either-sex tag in my pocket, I decided to shoot the biggest doe in the group if the opportunity presented itself. Moments later, my trusty old Winchester Model 1200 pump shotgun found its mark, dropping the mature doe in her tracks at 40 yards.

After the shot, I patiently remained in my stand for another 30 minutes in hopes that a buck might come along. When nothing appeared, I climbed down and walked over to begin the task of field-dressing the mature doe. Not taking any chances, I made sure that my shotgun was close by while I dressed out the doe. Just as I was finishing with the doe, I saw movement in the field. It was another doe and she was heading my way. I quickly realized through the doe's body language that she seemed to be overly concerned about something behind her.

"Could it be a buck?" I wondered.

Wisely, I removed my rubber gloves and took cover in a nearby deadfall. Within minutes, I caught sight of a large 6-pointer following the doe's trail. In my excitement, I fired a shot at the 6-pointer but missed cleanly. The buck disappeared. Disgusted with myself, I sat for a moment wondering how I could have missed the shot.

WHITETAIL DEER NON-TYPICAL ANTLERS
Third Award – 256 3/8

▼ ▼ ▼ ▼ ▼

STEVE WALLIS

Suddenly, I spotted the antlers of another buck coming over the ridgetop, also following in the footsteps of the doe. I instantly realized that this deer was no ordinary whitetail, this buck was a true monster, the kind of animal I have always dreamed about. The sight of his giant rack and his huge body size is the kind of vision that would make even the most seasoned hunter come unglued. Doing my best not to look at the buck's massive rack, I tried to line up the iron sights of my Winchester pump on the buck's vitals. The cherished old shotgun had been given to me by my dad, and it held a lot of family history. My mother had purchased the gun for my dad some 32 years earlier.

When the giant buck stepped within 40 yards and turned broadside, I aimed and squeezed off the shot. Unscathed, the huge buck just stood there motionless. I pumped another shell into the chamber and squeezed off a second shot. Oblivious to where the shots had come from, the buck turned and started walking to the north. After a few steps, the buck stopped giving me a quartering-away shot. I took aim and sent a third slug on its way. This time my shot hit a little farther back than I would have liked. The big buck took off and disappeared into a nearby ravine. I was now on an emotional roller-coaster.

After hearing the shots, my dad came over to see if I needed any help tracking a deer. Barely able to talk because of adrenaline overload, I used hand gestures to let Dad know I had just shot a monster buck. Dad and I soon began following a good blood trail across the pasture. Because of the rolling lay of the land, we carefully scrutinized the ground in front of us after every few steps. As the two of us crested a slight ridge, I said, "There he is, bedded down."

My dad looked at me and asked, "Where is he? Is he behind that bush bedded down?"

"That's not a bush; that's his rack sticking up above the grass!"

Realizing the buck had not expired, and not wanting the deer to get up and run, I quickly put him down for good with a final slug.

Just as light was giving way to darkness, everyone gathered around to get their first look at the giant whitetail that lay before us. Everyone was in awe; the high fives and congratulations were flying. We counted 22 points on the buck's massive rack and noticed at least one point that was partially broken off.

With good camera light fading, we took a few field photos and shot video footage of the deer. With everyone's deer loaded in the trailer, it was off to the check station to have our deer recorded for the state harvest totals.

Once at the check station, it didn't take long for my buck to cause a commotion. Hunters

Photograph courtesy of Steve Wallis

The Wallis Clan has been hunting whitetails in Illinois for almost 40 years. Steve Wallis, left, harvested this award-winning non-typical in 2004. He was hunting with his dad, also pictured above, and several other members of his family. Wallis' buck has a final score of 256-3/8 points.

surrounded the trailer, took pictures, and wanted to hear every detail of how I shot the buck. For over an hour, the line of trucks waiting to check deer in came to a complete standstill, but no one seemed to mind.

Most of the hunters at the check station had never seen a buck wearing a rack of this caliber before. It finally started to sink in that I had truly just shot a buck of a lifetime.

The 2004 Illinois shotgun season will be one we'll never forget. In addition to my great buck and doe, my brother shot the big 8-pointer mentioned earlier and a doe. My dad took a very nice 10-pointer and a doe, my cousin Tim Leitheit and Steve Malatia each shot does. Mark Matkovich, a new hunter in our group, shot a respectable 10-pointer and a doe.

Hunting whitetails for me, my family, and friends is a passion that burns deep; it is a big part of who we are. Words cannot express our gratitude to our families for allowing us to continue to pursue our passion. One man lit that fire almost 40 years ago — Don Leifheit. For that, we thank him; may God rest his soul.

Prior to November 20, 2004, when I shot him, no one in our group had ever seen the big buck before. One thing is for sure, you can bet your life the Wallis group will be out in the woods looking for the offspring of my great Illinois buck. ▲

B&C Photo Archives

The award-winning whitetail deer on display were among the most impressive to date. Two of the non-typical trophies tied at 295-3/8 points, which put them as the number 6 non-typical whitetail deer of all time – Jonathan R. Schmucker's buck (top center), and Scott R. Dexter's buck (top right). The other two non-typicals on display were David H. Jones' buck (bottom center) and Steve Wallis' (bottom right). Both of these bucks also rank high on the all-time list.

Photograph by Bill Honza

TROPHY STATS

▼ ▼ ▼ ▼ ▼

Category
Coues' Whitetail Deer – Typical Antlers

Score
122 $^4/_8$

Length of Main Beam
Right: 19 $^3/_8$ Left: 19

Circumference Between Burr and First Point
Right: 4 $^3/_8$ Left: 4 $^3/_8$

Number of Points
Right: 4   Left: 4

Inside Spread
18 $^2/_8$

Location
Sonora, Mexico – 2005

Hunter
Terry C. Hickson

COUES' WHITETAIL DEER TYPICAL ANTLERS
First Award – 122 ⁴/₈

▼ ▼ ▼ ▼ ▼ ▼ ▼ ▼ ▼

TERRY C. HICKSON

It was late December 2004, and I was busy dreaming about my next hunt. I was heading for Sonora, Mexico, to hunt mule deer and Coues' deer. I was particularly excited about this hunt because I was being joined by good friends Clay Woodward, Eric Ovens, and David May, who has been employed by Campillo Brothers Outfitters for the last ten years.

We flew to Phoenix, where David picked us up at the airport and drove us to Tucson. In Tucson, we were met by outfitter Bobby

Last Day Triumph

Campillo. I had hunted with Bobby many times and always had a great time in his camp. We traveled 80 miles west of Tucson and crossed into Mexico. We then proceeded southwest to Bobby's leases, located in the Altar Valley. We arrived in camp after dark and began to unpack and enjoy dinner. We spend the next several hours listening to hunting stories and dreaming about the next day's hunt.

The next several days were spent hunting mule deer, while David was scouting for Coues' deer. The weather was overcast and sometimes very miserable due to the hard rains, but hunters had already taken three good mule deer bucks. It was now New Year's Eve, and I had one more day to hunt because of prior commitments. I decided to spend my last day hunting Coues' deer with David and two of Bobby's other guides.

The next morning was clear and nice as we traveled about 10 miles to our hunting area. We unpacked and started glassing. During the next hour, we saw three nice bucks but decided to keep looking.

We walked half a mile down a brushy flat that was located between two ridges about a mile apart. We approached a small mound, and David told me that this was the spot where Bill Mills

Photograph by Jack Reneau

Terry C. Hickson accepting his plaque and medal from Buck Buckner, Vice President and Chairman of the Big Game Records Committee.

Photograph courtesy of Terry C. Hickson

Terry C. Hickson is joined by friend and guide David May (right) with Hickson's award-winning Coues' whitetail deer. Hickson's hunt was focused on mule deer, and he didn't start hunting for Coues' deer until the last day of his hunt. His buck scores 122-4/8 points.

took a monster buck that scored 123-6/8 B&C two years earlier.

As we were glassing, David turned to me and said, "Mr. Hickson, we have a deer that needs to be taken."

We moved about 10 yards and were looking in the opposite direction. We were facing a small hill that was extremely brushy, making the deer very hard to locate. The buck was lying broadside and facing us at 225 yards, but I didn't know that until 20 minutes later.

My first attempt to locate the buck failed miserably, as did the next several attempts. I was getting extremely frustrated when David said, "Relax my friend; he will betray himself."

I tried to relax and continue searching, and then I froze. I saw an ear twitch; I had finally located the buck! I aimed the gun and fired. The last thing I remember was the rack falling backwards and hearing that wonderful thump.

What a great feeling! With smiles on our faces, we approached the hill in time to see the deer being lifted out of the brush. I couldn't believe my eyes; this tremendous Coues' deer was truly the buck of a lifetime. I was speechless and, with a tear in my eye, I gave David a big hug!

I would like to thank Campillo Brothers for a great hunt. I would also like to thank my good friend, David May, who made this dream a reality. ▲

B&C Photo Archives

Thousands of visitors viewed the award-winning trophies highlighted in this book. The trophy display was open to the public at Cabela's Fort Worth store from May 2 through June 23, 2007.

Photograph courtesy of the Pope and Young Club

TROPHY STATS

▼ ▼ ▼ ▼ ▼

Category
Coues' Whitetail Deer – Typical Antlers

Score
120 $^2/_8$

Length of Main Beam
Right: 18 $^3/_8$ Left: 18

Circumference Between Burr and First Point
Right: 4 $^4/_8$ Left: 4 $^4/_8$

Number of Points
Right: 4   Left: 4

Inside Spread
15 $^2/_8$

Location
Pima Co., Arizona – 2006

Hunter
Eric C. Rhicard

COUES' WHITETAIL DEER
TYPICAL ANTLERS
Second Award – 120 ²/₈

▼ ▼ ▼ ▼ ▼ ▼ ▼ ▼ ▼

ERIC C. RHICARD

This deer hunting story really started in 2000, when my buddy got me interested in trying to focus on better-than-average deer. During the 2001 rifle season, after over 60 days of scouting, I shot a 96-inch Coues' deer. I continued scouting and did an extensive amount of backpacking to remote areas. Then in 2002, I bought a bow after listening to the same friend tell me about how fun spot-and-stalk elk hunting is. This enabled me to hunt elk, as well as trophy deer, during the rut. The learning curve was steep and challenging, with too many misses to mention, but I finally started to connect on some deer.

In Arizona, the season bag limit is one deer per calendar year. This means that you can kill a deer with a bow or rifle on December 31 and another with a bow on January 1. If a hunter takes a buck in January, his bag limit is reached and he must wait until the following year to hunt again. With a bow it's not such a bad deal, but rifle hunters have to wait almost two years. So, if you're going to kill a deer in January, it had better be the one you want.

In December 2005, I backpack hunted with my bow for two weeks. I was holding out for a big buck, but by the last day, I decided I would take what came to the waterhole I was sitting on. I knew all the ranges so when a forked horn wandered down, I thought it would be a "slam dunk, meat in the freezer" shot. I choked and missed, even though I knew the exact range. I beat myself up a lot and wondered out loud and to myself how I would ever kill a big buck when I seemed to have enough trouble killing a small one.

On January 3, 2006, after being home for only two and a half days, I decided I would head into the mountains close to home to see if I could find some deer in an area I hadn't visited in almost two years. My wife never missed a beat and wished me luck.

When I got to my ridge, I spotted a doe right away. I decided to hang around the area and see what else showed up before dark. As time passed, I decided to try calling. Within seconds, I had the biggest deer I had ever seen standing nine yards from me — tall tines and wide rack — a real beauty. He looked past me for the deer he had heard as I stayed frozen, hoping for a chance to draw and shoot. As he moved to my left, I thought to myself that I could have wedged a softball between his G-3 and the tip of his main beam. When I eventually tried for a shot, I spooked him. I was disappointed but thrilled since I had only ever seen two other deer that were B&C-class deer and neither had been nine yards away. I waited until dark then headed home, barely able to contain myself. I had a plan to hang a stand in a tree before first light the next morning.

Eric C. Rhicard harvested this award-winning typical Coues' whitetail with a bow in January of 2006. The buck, which scores 120-2/8 points, was taken in Pima County, Arizona.

With little sleep, I was up and at it well before dawn. Twisted, short oak trees are tough to set up stands in. I did win the race to first light, however, and began ranging other trees and rocks on the hillside. I was beginning the process of committing the distances to memory when I spotted a doe about 35 yards away. She was heading right toward me. Behind her I could just make out movement as a buck chased another deer down the hill. As he came back toward the doe that was now just below me, I saw that it was the same buck from the night before. As she fed below me, he stood at eye level on the hillside just 32 yards away. I didn't move a muscle.

After a few minutes he took off again after a smaller buck. The doe continued to feed to my left and a little behind me. When the big fella returned, he stopped behind a tree about 24 yards in front of me but lower on the hillside. I could see his nose, stomach, and haunches and was planning to draw as soon as he started to move.

After about five minutes, he moved, and I drew the bow. When he stopped, he was 18 yards from me. Interestingly, I wasn't overly excited as I had been when I missed the forked horn four days earlier. It felt more like a light coffee buzz. Since my miss, I had been drilling my shot sequence into my head — range, pick a spot, pin on the spot, release, follow through. As I put the pin just behind the shoulder, the buck turned his head back and began to lick his haunches, covering up my spot. As his head came back around, I settled the pin on the spot and released.

I never saw the arrow hit him, but the buck leapt forward and down the hill. I watched him for 50 yards, until he turned up a drainage and disappeared behind the oaks.

Then the shaking began, somewhere in the 8.0 range on the Richter Scale. I was pretty sure I had hit the deer of my dreams. I began to look for the arrow, which I thought should be sticking out of the ground. I was shaking so badly I couldn't hold the binoculars steady enough to see anything. For 15 minutes I tried to stop shaking and could not.

Arrows can be tough to find, as the drying blood turns even bright-colored vanes to dark brown fairly quickly. Also, two other deer were moving through the area, a doe and an

85-inch 4x4. They headed in the same direction the buck had gone and both got a little jumpy when they reached the bottom of the draw. The small buck actually followed the blood trail down the hill, eventually working his way back up the hill toward me then wandering off. Finally, the shakes had subsided enough for me to see through the binoculars and to spot some blood on the ground where the deer had been standing. I could only hope it was a good hit.

COUES' WHITETAIL DEER TYPICAL ANTLERS
Second Award – 120 ²/₈

▼ ▼ ▼ ▼ ▼

ERIC C. RHICARD

I climbed down from the tree and found the blood, but no arrow. How could I have hit him where I had aimed and not had a pass through? I was a little worried, but the blood sign was good and, as I reached the bottom of the draw, I spotted him ten yards away. He had dropped just after going out of view. All that anxiety could have been relieved if he had just dropped a second earlier! I did find the arrow. It had nicked the back edge of the scapula and must have hung up on the vanes of the arrow.

I hauled him to a spot I could just get my truck to, loaded him up, and headed home. I called my wife, who was absolutely thrilled. Then, of course, calls to my pals. As they got off work, they all headed to my house. My friend Cres Snyder got there first and gave me the standard, low key, "Nice deer."

I kept saying I thought it was going to make B&C minimum — hoping at least 110. Cres replied that he thought it would be. Then he would hold the antlers some more and say, "I think it's going to make it." It's a little game he plays.

I had not seen many 110-plus deer, and the animal's body size made the rack seem smaller than the ones I had seen mounted at the taxidermist's shop, so I didn't know for sure. After about an hour we got the tape out and Cres set to measuring. Finally, he announced, "118 and some change."

I was stunned. This deer was the buck of my dreams. A gorgeous 8-pointer and he was going to make B&C minimum. As it turned out, he was a little bigger than that. Cres always tries to measure a little more conservatively.

Meeting the B&C minimum was a goal I had set in 2002. Hundreds of hours of hiking, scouting, looking at maps, hunting in all kinds of conditions, and failing to connect on smaller deer had finally paid off. What a treat I have been given. I have to thank my wife who seemed unfazed as I headed out once again, just days after having being gone for two weeks, to check out one more area. ▲

Photograph courtesy of William P. Mattausch, Jr.

TROPHY STATS

▼ ▼ ▼ ▼ ▼

Category
Coues' Whitetail Deer – Typical Antlers

Score
120 1/8

Length of Main Beam
Right: 18 4/8   Left: 18 7/8

Circumference Between Burr and First Point
Right: 4   Left: 4

Number of Points
Right: 4   Left: 5

Inside Spread
17 3/8

Location
Pima Co., Arizona – 2006

Hunter
William P. Mattausch, Jr.

COUES' WHITETAIL DEER TYPICAL ANTLERS
Third Award – 120 ⅛

▼ ▼ ▼ ▼ ▼ ▼ ▼ ▼ ▼

WILLIAM P. MATTAUSCH, JR.

My family was lucky enough to be born and raised in Pima County, Arizona, home not only to some of the best Coues' deer hunting, but also to the World's Record typical Coues' deer, taken by Ed Stockwell in 1953. This buck stands alone as king of the Coues' deer.

Since the 1960s, we have been hunting his gene pool in search of a "Top 50"-class All-time buck. A quick glance at the records shows Pima County listed on the first page many times. Hard work and persistence would be the key to our goal.

120 Days and 120 Inches

My brother Ben, an Arizona guide with H and H Outfitters, has over 30 years experience with deer and desert sheep, and he has had notable success. Over the years, he has helped several hunters get bucks in the 110-inch class.

In February, he starts the year off by getting video of the rut's final stages. In late March and April, it's time to search for big shed antlers, both for fun and for trying to find big buck home ranges. This is the only time we will be seen walking where bucks live. As velvet antlers begin to appear, it's time for hard glassing and long-range video — times when you only get a brief glimpse at dawn and dusk.

All Arizona hunters are familiar with the challenges of summer — flies, mosquitoes, ants, bees, and ever-present rattlesnakes. From June until September, Ben gets footage every other day at this time to record growth and to make the final cut for bucks we will set up on. It is so important to get the buck's undisturbed natural movements. Tripod glassing must be done from far away (a mile or two is common) or you risk spooking a big deer.

Over the years, we have developed some rules that cover your conduct on stand and in the field.

Rule #1: Trophy class, mature bucks only! We did not work all summer for a small young buck.

Rule #2: Be still. No moving suddenly or making sounds with your equipment, tripods, backpack, or weapons, and be totally camouflaged at all times.

Rule #3: No leaving. Stay put on your stand or in the field until after dark before walking out to the pickup spot. The past three years I have missed out on some tremendous bucks by leaving my ground blind and trying to stalk them or cut the distance. Spooked bucks don't return anytime soon. I learned my lesson, and vowed to stay put this time, no matter what

Photograph courtesy of William P. Mattausch, Jr.

William P. Mattausch, Jr.'s, award-winning Coues' whitetail deer was taken in Pima County, Arizona, and scores 120-1/8 points.

happened around my blind!

It was late June and early July when we obtained the first video footage of the buck we would call "the wide buck," for obvious reasons. He was always with three other good bucks. One was "the proud buck." This 108-class buck was always posing and sparring. The other two were "the cookie cutters" — twin bucks with perfectly matching 110-inch racks.

The wide buck's antlers looked twice as big as any of the others. We could tell early in velvet that he was going to reach "buck-of-a-lifetime" status. We filmed him through the summer, up until he had strips of velvet hanging from his main beams. Then, about two weeks before the first rifle hunt, he promptly disappeared.

I scouted hard and saw many bucks over the next two months but could not locate the wide buck. Ben returned from a Tiburon Island sheep hunt as the 2006 bow season began and promptly found the wide buck on his first day back. The buck had relocated two canyons away from his last hangout. We both guessed he was about 118" or maybe even better. I was thankful a lion hadn't eaten him, and his rack was not broken up from fighting.

The next 20 days we spent hunting him from stands and ground blinds, coming very close but never being able to finish the job. The rut sends these bucks into a state of constant motion and relentless checking of scrapes or chasing off other bucks. It would be impossible to guess where he might be the next morning after we bedded him down the night before. But, we were getting closer every day. With persistence and a little luck things could still go our way.

On January 28, with only three days left in the season, we parked our truck on top of the overlook spot at 4:10 a.m. We got our packs and walking sticks and made our plan for the day. I would hunt the rock blind, and Ben would set up above me on a saddle that had a nice little flat with mesquite that formed a canopy. Out of caution, we arrived at our spots at least an hour before any light, and as the trail split to each of our stands Ben said, "Don't take any bad shots, and don't miss any good shots. Focus, and let's kill this buck."

It was about 5:05 a.m. and freezing cold when I made it to the rock blind. Looking up at the clear sky and bright crescent moon I wondered if today would be the day I would finally get a shot. The rock blind was just a pile of couch-sized boulders all stacked around two house-sized boulders, and was completely covered in thick cat claw and peanut cactus. I positioned myself back in a gap between the two house rocks behind some brush. I had about 15 feet of open shooting lane side-to-side, and 35 yards clear in front of me to a scrape that was all pawed up.

After a while, I could make out a doe about 80 yards in front of me standing in a clearing made by the black ants — nothing ever grows in the 8-foot circle around their hole. Ben was across the canyon about 300 yards, but we could see each other. By using hand signals we developed over the years we could keep in touch and ready.

I put up my 10x40 Zeiss binoculars and saw the proud buck moving over to the doe. Just as he got to her, I heard a loud snapping and popping of brush. I looked just in time to see the wide buck with a full head of steam. Soon, he had chased the proud buck over the rise. The doe followed slowly in the same direction over the rise and then all was quiet.

After about 30 minutes, I glassed Ben. He signaled that the wide buck was breeding the doe to my left out of sight. A few minutes later, I saw him motion me to get ready and draw my bow; they were both coming to me! I hooked my loop and slowly drew the PSE Intruder to anchor point and said to myself, "Don't look at the antlers."

The doe appeared first and was by my lane in a second, and then I saw the top of the buck's shoulders as he swung his head low to the ground sniffing her trail. I instantly moved back through the peep sight, stopped at a place just behind his shoulder, and then pressed the trigger of my release. The arrow flight looked perfect and the impact sounded like it hit meat. He tensed up for a second, but I could see no visible difference in his walk or his purpose; he was still hot on the doe. He went to my right and out of sight.

A flood of things went through my mind all at once. I had to have hit him, 22 yards and perfect broadside. I thought how all three of my brothers had passed on bucks in the 105 to 109 class so many times, telling me, "You can't kill a 120-incher if you don't let these go." I admired them for that; I never could let any pass that class. They deserved him more than I.

The early victory celebration was quickly canceled when I glassed Ben and he signaled that I had missed, and that the wide one had caught the doe and was breeding her again! I was sick and thought I missed my chance again.

A couple of hours passed by with no more deer movement. I glassed and glassed the brush where the arrow must have landed. Suddenly, I saw the fletching and nock and they appeared red in color! I started smiling and frantically waving at Ben. It took him a long time to come over, as he was sure I had missed. Judging from the buck's activity just after the shot, who would think otherwise?

The shuttle "T-Lock" had gone right through him, just a little high and a few inches back from where I would have liked. We found a blood trail but it got spotty after about 20 yards. Ben looked at me and said, "We are not pushing this one."

After another hour we started trailing him, slowly picking our way over and through some of the thickest manzanita and cat-claw brush you will ever encounter. A couple of times we spooked deer ahead of us, and held up not knowing if we had busted him out or if it was the cookie cutter bucks snorting and blowing. We continued to track him until we found his now expired body. He ended up traveling about half a mile from the rock blind to where he now lay dead.

In closing, I have to thank my parents and brothers for all their help and support. I could not have accomplished this goal without them. ▲

Photograph by Bill Honza

TROPHY STATS

▼ ▼ ▼ ▼ ▼

Category
Coues' Whitetail Deer –
Non-Typical Antlers

Score
134 4/8

Length of Main Beam
Right: 19 6/8   Left: 20 3/8

Circumference Between Burr and First Point
Right: 4 1/8   Left: 4

Number of Points
Right: 6   Left: 7

Inside Spread
15 6/8

Location
Sonora, Mexico – 2005

Hunter
James Schacherl

COUES' WHITETAIL DEER NON-TYPICAL ANTLERS
First Award – 134 4/8

▼ ▼ ▼ ▼ ▼ ▼ ▼ ▼ ▼

JAMES SCHACHERL

I have been very fortunate to hunt many different places in my life. I have hunted elk, mule deer, bear, and various other game in Colorado, New Mexico, and Texas. But growing up in south-central Texas, whitetails have always been my passion.

The year 2003 began as a very promising year on the south Texas deer lease I had been hunting for several years with some good friends from my hometown of Gonzales, Texas. We saw some very good bucks

Grey Ghosts of the Desert

including one buck that, with one more year to grow, would be a monster. In February of 2004 we all made a trip to the deer lease to work on the property. The following day I got a knock on the door. A good friend of mine and fellow hunter on the lease delivered the bad news. We had lost our lease to some "deep pockets" out of the city. Needless to say, we were all sick, feeling betrayed and confused, and wondering where we were going to hunt the next year.

A few weeks later I got a phone call from a good friend of mine in Colorado. He said he was thinking of putting together a Coues' deer hunt in Mexico and was wondering if I would be interested. Well, with the recent chain of events, it didn't take me long to accept his offer. During the next few months, we researched several different outfitters, finally deciding to book with B&K Outfitters based out of Tucson. None of the hunters in our group had ever hunted Coues' deer before, but we all knew they were very skittish little creatures that could vanish into thin air. Combining their wariness with the rugged desert terrain they lived in, we all knew this probably wouldn't be an easy hunt.

The next few months passed, and I made my annual trip to hunt mule deer and elk in Colorado. We had also found another lease in south Texas that helped pass the time, but I was eagerly anticipating the Coues' deer hunt that was booked for January 7-13, 2005. The day finally came and on the morning of January 5th, I left for Arizona. I drove straight through to Tucson, arriving about 9 p.m.

The next morning, I met up with Brandy Williams, Hank Williams, and Howard Hughes, my hunting partners from Colorado. Now I know what you are thinking, so let me clarify. Brandy is not a girl; Hank is not a singer; and Howard is not the "Aviator"; they also nicknamed me James "Brown" but I am not the Godfather of Soul. The outfitter got a kick out of it and called us the celebrity hunting group. We spent the rest of the day checking out taxidermy shops and sightseeing.

That evening I got a call from my dad. He said that my grandmother had been put in the hospital and was not doing well. My heart sank, and I questioned whether I should stay or just turn around and go home. He told me to stay and that he would keep me informed of her condition.

The next morning we met our guide in Nogales and began getting ready to cross the border into Mexico. I made a call to my dad to check on my grandmother. He said she was doing better and that I should go on to Mexico and not worry, so we began our journey across the border.

If any of you have ever crossed the border with guns you know what a hassle it can be. So, six hours later, we were finally on our way to the ranch near Hermosillo we would be hunting on for the next five days. We got to the camp a little after dark and unloaded our gear.

THE NEXT MORNING, I MET UP WITH BRANDY WILLIAMS, HANK WILLIAMS, AND HOWARD HUGHES, MY HUNTING PARTNERS FROM COLORADO. NOW I KNOW WHAT YOU ARE THINKING, SO LET ME CLARIFY. BRANDY IS NOT A GIRL; HANK IS NOT A SINGER; AND HOWARD IS NOT THE "AVIATOR"; THEY ALSO NICKNAMED ME JAMES "BROWN" BUT I AM NOT THE GODFATHER OF SOUL.

The hacienda was very comfortable. There was an older Mexican couple living there that greeted us and showed us where we would be staying. After a few broken words of Spanglish, we bedded down and rested up for the hunt the next morning.

Daylight came pretty early, and it was clear and cold. We were excited as we drove across the mule deer flats on the way to the mountains in the distance; our guide told us that the Coues' deer would primarily be found in the mountains.

As we got to the first mountain, we spotted some Coues' deer right off the bat, and there was a buck in the bunch! None of us knew what to expect on this hunt, so everyone began scrambling for guns and spotting scopes. I just wanted to get out of the way! As it turned out, the buck had a broken tine, and we all decided to pass on him. This was a good sign, though. The bucks were in rut, which added a great advantage to hunting these little "gray ghosts of the desert." It also gave us our first real look at a Coues' deer. They looked a lot like a miniature whitetail, with long ears, a long tail, and a sandy brown coat.

After a few more close encounters that morning, we split up into two groups. Brandy, Hank, and I went one way; Howard and the guide, Dave, went another. We hadn't gone far when Brandy, after a few misses, had our first Coues' deer buck on the ground. The buck was on top of a small mountain, so we scrambled up to the top as quickly as we could to take a look. It was a fine buck by Coues' deer standards — nine points, wide spread, good mass and length, and scoring well over 100 inches.

After we packed him back to the truck, Hank decided to do some walking and glassing, so Brandy and I headed back to camp to take care of his buck. When we got back to camp, the ranch owner and his nephew, Louis, met us. They congratulated us on Brandy's buck, and Louis said he would go out with us after we got Brandy's buck taken care of. We

COUES' WHITETAIL DEER NON-TYPICAL ANTLERS
First Award – 134 4/8
▼ ▼ ▼ ▼ ▼
JAMES SCHACHERL

gladly accepted his offer, knowing he had extensive knowledge of the ranch and had hunted these deer all his life.

As we headed back out, Louis suggested we try another part of the ranch near an abandoned silver mine. We drove about halfway to the mountain then got out and began hiking. The brush and cactuses were very dense in spots until we got out onto an old road that went to the mine.

We were working our way toward the brush-covered rocky hill when I spotted a deer down low on the side of the mountain. It was about 200 yards away but I could tell it was a nice buck. The deer disappeared back into the thick brush as quickly as it had appeared but it wasn't spooked, so we decided to get a little closer for a better look. Brandy stayed back to watch from where we had first spotted the buck, so Louis and I headed into the brush.

We made our way to a small creek bottom about 150 yards from the mountain and spotted a doe directly above where the buck had been. We stopped there, and I found a good rest on a palo verde tree. About ten minutes went by but nothing moved. The doe was just browsing on some brush, but no sign of the buck. Louis looked at me and said, "Something is wrong, man. The buck should have come back out by now. We must have spooked him."

No sooner than he had said that when I saw the buck to our far right. He was heading right toward the doe. I told Louis, "There he is!"

"Let me take a look at him before you shoot," Louis said.

As soon as he picked his binoculars up and looked at the buck, he said, "Shoot! Shoot! Shoot!"

I raised my .300 Weatherby Magnum, settled the crosshairs on the deer's shoulder, and tried not to look at the antlers. However, I couldn't help seeing a nice drop tine off the left main beam. Of course this didn't help my nerves at all, but I controlled my breathing and squeezed a round off. The bullet found its mark, and sent back a resounding "thud." The buck made it about ten yards and folded.

As Louis and I headed toward the buck, Brandy came running up at full throttle. We all reached the buck at the same time, but none of us were prepared for what we found. Lying there before us was an absolute "monster." A rush of emotion came over us. We couldn't believe how big this buck was. There were several kickers including a drop tine, long beams, and unbelievable mass. After a lot of celebration and congratulations, we loaded the buck up and headed back to camp.

Over the next few days, we saw several big bucks. Hank took a great typical 11-pointer that gross scored 111 B&C but just narrowly missed the record book. Howard hunted hard

James Schacherl is pictured above (right) with guide Luis Brisenio with Schacherl's award-winning non-typical Coues' whitetail deer. The buck, which scores 134-4/8 points, received a First Place Award at the 26th Big Game Awards Program in Fort Worth, Texas.

with his bow until the last day and then took out his rifle and got a very nice 8-pointer that gross scored 93 B&C. Brandy's buck gross scored 106 B&C. These were all excellent bucks by anyone's standards. A lot of people have hunted their entire life to kill a Coues' that will break 90 inches, and we had four of them.

This was truly a hunt of a lifetime, and I am glad to have shared it with such good friends. I was filled with many emotions, from great joy over the magnificent trophies we were taking home, to sadness with the constant thought of my ailing grandmother who I lost a few days after I got home. But I know that the memories of it all will live in my heart and in my mind forever, and that is the truest trophy of all. ▲

Mossy Oak Brand Camo has been a longtime supporter of the Club and most recently helped the Club to produce its very first television series, *Leupold Big Game Profiles* presented by the Boone and Crockett Club. Mossy Oak's Dustin Whitacre (right) is pictured accepting their Plaque of Appreciation as a 26th Big Game Awards sponsor from Keith Balfourd, the Club's Director of Marketing.

Photograph by Bill Honza

TROPHY STATS

▼ ▼ ▼ ▼ ▼

Category
Coues' Whitetail Deer –
Non-Typical Antlers

Score
121

Length of Main Beam
Right: 17 $^6/_8$ Left: 17 $^7/_8$

**Circumference Between
Burr and First Point**
Right: 4 $^1/_8$ Left: 4 $^2/_8$

Number of Points
Right: 6   Left: 7

Inside Spread
13 $^5/_8$

Location
Sonora, Mexico – 2006

Hunter
James G. Petersen

COUES' WHITETAIL DEER NON-TYPICAL ANTLERS
Second Award – 121

▼ ▼ ▼ ▼ ▼ ▼ ▼ ▼ ▼

JAMES G. PETERSEN

This story really begins at Boone and Crockett Club's 25th Big Game Awards. While my wife and I sat visiting with people, we met Kirk Kelso. As most of my conversations go, it didn't take long to get to the subject of hunting. We enjoyed Kirk's company and picked his mind about hunting. I decided to book a hunt with him.

In the spring of 2005, I made arrangements with Kirk to hunt antelope in New Mexico. The hunt was everything I expected — first class all the way. So when Kirk suggested a Coues' deer hunt in Mexico in January, I signed up.

Photograph courtesy of James G. Petersen

James G. Petersen was hunting in Sonora, Mexico, when he harvested this award-winning Coues' whitetail. The buck, which scores 121 points, received a Second Place Award at the 26th Big Game Awards Program Banquet in Fort Worth, Texas.

Kirk and Roxi met several other hunters and me in Tucson, where they escorted us across the border without a hitch. Sitting around the fire that first evening, I became aware of how most hunters in this group were experienced and enthusiastic Coues' deer hunters. Having never hunted Coues' deer before, I needed all the advice I could get.

The first day my guide, Raphael Jamie, and I went on a long hike. We saw several bucks. We even bumped one that got away before we could react. Raphael thought he was a good buck, but we just messed up, and didn't have an opportunity!

The next two days we spotted a lot of good bucks. I was told several were around the 100-inch mark.

On the fourth day, we went to the same area where we went the first day but from a different approach. We spotted several deer, and about midday we spotted a good buck headed away from us chasing a doe. Cautiously, we moved, glassed, and made our way toward where we had seen the buck. We glassed and glassed, but we couldn't find him.

In the afternoon, we finally spotted a good buck in the distance, so off we went for a closer look. Raphael and I made it to a rock outcropping and set up the spotting scope. We finally found the buck. Still wanting a better look, we closed the distance. Because it was getting late, I moved up by myself to make the final decision. The buck began chasing a doe.

As I got set up, another buck stood up. He had been hidden the whole time by grass and brush. He was noticeably bigger, even to this novice Coues' deer hunter. The buck began moving toward the doe. I ranged the buck at 377 yards. When he stopped, I fired the Bansner 7STW. The buck disappeared from view, but there were deer moving everywhere. As I watched several deer exit the little basin, Raphael shouted, "No shoot!"

He came over. There seemed to be some confusion as to where the buck went. As we walked, he went to the left side of the small basin and I went to the right side where I had last seen the buck. When I arrived at the spot, there he was.

I really didn't know what I had; I just knew he was the best I had seen so far. Since it was late and we didn't want to leave the buck overnight, we quickly caped and dressed the deer and began packing him out. We hustled; no photos, nothing, as we were about one and a half hours from the truck, and it was getting dark. Thank God for headlamps. After a long hike, we reached the truck and drove to camp.

The other hunters confirmed that I didn't know what I had. Raphael stated that he thought the buck was the one we bumped the first day. Kirk scored the buck and told me that I might have to attend another awards ceremony! ▲

Award-Winning Moments

The name Nosler and specialty big game hunting bullets are synonymous. N. Guy Eastman (right) accepts the Plaque of Appreciation on behalf of Nosler, recognizing them as an official sponsor of Boone and Crockett Club's 26th Big Game Awards Program and Trophy Display in Fort Worth, Texas. B&C's Keith Balfourd presented the plaque.

Photograph by Bill Honza

TROPHY STATS

▼ ▼ ▼ ▼ ▼

Category
Coues' Whitetail Deer –
Non-Typical Antlers

Score
111 $^6/_8$

Length of Main Beam
Right: 17 $^6/_8$ Left: 15

**Circumference Between
Burr and First Point**
Right: 3 $^7/_8$ Left: 3 $^6/_8$

Number of Points
Right: 4   Left: 6

Inside Spread
12 $^1/_8$

Location
Sonora, Mexico – 2005

Hunter
Keith D. Riefkohl

COUES' WHITETAIL DEER NON-TYPICAL ANTLERS
Third Award – 111 ⁶/₈

▼ ▼ ▼ ▼ ▼ ▼ ▼ ▼

KEITH D. RIEFKOHL

Coues' deer have the much-deserved reputation of being one of North America's toughest and most challenging big-game animals to hunt. The terrain they inhabit is desperately hot, rocky, rugged, and just generally inhospitable. Most things that grow there either bite, poke, sting, or burn.

Spotting Coues' deer can be an effort in futility. They have the sneakiness of their larger whitetail cousins, with a body color softer and dustier, just enough so that they are practically impossible to spot. If the hunter doesn't just happen to see an ear flicker or tail wag while the deer is in the field of view, it can be impossible.

Despite the constant difficulties and long odds, on January 14, 2005, Keith Riefkohl had his dream scenario unfold. He was looking through the scope of his .300 Remington Ultra-Mag. at a giant of a buck 425 yards away. At 5:15 p.m, with the squeeze of a finger, the 180-grain bullet was sent on its way, and Keith had made the most of a gift nothing short of divine.

This buck, with the unique 13-2/8-inch abnormal point resembling a third main beam, is truly a trophy as unique as they come. At 111-6/8, it was also large enough to receive the 3rd Award for non-typical Coues' deer at B&C's 26th Big Game Awards Banquet in 2007, in Fort Worth, Texas. ▲

Photograph by Bill Honza

TROPHY STATS

▼ ▼ ▼ ▼ ▼

Category
Canada Moose

Score
227 $^6/_8$

Greatest Spread
59 $^2/_8$

Length of Palm
Right: 45   Left: 46

Width of Palm
Right: 18   Left: 16 $^5/_8$

Normal Points
Right: 15   Left: 18

Location
Kawdy Mt., British Columbia – 2004

Hunter
Frank A. Hanks

CANADA MOOSE
First Award – 227 ⁶/₈

▼ ▼ ▼ ▼ ▼ ▼ ▼ ▼ ▼

FRANK A. HANKS

Written by Wade Hanks

On Christmas of 2003, mom and I decided to do something special for Dad. We arranged for him to go on a Canada moose hunt. He had already taken an Alaska-Yukon moose, but had been talking more and more about wanting to get his Shiras moose in Idaho. That, of course, is through a draw, so I thought it might be fun to get him one step closer to an all three categories "moose slam" by taking him on a moose hunt in Canada.

Dad's Moose

I had some good friends who had gone to northern British Columbia the previous year and had what I felt was an exceptional hunt on Canada moose. I contacted him and he helped me set up our 2004 hunt with Fletcher and Sherry Day, owners and operators of Tahltan Outfitters out of Dease Lake.

Dad and I have both been to Alaska numerous times and so the only preparation we made for the trip was to sight in our guns. We both took our tried and true .338 Winchester Magnums. I also took my bow, in hopes of finding an opportunity favorable for a good stalk.

We drove the 24-hour scenic trek straight through from northern Idaho and arrived in time to catch our floatplane into Fletcher's camp. Bruce, of Dease Lake Air Charters, flew us into camp in a prehistoric DeHaviland Beaver on floats. Sherry Day was accompanying us on the flight. She spends most of her time at home coordinating hunters and arranging hunts for upcoming years.

Fletcher met us at the lake with an Argo on a clear sunny day. There was snow on all of the peaks around us, and it just felt like a good time and place to hunt moose. Once the two-hour Argo ride was over I really felt ready to hunt.

Photograph by Jack Reneau

Frank A. Hanks accepting his plaque and medal from Buck Buckner, Vice President and Chairman of the Big Game Records Committee.

Little did I know that the next day we would again travel all day to our spike camp. This time it wasn't in a comfortable Chevy half-ton, or a floatplane, or an Argo; it was on horseback.

Vernon Marion and Chuck were to be our guides. They were cowboys in every sense. They were trained in moose hunting with horses; I had always hunted moose from a spike camp with a pack frame. The only thing we had in common was the fact that we had both glassed up a lot of moose in our lives, and had spent our fair share of time butchering and caping these enormous animals. I could tell that everything I thought I knew about moose hunting would be worthless to me in this new environment.

Though sore, I survived the 20-mile horseback ride. We awoke the next morning from a great night's sleep only to find fog and rain. We thought it would be fruitless but still trudged up to our knob (a hill providing the only vantage point in the area). After a couple of hours of unrelenting wind, rain, and fog, I suggested we return tomorrow. Relieved, Vernon and Chuck gave in, and we called it a day. This choice turned out to be the right one as the fog and rain continued all day and night.

WE APPROACHED THE FALLEN GIANT AND REALIZED THAT HE HAD ONLY TRAVELED FAR ENOUGH TO STUMBLE ONCE AND GO DOWN. WHAT A DAY — TWO TROPHY BULL MOOSE WITHIN 500 YARDS OF EACH OTHER, AND WITHIN 30 MINUTES! MY BULL WAS ALSO ABOUT 60 INCHES WIDE. IT HAD GOOD PALMS AND A TOTAL OF 23 POINTS. I KNEW INSTANTLY THAT I HAD BEEN OUTDONE BY MY FATHER, BUT I SUPPOSE I WOULDN'T HAVE WANTED IT ANY OTHER WAY.

Day two was a little bit better than day one, but there was still some snow in the air. We reached the top of the knob and the moose hunting started slow. Chuck was the first to spot a bull. It was a good one, just not a great one. Before long, we were spotting moose all over. Chuck saw another bull that appeared huge but was into the trees before we could get a better look. In the valley below us, we had spotted 13 different bull moose, including a bull with two cows that had potential, but he was staying in the trees as well. Thanks to his cows he was in and out of the trees and gave us enough of a look at him, so that we decided to take him.

He was over a mile away, so we had to ride the horses closer to start the stalk. Vernon led us across the tundra and through the spruce thickets to an opening where we hitched the horses. I wanted Dad to take this one, as he appeared to be around 60 inches wide with good palms and points. Since he would be shooting, I left my bow and only took my rifle as back up.

We began sneaking through the willow brush with a good wind in our face. The rain had momentarily stopped, and conditions were perfect. I was getting the feeling that this moose was in the bag. If he were still in the same place he had bedded 1-1/2 hours ago, it would be a cakewalk.

Just when we thought we should be able to see the moose with his cows, we were surprised by a spooked pair of moose. A different bull and cow had gotten between us and our target. It didn't take but a second to realize that this moose was bigger and better than our target bull. Both Vernon and I were telling Dad to shoot. He was struggling to find a rest and was going to miss out on the bull of a lifetime if he didn't hurry.

CANADA MOOSE
First Award – 227 6/8
▼ ▼ ▼ ▼ ▼
FRANK A. HANKS

I tried handing him my tripod, but it wasn't tall enough; he tried a willow bush or two but they were too short as well. Finally, after what seemed like forever to me, dad fired an offhand shot at the still curious moose.

The bull was hit and turned back to the safety of a small grove of spruce. The cow ran forward and out of sight into the thick black forest. Dad rushed to the partially hidden moose and prepared for another shot. The big bull, still unsure of what had just transpired, stepped back out of the trees to see what the commotion was all about. Dad fired again and the disoriented bull began running for safety in our direction.

I don't think he was charging us, but we were right in the middle of his exit strategy. Dad fired a couple more times before the giant came to a stop and finally collapsed 60 yards from us.

What a celebration we had when we realized just how big this trophy was! Dad was pleasantly surprised. During all the excitement he hadn't even looked at the rack. He simply had trusted his guide and his son. The bull was about 60 inches wide, with incredible palms, and had 33 points. We couldn't believe it.

As we were soaking up the moment, two cows appeared on the edge of the trees near where the original bull had been. Chuck and I decided it was worth a look, and took off in that direction. I knew at that moment I should have had my bow.

We jockeyed into position downwind and behind the two alert cows. We looked and looked for the bull. As we moved around seeking different angles, I finally spotted him. He was looking straight away and was directly upwind. There was a clear opening through the 150 yards of brush between us and the bull. I was sick that my bow was in the scabbard on the horse. I am not sure if I could have drawn a more perfect scenario for an archery stalk.

Chuck asked if I had a clear shot. I had found a scrubby spruce tree for a rest and felt comfortable with the shot. We knew there was only enough opening for one shot, so I caught my breath and calmly took the shot. At the crack of the rifle, the bull lunged forward. We watched the few openings in the direction they went but did not see the cows or the bull. Chuck questioned the shot, but it felt good to me. I was fairly confident the bull would be lying just out of sight.

We approached the fallen giant and realized that he had only traveled far enough to stumble once and go down. What a day — two trophy bull moose within 500 yards of each other, and within 30 minutes! My bull was also about 60 inches wide. It had good palms and a total of 23 points. I knew instantly that I had been outdone by my father, but I suppose I wouldn't have wanted it any other way.

Wade Hanks, left, is seated next to his dad Frank A. Hanks and Frank's award-winning Canada moose. Frank's moose scores 227-6/8 points and received the First Place Award.

After the bulls were down, the real work began. Daylight was fading, and we were still over an hour's ride from our camp. We prepared the bulls for their last evening in the wild and hoped no visitors would show up by morning. We told a couple of good campfire stories that night while dining on some fine stew.

Morning came with a rainstorm. We spent a miserable day in the field butchering and loading the horses. We did see a couple more bulls during the day, a big black grizzly bear, and a lot of wolf tracks, but nothing that compared with our two trophies.

With the two moose out of the way, we were ready to look for our mountain caribou. We made the journey back to the main camp with 24 horses laden with spike camp and moose. The long ride home was hard but pleasant as I followed the two horses carrying the antlers and floated on cloud nine. It was definitely the agony of victory.

Days later, from the comforts of the main camp, dad was able to harvest a respectable caribou. It was the biggest one we had seen the entire week. The weather had been cold but cooperative. I was being quite selective and did not take a caribou. As it turned out it was probably a good thing. We could not have fit one more pound of meat or another antler into the truck for the journey home.

Fletcher and the crew were happy for us and welcomed us back anytime. The camp and experience were spectacular. The two bulls both ended up qualifying for Boone and Crockett. My moose officially scored 203-2/8, placing around 300th all-time. Dad's bull, however, scored 227-6/8, placing it seventh all-time. Congratulations, Dad! ▲

B&C Photo Archives

A family visiting the Fort Worth area spends time in Boone and Crockett Club's 26th Big Game Awards Trophy Display at Cabela's. The moose exhibit was especially impressive due to the size of these great animals. Above, a mother points out Frank Hanks' Canada moose to her three sons. Hanks' bull received a First Place Award and has a final score of 227-6/8 points.

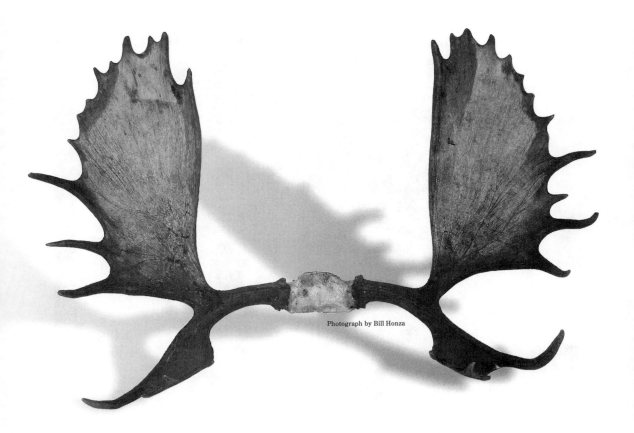

Photograph by Bill Honza

TROPHY STATS

▼ ▼ ▼ ▼ ▼

Category
Canada Moose

Score
216 $^2/_8$

Greatest Spread
61

Length of Palm
Right: 46 $^1/_8$ Left: 48 $^6/_8$

Width of Palm
Right: 14 $^2/_8$ Left: 14 $^4/_8$

Normal Points
Right: 11   Left: 10

Location
Lake Co., Minnesota – 2006

Hunter
D.C. Rengo & J.C. Rengo

Owner
Dennis C. Rengo

CANADA MOOSE
Second Award – 216 ²/₈
▼ ▼ ▼ ▼ ▼ ▼ ▼ ▼ ▼

HUNTERS – D.C. RENGO & J.C. RENGO
OWNER – DENNIS C. RENGO

I had been applying for the once-in-a-lifetime moose hunt in Minnesota for nearly 25 years, while my father Jim had been sending in his application for over 30 years. Our bad luck finally changed for the 2006 hunt. We applied together and were finally drawn.

We had selected a zone south of Ely and east of Babbit to hunt. My brother Jeff suggested this area. As a forester for the Minnesota DNR, he knows this area well and routinely travels it setting up timber sales. He had found many shed moose antlers and had seen much sign in his travels through this countryside. He assisted with some preseason scouting and in getting us familiar with the area.

My cousin Chuck Kovala was also lucky enough to draw a tag in the same zone as us on only his first time applying for the moose hunt. Chuck had a large wall tent that we used as our base camp. We set up camp the Friday before the season opened and then spent the afternoon doing some final scouting. We hoped to get an idea where the other moose hunters would be hunting on opening morning so we could avoid being too close to another group.

Jim and I selected a cutover area a couple of miles from camp for our hunt the first morning. The spot was about a half-mile off a dead end Forest Service road. We had seen some fresh sign the day before, so we were hopeful a bull would still be in the area. We arrived about 45 minutes before sunrise and decided to set up on a rocky and brushy hill where we could see 150 yards in every direction.

I started cow calling with a megaphone made out of some posterboard-type material. About five minutes later, I heard what I thought was another group of hunters making their own calls. I waited a couple of minutes and called again. This time I got a reply right away but from much closer, probably within a quarter of a mile. I realized quickly that this wasn't a hunter; it was a moose!

The wind was light and swirling, so I figured the moose wouldn't be able to pick up our scent right away. I kept calling intermittently for the next 20 minutes. Each time I stopped, we could hear him getting closer and closer. He was crashing through a dry cutover area and grunting as he walked.

We finally spotted him about 150 yards out. His body was jet black and the inside of his antler palms looked liked two canoe paddles being waved in the air. I whispered to my dad that I thought he was big enough to shoot. The bull kept slowly making his way toward us, weaving in and out of thick cover. He was now within 25 yards of us, all the while never

Jim Rengo, left, and his son, Dennis C. Rengo, harvested this award-winning Canada moose in Lake County, Minnesota. Both men had been applying individually for a moose permit for over 25 years before they applied together and were finally drawn. The bull scores 216-2/8 points.

letting us get a clear shot at him. We could see the young aspen trees shaking as he scraped them with his antlers.

He stayed close for a few minutes before he got nervous and started to slowly trot away from us. The bull was about 50 yards away when he turned broadside through a large opening. We both raised our .30-06s and each fired off one round. The moose went right down. We could hardly believe it. It wasn't even 7 a.m. on opening morning and we already had our moose!

I decided that I would head back to camp to get Jeff, my other brother Todd, and two of Todd's sons, Matt and Sam, while Jim started field-dressing our trophy animal. We were able to drive my ATV right up to the kill site. We lifted the head as high as we could and strapped it to the rear rack of the ATV. Jeff had to sit on the front rack so we could keep the front wheels on the ground to steer. We inched our way out over rocks and stumps with the 1,200-pound bull moose dragging behind. Once it was back at camp, it took us most of the afternoon to skin and quarter the beast.

Chuck had hunted an area south of camp the first morning without any luck. The second morning he decided to head about 10 miles south of camp to another area where we had seen good sign before the season. By 6:45 a.m. on Sunday morning, Chuck had shot a small bull, and our tags were all full for the season.

It was hard to believe less than two days of hunting and our season was over. It turned out that our moose scored an incredible 216-2/8 B&C points and is the second-largest to ever come from Minnesota. ▲

B&C Photo Archives

All of the trophies at the 26th Big Game Awards Program were shipped to Cabela's Fort Worth store in April of 2007. The crew spends several days carefully uncrating each trophy prior to the Judges Panel's arrival, at which point the final score verification process begins.

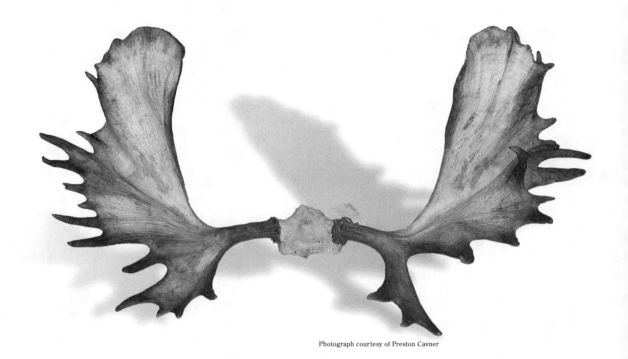

Photograph courtesy of Preston Cavner

TROPHY STATS

▼ ▼ ▼ ▼ ▼

Category
 Alaska-Yukon Moose

Score
 254 5/8

Greatest Spread
 70 7/8

Length of Palm
 Right: 46 4/8   Left: 48 2/8

Width of Palm
 Right: 22 2/8   Left: 23 1/8

Normal Points
 Right: 15   Left: 16

Location
 Kvichak River, Alaska – 2005

Hunter
 Franz Kohlroser

ALASKA-YUKON MOOSE
First Award – 254 ⁵/₈

▼ ▼ ▼ ▼ ▼ ▼ ▼ ▼ ▼

FRANZ KOHLROSER

Written by the guide on the hunt, Eric Lantzer

It was the last day of the hunt for my client, Franz Kohlroser. He had come all the way from Austria to hunt moose in Alaska, and I didn't want him to go home with an unfilled tag. It was cold, rainy, and windy — a typical Alaska day.

After glassing into the wind for an hour and a half, I sat down by Franz, and we had some hot tea. We talked and joked for a little while, and then glassed for a bit longer before going back to camp to have lunch. We'd had a good, hard hunt, but it looked like we might

Photograph courtesy of Preston Cavner

Franz Kohlroser, left, and his guide Eric Lantzer are pictured above with Franz's Alaska-Yukon moose taken near the Kvichak River in Alaska. The bull received a First Place Award at the 26th Big Game Award Program Banquet in Fort Worth, Texas.

The author packed out Franz's moose antlers, which have a greatest spread of 70-7/8 inches. The bull is the fifth largest ever taken by a hunter.

have to go home empty-handed. But hunting is hunting, and you never know when your luck can change.

I was trying to spot a cow that we had seen the night before. When a real nice set of antlers showed up in my binoculars, I put my spotting scope on them to take a closer look. I took a quick look and said, "Franz, I found what we're looking for!"

We watched as the bull stood up, looked around, and then lay back down. We then quickly and carefully planned our mile-long stalk. We hiked toward him, stopping at the edge of clearings to glass and call, just in case he had moved. It seemed like it took forever, but we soon came to the edge of the clearing we had seen him bedding in.

We took off our rain gear and continued on with our rifles. We happened to look back toward where we had spotted him from, and there was a huge rainbow. Now that's the sign of promise!

We slowly made our way down the clearing and then spotted his massive rack in exactly the same spot he had been when we spotted him. Only now, we were 100 yards away, instead of a mile. We crept up to 76 yards, keeping a black spruce between him and us.

We got Franz set up, and then I gave two moose grunts. We watched as the huge moose sprang to his feet, looking around for an intruder. I whispered, "Shoot him, Franz."

Franz obliged, and with two quick shots put the bull down in his bed for good. We knew when we walked up to him that he was an exceptional animal, but it's hard to imagine having an all-time giant right there in front of you. Franz's incredible bull ended up scoring 254-5/8 points, placing it as the fifth-largest Alaska-Yukon moose ever taken by a hunter. Hunting is about being in the right place at the right time, being ethical, and enjoying what you're doing. Franz's moose was a great reward for a great hunt. ▲

The second product ever to carry the Boone and Crockett name is a Remington Model 700 CDL Boone and Crockett Edition rifle. The Club is looking forward to a long and fruitful relationship with America's oldest gun maker. Remington's Press Relations and Conservation Sales Manager, Linda Powell, is pictured accepting a Plaque of Appreciation from B&C's Keith Balfourd for their support of the 26th Big Game Awards Program.

Photograph by Bill Honza

TROPHY STATS

▼ ▼ ▼ ▼ ▼

Category
Alaska-Yukon Moose

Score
244

Greatest Spread
75 $^2/_8$

Length of Palm
Right: 45 $^1/_8$ Left: 47 $^1/_8$

Width of Palm
Right: 20 $^6/_8$ Left: 18

Normal Points
Right: 15   Left: 14

Location
Pingston Creek, Alaska – 2004

Hunter
Jerry D. Whisenhunt

ALASKA-YUKON MOOSE
Second Award – 244
▼ ▼ ▼ ▼ ▼ ▼ ▼ ▼ ▼

JERRY D. WHISENHUNT

When most girls ask for an 18th birthday present, a car or oodles of money might come to mind as the leading requests. Not so in the Whisenhunt household. Jerry's daughter, Amber, asked for only one thing – she wanted to go moose hunting. Jerry and Amber have a close hunting relationship, and he quickly obliged.

The focus of the hunt was for Amber to get a moose, and possibly a grizzly. Jerry was there to hunt, too, but he really wanted Amber to fill her tag on the trip. Little did Jerry know

Photograph courtesy of Jerry D. Whisenhunt

Jerry D. Whisenhunt is pictured above with his award-winning Alaska-Yukon moose. The bull was taken near Alaska's Pingston Creek during the 2004 season while on a hunt with his daughter Amber. The moose has a final score of 244 points.

Photograph by Jack Reneau

Jerry D. Whisenhunt accepting his plaque and medal from Buck Buckner, Vice President and Chairman of the Big Game Records Committee.

that his generosity would soon lead to his own reward.

To give Amber the full run of all the best hunting areas, Jerry and his guide chose a remote and rugged location far away from Amber, so they would not interfere in her hunt. The hunt Jerry would undertake would demand all he and his guide had physically. They agreed they would not take a moose in that area unless it was the biggest animal they had ever imagined.

That proved to be exactly what happened. They made their way into the isolated spot, and soon spotted a huge bull. With a little luck and some calling, they had him pinpointed. A cow complicated things, but when she spooked, they followed her as closely as they could, hoping she would lead them to the big bull. It worked like a charm, and soon Jerry had the bull dreams are made of in his sights.

The adventure proved to be all Jerry and his guide could take; it took them a total of five days to retrieve and relocate the entire moose back to their camp. Looking at his prize, Jerry is positive it was worth it. His great Alaska-Yukon moose has a 75-2/8-inch greatest spread, and ranks among the best ever taken by a hunter.

Amber, whose hunt was the real focus of the trip, didn't get her moose, but Jerry has promised to take her bear hunting instead. Sounds like a great plan, Jerry. ▲

Each trophy that received a place award received a plaque and a B&C medal at the 26th Big Game Awards Banquet. Above Jerry D. Whisenhunt proudly displays his award after taking his place on stage.

Photograph by Bill Honza

TROPHY STATS

▼ ▼ ▼ ▼ ▼

Category
Shiras Moose

Score
187 $^1/_8$

Greatest Spread
59 $^5/_8$

Length of Palm
Right: 38 $^6/_8$ Left: 40 $^3/_8$

Width of Palm
Right: 11 $^4/_8$ Left: 12 $^4/_8$

Normal Points
Right: 7   Left: 8

Location
Shoshone Co., Idaho – 2005

Hunter
Chad Hammons

SHIRAS MOOSE
First Award – 187 ⅛

▼ ▼ ▼ ▼ ▼ ▼ ▼ ▼ ▼

CHAD HAMMONS

It all started out at a Little League game in June. A friend of mine told me he drew a moose tag for the unit I had applied for. He was rubbing it in pretty good, and I was getting pretty jealous, so the first thing I did when I got home was get on the computer. I looked up my application on the Idaho Fish & Game web site and, sure enough, I had also drawn a tag!

I spent the next couple of months looking up everything I could about moose on the internet. I knew several places where I had seen moose on previous elk and deer hunts, so I wasn't that concerned about finding a moose. My biggest concern was seeing a small one and being tempted to shoot it. Any bull would be legal on this hunt and I had almost three months to fill my tag. I knew I wanted to wait until the antlers were out of velvet, and hopefully until the weather cooled off. Sometimes in September the weather is still in the eighties in the daytime, and I didn't want to have to fight off flies and bees if I did connect with one.

About two weeks before the season started, I quit my job and went to work for my father-in-law. I told him I would need some time off for moose hunting because I had a once in a lifetime tag. He said we could work something out, and that was that.

The first week of season came, and it went without me stepping foot in the woods. Then one night my dad called and said a friend of his had seen a big bull up in one of my hunting areas while hunting for grouse. The next evening my dad Wayne and friend Roger O'Dwyer decided to go do a little scouting. I picked them up after work and we drove up Child's Creek to look for my moose. We went to the top of the mountain and walked out an old road to the area Roger and his wife had seen the bull a couple of days before, but unfortunately he wasn't there.

The next morning, my stepfather Dave and I went up the same drainage to look around but took a different road. We ended up seeing one bull that was 40-45 inches wide, but I felt confident I could find a bigger one. Dave had to

Photograph by Jack Reneau

Chad Hammons accepting his plaque and medal from Buck Buckner, Vice President and Chairman of the Big Game Records Committee.

be home early, so we decided to let that one go. As I dropped Dave off, my brother Dustin showed up, we decided to go for a scouting trip. We also ran into my other brother, Mark, and his four-year-old son, Brayden. We all decided to take a drive and see if we could find anything.

We went back up to the same area and arrived at a spot in the road where it forked. I decided to let my pickup cool off; it was running hot from the steep hill and a plugged radiator (I found out later). Everybody got out to stretch their legs, so I decided to walk down an old overgrown road. I grabbed my rifle and headed out while everyone else was still getting out.

I made it down the road a few corners when I decided to make a moose call down into the canyon. I had grunted a couple of times when I thought I heard something down in the brush. I grunted a few more times to try to locate where the noise was coming from. I looked up on the hillside above me and there, out of nowhere, stood the moose of my dreams!

At first I couldn't decide whether to run back to the pickup and get my brothers to see him and bring the camera, or just watch him. While I was deciding what to do, he turned his head to where I had a good view of his antlers. It only took me about two seconds to decide this scouting trip had just turned into a hunting trip!

I dropped onto one knee, raised my .300 Remington Winchester Magnum, aimed right behind his shoulder, and squeezed the trigger. He walked a few steps before I cycled the action and shot him again behind the shoulder. That was where he dropped.

I let out a big holler and my brothers and nephew came running around the corner to see what I was doing. I told them I just shot a huge moose, and he was down. I still don't know if they believed me or not, until they saw him. It was then when my nephew named him "Big John Dandy", which has been his name ever since.

After a few high-fives, the thought of how we were going to get him in the pickup sank in. He looked awfully big lying on the ground. We videotaped the field-dressing process and took a whole roll of pictures with a camera that didn't work. We ended up being able to drag the moose down to the road and slide him into the pickup whole. He weighed approximately 550 pounds at the meat processors. I'm guessing he weighed 1,500 pounds live weight. ▲

Chad Hammons stands in front of his Shiras moose during Press Day held at Cabela's in Fort Worth. Hammons' moose has a final score of 187-1/8 points and received a First Place Award.

Photograph by Bill Honza

TROPHY STATS

▼ ▼ ▼ ▼ ▼

Category
Shiras Moose

Score
183 $^6/_8$

Greatest Spread
54 $^6/_8$

Length of Palm
Right: 33 $^3/_8$ Left: 33 $^5/_8$

Width of Palm
Right: 12   Left: 12 $^2/_8$

Normal Points
Right: 13   Left: 13

Location
Stevens Co., Washington – 2005

Hunter
Marc W. Babiar

SHIRAS MOOSE
Second Award – 183 ⁶/₈

▼ ▼ ▼ ▼ ▼ ▼ ▼ ▼ ▼

MARC W. BABIAR

I've hunted public land mule deer (my favorite big game) in Washington every year since 1974, but I live a few hundred miles away from Washington's "moose country." Nonetheless, I tried unsuccessfully for nearly a decade to draw one of the state's coveted moose tags. Finally, in 2005, my luck changed, and I was drawn.

I spoke with some friends and Washington wildlife biologists about moose, moose habitats, and general areas to look for moose. By the time the season came, I was fairly confident that I had some good areas to hunt.

Lucky Charm

I always thought marshy wetlands would be where I'd be hunting; instead, my unit in Stevens County was mostly mountainous country. These animals seemed to hang out in clearcuts that had been opened up and provided great grazing opportunities.

I spoke with my friend Jeff, and he had a friend that had taken a nice bull moose in my unit a few years previous; he suggested I talk to him. When I called Jeff's friend Bill, things sounded promising. Bill had property in my hunting unit and had seen moose close by. Bill said I could camp on his property, and we made aarrangements to meet him late Wednesday night to set up camp. At that point, he would give my friend Dave and me a general layout of the land. He also said that he'd meet us Friday on the mountain to help me find some moose.

The hospitality that Bill extended to us was incredible. He and his girlfriend drove 1-1/2 hours to meet us at 11 p.m. to let us on his property, and then he had to drive back home that night to work the next day. Don't forget the fact that he had never even met me before.

On Thursday morning, Dave and I got up before light and headed out in search of a nice bull. After six hours of hunting, I spotted a dark shape in my binoculars moving on a ridgetop nearly a mile away. It looked like a nice bull.

Photograph by Jack Reneau

Marc W. Babiar accepting his plaque and medal from Buck Buckner, Vice President and Chairman of the Big Game Records Committee.

Marc W. Babiar is pictured above with his Shiras moose scoring 183-6/8 points. The award-winning bull was taken in Stevens County, Washington, during the 2005 season. Marc's moose is the largest Shiras moose ever taken in the state of Washington.

Dave kept low and would try to keep an eye on the bull while I moved up the ridge to head him off.

In the thick brush, I was able to get to within 30 yards but could never see the bull. I could only hear him grunt. We tried to call him out of the thick brush with grunt calls, but he wouldn't respond. Eventually, he must've winded us and took off down the valley.

As darkness approached, Dave and I saw a small bull that wasn't quite what we were looking for but still very fun to play with. After the bull ran up a hill into the brush, Dave and I started calling and thrashing the brush. The bull responded for a good 30 minutes.

The next day we left camp before light and hunted until noon without seeing any moose. Bill had better luck, however, and said he had one that I should check out. When we spotted the bull, he was on the run. We tried to get in position for a shot but it all happened too quickly.

We split up in an attempt to find him. I was on top of a ridge when I saw a dark shape moving up a steep hogback ridge. It was a different huge bull! This one was wide, with three tines on his brow palms. He bedded down, and I thought I might have a chance at him, but after less than a minute he got back up and went over the top of the mountain.

By the time we got up there (nearly two hours later) he was nowhere to be found.

I was sick knowing such a giant bull had escaped. We made our way back to camp in the dark, and Bill said he'd be up sometime around mid-morning the next day to see how I was doing.

SHIRAS MOOSE
Second Award – 183 6/8
▼　▼　▼　▼　▼
MARC W. BABIAR

Saturday morning I woke up and held my grandpa's old red-and-black checkered-wool hunting glove that both he and my dad had worn while hunting and wished myself good luck. Dave and I took off again before daylight.

At about 7 a.m., we spotted a bull with a small cow. Dave started calling when I heard him say there was a big bull on top. After about a two-second look, I knew it was the type of bull I had been looking for. I found a log to rest my rifle on and squeezed off a round from 178 yards from a .338 borrowed from my friend, Ray. The bull flinched but was still up. Two more shots for insurance, and he was down for good. The first shot was lethal, but I wanted the bull down right were it stood; 30 yards ahead of him was a thick, steep canyon that would have made packing him out difficult.

Dave and I were in awe as we finally got a close-up view of what a giant Shiras moose looked like. He had 13 points on each antler and was nearly 55 inches wide! To my surprise, it was the same bull I'd seen the day before on the hogback ridge — nearly five miles away. I guess that goes to show you what a hot cow moose will do to excited bulls.

Bill showed up later to help us with the celebrating. That night at camp, we had moose backstraps, and that's what it's all about. This moose hunt was a once-in-a-lifetime opportunity, with dad and grandpa getting me started in hunting, and my friends, my wife, and two daughters' help and support. ▲

Photograph by Bill Honza

TROPHY STATS

▼ ▼ ▼ ▼ ▼

Category
Mountain Caribou

Score
437 $^6/_8$

Inside Spread
40 $^2/_8$

Length of Main Beam
Right: 42 $^2/_8$ Left: 44 $^6/_8$

Width of Brow Palm
Right: 10 $^1/_8$ Left: 4 $^1/_8$

Normal Points
Right: 18   Left: 18

Location
Tucho Lake, British Columbia – 2004

Hunter
William F. Nye

MOUNTAIN CARIBOU
First Award – 437 ⁶/₈

▼ ▼ ▼ ▼ ▼ ▼ ▼ ▼ ▼

WILLIAM F. NYE

Once again, I was sitting back in the tent wondering if we will ever find a sheep. It was September 2004, and I was just up the valley from Tucho Lake in northern British Columbia. I was hunting with Jerry Geraci's Upper Stikine Adventures, and I had met Gene, my guide, 12 days earlier. I had tags for Stone's sheep, grizzly bear, mountain goat, and mountain caribou, and had dedicated 20 days to hunting them.

On the second day of the hunt we woke up to a foot and a half of snow — not exactly normal weather for early September. We had already covered a lot of area, and considering

Photograph courtesy of William F. Nye

William F. Nye is pictured above with his mountain caribou scoring 437-6/8 points. The award-winning bull was taken near Tucho Lake in British Columbia. On the thirteenth morning of his combo hunt, Nye took a grizzly bear and later tagged this bull while his guide was away gathering equipment.

William F. Nye accepting his plaque and medal from Buck Buckner, Vice President and Chairman of the Big Game Records Committee.

the conditions, I wasn't looking forward to yet another marathon horseback ride. On the morning of day 13, we walked up a valley where we had seen some grizzly sign the day before. As we peeked over the rise of the hill, we spotted a good grizzly about 160 yards away, not too much trouble for my 7mm STW. I settled into a good rest over my pack, and he was mine.

After the handshakes and high fives, Gene ran back to the tent (about a quarter of a mile away) to get his skinning knives while I glassed the surrounding valleys for sheep. I spotted a small group of caribou, among them a few cows, a smaller bull, and HIM. His antlers were blood red, having probably just shed his velvet a few hours before. As I watched him demolish a small tree, I knew we had to go after this one.

I could hardly contain myself when Gene returned. As we skinned the grizzly, I constantly watched the caribou to see where they were going. Much to my surprise, they bedded down. After packing the grizzly back to the tent, Gene asked what I wanted to do. So, off we went to find the big bull.

We had at least a two-mile hike down the valley and two hours of climbing to reach him. The hike down was easy, but the climb up was another story. The bottom held the thickest alders imaginable. Next were the spruce trees that gave us a little relief until we broke out and started climbing through ankle-breaking rocks covered in foot-deep snow. Once we reached the top, all I saw was snow, more snow, and caribou tracks. The caribou were nowhere to be seen, so Gene headed up the draw to look for sheep or goats.

I watched him go for about 600 yards before he turned around and headed back. When he was about 200 yards away I saw him waving his arms and pointing to the knob across from me. The caribou were coming back toward me, and my bull was the last one in line. I jumped up and tried to get the best rest I could off the rock I was sitting on. The bull was now about 220 yards away as I waited for him to turn broadside. The first shot was on the money. The second was a miss, but the third shot finally put him down.

As we approached, I could not believe the size of his body. His top points soon came into focus, and they were longer and more massive than anything I had ever seen.

I couldn't believe I was fortunate enough to harvest an animal like this. The day prior, I was wondering if I would ever see a sheep. On this great day, I had taken a beautiful grizzly bear in the morning and a magnificent mountain caribou in the afternoon. It was a magnificent day. ▲

B&C Photo Archives

Fourteen award-winning caribou were part of the 26th Big Game Awards Trophy Display at Cabela's.

Photograph by Bill Honza

TROPHY STATS

▼ ▼ ▼ ▼ ▼

Category
Mountain Caribou

Score
427 $^1/_8$

Inside Spread
36 $^2/_8$

Length of Main Beam
Right: 45 $^6/_8$ Left: 43 $^6/_8$

Width of Brow Palm
Right: 14 $^7/_8$ Left: 13 $^4/_8$

Normal Points
Right: 19   Left: 21

Location
Russell Range, Yukon Territory – 2005

Hunter
John S. Bell

BOONE AND CROCKETT CLUB'S

MOUNTAIN CARIBOU
Second Award – 427 ¹/₈
▼ ▼ ▼ ▼ ▼ ▼ ▼ ▼ ▼

JOHN S. BELL

Hunting caribou sometimes has a stereotype of being a comparatively easy hunt, with caribou roaming by the thousands and simply picking which ones to take. In fact, caribou represent a great challenge to the fair-chase hunter. The weather can vary from balmy to blizzards, the winds from calm to gale force, and the bugs from a just a few on a windy day to clouds and swarms so dense they seem to be their own storm.

John Bell left his home in the Midwest in early fall of 2005, very much excited about his upcoming North Country hunting adventure. He was to hunt with Bill Sandulak in the Russell Range of Yukon Territory.

They packed in on horses to a remote location and prepared for the hunt. It was beautiful and desolate country, somewhat open and with a fair amount of rock.

John was hoping to down a nice bull with his .50-caliber Traditions muzzleloader. He had been hunting with one for about four years, and liked the challenge.

At around 3 p.m. on September 6, he encountered a great bull with a beautiful, deep chocolate coat. The bull had a double shovel, handsome dark antlers, and tremendous tops, fully palmated. It was the kind of trophy that hunters dream of.

He was able to get to within 40 yards of the bull before he fire. It took two shots, but ultimately, John filled his tag with an incredible trophy.

John Bell's mountain caribou was not only an incredible souvenir from a memorable hunt; it was also one of the top caribou taken anywhere in North America during that period. Good enough, in fact, to receive the 2nd Award for mountain caribou at B&C's 26th Big Game Awards. ▲

Photograph courtesy of John S. Bell

John S. Bell pictured with his mountain caribou taken in 2005. The award-winning bull from Yukon Territory has a final score of 427-1/8 points

Photograph by Bill Honza

TROPHY STATS

▼ ▼ ▼ ▼ ▼

Category
Woodland Caribou

Score
384 $^2/_8$

Inside Spread
39 $^3/_8$

Length of Main Beam
Right: 39 $^2/_8$ Left: 39 $^1/_8$

Width of Brow Palm
Right: 10 $^2/_8$ Left: 17 $^3/_8$

Normal Points
Right: 16   Left: 19

Location
Sam's Pond, Newfoundland – 2005

Hunter
James H. Holt

252

WOODLAND CARIBOU
First Award – 384 ²/₈

▼ ▼ ▼ ▼ ▼ ▼ ▼ ▼ ▼

JAMES H. HOLT

Our plans for a hunt in Newfoundland started at the Eastern Sports & Outdoor Show in Harrisburg, Pennsylvania, in February of 2004. My girlfriend and hunting buddy Marcie Mott and I had thought about going to Newfoundland for some time. The thought of hunting three big game animals on one hunt sounded exciting. From what we read, the chances of seeing and bagging a woodland caribou, a moose, and a black bear were quite possible - "The Newfoundland Grand Slam." We also had some friends that had been to Newfoundland for moose with great success. They had also seen bear and caribou on their trips.

Going on hunts in distant places was nothing new for us. We had been on several deer hunts in a number of states including Mississippi, Illinois, and West Virginia, and spent every deer season in Pennsylvania for the last 40 years (me) and 22 years (Marcie). We have both taken our share of whitetails with bow and gun. We have also been on an archery elk hunt in Montana and several bear hunts in Ontario and Quebec, with good success on the bear hunts. I had been on a Northern Quebec hunt for caribou in 2001 and thought that taking a caribou with a bow could be quite possible.

We stopped at several booths at the show, asking questions and getting information. After talking to a number of Newfoundland outfitters, we found ourselves at Efford's Hunting Adventures. We liked their straight answers and the photo albums full of successful hunts. Marcie was asking about sleeping quarters, showers, toilet facilities, and meals. When a lady is planning a hunt, the accommodations are very important. She is 50 percent of the deciding factor on our hunts. A word of advice to the outfitters — when a lady asks a question, the answer should be directed to her, not the gentleman. This makes her feel welcome and wanted in camp. We have been pleased to see that more and more outfitters are realizing that women also want to go on hunting trips. Bob Efford made her feel very welcome, so after making a few reference calls from home, that's who we booked with.

Early Friday morning on September 23, 2005, we started our trip to "The Rock," as Newfoundland is known. We spent the first day driving through Pennsylvania, New York, Connecticut, Massachusetts, New Hampshire, and Maine. It was a beautiful, sunny day. We spent the night in Maine. We continued our drive on Saturday, crossing into New Brunswick and then Nova Scotia. We arrived in North Sydney and boarded the ferry for our seven-hour ride to Newfoundland. After arriving in Channel-Port aux Basques on Sunday morning, we had another six-hour drive to the eastern side of Newfoundland.

Finally, we met up with Bob Efford, who happens to be a pilot with his own plane. As we flew in to Sam's Pond Lodge, it was a beautiful sight looking down on the lakes, ponds, and

Photograph courtesy of James H. Holt

James H. Holt almost passed this woodland caribou up because it was the first caribou he saw on the first day of their hunt. The award-winning bull has a final score of 384-2/8 points and is largest woodland caribou taken in the last 39 years.

barren and wooded landscapes.

Soon, we were on the water taxiing up to the dock. There to meet us were the guides, Frank Lethbridge, Howie Lethbridge and Dwayne Tucker, as well as the cook, Mr. B. After introductions to everyone, including the other couple hunting (Dave and Becky Opatz), we were shown around camp. We then sat down to a great dinner. Afterward, we sat on the front porch overlooking Sam's Pond that evening. What a beautiful sight it was.

The first morning, after a good breakfast, we all went off in different directions. Marcie and I usually hunt together but were given the option to have separate guides, so we decided to try it and see how things went.

My guide, Frank, and I headed down the lake a few miles to a little cove. I carried my bow and Frank packed my 12-gauge slug gun. We secured the boat and headed to higher ground for some glassing. The ground is much like northern Quebec, with all the beautiful colors of lichen, moss, evergreens, and alders. You have to see it to really appreciate it.

We walked a few miles on a steady incline to a high vantage point. There, with our backs against a boulder, we could watch one valley for a while and then the other valley.

After about an hour, Frank spotted a white patch moving across the valley. The white patch was a sure sign of a mature bull caribou. Frank knew from years of experience that there was a good chance that the lone bull would cross the valley between two lakes below us.

We made our way down to the small stream that flowed from one lake into the other, making sure to move only when the bull lowered his head to feed. Sure enough, as we worked our way down so did the bull. As we neared the stream, a well-worn trail was there in front of us. We set up so the bull would be at 20 yards if he followed the trail he appeared to be on. The wind was in our face — a perfect set up. I couldn't believe how easy this was, or so I thought. As the bull got closer, he continued to look bigger. I was looking through the brush we were hiding behind; Frank was hunkered down to keep out of sight.

At about 70 yards, the bull made a left turn into some trees. I told Frank that the bull had turned and was heading away from us. I asked if he thought I could stalk to him within bow distance. His response was, "Only if you're an Olympic sprinter." When a caribou is on the move they can cover an amazing amount of ground.

WOODLAND CARIBOU
First Award – 384 ²/₈

▼ ▼ ▼ ▼ ▼

JAMES H. HOLT

I told him I would pass on this one because it was the first morning of the hunt and the first bull we had seen. Frank said it was a very good bull and would more than likely make the records book. I had to make a decision quickly because the bull was getting further away by the second. I grabbed my slug gun and headed around the patch of small trees the bull was headed through. I was able to get within 75 yards of the bull when he exited the thick cover. The slug gun did its job and the bull was down within seconds after the shot. Frank and I stood over the bull in awe while surveying the antlers. It was quite a sight with all that incredible mass and palmation.

After the caping and quartering chores, we headed back to the boat with a load, then returned for the rest of the animal. It took the rest of the day to get everything to the boat and back to camp. We arrived back at camp as the sun set.

My first day hunting on "the Rock" turned out to be very exciting. Bob flew in the next day and took the rack to have it green-scored. He called on Wednesday night and said that he believed it would likely be in the top five woodland caribou ever recorded.

Our hunt was far from being over, however. Marcie, Dave, and I each bagged a caribou and a bull moose. We had spotted a couple of bears but were unable to make a stalk because of rivers and streams, or we might have achieved our "Newfoundland Grand Slam" on our first trip.

My woodland caribou scores 384-2/8 and ranks number 4 all-time in B&C. It is also the largest of its kind killed in the last 39 years! And to think I almost passed him up because he was the first caribou I saw on my hunt. ▲

Photograph by Bill Honza

TROPHY STATS

▼ ▼ ▼ ▼ ▼

Category
Woodland Caribou

Score
353 $^2/_8$

Inside Spread
40 $^1/_8$

Length of Main Beam
Right: 41 $^5/_8$ Left: 40 $^7/_8$

Width of Brow Palm
Right: 11 $^5/_8$ Left: 14 $^4/_8$

Normal Points
Right: 15   Left: 17

Location
Northern Pen., Newfoundland – 2000

Hunter
Dale L. Hardy

WOODLAND CARIBOU
Second Award – 353 $^2/_8$

▼ ▼ ▼ ▼ ▼ ▼ ▼ ▼ ▼

DALE L. HARDY

September 9-13, 2000

This combination moose and caribou hunt was set up with Moose Country Adventures in Roddington, Newfoundland. The trip started out rainy and windy, both for the plane ride in and also the next day.

Monday changed to sunny and cool. Stanley, my guide, asked what I wanted to go after first. We started out for moose because the caribou were roaming around. As we were glassing for moose from a high ridge, I could see numerous large caribou. One, however, stood out above all the others. He was about a mile away on another ridge, moving in our direction.

Photograph courtesy of Dale L. Hardy

Dale L. Hardy is pictured above with his woodland caribou scoring 353-2/8 points. The award-winning bull was taken on Newfoundland's Northern Peninsula in the fall of 2000. Hardy took the bull on the first day of a five-day combo hunt.

Photograph by Jack Reneau

Dale L. Hardy accepting his plaque and medal from Buck Buckner, Vice President and Chairman of the Big Game Records Committee.

I asked Stanley what he thought about the bull. He replied, "About average."

As he got closer, I could see he had a double shovel. Again, I asked Stanley what he thought of the bull. Again, he replied, "About average."

I had been in Quebec on another caribou hunt two years earlier, and if this was average, I couldn't wait to see an above-average bull!

We kept glassing for moose. When the big caribou I had been preoccupied with was about 600 yards below us, I pointed it out to Stanley. His mood and voice then changed.

"Oh, by Jesus; that is much better than average!"

We moved and got into position. The caribou were angling up the ridge and away from us. I shot my trophy at 325 yards, and the rest is "on the wall."

That was on Monday of the five-day hunt. I finally did get a moose just two hours before the plane came in to pick us up on Friday! ▲

BOONE AND CROCKETT CLUB'S

B&C Photo Archives

Dale L. Hardy, left, and William F. Nye, right, both had award-winning caribou on display at Cabela's. Hardy's woodland caribou, which scores 353-2/8 points, received a Second Place Award, and Nye's mountain caribou received a First Place Award with a final score of 437-6/8 points.

Photograph by Bill Honza

TROPHY STATS
▼ ▼ ▼ ▼ ▼

Category
  Woodland Caribou

Score
  340 ⁵/₈

Inside Spread
  37 ¹/₈

Length of Main Beam
  Right: 49 ³/₈   Left: 49 ⁴/₈

Width of Brow Palm
  Right: 14 ⁷/₈   Left: 18 ⁷/₈

Normal Points
  Right: 10   Left: 14

Location
  Sam's Pond, Newfoundland – 2006

Hunter
  Scott A. Trujillo

WOODLAND CARIBOU
Third Award – 340 ⁵/₈
▼ ▼ ▼ ▼ ▼ ▼ ▼ ▼ ▼

SCOTT A. TRUJILLO

My two friends and I had been preparing for our hunting trip to Newfoundland all year. I have known Brad Sauve and Steve Gardner for most of my adult life, and we have hunted together in Colorado and Utah for several years for elk and mule deer. Brad had harvested a big caribou on a previous hunt in Quebec, so he was signed up for a moose and black bear combination hunt this year. Steve and I were preparing for woodland caribou.

Our outfitter, Bob Effords, was extremely helpful with all of the preparation for the trip. He spoke specifically of the wet conditions for which Newfoundland is famous. Per Bob's recommendation, we each invested in hip boots, new rain gear, and several other items that would help our equipment and our bodies survive and function in cold, rainy conditions.

When we arrived in St. Johns, however, it became clear that we were going to get conditions that none of us had prepared for — warm, beautiful weather! It seemed great on our first day. We spent that Sunday driving to Effords' headquarters, where Bob's team helped us pack our equipment into his floatplane.

At camp, we sighted in our rifles and demonstrated to our respective guides that we were familiar with our guns. We listened to amusing stories of hunters who came to camp having never shot their recently purchased rifles. The most common anecdote centered on hunters who came to camp with expensive, top-of-the-line hunting boots that barely covered their ankles. We would learn the importance of that lesson in days to come.

We listened while Brad hit bulls-eyes on a target he asked to set up about 600 yards away. Brad said he just wanted to make sure his gun was fine-tuned. I resisted the urge to explain to our hosts that Brad was the 2004 and 2006 United States National Marksmanship Champion in F-class shooting (scoped rifles). The rest of the evening was spent speculating

Photograph by Jack Reneau

Scott A. Trujillo accepting his plaque and medal from Buck Buckner, Vice President and Chairman of the Big Game Records Committee.

on how ironic and hilarious it would be if Brad missed a trophy animal that week. These guys were great fun and shared lots of hunting stories with us.

The next morning, Brad, Steve, and I took off in separate directions with our guides. My guide Craig and I took a boat across the lake and spent the day trudging through miles of bogs and rivers. The land is difficult to describe. It was like walking across stacks of soaking wet bed mattresses covered in grass, surrounded by gorgeous landscapes. Standing water seemed to exist at any elevation. It made walking difficult, and I was exhausted that first night, having covered so much area in warm weather. The most worrisome part was that none of us saw any animals that day. Like elk and deer, caribou preferred deep timber when the weather is dry and above 40°F. The weather was expected to remain like this all week. We all had some concerns.

The next day proved to be equally beautiful and equally void of wildlife. The following night, however, Steve came back to camp with his caribou. The next morning, Brad shot his moose. Yes, a perfect shot. I was still empty-handed and had only seen a cow and calf moose.

IN THE TIME IT TOOK THE CARIBOU TO MOVE 50 YARDS CLOSER, I HAD GONE FROM A POISED, CALM, EXPERIENCED HUNTER TO A NERVOUS PILE OF CAMOUFLAGE. I COULD FEEL EMBARRASSMENT AS I STRUGGLED TO KEEP MY GUN FROM SHAKING AND I KNEW BOB WAS POSITIONED PERFECTLY TO SEE THE END OF THE BARREL MOVING ALL OVER THE PLACE.

Craig explained that he had never seen the land so empty. When Bob flew into camp later that week, he spoke with Craig, who assured him that we were covering miles of area together, from morning through sunset, but the animals were in deep cover.

Then came a curve in the experience I had not expected. Unfortunately, Craig was not able to guide me through all of my hunting. Bob as the outfitter and owner of the operation, was dedicated to making sure I had an opportunity to see a decent caribou. He took me to an area I had not hunted earlier with Craig.

I soon realized why the guides supressed their laughter when Bob offered to guide me. We started our trek into the wilderness, and I struggled to keep up with him. Simply said, he walked very fast. The camp cook came along for the experience and struggled to keep up with Bob as well. We stopped for a minute when we reached some high ground about an hour from our starting point at the lake. The morning was cold but I was warm from the hike. I took out my spotting scope as an excuse to rest. About 10 minutes into our search, Bob nudged me and pointed to what looked like a sizeable herd about two miles away. I knew Bob was up for it and I was excited about seeing a whole herd, so I packed away my scope and prepared for the walk.

Bob asked me again before we got started if I was up for the walk. He explained that this area would be even more treacherous and rugged than the area I hunted with Craig. He was right. We trudged through wetlands, bogs and thick timber, unlike anything I had experienced in my 20 years of hunting. I stayed right behind Bob from the beginning, as I was too excited to be tired. Two hours later, however, I began to worry about finding this herd. We were weaving in and out of bogs and patches of timber

WOODLAND CARIBOU
Third Award – 340 ⁵/₈

▼ ▼ ▼ ▼ ▼

Scott A. Trujillo

and had not seen any signs of the herd since we left the area from where we spotted it. It had been about an hour since we were able to see more than 50-100 yards in any direction. I was convinced we had passed them or they had moved on to a different area. I looked for any indication that Bob was lost or confused about our location, relative to the animals, but saw no doubts on his face. The only time he looked back was when he checked on the cook, who was working to stay within sight of his boss. Bob was making no effort to be cautious or quiet during our hike. Then everything changed.

Without any indication of the herd, Bob told me to chamber a round from my clip, which I had not yet done for safety's sake. He started whispering for the first time since we left that morning. I kept looking around while he waited for the cook to catch up. I was convinced we had passed the herd an hour ago.

We followed Bob up to the next hill top and back down into a low area. Again, we saw nothing. Yet this time, he told me and the cook to move very quietly as we ascended the next hill. Even the cook looked around in confusion. At the top, Bob seemed almost surprised when we again saw nothing. I caught the cook looking back in the direction that we had come, as if he, too, thought we had passed the caribou. We followed Bob down the hill and this time he told me to get low as we approached the top of the next high area. I agreed, with forced enthusiasm on my face. I admit I was worried that he was just trying to keep my interest, having lost the caribou. Before we reached the top, Bob got down on all fours and crawled the last remaining distance to the crest of the hill. I put my gun on my back and did the same until I caught up with him.

I could not believe what I saw. There was the herd! I flattened out on the ground at the first glimpse of what must have been about 100 caribou on the next ridge. They were spread out all over. Females were bedded down on the next crest, while young caribou walked around feeding. Antlers were everywhere. I noticed that the cook stopped moving when he saw me flatten out, even though he couldn't see what we were hiding from. Bob signaled for him to quietly make his way up to us.

My first instinct was to ready my gun. In no time, I was looking through my riflescope as Bob directed the cook to take a position behind a bush to his left. Bob told me to crawl up a few yards to a small boulder where I could place my gun for stability. He suggested that we wait a while and scope the herd because they weren't aware of our presence, and it might take a while to spot the largest animal. I handed him my video camera to give to the cook. I continued looking though my riflescope as Bob retreated a few feet away to the bush where the cook was. When they were still and silent, I crawled up to the rock. My heart was pounding and I was convinced the caribou could hear my breathing. I slowly organized my position, moving twigs out of the way and adjusting myself on the hard gravel ground.

Scott A. Trujillo is pictured above with his award-winning woodland caribou taken near Sam's Pond, Newfoundland. The bull scores 340-5/8 points and was taken in 2006.

The next five minutes were spent scoping the herd and thinking to myself, "How did he do that?" We had traveled two and a half miles through thick wilderness, and he seemed to secretly know exactly where they would be two hours later. I felt guilty for doubting a man with such skill and experience.

I could hear Bob and the cook whispering while I looked for the best of the group. I strained to hear partial sound bites from them like "…what about that one on the right?" or "…the thick-antlered one toward the back is probably…"

I was calm now, having picked my animal. I spent the next several minutes scoping the different areas in front of me; frequently moving back to my favorite to make sure he was still there. I hadn't moved or taken my eye away from my scope in a while when I sensed intensity increase in the whispering behind me. I was sure I heard "@$#$^!" once or twice but I could not spot anything new. I swung my gun back and forth over the herd, looking for anything to justify the excitement. Seconds later, I could hear Bob crawling toward me. I hurriedly peeled my cheek off my gunstock for the first time in ten minutes and lifted my head, determined to see the what they spotted before Bob had to point it out to me. There he was, entering a low, open area in front of the herd.

If he didn't have such a white coat, I would have thought the rack belonged to a strange looking elk. I had not seen a real caribou before my visit to Newfoundland, but his antlers were tall and distinctive and I could tell by Bob choosing to crawl toward me that this was the beast he had been waiting for.

My binoculars have a built-in laser rangefinder, and I quickly scanned the caribou before Bob reached me. He was 255 yards away and I had my rifle settled on the ground in perfect firing position. I put my face back down and clicked my safety off. Bob said, "Hold your shot; he's moving toward us."

As we waited, however, I had to pick my gun off of my resting spot in order to keep him in my sights. Bob positioned himself right behind me as if he was hoping to look through my scope. He kept whispering, "Just a minute... he's still too far... "

A few seconds passed and I had to completely raise my gun to a kneeling position in order to stay on him. Finally the caribou stopped, and Bob gave the okay to shoot. In the time it took the caribou to move 50 yards closer, I had gone from a poised, calm, experienced hunter to a nervous pile of camouflage. I could feel embarrassment as I struggled to keep my rifle from shaking, and I knew Bob was positioned perfectly to see the end of the barrel moving all over the place. He was inches over my shoulder, whispering the common phrase, "Just calm down and take your time."

I actually started formulating excuses for a miss as I strained to keep the rifle steady. There wasn't the time to explain that I have been target shooting with the best in the country for the last several years and 250 yards from a stable, prone position was a "gimme" compared to a 200-yard shot from a strained kneeling position. Because of my nervous shaking, Bob even felt compelled to put his hand on my shoulder and said, "Hold off for a second... just get comfortable before you shoot."

I took a deep breath, whispered back to him (but really for my own benefit), "Don't worry; he'll be dropping in about two seconds."

I relaxed, took another breath, put the crosshairs on him, and pulled the trigger. My ears were still ringing when I heard the cook yell, "He's down! He's down!"

Bob yelled, "Perfect shot; you got him!"

I chambered another round while I searched for movement. There was none. I picked up my bullet casing, quickly gathered up my pack, and started walking down to him. I noticed the cook filming as we were walking. "Did you get all that on camera?" I asked.

"I think some parts," he responded.

Later I found out that the video wasn't on during the excitement. Who cares? He was a great cook.

We took the rest of the day getting the animal back to the lake. The door to the plane had to be left slightly ajar, as the antlers wouldn't fit completely inside. I held onto them the entire ride back to the Effords' Outfitters base.

Bob recommended that I contact Boone and Crockett Club to have the rack measured. I had never taken an animal thought to be large enough for the B&C records book. He ended up scoring 340-5/8, within the top 25 in the All-time B&C records book. He had several points broken off from fighting, including every point on his right bez, otherwise he may have scored closer to 350. He was truly a remarkable and distinctive animal. ▲

Photograph courtesy of the Pope and Young Club

TROPHY STATS
▼ ▼ ▼ ▼ ▼

Category
  Woodland Caribou

Score
  335 $^5/_8$

Inside Spread
  33 $^6/_8$

Length of Main Beam
  Right: 37 $^5/_8$ Left: 40 $^5/_8$

Width of Brow Palm
  Right: 12 $^2/_8$ Left: $^1/_8$

Normal Points
  Right: 18 Left: 12

Location
  Dolland Pond, Newfoundland – 2005

Hunter
  Larry A. Welchlen

BOONE AND CROCKETT CLUB'S

WOODLAND CARIBOU
Fourth Award – 335 ⅝
▼ ▼ ▼ ▼ ▼ ▼ ▼ ▼ ▼

LARRY A. WELCHLEN

October 8, 2006, was finally here. Four of us left on a flight to Gander International Airport in Newfoundland for a bow hunt for woodland caribou. Mark Turner, Kevin Martin, Ron Rockwell, and I would meet Roy Goodwin of Tag-Along Consultants at the floatplane base at Conne River. Roy set up the hunt and would be driving up from Massachusetts.

Everything was going smoothly until my bow case didn't show up at Gander. All I could do was fill out the lost baggage report and hope it would show up on the next flight.

We were met at Gander by the outfitter and his wife, who then drove us to Conne River about three hours away. They were flying supplies and guides to camp, and I hoped we would hear something about my bow before it was our turn to leave. One of the guides loaned me his bow just in case mine didn't show up before we left for camp. It didn't.

After a smooth flight over some beautiful country, we landed on Dollands Pond. Camp consisted of three main buildings — a guides' cabin, a hunters cabin, and the dining lodge — all very well kept and clean.

After getting settled in, my guide, Aubrey, and I went out to the target behind camp. I shoot fingers, and this bow was set up for a release shooter. After a few adjustments and losing one arrow, I felt like I could shoot it accurately if I could get close enough.

Monday, after a great breakfast, we paired up with our guides and headed out. The camp had two boats, so two guys went up the lake, and the rest of us headed in different directions from camp.

I had a couple of stalks on a couple nice bulls but couldn't close the gap to where I felt comfortable shooting with the borrowed bow. I kept hoping all day that my bow would be in camp when we returned. We saw a plane fly over in the afternoon, and when we got back to camp my bow case was there, so things were looking up. We also found out that Roy had shot a nice bull and everyone else had seen animals, so we

Photograph by Jack Reneau

Larry A. Welchlen accepting his plaque and medal from Buck Buckner, Vice President and Chairman of the Big Game Records Committee.

Photograph courtesy of Larry A. Welchlen

Larry A. Welchlen, right, was able to stalk within 45 yards before harvesting his award-winning woodland caribou. The bull has a final score of 335-5/8 points.

were off to a good start.

Tuesday we woke up to rain and fog. I didn't know if we should go out or not, but Aubrey was ready, so we took off. The rain turned to mist so it wasn't bad, but we couldn't glass far because of the fog. We tried calling moose and had one small one come in, but it was too small to try for. About mid-morning we decided to return to camp and wait out the weather.

It cleared early in the afternoon and everyone headed back out. Aubrey and I saw quite a few caribou and tried a couple stalks, but wind or open terrain was against us and wouldn't let me close the gap enough to take any shots.

Late that afternoon Aubrey spotted a herd bedded down. They were quite far away and he was worried about it getting dark before we could get to them. We took off as fast as we could and got there quicker than we thought we would. He didn't think there was enough cover to get close enough for a shot, so he decided he would let me stalk in on them alone. If I couldn't get close enough to shoot, he would circle around and come in above them, let them see or wind him, and hopefully they would move out between me and the nearby lake, giving me a shot.

I got to the last few bushes near them for cover, but it was too far for a shot. The biggest bull in the herd was lying in the middle of about 20 cows. All I could do was watch and wait to see what they would do when Aubrey came in above them. About 30 minutes later they were up and moving. They were going to go through closer to the lake than to me. When they went behind some bushes, I ran to get closer, and when they came out, I shot at that big bull. I connected, and he ran about 150 yards when I saw him go down.

I waited for Aubrey to come off the hill, and we went over to him and were elated! He had double shovels and good bezes. He was a little weak on top, but we were happy as could be. He was a great caribou, which later scored 288-4/8!

While we were standing over him, his harem was milling around 70 to 80 yards away. As we stood there, we looked to the south and saw five caribou, including a tremendous bull, come across a rise in our direction. His antlers were skylined and he was bigger than any we had seen. The bull was trying to round up the harem from my herd bull. Realizing what a great bull he was, and having no cover at all, I just ran toward him in hopes of getting a shot. I got within about 60 yards before he realized I was there. He turned to run, and was now too far to shoot.

WOODLAND CARIBOU
Fourth Award – 335 5/8

▼ ▼ ▼ ▼ ▼

LARRY A. WELCHLEN

I went back to Aubrey and the downed bull. Within a few minutes, though, the big one was back. This time there were a couple of bushes between us that I could use for cover. He herded one cow up the ridge and came down to get another. At that point, I'd run out of cover so I just ran toward him.

All his attention was focused on other things, so when he finally saw me I was about 45 yards away. He turned to leave, and I got an angling-away shot, hitting him right behind the shoulder. He ran about 100 yards, and I saw him go down.

I called out to Aubrey, and we got over to where he fell. We couldn't believe how big he was. We were so happy with the size of the first bull, and now this one made him look small. Talk about luck and being in the right place at the right time! We had it all — two magnificent animals in about 15 minutes.

The sun was setting fast and we needed to head back to camp. Before heading back to camp, we field-dressed them and draped some clothes over the antlers to keep predators away. Everyone was in the dining room finishing eating when we arrived and told our story. We were saying things like "big" and "bigger" but I'm sure the guys had no idea from our excited stories that the bulls were that big!

The next morning Aubrey, Ron, and I set out to get the bulls. Ron was going with us because his guide, Lee, had blown out his knee the day before and was unable to hunt. On our way out, we caught sight of a bull heading toward us, his antlers outlined against the sky. Ron thought he looked pretty good, so he got set up and shot him with his recurve at 28 yards.

The bull had everything — tops, bezes, and double shovels — but he was small. He looked a lot bigger skylined, but ground shrinkage was evident. However, Ron was still very happy.

At that point, we went to my bulls and Ron couldn't get over the size of them. Ron is B&C Official Measurer, and he's seen a lot of caribou. He was quite impressed.

We took pictures and caped them out. Then we went back to Ron's and caped it out and headed back to camp.

Also during that time, Ron took another caribou bigger than his first. It made Pope & Young Club's records book; Roy took a nice black bear at 15 yards; and Kevin got a nice bull that was his first with his long bow so he was very happy. Mark was not successful on this trip but had a great time, saw many animals, and got some great pictures.

It was quite an experience — a good camp, cooks, guides, animals, and hunting companions. A guy couldn't ask for anything more. ▲

Photograph by Bill Honza

TROPHY STATS

▼ ▼ ▼ ▼ ▼

Category
Woodland Caribou

Score
315 $^5/_8$

Inside Spread
34

Length of Main Beam
Right: 37 $^7/_8$ Left: 38 $^3/_8$

Width of Brow Palm
Right: 1 $^6/_8$ Left: 16

Normal Points
Right: 14   Left: 18

Location
Middle Ridge Pond, Newfoundland
– 2004

Hunter
Jay R. Wolfenden

WOODLAND CARIBOU
Honorable Mention – 315 ⁵/₈

▼ ▼ ▼ ▼ ▼ ▼ ▼ ▼ ▼

JAY R. WOLFENDEN

Jay Wolfenden has put his time in, and he has earned most of the game he has come by. For that reason, he has no reservations about laughing at the ease with which his hunt went for what became one of the biggest woodland caribou entered in the 26th Awards Program.

Jay had booked a woodland caribou hunt in Newfoundland. Upon his arrival, he found that the outfitter had been short one guide, and so had found a new person on short notice to come in and help. That didn't bother Jay; he

Blind Luck

Photograph courtesy of Jay R. Wolfenden

Jay R. Wolfenden was hunting near Middle Ridge Pond in Newfoundland when he harvested his woodland caribou, which scores 315-5/8 points. Jay was hunting with a guide who hadn't guided for caribou before, but felt that the bull looked "plenty good enough."

Photograph by Jack Reneau

Jay R. Wolfenden accepting his plaque from Buck Buckner, Vice President and Chairman of the Big Game Records Committee.

was there for the experience and still had confidence. The interesting part, though, was that as hunter and guide left to find caribou, neither had ever seen the area before.

They left camp, crossed a body of water on a boat, and were beginning to survey the area. It was generally a slightly corrugated country, full of bogs and small ponds, with scrubby-looking 15-foot high spruce. There were no major landmarks, just small knobs dotting the landscape.

They began to climb to a knob, where they ran into another guide with a client. As they stood there deciding who would go where, Jay looked over and saw what looked like the flash of a white pickup moving through the trees about 600 yards away. Then it hit him; they were far removed from the nearest road!

Jay looked over at his guide and said, "How about that one?"

Jay's guide, who had never guided for caribou before, thought it looked plenty good enough. They quickly ducked out of sight and began the stalk. They were able to eventually get to 100 yards and make a good shot, which Jay performed with his 7mm Weatherby.

Jay notes with a smile that there really wasn't much to it but blind luck. Either way, he says, they were still back to camp with a big caribou and having coffee by 9:30 a.m.!

Jay's caribou is a prime example of what a trophy these smaller, more compact caribou are. With great shovels and mass, they are unique and intriguing trophies. ▲

B&C Photo Archives

Many of the trophy owners receiving awards brought their families with them to help celebrate the occasion. Pictured above are Jay R. Wolfenden, left center, with his wife and daughters, Carol, Beth, and Emily. Andrew Seman, Jr., right center, was also joined by his wife Susie and their daughters Christie and Kelsie.

Photograph by Bill Honza

TROPHY STATS

▼ ▼ ▼ ▼ ▼

Category
Central Canada Barren
Ground Caribou

Score
406 $^2/_8$

Inside Spread
38 $^5/_8$

Length of Main Beam
Right: 55 $^2/_8$ Left: 54 $^4/_8$

Width of Brow Palm
Right: 8 $^5/_8$ Left: 14 $^1/_8$

Normal Points
Right: 15 Left: 15

Location
Bekere Lake, Northwest Territories
– 2005

Hunter
Robert F. Fairchild

CENTRAL CANADA BARREN GROUND CARIBOU
First Award – 406 $^2/_8$
Second Award – 392 $^2/_8$

▼ ▼ ▼ ▼ ▼ ▼ ▼ ▼ ▼

ROBERT F. FAIRCHILD

The twin Otter touched down on a brushy airstrip scratched out of the black spruce near Bekere Lake. I was in Canada's remote Northwest Territories about 300 miles east of the town of Inuvik. Upon arrival, I was greeted by the warm smile of Jonah Nakimayak who, along with his family, owns and operates Bekere Lake Lodge.

Returning to Bekere Lake seemed more like a homecoming than a guided caribou hunt. During the fall of 2004, I spent eight days hunting caribou and enjoying the Arctic. During that hunt, I formed a warm relationship with Jonah and his son, Herb. I saw hundreds of caribou and was able to harvest two beautiful bulls; the larger of the two scored 374 B&C points. I also had the opportunity to accompany another hunter on his musk ox hunt. Prior to this hunt, I had never even seen a caribou or a musk ox, and after experiencing what the Arctic had to offer, I was hooked. The people, scenery, remoteness, wildlife, and the vivid memories I had gathered beckoned my return to Bekere Lake.

My good friend, Roy Jacobs from Choteau, Montana, has spent every September for nine years at Bekere Lake Lodge. Roy doesn't really hunt much anymore, but he still loves to tag along. Roy is also a world-class taxidermist and receives a fair amount of business from the successful hunters at Bekere Lake lodge. He was also responsible for introducing me to the Arctic and my subsequent return.

I arrived at Bekere Lake Lodge on the evening of September 13, 2005, and had the next eight days to enjoy a fabulous hunt. My hunting partner for this trip was David Slikkers. The other hunters in camp were Ed Martin and Warner Freeze. I was only after caribou, but

Photograph by Jack Reneau

Robert F. Fairchild accepting his plaque and medal from Buck Buckner, Vice President and Chairman of the Big Game Records Committee.

Robert F. Fairchild holds up his Central Canada barren ground caribou taken on a hunt near Bekere Lake, Northwest Territories. The bull, which scores 406-2/8 points, received a First Place Award.

David, Ed, and Warner each also had musk ox tags in their pockets.

We stowed all of our gear at the lodge, which is actually a two-story house on the shore of Bekere Lake. The lodge is relatively new. All of the materials used to build it were hauled in by snow machines and sleds during the winter months when transportation over the numerous lakes is easier. The lodge is equipped with four bedrooms, a living room, and a modern kitchen. A generator provides electricity. There is hot running water, showers, and even satellite television! The outhouse is the only rustic living condition we had to endure!

The first morning of our hunt found David, Roy, Jonah's son Sonny, and me glassing for caribou from a slight rise a mile or two from the lodge. We spotted only a few caribou, including a couple of mature bulls. Since I was successful the previous year, and David had never killed a caribou, I told him that he could have the first choice at bagging a bull during our hunt. We were able to stalk within 200 yards of some good bulls, but David decided to pass on them.

When we returned to the lodge that evening, we learned that Warner had killed a beautiful bull, one that should score somewhere around 380 B&C. Over a delicious dinner cooked by Jonah's daughter Emma, Sonny decided we should head north of the lake the next morning. Sonny thought it would be a good place to look for caribou, and as equally important, we could also search for a musk ox for David.

The next morning found us hiking up a seismic line to glass for musk ox. We hiked and glassed but spotted no musk ox. Oddly, we didn't see any caribou either.

After a couple of hours of glassing, Roy spotted a band of caribou about two miles away moving along a sliver of land between two lakes. Their white manes and rumps were easy to spot. Looking through our binoculars, we could see one of the bulls was very large and decided to make a stalk. It is impossible to try to catch up with caribou moving at their ground-eating gait. Your only chance is to guess where they are going and attempt to head them off.

We figured the caribou would move through the bogs between the lakes and follow the contour of a low hill through a growth of willows and black spruce. With our plan in hand, Sonny, David, Roy, and I took off.

After about a mile, Sonny and David were ahead of me when Roy and I stopped to glass the openings in the timber at the base of the hill. We saw that the caribou had covered more distance than we expected and it appeared that Sonny and David would run into the very end of the band of about 30 cows and bulls. I tried to get their attention while Roy kept an eye on the caribou. Though we were only separated by about 150 yards, Sonny and David, intent on sneaking to where they thought the caribou were, could not hear my whistles. I caught glimpses of caribou in the timber, although the spruce mostly obscured the animals. I took off on a 50-yard sprint to make it to the edge of the timber and ended up in exactly the right spot.

At about 150 yards, I spotted a large bull between several other good bulls and cows. The bull I wanted was easy to spot, not only because of his massive antlers, but also because he had three feet of the top of a spruce tree sticking between his shovels. It looked as though he had a Christmas tree growing out of his nose!

At about 100 yards, the caribou spotted me and began to bolt. One shot from my rifle dropped the big bull in his tracks. A second later, another large bull actually jumped over his

CENTRAL CANADA BARREN GROUND CARIBOU
First Award – 406 $^2/_8$
Second Award – 392 $^2/_8$
▼ ▼ ▼ ▼ ▼ ▼ ▼ ▼ ▼
ROBERT F. FAIRCHILD

Photograph courtesy of Robert F. Fairchild

Robert is pictured above with his caribou, which received a Second Place Award. The bull has a final score of 392-2/8 points.

Photograph by Bill Honza

TROPHY STATS
▼ ▼ ▼ ▼ ▼

Category
Central Canada Barren
Ground Caribou

Score
392 $^2/_8$

Inside Spread
27 $^6/_8$

Length of Main Beam
Right: 45 $^3/_8$ Left: 44 $^7/_8$

Width of Brow Palm
Right: 14 $^2/_8$ Left: 11 $^4/_8$

Normal Points
Right: 20   Left: 17

Location
Bekere Lake, Northwest Territories
– 2005

Hunter
Robert F. Fairchild

fallen comrade and, as quick as I could jack another round in the chamber, I shot him at about 125 yards. I knew I had hit him as I watched him switch directions and run off into the willows. I then saw my first bull get to his feet, so I chambered another round and fired an insurance shot that hit the mark.

As fast as I could work the bolt of my rifle three times, my caribou hunt had ended! I walked up to the first bull and was in awe of his incredible length and mass. I then found my second bull on the edge of the willows about 75 yards from the first one. The tops of the second bull were massive, with numerous points and wide webbing. Both bulls sported large double shovels, with long main beams and heavy mass.

Soon, the guys and I relived the exciting seconds of the hunt. The customary handshaking and backslapping was followed by numerous photographs before the job of caping and butchering those magnificent animals began. I knew immediately that both of these fine bulls would qualify for the records book, but I got excited when Sonny said they were the biggest bulls he had ever seen. Roy said that he had seen thousands of caribou and has mounted dozens of them, but had not seen any larger than these!

Although my hunt was over, my Arctic adventure was just beginning. I was able to accompany David as he took a nice musk ox and caribou; I also watched as Warner and Ed took three more bulls after they filled their musk ox tags. I spent a lot of time helping around the lodge and getting to know the Nakimayaks better and enjoying the solitude of the Canadian Arctic.

The drone of the floatplane signaled the end of another great experience, saying farewell to good friends met through the common bond of the love of hunting, of wild places and the animals that live there. I will return to Bekere Lake but, in the meantime, I'll just have to dream of this wild and beautiful place.

After the required drying period, I took both racks to John Rappold, who is a B&C Official Measurer and the ranch manager of Boone and Crockett Club's Theodore Roosevelt Memorial Ranch located near Dupuyer, Montana. He confirmed that they would indeed qualify for "the book." The final scores of these trophies were 406-2/8 and 392-2/8. ▲

CENTRAL CANADA BARREN GROUND CARIBOU
First Award – 406 $^2/_8$
Second Award – 392 $^2/_8$

▼ ▼ ▼ ▼ ▼ ▼ ▼ ▼ ▼

ROBERT F. FAIRCHILD

Photograph by Jack Reneau

Fairchild accepting his First and Second Place Awards for his two caribou.

Photograph by Bill Honza

TROPHY STATS

▼ ▼ ▼ ▼ ▼

Category
Central Canada Barren
Ground Caribou

Score
382 ³/₈

Inside Spread
41 ⁶/₈

Length of Main Beam
Right: 52 ³/₈   Left: 53

Width of Brow Palm
Right: 3 ³/₈   Left: 15 ¹/₈

Normal Points
Right: 12   Left: 15

Location
Point Lake, Northwest Territories
– 2002

Hunter
N. Guy Eastman

CENTRAL CANADA BARREN GROUND CARIBOU
Third Award – 382 ³/₈

▼ ▼ ▼ ▼ ▼ ▼ ▼ ▼ ▼

N. GUY EASTMAN

As a young man, I had the unique opportunity to travel western North America and Alaska with my grandfather, the late Gordon Eastman, during my summer breaks from school. On these trips, as we traveled to our next location, Gordon would tell me story after story of his lifetime of adventures in the outdoors. Some

Bows on the Tundra

of my favorites were the tales of huge moose, caribou, and wolves of the Arctic in Canada's wild Northwest Territories.

I couldn't help but wonder if I would be fortunate enough to have some stories of my own to pass on to my grandchildren.

Perhaps I would now, I thought, as I sat in the airport with my brother Ike waiting for a flight to Yellowknife. We were filming the hunt for our television show, "Eastmans' Hunting Journal." Our destination was the wild Northwest Territories my grandfather had loved so much. Our bowhunting travels would take us a mere 20 miles short of the Arctic Circle in search of monster Central Canada barren ground caribou.

After our plane ride, my quest began near the head of Esker Bay. It was about three miles wide and covered with tundra in brilliant shades of red, orange, and yellow. The sparsely scattered patches of Arctic timber provided a subtle contrast of green.

After we tied up our boat, we gathered all our gear and began hiking up the bottom of the valley along a small, rocky creek. The sand on the edge of the creek was covered with grizzly tracks. There had been at least five or six different bears in this valley during the last couple weeks. We didn't relish the thought of running into one.

Photograph by Jack Reneau

N. Guy Eastman accepting his plaque and medal from Buck Buckner, Vice President and Chairman of the Big Game Records Committee.

N. Guy Eastman, right, and his brother Ike traveled to Northwest Territories in search of Central Canada barren ground caribou in 2002. Guy took the award-winning caribou pictured above after stalking to within 11 yards. The bull scores 382-3/8 points and was taken near Point Lake.

We had only gone a couple of miles when we spotted two caribou on the mountainside across the valley. I pulled the spotting scope from my pack, rested it on top of a rock, and focused on the two feeding animals. Immediately, I could see substantial racks on both feeding bulls. I then dialed the Swarovski to full power and told our guide Paul Jones he had better grab a look at these bulls. Paul had his eye to the scope for about five seconds before he started putting together a plan to stalk the bulls. As we frantically packed up our packs, Paul said, "The bull on the left is one we really need to go after."

Soon, we were off again, across the squishy tundra at full speed. The bulls were at least two miles away. We had to come down one side of the valley, cross the creek again and tromp up the other side. Fortunately, the big bull was in a perfect place for a stalk. He was feeding on a subtle ledge on the side of the mountain with the wind at his back. Just the sort of setup a bowhunter likes to see, because trophy animals seldom put themselves in a situation for a perfect stalk to within bow range. As we headed up the other side of the valley, we realized that because of the steep descent of the hillside, the bull could not see us coming from underneath him. It was going to be beautiful.

With 100 yards left to go, we shed our packs and all unnecessary items and stashed them in the brush. We put together a quick game plan, and I got Ike set up with the camera to film the action as it unfolded — good or bad!

Once we crept to within 50 yards, we began to see the velvet tops of his huge rack bobbing toward us in the skyline above the tundra. Ike started recording as the bull knocked another 25 yards off the distance between us. I knelt down and slowly drew my bow. The bull kept feeding closer and closer; his rack kept getting larger and larger. Paul ranged him at only 14 yards, but I didn't have a shot. He was coming straight at me, feeding with his head down. I knew we were going to have problems when his eyes rose to meet mine. I was a mere 11 yards from largest caribou I had ever seen, staring eye to eye with nothing between us but thin, crisp arctic air. I could almost see the wheels turning inside his head.

CENTRAL CANADA BARREN GROUND CARIBOU
Third Award – 382 3/8
▼ ▼ ▼ ▼ ▼
N. Guy Eastman

He then decided he'd had enough and instantly turned and ran. At about 40 yards, he suddenly stopped and turned broadside. I knew there was no time to range, so I estimated the distance, let the air out of my lungs, anchored my 40-yard pin behind his shoulder, and squeezed the release.

The shot felt good, and it sounded good when the arrow traveled cleanly through his body. The caribou turned and ran full blast across the tundra. His rack looked enormous as he was going away. I turned to Ike and gave him a slightly uncertain thumbs up.

Ike replied, "You hit him square behind the shoulder, and I got it all on film!"

It is a good thing the Arctic does not have much brush, because tracking a blood trail on the red tundra would have been a nightmare. Nonetheless, we had only walked about 60 yards before we found the huge bull piled up on the mountainside overlooking Esker Bay.

He was absolutely tremendous. His shovel was over 17 inches tall and hung out beyond his nose — so far beyond, in fact, that the points on the end were worn down from scraping the ground when he fed.

One of his most distinctive features is the 20-inch "back scratcher" on his right antler. It turned straight into the center of his rack, and his spread was well over four feet. He is my trophy of a lifetime. ▲

Photograph by Bill Honza

TROPHY STATS

▼ ▼ ▼ ▼ ▼

Category
Quebec-Labrador Caribou

Score
424 $^2/_8$

Inside Spread
45 $^6/_8$

Length of Main Beam
Right: 53 $^4/_8$ Left: 51 $^4/_8$

Width of Brow Palm
Right: 12 $^3/_8$ Left: 11

Normal Points
Right: 24   Left: 22

Location
Clearwater Lake, Quebec – 2005

Hunter
Woody Groves

QUEBEC-LABRADOR CARIBOU
First Award – 424 $^2/_8$

▼ ▼ ▼ ▼ ▼ ▼ ▼ ▼ ▼

WOODY GROVES

My trip started in the wee hours on a Saturday morning. I had a 6 a.m. flight out of Palm Beach into Atlanta, where I was connecting with my three hunting buddies. From there, we flew into Montreal and spent the night. The next day we flew a twin-engine prop plane another 1,000 miles northeast and landed on a gravel runway at our outfitter's camp. We loaded all of our gear into several Beaver and Otter floatplanes and waited for a break in the weather. We then flew another 300 miles north and landed at the Clear Lake Camp.

This hunt was touted as a trophy/rut hunt, and we were all excited about the possibilities of seeing record-class caribou. After shooting my bow a few times to make sure my sights were still on, we went into the main cabin for orientation. I was the only one in camp who had brought only archery equipment. After meeting our guide, I realized I should have paid more attention in that high school French class I took.

The main mode of transportation was small boats. We would go from island to island, get out and travel up to a vantage point and glass the hillsides for migrating caribou. The first day was successful, with over half the hunters in camp shooting nice animals. I, however, was not able to get close enough for a shot. I learned that caribou never stop; they move very fast even when they are walking. I was going to have to change my strategy if I was going to get close enough for a shot.

Late the next afternoon, we spotted a group of about 15 caribou on a nearby island. They were heading our way. The two other hunters I was with had already shot bulls with their rifles, so I was up to bat. I eased down the hillside to a spot I thought they would be coming up; I was dead on. As each caribou came up the bank, it would stop to shake off water.

The one I wanted was the fourth one back, so I had plenty of time to calm down and get situated. I made a 12-yard shot that penetrated right through the heart. He fell 30 yards away. This caribou was not the biggest one in camp

Photograph courtesy of Woody Groves

Woody Groves' hunting buddy snapped this photograph of the bull before Groves finally made the shot.

Photograph courtesy of Woody Groves

Woody Groves is pictured above with his award-winning Quebec-Labrador caribou taken from 40 yards with his bow. Despite receiving grief from his hunting partner for passing on numerous quality bulls, Groves held out and was rewarded with this fine bull, which scores 424-2/8 points.

(not by a long shot), but it took some pressure off, and now I could be extremely picky over the next four days of hunting.

That night the guides looked at the migration pattern and decided that we would leave early the next morning and travel about 20 miles north to see if we could catch the front edge of this large herd. This strategy paid off. We traveled across several ridges before spotting a very large group of caribou traveling across the next ridge a mile away. As we moved in that direction, the excitement began to build. There were thousands of them — or at least it seemed like thousands. Everywhere I looked there were caribou.

As the day wore on, everyone but me had shot a second bull. I had one of my buddies helping me glass and helping me pick the one I should shoot. We were set up in a little bowl with a triangle of trees in front of us. We could see about half a mile up the hillside. As the caribou came over the ridge toward us, they would split off at the trees ahead of us. Half would go to my left and half to my right. I ranged a big rock at 40 yards to my right; the shot to my left was only about 20 yards.

After an hour, we had seen hundreds of caribou come by, some so close we could grab their antlers. There had been a least a dozen bulls that would have made the book. I kept holding out because I knew as soon as I shot, it would be over. I didn't want the hunt to end. My buddy gave me grief every time one of those trophy bulls went by and I didn't shoot. He would look at me in disgust, mumble a few words, and bring his binoculars back to his eyes. He was just mad, because he had already shot both of his bulls, and it was torture for him.

QUEBEC-LABRADOR CARIBOU
First Award – 424 $^2/_8$

▼ ▼ ▼ ▼ ▼

WOODY GROVES

Then a massive bull came into view. We both saw this monster at the same time and knew this was the one. As he came over the hill and got closer, I began to get that adrenaline rush. It's funny how that happens. I had seen hundreds of whopper bulls in the past hour and didn't get the least bit nervous, but as soon as I see the one I want to shoot, I felt like I was 12 years old at my first school dance.

As he got closer, I started to take inventory of his headgear — long tops, heavy mass, wide inside spread, backscratchers, long and palmated bezes, and even a double shovel. Now I was really nervous.

Which way is he going to branch off, to my left or my right? I was set up further to the left and had a clear shooting lane all the way up to that big rock I had ranged at 40 yards. Well, he came to my left. Tom, my buddy, had traded his binoculars for his camera and was now taking pictures.

As the bull walked in front of the rock, I whistled three times. Did I mention that it's really hard to get them to stop? He stopped directly in front of the rock and looked down the hill at us. I was already drawn back and had my 40-yard pin right where it needed to be. When I released the arrow it was a pass through. The arrow ricocheted off the rock and flew about 30 feet in the air. Tom said, "You missed!"

I knew better. I knew it was a great shot as I watched the bull lunge over a small rise and stop. All we could see were the tops of his antlers as they began to weave back and forth. In ten seconds, he was on the ground.

I didn't realize how big he was until the taxidermist who met us at the airport said, "That's the biggest caribou I have ever seen."

It was a hunt of a lifetime, and I would highly recommend it to anyone. If you ever get a chance, you have to go. ▲

Photograph by Bill Honza

TROPHY STATS

▼ ▼ ▼ ▼ ▼

Category
Quebec-Labrador Caribou

Score
423 $^4/_8$

Inside Spread
46 $^1/_8$

Length of Main Beam
Right: 53 $^1/_8$ Left: 53 $^6/_8$

Width of Brow Palm
Right: 9 $^3/_8$ Left: 9 $^3/_8$

Normal Points
Right: 21   Left: 20

Location
Lac a L' Eau-claire, Quebec – 2005

Hunter
Stewart N. Shaft

QUEBEC-LABRADOR CARIBOU
Second Award – 423 4/8

▼ ▼ ▼ ▼ ▼ ▼ ▼ ▼ ▼

STEWART N. SHAFT

It is now October 10, 2005, and the second day of my fantastic hunt in far northwest Quebec near the shores of James Bay. The day before, I took a trophy bull caribou (see page 297). Upon arriving back in camp, I was told that I was experiencing the height of the Leaf River caribou herd migration. Game officials estimated that there are 330,000 caribou migrating in this corridor in scattered herds stretching over 40 miles long.

A Hunter's Dream Hunt

Photograph courtesy of Stewart N. Shaft

This is the second award-winning Quebec-Labrador caribou that Boone and Crockett Lifetime Associate Stewart N. Shaft took during his 2005 hunting trip. This bull scores 423-4/8 points and received a Second Place Award. Shaft's other bull is featured on page 297.

Photograph by Jack Reneau

Stewart N. Shaft accepting his plaque and medal from Buck Buckner, Vice President and Chairman of the Big Game Records Committee.

The outpost camp was to be closing its operations soon. I was one of the very last hunters still hunting.

That day found me once again on a high ridge overlooking a small lake and river. The caribou were still on their march streaming past me. Some of them were so close that I could easily touch them if I had chosen to do so. Unlike the day before, I could not observe them at a great distance. Rather, they were coming over a rocky hill and then continuing down low in front of me. Any decisions would have to be made quickly, as there was precious little time to do any field judging.

It was now midday and I was transfixed by the many hundreds of trophy-class bulls that were streaming by. Suddenly, a very tall and wide-antlered rack loomed on the skyline and came in my direction! However, he quickly disappeared. I was concerned that he might change directions and take a different route, as some of the animals had been doing. All of the sudden, the bull appeared and headed down a steep tree-strewn slope. He was certainly not going to slow down as I was glassing him with my binoculars. Already he was past me at nearly 200 yards and moving at a fast clip.

I put the crosshairs on the front shoulder and shot just as he was about to go behind a knoll. As fast as I could, I hurried in that direction to intercept him and was greatly relieved to see he was down. Walking over to him, I was awed by the shear size of this old monarch. It was obvious that I was fortunate to be able to take such a trophy animal. After taking photos, I returned to a hillside and continued to watch the caribou. It was an unbelievable, once-in-a-lifetime dream hunt!

As I lay there, a number of caribou continued to come by me. In fact, a cow and her calf actually came over and sniffed my now covered up head... awesome! These two back-to-back adventures will definitely rank among the top experiences I've had in my nearly 60 years of hunting! ▲

Trophy owners Stewart N. Shaft, left, and James F. Baichtal, right, enjoy the Friday night reception held at the Doral Tesoro Hotel and Golf Club in Fort Worth. Both gentlemen are long-time B&C Lifetime Associates and each had trophies in the 26th Big Game Awards Program.

Photograph by Bill Honza

TROPHY STATS

▼ ▼ ▼ ▼ ▼

Category
Quebec-Labrador Caribou

Score
413 $^6/_8$

Inside Spread
40 $^5/_8$

Length of Main Beam
Right: 45 $^5/_8$ Left: 48 $^1/_8$

Width of Brow Palm
Right: 14   Left: 16 $^6/_8$

Normal Points
Right: 22   Left: 21

Location
Minto Lake, Quebec – 2005

Hunter
Gordon G. Swenson

QUEBEC-LABRADOR CARIBOU
Third Award – 413 $^{6}/_{8}$

▼ ▼ ▼ ▼ ▼ ▼ ▼ ▼ ▼

GORDON G. SWENSON

September 19, 2005, began like the previous three days. A group of eight hunters, including me, were hunting caribou with Tuttulik Ouffitters. The hunt was near the famed Minto Lake, in the western sector of Quebec. We were in camp Oma on a lake called "Qullinaaraaluk" one ridge to the north of Minto Lake.

Our day would begin around 6 a.m. We would roll out of our sleeping bags, dress for the day's hunt, and then grab some breakfast before heading to the tundra. Our group consisted of five bowhunters, and there were three of us older guys using the rifle. Needless to say, the bowhunters were younger and always made it out of camp first. They were hard hunters.

The weather had been great! No wind to speak of, just a few sprinkles of rain now and then, accompanied by mild temperatures. Even with very little wind, there were no bugs! We were having ourselves a great hunt, and already had well over half our limit of caribou hanging in the meat house. As a group, we were seeing about 300 caribou per day, all of them being bulls.

Our plan for the day was the same as it had been since the very first day we hunted. We left camp in our 23-foot boat, crossed the lake, and entered a long narrow bay. We slowly motored the length of the bay, scanning the

AS SOON AS HE LAID EYES ON THE BULLS, HE SAID IN A COMPOSED TONE, "SHOOT THE ONE WITH THE TREE IN HIS RACK."

THE BULL HAD BEEN POLISHING HIS ANTLERS AND HAD TANGLED A TREE IN HIS RACK, AND WAS CARRYING IT AROUND WITH HIM. HE WASN'T HARD TO PICK OUT!

horizon with our binos looking for caribou racks silhouetted against the sky. This method was especially productive, considering the caribou would travel the ridgetops. If they were lying down, they would also lie on the ridgetops, I assume to catch the wind for protection against bugs, what few there were! In doing so, their racks would be highlighted against the sky. When we would find a good rack, the spot and stalk was indeed on! Our little group of three only needed two more bulls to fill out.

As we slowly motored along, we could see caribou to our south, quite some distance away. As quietly as we could, we worked the water's edge toward a point where we could beach the boat and get into position for an ambush. I was excited, considering it was my turn to shoot!

Photograph courtesy of Gordon G. Swenson

Gordon G. Swenson used his friend's 7mm Magnum to harvest this award-winning Quebec-Labrador caribou taken in 2005. The bull, which scores 413-6/8 points, was taken near Minto Lake.

When the boat was beached and I stepped out on the rocks, I spotted two ptarmigan only three feet from me. I thought to myself, please don't fly away and put those animals on red alert. As I was thinking this, they simply walked off, and didn't disturb a thing.

Once our group was ready, we all began moving toward the ridge that the caribou were on. We decided to position ourselves near a small patch of black spruce, where we thought the best vantage point was, and where we thought the caribou would eventually feed to. In no time at all, we were set up and ready.

I need to explain something real quick! I didn't bring my own rifle on this hunt. I had made arrangements with Jim Pearson to use his 7mm Magnum. I had helped him sight in his rifle during the summer months. Unfortunately, the previous day, Jim was crawling out of the boat and fell, catching himself with his rifle. I learned that this would affect my shot placements later on.

We were in position and things were beginning to come together perfectly! There were ten bulls in the group feeding in our direction. One of the bulls had incredibly massive tops. He was the one I wanted to take. However, I couldn't shoot because all the caribou were bunched together. It appeared as if they were going to change course and feed over to the top of the ridge. If they eventually wandered over the top, we would be able to change location and maybe get a better opportunity.

QUEBEC-LABRADOR CARIBOU
Third Award – 413 6/8
▼ ▼ ▼ ▼ ▼

GORDON G. SWENSON

At that time, our guide looked over to the right and spotted four bulls we hadn't previously seen because they were hidden in a draw. As soon as he laid eyes on the bulls, he said in a composed tone, "Shoot the one with the tree in his rack."

The bull had been polishing his antlers and had tangled a tree in his rack, and was carrying it around with him. He wasn't hard to pick out!

Right then, it seemed as if the bull wanted out of there. I'm not sure if the wind changed on us, and he caught our scent, or what, but I asked Jim to hand me his rifle so I could shoot the big caribou. My knees are really bad, so I couldn't kneel down to steady my shot. I was given no other choice than to take my shot in an offhand position. I got into position to shoot, and the bull offered me a quartering away shot. It was now time to shoot.

BOOM! The gun went off and delivered a heavy wallop to my shoulder. Before I could get refocused on the bull, he was on the ground! I slowly turned and was going to ask the guide how he liked that shot, when I heard Jim and our other hunting partner Mike Bohlsen mumbling something. I asked them what was going on, and they replied, "Hey! Your bull is trying to get away!"

I snapped my head around only to see that the news was true, my bull was indeed trying to run away! It took a few more shots, but I was finally able to anchor my trophy caribou. When we approached him, we were in awe of the size and admired him for the next few minutes. We were all in agreement that I was pretty darn lucky that this big bull decided to show up.

The eight of us all managed to fill our tags. Only two of our 16 caribou didn't make B&C or P&Y.

However, the interesting story was when Jim got home and shot his rifle. At 100 yards his rifle was six inches off. We estimated my caribou to be somewhere around 250 yards away from my first to last shot. Shooting offhand like I did, I guess I had to wiggle at just the right time to pull that one off! ▲

Photograph by Bill Honza

TROPHY STATS

▼ ▼ ▼ ▼ ▼

Category
Quebec-Labrador Caribou

Score
411 $^1/_8$

Inside Spread
45

Length of Main Beam
Right: 50 $^6/_8$ Left: 47 $^1/_8$

Width of Brow Palm
Right: 17   Left: 15 $^4/_8$

Normal Points
Right: 21   Left: 19

Location
Lac a L' Eau-claire, Quebec – 2005

Hunter
Stewart N. Shaft

QUEBEC-LABRADOR CARIBOU
Fourth Award – 411 ¹/₈

▼ ▼ ▼ ▼ ▼ ▼ ▼ ▼ ▼

STEWART N. SHAFT

October 9, 2005, found me sitting beside a mound of boulders perched high on a rocky ridge in far northwestern Quebec. I was hunting the Leaf River herd of Quebec-Labrador caribou. A few days earlier, I had no idea I would be there. I received a phone call from a fellow hunter asking me if I knew anyone that might like to go caribou hunting in Quebec. One of their party had to cancel at the last minute.

The call caught me off guard. All I could respond with was, "I'll check around."

The Dream Continues...

The last time I hunted caribou in Quebec was 1979, hunting the George River herd out of Schefferville. I must admit that in addition to sheep hunting, caribou are a real passion of mine! Having hunted all the North American caribou species starting back in 1968, the chance to once again hunt them haunted me all day long. Finally that evening, I returned the call. A few days later, I found myself flying to Montreal!

Soon we were aboard a chartered twin engine turbo prop landing 2-1/2 hours later at the LG-4 airstrip. Shortly after, we left our outfitter's beautiful main lodge alongside of the La Grande River in a floatplane. We flew to their remote Clearwater Lake outpost camp, many miles north. Upon arriving we were told that the migration and rut were in full swing. This was immediately confirmed by the quantity and quality of trophy racks lying by the dock.

Nestled by the boulders, I was able to see a large body of water in the distance and a narrow channel nearby. As the morning progressed, I started to see more and more strings of swimming caribou in the distance. Once on shore they climbed up a large snow-covered hill and disappeared. Soon they circled and appeared once again, this time swimming across the channel toward me!

As they came to shore, they would stop briefly and shake the water off their hides. They

Photograph by Jack Reneau

Stewart N. Shaft accepting the second of two plaques and medals from Buck Buckner, Vice President and Chairman of the Big Game Records Committee.

Photograph courtesy of Stewart N. Shaft

Stewart N. Shaft is pictured above with the first of two award-winning Quebec-Labrador caribou. Shaft was hunting near Lac a L' Eau-Claire, Quebec, when he harvested this bull, which has a final score of 411-1/8 points.

then filtered through the trees below me on their relentless migration trek.

They were now coming in wave after wave numbering well into the hundreds. Some came up onto the ridge near me and were so close I had difficulty getting them into my camera's viewfinder! Many of the caribou were bulls, with a number of handsome looking trophies scattered among them.

Finally, after about four hours of watching the steady stream of caribou through my binoculars, one bull really got my attention. He was with a number of other bulls, and definitely stood out. I had to make a decision quickly, as he was already passed me. I fired! Walking up to the downed bull, I knew he had all the necessary headgear to be a trophy-class caribou.

What a day, having had the privilege of witnessing hundreds, if not thousands, of caribou wandering by. I continued to watch and photograph animals the rest of the day, looking perhaps to fill my second tag. I saw many trophy caribou, but did not fire another shot — that would have meant the end of the hunt, and I did not want to stop this awesome adventure. ▲

Read about the conclusion to Stewart N. Shaft's Quebec-Labrador caribou hunt on page 289.

Photograph by Frederick J. King

Stewart N. Shaft harvested two award-winning Quebec-Labrador caribou on his 2005 hunt near Lac a L' Eau-claire in Quebec. The extraordinary bulls were mounted in tandem. Above B&C Director of Big Game Records Jack Reneau and a Dallas Safari Club volunteer uncrate the bulls to prepare them for their score verification.

Photograph by Bill Honza

TROPHY STATS

▼ ▼ ▼ ▼ ▼

Category
Rocky Mountain Goat

Score
54 $^4/_8$

Length of Horn
Right: 11 $^2/_8$ Left: 11 $^2/_8$

Circumference of Base
Right: 5 $^6/_8$ Left: 5 $^6/_8$

Greatest Spread
9

Location
Revillagigedo Island, Alaska – 2004

Hunter
Edward E. Toribio

ROCKY MOUNTAIN GOAT
First Award – 54 4/8
▼ ▼ ▼ ▼ ▼ ▼ ▼ ▼ ▼

EDWARD E. TORIBIO

Having fallen in love with the beautiful alpine country in southeast Alaska, I have made it a practice to pursue the mountain goats and Sitka blacktail deer on opening day of hunting season. We are lucky here in southeast Alaska to have a hunting season that begins on the first day of August and lasts for five months. My home in Ketchikan is the jumping-off point for many who choose to hunt the goats of Alaska. Misty Fiords National Monument is a popular flight-seeing destination for many tourists that visit Ketchikan. Those same scenic mountains are the home to many trophy goats.

On the evening of July 31, 2004, I took off from Ward Cove in a Supercub with my old friend, Earl Mossburg. Our destination was a small lake on the east side of Revillagigedo Island just inside the Monument boundary. I had hunted this lake on two previous occasions and had been successful on both goats and deer. Earl has been my mountain goat hunting mentor for more than 10 years and has been my pilot on a number of successful solo hunts. On this trip, Marcia Kirby would join me to share the beauty of the mountains.

After dropping me off, Earl returned to Ketchikan to pick up Marcia. I had the tent set up and a small fire going by the time they arrived. After discussing the pick-up date, we bid Earl farewell and went to scout the trail. We found the first few hundred yards to be a brush choked draw. I spent an hour cutting a trail up to an alpine bench while Marcia returned to camp to collect firewood. There was some evidence that a black bear had been feeding on berries nearby, so I reminded Marcia to keep the .44 pistol handy and not to wander far from camp without it.

I returned to camp and found that Marcia had supper ready and a good supply of wood. My hopes were high for good weather as we turned in beneath a sky full of stars.

I woke early to clear skies and made a hasty departure at first light, promising Marcia that I would return before dark. I did leave a radio with her in case of an emergency. I carried both

Photograph courtesy of Edward E. Toribio

Edward E. Toribio was joined by Marcia Kirby on his 2004 hunt on the east side of Revillagigedo Island.

Photograph by Edward E. Toribio

Edward E. Toribio is pictured above with his Rocky Mountain goat scoring 54-4/8 points. The billy received a First Place Award.

a radio and satellite phone in my pack. I made good time on the freshly cut trail and was in the wonderful alpine country within an hour.

I spotted a goat as soon as the mountaintop came into view. He was bedded just under the peak about half a mile away. I stopped to set up my spotting scope and immediately identified the goat as a good billy. He appeared to be alone, a good indication that he was an older trophy goat.

I hurriedly ate a snack and reloaded my pack. It would take me nearly two hours of climbing to reach the goat's elevation. I encountered some large deer tracks and wondered what I would do if I encountered a monster buck. Fortunately, I didn't have to choose. As I neared the mountaintop, I had to work sidehill, and only the roll of the slope separated me from the goat. I felt that I was within 100 yards with the wind coming up the hill from my right. I knew I was getting close and loaded a round in my chamber in case I had to act fast.

Just as I approached the final rise that would allow me to see him, I felt a breath of wind on the back of my neck. I immediately dropped my pack and hurried over the rise to look. He was gone. I spotted some tracks and droppings in a nearby snowfield and went to inspect. They were fresh and the goat appeared to be moving out. I raced in his tracks to the other side of the mountain and looked down the hill where he might have gone.

Then I spotted him, far below and headed for the low country. A quick shot with my rangefinder put him at 298 yards and moving steadily away. I dropped to the ground, took a quick rest and held for the hump and squeezed off a shot. I thought I heard the bullet connect, but the only indication I connected was that he started running faster. I shot again and saw his right leg go out. He was still on his feet and about to disappear from sight. I managed to get off two more shots and then he was gone.

Worried that he would continue into the deep canyon below and possibly end up on some difficult to access ledge, I nearly ran down the mountain to catch him. When I got to the spot that he had disappeared, I was almost startled and overjoyed to see him lying there taking his last breath. A final shot to the neck finished him. It was just after 9 a.m. on August 1st and I had filled my goat tag with a dandy. I was amazed at how big he was and estimated his horns to be at least 11 inches long and very heavy. I counted the rings and determined him to be 8-1/2-years old. This was the biggest goat I had ever taken on a solo hunt.

Having left my pack on the top of the mountain, I had to make the hike back up the hill to retrieve it. I gave Marcia a call on the radio to report my success. She said that she had heard the shots and hoped that I had scored.

Once back at the goat, I admired his size and rugged beauty. I took a couple of photos and set about the chore of caping and boning the meat. It was a struggle to get all of the meat and cape up to the top of the mountain. With a few difficult pitches in the trail, I decided it

ROCKY MOUNTAIN GOAT
First Award – 54 $^4/_8$

▼ ▼ ▼ ▼ ▼

EDWARD E. TORIBIO

would be better to make two loads for the trip down to camp. I split the load and buried some of the meat, the cape, and the skull in the snowfield.

I was back in camp by 5:30 p.m. with the first load, and happy to see that Marcia had kept the fire going for me. I called Earl on the satellite phone to schedule a pick-up for the next day. It started to rain that night, and I dreaded the trip back up the mountain in the morning. It actually wasn't too bad, since my pack was empty. The rain had slowed to a drizzle. I managed a three-hour round trip and had all of the meat, cape, and horns in camp. The weather had deteriorated and we were socked in with low clouds and rain. We kept the fire going and hoped for a clearing. I was just happy to be off the hill with all of meat and hide from my trophy goat.

The weather improved later in the day, and it was welcome noise to hear the hum of the Supercub echo through the mountains. Earl managed to sneak in under a low ceiling and made a gentle landing in our peaceful little lake. Earl would have to ferry us out in three loads to a lower and larger lake. Marcia went out with some of the gear on the first load.

Being alone on the shore of an alpine lake at the end of a hunt, there is nothing much to do, except wait and enjoy the scenery. A pair of loons kept me company. Alone in the mountains is one of my favorite times to reminisce about past hunts and remember my father, who taught me to hunt so many years ago. I hope to be able to do as well for my son, Andrew, who will be joining me in the mountains someday soon.

Before long, Earl was back. I helped him load the goat and most of the remaining gear into the plane. I would have to wait and ride out on the final trip. After another rendezvous with Marcia at the lower lake, I wished them a happy ride back to civilization. In a short time, I would be there, too.

Upon my return to Ketchikan, I took the horns to Boyd Porter, the area biologist for ADF&G. Boyd confirmed the goat's age and took some increment growth measurements for the records. I taped the horns and found them to be 11-3/8" long with 5-6/8" bases. I came up with a B&C green score of 54-6/8", which would tie the score of the monster billy that Ross Groben took with me in 2001. Ross' just happened to also receive the First Award at the 25th Big Game Awards Program Banquet three years earlier. I knew my bill's horns would shrink during the 60-day drying period, and secretly hoped he would at least equal the terrific goat Wally Grover and I shot in 1991 with Joe Nichols. That goat scored 54-2/8 at the final panel scoring. On October 1st, I sent my horns to Doug Larson in Juneau for an official Boone and Crockett score. Doug was happy to report that my billy scored 54-4/8 B&C. ▲

Photograph by Bill Honza

TROPHY STATS

▼　▼　▼　▼　▼

Category
Rocky Mountain Goat

Score
54 $^2/_8$

Length of Horn
Right: 9 $^5/_8$　Left: 9 $^4/_8$

Circumference of Base
Right: 6 $^3/_8$　Left: 6 $^3/_8$

Greatest Spread
7 $^4/_8$

Location
Duchesne Co., Utah – 2006

Hunter
Craig L. Rippen

ROCKY MOUNTAIN GOAT
Second Award – 54 ²/₈

▼ ▼ ▼ ▼ ▼ ▼ ▼ ▼ ▼

CRAIG L. RIPPEN

We opened our hunt on Thursday, October 5. It was overcast with rain showers. I was hunting with my longtime friend and guide Shawn Labrum of Wild Mountain Outfitters. Shawn had put me on a Boone and Crockett bull elk last year that was the most exciting hunt of my life. Little did I know, the best was yet to come.

Do You Love to Hunt? Try This One

After looking at approximately 30 goats on opening day, most of which were nannies, we spotted a fairly nice billy at about 3 p.m. We decided to get a better look at him, so we started up the mountain. As we got within range, the rain started pouring and the billy moved up and around the mountain. We were soaked and covered with mud when we arrived back at the truck. But, considering the weather, we still spotted many goats.

We awoke Friday to a record-setting downpour. It rained from the moment I got out of bed until approximately 3 a.m. Saturday morning. I don't mind hunting in the rain, but this was buckets from heaven!

Saturday was overcast with a few rain showers turning into snow. I started thinking it wasn't going to be fun looking for a white mountain goat in snow. White on white; could we make it any harder?

By mid-morning, we spotted a herd of goats with a couple of billies in it. Again, we decided to put the stalk on them to get a closer look. We were able to get within 225 yards of them. After looking them over, we decided to pass. Shawn knew we could do better.

We spent the next couple of hours trying to drive up the mountain, but the snow was just too deep and way too muddy. After lunch, we drove to another mountain range where Shawn had spotted a couple of nice goats the week before. Once again, we found several goats ranging from about halfway up the mountain to the very

Photograph by Jack Reneau

Craig L. Rippen accepting his plaque and medal from Buck Buckner, Vice President and Chairman of the Big Game Records Committee.

Craig L. Rippen climbed up one of the toughest, roughest, nastiest mountains that he had ever seen to get within shooting range of this award-winning Rocky Mountain goat. The billy scores 54-2/8 points and received the Second Place Award at the 26th Big Game Awards Program Banquet.

top of one of the tallest, roughest, nastiest mountains that I have ever seen. Wouldn't you know it? Right there at the top were two very nice large goats.

Shawn looked at me and said, "Are you ready?"

The more I looked at that mountain the more I knew I did not want to climb it. As we sat there glassing the goats, I happened to notice another goat on the opposite side of the mountain range. After getting a little closer and taking a good look, Shawn said, "This is the one we want!"

I thought to myself, "Gee, it's only about 1000 yards straight up the mountain; I should be able to handle that."

Well, after about 200 yards on all fours, I came to the conclusion that one of us had to be nuts to make this climb, and I'm sure you can figure out who I'm talking about. Shawn continued to encourage me up the mountain. With every step, every crawl, every fall, it kept getting harder and harder.

I remembered people telling me that hunting Rocky Mountain goat is one of the most difficult hunts in America. Well, they weren't kidding! We started up that mountain about 1:30 p.m. in the afternoon and finally got wihtin shooting range at about 5:45 p.m.

I was completely exhausted — to the point that I could not even stand up. There stood my goat about 240 yards above us. The monster billy was in thick timber with a very limited shooting lane. All he had to do was move 10 feet either way, and we would never see him again. I kept thinking I had one shot and one shot only because I knew I could not make another climb on another animal. This was it! As hard as I was breathing, it was all I could do to hold the crosshairs in place. With one deep breath I squeezed off the shot! I couldn't tell if I hit the mark because I got scope bite. How embarrassing is that?

ROCKY MOUNTAIN GOAT
Second Award – 54 ²/₈
▼ ▼ ▼ ▼ ▼
CRAIG L. RIPPEN

Shawn let out a yell. "He's down! He's down!"

My first thought wasn't, "Yes! I have my goat!"

It was, "Oh, my God. I have to climb another 240 yards straight up to get to him!"

Shawn got to the goat first and let out a yell that could have been heard in Salt Lake! He said, "Boone and Crockett, baby!"

It was getting dark fast, so we grabbed the cameras and took pictures. At this point, it was dark. We knew we would need to leave the goat on the mountain and head down. Thank God Shawn had a flashlight, and we had a full moon. I think I only fell a dozen times. It could have been worse.

As I looked back on the hunt, it was not only the most exciting, challenging hunt that I've ever experienced, but also a blessing. I was blessed with the Utah state record Rocky Mountain goat at 54-2/8. The hunt also took me to another level in my life! It showed me to never give up — it's 90 percent mental and only 10 percent physical.

What a magnificent animal. If you ever have the opportunity to hunt a Rocky Mountain goat, go knowing that it will be the hunt-of-a-lifetime. ▲

TROPHY STATS

▼ ▼ ▼ ▼ ▼

Category
Rocky Mountain Goat

Score
53 $^4/_8$

Length of Horn
Right: 10 $^4/_8$ Left: 10 $^4/_8$

Circumference of Base
Right: 5 $^6/_8$ Left: 5 $^7/_8$

Greatest Spread
7 $^7/_8$

Location
Kalum Lake, British Columbia – 2005

Hunter
Daryl K. Schultz

Photograph by Jack Reneau

Daryl K. Schultz accepting his plaque and
medal from Buck Buckner, Vice President
and Chairman of the Big Game Records
Committee.

ROCKY MOUNTAIN GOAT
Third Award – 53 ⁴/₈

▼ ▼ ▼ ▼ ▼ ▼ ▼ ▼ ▼

Daryl K. Schultz

It's been said that a good hunter has to create luck. This has become my personal motto, and I remind myself of it every time the alarm goes off at 4:30 a.m. A person can do everything right — you can own the best equipment, spend time scouting, have favorable wind, and the perfect stalk - but luck is the one thing no one can control. All we can do as hunters is put together the proper recipe for success and hope that lady luck pays a visit.

As Luck Would Have It

That's why looking back on my November 2005 goat hunt makes me chuckle at how sometimes lady luck does most of the work. Often you read of 10-day hunts that only bring success at the eleventh hour. In my case, things happened a little differently.

The week before the hunt I changed the course of my life forever and asked the woman of my dreams to marry me. Colleen said yes — hunting addictions and all. I had always wanted to take her to Terrace, British Columbia, to show her the magnificent beauty of this truly pristine area. We negotiated (i.e. Colleen *told* me) that we would go the weekend following our engagement. With only three days to work with, I decided to squeeze in a hunt the first day, spend the second with Colleen (taking her to the hot springs) and leave the final day for any unfinished hunting business. This is normally not a "recipe for creating luck."

I was familiar with the area I was hunting, having previously scouted it ahead for a limited time such as this. I awoke the first morning at 4 a.m., drove out of town with my friend, Todd, whom I had grown up since childhood. The year previous, he and I had shared a successful two-goat day. However, this year I was the only one with a Limited Entry Hunt tag, relegating him to Sherpa duty.

It was still dark out when we began our hike into the valley where we hoped to find a decent billy. A fresh six-inch blanket of snow greeted us, giving us optimism that nannies would be low on the cliffs. We also concluded that, with the rut in full swing, billies would be hanging around nearby.

After walking for nearly two hours, the light was slowly beginning to give us some perspective. When the sun finally climbed atop the mountains and bathed the valley in full light, I was speechless. We stopped and drank ourselves full of both water and scenery. I thanked God I could enjoy such breathtaking beauty.

Continuing up the valley, we immediately eyed some goats. Spotting scopes revealed that the billies were all heavily discolored; they were busy impressing the ladies by kicking up the soft ground with their front legs, throwing mud and soil all over themselves. Todd and

I began to stalk one billy, which ended up in the billy's favor.

It was now late in the day and we were trekking along a creek in the valley bottom when around a corner we noticed four goats on a cliff face only 250 yards away. Upon closer inspection, my heart rate suddenly accelerated. Dropping to our knees, I threw my spotting scope up to my eye. One goat was distinctly black! He looked respectable — maybe a little over nine inches with decent mass.

I PEERED FURTHER OVER THE EDGE AND SAW TWO GOATS MOVING CAUTIOUSLY UP THE SLOPE IN SINGLE FILE. THE GOAT IN THE REAR WAS DARK AND DIRTY, AND ON CLOSER INSPECTION MY HEART JUMPED WITH THE ADRENALIN SURGE THAT ONLY A TROPHY ANIMAL COULD BRING.

The goats were on to us and the billy was getting nervous. Decision time! With only a few minutes of legal light remaining in the day and the cliffy terrain in which he stood, I decided to pass on him.

Fast-forward two days. I was now back at the same spot where I had passed on the goat earlier. Todd couldn't make it that day, so I found myself with Marvin, another good friend. Marvin and I had hunted goats together in the past, and he has always been an exceptional hunting partner. On this bright morning, we did not spot the same billy, so we pressed deeper into the valley.

During the pre-dawn hike into the valley, I resolved that any billy close to nine inches would be in danger that day. Being my last opportunity of the season because of upcoming wedding plans, I had set my standard and drawn a line in the sand.

We glassed from the valley floor when farther up the drainage we spotted a few goats in a creek gorge; one goat was distinctly black. We began our stalk. A large spruce provided our visual landmark as we climbed alongside the creek gorge where the goats were feeding. It was strenuous work, moving through dense alder slides and slippery ground. We frequently came to the base of cliffs that proved impassable, requiring us to circle around. Two hours from the beginning of our stalk, we finally made it to our spruce tree. Offloading our packs, we devised a plan to turn 90 degrees, sneaking to the edge of the gorge. Marvin pulled out the video camera hoping to capture some good footage. I checked my rifle to make certain my Leupold scope was clear before proceeding.

We were now belly crawling the last few yards to the very edge of the gorge — finding ourselves in perfect position. As we eased our heads over the edge, we saw three unsuspecting goats only 150 yards away. One of the goats was a billy — a goat that we estimated was about nine inches. I quickly made a good rest for my .300 Weatherby in the snow and located him in the scope. With the camera rolling, I waited for the goat to give me a clean shot. He eventually stepped forward into the clear, and I slowly began the trigger squeeze. Then Marvin urgently whispered, "Hold on Daryl; there's something wrong with your camera! It says CONDENSATION ERROR, and it shuts off!"

I pulled back in disbelief of my lack of luck. As we were solving this problem the goat went back into a no-shoot feeding position. After Marvin figured out what was wrong and the camera was recording, I settled back into position, awaiting another chance. Every time the goat was in a shooting position the camera wasn't working and when the camera was cooperating the goat wasn't! I really wanted to get the shot on camera.

ROCKY MOUNTAIN GOAT
Third Award – 53 4/8

▼ ▼ ▼ ▼ ▼

DARYL K. SCHULTZ

Finally, after some pretty tense moments, both the camera and goat co-operated, and I was fully prepared to take the shot. Taking a deep breath and starting to squeeze the trigger, reaching within a fraction of a second from that point of no return, Marvin pipes up again, "Hold on!"

"Now what?" I thought to myself.

"I see movement from below," he whispered. Slowly moving my eyes downward, searching for the movement, I peered over the edge. "Whoa! That's a huge goat!" Marvin added.

I peered further over the edge and saw two goats moving cautiously up the slope in single file. The goat in the rear was dark and dirty, and on closer inspection my heart jumped with the adrenalin surge that only a trophy animal could bring. I was staring at the goat of a lifetime, only 150 yards away — and he was blissfully unaware of my presence. I had to act quickly. I found him in my scope and readied myself for the shot. Miraculously, this time the camera was rolling without issues.

At the bark of my Weatherby, the old billy just hunched his back as if he were ignoring I had shot him. He had roamed these mountains for many years, and it seemed as if he wasn't willing to go just yet. I was pretty confident my shot placement had been good, but I wanted to make sure, so I chambered another round and fired. He collapsed immediately and started to tumble down into the creek gorge. It was a moment I will never forget. Both of us were ecstatic!

Watching a big billy cartwheel into an area of very difficult recovery has a way of quickly snapping a person back into reality! We had some hard work ahead of us. We returned to our packs and decided we could only bring one camera, 50-feet of rope, and two knives. Unnecessary weight would need to stay behind. The two of us cautiously maneuvered ourselves down into the slippery and icy gorge. There were a few places where I could hear the roar of the creek below us and I knew that if one of us fell, there would be no stopping. This was not a position we would normally put ourselves into, but my trophy goat was down there, and we knew we had to get it out. We gingerly worked our way over ice and exposed rock, until we finally spotted the goat below. We tied the rope to a tree, using it to lower ourselves down, finding that the rope extended just inches above the creek bottom where the goat lay.

He was an amazing specimen with a huge body, but more importantly long in horn with good mass. I knelt down beside him, smiled, and shook the hand of my hunting partner. We had succeeded in harvesting an amazing trophy through some remarkable events.

Daryl K. Schultz and his hunting partner Marvin cautiously maneuvered down an icy, slippery gorge to retrieve Schultz's award-winning Rocky Mountain goat. The billy, was 13-1/2 years old and scores 53-4/8 points. Schultz was hunting near Kalum Lake, British Columbia, in 2005 when he harvested this magnificent goat.

The big billy was 13-1/2 years old and had only two half-worn teeth left — more than likely living out his last winter. We snapped field photos before caping and de-boning the meat, which was made easy by the abundant fresh water. Loading up our packs and climbing out of the gorge proved to be one of the hardest things I've ever done in my life. Marvin and I struggled against the elements to climb every inch. I can't express the value of good hunting partners in mountainous terrain, especially those partners willing to carry more than their share of a heavy burden. We finished the day hiking out to the truck by the light of our head-lamps. We were exhausted and wet, but both wore smiles we couldn't wipe off our faces.

Thinking back on that memorable week in November of 2005, I'm constantly reminded of how much luck played a part in those few short days. I was lucky to have a beautiful woman accept my marriage proposal. I was lucky to spend time hunting with good friends in breathtaking country. But perhaps, I was luckiest of all to experience a faulty video camera, ultimately allowing me to harvest a 53-4/8" Boone and Crockett goat. ▲

B&C Photo Archives

Three of the four hunters who took award-winning Rocky Mountain goats were in attendance at the 26th Big Game Awards Program in Fort Worth, Texas. Pictured above standing in front of their trophies are, from left to right, Craig L. Rippen (Second Place Award), Robert E. Reedy, Jr. (Honorable Mention), and Daryl K. Schultz (Third Place Award).

TROPHY STATS

▼ ▼ ▼ ▼ ▼

Category
Rocky Mountain Goat

Score
52

Length of Horn
Right: 10 $^1/_8$ Left: 10 $^1/_8$

Circumference of Base
Right: 5 $^5/_8$ Left: 5 $^5/_8$

Greatest Spread
9

Location
Tanzilla River, British Columbia
– 2004

Hunter
Robert E. Reedy, Jr.

Photograph by Bill Honza

BOONE AND CROCKETT CLUB'S

ROCKY MOUNTAIN GOAT
Honorable Mention – 52

▼ ▼ ▼ ▼ ▼ ▼ ▼ ▼ ▼

ROBERT E. REEDY, JR.

The time had come! It was October 2, 2004, and the hunt my partner Richard and I had booked over a year ago was now here. We drove from our home to Minneapolis, where we boarded a plane with a destination of Smithers, British Columbia, in mind. Richard and I rented a mini-van when we arrived at Smithers for the final leg of our trip to Dease Lake the following morning. After getting up early, we stopped in a small café for breakfast, and then we were on our way.

All in a Fall's Hunt

The scenery was simply breathtaking on our way up to Dease Lake. There were the Canadian Rockies, as well as multi-colored glaciers. We made a slight detour to Hyder, Alaska, so Richard could say he was in Alaska. We were anxiously hoping to see a brown bear by the river we crossed getting to Alaska, but all we saw were the skeletal remains of the salmon after the bears had been there – not a pleasant odor. After leaving Hyder, we were back on track to Dease Lake.

Upon arrival, we settled into a motel that evening, anticipating morning and the beginning of our long-awaited hunt. The next morning Richard and I met up with Rick McLean, of Eagle River Outfitters, and were off to his hunting camp. Richard was there to get a Canada moose and, if he had time, a goat. My goal was to get that magnificent Rocky Mountain goat.

Richard and his guide Keith, along with wrangler Megan, left for moose camp all on horseback. Rick, along with our singing wrangler Kevin and I, headed for our camp in search of goats. Our camp was located along the Tanzilla River, and consisted of a couple of tents. One tent was our mess hall; the other would be home for 10 days.

My horse was named Houdini, because he could escape from being tied up if not double knotted. We hunted what the locals call the "desert." The weather was always sunny and

Photograph by Jack Reneau

Robert E. Reedy, Jr. accepting his plaque from Buck Buckner, Vice President and Chairman of the Big Game Records Committee.

Photograph courtesy of Robert E. Reedy, Jr.

Robert E. Reedy, Jr., shot this Rocky Mountain goat at just 10 yards. He and his guide Rick were descending down a steep rock-faced mountainside when the billy stood up at close range. The goat scores 52 points.

windy. Here we saw some nice billies in the distance, on each side of the river. Every day those billies seemed to bed in the same location. We decided that we would have to cross the river with these large-bodied horses in order to get closer. Rick rode the horse in charge of the other horses. His name was "Haggard."

It wasn't until the fifth day of the hunt that we finally got close to a billy. Rick and I left camp early in the morning darkness, crossing the large, rapidly moving Tanzilla River, and running into the first obstacle of the day. As we got to the other side, Rick got poked in the eye with a twig. Shortly after, his eye began to swell and water. It really never stopped watering all day. Keeping a goat for me in mind, Rick did not want to turn back because of his eye, so we continued on our way.

We left the horses and walked for several miles. We scaled the mountainside for hours. Rick told me he could smell a billy as we were descending down the rock-faced mountainside. Steep was the only word for where we were. Then, all of the sudden, a billy stood up about ten yards in front of us! Rick said, "There's your goat!"

Shooting a .300 Winchester Magnum, I raised my rifle, filled the scope with white, and let a bullet go. Down the billy went. Thankfully, he got hung up on a group of evergreen trees, which kept him from sliding down the entire mountain.

Rick said, "If he moves, give him another one."

He didn't move, though. I was ecstatic! I had just harvested a fantastic billy that was everything I could have hoped for. I thanked Rick for a successful hunt and a most beautiful goat. What a magnificent animal.

Rick and I caped the billy out and made many trips up to the top of the mountain with the meat and cape. Before we left the harvest site, Rick left some gifts for the Spirits to thank them for the successful harvest.

It being dark now, we walked back to the horses with our headlamps lit. As we were walking, we could see eyes to the side of us. Rick figured them to probably be the eyes of

BOONE AND CROCKETT CLUB'S

bears. I was so exhausted by this time, I didn't even care. I was just glad to reach the horses and start our long way back to camp.

ROCKY MOUNTAIN GOAT
Honorable Mention – 52

▼ ▼ ▼ ▼ ▼

ROBERT E. REEDY, JR.

We loaded the meat and cape onto the horses, turned off the headlamps, and let Haggard lead us back to camp. We were then faced with another obstacle not anticipated. In a matter of only seconds, Haggard lost his footing and went sliding down the mountainside, pinning Rick's leg under him. I found out later that Rick had gotten his foot caught in the stirrup and couldn't get it loose. My horse, Houdini, being so close behind, got to the same location and down the mountain he began to slide, also! I jumped off Houdini on the uphill side and yelled to Rick that Houdini was also on his way down. It all happened so fast. I hustled down the darkened mountainside to see what had transpired. Luckily, Rick didn't get trapped between the two horses. This could easily have been a tragic situation. Rick did receive a season-ending knee injury from this incident. Houdini and Haggard were fine, and we managed to get the horses back up the mountain again. All of us arrived back at camp very late, exhausted, and a little worse for wear.

It must have been two days later when Richard came to goat camp after getting a very nice 57" Canada moose. We congratulated each other on our harvests. That evening Kevin got out his guitar and sang a few songs for us. Life just couldn't get any better. Then the rain came. It rained extremely hard all the next day.

A day later, Richard got his chance to shoot a goat. The billy that Richard found had only one eye and horns known as "Stove Pipes." After Richard had watched this billy for at least 20 minutes, at only 17 yards away, he shot and missed. What else can I say?

Our hunt was now nearing an end. Rick and I drove to a nearby town and I assisted him in getting some round bales for the horses. We did get to see a grizzly bear by the road on this jaunt.

Rick of Eagle River Outfitters is a great person to plan that dream hunt with, and his guides and wranglers help make that dream hunt become reality. Richard and I truly enjoyed our hunting experience with them. It was now time to head back to Wisconsin, with memories to remember, stories to tell, pictures to show, and animals to admire always.

There is one last note to mention about our hunt to British Columbia. Both Richard and I contracted "Beaver Fever" about a week after we got home. We had our kits and pills along for the water, but didn't think we would come down with it. The locals never get sick. So, after a trip to the doctor, we did get better and are ready to go again. ▲

New World's Record (tie)

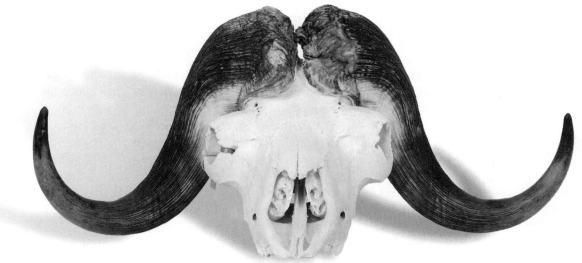

Photograph by Bill Honza

TROPHY STATS
▼ ▼ ▼ ▼ ▼

Category
Musk Ox

Score
129

Length of Horn
Right: 28 $^2/_8$ Left: 28 $^6/_8$

Width of Boss
Right: 12 $^1/_8$ Left: 11 $^3/_8$

Greatest Spread
31 $^4/_8$

Location
Coppermine River, Nunavut – 2006

Hunter
Jim Shockey

MUSK OX
First Award – 129

▼ ▼ ▼ ▼ ▼ ▼ ▼ ▼ ▼

JIM SHOCKEY

Journal Entry: April 13, 2006

It's snowing big, heavy flakes. Warmer than the last three days, though, and the wind has calmed a little, probably 10-15 miles an hour; pure white-out conditions. My Inuit guide Charlie Bolt has just gone out to chip some ice off the lake; we'll melt it for tea. Charlie and I have hunted together many times, hunts that have always been organized by Arctic outfitting legend Fred Webb.

The Old Master

Hard to get motivated to go out in this stuff when you know the odds are so low, but we've only got 2-1/2 days left before the musk ox season closes. I'm beat, but Charlie is insistent that we go out in this white out. Charlie's the boss.

We're in the sleds now, headed west, I think. Horrible conditions, snowing, no horizon, no perception of distance; we can see, but a rock can be two miles away or it can be two feet away, no way to tell. No way to know if there is a cliff in front of you. It's the oddest thing, everything is white. Even when you're walking, everything seems normal and then all of a sudden you step into a wall of snow, or step out into thin air and suddenly you're sliding down a hill.

According to the GPS, we're 16 miles from camp. Just bumped into a herd of caribou — 200 of them at least; it's eerie. Looks like they're walking through the sky! It's disconcerting, up is down, down is up, sideways is everywhere.

Musk ox! Eight or nine bulls, two that look good. They've started walking off so we're getting organized; we're going to go after these bulls. One of them looks like an ancient old bull with a really roughed-up boss.

We've walked 200 yards with our backs to the sleds, stepping out into a great white nothingness. It's disconcerting. The musk oxen are behind a rise now, less than a mile away.

There they are! We're behind a rock now, 80 yards from them, glassing. They're butting heads. I'm waiting for the one big one with the wide flare, shallow curls, but really heavy bosses, to step out into the clear; he's staying tucked in behind the rest. He's obviously the oldest bull in this batch, but there are several other good bulls in here. What a magnificent animal. Now he's stepping out into the open.

I've taken the shot now, and he has run out of sight over a snow ridge I didn't know was there, but I was dead on him. Had to be a good shot.

The other musk oxen have run off, but not far. I can see them on another knob. It looks like a half mile away, but could be two miles.

Photograph courtesy of Jim Shockey

Jim Shockey is pictured above with a musk ox that ties the current World's Record at 129 points. Shockey was hunting with a muzzleloader near Coppermine River, Nunavut, when he harvested the old bull in 2006.

My bull is huge! Big bosses all busted off and worn —— he's been rubbing on rocks! I've never seen a musk ox bull this old before; neither has Charlie. We're standing in awe, staring at the bull. His coat is tattered, hanging in rags, and there's a one-foot patch of actual skin pulled off and hanging. He was on his last legs for sure, this master of the musk ox living in this godforsaken land. I could stand here forever in reverence for this animal, but we can't. Here, forever is literally a moment of lingering away.

It's pitch black, and snowing. I have no idea what direction we're going. I'm lying on my back in the sled, on top of the musk ox quarters and hide, wrapped up in as much gear as I can cover myself in, and I'm still getting cold. The wooden sled is bumping along in the darkness, pulled by Charlie's snow machine. We're in the middle of nowhere traveling to another spot in the middle of nowhere, but I have no fear.

Charlie won't make a mistake. The Inuit are a living part of this land, an integral part of musk ox hunting. Without them, we from the south would die. Simple and final. ▲

320   BOONE AND CROCKETT CLUB'S

320 BOONE AND CROCKETT CLUB'S

Photograph by Frederick J. King

VP of the Club's Big Game Records Committee Eldon L. "Buck" Buckner discusses how to determine the starting point for the length of each horn on Jim Shockey's World's Record (tie) musk ox. Once the center point of the boss is determined, the length of horn measurement, which begins at the lowest point of horn material, can be measured.

TROPHY STATS

▼ ▼ ▼ ▼ ▼

Category
Musk Ox

Score
128 $^6/_8$

Length of Horn
Right: 29 $^4/_8$ Left: 30 $^4/_8$

Width of Boss
Right: 11 $^1/_8$ Left: 10 $^7/_8$

Greatest Spread
27 $^1/_8$

Location
Kugluktuk, Nunavut – 2004

Hunter
Tony L. Spriggs

Photograph by Bill Honza

MUSK OX
Second Award – 128 6/8
▼ ▼ ▼ ▼ ▼ ▼ ▼ ▼ ▼

TONY L. SPRIGGS

When Tony Spriggs and his friend Jess Forton went on a musk ox hunt in spring of 2004, it was anything but conventional. It was impromptu and booked on short notice. They were lucky and filled two spots with Fred Webb after a few cancellations. The hunts were booked in January for a March hunt.

In short order, they were headed north. At least Tony was. Jess forgot his passport, and Tony had to take both guns and hope somehow that Jess would find a way to meet him in Yellowknife. Jess made the rendezvous with only ten minutes to spare. Had he not made it in time, he would have missed their last flight and gone home with nothing more than bad memories and a dented checkbook.

Photograph courtesy of Tony L. Spriggs

Tony L. Spriggs, left, and his guide Roy with Tony's award-winning musk ox taken in 2004. The bull, which scores 128-6/8 points, received the Second Place Award and is the third largest musk ox ever taken by a hunter.

Tony L. Spriggs accepting his plaque and medal from Buck Buckner, Vice President and Chairman of the Big Game Records Committee.

For the first three days of the –45° F hunt, they were trapped in a whiteout. Tony says that it was bad enough that two of the men, from California, demanded to be taken back. They ended their hunt without even getting to the destination.

On the evening of the third day, Jess's Inuit guide Roy was gone for about seven hours. He returned long after dark, with simple words. "Four bulls. All good."

The next day, they found the tracks and followed, eventually catching up to the four bulls. Tony remarks that all four looked to be records-book animals.

Jess had the first shot, and capitalized, taking a huge 122 B&C bull. Tony's shot quickly followed on what he felt was the best bull remaining of the three, a bull that would later score an unbelievable 128-6/8. They quickly field-dressed the animals in the extreme cold and then laid plans for getting back to a warmer and more hospitable location.

In less than ten seconds on that great hunting day, two of the biggest musk oxen ever recorded had fallen to two friends. All on a hunt that three months earlier, Tony and Jess didn't even know would happen.

Hunting musk ox in the Arctic has to rate as one of the great adventures a hunter can take in North America. As Tony said, "When conditions are that bad, you're rootin' for everybody." ▲

Dedicated to Jess Forton's wife, Dixie Forton, who passed away in the fall of 2006.

B&C Photo Archives

Four award-winning musk oxen were on display for visitors at Cabela's Fort Worth store to see. Tony Spriggs' pedestal-mounted bull (center) scores 128-6/8 inches and received a Second Place Award. Ben F. Carter III's life-size mounted bull to the right scores 123-6/8 points and received a Fourth Place Award. Jim Shockey's Third Place European-mounted musk ox, which scores 128-2/8 inches, can be seen in the background.

Photograph by Bill Honza

TROPHY STATS

▼ ▼ ▼ ▼ ▼

Category
Musk Ox

Score
128 $^2/_8$

Length of Horn
Right: 31 $^5/_8$ Left: 31 $^7/_8$

Width of Boss
Right: 10 $^4/_8$ Left: 10 $^4/_8$

Greatest Spread
29 $^6/_8$

Location
Coppermine River, Nunavut – 2006

Hunter
Jim Shockey

MUSK OX
Third Award – 128 ²/₈

▼ ▼ ▼ ▼ ▼ ▼ ▼ ▼ ▼

JIM SHOCKEY

Journal Entry: April 15, 2006

We're getting ready to head out today, last day of the musk ox season. Fred Webb was concerned that the late spring might keep the barren ground grizzlies denned up, so he arranged for me to have a second musk ox tag when we left the village. He was definitely right about the weather; it's been bitter cold, snowing most days. No bears out of hibernation yet, at least not up here. The musk ox we took

A Day in the Life

two days ago was a brute, definitely the biggest of the five musk oxen I've taken over the years hunting with Fred.

Since there are no grizzlies out yet, Charlie and I have decided to use the second tag to try and find another musk ox, a bigger one than we already have. Fat chance. We'll head back to Kugluktuk tomorrow and try for a wolf along the way. Not sure if it's a good choice, though. Kind of wish I could be in town today, the Inuit are having a winter festival; snow machine races, all kinds of games, and even a Johnny Cash impersonation contest that I would love to enter!

We'll see what today brings. We're headed further east into big musk ox territory where we hope to find more rocks. Charlie says the musk ox will hang in the rockier country to keep away from the wolves. The sun's out! It's absolutely beautiful here, fresh powder snow, maybe 4 inches deep, great for tracking, and our world is white, white, white except for the sky, which is blue, blue, blue. The powder snow has covered everything, so the first wind will show the rocks again, but right now it's just one big white rolling expanse that goes on forever. Even the sled seems to be smoother today, not as bumpy.

Photograph courtesy of Jim Shockey

Jim Shockey with his award-winning musk ox taken near Coppermine River, Nunavut, in 2006. The bull has a final score of 128-2/8 points and received a Third Place Award.

We've just spotted our first herd of musk ox, probably 50 or 60 animals in the herd. There is a baby musk ox that's just been born. It can barely stand, so we're steering way clear. The baby will get lost or trampled if the herd spooks. Now we've spotted a wolverine! It came right by us and has seen us now and is loping off. Like a big weasel. It's pleasant today, sitting in the sled, I'm comfortable.

Have all the bugs worked out of my seat in this wooden box, so now I can position myself without getting hammered and whiplashed. It's not exactly warm, still have to have every part of my face covered when we travel. Charlie's just spotted another herd of musk ox, 15 or so animals, 5 or 6 miles distant. So we're headed off in that direction.

We've just crested a rise and there they are in front of us, 15 bulls and they all look the same — No, there is one that is really big! His horns hang down so far they look bizarre!

They've run off a couple miles and stopped, so we're making a stalk. We spooked them. This time we have to hike back to the snow machines and try to make a 10-mile circle to get in front of them.

We've left the machines and are climbing to the top of the ridge we think the musk oxen are behind. Charlie can't walk in this snow, it's too slippery for him, he's wearing mukluks and they're frozen on the bottom. Have to make the climb myself.

We've failed half a dozen stalks today, but this time we have them, I think. They're still not giving me a good muzzleloader shot. It's frustrating for Charlie; he can't understand why I would use the entire day up, sneaking up to the musk ox when it's so much easier to hunt the Inuit way, the practical way; just roar after the herd and shoot the animal you want. Can't do it that way, I've explained to him on every hunt we've been on together; I'm not an Inuit; it has to be done my way.

I've crawled in close now, they're on the skyline. The big one has just run off a smaller bull, and he's given me the shot. I've just taken it, and he's run about 20 yards and tipped over. He's down! One of the bulls is coming toward me, 30 yards away and I'm wide open, lying here in the snow. I don't have any cover and no chance to reload.

These musk oxen are dangerous; I know that from experience, but now he's curled back and gone and joined the herd. They've run off.

The bull is a giant, and we're excited. The bull is a big, big bull, easily over 30 inches long on his horns, as big as a musk ox gets. What a gorgeous animal, white boss and almost white horns, not as old as some of the other ones in the herd, though, and I kind of feel bad about that. It has the most beautiful perfect hide, long flowing hair. What a magnificent animal on a magnificent day.

But now we've noticed a big cloud of white on the horizon — blizzard. Snow is billowing up in the distance, and coming toward us. Time to get out of here.

We're back in camp now, thank goodness for that; the wind is starting to blow hard, picking up the powder snow. Inside our canvas tent, I put a tape on the bull, 31 inches on each horn. This is a giant musk ox; it'll be right up near the World's Record for sure. It's cold in the tent; the wind is blowing, so we've set up a porch in front to try and block the snow from blowing in. We're boiling up musk ox heart. It was a good day. ▲

The 26th Big Game Awards Trophy Display included this special case featuring the skulls of award-winning grizzly bears and Alaska brown bears. Above, Gary Darrah points out his Alaska brown bear skull to Chris Schultz.

Photograph by Bill Honza

TROPHY STATS

▼ ▼ ▼ ▼ ▼

Category
Musk Ox

Score
123 $^6/_8$

Length of Horn
Right: 29 $^2/_8$ Left: 29 $^2/_8$

Width of Boss
Right: 10 $^4/_8$ Left: 10 $^2/_8$

Greatest Spread
28 $^1/_8$

Location
Kugluktuk, Nunavut – 2004

Hunter
Ben F. Carter III

MUSK OX
Fourth Award – 123 6/8

▼ ▼ ▼ ▼ ▼ ▼ ▼ ▼ ▼

BEN F. CARTER III

In 2003, I attended the Guides and Outfitters of British Columbia Convention as a representative of the Dallas Safari Club, of which I am a past president. Fred Webb had donated an Arctic musk ox hunt from his trophy area for their convention's live auction. I was the lucky winning bidder of the hunt and didn't know what to expect, since that winter in Dallas I don't believe we ever had a temperature below freezing.

Hunt in the Arctic

The summer before the hunt I bought a Northern Outfitters setup for the hunt. I tried the parka and pants on at home but it was so hot that I couldn't keep it on for more than a few minutes. Frankly, I was apprehensive about the hunt because I do not like cold weather. I've been on a few Alberta whitetail hunts, and those were pretty cold. But, I was going, no matter what.

Right after the Dallas Safari Club Convention in January, I talked to my hunting buddy Dave Baxter, a Dallas veterinarian, about my upcoming hunt. He said he was interested in going. He called Fred, who had one opening available on the same hunt. Dave also bought Northern Outfitters gear but paid about half the price, finding his setup on the internet.

As our departure date in late March approached, I watched the weather in Kugluktuk. The average temperature was 40 to 50 degrees below zero. That was hard to comprehend in Dallas, where it was 65 degrees.

We took off as scheduled on March 28, landed in Edmonton, and then continued on to Yellowknife to spend the night. In Yellowknife, there was quite a bit of snow. It was around zero or just below.

The next morning we caught a flight to Kugluktuk, flying over nothing but snow and ice — quite a sight for a homegrown Texan. We landed in Kugluktuk on a frozen runway and went into the airport. Fred and his son Martin

Photograph by Jack Reneau

Ben F. Carter III accepting his plaque and medal from Buck Buckner, Vice President and Chairman of the Big Game Records Committee.

Ben F. Carter III took his award-winning bull after the others in camp had filled their tags. His musk ox, the biggest of the bunch, received a Fourth Place Award at the 26th Big Game Awards Program held in Fort Worth, Texas. The bull had a final score of 123-6/8 points.

met us and took us to his house in Kugluktuk, where we sorted through our gear and got dressed in our cold-weather clothing.

We loaded the sleds with all of our necessary gear. Our guides would pilot the snowmobiles across the Arctic Ocean then inland to our first camp. There were five hunters and five guides.

It was about -25°F, but the suit kept me toasty. I sat on all the gear on a foam pad and caribou skin. We rode for about six hours, taking breaks along the way, and made our first camp on a river. I didn't particularly care for riding down the river, with all its crushed ice and pressure ridges.

We had a dinner of freeze-dried noodles and beef that was quite good. My guide, Charlie Bolt, chopped a chunk of ice out of the river and melted it for water. I slept just fine in the sleeping bag, even though it was -30°F.

The next morning we continued upriver another seven hours to our hunting area. Several of the guides went up a nearby hill to glass and saw a herd of musk ox with several mature bulls in them. Two of the guides and hunters peeled off and went after that group. We continued upriver.

I was so comfortable in the back of the sled that I actually fell asleep, only waking up when the sled stopped. I saw the other two hunters already glassing a distant hill. I then saw a group of approximately 20 bulls. All looked very large to me; I believe there were several book-size animals in the herd.

MUSK OX
Fourth Award – 123 6/8
▼ ▼ ▼ ▼ ▼
Ben F. Carter III

It was about 4 p.m., so we took an hour and made our camp close to where we had stopped. As it began to snow, we got our guns and took off to find those bulls.

We looked for the herd without any luck. My guide and the other hunter went down a little valley, and we thought Dave and his guide had gone somewhere else. The remaining hunter and I found the musk ox on top of the hill. We made a stalk and were in shooting position, but we were having a hard time determining which was the best one to take. They all looked good. About the time I had picked one, there was a shot. The one I had picked had just been shot by Dave, who had been coming from the other side. The remainder of the herd took off. Dave's bull wound up scoring about 115 points.

It was almost dark, so we went back to camp. The next day was a whiteout, forcing us to stay in the tent all day. I read three books and took several naps.

Fred Webb runs a great operation. My guide Charlie had been guiding for more than 20 years with Fred, and even though we were in the harshest environment on the planet, I

I HAVE BEEN ON MANY HUNTS ALL OVER NORTH AMERICA, BUT THIS ONE WILL ALWAYS HOLD A SPECIAL PLACE IN MY HEART FOR THE SHEER VASTNESS AND SOLITUDE OF THE ARCTIC ICE AND SNOW!

never felt uneasy. We had a shortwave radio that the guides used each night to check in with Fred at base camp.

The following morning we awoke to snow drifted up on our tents. It looked clear enough to hunt, so we took off. After about an hour, we saw a herd of musk ox. Again, these all appeared to be large bulls. The other hunter and I made a stalk and slowly separated to opposite sides of the herd. We were within eyesight of each other the entire time.

Again, I picked what I thought was the largest bull and was about to shoot when I heard a shot. Again, I saw the one I was going to shoot go down. That bull wound up scoring about 119 points.

My guide Charlie and I began to pursue the herd of musk ox and got up on them for another stalk. I had a hard time picking which was the largest. One bull separated a bit from the rest. His horns swept very low and had a lot of mass. I decided he looked like a good one and shot. He wound up being the largest of the three and scored 123-6/8 points! I guess being the last to shoot is not always the worst thing.

I have been on many hunts all over North America, but this one will always hold a special place in my heart for the sheer vastness and solitude of the Arctic ice and snow! ▲

TROPHY STATS

▼ ▼ ▼ ▼ ▼

Category
  Bighorn Sheep

Score
  199

Length of Horn
  Right: 41 $^2/_8$ Left: 40 $^4/_8$

Circumference of Base
  Right: 17 $^5/_8$ Left: 17 $^3/_8$

Greatest Spread
  25

Location
  Fergus Co., Montana – 2004

Hunter
  Robert E. Seelye

BIGHORN SHEEP
First Award – 199

▼ ▼ ▼ ▼ ▼ ▼ ▼ ▼ ▼

ROBERT E. SEELYE

Twenty-five years after his initial attempt at drawing a tag for bighorn sheep in Montana, Robert Seelye was finally going to be chasing bighorns. He had drawn one of the most coveted bighorn sheep tags in Montana. After getting used to being disappointed so many years in a row, he almost couldn't believe it when it finally happened.

That summer, he spent about 18 days scouting, learning as much as he could about possible access points, and gearing up for the hunt. Hunting in the Missouri Breaks area can be challenging. Most of the roads are clay, which turns to what is locally known as "gumbo" when it rains. The mixture it creates acts like a muddy glue, sticking to whatever comes into contact with it. For all intents and purposes, these conditions make the roads non-negotiable. A person out on those road systems during bad weather often has no choice but to wait until the road dries enough to get them and their vehicles out.

The other main access is the Missouri River, so access to a jet boat is a big plus in opening up options for reaching areas holding sheep.

As an employee of PSE Archery, Robert was pretty well set on wanting to fill his sheep tag with a bow. This added both pressure and difficulty to the hunt because much of the terrain is open. It can be difficult to execute a good stalk.

As the season progressed, Robert continued to push as hard as he could. He had put in close to 20 hunting days now, and hadn't seen many big rams. There was one, but the wind was so strong that day that there was just no chance to do what needed to be done.

On his final trip to his hunting area, he set up camp and then glassed for the evening. He soon had his binoculars on three great-looking

Photograph courtesy of Robert E. Seelye

Robert E. Seelye is pictured above with his award-winning bighorn sheep, which scores 199 points. Seelye had applied for 25 years before he finally drew his tag in Montana.

rams, two of which he felt were nothing short of exceptional. He watched them until dark and then headed back to camp, crossing his fingers that the rams wouldn't move too far before morning.

That night in camp, he was joined by his friend Dan Moore. He told Dan about what he had seen, and both went to bed with visions of grandeur in their dreams.

They headed out early in the morning toward where Robert had last spotted the rams. Sure enough, they were still in the same general area. It wasn't long before Robert had the biggest of the three great rams at 25 yards! The only problem was that it was head on to him, giving him no shot opportunity. Robert was forced to watch as the rams went over the edge and out of sight. Robert was in anguish, hoping his best opportunity thus far wasn't going to go up in smoke.

He began to follow them, but was busted shortly thereafter. They ran around a sharp point in the ridge, and that's when Robert caught his luckiest break of the entire hunting season. The best ram of the bunch made a fatal mistake — he stopped.

Robert wasn't about to second-guess his luck. He drew his bow, placed the pin, and released. It was a fatal shot, one that would go down in history. Robert had just arrowed the second-largest bow-taken bighorn sheep in history.

He summed up his efforts with happiness and modesty: "It's not often that you get to take home the biggest that you've ever seen." ▲

B&C Photo Archives

B&C Official Measurer Curtis Smiley admires nearly a dozen wild sheep trophies at the 26th Big Game Awards Trophy Display at Cabela's. All four sheep species recognized by the Boone and Crockett Club were represented. In particular, the collection of desert sheep was one of the best ever.

Photograph by Bill Honza

TROPHY STATS

▼ ▼ ▼ ▼ ▼

Category
Bighorn Sheep

Score
198 $^3/_8$

Length of Horn
Right: 43 $^5/_8$ Left: 44 $^4/_8$

Circumference of Base
Right: 17 $^1/_8$ Left: 17 $^2/_8$

Greatest Spread
23 $^4/_8$

Location
Blaine Co., Montana – 2006

Hunter
Stephen C. Morrical

BOONE AND CROCKETT CLUB'S

BIGHORN SHEEP
Second Award – 198 ³/₈

▼ ▼ ▼ ▼ ▼ ▼ ▼ ▼ ▼

STEPHEN C. MORRICAL

Most successful hunts start with a lot of planning and preparation and end with a lot of luck. In the case of my 2006 Montana bighorn sheep hunt, a great deal of the luck took place before the hunt even happened.

For over 20 years, I had been applying for a bighorn sheep permit in my home state of Montana, with no success. Finally, this past year in June, I received notification from the Montana Department of Fish, Wildlife & Parks that I had finally drawn a tag. I didn't draw just any tag; I drew one of the coveted Missouri Breaks permits. This permit is highly desired by big game hunters because this district, home range to the now extinct Audubon sheep first recorded by the Lewis and Clark expedition, is known to contain a very healthy herd of transplanted Rocky Mountain bighorn sheep, with many older rams capable of scoring high in Boone and Crockett Club's records book.

Aerial surveys conducted by the Montana Department of Fish, Wildlife and Parks in the spring of 2006 reported the Missouri Breaks herd doing well. In addition to a healthy herd, biologists conducting the surveys observed many trophy-class rams.

With tag in hand and reports of excellent sheep populations, the stage was set. I could hardly contain my enthusiasm through the summer months. Being a first-time sheep hunter, I read as many books and articles on bighorn sheep hunting as I could get my hands on, focusing my study on field judging horn size. I knew this was going to be the best opportunity I would ever get to harvest a Boone and Crockett animal, so I set out to learn what a 180+ set of horns looked like.

Although I had not spent much time in the area I would be hunting sheep, I was no stranger to the Missouri Breaks. During the last 10 years, I had spent a lot of time bowhunting for elk, rifle hunting for mule deer, and exploring the terrain of the Missouri River Basin from my

Photograph by Jack Reneau

Stephen C. Morrical accepting his plaque and medal from Buck Buckner, Vice President and Chairman of the Big Game Records Committee.

jet boat. I was all too aware of the challenges hunting the Breaks can pose. As it is in much of the western United States, the weather here can be fickle. In the Breaks, however, rain or snow means "gumbo clay" which in turn means "You're not going anywhere until things dry out." My sheep district would be accessible by either the river or a network of unimproved BLM roads, totally at the mercy of the weather.

The Montana sheep hunting season is long (Sept. 15-Nov. 30) and the hunter can choose to hunt with either a bow or a firearm. Being both an avid bowhunter and a firearms hunter, selecting which method became a dilemma. In the end, I decided to conduct my early hunts with the bow, keeping my .30-06 in camp in case I felt the need to use it. Because my hunting district was about five hours travel time from my home, I set aside numerous vacation days with the intent of spending three to four days at a time hunting, distributing several of these hunts throughout the season.

> IN LISTENING TO MY ACCOUNT OF THE HUNT, ONE MAY THINK THAT MY ONLY MEASURE OF SUCCESS WAS TO HARVEST A "BOOK" ANIMAL. BUT HUNTING IS NOT ONLY ABOUT KILLING A TROPHY ANIMAL. IT'S THE THRILL OF THE HUNT, THE COMPANIONSHIP, AND THE TRUE CONNECTION THAT HUNTERS HAVE WITH THE NATURAL WORLD THAT REALLY MATTERS.

Opening weekend found my friend Mike Killian and me running 25 miles upriver in the jet boat to hunt the steep cliffs and lower coulees of the Missouri River. The weather was wet and miserable and fortunately we did not need to rely on vehicle travel to access the hunting areas because, as earlier mentioned, the roads were impassable due to the gumbo. Even the hiking proved difficult as, with every third step, five pounds of clay would be sticking to your boots.

Most of the hunting that weekend was confined to glassing from the river. Even the sheep seemed to be hanging low as we only spotted a few bands of rams over the course of the first three days, with nothing that appeared to be an eye-popper.

A few weeks later I was back at it again, this time solo, and hunting by truck off the BLM road system. The weather was more cooperative, and I did manage to spot a fair number of sheep, including one magnificent ram that I guessed would go in the high 180s. He was lounging with three smaller rams on a hanging bench in a steep canyon. I was still carrying my bow and planned a stalk that would put me within 50 yards but, as is often the case, something happened and the sheep slipped across the canyon, casually observing my stalk from a safe distance. I did get a great opportunity to sit and study this ram at 150 yards for over an hour, piecing together the aspects of horn size and learning a lot about judging a trophy-class sheep.

One of the highlights of my sheep hunting experience came on this trip when I awoke at 4 a.m. to a spectacular northern lights show. It was close to wake-up time, so I decided to brew coffee and sit in my camp chair watching the show and listening to the coyotes.

The 2006 sheep season was nearly at the midpoint when I embarked on the third hunt. On this trip, my very good friend, fishing buddy and bowhunting mentor Mike Ellig accompanied me. Although being a sheep-hunting novice like me, Mike has as much experience hunting North American big-game animals as anyone I know, and I looked forward to his help and companionship. We would again be hunting by vehicle but chose to hunt a part of the hunting district that had so far been tough to get to because of weather conditions.

On the evening of our first day, we spotted a lone ram feeding on a grassy knoll. He looked good at 800 yards through the spotting scope, so I decided to stalk in for a closer look. As I got closer, the ram moved just out of sight below the grassy knoll, a perfect condition for a bow stalk. I slipped off my pack, nocked an arrow and carefully closed to where I thought he should be.

At that moment I heard Mike, 500 yards away, whistle my attention. As I turned to see what he was telling me, I noticed a movement to my left. There he was, 40 yards away, head concealed by a juniper bush, body fully exposed. I didn't want to shoot because I wasn't sure how big he was. After about 15 seconds, the sheep had enough and bolted to about 70 yards before stopping and looking me over. I was heartbroken and awed at the same moment. He was a massive ram with huge bases, horn clearly below the jawline and mass extending along the horn length to the broomed ends. An interesting thing about this animal was that he carried a radio collar. We stared each other down for at least 30 minutes before he again had enough and disappeared down into a maze of steep clay cliffs and draws. The shot was too far for me to take with the bow, and my gun was safely stowed back in the truck. I learned a valuable lesson from this experience — decide whether or not you are going to shoot before getting too close, especially on sheep, where careful study is required if you want to be sure.

That night in camp I made a pivotal decision; I was going to start carrying the rifle. My main goal was to shoot a ram that would make the records book, and I didn't know how many opportunities I would get for a sheep like the collared ram. I love the challenge that archery presents but, more than that, I wanted a trophy sheep.

We spent most of the next day trying to find the collared ram with no success. Toward late afternoon, we glassed four rams in a jumbled canyon. As we looked them over, it became apparent that one looked exceptional. At 600 yards, you could see the length of horn and what appeared to be good mass. This sheep didn't appear to be broomed at all.

After some on-again, off-again decision making, I decided that he didn't look as massive as the collared ram and that we should keep looking. I had half the season ahead of me plus the rut so I was very nervous about making a hasty decision. Still, that night in camp I seriously wondered if I had not made yet another mistake.

The last full day of this hunt broke clear, cool, and calm. We again spent the day looking

BIGHORN SHEEP
Second Award – 198 ³/₈
▼ ▼ ▼ ▼ ▼
STEPHEN C. MORRICAL

Photograph courtesy of Stephen C. Morrical

Stephen C. Morrical is pictured above with his award-winning bighorn sheep taken in Blaine County, Montana, during the 2006 season. Morrical's ram has a final score of 198-3/8 points and received a Second Place Award at the 26th Big Game Awards Program in Fort Worth, Texas.

for the collared ram with no success, ending up the day back where we had seen the other big ram the evening before. After splitting up and doing some careful spotting, I found the band of rams seen the afternoon before about a mile across the canyon feeding. Mike and I decided that with only an hour of shooting light left, our best option was to jump in the truck, drive around to the opposite ridge, and try to approach these sheep from above. It took us 40 minutes to get to where we wanted to park, so time was dwindling fast.

As we stalked down off the ridgetop and closed in on landmarks guiding us to the last known whereabouts of the rams, I could feel my pulse quickening and throat tightening. The wind was dead calm, so every step was made as quietly as possible. As I inched closer to an overlook, I couldn't figure out where the sheep had disappeared to. Finally, on the last step, I noticed the back of a sheep no more than 45 yards straight below me. I quickly ducked, hand-signaled Mike the situation, and together we belly crawled to the edge of the overlook.

On the hanging bench, totally unaware of our presence, were three of the rams, including the biggest one I had agonized over. At such a close distance, I didn't need the binoculars or the scope to confirm horn size. His bases were much more massive than originally thought and the horn extended well below the jawline

BIGHORN SHEEP
Second Award – 198 ³/₈

▼ ▼ ▼ ▼ ▼

STEPHEN C. MORRICAL

and back up over the bridge of the nose. The mass at the midpoint appeared to be equal to the base. A lot of things were going through my mind those last few seconds, but foremost was the underlying question — was this going to be it?

A few seconds of viewing this tremendous animal and the answer was clear. I whispered to Mike that I was going to take him. The huge grin on his face was all I needed to confirm his approval. From our position above the sheep, I elected to take the shot straight down through the top of the back. The 180-grain Nosler partition bullet hit the mark, resulting in a clean, quick kill. The rangefinder verified the shot at 41 yards.

After waiting a few moments to make sure he wasn't going anywhere, we picked our way down to him. As we got closer, I couldn't believe the beautiful and massive animal before us. The horns were much heavier than we had first thought and the tips were hardly broomed, curling above the bridge of the nose. We spent those first several minutes just taking in the moment, admiring our trophy, and thanking our good fortune.

The next few hours were spent caping and skinning the ram by headlamp under a clear October night sky. We then ascended the canyon with the head and cape. We retrieved the quarters early the next morning and headed straight to the nearest ranch to contact Montana Department of Fish, Wildlife & Parks to obtain the necessary transport permit. The wardens that checked us were not only impressed with the size of my ram but were also awed by the fact that he was aged at 5-1/2 years old! What a tribute to the quality of habitat and genetics of this sheep population.

When I reflect back on my 2006 sheep hunting experience, I realize how fortunate I was to draw the permit and hunt such a magnificent animal in the unspoiled setting of the Missouri River Breaks. In listening to my account of the hunt, one may think that my only measure of success was to harvest a "book" animal. But hunting is not only about killing a trophy animal. It's the thrill of the hunt, the companionship, and the true connection that hunters have with the natural world that really matters. ▲

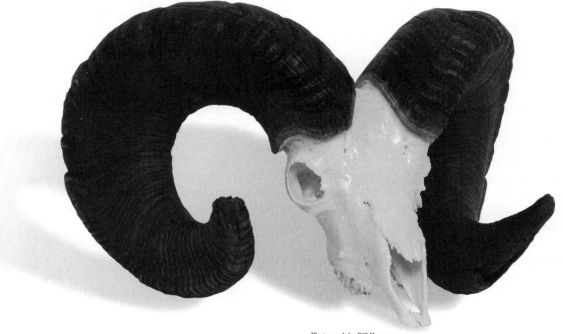

Photograph by Bill Honza

TROPHY STATS

▼ ▼ ▼ ▼ ▼

Category
Bighorn Sheep

Score
197 $1/8$

Length of Horn
Right: 41 $4/8$ Left: 40 $7/8$

Circumference of Base
Right: 16 $1/8$ Left: 16

Greatest Spread
22 $4/8$

Location
Ewin Creek, British Columbia – 2004

Hunter
Steven S. Bruggeman

BIGHORN SHEEP
Third Award – 197 ¹/₈
▼ ▼ ▼ ▼ ▼ ▼ ▼ ▼ ▼

STEVEN S. BRUGGEMAN

My hunt for a Rocky Mountain bighorn ram began in January 2004 at the National FNAWS convention in Reno, Nevada. I had a lengthy conversation with Bob Fontana of Elk Valley Bighorn Outfitters about the possibilities of taking a big ram with a muzzleloader. Based on Bob's optimism and previous success, I purchased the late-season permit and booked the hunt. I planned to travel to British Columbia in early November to search for a trophy ram.

In late July I received the tragic news that Bob had been killed by a charging cape buffalo while hunting in Tanzania. I immediately sent a note expressing my condolences to his wife, Anna, and was surprised to get a quick response saying, "Don't worry about your hunt; everything is well organized and will go on as planned."

Knowing that Bob would not be there, I asked my good friend, John Lewton, to join me on the hunt. John has spent more time locating, filming, and judging bighorn rams than anyone else I know. I was sure he would be a big help on my hunt.

On November 4, I flew to Kalispell, Montana. John picked me up and we drove from there to Fernie, B.C. There we met Anna and her guides, Jake Wiebe, Ryan Damstrom, and Malt Lewenberger.

Since the area we had to hunt was very large, we spread out and searched several areas each day, hoping to find a big ram. For the first few days we rode horses, hiked ridges through knee-deep snow, and covered some spectacular country, but found only a few small rams.

On the evening of the fourth day of the hunt, we heard that a friend of one of the guides had seen a big ram while deer hunting that day. Early the next morning we started glassing the area. About noon, we located two big rams with a bunch of ewes. They were near the top of a big south-facing ridge that had some exposed grass that the sheep were feeding on. We got a little closer and took a careful look through the spotting scopes. After comparing notes, everyone

Photograph by Jack Reneau

Steven S. Bruggeman accepting his plaque and medal from Buck Buckner, Vice President and Chairman of the Big Game Records Committee.

Photograph courtesy of Steven S. Bruggeman

Steven S. Bruggeman (second from right and holding the sheep) is pictured above with his award-winning bighorn sheep scoring 197-1/8 points. Also pictured are (from left to right) John Lewton, Matt Lewenberger, Jake Wiebe, and Ryan Damstrom.

agreed that the biggest ram was in the 190-plus category.

We planned the stalk and headed up the mountain. Three hours later we were on the ridgetop carefully peeking over and looking for the rams. Because I was hunting with a muzzleloader, I needed to get close. As we slowly crept forward, we started spotting ewes; then a bunch of cow elk came into view, and suddenly we were pinned down. I had taken off my jacket after overheating during the climb, but now lying in the snow, I was freezing.

As we lay watching and unable to move, the biggest ram came into view, but I was too low to get a shot. Daylight was starting to slip away, and I needed to do something or our chance would be gone. When the ram finally turned broadside and was isolated from the ewes and the elk, I rose to one knee and quickly took the shot at 145 yards. Smoke from the muzzleloader made it impossible to see where the ram went, but I was confident that the shot had been good. I reloaded, and we hurried down to where the ram had been standing. We followed his tracks a short distance to where he had fallen into the branches of a big pine tree.

As I put my hands on his horns to pull his head free, it was obvious I had taken the trophy of a lifetime. When someone suggested that we get out a tape measure, I said, "No, let's just enjoy the beauty of this magnificent ram and take some photos before we run out of light."

There was a lot of celebrating on the mountain and into the wee hours of the morning. The whole crew admired the ram, and many of their friends stopped by to see it. My only regret is that Bob Fontana was not there to enjoy our success, but I know that he was looking down on our hunt and was very proud of his wife and crew and the great job they all did. ▲

B&C Photo Archives

Trophy owner Steven S. Bruggeman, left, and his guest Doug Carlson, enjoy the Friday Night Welcoming Reception at the Doral Tesoro Hotel and Golf Club. Bruggeman's bighorn sheep received a Third Place Award at the 26th Big Game Awards Program.

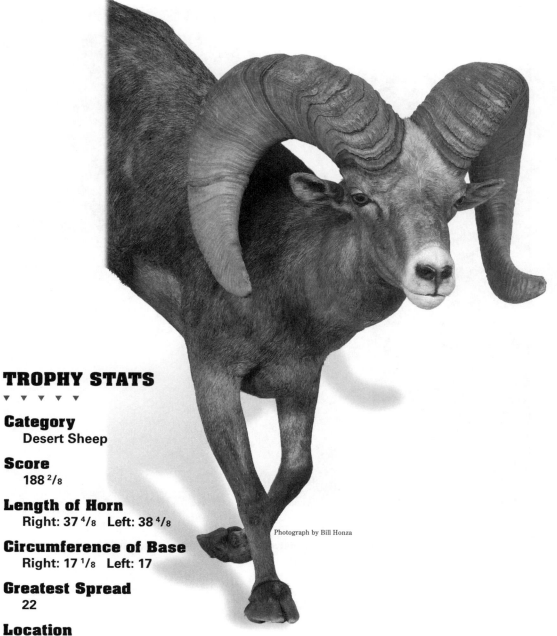

Photograph by Bill Honza

TROPHY STATS

▼ ▼ ▼ ▼ ▼

Category
Desert Sheep

Score
188 $^2/_8$

Length of Horn
Right: 37 $^4/_8$ Left: 38 $^4/_8$

Circumference of Base
Right: 17 $^1/_8$ Left: 17

Greatest Spread
22

Location
Hidalgo Co., New Mexico – 2006

Hunter
Russell A. Young

DESERT SHEEP
First Award – 188 ²/₈

▼ ▼ ▼ ▼ ▼ ▼ ▼ ▼ ▼

RUSSELL A. YOUNG

My hunt for desert sheep began in February 2006 when I acquired a coveted permit for New Mexico. I immediately called my friends Chris Harlow and Tyson Hatch, owners of Double H Outfitters out of Arizona. Both Chris and Tyson have extensive experience hunting desert sheep throughout the Southwest.

In 2005, they guided a hunter to the New Mexico State record for desert sheep. During their scouting for the 2005 hunt, they observed several exceptional rams in addition to the one they harvested. Our goal was to find and harvest one of these rams.

We would be hunting the Peloncio Mountains that run through the southwest corner of New Mexico. Our camp was set up west of the small town of Rodeo.

Chris and Tyson began scouting in March. Over the next five months they located several rams they thought would make Boone and Crockett. They named the largest ram "droopy" because of how far below the jaw his horns drooped. Tyson had first seen Droopy in 2004. Tyson said that he told his wife Misty that he found a ram that could score 190 in a few years.

I arrived in New Mexico on July 30 for the August 1 opener. I was met with monsoon rains that were causing flooding and washing out roads. The Peloncio Mountains were desperate for the rain. The area had been dry for almost a year.

It continued to rain for the next six days. The sheep that we had been scouting dispersed, and we were unable to locate Droopy. Chris and Tyson told me to go home for a few weeks while they continued to scout and things dried out.

Over the next six weeks it continued to rain, delivering 18 inches to the area. The desert was now in full bloom with flowers, snakes, gnats, and mosquitoes.

On September 14, Chris, Tyson, and I spoke by phone. They told me that they had seen more than 30 different rams since I left. They

Photograph by Jack Reneau

Russell A. Young accepting his plaque and medal from Buck Buckner, Vice President and Chairman of the Big Game Records Committee.

Russell A. Young with his award-winning desert sheep that is the largest hunter-taken desert ram in New Mexico history. The ram, which scores 188-2/8 points, was taken in Hidalgo County during the 2006 season.

also said that Droopy was the largest ram on the mountain. Chris said that the ram had the biggest bases and lowest drop below the jaw of any ram he had ever seen in more than 25 years of sheep hunting. He also said the ram could be the new state record.

I returned to New Mexico on September 17 to continue my hunt. Chris located Droopy too late on September 19 for a stalk.

We found Droopy traveling with two other rams and two ewes the next morning along with two other herds of sheep on the same mountain. We could not make a stalk without spooking one of the herds. At 10 a.m., the herds separated and moved in opposite directions. It was time for us to make our move.

Tyson and I would make the stalk while Chris stayed back to keep track of the sheep in case they moved on us. Tyson and I had to work our way up a narrow wash to get within range.

As we crawled up the wash, I heard a noise. I thought that it came from Tyson, who was behind me.

Tyson said, "Did you hear that?"

I looked back and said, "I heard something."

He said, "You just crawled within 18 inches of a rattlesnake in this bush!"

I said, "Well, it's your turn now."

We ran out of cover just within rifle range. From this location, I was able to successfully make the shot with my .30-378 Weatherby.

When we walked up to the ram, Chris said, "I think we are going to be pleasantly surprised with the score of this ram."

Chris is a big man with big hands that couldn't reach around the bases. I got down on my back and kicked my legs in the air like a kid.

The ram is officially the New Mexico state record for a hunter-taken trophy. It took the Gold Award and Rifle Award of Excellence at the Foundation for North American Wild Sheep Convention in Salt Lake City in January 2007.

I would like to offer special thanks to Chris Harlow and Tyson Hatch for their hard work helping me harvest this great ram. Also, I want to thank the New Mexico Game and Fish Department for its outstanding sheep management program. ▲

DESERT SHEEP
First Award – 188 $^2/_8$
▼ ▼ ▼ ▼ ▼
RUSSELL A. YOUNG

Photograph by Bill Honza

TROPHY STATS

▼ ▼ ▼ ▼ ▼

Category
Desert Sheep

Score
185 $^2/_8$

Length of Horn
Right: 38 $^4/_8$ Left: 37 $^6/_8$

Circumference of Base
Right: 16 Left: 16 $^2/_8$

Greatest Spread
20 $^4/_8$

Location
Sonora, Mexico – 2005

Hunter
K. Michael Ingram

DESERT SHEEP
Second Award – 185 $^2/_8$
▼ ▼ ▼ ▼ ▼ ▼ ▼ ▼ ▼

K. MICHAEL INGRAM

Hunting desert sheep is an incredibly exceptional opportunity. On the rare occasion the chance is presented, not many hunters take it lightly. Every resource available is often brought into play to make it the hunt of a lifetime.

Michael Ingram boarded his plane for his hunt destination, excited as a kid on his first hunting trip. From time to time, his thoughts drifted to desert sheep, and rams with yellowish-tinted horns contrasting against the stark desert landscape.

They headed out to their hunting area, a stark landscape full of loose rock and with little for vegetation. On the first day, they saw some rams but decided to pass. On the second day, they saw some of the same rams, but also saw the track of what looked like something a little bigger. That evening, they found him.

Mike took the shot with his .300 WSM and connected. He was both excited and nervous as they followed the track of the wounded ram. He and his guide continued to follow the occasional blood droplet and scuffed or displaced rock until it was dark. Not wanting to disturb any evidence by bumbling around in the dark, they backed off until morning.

The next morning they found the wounded ram again. He was not alone now, though. He had taken up with a band of ten other rams. They had to wait patiently, both to properly identify the ram and also to make sure they could make a clean shot on him.

At 1:30 p.m. on March 25, 2005, all of his hard work had culminated in this – the giant desert ram was there, 175 yards away. Michael shouldered his rifle and fired. As he approached, he couldn't believe his eyes. This ram surpassed even his highest hopes and expectations. It was a massive, massive ram, with a nice tight curl. Surely, he had to be one of the biggest rams for miles around.

Michael Ingram's 2005 desert ram is one of only 39 desert sheep in history to have ever been recorded with a score higher than 185 B&C points. With bases of 16" (right) and 16-2/8" (left), this ram is truly the trophy dreams are made of. This sheep received the 2nd Award for desert sheep at Boone and Crockett Club's 26th Big Game Awards Banquet. ▲

Photograph by Bill Honza

TROPHY STATS

▼ ▼ ▼ ▼ ▼

Category
Desert Sheep

Score
183 $^5/_8$

Length of Horn
Right: 36 $^6/_8$ Left: 36 $^3/_8$

Circumference of Base
Right: 15 $^6/_8$ Left: 15 $^6/_8$

Greatest Spread
24 $^6/_8$

Location
Brewster Co., Texas – 2005

Hunter
Terry J. Fricks

BOONE AND CROCKETT CLUB'S

DESERT SHEEP
Third Award – 183 ⁵/₈
▼ ▼ ▼ ▼ ▼ ▼ ▼ ▼ ▼

Terry J. Fricks

I raised my rifle and entertained fleeting thoughts of my Grand Slam. Quickly, I put that out of my mind and focused on the heaviest ram I'd ever seen.

I centered the crosshairs just behind the ram's shoulder. I asked Justin if he had the ram ranged. I heard Justin take a deep breath, followed by a long sigh. The range finder was not cooperating.

The big ram was unsettled, nervous. I needed to shoot. My rate of breathing increased, my pulse raced. I needed to make the shot now. I was about to squeeze the trigger, when Justin whispered, "258 yards."

As if in slow motion, my finger squeezed the trigger. I felt the 7mm Magnum's recoil, heard the shot. The Federal Premium 160-grain Nosler Partition bullet sped toward its target.

The ram's head instantly went down. It slid off the backside of the rock in slow motion and disappeared. Only two rams ran away. But every hunter knows—it's not over 'til it's over.

Sheep fever first struck me on a moose hunt in British Columbia in 1975. One of the guys in camp was there to hunt Stone's sheep. He took his sheep on his second day out, and I concluded sheep hunting was fun and must be pretty easy — little did I know.

After a pair of hunts in Alaska, two more in British Columbia, and one in Baja, I came to grasp the true realities of sheep hunting. In the early 1980s, however, I put sheep hunting on the back burner, raised a family and built a business. I was not to return to my passion for nearly 20 years.

In 2000, sheep hunting came back into focus. In 2003, I took a bighorn sheep in Alberta, and that was when I reconnected to my Grand Slam dream. Like so many others, I needed that elusive desert sheep. But getting the permit would prove no small task. After years of trying, when it looked like drawing a permit was

Photograph by Jack Reneau

Terry J. Fricks accepting his plaque and medal from Buck Buckner, Vice President and Chairman of the Big Game Records Committee.

unlikely, I began to give serious consideration to buying one. I found out that several states would have permits available at the 2005 FNAWS convention. I wound up with the Texas permit allowing me to hunt Elephant Mountain south of Alpine.

After I bought the permit, Texas Parks and Wildlife area manager Mike Pittman and I put our heads together and decided to start the hunt three weeks later, on Sunday, March 20, 2005. I had less than a month to prepare, but I work out regularly and stay in decent shape.

SHEEP FEVER FIRST STRUCK ME ON A MOOSE HUNT IN BRITISH COLUMBIA IN 1975. ONE OF THE GUYS IN CAMP WAS THERE TO HUNT STONE'S SHEEP. HE TOOK HIS SHEEP ON HIS SECOND DAY OUT, AND I CONCLUDED SHEEP HUNTING WAS FUN AND MUST BE PRETTY EASY — LITTLE DID I KNOW.

I wanted to improve my field-judging ability. This was to be my ninth sheep hunt, and I had a fair idea of what I wanted to shoot, but it never hurts to sharpen your skills. I have spent years hunting deer in that west Texas environment, but never desert sheep. The horn size of this species, in relation to its body, is different than the others I have taken. With its small body and short hair, the species' horns look enormous.

To round out my skills, I picked up several books by my favorite author, Jack O'Connor, and revisited the chapters on sheep hunting. I ordered videos on field judging, and I studied every sheep picture I could find in magazines. Finally, like flash cards, I had my wife show me pictures of sheep, and I tried to estimate their scores.

The Hunt

Day 1, Sunday, March 20, 2005

Mike met me in Alpine, and we drove the 25 miles south to Elephant Mountain. When we got to the big house, I met the Texas Parks and Wildlife staff who were there to assist me with my hunt. Justin Foster was to be my guide. Justin runs the Sierra Diablo Wildlife Management Area.

After lunch, Justin, Pat Latham, and I headed up the mountain to stretch our legs. We drove around the north side and up a jeep trail to a bench halfway up the mountain. As we drove, Justin and I talked about my sheep. Naturally, like everyone else, I wanted the biggest sheep on the mountain, but I told Justin I'd be happy with a mature ram with heavy, heavy horns. The actual score was secondary.

Toward the end of that trail, we looked up and spotted several sheep. When we stopped for a better look, they all turned out to be rams. The sheep were about halfway up the mountain. As we got closer, we saw several more animals scattered over the mountain. By the time we reached the end of the road, we had counted 26 rams.

We donned our backpacks and headed south, around the west side of the mountain. Staying on the bench, we glassed ahead and above. Now and then, Justin would separate and go down the mountain to glass the heads of draws toward the bottom. The plan was for Pat and me to continue walking and hook up with Justin later. We walked ahead over the rocks, the yucca and sotol brush all around us. And as a

DESERT SHEEP
Third Award – 183 ⁵/₈
▼ ▼ ▼ ▼ ▼
Terry J. Fricks

lechugilla thorn stuck me in my shin, I was taken back to a point in time when I hunted deer with my sons in the Apache Mountains. The boys and I had that lease for 15 years.

Not one day into my hunt, and I was already reminded how much I love to hunt that big country. The mountains in west Texas are unique. While the elevations are not as high as some, I believe the terrain is just as rough, in its own way, as any sheep country in the world. Each square inch seems to have a rock. Every place you step there is rock beneath your foot, from the size of a walnut to the size of a school bus, and they're all loose. Footing is treacherous, and everything that grows there is sharp and prickly. It's awesome country and a lot of fun to hunt.

We saw more than 30 rams, three or four of which were book sheep for sure — not a bad first half-day of hunting. I didn't have any second thoughts about passing up those sheep. I wanted a mature ram with heavy horns, and that was a priority over B&C score.

Over the next few days we spotted several very good rams and made stalks on a couple, but in both cases I decided to hold out.

Day 5, Thursday, March 24, 2005

We left the big house at 7 a.m. "Where are we going, Justin?" I asked.

Justin explained that we would drive around to the east side of the mountain, walk up the old jeep trail in Rough Canyon and work our way west.

The trail took us a third of the way up the side of the mountain, and we angled across to the west. About mid-morning, Justin spotted him first, about 450 yards ahead, a little bit below us on a bench. "Wow," Justin exclaimed, "that's one heavy ram."

I put my binoculars on the sheep and instantly knew this was the best ram we had seen on the trip — the best ram I had ever seen on any previous hunt. There was a smaller ram with him. Neither had seen us.

Carefully, we set up the spotting scope. At 40X, we saw an old mature ram with massive horns, but we couldn't tell for sure about his length. The left horn looked longer. Both tips were broomed well back, and flared slightly.

It was late morning and already the shimmering heat waves would not allow us a good look at the ram. Still, we agreed he was a shooter. The shot was too far, though, and we decided we would have to get closer. The ram was lying down, staring directly at us. Circling up and ahead was not an option because the wind was blowing back down the mountain.

Approaching from below was not an option either, because the other ram might see us. Were there other animals below that might see us if we attempted a stalk? Now it was a waiting game, waiting for the sheep to move.

Terry J. Fricks, left, and his hunting crew are pictured above with Terry's desert sheep taken in Brewster County, Texas. The award-winnning ram, which scores 183-5/8 points, is the new Texas state record.

There was a ridge just ahead. If we could get there, we could cut 150 yards off the shot. For that to work, the sheep would have to move or quit looking in our direction. We expected the rams to move down off the front edge of the bench, and the smaller ram did just that. The larger ram, however, got up and moved toward us. It was like a gift from above.

The big guy was soon out of sight below the brow of the hill. I looked to the right, along the ridge ahead. Now was the time to move. As we cautiously climbed up the ridge, we expected to see the ram feeding 200 yards below.

When we took a peek over the top, there were now three rams visible, and they were all headed down. When they reached the edge of the bench, they stopped. One of the rams went over the edge. We didn't get a good look at him, but we were pretty sure he wasn't anything to get too excited about.

The big ram was lying down on a rock the size of a truck. The third smallest ram just stood there looking at us. He had us pegged. At 300 yards, looking through the low brush, we couldn't be certain which ram was which. The big ram was broadside to us, but we could only see his left horn.

Justin asked if I felt comfortable with the shot. I replied emphatically, "No!"

I wanted to get above the brush and find a better rest. If this ram was everything we gauged him to be, he would be the trophy of my lifetime, and I didn't want to do anything stupid.

There was a good-sized rock about 30 yards ahead that would make a perfect rest. The only problem was we would have to crawl in full view of the rams most of the way, and one of the rams already had us pegged. We agreed that we should take another look through the spotting scope and make doubly sure the bedded ram was the same one we had previously spotted.

When we set up the scope, we saw the huge left horn. I wanted to confirm that the right horn was unbroken and comparable to the left, and I didn't want to move until the decision to take the shot was made.

Finally, the ram stood up, turned 360 degrees, and lay down in the same place. In that instant, we got a good look at both horns. Now we were certain, and I could advance to the rock and take up a shooting position. I handed my binocular/rangefinder combo to Justin and asked him to give me the yardage when we got into position.

As I approached the ram, I could not believe my eyes. He was more massive than we had imagined. The final B&C score, after drying, was 183-5/8 inches, a new Texas state record and a great tribute to all the good folks at Texas Parks and Wildlife and their outstanding sheep program. My hunt never would have happened without the dedication and long hours invested by all the volunteer members of the Texas Bighorn Society who have helped make the Texas Sheep Program the successful operation that it is today.

I can't say enough about the Texas Parks and Wildlife guys who helped on this once-in-a-lifetime hunt. They were as interested in my success as I was. Thank you all! You are a great bunch of guys, and you really made my hunt the most memorable, most enjoyable experience of my life. ▲

DESERT SHEEP
Third Award – 183 ⁵/₈
▼ ▼ ▼ ▼ ▼

Terry J. Fricks

Photograph by Bill Honza

TROPHY STATS
▼ ▼ ▼ ▼ ▼

Category
Desert Sheep

Score
182 $^6/_8$

Length of Horn
Right: 36 $^5/_8$ Left: 39 $^5/_8$

Circumference of Base
Right: 15 $^4/_8$ Left: 15 $^2/_8$

Greatest Spread
17

Location
Hidalgo Co., New Mexico – 2005

Hunter
Thomas D. Friedkin

DESERT SHEEP
Fourth Award – 182 6/8
▼ ▼ ▼ ▼ ▼ ▼ ▼ ▼ ▼

THOMAS D. FRIEDKIN

In September 2005, southwestern New Mexico was unseasonably warm — a charitable description perhaps, because in actuality it was extremely and painfully hot. Thomas D. "Dan" Friedkin had come to this region to hunt desert bighorn sheep, and the excessive heat made the hunting even more challenging than normal.

Despite the heat, the hunter and guide Chris Harlo were optimistic, and with good reason. One morning they spooked an especially big ram out of his bed and watched him disappeared over a distant mountaintop. One quick glance was all they needed to know that this was a ram worth following, no matter how far he might go.

They formulated a game plan that seemed simple enough — follow the ram. However, that would prove much more difficult than either hunter or guide would suspect. Decisions are made on what you see and know. Sometimes you can't anticipate what might happen. They knew it would be a long hike to the mountain but didn't anticipate just how much further the ram would go once it went over the other side.

Packing gun, gear, and spotting scopes on their backs, they set out. Just as fatigue from the long hike was starting to make them drop their guard, they heard the unmistakable rattle of a snake that was within striking distance of both of them. That brought them to full attention. A fresh rush of adrenaline now aided part of their climb up the next mountain.

Unfortunately, adrenaline wears off quickly under the 100-degree sun. By now it was midday, and the two-man team had traveled five miles. Even so, they were only halfway up the mountain that the ram had so easily crossed earlier that morning. Unspoken so far, but realized by both men, was that at this pace and in this heat, their small supply of water might not be sufficient to avoid dehydration. But thoughts of cold water rapidly disappeared as another rattlesnake set off its alarm just off of the narrow path the hunters were following. They gave the snake a wide berth and kept moving up the mountain.

> JUST AS FATIGUE FROM THE LONG HIKE WAS STARTING TO MAKE THEM DROP THEIR GUARD, THEY HEARD THE UNMISTAKABLE RATTLE OF A SNAKE THAT WAS WITHIN STRIKING DISTANCE OF BOTH OF THEM. THAT BROUGHT THEM TO FULL ATTENTION. A FRESH RUSH OF ADRENALINE NOW AIDED PART OF THEIR CLIMB UP THE NEXT MOUNTAIN.

With dry and parched mouths, a burning sun overhead, and snakes on their minds, they finally reached the top of the mountain. The crest revealed more walking to be done. They would need to reach the downslope of the other side of the mountain before they could reassess their plan.

A mile or so later they were overlooking the valley that lay below the downslope of the mountain they had just climbed. Quickly, they worked to set up their spotting scopes to scan the valley below. With a keen eye and a stroke of good luck, Dan spotted the ram in the shade under a slippery rock overhang on the side of the next mountain over. With open country between them and the ram, the new game plan was to sneak around the backside of the mountain and come over the top of him.

More than an hour had gone by as hunter and guide stalked around and above the big ram. They crept ever closer to the landmarks that told them where the ram had been bedded, and decided they were as close as they could get without spooking him. They waited 45 minutes, quietly discussing the distance covered that day. Their best guess was about eight miles. The conversation kept their minds off of their thirst, but all the while they were much more worried that the ram had walked off while they were on the backside of the mountain.

Their patience was rewarded when the ram suddenly leapt up only 20 yards away from the very overhang that they were on. The bighorn ran downhill, crossed a small river, and stopped. That was all the time Dan needed to find the sheep in his scope and release the bullet that would drop the desert ram in his tracks.

As they approached the animal, both hunter and guide realized what an exceptional trophy they had lying before them. They admired the size, color, and mass of the horns and the ram itself. Both felt that the only thing that could equal the quality of the ram was the quality of the hunt itself. ▲

B&C Photo Archives

Allan Naught holds the plaque for his father's award-winning typical Columbia blacktail deer while his guest, Ashley, looks on. Allan's father, Larry Naught, had taken his blacktail 52 years earlier. The buck is still proudly displayed in the family home today.

Photograph by Bill Honza

TROPHY STATS

▼ ▼ ▼ ▼ ▼

Category
Dall's Sheep

Score
178 $^4/_8$

Length of Horn
Right: 43 $^4/_8$ Left: 43 $^4/_8$

Circumference of Base
Right: 14 $^5/_8$ Left: 14 $^4/_8$

Greatest Spread
28 $^4/_8$

Location
Mackenzie Mts., Northwest
Territories – 2005

Hunter
Cody A. Miller

DALL'S SHEEP
First Award – 178 ⁴/₈

▼ ▼ ▼ ▼ ▼ ▼ ▼ ▼ ▼

CODY A. MILLER

By Cody Miller and Scotty Boyd

This hunt started over 20 years ago when my high school buddy, Dr. Rocky Crate, planted the "sheep fever" in me. Every time I stopped by his veterinary office he would spend most the time talking about sheep hunting and, in later years, about sheep hunting and FNAWS. He was also a good friend of my brother and my lifelong hunting partner, Jody Miller. I want to thank them both for getting me up the mountain and into sheep hunting.

This was Jody's third sheep hunt; I had joined him all three times. The first two were horseback hunts, but still very challenging physically. Jody says that backpack hunting is the only way to go. No backtracking to the horses, and make camp wherever you want. My thoughts are that you make camp wherever you collapse.

For our hunt, we decided on Stan Steven's Mackenzie Mountain Outfitters. From then on, it was time to get ready. In June and July, I walked around my neighborhood with a 40-pound pack on my back in 80-degree heat trying to get in sheep shape. I cussed Jody on a daily basis.

We left for Northwest Territories on August 4, 2005, and were in base camp a day later. When we got off the floatplane, we were met by Stan Stevens, his guides, and the departing hunters. We admired their trophies of old rams and nice caribou, and then moved our gear into the vacated cabins.

Stan stopped and chatted with each of us, getting to know us a little better so he could make guide assignments. I was assigned to Scotty Boyd and his wonderful pack dog, Moose. Scotty has been guiding for 20 years, and this was his 13th year with Stan. We are both real estate associates in different countries when we aren't hunting or guiding; it was an excellent mix of personalities, and it turned into a great friendship.

We sighted-in our rifles and then headed for the cook's house. We could smell a wonderful aroma, which turned out to be a roast of hindquarter Dall's sheep with all the fixings.

Stan had us up early the next morning, and Helen had a huge breakfast ready for us with fresh blueberry pancakes, bacon, eggs, and sausage. Stan was flying Scotty and me out last because Scotty mentioned that he had not hunted the front range for a few years. He said it's tougher hunting there, and the flies come at you like a million linebackers, but there are some good rams out there.

Stan landed us on a gravel bar next to a river, in a spot Scotty had not hunted before. Stan told us to really watch the wind here; the rams liked to get on the edge of the cliff face all the way up the valley. They stayed in the wind to keep the bugs away. He said these were "bush rams" and tough to get. He then got in the plane and took off empty in 80 yards. Those are amazing planes.

Scotty loaded about 25 pounds of supplies on Moose. We then shouldered our packs and headed up the valley. After camp was set up, we glassed for sheep, but only saw a few ewes and lambs.

After a while it started to rain, thunder, and lightning with a vengeance. We crawled in our tent, ate some of Helen's famous "guide bread" and read our books. We knew we couldn't hunt for 12 hours after flying but with the weather we were in, there was no hurry anyway.

> I TOLD JODY THAT SINCE HE TALKED ME INTO COMING THAT WE SHOULD COME BACK ON MAYBE A TWO-ON-ONE HUNT, AND THAT I'D BE ANOTHER SET OF EYES. I EVEN TOLD HIM HE COULD HAVE FIRST CHOICE. JODY LOOKED AT ME AND SAID, "CODY, FOR THE REST OF YOUR LIFE I HAVE FIRST CHOICE." AND, YOU KNOW, THAT'S OKAY BY ME.

I drifted off to sleep and awoke about 3:30 a.m. I looked over and Scotty was already awake. I asked him if we should get up now. "Why not?" He said. "I can't sleep with your snoring anyway." It's a good thing Scotty has a great sense of humor.

Scotty boiled some water for hot chocolate and his famous breakfast of ichbum soup with a can of Brunswick herring in teriyaki sauce; I ate oatmeal. He loaded up Moose with the spotting scope and some food for lunch, put our packs on, and headed out. The flies were out in full force. We took some pictures of the sunrise on our way up the cut in the mountain pass that would get us on top.

When we got to the top, the wind was wrong, so we had to circle around the cliff down in the timber. We hiked up another ridge and did some glassing for a while. Scotty spotted two sheep but they were out of view before we got the spotting scope out. We spotted a sheep by itself but it was too far away to make anything out.

We built a wind break under a thick, stunted spruce and waited to see if any more sheep came into view. After an hour, Scotty said that we should circle around to that ridge, and then climb up to the edge of the cliff face. That way we could hunt the cliff face back with a good wind in our face.

There was an ample amount of bugs chewing on us but when we got to the cliff face the wind was too strong for them. That's why the rams like lying on the edge; it was their only respite from the swarm.

Below the cliff edges, it was a 2,000-foot drop to the river bottom. There was a multitude of sheep sign and trails here. There was also enough feed and water to hold them along here for miles.

We hunted the cliff face slowly, expecting to see a ram at anytime. We were on the sheep trail when Scotty looked down and said, "That is the biggest sheep track I have ever seen!"

Scotty pulled out his camera and took a few pictures of a small bird called a plover. As he got closer, he peeked over the rise and spotted a small ram by himself 350 yards away. Scotty took a closer look and said, "A full curl ram,

DALL'S SHEEP
First Award – 178 4/8
▼ ▼ ▼ ▼ ▼
Cody A. Miller

Cody, but not big enough. There might be some more with him, though."

The ram was feeding, so we waited for him to go out of sight before we continued. When we reached the next hilltop, we couldn't see the small ram but spotted seven rams about 550 yards away. They were all lying down right on the edge of the cliff, and one of them really stood out. Scotty put him in the spotting scope and said, "Wow! Cody, you better have a look at this."

I looked through his Leupold scope and said, "He's the one on the right."

Scotty said, "Yup. Do you see the other ram on his left?"

I said, "Yes, the small one."

Scotty said, "Cody, that is not a small ram. We would shoot that ram. It's just that other one on the right is making him look small."

I then asked him how big he was. "Cody, he is big. Really, really big, and that's all you need to know."

Scotty didn't want to put any more pressure on me than I already had. We continued to glass him, and he continued to get bigger and bigger. After about 30 minutes the tension was almost unbearable. I walked 80 yards back to the packs and sat with Moose to calm down.

Scotty kept watching the rams in the spotting scope. It was too far to shoot, and we couldn't get any closer without being spotted. We couldn't shoot him there anyway or he would surely fall off the edge to a 2,000-foot freefall. The wind was good so all we could do was watch them and wait for them to move and feed. After 45 minutes the big ram got up and stretched. The second large ram rubbed his horns against the big boy.

They then started to feed away from the cliff face. They were 450 yards away but Scotty knew we could get closer. We circled around a couple of small hills out of sight, hoping to be right on top of them. We had to be careful that the little ram we saw earlier wasn't still there. If we spooked him, he would certainly take them all with him.

We looked at the rams one more time before starting our stalk. There were now nine in the group! Maybe the small one had joined them. We both felt that we couldn't wait any longer. We dropped our packs and tied Moose. Scotty told him to stay, be quiet, and to please not mess this up for us. It was only his third sheep hunt.

Scotty pulled out his camera in hopes of getting it on film. We crawled up to look over the edge. No sheep. We low-crawled 80 yards to another hill, peeked over the edge, and there they were.

They were feeding left to right through a grove of stunted spruce trees; we were above them with the wind in our face. Scotty and I were whispering to each other, making sure we

Photograph courtesy of Cody A. Miller

Cody A. Miller is pictured above with pack dog Moose and Miller's award-winning Dall's sheep. The ram, which has a final score of 178-4/8 points, was taken in Northwest Territories' Mackenzie Mountains in 2005.

were both targeting the same ram. We weren't getting a good look at them as they meandered through the spruce trees.

All of the sudden, the two big rams stepped out together. I was lying down, with my rifle pointed downhill. Scotty whispered that my barrel might not clear the rocks in front of me, so I slowly crawled another 15 feet to make sure I was clear. Scotty whispered, "150 yards."

My heart starting pumping fast. Here I was, with a firm rest, good wind, and the ram of a lifetime only 150 yards away. Scotty got his camera on the ram and whispered, "The one in the back; now he's trotting; now he's stopped. Wait for the broadside."

Just then the ram turned broadside. My Browning A-Bolt .30-06, a 50th birthday present from my brother Jody, seemingly went off by itself. I didn't hear or feel the recoil but I did hear the whack. My ram stumbled, trotted 20 yards, and fell over. The 150-grain Nosler did the job.

Scotty was hollering, "Great shot through the heart!"

The other rams moved about 50 yards from their downed leader, gathered in a semicircle and stood there for about 10 minutes. Then the oldest ram trotted off, and the rest all followed their new leader.

I just lay there, watching my ram, while Scotty went back for Moose and our gear. When he returned, I mentioned the new leader was a real good ram. Scotty replied, "Just wait 'til you see what you got."

DALL'S SHEEP
First Award – 178 4/8
▼ ▼ ▼ ▼ ▼
CODY A. MILLER

As we walked up on our ram, we were both in awe. Scotty mentioned that in 20 years of guiding this was truly the nicest looking and the biggest ram he had ever been a part of. We aged the ram at 8-1/2 years and were amazed that he could have that mass and length at that age. Scotty couldn't stop grinning. He had finally guided a hunter to a record-book ram, and not just a book ram but a ram of a lifetime. He said he sure hoped I was a good tipper. What a kidder that Scotty is.

We loaded up two hindquarters on Moose; back straps, tenderloins, and miscellaneous cuts went to me; the head, cape, two front quarters, and ribs went on Scotty, which sounded fine to me, since Scotty's a lot younger.

It took us eight hours to get to camp. We had been up and at 'em for about 21 hours. I was totally exhausted. I couldn't even eat; I just collapsed in my sleeping bag. Scotty said it was the loudest snoring he'd ever heard, even with his ear plugs.

We radioed Stan and asked for a pick-up, but the winds were too strong, so we had to wait 12 hours or so. Back at main camp, nobody could believe it. As Stan went and got the other hunters to tell them, no one would believe him until they saw it.

Everyone in camp got a good ram except Walter Ford, who passed on some fine-looking rams, deciding instead to wait for his once-in-a-lifetime ram.

My brother Jody took an excellent ram — full curl, nice spread, a definite shooter, but not like mine. I told Jody that since he talked me into coming that we should come back on maybe a two-on-one hunt, and that I'd be another set of eyes. I even told him he could have first choice. Jody looked at me and said, "Cody, for the rest of your life I have first choice." And, you know, that's okay by me.

Thanks again to Dr. Rocky Crate for starting me chasing sheep; my brother Jody Miller for talking me into the best hunt of my life; Stan and Helen Stevens, outstanding outfitters; Scotty Boyd, guide extraordinaire; the great strong pack dog Moose; and finally the most important one, my lovely wife Cynthia, who says, "Go hunt; it's good for you." ▲

Photograph by Bill Honza

TROPHY STATS

▼ ▼ ▼ ▼ ▼

Category
Dall's Sheep

Score
173 $4/8$

Length of Horn
Right: 43 $3/8$ Left: 43 $1/8$

Circumference of Base
Right: 13 $6/8$ Left: 13 $6/8$

Greatest Spread
24 $7/8$

Location
Chugach Mts., Alaska – 2006

Hunter
Nick J. Duncan

DALL'S SHEEP
Second Award – 173 4/8
▼ ▼ ▼ ▼ ▼ ▼ ▼ ▼ ▼

NICK J. DUNCAN

My hunting partner Adam and I caught a flight into hunting camp two days prior to the season opener to try to locate some good rams. We set up a base camp on the landing strip and started our trek up the mountain with food for five days and our spike camp on our backs.

The thick alder brush that blankets the valley floors in the Chugach Mountains lived up to its reputation, trying its hardest to keep us out of sheep country. Three hours later and not more than a half mile from the landing strip, we finally cleared the alder and reached the rocky, steep terrain in which we would be spending the next 11 days.

At the vantage point we spotted on the flight in, we set up our spike camp and began glassing. The first evening passed with no sheep sightings. The second morning was more of the same. That afternoon we set out to look into the head end of the basins that we could not see with our optics. We covered roughly 11 miles of country over the next three days with little success. We spotted a few bands of ewes with lambs and some small rams, but nothing we would consider shooting.

The fourth day, which was the second day of the season, the weather turned bad. Intense rain, with 25-mph winds, forced us to hole up in our two-man mountaineering tent for most of the day. We peeked our heads out once in a while to glass the hillsides as the clouds moved, with no success.

Photograph courtesy of Nick J. Duncan

Nick J. Duncan was hunting in the Chugach Mountains when he took his award-winning ram. Pictured above is Stevens Glacier.

Photograph courtesy of Nick J. Duncan

Nick J. Duncan is pictured above with his Dall's sheep that received a Second Place Award at the 26th Big Game Awards Program in Fort Worth, Texas. The ram, which scores 173-4/8 points, was taken during the 2006 season in Alaska.

With only one day's worth of food left, Adam and I decided that the day was a waste, and one of us should hike back to the landing strip and replenish our food supply. I volunteered for the descent that evening. I arrived back at the landing strip three hours later, soaking wet from the rain-drenched alder. I hung my clothes under a tarp to dry and called it a day.

The next morning the rain had quit, but the alder was still soaked. I decided to wait a few hours and let the wind dry the alder out before starting my ascent back up the mountain. While I was waiting, I set up my spotting scope and glassed some of the distant hills miles down the drainage. I spotted a band of rams feeding on a hillside about 1,500 feet above the river. These rams were safe from us; we would have no way to cross the runoff-swollen river to reach them. The sight of the mature rams reignited the fire I had the first couple of days, but which had been smothered by the cold, wet, unforgiving bush and lack of action.

I made my way back to spike camp and re-stocked with food for the remainder of the hunt. Our plan had been to head around the corner to look at some new country. When I arrived back at spike camp, Adam told me he had seen two nice rams come around the corner we planned on heading to; the only problem was two hunters followed them and harvested both rams while he was watching in his spotting scope over a mile away. We had an overwhelming feeling of disappointment.

We scratched our heads at what to do. The big corner trip was busted, and we had already covered everything we could in the other direction. We were beaten, not so much physically, but mentally.

After finishing dinner, I went back to glassing the country we had been looking at now for five days, when two mountain goats I had been watching for two days suddenly turned into four. The top two didn't seem to have that same boxy frame as the other two. I called Adam over to have a look. The light was beginning to fade, and we were looking a long way, but we both came to the conclusion they were rams. We just didn't know how big.

A quick pack job of our spike camp and we were off. We descended from our vantage point in 30 minutes, sidehilling around the alder on the valley floor to a spot where we could get a better look at the rams. We cut the distance in half before dark. We relocated the rams and were able to put them to bed about three quarters of the way up the hill across the canyon.

The next morning came early. We were up at 4:30 a.m. trying to locate the rams again. After an hour of glassing, we could only find one ram; he was about 250 yards higher on the hill than he was the night before and moving fast up and over the top. We packed up camp again and headed down the hill. As we got to the bottom near the creek, we dropped our packs, grabbed some water and snack bars, and took off after the rams.

We went about 100 yards when I thought we had better give this basin one last glance. I couldn't believe my eyes! Not more than a mile up in the head end of the basin were seven rams feeding just off the creek in a nice green patch of vegetation that had been just below our line of sight for the last couple of days. Our plans just changed!

Two deep, cold, and half-naked creek crossings later we were half a mile away from the rams. We decided to go straight up a nearly vertical cliff, using a small erosion path worn in the rock as our hand and footholds. Once we were above the rams we would have a very brisk wind blowing directly in our face.

Near the top of the rock outcropping, we could see the saddle we were heading for. All we had to do was cross a dreadfully steep avalanche chute still packed with snow. Suddenly, the sound of falling rocks right above us caught our attention. Adam said, "Ram!"

He was huge. I was in the lead, not giving Adam a clear shot. At 70 yards, with the ram running uphill and quartering away from us, I fired once. It connected, stopping him from going any further uphill. The ram turned, stumbled, and started running downhill right at us. I knew I hit him hard. I put another round in him and dropped him to the ground. I looked at Adam in disbelief at what just happened, and then I noticed the ram starting to get up again. I shot once more, trying to keep him down. His momentum carried him down the hill until his legs gave way. Then he went head first, burying his lamb tips into loose rock and skidding to a halt. Adam, thinking quickly, ran to secure the ram before his death kicks propelled him over the 500-foot ledge not 10 feet away.

It only took a glance, and I knew I had just taken what will probably prove to be the trophy of my lifetime. Adam was also able to harvest a trophy but not of the sheep variety. He took a bull moose that was over 60 inches wide.

We have been very fortunate to hunt this area unguided on general-season tags. It's rare these days to be so lucky in taking quality animals, as it seems that anymore, quality comes with either years of waiting to draw a coveted tag or a huge price tag! ▲

Photograph by Bill Honza

TROPHY STATS

▼ ▼ ▼ ▼ ▼

Category
Dall's Sheep

Score
173 $^3/_8$

Length of Horn
Right: 41 $^7/_8$ Left: 42 $^4/_8$

Circumference of Base
Right: 14   Left: 14

Greatest Spread
23 $^6/_8$

Location
Alaska Range, Alaska – 2004

Hunter
Cynthia Cassell

DALL'S SHEEP
Third Award – 173 ³/₈
▼ ▼ ▼ ▼ ▼ ▼ ▼ ▼

CYNTHIA CASSELL

This tremendous Dall's sheep is the greatest gift my husband ever gave me. Bob Cassell hiked 13 miles across wild Alaska mountain terrain, got a good long look at one of the largest rams he'd ever seen, and then hurried back home to tell me about it.

Instead of trying for it himself, this dedicated and driven sheep hunter decided to set his sights on persuading me — his wife — to take on the challenge. Even though it would be a huge physical and emotional effort for us both, he saved a once-in-a-lifetime-if-you're-lucky trophy for me.

The Biggest Gift

But I didn't understand all of this up front; I just wanted a safe, fun sheep hunt. While Bob was trying to convince me that he was arranging exactly that, I was obsessing about crashing our airplane, sliding into a crevasse, submitting to hypothermia....

So he flew back up into the mountains to improve our prospects. He found a better place to land on a river bar and then shoveled rocks for hours, smoothing and lengthening a strip. He hiked up the glacier again and memorized the best routes. He worked hard, and when he returned home with a revised description of the set up, my anxiety eased. I packed my gear, pulled myself into the back of the Cub, and put my fate in his hands.

For five days, I followed Bob's lead. I was never in any real danger, but there were four times when I lost my nerve: First, when I was overwhelmed by the steepness of the slope during the final stalk; then, two times after I shot the ram, when Bob had to leave me to climb into a scary, steep chute alone to recover it; and finally at the end of the hunt, when he flew away with half our gear, because the bush strip — even in its improved state — was still too short for a full load.

Aside from those intervals of fear, this was a blissful hunt. Bob showed me how to use strap-

Photograph by Jack Reneau

Cynthia Cassell accepting her plaque and medal from Buck Buckner, Vice President and Chairman of the Big Game Records Committee.

Cynthia Cassell and her husband Bob are shown above on the gravel bush strip before flying out. Cynthia's ram, which scored 173-3/8 points, received a Third Place Award at the 26th Big Game Awards Program in Fort Worth, Texas. They flew into the Alaska Range for the hunt.

on crampons, and we crunched along on sculpted ice for miles. We had clear, cool weather. At night, our headlamps beamed crystallized breath, and a lazy moon floated up, yellow and round, to expose the emptiness of the glacier and the fullness of our effort.

I finally got to hold the horns after Bob's second excursion to get the last of the ram. They were coarse for a Dall's, but symmetrical and beautifully worn. They were massive. Bob kept grinning and yelling, "HUUUGE!"

When he broke camp and took off with the first plane load, I was left with time to think, pacing around the gravel bar with only pebbles, mountains, and a ram skull to keep me company. That's when I realized that my husband gave me the biggest gift imaginable: an adventure to cherish and a trophy to treasure. ▲

Award-Winning Moments

B&C Photo Archives

Three women were recognized for their outstanding trophies at the 26th Big Game Awards Program. Pictured above from left to right are Cynthia Cassell (Dall's sheep – Third Place Award), B&C Lifetime Associate Myra S. Smith (typical mule deer – First Place Award), and Catherine E. Keene (non-typical mule deer – First Place Award).

Photograph by Bill Honza

TROPHY STATS
▼ ▼ ▼ ▼ ▼

Category
Stone's Sheep

Score
179 5/8

Length of Horn
Right: 42 7/8   Left: 43

Circumference of Base
Right: 15   Left: 15

Greatest Spread
22 6/8

Location
Hook Lake, British Columbia – 2005

Hunter
Jelindo A. Tiberti II

STONE'S SHEEP
First Award – 179 ⁵/₈

▼ ▼ ▼ ▼ ▼ ▼ ▼ ▼ ▼

JELINDO A. TIBERTI II

I flew into Whitehorse from Las Vegas to fulfill a sheep hunter's goal — a grand slam. It was August 11, 2005, when I arrived. I met up with some other hunters and went off to find my outfitter. After explaining that my Christensen Arms .300 Ultra Mag was missing, my outfitter assured me that it would be on the late night flight or that I could use his trusty .30-30. What a way to hunt Stone's sheep!

The next morning the van was there to take us to our floatplane some four hours away and, luckily, my gun was with me at that point. On the way, the other four sheep hunters and I were talking (the first liar had no chance), and I was in the front seat. After we were three-quarters of the way there, my outfitter asked if I could backpack. I told him I could, as I had gone last year on a ten-day hunt in Northwest Territories for my Dall's sheep hunt. He said that was good because he had a guide who had seen a ram last year in a backpack area. The thought started racing through my mind, as this was not my first rodeo, that this was supposed to be a horseback hunt and I had not trained for a forced-man-march.

To start, it was about 110°F at home when I left. Second, we were instructed to bring a day pack, and as an obedient husband of 22 years, I followed instructions well. I told him I would need a pack. He asked the other hunters in the van if anyone had brought a pack frame and one hunter said, "Yes." My legs became instantly tired.

As we waited for our floatplane, I packed my ten-day supply of gear in my unfitted pack frame. We landed at base camp just long enough to pick up my guide, Ryan Damstrom; then we were off to Tea Kettle Lake. After a smooth water landing, we made our way to the higher hills and set up camp. The first hike from the lake was through such thick trees that I lost my Swarovski scope covers, and I was concerned about the rain and how to keep my sights clear. Just another day for a sheep hunter.

Photograph by Jack Reneau

Jelindo A. Tiberti II accepting his plaque and medal from Buck Buckner, Vice President and Chairman of the Big Game Records Committee.

Jelindo A. Tiberti II is pictured above with his Stone's sheep scoring 179-5/8 points.

After we set up camp the bell rang and the bugs were released. If you go north, trust me about one thing; if you get there on a bad bug year there is nothing worse. I had Jungle Juice (an insect repellent) and that was the only thing that made it bearable. Ryan toughed it out for a while, but after his neck, hands, and ears were covered in bites he agreed to use some spray.

The next morning we were on the hunt with great excitement and expectations. It was a nice day, and we saw three bull moose, one caribou, and six Stone's sheep ewes and lambs.

On Saturday, August 13, we awoke and decided to move camp to the top of a saddle to get away from the bugs. The day before, all the other animals we saw were on the very top of the mountains for the same reason that we were going — to beat the bugs.

We packed for some 5-1/2 hours through the thickest forest and were headed for the top. Due to the unexpected type of hunt, I ended up with a silver-dollar-sized blister on my right foot. I was exhausted, but we made it to the top of our new camp.

At 1:45 p.m., we had a lunch of cheese and crackers along with a chocolate bar. I just started to glass, and I found a ram. My heart raced as I told Ryan. He pulled out the spotting scope, and we both were excited to see this beautiful ram. He was picture perfect, dark coat, white socks and face, and had terrific horns. Ryan asked me if I was ready to go. My heart said "Yes" but my feet screamed "No," so we were off. After a 2-1/2-hour descent and re-climb we were peeking over the edge. Ryan spotted the ram as I set up for the shot. I heard him say, "Don't shoot the ram we saw; shoot the ram on the right." One quick look and my hunt was over.

After the mandatory 60-day drying period, the ram gross-scored 180-1/8 and had a final B&C score of 179-5/8. It had 43-inch horns and 15-inch bases. All sheep hunts are tough but this one was special, my number 4.

I would like to thank Sandee, my wife and one special lady, for helping make all my hunting trips easy. I also want to thank my guide, Ryan Damstrom, one tough Canadian, who worked hard for a very meaningful hunt. ▲

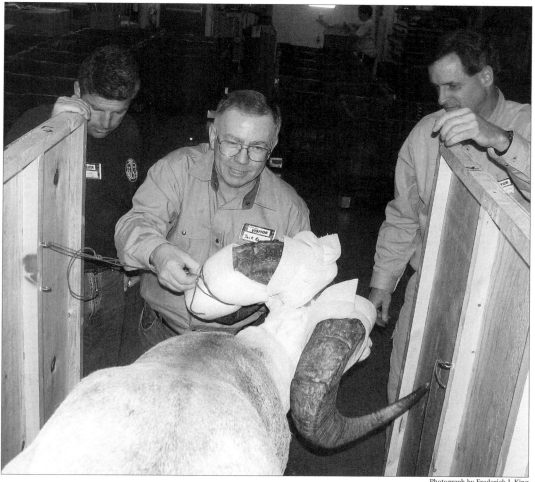

Photograph by Frederick J. King

Jelindo A. Tiberti II's First Place Award Stone's sheep is carefully uncrated by B&C's Director of Big Game Records Jack Reneau at Cabela's in Fort Worth, Texas. After the ram was uncrated and its score verified, it went on display to the general public for over six weeks.

TABULATIONS OF RECORDED TROPHIES 26TH AWARDS PROGRAM 2004-2006

TABULATIONS OF RECORDED TROPHIES IN THE 26TH AWARDS ENTRY PERIOD

The trophy data shown herein have been taken from score charts in the Records Archives of the Boone and Crockett Club for the 26th Awards Program, 2004-2006. Trophies listed are those that meet minimum score and other stated requirements of trophy entry for the period.

The final scores and rank shown in the book are official, except for trophies shown with an asterisk. An asterisk is assigned to trophies accepted in this Awards Program with entry scores that were subject to verification by the 26th Awards Program Judges Panel. The asterisk can be removed (except in the case of a potential new World's Record) by submitting two additional, independent scorings by Official Measurers of the Boone and Crockett Club. The Records Committee of the Club will review the three scorings available and determine which, if any, will be accepted in lieu of the Judges' Panel measurement.

When the score has been accepted as final by the Records Committee, the asterisk will be removed in future editions of the all-time records book, *Records of North American Big Game*, and other publications by the Boone and Crockett Club. In the case of a potential new World's Record, the trophy must come before an Awards Program Judges Panel or a Special Judges Panel, which is convened between Awards Program Judges Panels on an as-needed-basis to verify World's Record status in a timely manner. Only an Awards Program Judges Panel or a Special Judges Panel can certify a new World's Record and finalize its score. Asterisked trophies are shown at the end of the listings for their category. They are not ranked, as their final score is subject to revision by a Judges' Panel or by the submission of additional scorings, as described above.

Note that "PR" preceding the date of kill indicates "prior to" the year shown for kill.

B&C is pleased to announce that this is the first B&C book that lists a gross score for antlered, horned, and tusked animals. Gross score for antlered animals is basically the typical frame, without deductions for lack of symmetry, plus the total of the lengths of the abnormal points. Gross score for horned and tusked animals is the total of the left and right sides without any deductions for lack of symmetry. Trophies will continue to be listed and ranked in B&C publications by their final score, but the gross score is listed for informational and comparison purposes.

The scientific and vernacular names, and the sequence of presentation, follows that suggested in the *Revised Checklist of North American Mammals North of Mexico*, 1979 (J. Knox, et al; Texas Tech University, 14 December 1979.)

TROPHY BOUNDARIES

Many of the categories recognized in the Boone and Crockett Club's North American Big Game Awards Program are based upon subspecies differences. In nature, subspecies freely interbreed where their ranges overlap, thus necessitating the setting of geographic boundaries to keep them, as well as hybrids, separate for records-keeping purposes.

Geographic boundaries are described for a number of categories. These include: Alaska brown and grizzly bear; Atlantic and Pacific walrus; American, Roosevelt's, and tule elk; mule, Columbia, and Sitka blacktail deer; whitetail and Coues' deer; moose; and caribou. Pertinent information for several of these boundaries is included in the trophy data listings that follow, but the complete, detailed description for each is to be found in *Measuring and Scoring North American Big Game Trophies*, 2nd Edition, revised 2000, or on the Club's web site at www.booneandcrockettclub.com.

FIELD PHOTOS LISTED IN THIS BOOK

🎞 Denotes B&W field photo

🎞 Denotes color field photo

In addition to category specific boundaries, all trophies must be from North America, north of the south border of Mexico, to be eligible. For pelagic trophies such as walrus and polar bear, they must be from Canada, Greenland, and the United States of America side of the International Date Line to be eligible.

Trophy boundaries are set by the Boone and Crockett Club's Records of North American Big Game Committee, working with the latest and best available information from scientific researchers, guides, hunters, and other parties with serious interest in our big game resources. Boundaries are set so that it is highly unlikely specimens of the larger category or hybrids can be taken within boundaries set for the smaller category, thus upsetting the rankings of the smaller category. Trophy boundaries are revised as necessary to maintain this separation of the categories. ▲

Photograph by Frederick J. King

Members of the 26th Big Game Awards Judges Panel certified Jim Shockey's musk ox as a new World's Record (tie). Only an Awards Program Judges Panel or a Special Judges Panel can certify a new World's Record and finalize its score.

BLACK BEAR

Ursus americanus americanus and related subspecies

Minimum Score 20

World's Record 23 10/16

Final Score	Greatest Length of Skull Without Lower Jaw	Greatest Width of Skull	Locality	Hunter	Owner	Date Killed	Rank
23 3/16	14 9/16	8 10/16	Fayette Co., PA	Andrew Seman, Jr.	Andrew Seman, Jr.	2005	1
22 15/16	13 14/16	9 1/16	Monroe Co., PA	Jeremy Kresge	Jeremy Kresge	2004	2
22 11/16	14 3/16	8 8/16	Chippewa Co., WI	Duane Helland	Duane Helland	2003	3
22 11/16	13 15/16	8 12/16	Price Co., WI	Joseph T. Brandl	Joseph T. Brandl	2006	3
22 9/16	13 10/16	8 15/16	Goochland Co., VA	Stacy L. McLeod	Stacy L. McLeod	2003	5
22 9/16	14 4/16	8 5/16	Chippewa Co., WI	Picked Up	Mike Kuehnast	2005	5
22 7/16	14	8 7/16	Lake Co., CA	Scott M. Young	Scott M. Young	2004	7
22 7/16	14 1/16	8 6/16	Beaufort Co., NC	Charles A. Geer	Charles A. Geer	2005	7
22 4/16	14 1/16	8 3/16	Centre Co., PA	Joel J. Kuhns	Joel J. Kuhns	2005	9
22 3/16	13 5/16	8 14/16	Falcon Lake, MB	Paul D. Born	Paul D. Born	2003	10
22 3/16	13 12/16	8 7/16	Lebanon Co., PA	Lynn Horst	Lynn Horst	2004	10
22 3/16	14 2/16	8 1/16	Potter Co., PA	Ronald H. Landis	Ronald H. Landis	2005	10
22 3/16	13 12/16	8 7/16	Sussex Co., NJ	William Parchomcik	William Parchomcik	2005	10
22 2/16	13 14/16	8 4/16	Bayfield Co., WI	Paul Henthorn	Paul Henthorn	2003	14
22 2/16	13 15/16	8 3/16	Columbia Co., PA	Robert J. Maciejewski	Robert J. Maciejewski	2003	14
22 2/16	13 7/16	8 11/16	Cass Co., MN	Jerome P. Crimmins	Jerome P. Crimmins	2004	14
22 2/16	13 9/16	8 9/16	Marinette Co., WI	Steven M. Heroux	Steven M. Heroux	2004	14
22 2/16	13 14/16	8 4/16	Chippewa Co., WI	Brian M. McGinnis	Brian M. McGinnis	2004	14
22 1/16	13 9/16	8 8/16	Pike Co., PA	Thomas J. Young, Jr.	Thomas J. Young, Jr.	2003	19
22 1/16	13 10/16	8 7/16	Monroe Co., PA	William Graver	William Graver	2004	19
22 1/16	13 14/16	8 3/16	Clear Lake, MB	Robert Andjelic	Robert Andjelic	2006	19
22	13 7/16	8 9/16	Lackawanna Co., PA	Daniel J. Gregorsky	Daniel J. Gregorsky	2003	22
22	13 3/16	8 13/16	Menominee Co., MI	Donna L. Herson	Donna L. Herson	2006	22
21 15/16	13 11/16	8 4/16	Vilas Co., WI	Paul A. Reed	Paul A. Reed	2002	24
21 15/16	13 10/16	8 5/16	Camden Co., NC	Jason R. Meads	Jason R. Meads	2003	24
21 15/16	13 10/16	8 5/16	Warren Co., NJ	Kirk M. Lee	Kirk M. Lee	2005	24
21 15/16	13 13/16	8 2/16	Riding Mt., MB	Robert J. Evans	Robert J. Evans	2006	24
21 14/16	13 5/16	8 9/16	Prince of Wales Island, AK	Bruce P. Lavergne	Bruce P. Lavergne	2006	28
21 13/16	13 7/16	8 6/16	Tabusintac River, NB	Thomas R. Hatfield	Thomas R. Hatfield	2002	29
21 12/16	13 9/16	8 3/16	Spokane Co., WA	Lars C. Swartling	Lars C. Swartling	2001	30
21 12/16	13 8/16	8 4/16	Placer Co., CA	David A. Mussman	David A. Mussman	2003	30
21 12/16	13 6/16	8 6/16	Clarion Co., PA	Travis Schill	Travis Schill	2003	30
21 12/16	13 14/16	7 14/16	Loon Lake, SK	Jarred L. Faust	Jarred L. Faust	2004	30

21 12/16	13 6/16	8 6/16	Sullivan Co., PA	James L. Knosp	James L. Knosp	2004	30
21 12/16	13 8/16	8 4/16	Leaf Rapids, MB	Jerry D. Madsen	Jerry D. Madsen	2006	30
21 11/16	13 3/16	8 8/16	Barron Co., WI	Seth J. Bichler	Seth J. Bichler	2002	36
21 11/16	13 12/16	7 15/16	Barron Co., WI	Picked Up	Alan Dirkes	2002	36
21 11/16	13 4/16	8 7/16	Alcona Co., MI	Scott A. Bowles	Scott A. Bowles	2004	36
21 11/16	13 2/16	8 9/16	Tioga Co., PA	Gerald L. Everhart, Jr.	Gerald L. Everhart, Jr.	2004	36
21 11/16	13 9/16	8 2/16	Menominee Co., MI	Peter Granquist	Peter Granquist	2004	36
21 11/16	13 7/16	8 4/16	Brownson Bay, AK	Erik A. Johnson	Erik A. Johnson	2004	36
21 11/16	13 11/16	8	Utah Co., UT	Ben D. Lowder	Ben D. Lowder	2004	36
21 11/16	13 7/16	8 4/16	Huntingdon Co., PA	Richard James	Richard James	2005	36
21 10/16	13 10/16	8	Barron Co., WI	Kellie M. Amundson	Kellie M. Amundson	2004	44
21 10/16	13 4/16	8 6/16	Townsend Lake, SK	Mitch Bilokreli	Mitch Bilokreli	2005	44
21 10/16	13 10/16	8	Chippewa Co., WI	Michael P. Codere	Michael P. Codere	2005	44
21 10/16	13 8/16	8 2/16	Madera Co., CA	Henry J. Hines	Henry J. Hines	2005	44
21 10/16	13 9/16	8 1/16	Marinette Co., WI	Leonard S. Klarkowski	Leonard S. Klarkowski	2005	44
21 10/16	13 4/16	8 6/16	Schuylkill Co., PA	Steven T. Razzano	Steven T. Razzano	2005	44
21 9/16	13 4/16	8 5/16	Clinton Co., PA	James S. Watson	James S. Watson	2002	50
21 9/16	13 7/16	8 2/16	Washburn Co., WI	David Marker	David Marker	2003	50
21 9/16	13 12/16	7 13/16	Rainy Lake, ON	Tony C. Schuler	Tony C. Schuler	2004	50
21 9/16	13 1/16	8 6/16	Polk Co., WI	Thomas M. Aird	Thomas M. Aird	2005	50
21 9/16	13 7/16	8 2/16	Lycoming Co., PA	John J. Czerniakowski	John J. Czerniakowski	2005	50
21 8/16	13 7/16	8 1/16	Wayne Co., PA	Daniel Petroski	Daniel Petroski	1998	55
21 8/16	13	8 8/16	Wayne Co., PA	Andrew G. Box	Andrew G. Box	2003	55
21 8/16	13 8/16	8	Tobin Lake, SK	Reginald B. Coburn	Reginald B. Coburn	2003	55
21 8/16	13 5/16	8 3/16	Forest Co., WI	Dick Pluedeman	Dick Pluedeman	2003	55
21 8/16	13 12/16	7 12/16	Pelican Lake, MB	Tony A. Ruys	Tony A. Ruys	2003	55
21 8/16	13 9/16	7 15/16	Marinette Co., WI	Dustin M. Dunlap	Dustin M. Dunlap	2004	55
21 8/16	13 5/16	8 3/16	Marinette Co., WI	David A. Neuville	David A. Neuville	2004	55
21 8/16	13 8/16	8	Bayfield Co., WI	Jerry V. Waara	Jerry V. Waara	2004	55
21 8/16	13 2/16	8 6/16	Fergus Co., MT	Pat R. Descheemaeker	Pat R. Descheemaeker	2005	55
21 8/16	13 4/16	8 4/16	Menominee Co., MI	Michael S. Martin	Michael S. Martin	2005	55
21 7/16	13 7/16	8 1/16	Rusk Co., WI	Thomas A. Lutz	Thomas A. Lutz	2006	55
21 7/16	13 1/16	8 6/16	Gila Co., AZ	Shannon E. Thomas	Shannon E. Thomas	1992	66
21 7/16	12 13/16	8 10/16	Douglas Co., WI	Tim S. Kaufman	Tim S. Kaufman	2001	66
21 7/16	13 3/16	8 4/16	Prince of Wales Island, AK	Thomas G. Lamoree II	Thomas G. Lamoree II	2004	66
21 7/16	13 9/16	7 14/16	Chilliwack River, BC	J. Steven Mohr	J. Steven Mohr	2004	66
21 7/16	13 6/16	8 1/16	Forest Co., WI	Jade L. Ruechel	Jade L. Ruechel	2004	66
21 7/16	13 5/16	8 2/16	Duck Mountain, SK	Kevin R. Williams	Kevin R. Williams	2004	66
21 7/16	13 6/16	8 1/16	Pistol Lake, ON	Nicholas M. Farr	Nicholas M. Farr	2005	66
21 7/16	13 2/16	8 5/16	Forest Co., PA	Michael D. Hale	Michael D. Hale	2005	66
21 7/16	13 9/16	7 14/16	Duck Mt., MB	Stephen J. Shannon	Stephen J. Shannon	2005	66
21 7/16	13 5/16	8 2/16	Barron Co., WI	Jeffrey P. Tomesh	Jeffrey P. Tomesh	2005	66

BLACK BEAR

Ursus americanus and related subspecies

Final Score	Greatest Length of Skull Without Lower Jaw	Greatest Width of Skull	Locality	Hunter	Owner	Date Killed	Rank
21 7/16	13 2/16	8 5/16	Catron Co., NM	Donald E. Wenner	Donald E. Wenner	2005	66
21 7/16	13 5/16	8 2/16	Prince of Wales Island, AK	Bernard A. Chastain	Bernard A. Chastain	2006	66
21 6/16	13 7/16	7 15/16	Warren Co., PA	Shawn M. Gallagher	Shawn M. Gallagher	2003	78
21 6/16	13 11/16	7 11/16	Washburn Co., WI	Mike Johannes	Mike Johannes	2003	78
21 6/16	13 4/16	8 2/16	Union Co., GA	John M. Wood	John M. Wood	2003	78
21 6/16	13 10/16	7 12/16	Sawyer Co., WI	David A. Houzner	David A. Houzner	2004	78
21 6/16	13 4/16	8 2/16	Chautauqua Co., NY	Daniel C. Beres	Daniel C. Beres	2005	78
21 6/16	13 6/16	8	Rusk Co., WI	Ronald T. Locascio	Ronald T. Locascio	2005	78
21 6/16	13 6/16	8	Big River, SK	James G. Spencer	James G. Spencer	2005	78
21 6/16	13 14/16	7 8/16	Preston Co., WV	Thomas A. Teter II	Thomas A. Teter II	2005	78
21 5/16	13 1/16	8 4/16	Chippewa Co., WI	Dale Helland	Dale Helland	2002	86
21 5/16	13 6/16	7 15/16	Presque Isle Co., MI	Grant R. Dix	Grant R. Dix	2003	86
21 5/16	13 8/16	7 13/16	Burnett Co., WI	Bryan D. Kostuch	Bryan D. Kostuch	2003	86
21 5/16	13 8/16	7 13/16	Lassen Co., CA	Ian K. Chase-Dunn	Ian K. Chase-Dunn	2004	86
21 5/16	13 3/16	8 2/16	Bronson Lake, SK	Lynn Drechsel	Lynn Drechsel	2004	86
21 5/16	13 3/16	8 2/16	Rusk Co., WI	Austin Oleskow	Austin Oleskow	2005	86
21 4/16	13 8/16	7 12/16	Juneau Co., WI	Brian J. Baukin	Brian J. Baukin	2003	92
21 4/16	12 7/16	8 13/16	Carbon Co., MT	Joseph A. Krenzer	Joseph A. Krenzer	2003	92
21 4/16	13 4/16	8	Nez Perce Co., ID	Nick G. Manfull	Nick G. Manfull	2003	92
21 4/16	12 15/16	8 5/16	Leaf Rapids, MB	Steve M. Boulton	Steve M. Boulton	2004	92
21 4/16	13 4/16	8	Apache Co., AZ	Trisha R. Chancellor	Trisha R. Chancellor	2004	92
21 4/16	13 7/16	7 13/16	Sawyer Co., WI	Carl D. Saueressig	Carl D. Saueressig	2004	92
21 4/16	13 1/16	8 3/16	Prince of Wales Island, AK	Richard A. Hurd	Richard A. Hurd	2005	92
21 4/16	13 8/16	7 12/16	Clear River, AB	Malcolm R. Reese	Malcolm R. Reese	2005	92
21 4/16	13 8/16	7 12/16	Marathon Co., WI	Allan Vogel	Allan Vogel	2005	92
21 4/16	13	8 4/16	Trinity Co., CA	Bryan W. Yoder	Bryan W. Yoder	2005	92
21 4/16	14 1/16	7 3/16	Sevier Co., UT	Jed M. Hansen	Jed M. Hansen	2006	92
21 4/16	13 5/16	7 15/16	Graham Co., AZ	John P. Hickcox	John P. Hickcox	2006	92
21 4/16	13 10/16	7 10/16	Barron Co., WI	Matthew W. McDonough	Matthew W. McDonough	2006	92
21 3/16	13 4/16	7 15/16	Idaho Co., ID	Dustin G. Derrick	Dustin G. Derrick	2004	105
21 3/16	13 7/16	7 12/16	Charlton Co., GA	Jason Lederman	Jason Lederman	2004	105
21 3/16	12 13/16	8 6/16	Ashland Co., WI	Robert C. Meske	Robert C. Meske	2004	105
21 3/16	13 1/16	8 2/16	Indiana Co., PA	Richard W. Bishop	Richard W. Bishop	2005	105

Score	Length	Width	Locality	Hunter	Owner	Date	Rank
21 3/16	13 10/16	7 9/16	Pleasant Valley Creek, MB	Laurence J. Eaton	Laurence J. Eaton	2005	105
21 3/16	12 15/16	8 4/16	Orange Co., NY	Paul R. Gale	Paul R. Gale	2005	105
21 3/16	12 12/16	8 7/16	Marathon Co., WI	Ronald H. Roth	Ronald H. Roth	2005	105
21 3/16	13 7/16	7 12/16	Kehiwin Lake, AB	Bernard W. Yonkman	Bernard W. Yonkman	2005	105
21 2/16	13 1/16	8 1/16	Thurston Co., WA	Terry Sherrill	Terry Sherrill	1996	113
21 2/16	13	8 2/16	Prince of Wales Island, AK	Robert E. Vlach, Jr.	Robert E. Vlach, Jr.	2002	113
21 2/16	13 4/16	7 14/16	Fond du Lac River, SK	Andy Carpenter	Andy Carpenter	2003	113
21 2/16	12 14/16	8 4/16	Clarion Co., PA	Brandon S. Carson	Brandon S. Carson	2003	113
21 2/16	13 4/16	7 14/16	Prince of Wales Island, AK	Jeff J. Haynie	Jeff J. Haynie	2004	113
21 2/16	13 4/16	7 14/16	Dauphin Co., PA	Ryan C. Hornung	Ryan C. Hornung	2004	113
21 2/16	12 14/16	8 4/16	Delta Co., MI	Gaylord M. Jones	Gaylord M. Jones	2004	113
21 2/16	12 15/16	8 3/16	Dauphin Co., PA	Fran L. Miller	Fran L. Miller	2004	113
21 2/16	13 3/16	7 15/16	Prince of Wales Island, AK	Jason Snell	Jason Snell	2004	113
21 2/16	13	8 2/16	Prince of Wales Island, AK	Gary R. Stancil	Gary R. Stancil	2004	113
21 2/16	13 6/16	7 12/16	Codette Lake, SK	Steve Clifford	Steve Clifford	2005	113
21 2/16	13 6/16	7 12/16	Nimpkish River, BC	Robert V. Gothier, Jr.	Robert V. Gothier, Jr.	2005	113
21 2/16	12 10/16	8 3/16	N. Saskatchewan River, AB	Robert B. Hutton	Robert B. Hutton	2005	113
21 2/16	13 4/16	7 14/16	Sussex Co., NJ	John P. Noon, Sr.	John P. Noon, Sr.	2005	113
21 2/16	13 4/16	7 14/16	Gila Co., AZ	Lynn A. Pariso	Lynn A. Pariso	2005	113
21 2/16	13 2/16	8	Berkshire Co., MA	Richard B. Phair	Richard B. Phair	2005	113
21 2/16	13	8 2/16	Prince of Wales Island, AK	Robert L. Elliott	Robert L. Elliott	2006	113
21 2/16	13 6/16	7 12/16	Hudson Bay, SK	Toby Lawrence	Toby Lawrence	2006	113
21 2/16	13 3/16	7 15/16	Prince of Wales Island, AK	Charles D. Pollansky	Charles D. Pollansky	2006	113
21 1/16	13	8 1/16	Ochre River, MB	James B. Faller	James B. Faller	1982	132
21 1/16	13 2/16	7 15/16	Frederick Co., VA	David S. Iser	David S. Iser	2003	132
21 1/16	13 1/16	8 2/16	Clark Co., WI	Mark J. Wickham	Mark J. Wickham	2003	132
21 1/16	13 5/16	8	Potter Co., PA	Raymond C. Bobb III	Raymond C. Bobb III	2004	132
21 1/16	13 7/16	7 12/16	Hyde Co., NC	Dake A. Esposito	Dake A. Esposito	2004	132
21 1/16	13 5/16	7 10/16	Heron Creek, MB	E. Kevin Harmon	E. Kevin Harmon	2004	132
21 1/16	13 6/16	7 12/16	Alger Co., MI	Scott D. LaChonce	Scott D. LaChonce	2004	132
21 1/16	13 3/16	7 11/16	Carrot River, SK	Dana Morrison	Dana Morrison	2004	132
21 1/16	12 15/16	7 14/16	Tioga Co., PA	Melvin C. Nace	Melvin C. Nace	2004	132
21 1/16	13 5/16	8 2/16	Socorro Co., NM	Terry L. Diedrick	Terry L. Diedrick	2005	132
21 1/16	13 5/16	7 12/16	Carteret Co., NC	Ronald H. Odom, Jr.	Ronald H. Odom, Jr.	2005	132
21 1/16	13 6/16	7 12/16	Spirit River, AB	Randal K. Pierson	Randal K. Pierson	2005	132
21 1/16	13 7/16	7 11/16	Lewis Co., NY	Timothy P. Acoveno	Timothy P. Acoveno	2006	132
21 1/16	12 15/16	7 10/16	Prince of Wales Island, AK	Donald L. Fleming, Jr.	Donald L. Fleming, Jr.	2006	132
21 1/16	13 9/16	7 8/16	Onanole, MB	David J. Hall	David J. Hall	2006	132
21 1/16	13 1/16	8	Montrose Co., CO	James A. Washam	James A. Washam	2006	132
21	13	8	Gull Pond, NL	Dean Crocker	Dean Crocker	1994	148
21	13	8	Shasta Co., CA	Barry Wade	Barry Wade	1999	148
21	12 14/16	8 2/16	La Plata Co., CO	Thadius Countess	Thadius Countess	2002	148

BLACK BEAR

Ursus americanus americanus and related subspecies

Final Score	Greatest Length of Skull Without Lower Jaw	Greatest Width of Skull	Locality	Hunter	Owner	Date Killed	Rank
21	12 14/16	8 2/16	La Plata Co., CO	Picked Up	John L. Gardner	2002	148
21	13 6/16	7 10/16	Cheboygan Co., MI	Joe Baumgarten	Joe Baumgarten	2003	148
21	13 2/16	7 14/16	Hyde Co., NC	Zachary J. Davis	Zachary J. Davis	2003	148
21	13 5/16	7 11/16	St. Croix Co., WI	David DeJong	David DeJong	2003	148
21	13 6/16	7 10/16	Juneau Co., WI	Dennis E. Dodge	Dennis E. Dodge	2003	148
21	12 15/16	8 1/16	Prince of Wales Island, AK	John B. Levert, Jr.	John B. Levert, Jr.	2003	148
21	13 2/16	7 14/16	Morgan Co., WV	Edward T. Powers	Edward T. Powers	2003	148
21	12 15/16	8 1/16	Spanish River, ON	Randy D. Raymond	Randy D. Raymond	2003	148
21	13 2/16	7 14/16	Camden Co., NC	William E. Rose	William E. Rose	2003	148
21	13	8	Tioga Co., PA	Carol S. Broadbent	Carol S. Broadbent	2004	148
21	13	8	Burnt River, AB	Robert B. Couce	Robert B. Couce	2004	148
21	13	8	Coffman Cove, AK	Stephen C. Dwyer	Stephen C. Dwyer	2004	148
21	13	8	Oconto Co., WI	Gerald L. Fabry	Gerald L. Fabry	2004	148
21	13 2/16	7 14/16	Clearfield Co., PA	Bradley L. Walters	Bradley L. Walters	2004	148
21	13 8/16	7 8/16	Hyde Co., NC	Evan J. Williams	Evan J. Williams	2004	148
21	13 3/16	7 13/16	Sevier Co., UT	Richard L. Bagley	Richard L. Bagley	2005	148
21	13 7/16	7 9/16	Bayfield Co., WI	Dale R. Krajenka, Sr.	Dale R. Krajenka, Sr.	2005	148
21	13 6/16	7 11/16	Gila Co., AZ	David H. Scott	David H. Scott	2005	148
21	12 13/16	8 3/16	Berks Co., PA	Darryl L. Uhrig	Darryl L. Uhrig	2005	148
21	13 1/16	7 15/16	Crow Wing Co., MN	William D. Bright	William D. Bright	2006	148
21	12 8/16	8 8/16	Marinette Co., WI	Thomas S. Dyer	Thomas S. Dyer	2006	148
21	13 1/16	7 15/16	Klakas Inlet, AK	Shane A. Mathill	Shane A. Mathill	2006	148
20 15/16	13 3/16	7 12/16	Armstrong Co., PA	Kevin G. Bussard	Kevin G. Bussard	2003	173
20 15/16	12 13/16	8 2/16	Ashland Co., WI	Paul J. Tessmer	Paul J. Tessmer	2003	173
20 15/16	13	7 15/16	Pickens Co., SC	Randall G. Brock	Randall G. Brock	2004	173
20 15/16	13	7 15/16	Fond du Lac River, SK	Brian S. Hotze	Brian S. Hotze	2004	173
20 15/16	13 5/16	7 10/16	Nut Mt., SK	Ken Corley	Ken Corley	2005	173
20 15/16	12 15/16	8	Alger Co., MI	Paul D. Kelto	Paul D. Kelto	2005	173
20 15/16	12 13/16	8 2/16	Montrose Co., CO	James E. Maham	James E. Maham	2006	173
20 14/16	13 3/16	7 11/16	Washburn Co., WI	Melvin Kusilek	Melvin Kusilek	2000	180
20 14/16	13 4/16	7 10/16	Kittitas Co., WA	Ray J. Owens	Ray J. Owens	2002	180
20 14/16	13 6/16	7 8/16	Lycoming Co., PA	Galen G. Campbell	Galen G. Campbell	2003	180
20 14/16	13 4/16	7 10/16	Vilas Co., WI	Anthony J. Klima	Anthony J. Klima	2004	180

		Location	Hunter	Year	Score
20 14/16	12 14/16	Alpine Co., CA	Dale M. Shirley	2004	180
20 14/16	13	Yakoun River, BC	Ronny Bohrmann	2005	180
20 14/16	13 4/16	Eau Claire Co., WI	David E. Willert	2006	180
20 13/16	12 4/16	Rio Arriba Co., NM	Dustin S. Boyd	2001	187
20 13/16	12 15/16	Nushagak River, AK	Brian D. Pauls	2002	187
20 13/16	13 1/16	Koochiching Co., MN	Paul D. Duesterhoeft	2003	187
20 13/16	13 5/16	Price Co., WI	Dennis L. Jones	2003	187
20 13/16	13 1/16	Bayfield Co., WI	Kevin Meierotto	2003	187
20 13/16	13 2/16	Potter Co., PA	Todd E. Wiest	2003	187
20 13/16	12 12/16	Clark Co., WI	Roger N. Getter	2005	187
20 13/16	13	Wilkes Co., NC	Brian C. Johnson	2005	187
20 13/16	12 11/16	Tehama Co., CA	Mark W. Odenkirchen	2005	187
20 13/16	13 1/16	Beltrami Co., MN	Max D. Roszkowski	2005	187
20 13/16	12 9/16	Lincoln Co., OR	William L. Mulder	2006	187
20 12/16	8	Aitkin Co., MN	Leonard L. Lewis	1998	198
20 12/16	12 12/16	Braxton Co., WV	John A. Barker	2003	198
20 12/16	12 15/16	Sullivan Co., PA	Lowell T. Ditzler	2003	198
20 12/16	12 12/16	Vilas Co., WI	Marty Macco	2003	198
20 12/16	12 7/16	Skowl Arm, AK	George A. Pickel	2003	198
20 12/16	12 14/16	Bayfield Co., WI	Andrew R. Thyssen	2003	198
20 12/16	12 14/16	Barrage Gouin, QC	Samuel F. Warrender, Jr.	2003	198

BLACK BEAR
FINAL SCORE: 20-2/16
HUNTER: Wayne E. Umlor

BLACK BEAR
FINAL SCORE: 20-5/16
HUNTER: Julie M. James

BLACK BEAR
FINAL SCORE: 20
HUNTER: Eric H. Boley

BLACK BEAR
FINAL SCORE: 21-2/16
HUNTER: Jeff J. Haynie

Ursus americanus and related subspecies

Final Score	Greatest Length of Skull Without Lower Jaw	Greatest Width of Skull	Locality	Hunter	Owner	Date Killed	Rank
20 12/16	13	7 12/16	Sierra Co., NM	Nathan H. Wenner	Nathan H. Wenner	2003	198
20 12/16	13 1/16	7 11/16	Eau Claire Co., WI	Richard L. Price	Richard L. Price	2004	198
20 12/16	12 13/16	7 15/16	Prince of Wales Island, AK	Daniel E. Sample	Daniel E. Sample	2004	198
20 12/16	12 15/16	7 13/16	Sevier Co., UT	Peter H. Chinnici, Jr.	Peter H. Chinnici, Jr.	2005	198
20 12/16	13 2/16	7 10/16	Cass Co., MN	Linda M. Krueger	Linda M. Krueger	2005	198
20 12/16	12 14/16	7 14/16	Prince of Wales Island, AK	David W. Monke	David W. Monke	2005	198
20 12/16	12 10/16	8 2/16	Price Co., WI	Jared W. Richert	Jared W. Richert	2005	198
20 12/16	12 14/16	7 14/16	McKean Co., PA	Gary L. Senderling	Gary L. Senderling	2005	198
20 12/16	13 1/16	7 11/16	Passaic Co., NJ	Thomas J. Wardlaw	Thomas J. Wardlaw	2005	198
20 11/16	12 14/16	7 13/16	Stanislaus Co., CA	Michael J. Battin	Michael J. Battin	2000	214
20 11/16	13	7 11/16	Montezuma Co., CO	Picked Up	Woody Ott	2002	214
20 11/16	12 12/16	7 15/16	Dauphin Co., PA	Steven L. Bender	Steven L. Bender	2003	214
20 11/16	12 15/16	7 12/16	Desha Co., AR	William B. Hawthorne	William B. Hawthorne	2003	214
20 11/16	12 3/16	8 8/16	Okanogan Co., WA	Jeff Bishop	Jeff Bishop	2004	214
20 11/16	12 15/16	7 12/16	Langlade Co., WI	Charles H. Koch	Charles H. Koch	2004	214
20 11/16	13 1/16	7 10/16	Josephine Co., OR	Thad C. Lambert	Thad C. Lambert	2004	214
20 11/16	13 2/16	7 9/16	Marinette Co., WI	Rocky L. Anderson	Rocky L. Anderson	2005	214
20 11/16	12 12/16	7 12/16	Clinton Co., PA	Herman J. Erickson	Herman J. Erickson	2005	214
20 11/16	12 15/16	7 12/16	Kosciusko Island, AK	William A. Keebler	William A. Keebler	2005	214
20 11/16	12 13/16	7 14/16	Jackson Co., OR	Michael W. Herzog	Michael W. Herzog	2006	214
20 10/16	13	7 10/16	Lewis Co., ID	Bradley J. Zenner	Bradley J. Zenner	2003	225
20 10/16	13 2/16	7 8/16	El Dorado Co., CA	Gregory G. Childers	Gregory G. Childers	2005	225
20 10/16	13	7 10/16	Kehiwin Lake, AB	Jason Gamracy	Jason Gamracy	2005	225
20 10/16	13 1/16	7 9/16	Porcupine Plain, SK	Craig S. Lemon	Craig S. Lemon	2005	225
20 10/16	12 10/16	8	Vermilion Lake, SK	Bob J. Spooner	Bob J. Spooner	2005	225
20 10/16	12 13/16	7 13/16	Forest Co., WI	Joseph A. Steger	Joseph A. Steger	2005	225
20 10/16	12 14/16	7 12/16	Saddle Hills, AB	Brent Watson	Brent Watson	2005	225
20 10/16	13 6/16	7 4/16	Baker Co., OR	Brandon A. Briels	Brandon A. Briels	2006	225
20 10/16	12 13/16	7 13/16	Sheffield Lake, NL	Richard D. Collins, Jr.	Richard D. Collins, Jr.	2006	225
20 10/16	12 15/16	7 11/16	Green Lake, SK	Leads M. Du Bois	Leads M. Du Bois	2006	225
20 9/16	12 9/16	8	Fremont Co., CO	Charles R. Rupp	Charles R. Rupp	1979	235
20 9/16	12 12/16	7 13/16	Lincoln Co., WI	Gordan L. McMillen	Gordan L. McMillen	2001	235
20 9/16	12 6/16	8 3/16	Echo Bay, ON	Rene Cescon	Rene Cescon	2002	235

20 9/16	12 15/16	Belknap Co., NH	Joseph A. Santucci	Joseph A. Santucci	2002	235
20 9/16	13	Wasatch Co., UT	Rod J. Cassity	Rod J. Cassity	2003	235
20 9/16	13 3/16	Oscoda Co., MI	Jeffrey L. Heiden	Jeffrey L. Heiden	2003	235
20 9/16	12 14/16	Potter Co., PA	Roger E. Hunter	Roger E. Hunter	2003	235
20 9/16	12 15/16	Price Co., WI	Joseph L. Sprangers	Joseph L. Sprangers	2003	235
20 9/16	13	Langlade Co., WI	Richard E. Nelsen	Richard E. Nelsen	2005	235
20 9/16	13 1/16	Caribou Co., ID	Travis G. Ostler	Travis G. Ostler	2005	235
20 9/16	12 12/16	Iron Co., MI	Paul Baumann	Paul Baumann	2006	235
20 9/16	12 15/16	Prince of Wales Island, AK	Tate W. Myers	Tate W. Myers	2006	235
20 8/16	12 11/16	Burnett Co., WI	Jeff Holdt	Jeff Holdt	1989	247
20 8/16	12 15/16	Rusk Co., WI	Eric Lundmark	Eric Lundmark	2000	247
20 8/16	13 1/16	Bedford Co., PA	Jon D. Cornell	Jon D. Cornell	2003	247
20 8/16	12 6/16	Ulster Co., NY	Carlo Ferraiolo	Carlo Ferraiolo	2003	247
20 8/16	12 12/16	Marinette Co., WI	Kenneth A. Guenther	Kenneth A. Guenther	2003	247
20 8/16	13	Iron Co., WI	Jere J. Hamel	Jere J. Hamel	2003	247
20 8/16	12 15/16	McKean Co., PA	Randy J. Ours, Sr.	Randy J. Ours, Sr.	2003	247
20 8/16	12 12/16	Yakima Co., WA	Jerry W. Reynolds	Jerry W. Reynolds	2003	247
20 8/16	12 12/16	Fremont Co., CO	Deborah J. Walker	Deborah J. Walker	2003	247
20 8/16	12 13/16	Prince of Wales Island, AK	Greg G. Abdallah	Greg G. Abdallah	2004	247
20 8/16	13 1/16	Cass Co., MN	Rusty Lilyquist	Rusty Lilyquist	2004	247
20 8/16	12 15/16	Kuiu Island, AK	Frank S. Noska IV	Frank S. Noska IV	2004	247
20 8/16	12 10/16	Prince of Wales Island, AK	Dwayne T. O'Cull	Dwayne T. O'Cull	2004	247
20 8/16	12 12/16	Wahkiakum Co., WA	Ken F. Smith	Ken F. Smith	2004	247
20 8/16	12 12/16	Price Co., WI	Jessica A. Trochinski	Jessica A. Trochinski	2004	247
20 8/16	13	Van Buren Co., AR	Jason L. Vaughn	Jason L. Vaughn	2004	247
20 7/16	12 14/16	Clearwater Co., MN	Rex T. Kemmer	Rex T. Kemmer	2005	247
20 7/16	12 15/16	Eau Claire Co., WI	Sarah E. Wiggins	Sarah E. Wiggins	2005	247
20 7/16	12 14/16	Halibut Cove, AK	Henry F. Abel, Jr.	Henry F. Abel, Jr.	2006	247
20 7/16	12 14/16	Rusk Co., WI	Jerome J. Kalal	Jerome J. Kalal	2006	247
20 7/16	12 12/16	Beaver River, AB	Coral VanDerVoort	Coral VanDerVoort	2006	247
20 7/16	12 11/16	Nez Perce Co., ID	Chris Brown	Chris Brown	1998	268
20 7/16	13	Bedford Co., PA	Richard L. Miller	Richard L. Miller	2002	268
20 7/16	12 10/16	Morris Co., NJ	Robert P. Conover	Robert P. Conover	2003	268
20 7/16	13 1/16	Dunn Co., WI	Terry Crosby	Terry Crosby	2003	268
20 7/16	12 6/16	Sullivan Co., NH	Richard C. Muller	Richard C. Muller	2003	268
20 7/16	12 14/16	Jefferson Co., PA	James H. Dougherty, Jr.	James H. Dougherty, Jr.	2004	268
20 7/16	12 13/16	Ministikwan Lake, SK	Thomas Giordano	Thomas Giordano	2004	268
20 7/16	13	Prince of Wales Island, AK	Bernard J. Hickenbotham	Bernard J. Hickenbotham	2004	268
20 7/16	12 8/16	Aroostook Co., ME	David M. Pierce	David M. Pierce	2004	268
20 7/16	12 9/16	Aroostook Co., ME	Paul H. Demerchant	Paul H. Demerchant	2005	268
20 7/16	12 9/16	Duck Mt., MB	Daniel J. Harty	Daniel J. Harty	2005	268
20 7/16	12 13/16	Washburn Co., WI	Larry R. Melton	Larry R. Melton	2005	268

BLACK BEAR

Ursus americanus americanus and related subspecies

Final Score	Greatest Length of Skull Without Lower Jaw	Greatest Width of Skull	Locality	Hunter	Owner	Date Killed	Rank
20 7/16	12 12/16	7 11/16	Tioga Co., PA	Duane F. Raber	Duane F. Raber	2005	268
20 7/16	12 5/16	8 2/16	Warren Co., PA	Alfred F. Vogt	Alfred F. Vogt	2005	268
20 7/16	12 10/16	7 13/16	Fair Harbour, BC	Adam H. Bartsch	Adam H. Bartsch	2006	268
20 7/16	12 9/16	7 14/16	Sandilands, MB	Nathan K. Cropper	Nathan K. Cropper	2006	268
20 7/16	12 8/16	7 15/16	Thorne Bay, AK	P.R. Potts	P.R. Potts	2006	268
20 6/16	12 11/16	7 11/16	Forest Co., WI	Charles F. Dreher	Charles F. Dreher	1997	285
20 6/16	12 14/16	7 8/16	Klakas Inlet, AK	Andrew J. Fierro	Andrew J. Fierro	1999	285
20 6/16	12 10/16	7 12/16	Prince of Wales Island, AK	Lyle E. Israelsen	Lyle E. Israelsen	2001	285
20 6/16	12 7/16	7 15/16	Madera Co., CA	Fred R. Blevins	Fred R. Blevins	2003	285
20 6/16	13 1/16	7 5/16	Marshall Co., MN	Troy A. Edberg	Troy A. Edberg	2003	285
20 6/16	12 10/16	7 12/16	Bayfield Co., WI	Bradford J. Hilton	Bradford J. Hilton	2003	285
20 6/16	12 10/16	7 12/16	Prince of Wales Island, AK	Jon E. Lueck	Jon E. Lueck	2003	285
20 6/16	13	7 6/16	Sullivan Co., NY	Steven Pecora	Steven Pecora	2003	285
20 6/16	12 11/16	7 11/16	Clinch Co., GA	Robert Tanner	Robert Tanner	2003	285
20 6/16	12 10/16	7 12/16	Little Barachois Brook, NL	Bob Ackerman	Bob Ackerman	2004	285
20 6/16	12 13/16	7 9/16	Pasqua Hills, SK	H. Robert Foster	H. Robert Foster	2004	285
20 6/16	12 10/16	7 12/16	Bayfield Co., WI	Gordon N. Gibbons	Gordon N. Gibbons	2004	285
20 6/16	12 6/16	8	Marinette Co., WI	Eric M. Guenther	Eric M. Guenther	2004	285
20 6/16	12 9/16	7 13/16	Candle Lake, SK	Brian Pierce, Jr.	Brian Pierce, Jr.	2004	285
20 6/16	12 8/16	7 14/16	Bayfield Co., WI	Gary L. Shruck	Gary L. Shruck	2004	285
20 6/16	12 10/16	7 12/16	Portage Creek, AK	Mark S. Wade	Mark S. Wade	2004	285
20 6/16	12 13/16	7 9/16	Jefferson Co., PA	Raymond G. Cessna	Raymond G. Cessna	2005	285
20 6/16	13 1/16	7 5/16	Indiana Co., PA	Cecil S. Lindsey	Cecil S. Lindsey	2005	285
20 6/16	12 12/16	7 10/16	Sugar Lake, ON	Randy D. Raymond	Randy D. Raymond	2005	285
20 6/16	12 13/16	7 9/16	Yuba Co., CA	David E.P. Ver Linden	David E.P. Ver Linden	2005	285
20 6/16	12 15/16	7 7/16	Moose Creek, MB	John M. Sarno	John M. Sarno	2006	285
20 5/16	13 1/16	7 4/16	Chippewa Co., WI	Sidney Larson, Jr.	Sidney Larson, Jr.	2001	306
20 5/16	12 12/16	7 9/16	Pike Co., PA	Daniel Z. Chung	Daniel Z. Chung	2003	306
20 5/16	12 8/16	7 13/16	Coos Co., OR	Ray Herning	Ray Herning	2003	306
20 5/16	12 14/16	7 7/16	Sussex Co., NJ	William C. McNamara	William C. McNamara	2003	306
20 5/16	13 1/16	7 4/16	Barron Co., WI	Richard J. Wenk	Richard J. Wenk	2003	306
20 5/16	13 2/16	7 3/16	Boone Co., WV	Millard W. Broughton	Millard W. Broughton	2004	306
20 5/16	12 10/16	7 11/16	Mesa Co., CO	Christopher D. Crites	Christopher D. Crites	2004	306

20 5/16	12 14/16	7 7/16	Prince of Wales Island, AK	Thomas J. Frane	Thomas J. Frane	2004	306
20 5/16	12 9/16	7 12/16	Carlton Co., MN	William J. Schmitz	William J. Schmitz	2004	306
20 5/16	12 8/16	7 13/16	Sullivan Co., PA	Jeffrey J. Blatt	Jeffrey J. Blatt	2005	306
20 5/16	12 12/16	7 9/16	Gilpin Co., CO	Julie M. James	Julie M. James	2005	306
20 5/16	13 1/16	7 4/16	Sawyer Co., WI	Fred Kotulski	Fred Kotulski	2005	306
20 5/16	12 13/16	7 8/16	Apache Co., AZ	Lauren Claxton	Lauren Claxton	2006	306
20 5/16	12 12/16	7 9/16	Prince of Wales Island, AK	Brent K. Jenson	Brent K. Jenson	2006	306
20 4/16	12 8/16	7 13/16	Prince of Wales Island, AK	Howard F. McCloy	Howard F. McCloy	2006	321
20 4/16	12 9/16	7 9/16	Canoose Stream, NB	Robert A. Eisele, Sr.	Robert A. Eisele, Sr.	2002	321
20 4/16	13	7 4/16	Mesa Co., CO	James E. Brandt	James E. Brandt	2003	321
20 4/16	12 7/16	7 13/16	Thunder Bay, ON	Michael Brozek	Michael Brozek	2003	321
20 4/16	12 12/16	7 12/16	Tulare Co., CA	Vernard A. Craven	Vernard A. Craven	2003	321
20 4/16	12 8/16	7 12/16	Spokane Co., WA	Doug Flory	Doug Flory	2003	321
20 4/16	12 8/16	7 12/16	Jackson Co., OR	Jesse Holcomb	Jesse Holcomb	2003	321
20 4/16	12 6/16	7 14/16	Washington Co., ME	Chad A. Thompson	Chad A. Thompson	2003	321
20 4/16	13	7 4/16	Chippewa Co., WI	Lukas C. Hoel	Lukas C. Hoel	2005	321
20 4/16	12 8/16	7 12/16	Caniapiscau Lake, QC	Randall S. Moyer	Randall S. Moyer	2005	321
20 4/16	12 15/16	7 5/16	Oconto Co., WI	Dan J. Peterson	Dan J. Peterson	2005	321
20 4/16	12 8/16	7 12/16	Gallop Lake, NB	Michael Petschauer	Michael Petschauer	2005	321
20 4/16	12 11/16	7 9/16	Teton Co., ID	Kirk L. Reynolds	Kirk L. Reynolds	2005	321
20 4/16	12 12/16	7 8/16	Monroe Co., PA	Thomas P. Rode, Jr.	Thomas P. Rode, Jr.	2005	321
20 4/16	13 1/16	7 3/16	Riding Mt., MB	Ricky J. Suire	Ricky J. Suire	2005	321
20 4/16	12 12/16	7 8/16	Langlade Co., WI	William F. Vander Weyst	William F. Vander Weyst	2005	321
20 4/16	12 8/16	7 12/16	Kirkland, ON	Troy T. Bishop	Troy T. Bishop	2006	321
20 4/16	12 8/16	7 12/16	Snipe Lake, AB	Thomas H. Burts	Thomas H. Burts	2006	321
20 4/16	12 7/16	7 13/16	Uintah Co., UT	Ronald L. Ewell	Ronald L. Ewell	2006	321
20 3/16	12 8/16	7 12/16	Jackson Co., OR	Clinton Pietsch	Seth T. Pietsch	2006	321
20 3/16	12 4/16	8	Marquette Co., MI	Walter R. Scanlon, Jr.	Walter R. Scanlon, Jr.	2006	321
20 3/16	12 11/16	7 9/16	Iron Co., WI	Steven B. Zwicke	Steven B. Zwicke	2006	321
20 3/16	12 8/16	7 11/16	Wallowa Co., OR	Fred L. Hornshuh, Jr.	Fred L. Hornshuh, Jr.	2002	342
20 3/16	12 11/16	7 8/16	Staney Creek, AK	Kyle J. Marinoff	Kyle J. Marinoff	2003	342
20 3/16	12 4/16	7 15/16	Westmoreland Co., PA	Jack D. Williams	Jack D. Williams	2003	342
20 3/16	12 15/16	7 4/16	Collister Lake, MB	Tom Wyatt	Tom Wyatt	2003	342
20 3/16	12 6/16	7 13/16	Sheridan Co., WY	Jim Aksamit	Jim Aksamit	2004	342
20 3/16	12 6/16	7 13/16	Dolores Co., CO	Amber A. Daves	Amber A. Daves	2004	342
20 3/16	12 13/16	7 6/16	Santa Cruz Co., AZ	Stanley W. Gaines	Stanley W. Gaines	2004	342
20 3/16	12 8/16	7 11/16	Jefferson Co., NY	Kurt Neibacher	Kurt Neibacher	2004	342
20 3/16	13	7 8/16	Crow Wing Co., MN	Craig A. Schroeder	Craig A. Schroeder	2004	342
20 3/16	12 10/16	7 3/16	Muskeg Lake, SK	Milton J. Shimek	Milton J. Shimek	2004	342
20 3/16	12 8/16	7 9/16	Tioga Co., PA	John W. Beiler	John W. Beiler	2005	342
20 3/16	12 5/16	7 11/16	Rusk Co., WI	Brian D. Nies	Brian D. Nies	2005	342
20 3/16	12 7/16	7 14/16	Big Creek, AK	Kurt J. Snapper	Kurt J. Snapper	2005	342

BLACK BEAR

Ursus americanus americanus and related subspecies

Final Score	Greatest Length of Skull Without Lower Jaw	Greatest Width of Skull	Locality	Hunter	Owner	Date Killed	Rank
20 3/16	12 14/16	7 5/16	Riding Mt., MB	Douglas W. VanWyk	Douglas W. VanWyk	2005	342
20 3/16	12 9/16	7 10/16	Douglas Co., OR	Tom Lusby	Tom Lusby	2006	342
20 2/16	12 8/16	7 10/16	Wyoming Co., PA	A.J. Manganiello & C. Richter	Alfred J. Manganiello	2001	357
20 2/16	12 9/16	7 9/16	Schoolcraft Co., MI	Tim A. Salisbury	Tim A. Salisbury	2002	357
20 2/16	12 11/16	7 7/16	Gila Co., AZ	Michael E. Schlotman	Michael E. Schlotman	2002	357
20 2/16	12 9/16	7 12/16	Taylor Co., WI	Troy L. Davis	Troy L. Davis	2003	357
20 2/16	12 9/16	7 12/16	Sierra Co., NM	Jeff A. Mund	Jeff A. Mund	2003	357
20 2/16	12 14/16	7 4/16	Clinton Co., PA	Robert M. Shrader	Robert M. Shrader	2003	357
20 2/16	12 2/16	8	Carswell Lake, SK	Richard P. Smith	Richard P. Smith	2003	357
20 2/16	12 12/16	7 6/16	Morrison Co., MN	Dennis A. Wenzel	Dennis A. Wenzel	2003	357
20 2/16	12 11/16	7 7/16	Bradford Co., PA	Dennis Witiak	Dennis Witiak	2003	357
20 2/16	12 10/16	7 8/16	Fair Harbour, BC	Adam H. Bartsch	Adam H. Bartsch	2004	357
20 2/16	12 10/16	7 8/16	Lycoming Co., PA	Scott M. Chieffo	Scott M. Chieffo	2004	357
20 2/16	12 4/16	7 14/16	Jefferson Co., MT	Kenneth L. Senst	Kenneth L. Senst	2004	357
20 2/16	12 11/16	7 7/16	St. Louis Co., MN	John Tanski	John Tanski	2004	357
20 2/16	12 13/16	7 5/16	Delta Co., MI	Wayne E. Umlor	Wayne E. Umlor	2004	357
20 2/16	12 9/16	7 9/16	La Plata Co., CO	Normand H. Birtcher	Normand H. Birtcher	2005	357
20 2/16	12 8/16	7 10/16	Kaminni Lake, ON	Jim C. DeHoey	Jim C. DeHoey	2005	357
20 2/16	12 12/16	7 6/16	Tioga Co., PA	Dennis L. Kline, Sr.	Dennis L. Kline, Sr.	2005	357
20 2/16	12 6/16	7 12/16	Teton Co., WY	Jeffrey M. Santangelo	Jeffrey M. Santangelo	2005	357
20 2/16	12 5/16	7 13/16	Polk Co., WI	Lawrence A. Weston	Lawrence A. Weston	2005	357
20 2/16	12 4/16	7 14/16	Pitkin Co., CO	Bradley C. Knotts	Bradley C. Knotts	2006	357
20 1/16	12 15/16	7 2/16	Mille Lacs Co., MN	Kevin H. Keck	Kevin H. Keck	2001	377
20 1/16	12 9/16	7 8/16	Bayfield Co., WI	Jeff Adank	Jeff Adank	2002	377
20 1/16	12 11/16	7 6/16	La Plata Co., CO	Wes S. Akers	Wes S. Akers	2003	377
20 1/16	12 12/16	7 5/16	La Plata Co., CO	David E. Longenette	David E. Longenette	2003	377
20 1/16	12 13/16	7 4/16	Washburn Co., WI	JoDee V. Mittlestadt	JoDee V. Mittlestadt	2003	377
20 1/16	12 13/16	7 4/16	Koochiching Co., MN	Joel W. Pagnac	Joel W. Pagnac	2003	377
20 1/16	12 2/16	7 15/16	Hood River Co., OR	Jamie Stencil	Jamie Stencil	2003	377
20 1/16	12 9/16	7 8/16	Little Saskatchewan River, MB	John G. Wooldridge	John G. Wooldridge	2003	377
20 1/16	12 6/16	7 11/16	Aitkin Co., MN	Rosemarie E. Andresen	Rosemarie E. Andresen	2004	377
20 1/16	12 6/16	7 11/16	Catron Co., NM	Ken Castaneda	Ken Castaneda	2004	377

20 1/16	12 8/16	7 9/16	English River, ON	Todd M. Christian	Todd M. Christian	2004	377
20 1/16	12 6/16	7 11/16	Wolseley Bay, ON	Steve M. Estep	Steve M. Estep	2004	377
20 1/16	12 10/16	7 7/16	Prince of Wales Island, AK	Erik N. Palle	Erik N. Palle	2004	377
20 1/16	12 9/16	7 8/16	Dufferin Lake, SK	Donald L. Roxby	Donald L. Roxby	2004	377
20 1/16	12 11/16	7 6/16	Graham Co., AZ	Karl W. Thorn	Karl W. Thorn	2004	377
20 1/16	12 10/16	7 7/16	Wallowa Co., OR	Chad H. Adams	Chad H. Adams	2005	377
20 1/16	12 5/16	7 12/16	Shawano Co., WI	Kenneth G. Hafferman	Kenneth G. Hafferman	2005	377
20 1/16	12 11/16	7 6/16	Lake Co., MI	Norm Hunderman	Norm Hunderman	2005	377
20 1/16	12 8/16	7 9/16	Hudson Bay, SK	Toby Lawrence	Toby Lawrence	2005	377
20 1/16	12 4/16	7 13/16	Sullivan Co., PA	Harold G. Lohmiller	Harold G. Lohmiller	2005	377
20 1/16	12 7/16	7 10/16	Lake Nipigon, ON	Frederic F. Nowak	Frederic F. Nowak	2005	377
20 1/16	12 12/16	7 5/16	Barron Co., WI	Donavan V. Robarge	Donavan V. Robarge	2005	377
20	12 5/16	7 11/16	Otero Co., NM	William S. Pickett III	William S. Pickett III	1994	399
20	12 5/16	7 11/16	Fremont Co., WY	Alvin G. Grospiron	Alvin G. Grospiron	2002	399
20	12 6/16	7 10/16	Peel Inlet, BC	Greg T. Nelson	Greg T. Nelson	2002	399
20	12 10/16	7 6/16	Sheldens Bay, BC	Greg T. Nelson	Greg T. Nelson	2002	399
20	12 5/16	7 11/16	Prince of Wales Island, AK	Jeffrey D. Folsom	Jeffrey D. Folsom	2003	399
20	12 8/16	7 8/16	Garfield Co., UT	Eric H. Boley	Eric H. Boley	2004	399
20	12 14/16	7 2/16	Jefferson Co., PA	Rick G. Byerly	Rick G. Byerly	2004	399
20	11 7/16	8 9/16	Namur Lake, AB	Stephen R. Haufsk	Stephen R. Haufsk	2004	399
20	12 2/16	7 14/16	Judith Basin Co., MT	Jamey R. Linn	Jamey R. Linn	2004	399
20	12 4/16	7 12/16	Clearwater Co., ID	Nathan Manfull	Nathan Manfull	2004	399
20	12 11/16	7 5/16	Price Co., WI	Joseph C. Marx	Joseph C. Marx	2004	399
20	12 1/16	7 15/16	Aroostook Co., ME	Jerry McLaughlin	Jerry McLaughlin	2004	399
20	12 5/16	7 11/16	Dungarvon River, NB	Ronald L. Klier	Ronald L. Klier	2005	399
20	12 8/16	7 8/16	Pierce Co., WA	Herman Maag	Herman Maag	2005	399
20	12 9/16	7 7/16	Nahmint River, BC	Carroll Moran	Carroll Moran	2005	399
20	12 7/16	7 9/16	Grey River, NL	David E. Stonestreet	David E. Stonestreet	2005	399
20	12 11/16	7 5/16	King Co., WA	Stanley M. Weeks	Stanley M. Weeks	2005	399
20	12 5/16	7 11/16	Westmorland Co., NB	Rudolph Carastro	Rudolph Carastro	2006	399
20	12 9/16	7 7/16	Riding Mt., MB	Brenden P. Cox	Brenden P. Cox	2006	399
20	12 1/16	7 15/16	Penobscot Co., ME	Walter J. Donohue	Walter J. Donohue	2006	399
20	12 6/16	7 10/16	Madison Co., ID	Stetson T. Perry	Stetson T. Perry	2006	399
20	12 4/16	7 12/16	Dore Lake, SK	John P. Snyder	John P. Snyder	2006	399
22 14/16*	14 2/16	8 12/16	Carbon Co., PA	Brian J. Coxe	Brian J. Coxe	2003	399
22 10/16*	14 2/16	8 8/16	Marinette Co., WI	Greg J. Kobus	Greg J. Kobus	2004	399

* Final score subject to revision by additional verifying measurements.

GRIZZLY BEAR

Ursus arctos horribilis

Minimum Score 23

Final Score	Greatest Length of Skull Without Lower Jaw	Greatest Width of Skull	Locality	Hunter	Owner	Date Killed	Rank
27 13/16	17 4/16	10 9/16	Lone Mt., AK	Picked Up	Gordon E. Scott	1976	1
26 13/16	16 5/16	10 8/16	Otter Creek, AK	James C. Blanchard	James C. Blanchard	2001	2
26 5/16	16 2/16	10 3/16	Klikitarik Bay, AK	Dennis H. Dunn	Dennis H. Dunn	2004	3
26 4/16	16 4/16	10	Radio Creek, AK	Matthew J. Williams	Matthew J. Williams	2003	4
25 13/16	16 3/16	9 10/16	Fox River, AK	Earl W. Wellen	Earl W. Wellen	2005	5
25 12/16	16 7/16	9 5/16	Kimsquit River, BC	Kevin D. Kniert	Kevin D. Kniert	2004	6
25 9/16	15 13/16	9 12/16	Noatak River, AK	Christopher W. Kirchhof	Christopher W. Kirchhof	2004	7
25 8/16	16 2/16	9 6/16	Buckland River, AK	Mike Wieser	Mike Wieser	2006	8
25 6/16	15 13/16	9 9/16	Brimstone Creek, BC	Jerry R. Kolke, Jr.	Jerry R. Kolke, Jr.	2005	9
25 6/16	15 13/16	9 9/16	Christmas Creek, AK	Lewie D. Sagner	Lewie D. Sagner	2005	9
25 2/16	15 10/16	9 8/16	Ungalik River, AK	David A. Fait	David A. Fait	1977	11
25 2/16	15 11/16	9 7/16	Anvik River, AK	Robert L. Nelson	Robert L. Nelson	2005	11
25 2/16	15 14/16	9 4/16	Takhanne River, YT	Leonard R. Beecher	Leonard R. Beecher	2006	11
24 15/16	15 8/16	9 7/16	Graham River, BC	Bennie J. Rossetto	Bennie J. Rossetto	2005	14
24 13/16	15 6/16	9 7/16	Eaglet Lake, BC	Alan W. Anderson	Alan W. Anderson	2004	15
24 13/16	15 8/16	9 5/16	Anvik River, AK	Peter J. Bausone	Peter J. Bausone	2006	15
24 10/16	15 4/16	9 6/16	Moody Creek, AK	John R. Marshall	John R. Marshall	2003	17
24 10/16	15 7/16	9 3/16	Kawdy Creek, BC	Todd Davis	Todd Davis	2005	17
24 10/16	15 2/16	9 8/16	Kougarok River, AK	M.W. Smith & L.M. Smith	M.W. Smith & L.M. Smith	2005	17
24 8/16	15 10/16	8 14/16	Kuzitrin River, AK	Benjamin N. Peterson	Benjamin N. Peterson	2003	20
24 8/16	15	9 8/16	Squirrel River, AK	Kenneth R. Ruffner	Kenneth R. Ruffner	2004	20
24 8/16	15 1/16	9 7/16	Babine Lake, BC	Patrick S. Stuart	Patrick S. Stuart	2006	20
24 7/16	15 7/16	9	Cub Lake, BC	Halliet L. Brooks	Halliet L. Brooks	2005	23
24 7/16	14 15/16	9 8/16	Ogilvie Mts., YT	Gordon D. Crawford	Gordon D. Crawford	2005	23
24 6/16	15 15/16	8 7/16	Swift River, AK	Tony R. Milliken, Sr.	Tony R. Milliken, Sr.	2006	25
24 4/16	15 3/16	9 1/16	Big River, AK	Bronko A. Terkovich	Bronko A. Terkovich	2002	26
24 4/16	14 13/16	9 7/16	Moon Lake, BC	Craig T. Main	Craig T. Main	2003	26
24 4/16	15 4/16	9	Kechika River, BC	Frank R. Reynolds	Frank R. Reynolds	2003	26
24 4/16	15 4/16	9	Rabbit River, BC	Steve Hornady	Steve Hornady	2004	26
24 4/16	15	9 4/16	Meziadin Lake, BC	Susan G. Beebe	Susan G. Beebe	2005	26
24 3/16	15 10/16	8 9/16	Talbot Creek, BC	Robert Foster	Robert Foster	2003	31
24 3/16	15 2/16	9 1/16	Meachen Creek, BC	Joseph D. Galandy	Joseph D. Galandy	2004	31
24 3/16	14 11/16	9 8/16	Healy River, AK	Rhett S. Gorda	Rhett S. Gorda	2005	31

Score	Length of Skull	Width of Skull	Hunter	Locality	Date Killed	Rank
24 3/16	15 3/16	9	Kenneth D. Wiebe	Keele River, NT	2005	31
24 2/16	15 3/16	8 15/16	Darryl E. Barker	Bullmoose Mt., BC	1965	35
24	14 10/16	9 6/16	Gregory D. Pisk	Tay Lake, YT	2004	36
23 15/16	15 3/16	8 12/16	David Novak	Moberly Lake, BC	2002	37
23 15/16	14 13/16	9 2/16	Chuck T. Hanson	Kobuk River, AK	2003	37
23 13/16	14 13/16	9	Enzo V. Caccavo	Duncan River, BC	2005	39
23 13/16	14 8/16	9 5/16	Boyd L. Mothe, Jr.	Taku River, BC	2005	39
23 12/16	14 13/16	8 15/16	Michael G. Adams	Taku River, BC	2005	41
23 11/16	15	8 11/16	David P. Rivers	Bell-Irving River, BC	2006	42
23 9/16	14 15/16	8 10/16	James D. Unrein	Cape Lisburne, AK	2004	43
23 8/16	14 11/16	8 13/16	Patrick J. Lefemine	Joe Poole Creek, BC	2002	44
23 7/16	14 7/16	9	Max G. Morgan	Ungalik River, AK	1998	45
23 6/16	14 11/16	8 11/16	Dale A. Boorsma	Kaiyuh Mts., AK	2006	46
23 5/16	14 3/16	9 2/16	Bryan L. McGregor	Twin Lakes, AK	2005	47
23 3/16	14 6/16	8 13/16	Greg Hocevar	Quesnel Lake, BC	2004	48
23 2/16	15	8 2/16	Charles F. Seibold	Owikeno Lake, BC	1985	49
26 12/16*	16 14/16	9 14/16	Gary Egrass	Bear Creek, AK	2002	

* Final score subject to revision by additional verifying measurements.

GRIZZLY BEAR
FINAL SCORE: 23-15/16
HUNTER: Chuck T. Hanson

ALASKA BROWN BEAR
FINAL SCORE: 28-5/16
HUNTER: David A. Ratiff

ALASKA BROWN BEAR
FINAL SCORE: 26-8/16
HUNTER: Robert J. Kaleta

GRIZZLY BEAR
FINAL SCORE: 23-12/16
HUNTER: Michael G. Adams

ALASKA BROWN BEAR

Ursus arctos middendorffi and certain related subspecies

Minimum Score 26   World's Record 30 12/16

Final Score	Greatest Length of Skull Without Lower Jaw	Greatest Width of Skull	Locality	Hunter	Owner	Date Killed	Rank
29 7/16	18 4/16	11 3/16	Meshik River, AK	Scott Weisenburger	Scott Weisenburger	2004	1
29 5/16	17 13/16	11 8/16	Bear Lake, AK	James H. Doyle	James H. Doyle	2006	2
29 3/16	18 2/16	11 1/16	Lake Iliamna, AK	Jack G. Brittingham	Jack G. Brittingham	2004	3
29 3/16	17 8/16	11 11/16	Buskin Lake, AK	Gary Darrah	Gary Darrah	2004	3
29 1/16	17 14/16	11 3/16	Russian Harbor, AK	Robert L. Hales	Robert L. Hales	2004	5
29 1/16	17 11/16	11 6/16	Aliulik Pen., AK	Donald F. Gould	Donald F. Gould	2005	5
28 14/16	17 14/16	11	Meshik River, AK	Glenn K. Kennedy	Glenn K. Kennedy	2004	7
28 13/16	17 15/16	10 14/16	Bear Lake, AK	Fred C. Bryant	Fred C. Bryant	2003	8
28 13/16	18 7/16	10 6/16	Coal Creek, AK	Silvio J. Rossi	Silvio J. Rossi	2006	8
28 12/16	17 2/16	11 10/16	Kupreanof Pen., AK	Robert L. Shafer	Robert L. Shafer	2002	10
28 10/16	17 11/16	10 15/16	Copper River, AK	Martin M. Killinger	Martin M. Killinger	2003	11
28 10/16	17 8/16	11 2/16	Pavlof Bay, AK	John P. Harr, Sr.	John P. Harr, Sr.	2004	11
28 8/16	17 15/16	10 9/16	Bearskin Gulch, AK	Fred J. Graybill	Fred J. Graybill	1997	13
28 8/16	17 12/16	10 12/16	Pumice Creek, AK	Dave Melchert	Dave Melchert	2003	13
28 8/16	17 2/16	11 6/16	Halibut Bay, AK	James L. Briggs	James L. Briggs	2004	13
28 8/16	17 6/16	11 2/16	Tsiu River, AK	Frank J. Tritz, Jr.	Frank J. Tritz, Jr.	2006	13
28 6/16	17 12/16	10 10/16	Port Heiden, AK	Terry Andres	Terry Andres	2001	17
28 6/16	17 14/16	10 8/16	Terror Bay, AK	Kelly T. Boyle	Kelly T. Boyle	2004	17
28 6/16	17 2/16	11 4/16	Ugak Bay, AK	Robert G. Callender	Robert G. Callender	2004	17
28 6/16	17 12/16	10 10/16	Joshua Green River, AK	Craig S. Pfent	Craig S. Pfent	2004	17
28 6/16	17 4/16	11 2/16	Aliulik Pen., AK	Bronko A. Terkovich	Bronko A. Terkovich	2004	17
28 5/16	17 10/16	10 11/16	Unimak Island, AK	Reed Mellor	Reed Mellor	2003	22
28 5/16	17 8/16	10 13/16	Sturgeon River, AK	David A. Ratliff	David A. Ratliff	2003	22
28 5/16	17 2/16	11 3/16	Zachar Bay, AK	Darrel E. Gusa	Darrel E. Gusa	2005	22
28 5/16	17 4/16	11 1/16	Karluk Lake, AK	Buck Siler	Buck Siler	2005	22
28 4/16	17 9/16	10 11/16	Pavlof Bay, AK	W. Carlyle Blakeney, Jr.	W. Carlyle Blakeney, Jr.	2004	26
28 4/16	17	11 4/16	Aliulik Pen., AK	Keith C. Halstead	Keith C. Halstead	2006	26
28 4/16	17 6/16	10 14/16	Red Lake, AK	Robin T. Wilson	Robin T. Wilson	2006	26
28 3/16	17 6/16	10 13/16	Meshik River, AK	Scott J. Collins	Scott J. Collins	2004	29
28 3/16	17 11/16	10 8/16	Balboa Bay, AK	H. James LeBoeuf, Jr.	H. James LeBoeuf, Jr.	2004	29
28 3/16	17 5/16	10 14/16	Bluff Creek, AK	Roger W. Robinson	Roger W. Robinson	2004	29
28 3/16	17 10/16	10 9/16	Johnson River, AK	Robert E. Weaver	Robert E. Weaver	2004	29
28 2/16	17 8/16	10 10/16	Wildman Lake, AK	John B. Bowman	John B. Bowman	2001	33

		Location	Hunter	Owner	Year	Page
28 2/16	16 12/16	Kodiak Island, AK	Victor C. Tortorici	Victor C. Tortorici	2006	33
28 1/16	17 12/16	Kodiak Island, AK	Jason D. Garrison	Jason D. Garrison	2002	35
28 1/16	16 12/16	Ugak Bay, AK	Ken R. Dionne	Ken R. Dionne	2003	35
28 1/16	17 9/16	Cold Bay, AK	Mel J. Tenneson	Mel J. Tenneson	2003	35
28 1/16	17 9/16	Meshik River, AK	Brad A. Lien	Brad A. Lien	2004	35
28 1/16	17 6/16	Izhut Bay, AK	Marc Van Dongen	Marc Van Dongen	2004	35
28 1/16	17 4/16	Littlejohn Lagoon, AK	David C. Haven	David C. Haven	2006	35
28	17 12/16	Lenard Harbor, AK	Robert A. Kuntz	Robert A. Kuntz	2002	35
28	17 8/16	Becharof Lake, AK	James A. Bibler	James A. Bibler	2005	41
27 13/16	17 6/16	Sandy River, AK	Robert C. Schulz	Robert C. Schulz	2005	41
27 12/16	17 6/16	Kakhonak Bay, AK	John D. Martin	John D. Martin	2006	43
27 11/16	16 15/16	Mallard Duck Bay, AK	Mark J. Yost	Mark J. Yost	2006	44
27 8/16	16 11/16	Aliulik Pen., AK	Luke A. Terkovich	Luke A. Terkovich	2004	45
27 7/16	17 6/16	Bear Lake, AK	Mark W. McKinnon	Mark W. McKinnon	2004	46
27 5/16	16 8/16	Kodiak Island, AK	Rocky A. Hall	Rocky A. Hall	2003	47
27 4/16	17 4/16	Cold Bay, AK	John R. Garr	John R. Garr	2002	48
27 3/16	16 12/16	Wernicke River, AK	Ray Aderholt	Ray Aderholt	2004	49
27 2/16	17 7/16	Agripina Bay, AK	Nicholas A. Unrein	Nicholas A. Unrein	2004	50
27 1/16	17 2/16	Caribou River, AK	Tony L. Reichter	Tony L. Reichter	2003	51
27 1/16	16 11/16	Lake Clark Pass, AK	Doug J. Roffers	Doug J. Roffers	2004	52
27	17 1/16	Cinder River, AK	Mark A. Wayne	Mark A. Wayne	2004	52
27	16 8/16	Sharatin Bay, AK	James R. Cowhy	James R. Cowhy	2006	54
26 15/16	16 9/16	Cabin Bay, AK	Tim E. Hunt	Tim E. Hunt	2005	54
26 14/16	17	Brown Peak, AK	Mark W. John	Mark W. John	2005	56
27	16 8/16	Dream Creek, AK	Robert W. Reed, Jr.	Robert W. Reed, Jr.	2002	57
26 12/16	16 6/16	Iliamna Lake, AK	Gonzalo E. Vázquez	Gonzalo E. Vázquez	2003	58
26 12/16	17 4/16	Black River, AK	Jim C. Grisham	Jim C. Grisham	2005	58
26 12/16	16 5/16	Terror Bay, AK	Len H. Guldman	Len H. Guldman	1988	58
26 8/16	16 10/16	Sheep Bay, AK	Robert J. Kaleta	Robert J. Kaleta	2005	61
26 8/16	16 9/16	Chicago Bay, AK	Loren M. Grosskopf	Loren M. Grosskopf	2004	61
26 6/16	16 5/16	Weasel Creek, AK	C. Michael Morrow	C. Michael Morrow	2005	63
26 6/16	16 5/16	Russell Fjord, AK	J. Mack Barham	J. Mack Barham	1997	63
26 3/16	16 5/16	Chichagof Island, AK	Ben L. Hogevoll	Ben L. Hogevoll	1990	65
26 1/16	16 4/16	Sheep Bay, AK	Heath Sisk	Heath Sisk	2004	66
29 5/16*	17 13/16	Kaguyak Bay, AK	David O. Handel	David O. Handel	2005	66
29 4/16*	17 13/16	Fraser Lake, AK	John D. Todd	John D. Todd	2004	66

* Final score subject to revision by additional verifying measurements.

COUGAR

Felis concolor hippolestes and related subspecies

Minimum Score 14 8/16   World's Record 16 4/16

Final Score	Greatest Length of Skull Without Lower Jaw	Greatest Width of Skull	Locality	Hunter	Owner	Date Killed	Rank
16 2/16	9 8/16	6 10/16	Sundance Lake, AB	Joseph Gore, Jr.	Joseph Gore, Jr.	2005	1
15 6/16	9 1/16	6 5/16	Jackfish Lake, AB	Darryl L. Kublik	Darryl L. Kublik	2003	2
15 6/16	9	6 6/16	Archuleta Co., CO	Dick Ray	Dick Ray	2004	2
15 5/16	8 14/16	6 7/16	Umatilla Co., OR	Mike L. Cornell	Mike L. Cornell	2003	4
15 5/16	9 1/16	6 4/16	Battle Creek, BC	Malcolm R. Bachand	Malcolm R. Bachand	2004	4
15 5/16	9	6 5/16	Mineral Co., MT	Martin Desapio	Martin Desapio	2005	4
15 4/16	8 15/16	6 5/16	Sevier Co., UT	Donald E. Perrien	Donald E. Perrien	2003	7
15 4/16	9 1/16	6 3/16	Rio Blanco Co., CO	Jeff J. Thomas	Jeff J. Thomas	2003	7
15 4/16	9	6 4/16	Windfall Creek, AB	Dale A. Fournier	Dale A. Fournier	2004	7
15 3/16	8 13/16	6 6/16	Baker Co., OR	Harry J. Galloway	Harry J. Galloway	2000	10
15 3/16	9 1/16	6 2/16	Clark Co., ID	Cameron T. Ballard	Cameron T. Ballard	2003	10
15 3/16	9	6 3/16	Wildhay River, AB	Kyla Carter	Kyla Carter	2003	10
15 3/16	8 14/16	6 5/16	Bigoray River, AB	Chad Lenz	Chad Lenz	2003	10
15 3/16	8 13/16	6 6/16	Idaho Co., ID	Nathan Manfull	Nathan Manfull	2003	10
15 3/16	9	6 3/16	Yakima Co., WA	Michael L. McIntyre	Michael L. McIntyre	2003	10
15 3/16	8 13/16	6 6/16	Chelan Co., WA	Sarah E. Flickinger	Sarah E. Flickinger	2004	10
15 3/16	8 14/16	6 5/16	Nicola River, BC	Dean J. Ficociello	Dean J. Ficociello	2005	10
15 3/16	8 14/16	6 5/16	Umatilla Co., OR	William M. O'Loughlin	William M. O'Loughlin	2005	10
15 3/16	9 1/16	6 2/16	Rio Arriba Co., NM	Robert J. Seeds	Robert J. Seeds	2005	10
15 3/16	8 12/16	6 7/16	Elk River, BC	Kent E. Fraser	Kent E. Fraser	2006	10
15 3/16	8 13/16	6 6/16	Flat Creek, AB	Peter S. Wambeke	Peter S. Wambeke	2006	10
15 2/16	8 14/16	6 4/16	Nimpkish Lake, BC	Jim Shockey	Jim Shockey	1994	22
15 2/16	8 11/16	6 7/16	Bonner Co., ID	Michael S. Dotson	Michael S. Dotson	1998	22
15 2/16	8 14/16	6 4/16	Weigert Creek, BC	Shawn M. Bevilacqua	Shawn M. Bevilacqua	2004	22
15 2/16	8 14/16	6 4/16	Valley Co., ID	Stuart C. Derrick	Stuart C. Derrick	2004	22
15 2/16	8 14/16	6 4/16	Swan Creek, AB	Scott L. Burnett	Scott L. Burnett	2005	22
15 2/16	8 15/16	6 3/16	Missoula Co., MT	David W. Hoback	David W. Hoback	2005	22
15 2/16	8 14/16	6 4/16	Dog Creek, BC	Lori J. Ginn	Lori J. Ginn	2006	22
15 2/16	8 13/16	6 3/16	N. Saskatchewan River, AB	Thomas Radcliffe	Thomas Radcliffe	2006	22
15 2/16	8 13/16	6 5/16	Missoula Co., MT	Deloit R. Wolfe	Deloit R. Wolfe	2006	22
15 1/16	8 14/16	6 3/16	Kittitas Co., WA	Daniel J. Jonassen	Daniel J. Jonassen	1999	31
15 1/16	8 12/16	6 5/16	Emery Co., UT	Edward A. Conway	Edward A. Conway	2003	31
15 1/16	8 15/16	6 2/16	Adams Co., ID	Dennis B. Shennard II	Dennis B. Shennard II	2003	31

15 1/16	8 14/16	Sanders Co., MT	Terry K. Turner	2003	31
15 1/16	8 14/16	Idaho Co., ID	Nicola A. Johnson	2004	31
15 1/16	9	Mesa Co., CO	Randy St. Ores	2004	31
15 1/16	9	Mesa Co., CO	Christopher D. Crites	2005	31
15 1/16	9 1/16	Rio Grande Co., CO	Clinton W. Wilson	2005	31
15 1/16	8 12/16	Ravalli Co., MT	Robert S. Wood	2005	31
15 1/16	8 14/16	Missoula Co., MT	James M. Lamphier	2006	31
15	8 15/16	Elko Co., NV	Cecil R. Bell	1994	41
15	8 10/16	Kootenay Lake, BC	Dean J. Ficociello	1995	41
15	8 12/16	Gila Co., AZ	John L. Hughes	2003	41
15	8 10/16	Missoula Co., MT	Paul L. Walhood	2003	41
15	8 14/16	Lincoln Co., WY	Rachelle L. Hyde	2004	41
15	9	Idaho Co., ID	Frank A. Staab	2006	41
14 15/16	8 11/16	Idaho Co., ID	Kassem Meiss	2006	47
14 14/16	8 12/16	Rio Arriba Co., NM	Bill J. Lewellen	2003	48
14 14/16	8 14/16	Utah Co., UT	Tammy Coburn	2004	48
14 14/16	9	Cowlitz Co., WA	Chad Coburn	2004	48
14 14/16	8 13/16	Latah Co., ID	Robert T. Ferry	2005	48
14 13/16	8 11/16	Idaho Co., ID	Timothy B. Johnston	2005	52
14 13/16	8 11/16	Morgan Co., UT	David F. Bier	2005	52
14 13/16	8 12/16	Rio Blanco Co., CO	Glen O. Hallows	2005	52
	8 12/16		Roger Sermersheim	2005	52

COUGAR
FINAL SCORE: 15-2/16
HUNTER: Michael S. Dotson

COUGAR
FINAL SCORE: 14-9/16
HUNTER: John P. Schreiner

COUGAR
FINAL SCORE: 14-9/16
HUNTER: Greg M. Hartman

COUGAR

Felis concolor hippolestes and related subspecies

Final Score	Greatest Length of Skull Without Lower Jaw	Greatest Width of Skull	Locality	Hunter	Owner	Date Killed	Rank
14 12/16	8 10/16	6 2/16	Little Timothy Mt., BC	Michael Porcelli	Michael Porcelli	2001	55
14 12/16	8 9/16	6 3/16	Chilcotin Ranges, BC	Gary L. Bailey	Gary L. Bailey	2003	55
14 12/16	8 11/16	6 1/16	Utah Co., UT	Bryan C. Darling	Bryan C. Darling	2003	55
14 12/16	8 10/16	6 2/16	Grant Co., OR	Geraldine Emerson	Geraldine Emerson	2004	55
14 12/16	8 10/16	6 2/16	Mesa Co., CO	Werner H. Schmiesing	Werner H. Schmiesing	2004	55
14 11/16	8 10/16	6 1/16	Idaho Co., ID	David E. Lucas	David E. Lucas	1992	60
14 11/16	8 10/16	6 1/16	Rio Arriba Co., NM	Dustin S. Boyd	Dustin S. Boyd	2003	60
14 11/16	8 10/16	6 1/16	Utah Co., UT	Paul H. Peterson	Paul H. Peterson	2003	60
14 11/16	8 11/16	6	Rio Blanco Co., CO	Matt E. Vaughn	Matt E. Vaughn	2003	60
14 11/16	8 10/16	6 3/16	Saguache Co., CO	Virgil L. Hannig	Virgil L. Hannig	2004	60
14 11/16	8 8/16	6 2/16	Kootenai Co., ID	W. Thexton & B. Gonzales	William Thexton	2004	60
14 10/16	8 9/16	6 1/16	Montezuma Co., CO	Branko Terkovich	Luke A. Terkovich	2002	66
14 10/16	8 8/16	6 2/16	Idaho Co., ID	Dan D. Drover	Dan D. Drover	2004	66
14 10/16	8 9/16	6 1/16	Elmore Co., ID	Mark T. Lacosse	Mark T. Lacosse	2004	66
14 10/16	8 10/16	6	Lincoln Co., MT	Gary A. Crowe	Gary A. Crowe	2005	66
14 10/16	8 8/16	6 2/16	Las Animas Co., CO	Billy B. Sanders	Billy B. Sanders	2006	66
14 9/16	8 11/16	5 14/16	Mineral Co., MT	Robert R. Wiesner	Robert R. Wiesner	1976	71
14 9/16	8 10/16	5 15/16	Saguache Co., CO	Marc T. Crumpton	Marc T. Crumpton	2003	71
14 9/16	8 7/16	6 2/16	Bear Lake Co., ID	James W. Brower	James W. Brower	2004	71
14 9/16	8 10/16	5 15/16	Tatla Lake, BC	Michael E. Burkman	Michael E. Burkman	2004	71
14 9/16	8 7/16	6 2/16	Castle River, AB	William R. Messum	William R. Messum	2004	71
14 9/16	8 9/16	6	Sheridan Co., WY	Greg M. Hartman	Greg M. Hartman	2005	71
14 9/16	8 10/16	5 15/16	Big Horn Co., WY	John P. Schreiner	John P. Schreiner	2005	71
14 9/16	8 10/16	5 15/16	Duchesne Co., UT	Jeremy J. Starr	Jeremy J. Starr	2005	71
14 9/16	8 8/16	6 1/16	Lincoln Co., WY	Brian D. Tallerico	Brian D. Tallerico	2005	71
14 8/16	8 9/16	5 15/16	Eureka Co., NV	Chad D. Bliss	Chad D. Bliss	2004	80
14 8/16	8 6/16	6 2/16	Rosebud Co., MT	Shawn Hayes	Shawn Hayes	2005	80
14 8/16	8 8/16	6	Emery Co., UT	Richard Riggle	Richard Riggle	2005	80
14 8/16	8 8/16	6 1/16	Storey Co., NV	Mitchell G. Bailey	Mitchell G. Bailey	2006	80
14 8/16	8 7/16	6 1/16	Saguache Co., CO	Thomas D. Lundgren	Thomas D. Lundgren	2006	80
15 6/16*	9	6 6/16	Sevier Co., UT	Brady Baker	Brady Baker	2004	
15 6/16*	9	6 6/16	Dismal Creek, AB	Robert Garcia	Robert Garcia	2004	

* Final score subject to revision by additional verifying measurements.

PACIFIC WALRUS

Odobenus rosmarus divergens

Minimum Score 100

World's Record 147 4/8

The geographical boundary for Pacific walrus is: That portion of the Bering Sea east of the International Dateline; south along coastal Alaska, including the Pribilof Islands and Bristol Bay; extending eastward into Canada to the southwest coasts of Banks and Victoria Islands and the mouth of Bathurst Inlet in Nunavut Province (formerly the northwest portion of Northwest Territories).

Final Score	Gross Score	Entire Length of Loose Tusk R.	L.	Circumference of Base R.	L.	Circumference at the Third Quarter R.	L.	Locality	Hunter	Owner	Date Killed	Rank
119 4/8	120 4/8	32 7/8	33 4/8	7 2/8	7 3/8	5 2/8	5 2/8	Cape Nome, AK	Picked Up	M. Wayne Carey	2003	1
119	124 2/8	31	26 7/8	8 5/8	8 4/8	6 7/8	6 4/8	Cape Seniavin, AK	Picked Up	Remo Pizzagalli	2005	2
114 2/8	116 7/8	31 2/8	30 3/8	7 7/8	8 4/8	5 1/8	4 5/8	Point Hope, AK	Unknown	Richard O. Turner	PR 1985	3

AMERICAN ELK - TYPICAL ANTLERS

Cervus elaphus nelsoni and certain related subspecies

Minimum Score 360   World's Record 442 5/8

Final Score	Gross Score	Length of Main Beam R.	L.	Inside Spread	Circumference at Smallest Place Between First & Second Points R.	L.	Number of Points R.	L.	Locality	Hunter	Owner	Date Killed	Rank
412 7/8	417 7/8	54 7/8	54 4/8	53 5/8	9 7/8	10 4/8	6	6	Utah Co., UT	Doug Degelbeck	Doug Degelbeck	2006	1
410 5/8	419 1/8	63 1/8	66 3/8	39 7/8	8 3/8	8 2/8	6	6	Gila Co., AZ	Dan J. Agnew	Dan J. Agnew	2003	2
403 4/8	416 3/8	56 2/8	56 1/8	54 2/8	8 6/8	9 6/8	6	6	Garfield Co., UT	Shan J. Ogden	Shan J. Ogden	2006	3
402 5/8	427 4/8	52 2/8	52 3/8	36 6/8	8 4/8	8 1/8	8	7	Athabasca River, AB	William J. Huppertz	William J. Huppertz	2004	4
402 2/8	413 7/8	51 1/8	51 1/8	47 3/8	10 2/8	10 5/8	7	6	Catron Co., NM	Picked Up	Travis R. Kiehne	1997	5
401	407 7/8	59	59	41	10 2/8	10 3/8	6	6	Garfield Co., UT	Larry L. Ball	Larry L. Ball	2004	6
399 7/8	409	52 6/8	53 5/8	47 7/8	10 4/8	10 4/8	7	6	White Pine Co., NV	Chris R. Knapp, Sr.	Chris R. Knapp, Sr.	2003	7
398 3/8	407 7/8	52 6/8	52 6/8	40 1/8	8 1/8	8 4/8	7	7	Rio Arriba Co., NM	Robert North	Robert North	2004	8
397 7/8	419 6/8	57	57 5/8	53 6/8	8 7/8	8 4/8	9	8	Powder River Co., MT	Picked Up	W.A. Buck Titus	2004	9
396 7/8	415 3/8	58	57 1/8	48 1/8	9 4/8	10 1/8	7	8	Navajo Co., AZ	Gary W. Crowe	Gary W. Crowe	2004	10
396 2/8	404 7/8	58 2/8	57 5/8	39	9 7/8	9 2/8	6	6	Socorro Co., NM	Bill L. Clark	Bill L. Clark	2006	11
395 5/8	410 6/8	60 7/8	60 1/8	45 1/8	9 6/8	10	7	8	Park Co., WY	Keith Hamilton	Keith Hamilton	2005	12
394 6/8	401 7/8	53 3/8	52 7/8	49	9 5/8	9 1/8	6	6	Garfield Co., UT	Brent D. Lowry	Brent D. Lowry	2004	13
394 2/8	407 7/8	57	56 5/8	50 6/8	9 6/8	9 5/8	7	7	Beaver Co., UT	Garry D. Matson	Garry D. Matson	2005	14
394 1/8	406 7/8	52 4/8	53	48 1/8	9 1/8	9 7/8	6	7	Wayne Co., UT	Victor K. Jones	Victor K. Jones	2005	15
394	405	54 1/8	53 5/8	45 2/8	11	10 3/8	6	6	Douglas Co., CO	John T. McCord	John T. McCord	2002	16
392 7/8	399 3/8	57 1/8	53 5/8	54 1/8	10 1/8	10 3/8	6	6	Cibola Co., NM	Paul L. Cool	Paul L. Cool	2005	17
392 6/8	403 4/8	55 7/8	57 1/8	40 6/8	10 6/8	10 2/8	6	7	Yellowstone Co., MT	Walter A. Tate	Walter A. Tate	2006	18
392 1/8	401 4/8	55 6/8	55 4/8	50 3/8	10 3/8	10 5/8	6	6	Teller Co., CO	Duane M. Bakke	James D. Bakke	1962	19
391 3/8	404	59 4/8	59 3/8	42 5/8	8 2/8	8 2/8	7	7	Navajo Co., AZ	Dennis K. Frandsen	Dennis K. Frandsen	2001	20
391	404 5/8	56 6/8	58 2/8	48 2/8	10 6/8	10 6/8	6	7	Beaver Co., UT	Aaron W. Cox	Aaron W. Cox	2006	21
390 3/8	399 1/8	58	57	50 1/8	9 2/8	9 2/8	6	7	Sioux Co., NE	Robert L. Marsteller	Robert L. Marsteller	2004	22
390 3/8	398 5/8	58	59 3/8	50 7/8	8	9 4/8	6	6	Garfield Co., UT	K'Dee Gardner	K'Dee Gardner	2006	22
389 5/8	397 5/8	54 5/8	55 3/8	40 7/8	9	8 4/8	6	6	White Pine Co., NV	Tim A. Horn	Tim A. Horn	2005	24
389 1/8	402 1/8	58 5/8	59	41 1/8	9 4/8	9	7	7	Cache Co., UT	Lewis K. Winward	Lewis K. Winward	2004	25
388 7/8	397	50 4/8	52 7/8	42 5/8	7 7/8	8 6/8	6	6	Golden Valley Co., MT	Janna M. Heiken	Janna M. Heiken	2005	26
388 5/8	400 7/8	60	59 2/8	43 3/8	8 1/8	7 6/8	7	7	Larimer Co., CO	Mark J. Unger	Mark J. Unger	2004	27
388 4/8	400 4/8	57 2/8	55 4/8	47 2/8	8 2/8	9	6	6	Elko Co., NV	John Hildebrand	John Hildebrand	2004	28
387 6/8	390 3/8	57 2/8	57 2/8	49 2/8	7 7/8	7 7/8	6	6	Garfield Co., UT	Clint Fullmer	Clint Fullmer	2005	29
387 3/8	396 1/8	57 1/8	57 1/8	41 1/8	8 5/8	8 5/8	7	7	Mohave Co., AZ	Dorothy J. Harber	Dorothy J. Harber	2004	30
386 5/8	402 1/8	55 3/8	49 7/8	49 7/8	9 6/8	9 6/8	7	6	Goshen Co., WY	David A. Stenson	David A. Stenson	2005	31
386 2/8	401 3/8	58 2/8	56 7/8	50 4/8	8 5/8	7 6/8	7	8	Lincoln Co., NV	Daniel L. Evans	Daniel L. Evans	2005	32
386 2/8	396 5/8	54 3/8	54 2/8	48 6/8	10 4/8	10 1/8	6	6	White Pine Co., NV	Edward M. Neilsen	Edward M. Neilsen	2005	32

385 6/8	395 5/8	58 5/8	59 6/8	42	9 5/8	6	8 7/8	6	Dennis L. Cummins	Coconino Co., AZ	Dennis L. Cummins	2005	34
385 6/8	399 6/8	55 5/8	56 4/8	40 6/8	7 6/8	7	9 1/8	6	Danny L. Moore	Coconino Co., AZ	Danny L. Moore	2005	34
385 4/8	394 6/8	53 1/8	53	40	7 6/8	7	8 4/8	7	Ren D. Gardner	Powder River Co., MT	Ren D. Gardner	2005	36
385 4/8	392 1/8	53 6/8	53 3/8	45 4/8	9 2/8	7	8 4/8	7	Jeremy C. Joyner	Wasatch Co., UT	Jeremy C. Joyner	2005	36
385 2/8	392 1/8	58 6/8	59 3/8	47 4/8	7 7/8	6	8 1/8	6	Karl R. Hirst	San Juan Co., UT	Karl R. Hirst	2005	38
385 2/8	400 1/8	53 6/8	55 4/8	53	9 1/8	7	9 1/8	6	Stewart W. Stone	Larimer Co., CO	Stewart W. Stone	2005	38
384 6/8	389 7/8	52 2/8	51	43 4/8	8 6/8	6	8 4/8	6	Dustin S. Pexton	Converse Co., WY	Dustin S. Pexton	2005	40
384 6/8	409	56 4/8	53 2/8	58 4/8	8 4/8	7	8 1/8	6	Frisco Tsosie	Coconino Co., AZ	Frisco Tsosie	2005	40
383 7/8	389 7/8	52 6/8	54 4/8	39 3/8	7 7/8	6	8 1/8	6	William M. Kain	Catron Co., NM	William M. Kain	2003	42
383 2/8	405 7/8	52 7/8	52 2/8	48 1/8	9	7	9 2/8	7	Russell I. Marion	Colfax Co., NM	Wayne R. Marion	1968	43
383 1/8	394 5/8	54 1/8	54	43 3/8	9 4/8	6	9 7/8	6	Andy B. Durrett	Navajo Co., AZ	Andy B. Durrett	2005	44
383	395 6/8	59 2/8	59 2/8	41 1/8	9 6/8	6	9 4/8	6	Kenneth I. Farber	Cascade Co., MT	Kenneth I. Farber	2003	45
382 7/8	392 5/8	55 6/8	56 4/8	40 1/8	8 7/8	7	9	6	James R. Boldt	Gila Co., AZ	James R. Boldt	2005	46
382 1/8	391 5/8	52	54 4/8	37 7/8	9 1/8	6	9 1/8	6	Kenny Rhodes	San Juan Co., UT	Kenny Rhodes	2004	47
382	393 1/8	53 6/8	55 3/8	43 4/8	8 1/8	7	8 1/8	7	Jeannine Ray	Las Animas Co., CO	Jeannine Ray	1979	48
382	387 4/8	53 2/8	52 1/8	43 2/8	7 6/8	6	8	6	Gabe Grant	Glacier Co., MT	Gabe Grant	2005	48
381 7/8	394 3/8	56 1/8	55 5/8	42 7/8	8 4/8	7	9 6/8	7	Keith D. Argyle	Coconino Co., AZ	Keith D. Argyle	2005	50
381 5/8	391 4/8	56	55 4/8	46 5/8	9 4/8	7	9 1/8	6	C. Emery Link	Park Co., WY	Daniel J. Darnall	1956	51
381 5/8	391 2/8	56 1/8	54	49 7/8	8 6/8	6	8 3/8	6	Curt L. Stegelmeier	Fremont Co., ID	Curt L. Stegelmeier	1997	51
381 5/8	391	57 7/8	58 4/8	47 1/8	8 5/8	6	9 1/8	6	Martin J. Mattson	Beaverhead Co., MT	Martin J. Mattson	2005	51
381 3/8	407 1/8	54 4/8	54 4/8	37	7 4/8	6	7 3/8	8	Aaron U. Jones	Coconino Co., AZ	Aaron U. Jones	2003	54

NON-TYPICAL AMERICAN ELK
FINAL SCORE: 385-3/8
HUNTER: Jill F. Plese

NON-TYPICAL AMERICAN ELK
FINAL SCORE: 394-1/8
HUNTER: Russel A. Young

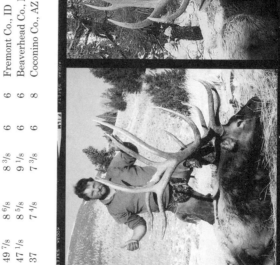

NON-TYPICAL AMERICAN ELK
FINAL SCORE: 389-7/8
HUNTER: Stan C. Gorsh

TYPICAL AMERICAN ELK
FINAL SCORE: 380-7/8
HUNTER: Timothy D. Metzler

AMERICAN ELK - TYPICAL ANTLERS

Cervus elaphus nelsoni and certain related subspecies

Final Score	Gross Score	Length of Main Beam R.	L.	Inside Spread	Circ. at Smallest Place Between First & Second Points R.	L.	Number of Points R.	L.	Locality	Hunter	Owner	Date Killed	Rank
381 3/8	388 7/8	54 7/8	55 6/8	49 6/8	8 5/8	8 4/8	7	7	Park Co., WY	Arlene G. Fischer	Arlene G. Fischer	2005	54
381 3/8	391 6/8	52 3/8	52 6/8	51 1/8	8 4/8	9 2/8	6	7	Apache Co., AZ	Ben Hollingsworth, Jr.	Ben Hollingsworth, Jr.	2005	54
381 1/8	395	49 5/8	50	36 1/8	8 4/8	8	7	7	Boulder Co., CO	Paul A. Hames	Paul A. Hames	2006	57
381	398 6/8	50 1/8	51 1/8	44	9 1/8	9 4/8	6	7	Park Co., WY	Jeff L. Stocklin	Jeff L. Stocklin	2004	58
381	397 3/8	57 2/8	57 4/8	60 4/8	8 5/8	8	6	7	Cibola Co., NM	Ronnie Metcalf	Ronnie Metcalf	2006	58
380 7/8	389	49	49 3/8	40 5/8	9 1/8	9 2/8	6	6	Park Co., WY	Timothy D. Metzler	Timothy D. Metzler	2005	60
380 7/8	388 1/8	60	60 1/8	43 5/8	10 3/8	10 2/8	6	6	Elko Co., NV	Tracy R. Mitton	Tracy R. Mitton	2005	60
380 2/8	392 6/8	57 4/8	59	41	8 6/8	8 4/8	6	6	Garfield Co., UT	Jerry L. Fronk	Jerry L. Fronk	2006	62
380 1/8	385 2/8	53 4/8	54 3/8	44 1/8	8 7/8	8 4/8	6	6	Utah Co., UT	Jack Stethem	Jack Stethem	2005	63
380	392 6/8	51 6/8	53 1/8	47 2/8	8 2/8	8 1/8	6	6	Lincoln Co., NV	Kurt W. Jensen	Kurt W. Jensen	2005	64
379 6/8	395 3/8	60 2/8	56 7/8	41 6/8	10	9 2/8	6	6	Millard Co., UT	Victor O. Pickett	Victor O. Pickett	2003	65
379 4/8	396 4/8	60 5/8	60 2/8	39 2/8	8 6/8	8 1/8	7	8	San Juan Co., UT	Robert S. Smith	Robert S. Smith	2005	66
379	393 4/8	59 4/8	63 1/8	44 6/8	9 7/8	10	6	6	Sevier Co., UT	Harlan J. Nielson	Harlan J. Nielson	2006	67
378 7/8	391 3/8	51 7/8	49 6/8	49 1/8	7 6/8	8 5/8	6	7	Moffat Co., CO	Alan L. Black	Alan L. Black	2005	68
378 6/8	388	57 2/8	57 5/8	41 2/8	10 1/8	10 3/8	7	7	Park Co., MT	David E. Brooks	David E. Brooks	2005	69
378 6/8	388 4/8	61 1/8	58 6/8	46 2/8	10 2/8	10 7/8	6	6	Tooele Co., UT	Jacob C. Holm	Jacob C. Holm	2005	69
378 5/8	388 2/8	53	53 7/8	51 3/8	9 6/8	8 6/8	7	6	Iron Co., UT	Keith D. Harrow	Keith D. Harrow	2006	71
378 3/8	397 5/8	55 4/8	54	42 5/8	9	9 3/8	6	7	Pine River, BC	Mark A. Guglielmini	Mark A. Guglielmini	2006	72
378 1/8	404 4/8	59 7/8	58	41 6/8	10 4/8	10	7	8	Carbon Co., WY	Elmer Wick	Dennis M. Wick	1929	73
378 1/8	390 5/8	53 3/8	53 2/8	47 1/8	8 3/8	8 5/8	7	6	Sanpete Co., UT	Ronald L. Clark	Ronald L. Clark	2004	73
378	393 5/8	53 4/8	54 2/8	47 2/8	7 2/8	8 6/8	7	6	White Pine Co., NV	Nathan T. Conk	Nathan T. Conk	2003	75
378	386 5/8	58	56 3/8	47 6/8	8 6/8	8 5/8	6	6	Golden Valley Co., ND	Dwight Ormiston	Dwight Ormiston	2005	75
377 5/8	386 7/8	53 5/8	55 3/8	43 1/8	9 6/8	9 7/8	6	6	San Juan Co., UT	Phillip P. Palmer	Phillip P. Palmer	2004	77
376 7/8	388 4/8	56 6/8	54 3/8	33 1/8	7 7/8	7 5/8	6	6	Shoshone Co., ID	Roger Johnson	Roger Johnson	1980	78
376 7/8	383 3/8	60 1/8	57 3/8	38 1/8	9 6/8	10 2/8	6	6	Navajo Co., AZ	Robert L. Earthman, Jr.	Robert L. Earthman, Jr.	2003	78
376 7/8	393 1/8	56 5/8	52 3/8	36 2/8	9 4/8	9 3/8	7	6	San Juan Co., UT	Frederick L. Bennetts	Frederick L. Bennetts	2005	78
376 7/8	390 7/8	54 7/8	55 5/8	43 5/8	8 1/8	8 6/8	7	7	Park Co., MT	Pete J. Salle	Pete J. Salle	2005	78
376 6/8	386 2/8	59 3/8	60 6/8	49	9 4/8	9 4/8	5	6	Lincoln Co., NV	Eric Merritt	Eric Merritt	2006	82
376 5/8	385 6/8	54 2/8	54	41 5/8	9 2/8	9 2/8	6	6	Garfield Co., MT	Linda A. Reder	Linda A. Reder	2005	83
376 4/8	397 6/8	54 7/8	53 4/8	39 6/8	8 5/8	8 5/8	8	6	Park Co., WY	Stanley R. Strike	Stanley R. Strike	2004	84
376 4/8	392 5/8	52 6/8	47 2/8	40	9 1/8	8 5/8	8	7	Douglas Co., CO	Glen Summers	Glen Summers	2004	84
376 4/8	393 6/8	56 6/8	56 5/8	45 6/8	8 4/8	9	7	8	Iron Co., UT	Richard E. Jessop	Richard E. Jessop	2006	84

376 3/8	393	59 1/8	62	39 4/8	9 7/8	9 4/8	6	8	Columbia Co., WA	John R. Appel	John R. Appel	2005	87
376 2/8	395 2/8	49 3/8	48 6/8	36 7/8	8	7 7/8	6	7	Yavapai Co., AZ	Everett W. Barber	Everett W. Barber	2004	88
376 1/8	382 2/8	48 4/8	48 3/8	39 5/8	9 3/8	9 2/8	7	7	Park Co., WY	Brent E. Wood	Brent E. Wood	2004	89
376	382 6/8	54 2/8	53 2/8	53 6/8	7 7/8	7 5/8	6	6	Piute Co., UT	Stan Hendrickson	Stan Hendrickson	2004	90
376	383 4/8	50	52	45	8 3/8	8 1/8	6	6	Piute Co., UT	Cloys D. Seegmiller	Cloys D. Seegmiller	2005	90
376	388 2/8	56 6/8	56 4/8	50 2/8	10	9 6/8	8	8	Elko Co., NV	Daniel L. Evans	Daniel L. Evans	2006	90
375 7/8	385 6/8	56 2/8	52	39 5/8	9 3/8	8 7/8	7	7	Park Co., MT	Randy J. Koliha	Randy J. Koliha	2005	93
375 4/8	383 4/8	54 2/8	55 3/8	46 6/8	9 3/8	9 3/8	7	6	Fergus Co., MT	Randall S. Ulmer	Randall S. Ulmer	2004	94
375 4/8	389 5/8	53 2/8	54 4/8	40 4/8	8 5/8	9 3/8	6	6	Elko Co., NV	Ralph S. Pinkston	Ralph S. Pinkston	2005	94
375 4/8	390 4/8	51 2/8	50 2/8	50 2/8	9 2/8	9 2/8	7	6	Spokane Co., WA	Trevor W. Smith	Trevor W. Smith	2005	94
375 3/8	384 2/8	51 2/8	49 2/8	44 1/8	10 1/8	9 7/8	6	6	Navajo Co., AZ	Randy L. Callison	Randy L. Callison	2005	97
375 2/8	391 3/8	56 2/8	55 6/8	43 2/8	9 7/8	9 2/8	7	6	Bonner Co., ID	Barry D. Nelson	Barry D. Nelson	1967	98
375 2/8	381 7/8	54 7/8	55	41 6/8	8 7/8	8 4/8	6	6	Socorro Co., NM	Jan H. Ohlander	Jan H. Ohlander	2003	98
375 2/8	399	54 2/8	52	38 7/8	10 3/8	10	6	6	Coconino Co., AZ	Tod L. Reichert	Tod L. Reichert	2005	98
375	388 7/8	57 4/8	56	33 4/8	9 2/8	9 1/8	9	7	Owyhee Co., ID	Don J. Burch	Don J. Burch	2005	101
375	383 4/8	58 1/8	59 5/8	44	8 4/8	8 4/8	8	6	Garfield Co., UT	Dirk C. Rasmussen	Dirk C. Rasmussen	2005	101
375	385 5/8	57 7/8	56 5/8	43 6/8	8 4/8	8 4/8	8	7	Millard Co., UT	Ryan T. Wood	Ryan T. Wood	2005	101
374 6/8	385 3/8	48 4/8	52	33 4/8	9 6/8	10 3/8	8	6	Jefferson Co., CO	Phil R. Parker	Phil R. Parker	2005	104
373 7/8	402 6/8	55	56 4/8	43 1/8	9 1/8	8 7/8	7	7	Gallatin Co., MT	Ralph C. Wermers	Ralph C. Wermers	2005	105
373 2/8	395	51 7/8	52 5/8	42 2/8	8 5/8	8 6/8	7	6	White Pine Co., NV	Larry D. Stahlheber	Larry D. Stahlheber	2003	106
372 6/8	379 5/8	55 3/8	55 2/8	37 3/8	8 2/8	8 4/8	6	6	Idaho	Ben Howland	Rick E. States	1929	107
372 5/8	380 4/8	60 3/8	61	39 1/8	7 7/8	7 6/8	7	7	Sevier Co., UT	Roy L. Wheeler, Sr.	Roy L. Wheeler, Sr.	2005	108
372 5/8	382 5/8	57 2/8	55 1/8	39 3/8	8	7 6/8	6	6	White Pine Co., NV	Arthur J. Phillips	Arthur J. Phillips	2006	108
372 2/8	384 6/8	51 6/8	52 5/8	47 2/8	8 3/8	8 4/8	8	7	Bonner Co., ID	George Agar	George Agar	1955	110
371 6/8	385 1/8	51 4/8	53 2/8	39 2/8	8 4/8	8 7/8	7	6	Diefenbaker Lake, SK	Ronald B. Munter	Ronald B. Munter	2005	111
371 5/8	376 1/8	55 3/8	55	40 7/8	8 7/8	7 7/8	6	6	Park Co., MT	Steven R. Halmi	Steven R. Halmi	2005	112
371 3/8	379 6/8	56 2/8	56 2/8	52 1/8	7 7/8	8 2/8	7	6	Custer Co., ID	David D. Lee	David D. Lee	1977	113
370 6/8	381 7/8	47	49 6/8	47 2/8	9 1/8	9 6/8	6	7	Navajo Co., AZ	Raymond M. Ramirez	Raymond M. Ramirez	2003	114
370 5/8	391 1/8	56	55 1/8	45 4/8	11 1/8	7 7/8	6	7	Millard Co., UT	Gayle Peterson	Gayle Peterson	2003	115
370 1/8	380 4/8	49 5/8	54 3/8	44 3/8	8 6/8	8 4/8	7	7	Teton Co., WY	David L. Pittman	David L. Pittman	2003	116
370	376 4/8	50 4/8	49 6/8	36 2/8	9 1/8	8 1/8	7	7	Benewah Co., ID	Aaron C. Robinson	Aaron C. Robinson	1961	117
369 7/8	379	57 3/8	56 4/8	37 1/8	9 3/8	9 3/8	7	7	Hot Springs Co., WY	Zachary I. Walker	Zachary I. Walker	2006	118
369 4/8	389 3/8	57 5/8	56 7/8	40 3/8	8 2/8	8 2/8	7	6	Cameron Co., PA	Dale McElheny	Dale McElheny	2003	119
369 3/8	382 3/8	48 1/8	42 5/8	42 5/8	9 5/8	8 1/8	6	7	Juab Co., UT	Jason Worwood	Jason Worwood	2003	120
369 3/8	385 3/8	50 5/8	47 6/8	34 1/8	9 6/8	10 1/8	7	6	Elko Co., NV	Timothy J. Naveran	Timothy J. Naveran	2004	120
369 3/8	375 7/8	60 3/8	49 2/8	40 7/8	9	10 1/8	7	7	Piute Co., UT	Bob J. Dickinson	Bob J. Dickinson	2006	120
368 6/8	385 3/8	54 4/8	60 2/8	46 4/8	8 4/8	8 4/8	6	6	Mesa Co., CO	Patrick R. Rish	Patrick R. Rish	2004	123
368 6/8	378	52 7/8	54 4/8	47	7 5/8	7 5/8	6	7	Coconino Co., AZ	Cathy Grgas	Cathy Grgas	2005	123
368 4/8	376 7/8	56 1/8	53 7/8	43 2/8	9 6/8	9 6/8	6	6	Gallatin Co., MT	Charles P. Teague	Charles P. Teague	2003	125
368 4/8	390 3/8	57 3/8	57 3/8	45	9 2/8	8 6/8	7	6	Washakie Co., WY	Dan G. Rice	Dan G. Rice	2005	125
368 2/8	376 4/8	55 3/8	53 5/8	38 2/8	8 2/8	8 2/8	6	6	Navajo Co., AZ	Jay A. Kellett	Jay A. Kellett	2003	127
368 2/8	377 1/8	52 2/8	50 4/8	46	9 3/8	7 1/8	6	6	Teton Co., WY	Ty W. Harding	Ty W. Harding	2005	127

AMERICAN ELK - TYPICAL ANTLERS

Cervus elaphus nelsoni and certain related subspecies

Final Score	Gross Score	Length of Main Beam R	L	Inside Spread	Circumference at Smallest Place Between First & Second Points R	L	Number of Points R	L	Locality	Hunter	Owner	Date Killed	Rank
368 1/8	378 3/8	53 2/8	50 3/8	40 1/8	9 1/8	8 7/8	6	6	Spionkop Creek, AB	Philip M. Browne	Philip M. Browne	2005	129
367 7/8	384 2/8	58 1/8	57 3/8	38 7/8	7 1/8	7 7/8	7	8	Kittitas Co., WA	Thomas J. Little	Thomas J. Little	2005	130
367 6/8	387	50 1/8	52 4/8	43 3/8	9 5/8	9 1/8	6	8	Idaho Co., ID	Don Ruark	Cindy Worth	1964	131
367 5/8	373 1/8	53 3/8	52 5/8	46 5/8	8	7 5/8	7	7	Fremont Co., ID	A. Nelson & G. Nelson	Alma Nelson	1960	132
367 5/8	373 2/8	54 4/8	52	45 5/8	8 5/8	8 4/8	6	6	Campbell Co., WY	Michael J. Halter	Michael J. Halter	2003	132
367 3/8	377 4/8	50 7/8	51 3/8	38 3/8	9 4/8	9 4/8	6	6	Garfield Co., UT	Scott W. Healy	Scott W. Healy	2004	134
367 3/8	385 1/8	50 3/8	55 7/8	43 3/8	9 2/8	10 6/8	6	7	Duchesne Co., UT	S. Trent Nelson	S. Trent Nelson	2004	134
367 1/8	379 1/8	52 2/8	50 3/8	36 1/8	10 2/8	9 6/8	7	7	Fergus Co., MT	Stephen Lalum	Stephen Lalum	2003	136
367	377 6/8	59 7/8	60 7/8	38 4/8	7	7	6	6	White Pine Co., NV	Robert A. Bailey	Robert A. Bailey	2005	137
366 7/8	373 6/8	51 6/8	52 6/8	42 3/8	7 7/8	8 4/8	6	6	Moffat Co., CO	Gary R. Edlin	Gary R. Edlin	2003	138
366 6/8	375 5/8	49	47 4/8	40 2/8	10 1/8	10	6	6	Natrona Co., WY	Aaron D. Zuhlke	Aaron D. Zuhlke	2006	139
366 4/8	375 5/8	55 1/8	55 3/8	49 2/8	7 4/8	7 7/8	6	6	Park Co., MT	Picked Up	Ronald D. Kuntz	1974	140
366 4/8	376 3/8	52	51 5/8	44 4/8	9 4/8	8 7/8	6	6	Rich Co., UT	Raymond D. Hlavaty	Raymond D. Hlavaty	2005	140
366 4/8	372 3/8	55 5/8	53 4/8	40 4/8	8	8	6	6	Crook Co., OR	Tim W. Koester, Jr.	Tim W. Koester, Jr.	2005	140
366 3/8	399 3/8	53 3/8	54 6/8	39 5/8	10	9 6/8	7	8	San Juan Co., UT	John S. Dowell	John S. Dowell	2004	143
366 2/8	376 2/8	53 5/8	52 1/8	35 6/8	8 7/8	9	6	7	Idaho Co., ID	Picked Up	B. McClure & G. McClure	1995	144
366 2/8	372 3/8	55 6/8	57 4/8	37 4/8	9	9 3/8	6	6	White Pine Co., NV	Lynne D. Brown	Lynne D. Brown	2003	144
366 2/8	389 7/8	56 1/8	54	41 6/8	8 4/8	8 7/8	8	7	Treasure Co., MT	Jeffery T. Llewellyn	Jeffery T. Llewellyn	2006	144
366 1/8	375 2/8	53	52 4/8	42 7/8	8 6/8	8 7/8	6	6	Duchesne Co., UT	Craig L. Rippen	Craig L. Rippen	2005	147
365 6/8	375 2/8	56 4/8	54 4/8	39 2/8	10	10 1/8	6	6	Missoula Co., MT	Chad M. Bauer	Chad M. Bauer	2003	148
365 5/8	375 5/8	52 6/8	50 6/8	34 3/8	9 3/8	9	6	6	Navajo Co., AZ	John T. Dardis II	John T. Dardis II	2005	149
365 4/8	392 7/8	51 4/8	48 1/8	41 6/8	9 1/8	9 1/8	7	7	Clearwater Co., ID	James R. Brian	James R. Brian	1970	150
365 1/8	389 4/8	53 4/8	52	40 2/8	7 5/8	8 1/8	7	7	Converse Co., WY	John C. Stewart	John C. Stewart	2005	151
364 5/8	388 3/8	51 2/8	57 1/8	44 6/8	9 5/8	10 1/8	8	6	Elk Co., PA	Edward S. Polashenski	Edward S. Polashenski	2003	152
364 3/8	385 3/8	57 2/8	51 6/8	37 3/8	9 3/8	9 3/8	8	7	Kootenai Co., ID	Curtis Yanzick	Curtis Yanzick	1990	153
364 2/8	377 3/8	57 3/8	58	44 4/8	9 3/8	9 3/8	7	6	Kittitas Co., WA	Colleen M. Akerblade	Colleen M. Akerblade	2003	154
363 6/8	371 6/8	51 2/8	50 2/8	51 5/8	8	7 2/8	6	6	Battle River, AB	Peter S. Litwinow	Peter S. Litwinow	2005	154
363 6/8	369 2/8	58 2/8	56 4/8	40 6/8	8 6/8	8 1/8	6	6	Park Co., WY	Randy A. Cragoe	Randy A. Cragoe	2006	154
363 3/8	375 2/8	50 7/8	53 1/8	38 5/8	9 4/8	9 2/8	7	7	Piute Co., UT	Stanley Sessions	Stanley Sessions	2004	157
362 6/8	364 6/8	57	56 2/8	39 4/8	9 5/8	9 5/8	6	6	Elmore Co., ID	Cary G. Cada	Cary G. Cada	2005	158
362 5/8	376 3/8	55 1/8	54	41 3/8	10 4/8	10 1/8	7	7	Colfax Co., NM	Douglas T. Price	Douglas T. Price	2005	159
362 4/8	371 1/8	54 2/8	52 6/8	39 6/8	7 7/8	7 7/8	6	6	Catron Co., NM	Robert R. Scaife	Robert R. Scaife	2004	160

Score									Locality	Hunter	Owner	Date	Rank
362 3/8	371	53 4/8	52 3/8	37 1/8	9 2/8	8 4/8	6	6	Johnson Co., WY	Terry L. Ridgeway	Terry L. Ridgeway	2001	161
362 1/8	375 5/8	50 1/8	52	41 3/8	9 5/8	9 3/8	7	7	Walla Walla Co., WA	Mark L. Pankey	Mark L. Pankey	2005	162
362	371 5/8	54 4/8	54 3/8	40 6/8	7 5/8	8	6	7	Yellowstone Co., MT	Randy Peterson	Randy Peterson	1958	163
361 5/8	376 3/8	52 1/8	49	41 3/8	8 6/8	8 2/8	7	7	Coconino Co., AZ	Darren G. Tucker	Darren G. Tucker	2001	164
361 4/8	378 2/8	55 6/8	55 6/8	48 4/8	8	7 6/8	6	6	Jefferson Co., MT	Tyler J. Maxwell	Tyler J. Maxwell	2005	165
361 3/8	378 2/8	53 6/8	55 2/8	38 1/8	8 6/8	9 2/8	6	7	Johnson Co., WY	Tammy L. Severeide	Tammy L. Severeide	2004	166
361 3/8	368 2/8	55 3/8	56 5/8	43 1/8	9	9 5/8	7	6	San Miguel Co., CO	Preston B. Gardner	Preston B. Gardner	2005	166
361 1/8	376 1/8	55 2/8	54 6/8	49 6/8	9 2/8	9 2/8	6	7	Garfield Co., UT	Brent M. Rowley	Brent M. Rowley	2004	168
361 1/8	374 2/8	52 6/8	52 6/8	46 3/8	8 1/8	7 7/8	7	7	Wasatch Co., UT	Trevor A. Kochevar	Trevor A. Kochevar	2005	168
361	385	49 4/8	50 3/8	41 1/8	9 3/8	9 6/8	7	6	Fremont Co., ID	Wilbur Chitwood	Wilbur Chitwood	1956	170
361	366 3/8	51 6/8	51 2/8	41 6/8	8 7/8	9 3/8	6	6	Garfield Co., UT	Kenneth T. Calton	Kenneth T. Calton	2006	170
360 7/8	368 6/8	56	54 4/8	48 3/8	8	8 4/8	6	6	Socorro Co., NM	James P. Bredy	James P. Bredy	2005	172
360 6/8	367 1/8	54	53 3/8	36 6/8	8	8 3/8	6	6	Elko Co., NV	William L. Leever	William L. Leever	2005	173
360 3/8	385	54 2/8	54 2/8	37 5/8	9 2/8	10 3/8	6	6	Sanpete Co., UT	Kim D. Lund	Kim D. Lund	2005	174
360 2/8	385	53 4/8	49 2/8	42 2/8	9 1/8	9	6	6	Coconino Co., AZ	Tim J. Suder	Tim J. Suder	2004	175
360 2/8	371 3/8	55 4/8	51	35 6/8	9 1/8	9	6	6	Teton Co., MT	Kyle L. Horn	Kyle L. Horn	2005	175
411 3/8*	416 7/8*	53	52 4/8	43 1/8	9 7/8	9 7/8	6	6	Millard Co., UT	Denny Austad	Denny Austad	2006	
408 4/8*	427	54 5/8	56 5/8	44 4/8	10 1/8	10 1/8	7	6	Millard Co., UT	Lloyd R. Jacobsen	Lloyd R. Jacobsen	2005	
404 4/8*	427 4/8*	60	58 1/8	45 1/8	9 1/8	9 6/8	7	8	Gila Co., AZ	Jay Scott	Jay Scott	2005	

* Final score subject to revision by additional verifying measurements.

TYPICAL AMERICAN ELK
FINAL SCORE: 376
HUNTER: Cloys D. Seegmiller

NON-TYPICAL AMERICAN ELK
FINAL SCORE: 387-1/8
HUNTER: Jeff L. Lundahl

TYPICAL AMERICAN ELK
FINAL SCORE: 378-3/8
HUNTER: Mark A. Guglielmini

TYPICAL AMERICAN ELK
FINAL SCORE: 381-3/8
HUNTER: Arlene G. Fischer

AMERICAN ELK - NON-TYPICAL ANTLERS

Cervus elaphus nelsoni and certain related subspecies

Minimum Score 385   World's Record 465 2/8

Final Score	Gross Score	Length of Main Beam R.	L.	Inside Spread	Circumference at Smallest Place Between First & Second Points R.	L.	Number of Points R.	L.	Locality	Hunter	Owner	Date Killed	Rank
433 1/8	439 4/8	50 4/8	51 1/8	44 5/8	7	7 2/8	11	12	Latah Co., ID	Peter J. Orazi, Jr.	Peter J. Orazi, Jr.	1977	1
429 1/8	435 6/8	49 3/8	48 2/8	47 6/8	8	8 1/8	10	9	Granite Co., MT	John Luthje	Rocky Mountain Elk Foundation	1971	2
417 1/8	426 4/8	47 3/8	47 6/8	40	10 6/8	11	6	8	Apache Co., AZ	Lynn H. Stinson	Lynn H. Stinson	2004	3
415 6/8	421 6/8	57 3/8	58 1/8	46	7 5/8	7 5/8	7	7	Nye Co., NV	Ted L. Wehking	Ted L. Wehking	2005	4
413 5/8	427 2/8	57 3/8	57 5/8	40	9 4/8	9 6/8	7	9	Kern Co., CA	Raymond G. Schaeffer	Raymond G. Schaeffer	2003	5
411 7/8	419 4/8	56 5/8	57 5/8	45 1/8	9 5/8	10 1/8	8	7	Coconino Co., AZ	Mike J. Drake	Mike J. Drake	2005	6
409 7/8	419 6/8	50 1/8	50 1/8	46 4/8	9 2/8	8 6/8	7	7	White Pine Co., NV	Randall S. Ulmer	Randall S. Ulmer	2003	7
409 6/8	425 2/8	54	56 4/8	42 6/8	9 2/8	10 6/8	7	6	Garfield Co., MT	Dennis R. Mangold	Dennis R. Mangold	2003	8
409 2/8	457 4/8	55 2/8	56 4/8	48 6/8	14 4/8	10 6/8	7	8	Coconino Co., AZ	Robert D. Hartwig	Robert D. Hartwig	2004	9
408 6/8	421	60 5/8	59 7/8	41 2/8	9 4/8	10 6/8	9	7	Gila Co., AZ	Kevin L. Christianson	Kevin L. Christianson	2004	10
406 7/8	417 4/8	55 3/8	56 3/8	45 6/8	9 2/8	9 5/8	8	7	Elko Co., NV	Jeffrey K. Rahbeck	Jeffrey K. Rahbeck	2003	11
404 6/8	421 4/8	51 6/8	47 2/8	40 7/8	8 7/8	9 1/8	8	9	Cibola Co., NM	Lacy J. Harber	Lacy J. Harber	2005	12
404 5/8	421 5/8	44	46 4/8	38 7/8	9 5/8	9 5/8	7	7	Navajo Co., NM	Richard Corbett	Richard Corbett	2004	13
404 2/8	430 6/8	56 5/8	57 2/8	47 1/8	8 4/8	7 5/8	10	9	Modoc Co., CA	Ron L. Beggs	Ron L. Beggs	2004	14
404	411 7/8	56 4/8	55 3/8	44 6/8	9	9	7	7	Elko Co., NV	Mike D. Popejoy	Mike D. Popejoy	2005	15
403 2/8	422 4/8	56 4/8	52 3/8	47 4/8	9 5/8	9 6/8	8	9	Piute Co., UT	Greg Holman	Greg Holman	2006	16
401 4/8	413 4/8	52 4/8	54 1/8	43 2/8	10 7/8	9 5/8	7	7	Apache Co., AZ	Thomas D. Friedkin	Thomas D. Friedkin	2005	17
400 5/8	415 1/8	52 5/8	51 3/8	44	9 4/8	10 1/8	8	7	Fremont Co., ID	Ernest H. Paskett	Ernest H. Paskett	1964	18
400 2/8	420 4/8	51	50	42 6/8	8 2/8	8 1/8	8	8	Elk Co., PA	Barry L. Klusewitz	Barry L. Klusewitz	2005	19
399 2/8	404 3/8	55 4/8	56 3/8	43 1/8	9 6/8	9 2/8	7	8	Emery Co., UT	Todd Pedersen	Todd Pedersen	2006	20
398 2/8	412 2/8	54 1/8	56 4/8	40 1/8	8 4/8	9	8	9	Navajo Co., AZ	Glen W. Morgan	Glen W. Morgan	2005	21
398	407 1/8	50 5/8	50 3/8	39	9 5/8	9 6/8	9	9	White Pine Co., NV	James R. Anderson III	James R. Anderson III	2005	22
397 5/8	421 1/8	47 7/8	56 4/8	37	10 2/8	10 3/8	8	8	Sierra Co., NM	Neil L. Lawson	Neil L. Lawson	2005	23
394 2/8	403 1/8	54 3/8	55 4/8	34 6/8	11 2/8	9 6/8	7	7	Natrona Co., WY	Steve R. Lamb	Steve R. Lamb	2006	24
394 1/8	408	52 1/8	52 2/8	35 4/8	9 1/8	9 5/8	7	7	Lincoln Co., NV	Russell A. Young	Russell A. Young	2003	25
393 7/8	406 7/8	59 2/8	59 7/8	43 2/8	9 2/8	10	6	7	Garfield Co., UT	Paul R. Jibson	Paul R. Jibson	2006	26
393 4/8	409 7/8	56 1/8	55 5/8	45 3/8	11 2/8	12	8	7	Modoc Co., CA	Robert R. Pinoli	Robert R. Pinoli	2005	27
393 3/8	403 1/8	45	44 7/8	41 4/8	9 2/8	8 7/8	8	8	Moose Mt. Prov. Park, SK	Vernon H. Muford	Vernon H. Muford	2006	27
392 6/8	423 7/8	54 7/8	49 1/8	34 4/8	8 4/8	8 6/8	9	10	San Juan Co., UT	Zane R. Bassett	Zane R. Bassett	2005	29
392 1/8	403 6/8	60 4/8	64	42 1/8	8 4/8	9 1/8	7	8	Coconino Co., AZ	Ralph E. Purvis, Jr.	Ralph E. Purvis, Jr.	2005	30
391	406 6/8	49 2/8	52 3/8	40 1/8	9 2/8	9 1/8	6	8	Gila Co., AZ	Jay Scott	Jay Scott	2006	31

389 7/8	399 1/8	47 6/8	47 3/8	37 5/8	9	8 7/8	7	7	Park Co., WY	Stan C. Gorsh	Stan C. Gorsh	2005	32
389 3/8	419 1/8	53	50 4/8	41 5/8	8	8 4/8	8	7	Socorro Co., NM	Mike Osborne	Mike Osborne	2004	33
389	403	53 6/8	55 1/8	42 4/8	10 1/8	10 2/8	6	10	Iron Co., UT	Tyson T. Thompson	Tyson T. Thompson	2006	34
387 6/8	406 1/8	50 3/8	53	39 3/8	9 3/8	9 2/8	8	7	Gila Co., AZ	Brandon R. Peddie	Brandon R. Peddie	2004	35
387 2/8	399 1/8	50 3/8	48 7/8	38 6/8	8 5/8	9	8	8	Navajo Co., AZ	Dennis K. Frandsen	Dennis K. Frandsen	2003	36
387 1/8	396 3/8	51 5/8	50 2/8	36 4/8	12	11	9	7	Otero Co., NM	Jeffery L. Lundahl	Jeffery L. Lundahl	2003	37
386 5/8	396 4/8	53 3/8	53 2/8	43 4/8	10 5/8	10	8	7	Millard Co., UT	Bonnie B. Moore	Bonnie B. Moore	2004	38
386 2/8	399 3/8	47 4/8	47 7/8	35 6/8	9 6/8	10 6/8	8	9	Idaho Co., ID	Daniel R. McClure	Daniel R. McClure	2005	39
386 2/8	400 1/8	49 6/8	51 4/8	44 2/8	10	9 2/8	6	8	Socorro Co., NM	William H. Williams III	William H. Williams III	2005	39
386 1/8	411 1/8	56 7/8	55 6/8	48 6/8	7 3/8	7 4/8	8	6	Unknown	Unknown	Stephen W. Blackwell	1940	41
386	401 6/8	51 6/8	48 6/8	44 4/8	8 1/8	8	8	7	Elk Co., PA	Damien Ramondo	Damien Ramondo	2005	42
385 5/8	397	47 7/8	46 1/8	32	9 5/8	9	8	9	Adams Co., ID	Richard L. Hansen	Richard L. Hansen	1978	43
385 4/8	394 3/8	52 2/8	53 3/8	45 2/8	9 2/8	8 7/8	8	7	Garfield Co., UT	Dallen M. Baugh	Cabela's, Inc.	2004	44
385 3/8	397 2/8	49 7/8	54 2/8	36 2/8	9 6/8	8 6/8	7	7	Elk Co., PA	Albert C. Erich	Albert C. Erich	2004	45
385 3/8	395 3/8	52 6/8	52 2/8	40 6/8	8 5/8	7 7/8	8	8	Garfield Co., UT	Jill F. Plese	Jill F. Plese	2004	45
385 2/8	397 5/8	50 4/8	52 5/8	41 4/8	9 5/8	9 5/8	7	8	Apache Co., AZ	R. Douglas Isbell	R. Douglas Isbell	2005	47
385 1/8	396 3/8	50 7/8	49 7/8	48 6/8	9 3/8	8 4/8	8	9	Catron Co., NM	David G. Weihl	David G. Weihl	2004	48
385	393	55	56 4/8	47 5/8	8 7/8	9 2/8	7	9	Cassia Co., ID	John Spratling	John Spratling	2001	49
385	392 4/8	55 4/8	54 4/8	39 7/8	9 6/8	9 6/8	10	8	Coconino Co., AZ	Picked Up	Cabela's, Inc.	2005	49
430 2/8*	438 4/8	54 2/8	54 3/8	43 1/8	10 1/8	8 5/8	8	8	Catron Co., NM	Chris Robb	Chris Robb	1998	
426 *	437 5/8	52 6/8	51 4/8	44 4/8	8 5/8	7 7/8	9	8	Ribstone Creek, AB	Hubert L. Rieland	Hubert L. Rieland	2005	

* Final score subject to revision by additional verifying measurements.

ROOSEVELT'S ELK

Cervus elaphus roosevelti

Minimum Score 275

World's Record 404 6/8

Roosevelt's elk includes trophies from: west of Interstate Highway I-5 in Oregon and Washington; Del Norte, Humboldt, and Trinity Counties, California, as well as that portion of Siskiyou County west of I-5 in Northern California; Afognak and Raspberry Islands of Alaska; and Vancouver Island, British Columbia.

Final Score	Gross Score	Length of Main Beam R.	Length of Main Beam L.	Inside Spread	Circumference at Smallest Place Between First & Second Points R.	Circumference at Smallest Place Between First & Second Points L.	Number of Points R.	Number of Points L.	Locality	Hunter	Owner	Date Killed	Rank
371 2/8	394 1/8	49 5/8	50 4/8	35 1/8	8 7/8	9 7/8	9	8	Gold River, BC	James V. Stewart	James V. Stewart	2003	1
346	360 1/8	47 7/8	49 2/8	34 2/8	9 6/8	10	8	7	Del Norte Co., CA	Picked Up	CA Dept. Fish & Game	2004	2
344 1/8	352 5/8	53 4/8	53 6/8	40 2/8	9 5/8	9 5/8	6	7	Clallam Co., WA	William R. Treese	William R. Treese	2005	3
340 3/8	345 3/8	46 7/8	47 5/8	38 6/8	8 1/8	8 3/8	7	8	Humboldt Co., CA	Jeffery C. Pierce	Jeffery C. Pierce	2005	4
336	348 2/8	53 7/8	48 7/8	36	9 3/8	8 6/8	7	7	Coos Co., OR	Rich L. Rounds	Rich L. Rounds	2004	5
329	335	51 2/8	51 2/8	36 1/8	10 6/8	10 2/8	6	6	Clallam Co., WA	Eric T. Hawkins	Eric T. Hawkins	2004	6
327 4/8	331 3/8	47 2/8	47 7/8	38 6/8	8 4/8	8 1/8	7	7	Grays Harbor Co., WA	Daryl E. Bartholomew	Daryl E. Bartholomew	1945	7
326 7/8	332 4/8	42 5/8	44 4/8	42 6/8	8 4/8	8 6/8	7	6	Pacific Co., WA	James Rettinghouse	Dale C. Rettinghouse	1948	8
326 5/8	337 2/8	57	53 6/8	38 4/8	10	9 5/8	6	7	Siskiyou Co., CA	Gary L. Cates	Gary L. Cates	2005	9
325 5/8	338 1/8	45 3/8	45 4/8	38 3/8	9 2/8	9 6/8	8	7	Douglas Co., OR	Bill Priest	Manford Amos	1941	10
324 2/8	329	48	48 4/8	33	8 6/8	8 2/8	7	6	Coos Co., OR	Ken Wilson	Ken Wilson	1969	11
323 2/8	326 7/8	47 6/8	47 4/8	42 3/8	7 3/8	7 4/8	7	6	Humboldt Co., CA	Tessa R. Wilburn	Tessa R. Wilburn	2004	12
321 4/8	334	48	48 3/8	32 6/8	10 7/8	11 1/8	7	6	Siskiyou Co., CA	Darrel C. Polasek	Darrel C. Polasek	2002	13
317 7/8	323	48 7/8	47 7/8	38 7/8	8 4/8	8 5/8	7	6	Douglas Co., OR	Kenneth W. Coe	Kenneth W. Coe	2005	14
317 2/8	328 6/8	44 5/8	44 4/8	41 7/8	9	9 1/8	8	8	Washington Co., OR	Matthew D. Schmidlin	Matthew D. Schmidlin	2006	15
314 3/8	319 6/8	45 1/8	45 6/8	44 4/8	9 7/8	9 3/8	6	6	Coos Co., OR	Kirk E. Winward	Kirk E. Winward	2005	16
311	324	53 1/8	52 1/8	41	7 7/8	8 3/8	7	6	Siskiyou Co., CA	Shawn E. Copper	Shawn E. Copper	2006	17
310 5/8	318 3/8	49	49 3/8	35 3/8	8 7/8	9 2/8	7	8	Yamhill Co., OR	Cindy Crowe	Cindy Crowe	2003	18
310 4/8	322 2/8	49 7/8	48 2/8	42	9 1/8	8 7/8	7	7	Curry Co., OR	R. Scott Knox	R. Scott Knox	2004	19
309 6/8	320 1/8	46 5/8	48 7/8	35	9 7/8	9 5/8	6	6	Jefferson Co., WA	Wes C. Cummings	Wes C. Cummings	2004	20
309 1/8	314 1/8	43 4/8	43 6/8	39 1/8	8 7/8	8 6/8	6	6	Powell River, BC	Dennis C. Campbell	Dennis C. Campbell	2004	21
307 3/8	311	47 3/8	49	41 3/8	9 4/8	9 1/8	6	5	Grays Harbor Co., WA	Todd F. Hubble	Todd F. Hubble	2001	22
307 2/8	313 4/8	50 1/8	49	43 4/8	8	8 2/8	6	6	Coos Co., OR	Racheal Smith	Racheal Smith	2005	23
306 7/8	317 4/8	49 6/8	51 3/8	42 6/8	9 3/8	9 2/8	6	7	Del Norte Co., CA	Dan E. Fox	Dan E. Fox	2006	24
306 1/8	315 6/8	49 5/8	46	41	8 6/8	9 1/8	6	6	Clallam Co., WA	Arnold J. LaGambina	Arnold J. LaGambina	2005	25
305 5/8	308 2/8	46 1/8	46	33 3/8	8 7/8	9 4/8	6	6	Trinity Co., CA	Robert J. King	Robert J. King	2005	26
304 6/8	314 7/8	48 2/8	47 6/8	32 4/8	10 6/8	11 1/8	5	6	Siskiyou Co., CA	Gearen L. Nugent	Gearen L. Nugent	2004	27
304	316 7/8	45 4/8	49 1/8	37	10 2/8	10	6	6	Clallam Co., WA	Timothy D. Seachord	Timothy D. Seachord	2004	28
303 2/8	311 5/8	42 5/8	47 3/8	35 2/8	8 1/8	8 3/8	7	6	Campbell River, BC	Randy A. Nelson	Randy A. Nelson	2005	29
302 4/8	307 5/8	42 3/8	42 1/8	37	8 1/8	7 3/8	6	6	Lincoln Co., OR	Ben L. Hogevoll	Ben L. Hogevoll	2004	30
300 5/8	311	43 1/8	45 5/8	34 6/8	8	8 1/8	7	7	Lincoln Co., OR	Keith W. Mitchell	Keith W. Mitchell	2005	31

Score								Locality	Hunter	Owner	Date	Rank
300 1/8	306 5/8	41 3/8	43 1/8	33 3/8	8 7/8	7	7	Columbia Co., OR	Cody W. Ogle	Cody W. Ogle	2006	32
297 1/8	302 5/8	44	42 4/8	36 2/8	9 1/8	5	5	Grilse Creek, BC	Marty C. Loring	Marty C. Loring	2005	33
296 3/8	303 2/8	48 4/8	45 7/8	29 2/8	9	7	6	Tillamook Co., OR	Dan Robeson	Dan Robeson	2003	34
296 1/8	309 2/8	46 5/8	47 1/8	31 5/8	8 7/8	6	6	Coos Co., OR	Jared Reeves	Jared Reeves	2006	35
295 3/8	315 7/8	42 6/8	42 6/8	38 1/8	8 5/8	8	8	Lincoln Co., OR	Mr. Ridenour	Darryl E. Barker	1905	36
294	300	39 2/8	41 2/8	33	8 2/8	6	6	Lewis Co., WA	Aaron Evans	Aaron Evans	2004	37
292 1/8	323 5/8	45 5/8	45 2/8	35 1/8	11	6	7	Clallam Co., WA	Chad R. Wilson	Chad R. Wilson	1999	38
292	300 5/8	42 6/8	41 5/8	42 2/8	8 3/8	6	6	Clallam Co., WA	Mike Rex	Mike Rex	2004	39
291	297 6/8	45 4/8	44 3/8	35 7/8	7 4/8	6	7	Coos Co., OR	Steven J. Martinez	Steven J. Martinez	2003	40
289	294 4/8	44 1/8	44 4/8	34	8 4/8	7	7	Columbia Co., OR	Andrew Morris	Andrew Morris	2004	41
286 1/8	301 5/8	43 4/8	40 2/8	31 7/8	9 1/8	8	7	Tillamook Co., OR	Jacob Thiemons	Jacob Thiemons	2005	42
282 4/8	291 2/8	41 2/8	43 5/8	35 3/8	8 5/8	7	6	Columbia Co., OR	Brandon L. Warren	Brandon L. Warren	2005	43
281 6/8	290	45 6/8	43 7/8	40 4/8	7 6/8	6	7	Tillamook Co., OR	Wilbur Barker	Darryl E. Barker	1961	44
281 1/8	286 3/8	41 2/8	40 1/8	39	7	7	7	Lincoln Co., OR	Timothy R. Taylor	Timothy R. Taylor	2005	45
280 5/8	293 6/8	40 6/8	42 4/8	39 7/8	7 6/8	8	8	Clatsop Co., OR	William J. Brown	William J. Brown	2000	46
278 4/8	288 1/8	42 5/8	42 3/8	33 3/8	9 3/8	7	7	Del Norte Co., CA	John R. Garr	John R. Garr	2001	47
275 4/8	279 5/8	39 4/8	37 6/8	42	9 1/8	6	6	Coos Co., OR	Randy Van Day	Randy Van Day	2004	48
355 3/8*	362 4/8	51 3/8	51 4/8	35 4/8	8 5/8	8	8	Benton Co., OR	David A. Kundert	David A. Kundert	2003	
348 *	355 6/8	51 6/8	52 2/8	41 2/8	8 4/8	7	7	Bonanza Lake, BC	Jim Shockey	Jim Shockey	2002	
347 3/8*	354 2/8	44 5/8	43 2/8	36 2/8	10 1/8	9	8	Salmon River, BC	Jesse Johnson	Jesse Johnson	2000	

* Final score subject to revision by additional verifying measurements.

ROOSEVELT'S ELK
FINAL SCORE: 306-7/8
HUNTER: Dan E. Fox

ROOSEVELT'S ELK
FINAL SCORE: 311
HUNTER: Shawn E. Copper

ROOSEVELT'S ELK
FINAL SCORE: 297-4/8
HUNTER: Marty C. Loring

ROOSEVELT'S ELK
FINAL SCORE: 347-3/8*
HUNTER: Jesse Johnson

TULE ELK

Cervus elaphus nannodes

Minimum Score 270   New World's Record 379

Tule elk are from selected areas in Calfiornia. For a complete description of the boundary, check the Official Measurer's manual, *Measuring and Scoring North American Big Game Trophies*, or visit the Club's web site at www.booneandcrockettclub.com.

Final Score	Gross Score	Length of Main Beam R.	L.	Inside Spread	Circumference at Smallest Place Between First & Second Points R.	L.	Number of Points R.	L.	Locality	Hunter	Owner	Date Killed	Rank
379	390 1/8	47 2/8	51	39 3/8	9 4/8	8 7/8	8	8	Glenn Co., CA	Picked Up	J. & J. Lopeteguy	2005	1
341 4/8	359 1/8	45 7/8	46	43 7/8	8 2/8	8 3/8	9	9	Colusa Co., CA	Val O. Olenski	Val O. Olenski	2004	2
331	351 7/8	42 2/8	41	36 7/8	9	9 4/8	8	9	Colusa Co., CA	Todd A. Robillard	Todd A. Robillard	2005	3
325 1/8	340 3/8	44 6/8	47 4/8	46 1/8	9 7/8	9 1/8	10	7	Solano Co., CA	Reed Mellor	Reed Mellor	2006	4
314 1/8	330 4/8	45	41 7/8	42 6/8	8 5/8	8 4/8	8	7	Colusa Co., CA	Mathew J. Garcia	Mathew J. Garcia	2006	5
312 5/8	321 5/8	45 6/8	44 4/8	41 7/8	8 1/8	8	7	9	Solano Co., CA	Richard R. Childress	Richard R. Childress	2003	6
312 5/8	321 2/8	45 4/8	45 2/8	42	8 4/8	8 3/8	7	8	Inyo Co., CA	Michael M. McCall	Michael M. McCall	2006	6
312 2/8	325 1/8	45	43 1/8	48	7 2/8	7 2/8	7	11	Monterey Co., CA	Kevin S. Small	Kevin S. Small	2005	8
303 6/8	309 2/8	43 2/8	44 4/8	39 5/8	8 4/8	9 1/8	7	7	Inyo Co., CA	Edward L. Fanchin	Edward L. Fanchin	2005	9
302 4/8	310 3/8	41	42 6/8	39	8 4/8	7 7/8	7	7	Monterey Co., CA	Eric C. Davis	Eric C. Davis	2005	10
295 7/8	306 5/8	44 6/8	45 7/8	44 5/8	7 2/8	7 7/8	7	7	Solano Co., CA	Daniel P. Connelly	Daniel P. Connelly	1999	11
295 7/8	298 6/8	44 1/8	44	48 1/8	7 4/8	7 1/8	8	7	Solano Co., CA	Todd J. Dorworth	Todd J. Dorworth	2004	11
294 2/8	298 5/8	40	40 1/8	44 6/8	7 3/8	7 4/8	7	7	Santa Clara Co., CA	Justin D. Fox	Justin D. Fox	2005	13
286 1/8	294 6/8	41 5/8	42 2/8	44	7 5/8	7 5/8	7	6	Mendocino Co., CA	Darrel C. Polasek	Darrel C. Polasek	2003	14
286 1/8	293 2/8	41 6/8	42 1/8	44 4/8	7 3/8	7 5/8	7	6	Monterey Co., CA	Tim S. Sharpe	Tim S. Sharpe	2005	14
283 3/8	296	41 1/8	42 2/8	41 3/8	8 4/8	8	7	7	Santa Clara Co., CA	Case B. Swenson	Case B. Swenson	2005	16
276 1/8	296 5/8	36 4/8	39	41	8 2/8	8 5/8	8	6	San Luis Obispo Co., CA	Jeffrey B. Buck	Jeffrey B. Buck	2005	17
272	277 6/8	37 5/8	37 1/8	39	7 6/8	7 4/8	6	8	San Luis Obispo Co., CA	Rebekah A.W. Bieber	Rebekah A.W. Bieber	2006	18

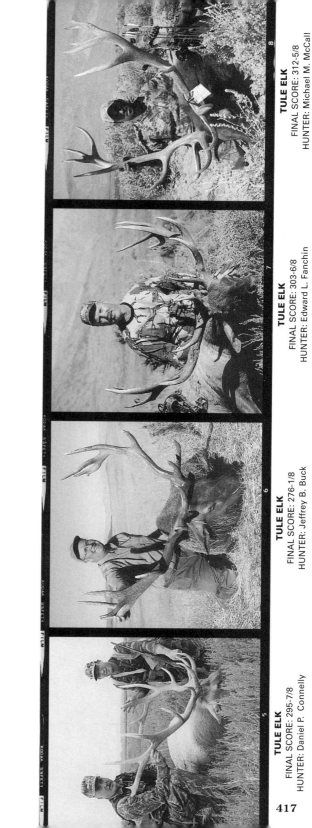

TULE ELK
FINAL SCORE: 312-5/8
HUNTER: Michael M. McCall

TULE ELK
FINAL SCORE: 303-6/8
HUNTER: Edward L. Fanchin

TULE ELK
FINAL SCORE: 276-1/8
HUNTER: Jeffrey B. Buck

TULE ELK
FINAL SCORE: 295-7/8
HUNTER: Daniel P. Connelly

MULE DEER - TYPICAL ANTLERS

Odocoileus hemionus hemionus and certain related subspecies

Minimum Score 180   World's Record 226 4/8

Final Score	Gross Score	Length of Main Beam R.	L.	Inside Spread	Circumference at Smallest Place Between Burr & First Point R.	L.	Number of Points R.	L.	Locality	Hunter	Owner	Date Killed	Rank
210 2/8	213 5/8	26 7/8	27 2/8	28 6/8	5 1/8	5	5	5	Sonora, MX	Myra S. Smith	Myra S. Smith	2006	1
208 4/8	226 4/8	27 5/8	28 1/8	25 2/8	5 5/8	5 4/8	8	6	Unknown	Unknown	Kevin Asbury	PR 2005	2
207 7/8	212 6/8	23 6/8	23 7/8	25 4/8	5 4/8	5 3/8	5	5	Teton Co., MT	Picked Up	MT Dept. Fish, Wildl., & Parks	2004	3
207 6/8	212 2/8	25 6/8	25 7/8	22 3/8	5 4/8	5 6/8	6	5	Eagle Co., CO	Robbie K. Cassett	Robbie K. Cassett	2006	4
207 5/8	210 6/8	25 1/8	26 6/8	22 7/8	5	5 1/8	5	5	Rio Arriba Co., NM	Unknown	Robert J. Seeds	PR 2003	5
206 6/8	216 1/8	27 5/8	27 3/8	26 4/8	4 3/8	4 4/8	5	5	Lincoln Co., WY	Gavin S. Lovell	Gavin S. Lovell	2004	6
206	230 7/8	29 4/8	30	26 3/8	5 5/8	5 5/8	6	5	Summit Co., UT	Kendal Kiesel	Kendal Kiesel	1966	7
205 3/8	209 5/8	25 4/8	27	22 7/8	5	4 7/8	5	5	Sounding Creek, AB	Dean G. Herron	Dean G. Herron	2003	8
204 6/8	210	26 2/8	26 2/8	24 6/8	4 7/8	4 6/8	5	5	Elko Co., NV	Donnie Thompson	Tamala D. Kraft	1982	9
204 5/8	208 5/8	25 1/8	25 5/8	26 4/8	5 2/8	5 2/8	5	5	Carbon Co., WY	Rich L. McKee	Rich L. McKee	2006	10
204 3/8	216	22 4/8	23 1/8	26 5/8	6 4/8	6 4/8	6	5	Sonora, MX	Donald E. Perrien	Donald E. Perrien	2006	11
203 7/8	214 1/8	26 1/8	25 3/8	23 5/8	5 5/8	5 2/8	5	5	Frenchman River, SK	Troy Hansen	Troy Hansen	2003	12
203 7/8	211 2/8	29 6/8	29 1/8	25 1/8	5 5/8	5 6/8	5	6	Franklin Co., WA	Thomas E. Adrian	Thomas E. Adrian	2004	12
203 7/8	208 2/8	26 1/8	27	22 5/8	5 2/8	5 3/8	5	5	Rio Arriba Co., NM	Unknown	Robert J. Seeds	PR 2004	12
203 5/8	215 1/8	26 5/8	27 4/8	22 6/8	4 6/8	4 6/8	5	7	Ravalli Co., MT	Keith Balfourd	Keith Balfourd	2005	15
202 2/8	207 1/8	26 6/8	27	29 2/8	6 1/8	6 1/8	6	5	Malheur Co., OR	James A. Hayhurst	James A. Hayhurst	2005	16
202	207 5/8	28 3/8	27 3/8	23 6/8	4 7/8	5	5	5	Montrose Co., CO	Leland J. Cox	Leland J. Cox	2004	17
201 3/8	209 5/8	26 3/8	25 6/8	31 4/8	5 4/8	5 7/8	5	6	Sonora, MX	Charles Tapia	Charles Tapia	2006	18
201 2/8	205	24 7/8	23 6/8	24	4 4/8	4 4/8	5	5	Weber Co., UT	Wayne R. Prevedel	Wayne R. Prevedel	2005	19
200 5/8	211 7/8	26 7/8	27 7/8	24 5/8	4 6/8	5	6	6	Timothy Mt., BC	Nolan Perchie	Nolan Perchie	2001	20
200 4/8	206 2/8	26 2/8	26 2/8	22 2/8	5 1/8	5 2/8	5	5	Delta Co., CO	Raymond R. Streily III	Raymond R. Streily III	1971	21
200 2/8	205 7/8	23 6/8	25 6/8	22 2/8	4 6/8	4 6/8	5	5	Routt Co., CO	Arthur L. Wyman	Arthur L. Wyman	1973	22
200	204 5/8	25 1/8	24 4/8	22 6/8	5	4 7/8	5	5	Billings Co., ND	John Stuchlik, Jr.	John Stuchlik, Jr.	2004	23
199 7/8	203	27	26 2/8	26 4/8	5 1/8	5 2/8	5	7	Rio Arriba Co., NM	Ryan L. Panzy	Ryan L. Panzy	2005	24
199 6/8	205 5/8	24 5/8	23 2/8	24 5/8	5 6/8	5 7/8	5	5	Sonora, MX	Ralph E. Purvis, Jr.	Ralph E. Purvis, Jr.	2006	24
199 5/8	205 5/8	26 4/8	28 1/8	19 6/8	6	6	5	5	Unknown	Unknown	Curtis P. Smiley	PR 1975	26
199 5/8	204 1/8	27 3/8	27 7/8	20 7/8	5 5/8	5 2/8	5	5	Gunnison Co., CO	Robert H. Hensarling	Robert H. Hensarling	2003	27
199 5/8	211 7/8	25 5/8	26 2/8	24 3/8	5 7/8	5 5/8	6	6	Mesa Co., CO	Timothy R. Viele	Timothy R. Viele	2005	27
199 3/8	200 7/8	27 3/8	27 3/8	23 1/8	4 6/8	4 6/8	5	5	Duchesne Co., UT	Charles H. Bird	Daniel C. Bird	1945	29
199 3/8	227 7/8	28	27	26 4/8	5 1/8	5 2/8	5	7	Lake Diefenbaker, SK	Darryll Helmeczi	Darryll Helmeczi	2003	29
199 1/8	204 3/8	27 5/8	26 7/8	31	5 3/8	5 3/8	5	5	Conejos Co., CO	Charles O. Handrahan	Roger A. Handrahan	1968	31
199	203 3/8	28 1/8	28 3/8	27 2/8	5 6/8	5 6/8	5	5	Fremont Co., WY	Bruce E. Davison	Bruce E. Davison	2004	32

Score									Locality	Hunter	Owner	Date	
198 7/8	203 2/8	26 1/8	24 4/8	25 3/8	5 5/8	5 2/8	5	5	Garfield Co., CO	A.C. Winnett	Bruce G. Barnett	1966	33
198 7/8	211 4/8	26 5/8	25 5/8	21 3/8	4 6/8	4 6/8	6	5	Franklin Co., ID	Herb G. Voyles, Jr.	Herb G. Voyles, Jr.	1973	33
198 6/8	202 3/8	26 2/8	27 1/8	26	4 6/8	4 7/8	5	5	Sonora, MX	Luis M. Garcia	Luis M. Garcia	2004	35
198 6/8	212 1/8	27 1/8	27 3/8	25 4/8	6	6 1/8	7	6	Montrose Co., CO	Andy R. Company IV	Andy R. Company IV	2005	35
198 6/8	211 1/8	26 5/8	26 2/8	24 2/8	5	4 7/8	5	6	Bow River, AB	Ervin L. Phipps	Ervin L. Phipps	2005	35
198 4/8	211 5/8	26	25 1/8	21 1/8	4 6/8	4 6/8	6	5	Pitkin Co., CO	Eugene B. Auten	Eugene B. Auten	2004	38
198 3/8	204 1/8	26	25 6/8	21 3/8	5 4/8	5 6/8	5	5	Rio Arriba Co., NM	Martha Loretto	Martha Loretto	2004	39
198 2/8	207 5/8	28	27 3/8	26 1/8	5 6/8	6	5	6	New Mexico	Joe J. Ulm	Richard L. DeChambeau	1977	40
198 1/8	208 4/8	25 7/8	28 3/8	24 3/8	5	5 1/8	6	5	Carbon Co., WY	Austin W. Patzer	Austin W. Patzer	2005	41
197 6/8	208 7/8	28 3/8	28 1/8	20 5/8	5 5/8	5 5/8	5	5	Bow Island, AB	Dave E. Trotter	Dave E. Trotter	2003	42
197 5/8	218 3/8	25 4/8	25 5/8	26 2/8	5 2/8	5 2/8	6	6	Gunnison Co., CO	Daniel J. Ampietro	Daniel J. Ampietro	2003	43
197 4/8	232 1/8	27 6/8	27 3/8	27	5 2/8	5 1/8	7	7	Eagle Co., CO	Michael S. McGee	Michael S. McGee	2004	44
197 4/8	202 7/8	25 5/8	25 4/8	23 7/8	5 2/8	5 3/8	6	5	La Plata Co., CO	Charles A. Thompson, Sr.	Charles A. Thompson, Sr.	2005	44
197 3/8	201 3/8	29 1/8	29	34	4 6/8	4 7/8	5	5	La Plata Co., CO	Boyd Freeman, Jr.	Boyd Freeman, Jr.	2004	46
197 3/8	205 2/8	25 6/8	25 5/8	23 6/8	5 2/8	5 3/8	6	5	Eagle Hills, SK	John R. MacDonald	John R. MacDonald	2004	46
197 1/8	202 6/8	27 3/8	28 3/8	26 3/8	4 5/8	4 6/8	5	5	La Plata Co., CO	James J. McCreery	James J. McCreery	2005	48
197	211 3/8	27 1/8	27	23 7/8	5	5	6	6	Teton Co., MT	Eugene G. Nelson	Eugene G. Nelson	1970	49
196 7/8	221 3/8	27 1/8	26 1/8	20 7/8	5 4/8	5 3/8	7	5	Mohave Co., AZ	Glenn Koch	Glenn Koch	2003	50
196 7/8	215 4/8	23 5/8	25 5/8	25 5/8	5 1/8	5 3/8	6	6	Douglas Co., CO	Ronald K. Milford	Ronald K. Milford	2003	50
196 7/8	201	23 5/8	23 2/8	22 3/8	4 7/8	5 1/8	5	5	Valley Co., ID	Joel Bender	Joel Bender	2004	50
196 7/8	223 3/8	26 7/8	27 4/8	22 1/8	5 1/8	5 2/8	5	6	Gunnison Co., CO	Willard B. Robbins III	Willard B. Robbins III	2004	50
196 6/8	210 3/8	26 4/8	26	24 1/8	5 2/8	5 3/8	6	5	Garfield Co., CO	Timothy P. Pedrick, Jr.	Timothy P. Pedrick, Jr.	2003	54
196 6/8	200 5/8	25	25 6/8	19 4/8	5	5	5	5	Mt. Bowman, BC	David Manderson	David Manderson	2004	54
196 5/8	201 6/8	23 5/8	24 4/8	20 3/8	5 4/8	5	6	6	Garfield Co., CO	Ronald L. Garcia	Ronald L. Garcia	1982	56
196 1/8	202 5/8	26 5/8	25 6/8	21 5/8	5 4/8	5 4/8	5	5	Deschutes Co., OR	William F. McGregor, Sr.	Scotty M. McGregor	1961	57
196 1/8	203 1/8	27 3/8	27 1/8	27	4 4/8	4 5/8	5	6	Okanogan Co., WA	James B. Wright	James B. Wright	1976	57
196	217	27 4/8	25	23 5/8	6 1/8	5 6/8	6	5	Wyoming	Unknown	William King	PR 1999	59
195 7/8	201 3/8	26 4/8	25 4/8	26 3/8	5 3/8	5 4/8	5	5	Cache Co., UT	Bobby Jo Cronquist Dansie	Bobby Jo Cronquist Dansie	2004	60
195 7/8	207 1/8	25 7/8	28	21	5 3/8	5 6/8	4	4	Grand Co., CO	Blaine J. Miller, Jr.	Blaine J. Miller, Jr.	2004	60
195 6/8	205 7/8	26 3/8	25 7/8	23 3/8	5 2/8	5 2/8	5	6	Missoula Co., MT	Obadiah M. Schulz	Obadiah M. Schulz	2004	62
195 6/8	202 1/8	26 5/8	26 6/8	26 2/8	5 3/8	5 2/8	6	6	S. Saskatchewan River, SK	Barry D. Miller	Barry D. Miller	2006	62
195 5/8	203 6/8	25	24 7/8	24 4/8	4 7/8	5 1/8	6	6	Kane Co., UT	Lloyd R. Jacobsen	Lloyd R. Jacobsen	1994	64
195 5/8	204 7/8	23 7/8	26 2/8	19 5/8	5	5	6	5	Lake Diefenbaker, SK	Neil Fornwald	Neil Fornwald	2003	64
195 5/8	204 1/8	23 6/8	26	26 3/8	4 4/8	4 3/8	5	6	Unknown	Unknown	Cabela's, Inc.	PR 2006	64
195 4/8	211	28 4/8	27	22 1/8	5 2/8	5 1/8	8	5	Madison Co., MT	David W. Hunt	Cabela's, Inc.	1964	67
195 4/8	206 2/8	26 4/8	28 1/8	26 5/8	5 1/8	5	6	5	Badger Lake, MT	Domenico Comita	Domenico Comita	2005	67
195 2/8	197 4/8	23 4/8	23 6/8	25 2/8	5	5	5	5	Sublette Co., WY	Frank D. Nataros	Frank D. Nataros	2004	69
195 2/8	198 3/8	26 2/8	24 6/8	24	5 6/8	5 5/8	5	5	Windy Mt., BC	Mark R. Scheid	Mark R. Scheid	2004	69

MULE DEER - TYPICAL ANTLERS

Odocoileus hemionus hemionus and certain related subspecies

Final Score	Gross Score	Length of Main Beam R.	L.	Inside Spread	Circumference at Smallest Place Between Burr & First Point R.	L.	Number of Points R.	L.	Locality	Hunter	Owner	Date Killed	Rank
195 1/8	200	24 1/8	24 6/8	23 7/8	5 2/8	5 1/8	5	5	Garfield Co., CO	Bernard F. Hueske	James B. Hueske	1942	71
195 1/8	214 6/8	27 6/8	25 3/8	27	5 1/8	5 1/8	6	7	Lemhi Co., ID	William D. Arbuckle	William D. Arbuckle	1969	71
195 1/8	199 1/8	23 4/8	23 3/8	20 3/8	5 3/8	5 3/8	5	5	Montrose Co., CO	Michael R. Davis	Michael R. Davis	2004	71
195	213	25 7/8	26 4/8	25 5/8	4 7/8	4 7/8	6	5	Garfield Co., CO	Ned H. Prather	Ned H. Prather	2004	74
195	222 5/8	27 3/8	27 6/8	23 2/8	4 6/8	4 6/8	7	7	Flathead Co., MT	Max G. Sutton	Max G. Sutton	2005	74
194 7/8	233 7/8	27 6/8	27 2/8	23 5/8	5 1/8	5 2/8	8	7	Ootsa Lake, BC	Michel G. Martin	Michel G. Martin	2005	76
194 5/8	221 1/8	28 3/8	27 2/8	24 5/8	4 6/8	5	6	7	Bear Lake Co., ID	Bobette Phelps	Bobette Phelps	2005	77
194 4/8	211 7/8	24 7/8	26 5/8	29 5/8	5 6/8	5 6/8	6	6	Lassen Co., CA	Ronald L. Peacock	Ronald L. Peacock	2006	78
194 3/8	225 5/8	28 7/8	27 5/8	23 1/8	4 6/8	4 5/8	7	8	La Plata Co., CO	Kevin R. Faddis	Kevin R. Faddis	2005	79
194 2/8	196 6/8	24 6/8	24 5/8	20	4 6/8	4 6/8	5	5	Grant Co., OR	Gary H. Purdy	Gary H. Purdy	2001	80
194 2/8	216 4/8	26 2/8	27 3/8	28	5 7/8	6	7	8	Rio Arriba Co., NM	Picked Up	Harold Vigil	PR 2006	80
194 2/8	204 6/8	26 1/8	29	25 6/8	6	6	5	5	Unknown	Unknown	Cabela's, Inc.	PR 2006	80
194 1/8	197 4/8	23 7/8	24 2/8	21 7/8	5 2/8	5 2/8	5	5	Moffat Co., CO	Jeffrey A. Larson	Jeffrey A. Larson	2004	83
194 1/8	210 6/8	27 6/8	28 5/8	22 4/8	4 6/8	4 6/8	7	7	Wallowa Co., OR	Kenneth L. Faircloth	Kenneth L. Faircloth	2005	83
194	198 3/8	25 1/8	23 4/8	22 6/8	4 7/8	5	5	5	Summit Co., UT	James E. King, Jr.	James E. King, Jr.	2006	85
193 7/8	200 7/8	26 6/8	25 3/8	23 1/8	4 3/8	4 2/8	4	5	Pitkin Co., CO	Danny P. Strickland	Danny P. Strickland	2005	86
193 5/8	199 3/8	23 7/8	23 6/8	21 1/8	4 7/8	4 4/8	5	5	Summit Co., UT	Hunter C. Dresden	Hunter C. Dresden	2004	87
193 4/8	198	21 7/8	23 6/8	23 7/8	5 1/8	5	5	5	Saguache Co., CO	Morris L. Pickel, Jr.	Morris L. Pickel, Jr.	1986	88
193 3/8	197 3/8	26 4/8	26 1/8	22 1/8	5 1/8	5 2/8	5	5	Eagle Co., CO	Jonathan D. Blotter	Jonathan D. Blotter	2004	89
193 2/8	203 5/8	27 7/8	26 4/8	25 7/8	5 1/8	5 1/8	5	6	Frenchman River, SK	Ronald Salter	Ronald Salter	2005	90
193 1/8	199 4/8	24	23 5/8	24 1/8	5 1/8	5 1/8	5	6	Archuleta Co., CO	Bill Moye	Bill Moye	1975	91
193 1/8	196 7/8	23 4/8	23 5/8	21 5/8	5 1/8	5 1/8	5	5	Malheur Co., OR	James A. Hayhurst	James A. Hayhurst	2004	91
193 1/8	199 7/8	24 5/8	26 4/8	23 7/8	5 2/8	5 1/8	5	5	Owyhee Co., ID	Jeremy C. Cunningham	Jeremy C. Cunningham	2005	91
193 1/8	213 4/8	25 1/8	25 1/8	25	5	5 2/8	6	6	Montrose Co., CO	David J. Gray	David J. Gray	2005	91
192 7/8	200 2/8	27 1/8	24 6/8	17 5/8	5	5 1/8	5	5	Colorado	Samuel O. Newell	D. & K. Stevens	1950	95
192 7/8	215 1/8	27 5/8	26 4/8	23 6/8	5 1/8	5	6	7	Adams Co., ID	Alvin Cheever	Donna Cheever	1992	95
192 6/8	203 4/8	25 6/8	23 7/8	19 5/8	5 1/8	5 1/8	6	6	Unknown	Unknown	Cabela's, Inc.	PR 2006	97
192 4/8	204 7/8	27 1/8	27 2/8	27 7/8	5 5/8	5 4/8	7	6	Mesa Co., CO	Cy Moore	Cy Moore	1974	98
192 4/8	200	25 3/8	25 3/8	22 2/8	5 2/8	5 1/8	6	5	Lake Diefenbaker, SK	Herb F. Siegele	Herb F. Siegele	2003	98
192 4/8	194 5/8	24 5/8	25 1/8	22 2/8	5 1/8	5	5	5	Salt Lake Co., UT	Bryan W. Grant	Bryan W. Grant	2004	98
192 3/8	209 3/8	25 5/8	25	22 5/8	5	5	7	6	Coconino Co., AZ	William H. Geare	William H. Geare	1949	101
192 3/8	197 1/8	24 4/8	25 2/8	24 5/8	5 2/8	5 1/8	5	4	Montrose Co., CO	Billy B. Batty	Billy B. Batty	2003	101
192 3/8	209 7/8	24 6/8	22 3/8	20 1/8	5 1/8	5 1/8	5	6	Delta Co., CO	Steve V. White	Steve V. White	2005	101

Score							Points R	Points L	Locality	Hunter	Owner	Date Killed	Rank
192 2/8	197 7/8	24 7/8	26	19 6/8	5 1/8	5 2/8	5	5	Unknown	Unknown	Cabela's, Inc.	PR 2006	104
192 2/8	196	25 6/8	27 2/8	22 2/8	5	5 1/8	5	5	Unknown	Unknown	Cabela's, Inc.	PR 2006	104
192 1/8	195 7/8	27	26 7/8	24 7/8	5 7/8	5 7/8	5	5	Hinsdale Co., CO	Jay L. David	Jay L. David	1975	106
192 1/8	203 1/8	28 6/8	26 4/8	23 7/8	6 3/8	6 1/8	6	5	Rio Arriba Co., NM	Jerry E. Sondag	Jerry E. Sondag	2003	106
192 1/8	197 3/8	27 6/8	28	24 7/8	5 1/8	5	5	5	Park Co., CO	James R. VanMeter	James R. VanMeter	2005	106
192 1/8	197 2/8	26	24 6/8	22 3/8	5	5 4/8	5	6	Great Sand Hills, SK	Morley J. Clary	Morley J. Clary	2006	106
192	216 4/8	27 3/8	28 6/8	27 4/8	4 5/8	5 2/8	7	5	Emery Co., UT	Unknown	Nathan W. Jacobson	1967	110
192	196 5/8	25 2/8	23 2/8	24 2/8	4 6/8	4 5/8	5	6	Montezuma Co., CO	Kirby Weaver	Kirby Weaver	1968	110
192	194 4/8	23	23 1/8	19 4/8	4 5/8	4 5/8	5	6	Fremont Co., ID	Kevin B. Calaway	Kevin B. Calaway	1986	110
192	202 4/8	24 2/8	24 7/8	24 6/8	5 1/8	4 5/8	6	6	Chelan Co., WA	Russell R. Esparza	Russell R. Esparza	2003	110
192	195 6/8	24 7/8	24	24	5 1/8	5	6	6	Pennington Co., SD	Scott Sharpe	Scott Sharpe	2003	110
192	208 7/8	25 7/8	23 6/8	22 2/8	5 5/8	5 3/8	5	5	Camas Co., ID	John E. Anderson	John E. Anderson	2005	110
191 7/8	212 6/8	23 5/8	22 4/8	20 7/8	5 3/8	5 6/8	5	5	Lincoln Co., NV	Robert J. Lee	Robert J. Lee	2005	117
191 7/8	208 7/8	27 7/8	26	25 2/8	5 1/8	5 2/8	5	5	Boundary Co., ID	Vic L. McGary	Vic L. McGary	2004	117
191 6/8	197 1/8	26 3/8	25 7/8	25 5/8	5 3/8	5	4	4	Sonora, MX	Jay R. Bollinger	Jay R. Bollinger	2006	119
191 5/8	194 6/8	24 4/8	24 3/8	25 6/8	4 6/8	5 2/8	5	6	Archuleta Co., CO	Kenneth J. Pena	Kenneth J. Pena	2004	120
191 5/8	196 7/8	25 2/8	25 3/8	24 7/8	4 4/8	4 6/8	5	5	Klamath Co., OR	Alden Hughes	Ray A. Wiser	1931	120
191 5/8	199 5/8	26 6/8	26 5/8	23 7/8	6 2/8	4 5/8	5	5	Idaho	Unknown	Arthur L. Wyman	1955	120
191 4/8	198 2/8	23 6/8	23 1/8	19 5/8	4 5/8	6 1/8	7	7	Old Wives Lake, SK	Kevin E. Tondevold	Kevin E. Tondevold	2004	124
191 4/8	205 3/8	23 3/8	23 7/8	23 7/8	5 6/8	4 5/8	6	6	Redwillow River, AB	Brent V. Trumbo	Brent V. Trumbo	2005	124
191 3/8	199 2/8	25 3/8	23 6/8	25 5/8	4 7/8	5 5/8	6	7	Montezuma Co., CO	Steve Perry	Steve Perry	2004	126
191 3/8	211 6/8	26 3/8	28 1/8	24 5/8	5 2/8	4 7/8	5	6	Carbon Co., WY	John A. McCall, Jr.	John A. McCall, Jr.	2005	126
191 3/8	209	26 4/8	27 1/8	27	5 4/8	5 1/8	5	5	Dolores Co., CO	John A. Garchar	Andrew E. Garchar	1950	126
191 3/8	199 6/8	27 4/8	27 3/8	25	4 6/8	5 4/8	5	5	Mesa Co., CO	William H. Bagby	William H. Bagby	1958	126
191 3/8	193 6/8	24 5/8	24 6/8	20 7/8	4 6/8	5	6	5	Dolores Co., CO	Victor S. Constantine	Victor S. Constantine	1996	126
191 3/8	197 2/8	25 3/8	23 2/8	22 5/8	5 4/8	4 4/8	6	5	Eagle Co., CO	David W. Long	David W. Long	2003	126
191 3/8	200	25 7/8	25 5/8	21 5/8	5 6/8	5 6/8	5	5	Pueblo Co., CO	William A. Fleming	William A. Fleming	2004	126
191 2/8	220 7/8	27 2/8	25 3/8	21 5/8	4 7/8	5 2/8	5	6	Gunnison Co., CO	James A. Vannorsdel	James A. Vannorsdel	2005	126
191 1/8	199	24 5/8	26 2/8	26 4/8	4 7/8	5	8	5	Unknown	Unknown	Cabela's, Inc.	PR 2006	126
191 1/8	194 2/8	24	25	25 5/8	5 2/8	4 7/8	6	8	Coconino Co., AZ	Glenn E. Thompson	Glenn E. Thompson	2004	133
191	212 6/8	28 5/8	25	18 6/8	5 3/8	5 5/8	5	6	Clear Creek Co., CO	Gregg J. Richter	Gregg J. Richter	2003	134
190 7/8	211 1/8	26 6/8	26 1/8	25 7/8	4 7/8	5 4/8	6	6	Souris River, SK	Cory D. Rucks	Cory D. Rucks	2005	134
190 7/8	191	25	24 3/8	22 7/8	5 2/8	5 1/8	5	6	Carbon Co., WY	Brad A. Bartlett	Brad A. Bartlett	2005	136
190 7/8	202 6/8	24 3/8	26	25 5/8	5 3/8	5 1/8	6	5	Trego Co., KS	Chris E. Unrein	Chris E. Unrein	2003	137
190 6/8	216 3/8	25 2/8	23 1/8	23 1/8	4 5/8	6	5	5	Las Animas Co., CO	Wayne R. Detmar	Wayne R. Detmar	2006	137
190 6/8	196 7/8	24 2/8	22 1/8	22 1/8	4 6/8	4 6/8	5	5	Sublette Co., WY	Charles E. Thomas	Charles E. Thomas	2006	137
190 5/8	193 5/8	25 4/8	26	23	5 1/8	4 7/8	7	7	Dolores Co., CO	Ted R. Holgate	Ted R. Holgate	2005	140
190 5/8	204	26	26	23 2/8	5 2/8	5 1/8	6	6	Dolores Co., CO	Bryan L. Sutch	Bryan L. Sutch	2005	140
190 5/8	201 1/8	25 6/8	25 2/8	22 7/8	5 3/8	5 2/8	6	5	Flathead Co., MT	Fred Watson	Ron Russell	1955	142
190 5/8	201 6/8	25	25 1/8	26 1/8	5 6/8	5 2/8	5	5	Idaho Co., ID	Justin E. Cagle	Justin E. Cagle	2004	142
190 5/8	194 5/8	25 7/8	25 5/8	22 6/8	5 2/8	5 2/8	6	6	Camas Co., ID	Howard J. Vander Poppen	Howard J. Vander Poppen	2004	142
190 5/8	202 1/8	26 2/8	26		5 1/8	5 1/8			Goshen Co., WY			2004	142

MULE DEER - TYPICAL ANTLERS

Odocoileus hemionus hemionus and certain related subspecies

Final Score	Gross Score	Length of Main Beam R.	L.	Inside Spread	Circumference at Smallest Place Between Burr & First Point R.	L.	Number of Points R.	L.	Locality	Hunter	Owner	Date Killed	Rank
190 5/8	200 5/8	27 4/8	26 7/8	24 1/8	5 4/8	5 2/8	5	6	Unknown	Unknown	Cabela's, Inc.	PR 2006	142
190 4/8	199 1/8	25 2/8	25	21 4/8	4 7/8	4 6/8	6	6	Okanogan Co., WA	Unknown	Cabela's, Inc.	1955	146
190 4/8	211 4/8	26	25 4/8	25 6/8	5	5 1/8	6	6	Great Sand Hills, SK	Jim Clary	Jim Clary	2004	146
190 4/8	194 7/8	23 7/8	24 4/8	22 2/8	5	5 1/8	5	5	Summit Co., UT	Harry M. Galloway	Harry M. Galloway	2006	146
190 3/8	193 6/8	24 4/8	25 4/8	21 5/8	5	5	5	5	Blaine Co., ID	Brian N. Ellway	Brian N. Ellway	2003	149
190 3/8	214 6/8	26 2/8	26	18 6/8	5 4/8	5 4/8	6	7	Rio Arriba Co., NM	John A. Busic	John A. Busic	2004	149
190 3/8	195 6/8	26	25 4/8	25 3/8	5 1/8	5 1/8	5	5	Sonora, MX	Julian E. Pylant	Julian E. Pylant	2004	149
190 2/8	212 1/8	27 1/8	24 6/8	28	4	4 2/8	8	5	Lincoln Co., WY	Ralph Spencer	Ralph Spencer	1998	152
190 2/8	210 2/8	25 4/8	25 5/8	21 2/8	5 2/8	5 4/8	5	8	Uintah Co., UT	Sybil Phillips	Sybil Phillips	2003	152
190 2/8	194 5/8	24	25 5/8	23 6/8	4 4/8	4 4/8	5	5	Idaho Co., ID	Rod E. Bradley	Rod E. Bradley	2004	152
190 2/8	211 5/8	23 4/8	26 4/8	22	5 5/8	5 5/8	7	6	Montezuma Co., CO	Samuel P. Sparks	Samuel P. Sparks	2004	152
190 1/8	197 1/8	24 2/8	24 5/8	20 5/8	4 6/8	5 1/8	5	6	Colorado	Unknown	Curtis P. Smiley	1982	156
190 1/8	196	25 2/8	27 1/8	28 5/8	4 6/8	4 6/8	6	5	Pitkin Co., CO	Walter D. Otwell	Walter D. Otwell	1990	156
190 1/8	225	26 1/8	26 6/8	23 7/8	5 4/8	5 6/8	8	8	Cypress Hills, SK	James D. Wright	James D. Wright	2005	156
190 1/8	196 2/8	24 3/8	26 2/8	23 1/8	4 3/8	4 3/8	4	5	Unknown	Unknown	Cabela's, Inc.	PR 2006	156
190	211 2/8	25 3/8	24 3/8	24 3/8	5 1/8	5 1/8	6	6	Moffat Co., CO	Elmer W. Gomes	Elmer W. Gomes	1961	160
190	224 2/8	31 5/8	29 6/8	28 3/8	6 5/8	7	5	6	Twin Falls Co., ID	Gary Redd	Raymond R. Cross	1978	160
189 7/8	228 3/8	27 7/8	25 6/8	26 6/8	6 2/8	6 1/8	7	7	Rio Blanco Co., CO	Sammy M. Baca	Sammy M. Baca	2004	162
189 6/8	198 5/8	24 6/8	24 5/8	23 7/8	5 1/8	5	6	5	Montrose Co., CO	LeRoy J. Gutierrez	LeRoy J. Gutierrez	2004	163
189 5/8	205 3/8	25 5/8	25 1/8	23	4 7/8	4 7/8	6	6	Boise Co., ID	Argolis Hyatt	Argolis Hyatt	1967	164
189 5/8	192 1/8	24 1/8	24 6/8	20 5/8	5 1/8	5 2/8	5	5	Jefferson Co., CO	Michelle L. Gaccetta	Michelle L. Gaccetta	2004	164
189 4/8	192 4/8	27 1/8	27 1/8	25	4 3/8	4 3/8	5	5	Pitkin Co., CO	Joseph J. Stroh	Joseph J. Stroh	2004	166
189 4/8	195 1/8	25 1/8	25 6/8	23 2/8	5 3/8	5 3/8	5	5	Elko Co., NV	Michael V. Terry	Michael V. Terry	2005	166
189 3/8	194 7/8	26	25 7/8	26	5 1/8	5 1/8	5	6	Big Muddy Lake, SK	Derek H. Hall	Derek H. Hall	2006	168
189 2/8	196 4/8	26	25 1/8	26 5/8	5 2/8	5	4	5	Delta Co., CO	Timothy G. Hovatter	Timothy G. Hovatter	1974	169
189 2/8	196 4/8	26	25 3/8	28 1/8	5 2/8	5 1/8	6	5	Great Sand Hills, SK	Chris E. Patenaude	Chris E. Patenaude	2004	169
189 1/8	229 5/8	29	29	24 6/8	5	5 7/8	8	8	Dolores Co., CO	Dale Eberharter	Dale Eberharter	1974	171
189 1/8	195 7/8	26 2/8	25 2/8	23 1/8	5 5/8	4 3/8	5	4	Pitkin Co., CO	Troy W. Walker	Troy W. Walker	2004	171
189 1/8	191 5/8	23 5/8	23 5/8	22 1/8	4 6/8	5 6/8	5	5	Lincoln Co., WY	Joseph D. Wiggs	Joseph D. Wiggs	2004	171
189	191 5/8	24 6/8	24 3/8	24 6/8	5 7/8	5 1/8	5	5	Mohave Co., AZ	Stevens D. Armstrong	Stevens D. Armstrong	2003	174
189	194 5/8	26 5/8	26 3/8	25 6/8	5	5 1/8	5	5	San Miguel Co., CO	Chris Ruff	Chris Ruff	2004	174
188 7/8	192 5/8	25 5/8	24 3/8	25 3/8	5 2/8	5 2/8	5	5	Nez Perce Co., ID	William J. Braun	William J. Braun	1963	176
188 5/8	194 6/8	24 1/8	25 5/8	20 3/8	5 2/8	5 1/8	5	5	Archuleta Co., CO	Melissa F. Snarr	Melissa F. Snarr	2005	177
188 4/8	195 5/8	22 5/8	22 6/8	24 2/8	5 4/8	5 4/8	6	5	Jefferson Co., CO	Art Espinosa	Art Espinosa	2003	178

Score	Gross Score	R. Main Beam	L. Main Beam	Inside Spread	Circumference	R. Points	L. Points	Locality	Hunter	Owner	Date	Rank
188 3/8	196 2/8	26 2/8	24 6/8	20 1/8	4 5/8	5	5	Delta Co., CO	William J. Madaris	William J. Madaris	1976	179
188 3/8	209 3/8	25 3/8	24 3/8	23 3/8	4 6/8	6	7	Rosebud Co., MT	Craig A. Connelly	Craig A. Connelly	2004	179
188 2/8	196 6/8	26 1/8	26 3/8	26 3/8	4 6/8	6	5	Franklin Co., ID	Larry W. Cross	Larry W. Cross	1981	181
188 2/8	199 6/8	27	26 6/8	20 2/8	4 4/8	5	6	Rio Arriba Co., NM	Joseph Griego	Joseph Griego	2004	181
188 2/8	194 6/8	24 6/8	27 6/8	23 2/8	5 1/8	5	5	Elko Co., NV	Ken M. Etchemendy	Ken M. Etchemendy	2005	181
188 2/8	193 2/8	26 2/8	26 2/8	23	6 2/8	5	5	Great Sand Hills, SK	Curtis M. Melnechenko	Curtis M. Melnechenko	2005	181
188 1/8	191 4/8	26	26 2/8	21 3/8	5 3/8	5	5	San Miguel Co., CO	David A. Thatcher	David A. Thatcher	2004	185
188 1/8	204 5/8	24 1/8	25 4/8	23 5/8	5 4/8	6	5	Unknown	Unknown	Brian J. Balfour	PR 2006	185
188	196 3/8	27 2/8	27	28 4/8	4 6/8	5	6	Sonora, MX	James A. Greer	James A. Greer	2003	187
187 7/8	196 2/8	24 4/8	24 5/8	25 6/8	5 1/8	6	5	Eagle Co., CO	Richard J. Cooke	Richard J. Cooke	2004	188
187 6/8	208 3/8	27 1/8	25 3/8	20 7/8	5	6	5	Baker Co., OR	Craig A. Briggs	Craig A. Briggs	2003	189
187 6/8	192 7/8	27 6/8	27	22	5 2/8	5	5	Douglas Co., CO	Matthew L. Clough	Matthew L. Clough	2004	189
187 5/8	203 7/8	28 2/8	28 4/8	23	5 7/8	6	7	San Miguel Co., CO	William E. Garland, Sr.	William E. Garland, Sr.	1967	191
187 5/8	212 5/8	25 4/8	26 3/8	26 5/8	5 6/8	7	7	Bonneville Co., ID	John J. Maggini	John J. Maggini	1987	191
187 5/8	197 1/8	24 6/8	24 3/8	25 3/8	4 6/8	6	5	Bonneville Co., ID	Randy J. Lambert	Randy J. Lambert	2004	191
187 4/8	199 6/8	26 2/8	22 6/8	24 2/8	4 7/8	6	5	Garfield Co., UT	Dale A. Jennings	Dale A. Jennings	2005	194
187 3/8	191 3/8	24 4/8	23 4/8	22 3/8	4 5/8	5	5	Bonneville Co., ID	Louis G. Nelson	Louis G. Nelson	2003	195
187 2/8	205 3/8	25 2/8	24 1/8	27 5/8	5 5/8	6	5	Montezuma Co., CO	Richard P. Munson	Richard P. Munson	2004	196
187 1/8	216 7/8	25	22 2/8	24 3/8	5 4/8	6	7	Wasatch Co., UT	William B. Prettyman	Warren Naillon, Jr.	1957	197
187 1/8	194	26 3/8	28 1/8	28 3/8	4 6/8	4	4	Elmore Co., ID	James H. Rainey, Sr.	Mike Rainey	1960	197
187 1/8	192 7/8	24 3/8	22 3/8	20 5/8	4 7/8	5	5	Dolores Co., CO	Margret L. Daves	Margret L. Daves	1990	197

TYPICAL MULE DEER
FINAL SCORE: 192-1/8
HUNTER: Morley J. Clary

TYPICAL MULE DEER
FINAL SCORE: 203-5/8
HUNTER: Keith Balfourd

TYPICAL MULE DEER
FINAL SCORE: 197-4/8
HUNTER: Michael S. McGee

TYPICAL MULE DEER
FINAL SCORE: 207-6/8
HUNTER: Robbie K. Cassett

MULE DEER - TYPICAL ANTLERS

Odocoileus hemionus hemionus and certain related subspecies

Final Score	Gross Score	Length of Main Beam R.	L.	Inside Spread	Circumference at Smallest Place Between Burr & First Point R.	L.	Number of Points R.	L.	Locality	Hunter	Owner	Date Killed	Rank
187 1/8	193 2/8	24 4/8	26	23 7/8	5	4 7/8	4	5	Sherman Co., KS	Rodney A. Lindsten	Rodney A. Lindsten	1996	197
187 1/8	189 1/8	24 5/8	24 6/8	21 7/8	5 1/8	5 1/8	5	5	Carbon Co., WY	Marty E. Killion	Marty E. Killion	2003	197
187 1/8	200 3/8	25 3/8	26 5/8	20 3/8	4 6/8	4 5/8	7	5	Morrill Co., NE	Jack L. Nelson	Jack L. Nelson	2004	197
187 1/8	192 7/8	20 7/8	23 2/8	21 3/8	5	5	5	5	Lincoln Co., NV	Franklin G. Grosch, Jr.	Franklin G. Grosch, Jr.	2005	197
187 1/8	191 1/8	24 1/8	25 4/8	22 5/8	4 6/8	4 6/8	5	5	San Juan Co., NM	Anthony J. Martins	Anthony J. Martins	2005	197
187	193 4/8	26 2/8	26	23 6/8	4 4/8	4 4/8	4	4	Green River, WY	Ray Marshall	Curtis P. Smiley	1959	205
187	201 3/8	24 7/8	24 3/8	25 1/8	4 7/8	5	6	5	Garfield Co., CO	Glen E. Street	Glen E. Street	2004	205
186 7/8	198 7/8	25 6/8	25 5/8	23 3/8	4 7/8	4 7/8	6	6	Gunnison Co., CO	Matthew Golla	Matthew Golla	2004	207
186 7/8	201	27 7/8	27 6/8	27	4 5/8	4 6/8	6	6	Malheur Co., OR	Richard J. McAbee	Richard J. McAbee	2004	207
186 5/8	201	25 5/8	24 3/8	18	5 5/8	5 5/8	5	6	Baker Co., OR	Karen L. Gillespie	Karen L. Gillespie	2005	209
186 4/8	195 1/8	27	26 2/8	25 6/8	5 2/8	5 3/8	6	5	Boise Co., ID	Rick L. Beck	Rick L. Beck	2004	210
186 2/8	191 6/8	23 7/8	23 6/8	23 6/8	4 6/8	4 5/8	5	5	Boise Co., ID	Wesley M. Shaw	Leah C. Shaw	1983	211
186 2/8	189 6/8	23 4/8	23	22 6/8	5 2/8	5	5	5	Dolores Co., CO	Rodney J. Daves	Rodney J. Daves	1984	211
186 2/8	193 6/8	25 4/8	24 4/8	24 1/8	4 7/8	5	6	5	S. Saskatchewan River, SK	Morris I. Fediash	Morris I. Fediash	2003	211
186 1/8	191 4/8	26 6/8	26	22 3/8	4 6/8	4 5/8	5	5	Rio Arriba Co., NM	Dominick J. Panzy	Dominick J. Panzy	2006	214
186	193 7/8	24 1/8	23 6/8	23 3/8	4 4/8	4 5/8	5	7	Park Co., WY	Rex G. Abelein	Rex G. Abelein	1961	215
186	193 3/8	26 1/8	25 6/8	23 4/8	5 1/8	5 1/8	5	5	Las Animas Co., CO	William S. Pickett III	William S. Pickett III	1995	215
186	191 7/8	22 4/8	23 2/8	25 5/8	5	5	5	5	Idaho Co., ID	Rickey M. Davis	Rickey M. Davis	2004	215
186	190 5/8	23 7/8	23 1/8	17 6/8	5 1/8	5	5	5	Weber Co., UT	Jack E. Peck, Jr.	Jack E. Peck, Jr.	2004	215
186	194 1/8	26	26 1/8	19 4/8	5	4 7/8	6	6	Terrace Mt., BC	Ryan M. Schleppe	Ryan M. Schleppe	2005	215
185 7/8	196 5/8	25 1/8	23 2/8	22 7/8	5 1/8	5 4/8	5	5	Chaves Co., NM	Gary C. Good	Gary C. Good	1968	220
185 7/8	193 1/8	24 2/8	24 4/8	20 1/8	4 7/8	4 4/8	5	5	Eagle Co., CO	Christopher McGrath	Christopher McGrath	2003	220
185 5/8	189 6/8	23 7/8	22 7/8	24 4/8	5	5 1/8	5	5	McKenzie Co., ND	Toby S. Gerhardt	Toby S. Gerhardt	2003	222
185 5/8	205 6/8	24 3/8	25 6/8	19 1/8	4 6/8	5	6	8	Carbon Co., WY	Dan E. McBride	Dan E. McBride	2004	222
185 5/8	192 3/8	22	24 2/8	17 5/8	4 3/8	4 7/8	5	5	Oregon	Unknown	Curtis P. Smiley	PR 2004	222
185 4/8	196 5/8	24 4/8	24 5/8	22 4/8	4 3/8	4 7/8	5	6	Oneida Co., ID	Bryce L. Bair	Bryce L. Bair	2003	225
185 4/8	189 7/8	25	25 2/8	24	4 6/8	4 5/8	6	5	Umatilla Co., OR	Tom Keen	Tom Keen	2004	225
185 3/8	192 5/8	24 4/8	23 5/8	21 7/8	5 1/8	5	5	6	Routt Co., CO	Alan Butts	Alan Butts	2004	227
185 2/8	187 6/8	28	27	31 4/8	4 6/8	4 7/8	5	5	Dolores Co., CO	Picked Up	Eugene Willett	1980	228
185 2/8	192	25	23 5/8	20	5 1/8	5 1/8	6	5	Owyhee Co., ID	Jerry McKague	Jerry McKague	1985	228
185 2/8	193 2/8	26 7/8	28 2/8	22 5/8	5	5	6	6	Lemhi Co., ID	Richard A. Barany	Richard A. Barany	2004	228
185 2/8	188 7/8	23 4/8	21 6/8	22 2/8	5	5	5	5	Teller Co., CO	Amber N. Edwards	Amber N. Edwards	2004	228
185 1/8	190 7/8	24 7/8	24 4/8	22 7/8	4 4/8	4 3/8	5	5	Franklin Co., ID	Herb G. Voyles, Jr.	Herb G. Voyles, Jr.	1970	232

Score	Gross Score	Length R	Length L	Inside Spread	Circ. R	Circ. L	Points R	Points L	Locality	Hunter	Owner	Date	Page
185 1/8	204 5/8	26 3/8	26 2/8	19 1/8	4 6/8	4 5/8	5	7	Battle River, AB	John C. Pitts	John C. Pitts	2005	232
185	187 5/8	26 6/8	26 4/8	24 4/8	5 2/8	5 2/8	4	4	Eagle Co., CO	Theodore P. Alegria	Theodore P. Alegria	1986	234
185	192 5/8	25 1/8	24 1/8	22 1/8	5 3/8	5 4/8	6	5	Childress Co., TX	Frankie Keller	Frankie Keller	2004	234
184 7/8	201 4/8	23 6/8	26 2/8	25	5 3/8	5 2/8	7	6	Coconino Co., AZ	Glenn J. Ashbrook	Glenn J. Ashbrook	1970	236
184 7/8	202 6/8	24 2/8	24 2/8	19 7/8	4 6/8	4 5/8	6	5	Uinta Co., WY	Tom W. Wheeler	Tom W. Wheeler	2003	236
184 7/8	200 7/8	25 2/8	23 1/8	26 2/8	4 7/8	5	6	6	Clear Creek Co., CO	Julie M. James	Julie M. James	2004	236
184 6/8	219 5/8	26 5/8	27	21 5/8	5	5 1/8	6	9	Lincoln Co., NV	Shane McDonald	Shane McDonald	2004	240
184 5/8	189 3/8	24	24	24	4 7/8	5 1/8	5	5	Weston Co., WY	Donald A. Oatman, Jr.	Donald A. Oatman, Jr.	2003	241
184 5/8	189 6/8	25 5/8	24 2/8	24	5	5 3/8	5	5	Valley Co., ID	John L. Lyon	John L. Lyon	1965	241
184 5/8	200 7/8	24 6/8	24 3/8	21 7/8	4 7/8	4 7/8	5	5	Montezuma Co., CO	Jack Willett	Jack Willett	1965	241
184 4/8	197 6/8	22 7/8	22 6/8	22 5/8	5	5	7	7	Guadalupe Co., NM	Wayne Martinez	Wayne Martinez	1995	244
184 4/8	188 1/8	23 6/8	23 7/8	21 7/8	5 4/8	5 3/8	5	6	La Plata Co., CO	Normand H. Birtcher	Normand H. Birtcher	2005	244
184 3/8	196 7/8	26	26 1/8	22 6/8	5 4/8	5 6/8	6	5	Three Hills, AB	Lloyd D. Whaley	Lloyd D. Whaley	2005	246
184 2/8	200 4/8	24 6/8	23 6/8	24 1/8	5	5	5	6	Montezuma Co., CO	Lora L. McEwen	Lora L. McEwen	2004	247
184 2/8	192 7/8	23 6/8	24 3/8	24 5/8	4 7/8	4 6/8	6	6	Graham Co., KS	Tim E. Kline	Tim E. Kline	1994	247
184 2/8	196 7/8	25 2/8	25 2/8	21	5 5/8	5 3/8	6	6	Moffat Co., CO	Warren J. Leek	Warren J. Leek	2003	247
184 2/8	190 5/8	21 6/8	20 4/8	21	5 3/8	5 2/8	5	5	San Juan Co., UT	Frederick L. Bennetts	Frederick L. Bennetts	2004	247
184 1/8	188 1/8	27	26 2/8	19 4/8	4	4 1/8	4	4	Summit Co., UT	Matthew J. McCormick	Matthew J. McCormick	2005	251
184 1/8	187 3/8	25 3/8	25 1/8	19 4/8	4 1/8	4 2/8	4	4	Carbon Co., WY	Gerald A. Steele	Gerald A. Steele	1995	251
184 1/8	199 3/8	24 4/8	24	24 5/8	6 4/8	6 4/8	6	7	Okanogan Co., WA	Kyle R. Tullar	Kirk D. Tullar	2004	251
184	192 6/8	23 3/8	24	23	5 4/8	5 4/8	6	6	Garfield Co., CO	Jeffrey S. Hoover	Jeffrey S. Hoover	2005	254
184	189 1/8	24	25 6/8	22	4 7/8	5	5	5	Cache Co., UT	Ian K. Chase-Dunn	Ian K. Chase-Dunn	1976	254
184	189 6/8	27 6/8	28 1/8	26 2/8	5 2/8	5 1/8	6	5	Mesa Co., CO	Jim J. O'Neal	Jim J. O'Neal	1979	254
184	192 6/8	22 6/8	22 3/8	22 3/8	4 3/8	4 3/8	5	5	Montezuma Co., CO	E. Scott Magness	E. Scott Magness	2003	254
183 7/8	191 5/8	25 7/8	24 2/8	22	5 5/8	5 6/8	6	5	Eagle Co., CO	William J. McEwen	William J. McEwen	2005	254
183 7/8	185 7/8	26 1/8	23 5/8	24 2/8	4 4/8	4 5/8	5	5	Routt Co., CO	Duane Remington	Duane Remington	2004	258
183 6/8	187 7/8	24 7/8	24 6/8	23 5/8	5 1/8	5 2/8	5	5	Pitkin Co., CO	Eric A. Alexander	Eric A. Alexander	2003	259
183 6/8	192 6/8	26 4/8	28 1/8	22 4/8	4 6/8	4 6/8	5	5	Tay River, AB	Peter S. Litwinow	Peter S. Litwinow	2003	259
183 6/8	202 5/8	23 5/8	21 4/8	28 1/8	4 4/8	4 4/8	6	6	Rio Arriba Co., NM	Brandon Layman	Brandon Layman	2006	259
183 4/8	191 6/8	24 4/8	23 1/8	18 7/8	4 6/8	4 6/8	5	5	La Plata Co., CO	Picked Up	John H. Ott	2004	262
183 3/8	198 3/8	22 3/8	24 2/8	25 7/8	4 5/8	4 5/8	6	6	Eagle Co., CO	Bruce D. Foster	Bruce D. Foster	2004	263
183 2/8	199	26 7/8	26 7/8	22	4 7/8	5 1/8	6	6	Eagle Co., CO	Bill N. Ceaglio	Bill N. Ceaglio	2004	264
183 2/8	190 5/8	23 2/8	23 2/8	26	4 7/8	4 4/8	5	4	Navajo Co., AZ	Mark L. Dunham	Mark L. Dunham	2005	264
183 1/8	186 1/8	22 4/8	23 6/8	22	4 5/8	5	5	5	Millard Co., UT	William G. Brockman	William G. Brockman	2003	266
183 1/8	199	22 7/8	23 6/8	20 3/8	4 4/8	4 4/8	7	5	Mesa Co., CO	David J. Yates	David J. Yates	2004	266
183	193 2/8	22 2/8	21 4/8	24	4 6/8	4 5/8	5	5	Park Co., WY	William E. Gibson, Jr.	William E. Gibson, Jr.	2004	268
183	188 4/8	23 7/8	22 6/8	22 5/8	4 7/8	4 7/8	6	5	Okanogan Co., WA	Scott S. Fuhrman	Scott S. Fuhrman	2005	268
183	206 4/8	26 2/8	23 5/8	16 6/8	4 7/8	4 7/8	5	5	La Plata Co., CO	D. Bradley McWilliams	D. Bradley McWilliams	2005	268
182 7/8	186 4/8	23 7/8	23 7/8	26 3/8	4 5/8	4 5/8	6	6	Unknown	Curtis P. Smiley	Unknown	PR 1996	271
182 7/8	187 2/8	25 6/8	21 4/8	23 7/8	5 2/8	5 2/8	5	5	Jefferson Co., CO	Kyle J. Burbach	Kyle J. Burbach	2003	271
182 7/8	203 5/8	23	21 3/8	21 4/8	5	5	6	6	Sonora, MX	Keith A. Johnson	Keith A. Johnson	2004	271
182 6/8	185	24 2/8	23 6/8	23 6/8	4 7/8	4 6/8	5	5	Garfield Co., UT	Roy H. Pfander	Roy H. Pfander	2004	274

MULE DEER - TYPICAL ANTLERS

Odocoileus hemionus hemionus and certain related subspecies

Final Score	Gross Score	Length of Main Beam R	L	Inside Spread	Circumference at Smallest Place Between Burr & First Point R	L	Number of Points R	L	Locality	Hunter	Owner	Date Killed	Rank
182 5/8	187 3/8	22 7/8	23 2/8	22 1/8	4 4/8	4 6/8	5	5	Cheyenne Co., CO	David C. Mulligan	David C. Mulligan	2003	275
182 5/8	189 2/8	27	27 1/8	29 6/8	5 4/8	5 1/8	5	4	Yuma Co., CO	John E. Blume	John E. Blume	2005	275
182 4/8	186 2/8	24 4/8	25 1/8	21 2/8	4 3/8	4 3/8	6	5	Ravalli Co., MT	Carissa Shima	Carissa Shima	2003	277
182 4/8	206 2/8	23 1/8	23	20 4/8	5 3/8	5 1/8	6	7	Unknown	Unknown	Cabela's, Inc.	2006 PR	277
182 3/8	189 7/8	25 5/8	25 4/8	24 2/8	5 4/8	5 4/8	6	5	Routt Co., CO	Homer W. Hale	Homer W. Hale	1979	279
182 3/8	190 1/8	22 4/8	22	21 7/8	6	5 6/8	5	5	El Paso Co., CO	Picked Up	Dennis K. Hess	1997	279
182 3/8	195 5/8	24 1/8	24 2/8	17 4/8	4 2/8	4 3/8	5	7	Mesa Co., CO	Roy H. Rominger	Roy H. Rominger	2004	279
182 3/8	201	24 5/8	22 6/8	22 4/8	5 3/8	5 6/8	6	9	Pine Lake, AB	Dennis R. Wilson	Dennis R. Wilson	2004	279
182 2/8	191 3/8	26 4/8	26 4/8	25 1/8	4 7/8	4 7/8	6	5	Santa Fe Co., NM	Joseph V. Repa	Joseph V. Repa	1982	283
182 2/8	184 7/8	24	23 7/8	21 2/8	4 7/8	5	5	5	Rio Arriba Co., NM	Curtis L. Tobias	Curtis L. Tobias	1998	283
182 2/8	186 1/8	26	25 6/8	29 3/8	4 4/8	4 3/8	5	5	McKenzie Co., ND	Samantha K. Johnson	Samantha K. Johnson	2003	283
182 1/8	186 6/8	22 3/8	23 1/8	25 3/8	5 1/8	5 2/8	5	5	Coconino Co., AZ	J. Douglas Moore	J. Douglas Moore	2004	286
182 1/8	196 4/8	23 1/8	23 1/8	22 1/8	5 4/8	5 4/8	7	8	Nye Co., NV	KayCee L. Otteson	KayCee L. Otteson	2006	286
182	190 4/8	25 2/8	24 1/8	22 1/8	4 7/8	5	5	6	Eagle Co., CO	Lawrence L. Lang	Lawrence L. Lang	2003	288
182	186 2/8	23 4/8	22 6/8	24 3/8	5	4 6/8	5	5	La Plata Co., CO	Joseph T. Allen	Joseph T. Allen	2005	288
182	191 6/8	21	21 1/8	21 1/8	5 3/8	5 1/8	6	6	La Plata Co., CO	Mike A. Gomez	Mike A. Gomez	2005	288
181 7/8	184 2/8	24	24 2/8	22 1/8	4 2/8	4 3/8	5	5	Iron Co., UT	Nathan B. Yorgason	Nathan B. Yorgason	2003	291
181 7/8	189 4/8	23 1/8	23 4/8	21 7/8	5 3/8	5 3/8	5	5	Montezuma Co., CO	Picked Up	Brian J. Balfour	2004	291
181 7/8	203 5/8	25 6/8	25	23 7/8	5 1/8	5 1/8	7	7	White Pine Co., NV	Joseph J. Timko	Joseph J. Timko	2005	291
181 6/8	191 3/8	23 6/8	23	20 6/8	4 4/8	4 4/8	6	6	Garfield Co., CO	Joey E. Greene	Jack A. Greene	1996	294
181 6/8	188 6/8	25 7/8	24 3/8	21 2/8	5 3/8	5 4/8	5	5	Montezuma Co., CO	Eddie D. Huber	Eddie D. Huber	2005	294
181 6/8	206	23 5/8	22 6/8	22	4 3/8	4 4/8	7	6	Washoe Co., NV	Patricia A. Lowery	Patricia A. Lowery	2005	294
181 6/8	187 4/8	22 6/8	23 6/8	21	5	4 4/8	5	5	Gooding Co., ID	Jeffrey S. Wallace	Jeffrey S. Wallace	2005	294
181 6/8	186 3/8	21 6/8	20 5/8	21 7/8	5 2/8	5 2/8	5	5	Sonora, MX	James E. King, Jr.	James E. King, Jr.	2006	294
181 5/8	198	25 2/8	24 2/8	19 1/8	5 2/8	5 4/8	6	5	Grand Co., CO	Samijean A. Lechman	Samijean A. Lechman	2004	299
181 5/8	196 2/8	26 2/8	25 7/8	21 6/8	5	5 2/8	6	6	S. Saskatchewan River, SK	Glen A. Miller	Glen A. Miller	2004	299
181 4/8	204	26	25 6/8	22 7/8	5 2/8	5 4/8	7	7	Larimer Co., CO	Picked Up	William E. York	1991	301
181 4/8	198	24 7/8	24 2/8	18 4/8	5 2/8	5 4/8	6	5	Blackwater River, BC	Ron A. Elliott	Ron A. Elliott	2005	301
181 3/8	201 1/8	25 1/8	27 7/8	23 3/8	4 5/8	4 6/8	7	6	Idaho Co., ID	Jerry Sutton	Dale R. Turner	1970	303
181 2/8	187 7/8	24 6/8	22 4/8	24	4 6/8	4 6/8	4	4	Rio Blanco Co., CO	Harold G. Walkley	Richard M. Noonan	1960	304
181 2/8	194 4/8	25 6/8	26 1/8	24 1/8	5 2/8	5 3/8	6	5	Reid Lake, SK	Elgin E. Bracken	Elgin E. Bracken	2004	304
181 2/8	196 6/8	26 1/8	25 1/8	23 4/8	4 7/8	5	5	7	Mesa Co., CO	Robert D. Hillis	Robert D. Hillis	2005	304

Score	Gross	Main Beam R	Main Beam L	Inside Spread	Circ. R	Circ. L	Pts R	Pts L	Locality	Hunter	Owner	Date	Rank
181 1/8	190 4/8	27 1/8	27 1/8	22 2/8	5	5	6	6	Sierra Co., CA	Knute D. Adcock	Knute D. Adcock	2003	307
181 1/8	185 7/8	23 6/8	24 3/8	26 6/8	5 5/8	6	5	5	Rosebud Co., MT	Art F. Hayes III	Art F. Hayes III	2005	307
181 1/8	195 4/8	24 5/8	23 7/8	27 4/8	4 6/8	4 7/8	6	5	Cascade Co., MT	Gary Hitchcock	Gary Hitchcock	2005	307
181 1/8	191 4/8	25	24	26	4 4/8	4 7/8	6	5	Unknown	Unknown	Brian J. Balfour	PR 2006	307
181	195	24 6/8	26	25 4/8	5 1/8	4 6/8	5	6	Baca Co., CO	William G. Harper	Robert G. Harper, Jr.	1936	311
181	188 7/8	22 2/8	22 3/8	16 7/8	5	5	5	5	Las Animas Co., CO	William S. Pickett III	William S. Pickett III	1998	311
181	186	24 3/8	23 5/8	24 1/8	4 7/8	4 6/8	6	6	Dolores Co., CO	Eric Garchar	Eric Garchar	2003	311
181	182 1/8	21 7/8	22 1/8	20 2/8	4 3/8	4 4/8	5	5	Montezuma Co., CO	Mike J. Ellig	Mike J. Ellig	2004	311
181	185 5/8	25 1/8	23 6/8	22 4/8	4 6/8	4 6/8	5	5	Converse Co., WY	Frankie L. Chapman	Frankie L. Chapman	2005	311
180 7/8	217 2/8	25	24 5/8	21 3/8	5 2/8	5 1/8	9	8	Carbon Co., WY	Roy D. Collins	Roy D. Collins	2005	316
180 6/8	183 3/8	24 7/8	24 7/8	20 2/8	4 6/8	4 6/8	5	5	Elko Co., NV	Chance M. Santina	Chance M. Santina	2005	317
180 5/8	188 3/8	24 7/8	25	25	4 4/8	4 4/8	5	5	Montezuma Co., CO	Gay Balfour	Gay Balfour	1980	318
180 5/8	196 1/8	24 3/8	25 7/8	19 7/8	5 2/8	5	8	5	Montezuma Co., CO	Judy Balfour	Judy Balfour	1981	318
180 5/8	204	28 2/8	25 3/8	23 1/8	4 7/8	5	6	8	Montezuma Co., CO	Vaughn D. Fairbanks	Vaughn D. Fairbanks	1986	318
180 5/8	183 3/8	23 1/8	24 1/8	25 1/8	4 7/8	4 7/8	5	6	Grant Co., OR	Ralph Harwood	Ralph Harwood	2003	318
180 5/8	185 3/8	24 4/8	26 2/8	24 7/8	4 4/8	4 5/8	5	5	Jackson Co., CO	William J. Millard, Jr.	William J. Millard, Jr.	2003	318
180 5/8	213 4/8	27 7/8	27 4/8	29 1/8	5	5 1/8	6	5	Rio Arriba Co., NM	Paul M. Bender	Paul M. Bender	2004	318
180 5/8	208 3/8	24	23 5/8	20 5/8	5 5/8	5 6/8	6	6	Lassen Co., CA	Dare T. Stolba	Dare T. Stolba	2004	318
180 5/8	186 1/8	26 1/8	26 2/8	25 1/8	4 5/8	4 5/8	5	6	Baker Co., OR	Benson L. Hogevoll	Benson L. Hogevoll	2005	318
180 5/8	190 2/8	26 1/8	26 1/8	26 2/8	5	4 7/8	4	5	Sonora, MX	Grady L. Miller	Grady L. Miller	2005	318
180 4/8	189 2/8	22 3/8	22 5/8	21 7/8	5 1/8	5 7/8	5	4	Rosebud Co., MT	Kenneth R. Bailey	Kenneth R. Bailey	2003	327
180 4/8	183 3/8	24	24 4/8	25	4 7/8	5	5	5	Meade Co., SD	Steven L. Yost	Steven L. Yost	2003	327
180 4/8	186 3/8	23 4/8	21 4/8	21 1/8	4 6/8	4 6/8	5	5	Modoc Co., CA	Daniel B. Beck	Daniel B. Beck	2004	327
180 4/8	194 1/8	23 4/8	23 4/8	25 1/8	5 5/8	5 6/8	5	5	Summit Co., UT	Harold A. Bries	Harold A. Bries	2004	327
180 4/8	189	28 4/8	26 7/8	26 7/8	4 4/8	4 3/8	5	5	Montezuma Co., CO	Ladelda Price	Ladelda Price	2004	327
180 3/8	206 3/8	26	26	23 6/8	5 4/8	5 2/8	6	5	Sonora, MX	Luis G. Guerra, Jr.	Luis G. Guerra, Jr.	2004	332
180 3/8	197 1/8	25 6/8	25 1/8	22 7/8	6 1/8	6 1/8	6	5	S. Saskatchewan River, SK	Taylor Andreas	Taylor Andreas	2005	332
180 3/8	194 1/8	22 5/8	23 4/8	22 5/8	5 1/8	4 7/8	7	6	Montrose Co., CO	Stephen A. Gray	Stephen A. Gray	2005	332
180 2/8	207 1/8	25 5/8	24 7/8	24 7/8	5 2/8	5 1/8	6	7	Mineral Co., MT	Hugh W. Magone	E. Lee Magone	1941	335
180 2/8	189	24 4/8	26	26	4 6/8	4 5/8	5	6	Granite Co., MT	Tom Harris	Tom Harris	1965	335
180 2/8	192 2/8	26 6/8	24 3/8	27 5/8	5 2/8	5 2/8	6	6	Eagle Co., CO	Allan W. Mitchell	Allan W. Mitchell	2004	335
180 2/8	202	22 3/8	22 3/8	22 3/8	4 5/8	4 5/8	6	6	Gunnison Co., CO	Jay M. Woffinden	Jay M. Woffinden	2004	335
180 1/8	199 7/8	27	27 2/8	27 2/8	4 4/8	4 4/8	7	7	Tooele Co., UT	Frank L. Barking, Sr.	Frank L. Barking, Sr.	1970	339
180 1/8	194	25 5/8	25	22	4 6/8	4 5/8	4	4	Bonneville Co., ID	John J. Maggini	John J. Maggini	1975	339
180 1/8	185 3/8	22 3/8	21 6/8	21 6/8	4 5/8	4 5/8	5	5	Lincoln Co., WY	Anthony Scarlin	Anthony Scarlin	1992	339
180 1/8	185 6/8	26 2/8	26 2/8	26 2/8	4 7/8	5	5	5	Ravalli Co., MT	David E. Lucas	David E. Lucas	2005	339
213 4/8*	217	26 2/8	24 2/8	24 2/8	6 4/8	6 4/8	5	6	Rio Arriba Co., NM	Unknown	Robert J. Seeds	PR 2004	
210 2/8*	220	28 3/8	25 1/8	25 1/8	5 5/8	5 6/8	6	6	Dewar Lake, SK	Jamie A. Gerein	Jamie A. Gerein	2005	
209 7/8*	221 4/8	28 5/8	31 2/8	33 6/8	5	5	5	5	Rich Co., UT	Denny Austad	Denny Austad	2004	
209*	219 5/8	29 4/8	29	24	4 5/8	4 5/8	5	5	Kiskatinaw River, BC	Randy Bedell	Randy Bedell	2005	

* Final score subject to revision by additional verifying measurements.

MULE DEER - NON-TYPICAL ANTLERS

Odocoileus hemionus hemionus and certain related subspecies

Minimum Score 215

World's Record 355 2/8

Final Score	Gross Score	Length of Main Beam R.	L.	Inside Spread	Circumference at Smallest Place Between Burr & First Point R.	L.	Number of Points R.	L.	Locality	Hunter	Owner	Date Killed	Rank
285 4/8	291 5/8	26 2/8	27 6/8	27 2/8	4 7/8	4 6/8	17	16	Fremont Co., WY	Catherine E. Keene	Catherine E. Keene	2004	1
275	285 3/8	24 6/8	24 5/8	21 5/8	5 3/8	5 5/8	17	20	Utah	Unknown	Cabela's, Inc.	1947	2
272 1/8	279 1/8	24 3/8	26 2/8	25 3/8	5 7/8	6	14	10	Mohave Co., AZ	Thomas D. Friedkin	Thomas D. Friedkin	2004	3
269 4/8	274 7/8	25 5/8	27 3/8	23 1/8	4 6/8	4 7/8	12	9	Unknown	Unknown	Cabela's, Inc.	PR 1994	4
265 5/8	272 3/8	25 3/8	24 6/8	23 1/8	5	5	12	16	Park Co., WY	John K. Corbett	John J. Corbett	1943	5
263 1/8	270 2/8	25 3/8	25 6/8	31 6/8	6 2/8	7	17	13	Yakima Co., WA	Robert D. Ward	Robert J. Ward	1936	6
259 1/8	266 5/8	24 7/8	24 1/8	23 2/8	4 4/8	4 4/8	12	14	Idaho	Unknown	Raymond R. Cross	PR 1992	7
258 4/8	262 7/8	27 4/8	28	27	5 4/8	5 5/8	15	14	Beaver Co., UT	Bill Walgren	Ryan Burke	1932	8
254 6/8	260	25 7/8	24 5/8	26 5/8	4 5/8	5	22	17	Boise Co., ID	Ted J. Simpson	Ted J. Simpson	2005	9
254	257 1/8	26 6/8	26 6/8	22 3/8	5 1/8	4 7/8	11	12	Mesa Co., CO	William C. Byrd, Jr.	William C. Byrd, Jr.	1968	10
251 6/8	257	27 6/8	27 4/8	22 4/8	5 2/8	5 2/8	14	13	Stillwater Co., MT	William Guthrie	Raymond Guthrie	1953	11
251 5/8	259 6/8	26 4/8	27	24	5 1/8	5 2/8	9	10	Camas Co., ID	Harry Woody	Garland E. Sawyers	1958	12
251 3/8	259 1/8	24 4/8	24 3/8	23 3/8	6 1/8	6 4/8	11	13	Great Sand Hills, SK	Clark J. Ehnisz	Clark J. Ehnisz	2006	13
250 4/8	255 3/8	27 3/8	27 4/8	28 1/8	5 3/8	5 3/8	11	11	Eagle Co., CO	Neil J. O'Neill	Neil J. O'Neill	1986	14
250 2/8	256 3/8	24 3/8	24 3/8	22 7/8	5 7/8	5 5/8	13	16	Adams Co., ID	Herbie Glenn	Georgianna Parker	1938	15
248 2/8	258 1/8	30 3/8	27 6/8	28 5/8	5 2/8	5 1/8	16	10	Wyoming	Unknown	Raymond R. Cross	PR 1995	16
247 6/8	254 6/8	24 5/8	21 5/8	18 1/8	5	5 2/8	10	13	Delta Co., CO	Linda L. Gaines	Linda L. Gaines	2003	17
247 6/8	249 7/8	25 3/8	25 3/8	22 2/8	4 5/8	4 5/8	12	10	Unknown	Unknown	Raymond R. Cross	PR 2004	17
247	251 4/8	28 5/8	28 4/8	27 2/8	6 1/8	5 7/8	8	9	Kaibab, AZ	Unknown	Aly M. Bruner	PR 1960	19
247	251 7/8	26 7/8	28	27 6/8	4 7/8	5	6	10	Adams Co., ID	Jack D. Noble	Jack D. Noble	1979	19
246 6/8	252 4/8	26 6/8	25 7/8	23 1/8	5 2/8	5 2/8	9	10	Delta Co., CO	Seth M. Ahlberg	Seth M. Ahlberg	2004	21
246 3/8	255 5/8	26 5/8	27 4/8	27 6/8	5 1/8	5 1/8	10	8	Adams Co., ID	Ronald C. Hamilton	Ronald C. Hamilton	1970	22
246 2/8	255 1/8	25 5/8	24 6/8	20 7/8	4 6/8	4 4/8	10	9	Millard Co., UT	Evan G. Bond	Cabela's, Inc.	2004	23
246 1/8	251 6/8	23 6/8	23 1/8	25 4/8	5 7/8	5 4/8	14	11	Yuma Co., CO	Rodney A. Lindsten	Rodney A. Lindsten	2005	24
246	251 3/8	24 6/8	24 2/8	23 5/8	5 1/8	5 1/8	13	14	Peace River, AB	Cory J. Yaremko	Cory J. Yaremko	2004	25
245 7/8	250 7/8	24 7/8	24 6/8	23 4/8	5 3/8	5 2/8	9	11	Ribstone Creek, AB	Hugh J. Bolton	Hugh J. Bolton	2003	26
245 6/8	248 4/8	28 3/8	28 3/8	33 7/8	5 1/8	5 3/8	8	10	Caribou Co., ID	Kelvin C. Burton	Kelvin C. Burton	1987	27
245 5/8	250 2/8	26 5/8	27	26	5 3/8	5 5/8	8	11	Gem Co., ID	Samuel L. Canite	Samuel L. Canite	2001	28
245 1/8	251 3/8	26 7/8	26 3/8	23 1/8	5 2/8	5 6/8	8	15	Luck Lake, SK	Rick W. Couch	Rick W. Couch	2005	29
244 2/8	251 2/8	24 2/8	26 6/8	20 4/8	4 5/8	5	15	14	Idaho	Unknown	Raymond R. Cross	PR 2004	30
244	249 3/8	23 3/8	26 5/8	22 4/8	5	5	9	9	Grand Co., CO	Marion L. Moore	Ernest E. Teague	1951	31
243 7/8	245 2/8	25 1/8	25 2/8	26 6/8	4 5/8	4 3/8	13	9	Adams Co., ID	John & Richard Stinnett	Bob Stinnett	1978	32

Score									Locality	Hunter	Owner	Date	Rank
243 4/8	247 7/8	26 7/8	22 4/8	26 4/8	5	5	13	10	Wallowa Co., OR	Nancy McCrae	Norman M. McCrae	1950	33
243 2/8	253 5/8	27 7/8	24 6/8	27 5/8	6	6 2/8	8	9	Great Sand Hills, SK	Darrell M. Stan	Darrell M. Stan	2005	34
243 1/8	245	24 5/8	21 2/8	24 2/8	5 4/8	5 3/8	14	9	Sevier Co., UT	Calvin J. Nielson	Douglas L. Nielson	1936	35
242 5/8	244 7/8	24 4/8	22 4/8	24 3/8	4 6/8	4 5/8	7	10	S. Saskatchewan River, SK	Sheldon L.D. Coderre	Sheldon L.D. Coderre	2003	36
242 4/8	249 1/8	27	20 4/8	27 1/8	5 6/8	5 6/8	9	10	Colorado	Unknown	William D. Lancaster	PR 2005	37
242 2/8	249 1/8	27 1/8	22 5/8	26 4/8	5 4/8	5 4/8	11	11	Tramping Lake, SK	Glen J. Mock	Glen J. Mock	2004	38
242	247 4/8	27 1/8	28 4/8	28 4/8	6	6	8	10	Gunnison Co., CO	Chad W. Harris	Chad W. Harris	2003	39
242	247 5/8	25 2/8	26 1/8	25 4/8	5 7/8	5 6/8	10	10	Crane Valley, SK	Heath Jordison	Heath Jordison	2003	39
241 2/8	250 3/8	25 4/8	25 4/8	27 1/8	5 4/8	5 4/8	8	10	San Juan Co., NM	Picked Up	NM Dept. Game & Fish	2003	41
241	252 6/8	24 6/8	17 2/8	21 2/8	6 1/8	5 4/8	12	18	Montrose Co., CO	Vicki L. Lakin	Vicki L. Lakin	2005	42
240 6/8	249 7/8	23	27 3/8	25 3/8	4 4/8	4 4/8	13	7	Kit Carson Co., CO	Ralph J. Holsclaw	Ralph J. Holsclaw	2005	43
240 5/8	249 3/8	25 5/8	18	25 5/8	5 3/8	5 1/8	9	10	Tea Lake, SK	A. Elliott & D. Elliott	A. Elliott & D. Elliott	2005	44
240	246 5/8	27	21 4/8	26 4/8	5 3/8	5 3/8	12	9	Garfield Co., CO	Tommy R. Cupit	Tommy R. Cupit	2005	45
239 4/8	248 5/8	27	22 5/8	26 6/8	5 1/8	5 1/8	16	11	Camas Co., ID	Charles Strickland	Tony Perdue	1971	46
239 4/8	242 2/8	27 4/8	23 3/8	27 3/8	5 4/8	5 6/8	14	15	Lower Arrow Lake, BC	Glenn H. Seaton	Paul Seaton	2003	46
239 3/8	256 3/8	27 3/8	18 1/8	25	5 6/8	5 1/8	7	14	Pitkin Co., CO	Cade Crawford	Cade Crawford	2003	48
239 2/8	243 3/8	25 2/8	23 6/8	24 3/8	5 1/8	4 7/8	8	7	Idaho Co., ID	Joey A. Travis	Joey A. Travis	1973	49
239 1/8	244 3/8	24 3/8	24 5/8	26 2/8	4 7/8	4 5/8	9	8	Garfield Co., UT	Kevin Fisher	Kevin Fisher	2005	50
239	244 1/8	28	24 5/8	22 7/8	5	4 5/8	13	15	Baker Co., OR	Roy Hunt	Jeffrey F. Phillips	1928	51
238 7/8	243 7/8	24	24 2/8	24 3/8	4 3/8	4 4/8	13	16	Unknown	Unkown	David Hobson	PR 1994	52

TYPICAL MULE DEER
FINAL SCORE: 194-4/8
HUNTER: Ronald L. Peacock

TYPICAL MULE DEER
FINAL SCORE: 180-5/8
HUNTER: Grady L. Miller

NON-TYPICAL MULE DEER
FINAL SCORE: 237-3/8
HUNTER: Jory D. Miller

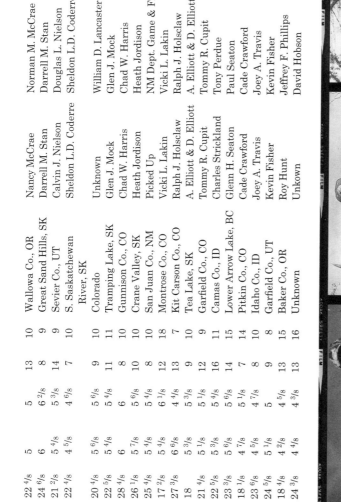

NON-TYPICAL MULE DEER
FINAL SCORE: 246
HUNTER: Cory J. Yaremko

MULE DEER - NON-TYPICAL ANTLERS

Odocoileus hemionus hemionus and certain related subspecies

Final Score	Gross Score	Length of Main Beam R.	L.	Inside Spread	Circumference at Smallest Place Between Burr & First Point R.	L.	Number of Points R.	L.	Locality	Hunter	Owner	Date Killed	Rank
238 5/8	242 2/8	25 2/8	26	23 2/8	5	5	9	10	Bull River, BC	Karl S. Schmieder	Karl S. Schmieder	1982	53
238 4/8	257 3/8	27 5/8	24 2/8	28 2/8	5 7/8	6	10	9	Power Co., ID	Jim Nilsson	Raymond R. Cross	1985	54
238 3/8	243 7/8	26 6/8	26 1/8	25 7/8	5 4/8	5 2/8	11	11	Adams Co., ID	C. Henry Daniels	Ryan B. Hatfield	1967	55
238	241 7/8	25 7/8	26 6/8	22 3/8	5 4/8	5 4/8	10	12	Great Sand Hills, SK	Gene T. Lennox	Gene T. Lennox	1969	56
237 7/8	240 1/8	24 3/8	24 4/8	22 6/8	5	4 7/8	9	12	Unknown	Emil Feidt	John J. Feidt III	1900	57
237 6/8	244	26 3/8	27 6/8	26 5/8	6 1/8	6	11	10	Garfield Co., CO	Robert W. Flewelling	Robert W. Flewelling	1962	58
237 3/8	250 4/8	25 3/8	26 3/8	21 1/8	5 3/8	5 1/8	10	10	Yuma Co., CO	Kerry S. Smith	Kerry S. Smith	2003	59
237 3/8	245 6/8	24 6/8	25 2/8	21	5	4 7/8	11	16	S. Saskatchewan River, SK	Jory D. Miller	Jory D. Miller	2006	59
236 6/8	240 4/8	26 2/8	26 6/8	20 1/8	5 3/8	5 1/8	7	11	Mesa Co., CO	Alan Pennington	Alan Pennington	2004	61
236 5/8	243 7/8	27	25 4/8	25 1/8	5 4/8	5 4/8	10	10	Saguache Co., CO	George Stoddart	Kenneth Thorson	1938	62
236	241 4/8	24 2/8	25 5/8	21 7/8	4 4/8	4 4/8	9	12	Oregon	Unknown	William D. Lancaster	1955	63
235 7/8	238 7/8	24	24 2/8	20 1/8	5 2/8	5 1/8	9	7	Mesa Co., CO	James R. March	James R. March	2003	64
235 4/8	242 2/8	26	25 5/8	28 5/8	5 3/8	5	13	11	Unknown	Unknown	William D. Lancaster PR	2003	65
235 1/8	245 3/8	25 2/8	26 7/8	20 3/8	6	5 7/8	13	11	Saskatchewan	Forrest Buckmaster	Larry L. Huffman	1942	66
234 7/8	244 3/8	22 2/8	22 6/8	20 6/8	5 4/8	5	6	12	Gove Co., KS	Tyler R. Remington	Tyler R. Remington	2003	67
234 7/8	240 7/8	26 2/8	26	27 4/8	5	4 4/8	8	11	Trego Co., KS	N. Guy Eastman	N. Guy Eastman	2004	67
234 2/8	241 5/8	23 4/8	23 1/8	21	5	5 2/8	15	16	Washoe Co., NV	Unknown	Marty Holley	1943	69
233	236 4/8	26 6/8	25 7/8	34	4 5/8	4 6/8	9	8	Gunnison Co., CO	David G. Bjorkman	David G. Bjorkman	2004	70
233	239 4/8	25 7/8	25 3/8	23 2/8	5	5 2/8	8	7	Mohave Co., AZ	Thomas D. Friedkin	Thomas D. Friedkin	2004	70
232 4/8	242 4/8	26 5/8	26 1/8	23 4/8	4 4/8	5 1/8	9	12	Carbon Co., WY	Melvin Peters	Melvin Peters	1963	72
232 1/8	239 6/8	27 5/8	23 3/8	24 6/8	4 3/8	4 4/8	9	12	Gem Co., ID	Cliff Knotts	William D. Lancaster	1982	72
231 7/8	238 5/8	24 6/8	25 5/8	22	5 6/8	5 3/8	13	11	Utah	Unknown	Nathan W. Jacobson PR	2006	74
231 4/8	242 4/8	26 5/8	27 4/8	24 6/8	4 6/8	4 7/8	13	8	Colorado	Unknown	Raymond R. Cross PR	2000	75
231 4/8	235 4/8	26 3/8	25 1/8	26 6/8	4 6/8	5 1/8	8	9	Rio Grande Co., CO	Leroy J. Quintana	Leroy J. Quintana	2005	75
231 3/8	238 1/8	26 3/8	25 6/8	22 4/8	5 2/8	4 6/8	9	9	Deschutes Co., OR	Leslie W. Wallace	Willy & Larry Wallace	1946	77
231 3/8	236 1/8	26 2/8	28	22 5/8	5 3/8	5 2/8	9	9	Fremont Co., WY	John Russell	James Russell	1954	77
231	234 7/8	29 7/8	29 3/8	28 1/8	5 2/8	5 2/8	8	8	White Pine Co., NV	Shawn R. Gregory	Shawn R. Gregory	2005	79
230 7/8	238 6/8	23 5/8	22 7/8	26 7/8	5 4/8	6	10	12	Coconino Co., AZ	Donald I. Hahnenkratt	Donald I. Hahnenkratt	1978	80
230 6/8	234	27 4/8	27 6/8	22 5/8	5 2/8	5 1/8	9	12	Caribou Co., ID	Von Adams	Von Adams	1966	81
230 6/8	233 6/8	22 7/8	23 6/8	18 7/8	5 2/8	4 3/8	9	11	Uinta Co., WY	N. Guy Eastman	N. Guy Eastman	2004	81
230 6/8	234 2/8	25 4/8	26 1/8	24 2/8	5 2/8	5 2/8	8	10	Chase Co., NE	Owen P. Madden	Owen P. Madden	2005	81

430

Score	Length R	Length L	Spread	Circ. R	Circ. L	Pts R	Pts L	Locality	By Whom Killed	Owner	Date	Rank
230 3/8	25 6/8	26	16 4/8	5 1/8	5 1/8	6	11	Boulder Co., CO	Raymond Dahl	Cabela's, Inc.	1957	84
230 2/8	25	27 6/8	23 2/8	5 7/8	5 6/8	10	11	Mesa Co., CO	Billy W. Teague	Billy W. Teague	2004	85
230 1/8	26 4/8	24 6/8	25 2/8	4 3/8	4 4/8	10	9	Lane Co., KS	Roger Schieb	Roger Schieb	1993	86
230 1/8	24 7/8	25 5/8	21 5/8	5 2/8	5 5/8	10	9	Truax, SK	Les A. Herle	Les A. Herle	2002	86
230	26 3/8	26 1/8	24 7/8	4 4/8	4 4/8	10	9	Utah Co., UT	Allen B. Williams	Ryan B. Barber	1939	88
229 6/8	23 7/8	23 7/8	17 7/8	5 2/8	5	13	16	Badger Creek, BC	Paul Moody	Paul Moody	1997	89
229	24 7/8	24 3/8	24 3/8	5 2/8	5 1/8	10	9	Owyhee Co., ID	Alburn Sayers	William D. Lancaster	1968	90
228 7/8	29 5/8	30 4/8	26 6/8	5 1/8	5 2/8	8	7	Grant Co., OR	Ralph Holman	Reina V. Holman	1942	91
228 1/8	25 7/8	26 3/8	24 4/8	5 2/8	5 1/8	14	8	Powder River Co., MT	Joe C. Masin	Joe C. Masin	1991	92
228	25	26 6/8	26 4/8	5	6	8	7	Eagle Co., CO	William J. McEwen	William J. McEwen	2003	93
227 7/8	25 7/8	25 7/8	25 2/8	6 2/8	6	8	11	Washington Co., ID	Jim Bumgarner	Jim Bumgarner	1969	94
227 1/8	25	25 3/8	23	6	6 4/8	9	8	Washington Co., ID	Warren R. Constans	Daniel M. Constans	1947	95
227 1/8	26 5/8	27	22 1/8	5 1/8	5	8	9	Rio Arriba Co., NM	Roland N. Chavez	Roland N. Chavez	2005	95
226 5/8	25 2/8	25 6/8	23 3/8	5 1/8	5 2/8	11	12	Garfield Co., UT	Kevin Fisher	Kevin Fisher	2004	97
225 7/8	24	25	18 5/8	5	5 1/8	13	11	San Juan Co., UT	Lon J. Bess	Lon J. Bess	2004	98
224 5/8	21 5/8	24 5/8	21	6 3/8	5 6/8	14	8	Washington Co., ID	Robert Jackson	Daniel M. Constans	1955	99
224	25 1/8	25 1/8	18 3/8	5 2/8	5 2/8	11	10	Fremont Co., CO	Chris D. Goodwin	Chris D. Goodwin	2004	100
224	26 3/8	27 1/8	20 3/8	5 5/8	5 6/8	13	6	Revelstoke Lake, BC	Steven A. Krossa	Steven A. Krossa	2005	100
223 5/8	24 2/8	23 7/8	19 7/8	4 6/8	4 5/8	9	12	Beaverhead Co., MT	Carl J. Guse	Robert W. Harwood	1963	102
223 3/8	22 7/8	24 2/8	20 6/8	4 6/8	4 6/8	12	9	Madison Co., ID	Val D. Grover	Val D. Grover	1978	103
223 3/8	25 1/8	25 1/8	21 5/8	6	5 7/8	6	12	Jackson Co., CO	Tom R. Herrick	Tom R. Herrick	2005	103
223 2/8	27 4/8	27 4/8	26 3/8	5 1/8	5 2/8	10	7	Coconino Co., AZ	Boyd Owens	Steven W. King	1965	105
223 1/8	25	20 5/8	20 1/8	4 6/8	4 7/8	11	8	Carbon Co., WY	Brandon C. Palicki	Brandon C. Palicki	2001	106
222 7/8	27 6/8	27 6/8	29 4/8	6 1/8	6 2/8	7	8	Owyhee Co., ID	Eric Tennant	Eric Tennant	2004	107
222 3/8	27 3/8	27 7/8	23 3/8	5 4/8	5 5/8	8	8	Montrose Co., CO	Joseph F. Lynn Moore	Joseph F. Lynn Moore	1959	108
222	26	26 4/8	26 4/8	5 4/8	5 6/8	6	8	Dolores Co., CO	Olive Truelsen	Val Truelsen	1957	109
222	26 6/8	25 5/8	25 5/8	5 3/8	5 2/8	9	9	Coconino Co., AZ	James R. Kowalski	James R. Kowalski	2004	109
221 6/8	25 5/8	24 7/8	28 1/8	5 2/8	5 2/8	9	9	Rio Blanco Co., CO	Ralph A. Schuette	Ralph A. Schuette	2005	111
221 3/8	22 5/8	21 6/8	22 6/8	7 6/8	7 7/8	8	9	Mesa Co., CO	Matthew R. Richardson	Matthew R. Richardson	2004	112
221	21 6/8	21	16 7/8	5	5	7	8	Montezuma Co., CO	Robert E. Weitzel	Robert E. Weitzel	2005	113
220 4/8	25 4/8	23 6/8	23	4 5/8	4 4/8	10	7	Routt Co., CO	Joe B. Essex	Joe B. Essex	1963	114
220 3/8	25 4/8	25 1/8	24 1/8	4 4/8	4 4/8	8	10	Elko Co., NV	Steven P. Feasel	Steven P. Feasel	2006	115
219 5/8	22 5/8	23 4/8	21 2/8	4 6/8	4 6/8	8	8	Pitkin Co., CO	Zac T. Hendricks	Zac T. Hendricks	2003	116
219 2/8	26	24 6/8	24 6/8	5 2/8	4 6/8	8	7	Kiowa Co., CO	Paul Weyand	Paul Weyand	2003	117
218 7/8	24 2/8	22 4/8	22 4/8	4 7/8	5 2/8	7	9	Flathead Co., MT	Robert P. Barnaby	Robert P. Barnaby	2004	118
218 6/8	24 5/8	24 2/8	21 7/8	5 3/8	4 7/8	9	10	Mohave Co., AZ	Bob Hall	Bob Hall	1979	119
218 5/8	28 1/8	27	25 7/8	5 2/8	5 3/8	10	8	Ouray Co., CO	Sophie N. Golden	Aaron W. Galloway	1911	120
218 2/8	25	24 5/8	26 2/8	5 2/8	5 2/8	8	11	Loon Lake, BC	Yogi Sharma	Yogi Sharma	1987	121
217 6/8	25 4/8	22 5/8	16 3/8	5 3/8	5 2/8	12	12	Oneida Co., ID	Donald T. Jenkins	Donald T. Jenkins	2005	122
217 1/8	22 5/8	24	27 1/8	4 3/8	4 4/8	11	11	Garfield Co., CO	Wiley Moore	Michael C. Moore	1962	123
215 5/8	23 3/8	29 7/8	26	5 4/8	5 4/8	7	7	La Plata Co., CO	Carlton J. Bertrand, Jr.	Carlton J. Bertrand, Jr.	1998	124
215 3/8	23 2/8	23 6/8	28 2/8	6 7/8	6 2/8	10	12	Inyo Co., CA	Darryl L. Coe	Darryl L. Coe	2005	125

MULE DEER - NON-TYPICAL ANTLERS

Odocoileus hemionus hemionus and certain related subspecies

Final Score	Gross Score	Length of Main Beam R.	Length of Main Beam L.	Inside Spread	Circumference at Smallest Place Between Burr & First Point R.	Circumference at Smallest Place Between Burr & First Point L.	Number of Points R.	Number of Points L.	Locality	Hunter	Owner	Date Killed	Rank
215 2/8	218	25	24 6/8	23 4/8	5 1/8	5	7	7	Sounding Creek, AB	Scott B. Olsen	Scott B. Olsen	2006	126
215 1/8	222 6/8	21 5/8	22 5/8	21 4/8	4 4/8	4 3/8	7	6	Tooele Co., UT	James D. Jensen	James D. Jensen	1980	127
283 *	293 5/8	27 7/8	27 7/8	23 2/8	5 6/8	5 2/8	16	15	Oneida Co., ID	Robert M. Phelps	Robert M. Phelps	1975	
278 *	285	22 2/8	23	17	6 2/8	5 5/8	17	14	Owyhee Co., ID	Charles W. Burden	B.R. Burden & C. Winkler	1955	
271 6/8*	280 7/8	27	27 3/8	25 5/8	5 1/8	5 1/8	10	10	Eagle Co., CO	Bob Galpin	Shirley Galpin	1945	

* Final score subject to revision by additional verifying measurements.

432

BOONE AND CROCKETT CLUB'S

NON-TYPICAL MULE DEER
FINAL SCORE: 239-1/8
HUNTER: Kevin Fisher

NON-TYPICAL MULE DEER
FINAL SCORE: 240
HUNTER: Tommy R. Cupit

NON-TYPICAL MULE DEER
FINAL SCORE: 221-6/8
HUNTER: Ralph A. Schuette

NON-TYPICAL MULE DEER
FINAL SCORE: 242
HUNTER: Chad W. Harris

COLUMBIA BLACKTAIL - TYPICAL ANTLERS

Odocoileus hemionus columbianus

Minimum Score 125 World's Record 182 2/8

Final Score	Gross Score	Length of Main Beam R.	L.	Inside Spread	Circumference at Smallest Place Between Burr & First Point R.	L.	Number of Points R.	L.	Locality	Hunter	Owner	Date Killed	Rank
170 6/8	179 7/8	24 2/8	24 3/8	20 7/8	5 1/8	5 2/8	5	4	Clatsop Co., OR	Larry Naught	Allan Naught	1955	1
170 6/8	174 4/8	24 2/8	23 7/8	21	4 1/8	4 3/8	5	5	Siskiyou Co., CA	Frank G. Merz	Frank G. Merz	1979	1
160 5/8	164 3/8	25 3/8	25 2/8	19 7/8	4 4/8	4 4/8	5	5	Tillamook Co., OR	Xavier B.P. Lopez	Xavier B.P. Lopez	2003	3
160 1/8	171 2/8	20 7/8	20 4/8	16 7/8	4	4 1/8	5	6	Trinity Co., CA	Bernard Lopez	Timothy Lopez	1978	4
158 5/8	164	21 2/8	21 6/8	17 3/8	5 1/8	5 1/8	5	5	Clark Co., WA	Johnny Alderman	Johnny Alderman	2003	5
158 4/8	160 2/8	20 6/8	20 6/8	17 4/8	4 6/8	4 3/8	5	5	Tehama Co., CA	Billy D. Waters	Billy D. Waters	2004	6
157 6/8	164 5/8	23	25 4/8	19 2/8	4 6/8	4 6/8	5	5	Marion Co., OR	Dennis A. Bleakney	Dennis A. Bleakney	2005	7
157 4/8	165 3/8	22 4/8	24	19 6/8	4 1/8	4 1/8	5	5	Stanislaus Co., CA	Picked Up	Scott A. Wilkinson	2004	8
156 5/8	164 2/8	21 6/8	21 7/8	18 1/8	5	4 7/8	6	6	Tehama Co., CA	Donald R. Meeder	Donald R. Meeder	2004	9
155 4/8	160 5/8	21 6/8	22 5/8	19 4/8	4 1/8	4 2/8	5	5	Clackamas Co., OR	Ed Weidman	Tom Gengler	1955	10
155	157 1/8	19	21	20 6/8	5 1/8	5 1/8	5	5	Mendocino Co., CA	Frank J. Lucchetti	Frank J. Lucchetti	2005	11
153 1/8	163 4/8	23 4/8	21 6/8	22 1/8	4 3/8	4 6/8	5	5	Mendocino Co., CA	Ken H. Fuller	Ken H. Fuller	2004	12
152 7/8	156 3/8	19 7/8	20 3/8	17 1/8	4 3/8	4 3/8	5	5	Stanislaus Co., CA	Picked Up	H. James Tonkin, Jr. PR	2005	13
152 5/8	157	22 6/8	22 3/8	13 1/8	5 3/8	5 4/8	5	5	Clackamas Co., OR	Rory L. Cramer	Rory L. Cramer	2004	14
152 2/8	155 5/8	22 2/8	21 4/8	16	4 7/8	4 7/8	5	5	Tillamook Co., OR	Roy Harris	Roy Harris	2003	15
151 3/8	157 6/8	21 6/8	22 5/8	19 1/8	5	5 3/8	5	5	Lewis Co., WA	Howard Koher	Dean Koher	1969	16
150 6/8	167 7/8	24 4/8	22 6/8	16 5/8	4 4/8	4 7/8	6	6	Trinity Co., CA	Brian W. Maple	Brian W. Maple	2005	17
150 4/8	159	22 5/8	23	22	4 6/8	5	5	5	Mendocino Co., CA	Joshua D. Powell	Joshua D. Powell	2003	18
149 4/8	152 2/8	20 5/8	20	17	3 6/8	3 7/8	5	5	Cowlitz Co., WA	Donald Rismoen	Donald Rismoen	1959	19
149 1/8	151 1/8	20 4/8	20 1/8	15 5/8	4 6/8	4 5/8	5	5	Douglas Co., OR	Randy Ellington	Randy Ellington	1994	20
148 6/8	153 4/8	20 2/8	20 4/8	20 2/8	4	4 4/8	5	5	Mendocino Co., CA	Ronald L. Christensen	Ronald L. Christensen	2005	21
148 4/8	151 1/8	20 1/8	20	19 6/8	4 2/8	4 3/8	5	5	Siskiyou Co., CA	Edward F. Smith	Edward F. Smith	2004	22
146 3/8	148	20 2/8	20	19 7/8	4 1/8	4 1/8	5	5	Mendocino Co., CA	Allen Z. La Delle	Allen Z. La Delle	1979	23
145 7/8	151 4/8	19 3/8	20 3/8	20 4/8	4 2/8	4 2/8	5	5	Glenn Co., CA	Ed Moore	Ed Moore	2003	24
145 7/8	152 5/8	20 6/8	21 7/8	16 3/8	4	3 6/8	5	5	Siskiyou Co., CA	Charles C. Kays	Charles C. Kays	2004	24
145 2/8	148 1/8	21 2/8	21 3/8	16	4 1/8	4 1/8	5	5	Polk Co., OR	Michael L. Farmer	Michael L. Farmer	2003	26
144 7/8	152 4/8	20	20 2/8	17 3/8	4 6/8	4 4/8	5	5	Trinity Co., CA	Josh L. Smith	Josh L. Smith	2004	27
144 5/8	150 5/8	21 3/8	21 5/8	19 3/8	4	4 1/8	5	5	Trinity Co., CA	Lew E. Wade	Lew E. Wade	1992	28
144 3/8	153 1/8	22 7/8	23	16 3/8	5 1/8	4 7/8	6	4	Trinity Co., CA	Autumn L. Brown	Autumn L. Brown	2004	29
144	147 3/8	20 3/8	20 6/8	19 6/8	4 5/8	4 6/8	5	5	Snohomish Co., WA	Leonard M. Patricelli	Leonard M. Patricelli	2005	30
143 7/8	153 7/8	21 4/8	23	19	4 4/8	4 3/8	6	5	Tehama Co., CA	E. Stephen Maloney III	E. Stephen Maloney III	2005	31
143 5/8	148 2/8	22 7/8	22 3/8	19 7/8	4 3/8	4 3/8	5	5	Trinity Co., CA	Cameron L. Brown	Cameron L. Brown	2005	32
143 2/8	146 7/8	21 7/8	21 3/8	18	4	4 1/8	5	5	Clackamas Co., OR	Nathan Boos	Nathan Boos	2004	33

Score	Beam R	Beam L	Inside Spread	Circ R	Circ L	Points R	Points L	Locality	Owner	By Whom Killed	Date	Rank
143 1/8	23 3/8	23 2/8	20 5/8	4 2/8	4 2/8	5	5	Mendocino Co., CA	William J. Gardner	William J. Gardner	2004	34
143	22 4/8	22 4/8	18 7/8	4 7/8	5	5	6	Trinity Co., CA	Darin Slote	Darin Slote	2005	35
142 7/8	22 7/8	22 5/8	21 4/8	4 1/8	4 1/8	6	5	Mendocino Co., CA	Nate Allsup	Nate Allsup	2004	36
142 2/8	23 2/8	23 5/8	19 2/8	5	5 1/8	5	4	Trinity Co., CA	Carroll L. Sherman	Carroll L. Sherman	2004	37
142 2/8	21 4/8	21 4/8	21 4/8	4 5/8	4 5/8	4	4	Trinity Co., CA	Richard J. Banko, Jr.	Richard J. Banko, Jr.	2005	37
142	21 2/8	21 1/8	16	3 6/8	3 6/8	5	5	Trinity Co., CA	Brad W. Criner	Brad W. Criner	2004	39
141 6/8	22 7/8	23	19 6/8	5	5	6	5	Grays Harbor Co., WA	Unknown	Brett A. Chalcraft	1967	40
141 4/8	21 2/8	20 4/8	18	4 1/8	4 2/8	5	5	Mendocino Co., CA	Brett C. Gomes	Brett C. Gomes	2003	41
141 4/8	22 7/8	23 2/8	23 4/8	5	5	5	4	Trinity Co., CA	Brian M. Hall	Brian M. Hall	2005	41
141 1/8	20 5/8	21 5/8	18 1/8	4 4/8	4 4/8	5	5	Columbia Co., OR	Russ A. Scholl	Russ A. Scholl	2004	43
141 1/8	22 4/8	20 5/8	19 7/8	4 3/8	4 5/8	5	5	Mendocino Co., CA	Nate Allsup	Nate Allsup	2006	43
140 4/8	23 2/8	23 3/8	19 3/8	4 2/8	4 2/8	6	6	Siskiyou Co., CA	Robert L. Thomas	M.L. James Thomas	1946	45
140 3/8	22 2/8	23 4/8	17 7/8	4 3/8	4 1/8	5	5	Colusa Co., CA	Knute M. Myers	Knute M. Myers	2005	46
140 1/8	21	21	16 3/8	4 1/8	4 1/8	5	5	Mendocino Co., CA	Redhawk R. Pallesen	Redhawk R. Pallesen	1997	47
140 1/8	20 3/8	21 7/8	18 4/8	4 5/8	4 4/8	7	7	Humboldt Co., CA	Carl L. Schoenhofer	Carl L. Schoenhofer	2003	47
140 1/8	20 7/8	20 7/8	16 3/8	5	5	5	5	Humboldt Co., CA	Timothy J. Silva	Timothy J. Silva	2004	47
139 6/8	20 5/8	20 4/8	19	4 2/8	4 2/8	5	5	Humboldt Co., CA	John M. Higley	John M. Higley	2004	50
139 4/8	20 4/8	20	18	4 5/8	4 5/8	5	5	Humboldt Co., CA	Timothy J. Silva	Timothy J. Silva	2002	51
139	22 6/8	21 6/8	19 5/8	5 1/8	5	7	7	Mendocino Co., CA	Steven M. Gollnick	Steven M. Gollnick	2003	52
139	23 4/8	22 5/8	22	3 6/8	3 6/8	5	4	Trinity Co., CA	John E. Pryor	John E. Pryor	2005	52
138 7/8	20 6/8	19 7/8	18 5/8	4 3/8	4 3/8	5	5	Mendocino Co., CA	Dennis J. Deaton	Dennis J. Deaton	1986	54
138 7/8	20 2/8	20 7/8	17 7/8	4 6/8	4 5/8	5	5	Clackamas Co., OR	Randell J. MacDonald	Randell J. MacDonald	2004	54
138 5/8	19 4/8	21 5/8	16 1/8	4 2/8	4 2/8	5	5	Trinity Co., CA	Kirk D. Younker	Kirk D. Younker	2004	56
138 4/8	22 2/8	22 2/8	18 4/8	3 6/8	3 7/8	4	4	Polk Co., OR	Jerry W. Howard	Jerry W. Howard	2004	57
138 3/8	21 1/8	21 4/8	16 5/8	4 2/8	4 3/8	5	5	Clackamas Co., OR	Richard J. Gibboney	Richard J. Gibboney	2004	58
138 2/8	23 2/8	23 5/8	15 4/8	4 3/8	4 1/8	5	5	Polk Co., OR	Michael L. Farmer	Michael L. Farmer	2004	59
137 7/8	20 5/8	21 5/8	17 3/8	4 1/8	4 1/8	5	5	Clackamas Co., OR	Kenneth C. Hostetler	Kenneth C. Hostetler	2004	60
137 5/8	19 6/8	19 6/8	17 1/8	4 7/8	4 7/8	5	5	Humboldt Co., CA	Nick Albert	Nick Albert	2004	61
137 4/8	21 2/8	20 6/8	18 7/8	4 3/8	4 2/8	6	5	Jackson Co., OR	Don Wolfe	Don Wolfe	2004	62
137 3/8	21 1/8	21 4/8	18 3/8	4 7/8	4 7/8	5	4	Mendocino Co., CA	Logan R. Nuberg	Logan R. Nuberg	2002	63
137 3/8	21 6/8	22 3/8	16 1/8	4 4/8	4 2/8	5	5	Humboldt Co., CA	David G. Lungi, Jr.	David G. Lungi, Jr.	2006	63
137 2/8	21 2/8	21 4/8	17 2/8	4 1/8	3 7/8	5	5	Lane Co., OR	Alvin D. Bean	Ken Halbert	1960	65
137 2/8	20 7/8	22	17 6/8	4 4/8	4 3/8	6	6	Jackson Co., OR	Dusty S. McGrorty	Dusty S. McGrorty	2003	65
137	21	20 6/8	15 4/8	4 5/8	4 4/8	6	5	Trinity Co., CA	Dave B. Newton	Dave B. Newton	2006	67
136 6/8	22 1/8	23 6/8	18	5 5/8	5 3/8	5	4	Mendocino Co., CA	Brendan W. Graves	Brendan W. Graves	2005	68
136 6/8	19 4/8	19 6/8	18 4/8	4 5/8	4 4/8	5	5	Mendocino Co., CA	Robert K. Browning	Robert K. Browning	2006	68
136 5/8	21 1/8	21 4/8	16 1/8	4 6/8	4 6/8	4	4	Linn Co., OR	Stephen P. Zaina	Stephen P. Zaina	2004	70
136 3/8	21	18 2/8	16 3/8	5 1/8	5 1/8	4	4	Jackson Co., OR	Lloyd Hickam	Ken Wilson	1984	71
136 2/8	20 7/8	21	17 4/8	4 4/8	4 4/8	5	5	Coos Co., OR	David C. Martin	David C. Martin	1962	72
136	21 6/8	21 4/8	17 2/8	4	4	5	5	Skamania Co., WA	J.L. Foyt, Jr., & C.W. Foyt	J.L. Foyt, Jr.	1990	73
135 7/8	22 3/8	22 4/8	19 5/8	4 4/8	4 4/8	5	5	Mendocino Co., CA	Jack D. Jordan	Jack D. Jordan	2005	74

COLUMBIA BLACKTAIL - TYPICAL ANTLERS

Odocoileus hemionus columbianus

Final Score	Gross Score	Length of Main Beam R.	L.	Inside Spread	Circumference at Smallest Place Between Burr & First Point R.	L.	Number of Points R.	L.	Locality	Hunter	Owner	Date Killed	Rank
135 5/8	141 7/8	21 7/8	20 3/8	17 3/8	4 5/8	4 5/8	5	5	Colusa Co., CA	Brett C. Gomes	Brett C. Gomes	2004	75
135 5/8	150 2/8	20 1/8	21 7/8	15 2/8	5 3/8	5 6/8	5	7	Washington Co., OR	Michael J. Seavey	Michael J. Seavey	2005	75
135 4/8	138 4/8	21 2/8	21 4/8	16 2/8	4 3/8	4 3/8	5	5	Douglas Co., OR	Richard L. Baumgartner	Richard L. Baumgartner	2005	77
135 3/8	146 3/8	20 6/8	20 2/8	14 3/8	4 2/8	4 1/8	6	6	Cowlitz Co., WA	Randy D. McCall	Randy D. McCall	2004	78
135 2/8	138 4/8	22	21 5/8	20 2/8	3 5/8	3 5/8	4	4	Trinity Co., CA	Daniel K. Dodson	Daniel K. Dodson	2004	79
135 2/8	146 2/8	21 4/8	18 4/8	16 2/8	4 5/8	4 4/8	6	5	Jackson Co., OR	Robert Jones	Robert Jones	2004	79
135 2/8	143 1/8	20 1/8	20 5/8	15	3 6/8	3 7/8	5	6	Trinity Co., CA	David A. Rosin	David A. Rosin	2005	79
135 1/8	146	21	21 4/8	18 5/8	3 5/8	3 7/8	4	6	Humboldt Co., CA	Kenneth W. Springer	Kenneth W. Springer	1976	82
135 1/8	140 2/8	19 3/8	18 4/8	16 5/8	4 5/8	4 5/8	5	5	Yamhill Co., OR	James T. Hallock	James T. Hallock	2004	82
135	143 7/8	20	20 4/8	20 1/8	4 4/8	5	6	5	Lane Co., OR	Glen E. Johnston	Glen E. Johnston	2001	84
134 6/8	139 3/8	18 7/8	19	17	4	4	5	5	Stanislaus Co., CA	Picked Up	H. James Tonkin, Jr. PR	2005	85
134 3/8	140 1/8	20 4/8	19 1/8	16 3/8	3 7/8	3 7/8	4	5	Trinity Co., CA	John R. Clark	John R. Clark	1978	86
134	139	22 2/8	23	21 1/8	4 7/8	4 6/8	4	5	Alameda Co., CA	Steve A. Fields	Steve A. Fields	2004	87
134	137	20 3/8	20 4/8	16 4/8	4 6/8	4 5/8	5	5	Humboldt Co., CA	David E. Evanow	David E. Evanow	2006	87
133 5/8	139	22 1/8	21 3/8	13 3/8	4 3/8	4 5/8	5	5	Jackson Co., OR	Michael C. McNall	Michael C. McNall	2002	89
133 5/8	144 4/8	22 4/8	23	20 3/8	4 7/8	4 6/8	5	4	Santa Clara Co., CA	Vince P. Bobba	Vince P. Bobba	2003	89
133	137 2/8	20 3/8	20 1/8	15 4/8	4	4	5	5	Siskiyou Co., CA	Dale W. Davis	Dale W. Davis	1995	91
133	138 6/8	19 5/8	21	19 6/8	4 1/8	4 3/8	5	5	Yamhill Co., OR	Wayne Stocks	Wayne Stocks	2004	91
132 2/8	139	19 6/8	18 7/8	15	5 1/8	5 2/8	5	6	Marion Co., OR	Chris Bischoff	Chris Bischoff	2003	93
132 2/8	135 7/8	19 7/8	19 6/8	18	4 2/8	4 2/8	5	5	Humboldt Co., CA	Greg A. Mullins	Greg A. Mullins	2005	93
132	140 6/8	20	21 4/8	15 1/8	5 3/8	5 3/8	5	6	Clallam Co., WA	Kameron K. Thompsen	Kameron K. Thompsen	2003	95
131 1/8	155 1/8	20 7/8	22 1/8	13 3/8	4 2/8	4 2/8	6	6	Lane Co., OR	Marsten E. Miller	Marsten E. Miller	1990	96
131	135 3/8	21 4/8	22 2/8	16	4	4 2/8	4	4	Mendocino Co., CA	Richard M. Noonan	Richard M. Noonan	1992	97
130 5/8	143 1/8	18 7/8	19 4/8	20 7/8	4 6/8	5	6	6	Lane Co., OR	Darryl W. Williams	Darryl W. Williams	2006	98
130 2/8	145 5/8	21 7/8	21 1/8	18	4 3/8	4 2/8	6	5	Glenn Co., CA	Mathew J. Garcia	Mathew J. Garcia	2004	99
129 4/8	158 3/8	23 1/8	23 4/8	17 1/8	5 3/8	5 4/8	7	6	Trinity Co., CA	Floyd E. Hecker	Floyd E. Hecker	2004	100
129 3/8	138 7/8	19 3/8	19 5/8	15 6/8	4 2/8	4 1/8	6	6	Marion Co., OR	Mark J. Overfield	Mark J. Overfield	2003	101
129 2/8	131 1/8	19 1/8	19 1/8	14	3 6/8	3 7/8	5	5	Jackson Co., OR	Michael J. Borel	Michael J. Borel	2004	102
128 3/8	129 4/8	20 5/8	20 4/8	23 2/8	4 4/8	4 3/8	4	4	Glenn Co., CA	Lowell R. King, Jr.	Lowell R. King, Jr.	2005	103
127 5/8	130 6/8	17 1/8	18 5/8	14 3/8	4 3/8	4 1/8	5	5	Coos Co., OR	Chris L. Mundell	Chris L. Mundell	2004	104
127 3/8	130 4/8	17 7/8	18 1/8	12 3/8	4 6/8	4 6/8	5	5	Clackamas Co., OR	Howard D. Bunnell, Jr.	Howard D. Bunnell, Jr.	2000	105
127 2/8	132 2/8	20 5/8	20 5/8	15 4/8	5	4 4/8	5	5	Lincoln Co., OR	A.A. Reed & G.F. Siniscal	George F. Siniscal	1964	106

Score								Locality	Hunter	Owner	Date	Rank
126 7/8	20 1/8	19 1/8	15 1/8	4 3/8	4 2/8	5	5	Tillamook Co., OR	Mallory R. Murphy	Mallory R. Murphy	2005	107
126 5/8	18 5/8	19 1/8	17 7/8	4	3 7/8	5	5	Sonoma Co., CA	Ronald C. Murray	Ronald C. Murray	2000	108
125 7/8	21 4/8	21 2/8	14 5/8	4	4 1/8	4	5	Tehama Co., CA	JayDee Flournoy	JayDee Flournoy	2006	109
125 6/8	21	21 2/8	16 4/8	4 3/8	4 2/8	5	4	Lewis Co., WA	Rodger H. Fritz	Rodger H. Fritz	2004	110
176 7/8*	25 6/8	25 7/8	21 4/8	6	5 7/8	6	6	Pacific Co., WA	Don Sowell, Sr.	Adam Burhop	1950	
170 4/8*	24 1/8	23 3/8	21 6/8	4 6/8	4 7/8	5	6	Mendocino Co., CA	Mike Thompson	Mike Thompson	2004	
164 1/8*	22 6/8	22 5/8	16 1/8	4 6/8	4 7/8	5	4	Linn Co., OR	Hollie Blankenship	Hollie Blankenship	2004	

* Final score subject to revision by additional verifying measurements.

COLUMBIA BLACKTAIL - NON-TYPICAL ANTLERS

Minimum Score 155   *Odocoileus hemionus columbianus*   World's Record 208 1/8

Final Score	Gross Score	Length of Main Beam R.	L.	Inside Spread	Circumference at Smallest Place Between Burr & First Point R.	L.	Number of Points R.	L.	Locality	Hunter	Owner	Date Killed	Rank
185 1/8	189 1/8	23 5/8	24 5/8	16 1/8	3 7/8	4	8	8	Trinity Co., CA	J. Peter Morish	J. Peter Morish	2005	1
168 3/8	178 5/8	22 2/8	22 5/8	18 3/8	4 2/8	4	9	11	Trinity Co., CA	Tim A. Nickols	Tim A. Nickols	2004	2
168	172	22 7/8	22 2/8	19 1/8	4 2/8	4 1/8	6	8	Mendocino Co., CA	Kevin Byler	Kevin Byler	2005	3
162	164 4/8	20 7/8	21	18 5/8	5 1/8	4 6/8	7	5	Lane Co., OR	Elwyn Bales	Robert Burrus	1937	4
159	165 5/8	21 5/8	20 5/8	14 4/8	4 5/8	4 1/8	10	6	Josephine Co., OR	John Donovan, Jr.	John Donovan, Jr.	2002	5
184 2/8*	189 6/8	20 3/8	19 2/8	16 1/8	4 6/8	4 5/8	13	13	Lincoln Co., OR	J. Robert Irelan	Kevin Irelan	1953	
177 4/8*	185 5/8	23 1/8	23 6/8	21 6/8	5	5	8	8	Humboldt Co., CA	Ernest Baxter	D.M. & J. Phillips	1972	
170 7/8*	175 3/8	22 1/8	22 1/8	19 2/8	4 4/8	4 6/8	8	9	Mendocino Co., CA	Jack M. Campbell	Jack M. Campbell	1986	

* Final score subject to revision by additional verifying measurements.

438

TYPICAL COLUMBIA BLACKTAIL
FINAL SCORE: 143-5/8
HUNTER: Cameron L. Brown

TYPICAL COLUMBIA BLACKTAIL
FINAL SCORE: 143-7/8
HUNTER: E. Stephen Maloney III

TYPICAL COLUMBIA BLACKTAIL
FINAL SCORE: 141-1/8
HUNTER: Nate Allsup

TYPICAL COLUMBIA BLACKTAIL
FINAL SCORE: 139
HUNTER: John E. Pryor

SITKA BLACKTAIL - TYPICAL ANTLERS

Odocoileus hemionus sitkensis

Minimum Score 100

Sitka blacktail deer includes trophies from coastal Alaska and the Queen Charlotte Islands of British Columbia.

Final Score	Gross Score	Length of Main Beam R.	Length of Main Beam L.	Inside Spread	Circumference at Smallest Place Between Burr & First Point R.	L.	Number of Points R.	L.	Locality	Hunter	Owner	Date Killed	Rank
122 5/8	127 5/8	18 1/8	19 2/8	15 1/8	3 6/8	3 6/8	5	5	Prince of Wales Island, AK	Picked Up	James F. Baichtal	2004	1
120 7/8	124 5/8	17 3/8	17 4/8	14 7/8	4	4 1/8	5	5	Wrangell Island, AK	Dave L. Brown	Dave L. Brown	2006	2
120 1/8	123 4/8	18 2/8	17 3/8	15 3/8	3 6/8	3 6/8	5	5	Prince of Wales Island, AK	James A. Sharpe	James A. Sharpe	2004	3
118 2/8	124 4/8	17 2/8	17 6/8	14 4/8	4 6/8	4 4/8	5	5	Prince of Wales Island, AK	Tim Koentopp	Tim Koentopp	2003	4
117 6/8	119 6/8	19 1/8	19 3/8	16 2/8	4	4 1/8	5	5	Etolin Island, AK	Davey W. Brown	Davey W. Brown	2004	5
116 6/8	119 4/8	18 3/8	18 5/8	15 6/8	4	4	5	5	Wild Creek, AK	George R. Gonsalves	George R. Gonsalves	2003	6
116 3/8	121 4/8	16 5/8	17 1/8	14 1/8	4 1/8	3 7/8	5	5	Prince of Wales Island, AK	Clifford L. Adamson	Clifford L. Adamson	2004	7
115 1/8	119 7/8	18 2/8	17 6/8	17 3/8	4 2/8	4 2/8	5	5	Prince of Wales Island, AK	Charles D. Johnson	Charles D. Johnson	2005	8
111 7/8	115 6/8	17 7/8	17 4/8	13 5/8	3 6/8	4	5	5	Kodiak Island, AK	Dana P. Bertolini	Dana P. Bertolini	2004	9
111 1/8	114 2/8	17 5/8	18 2/8	15 1/8	4 1/8	4 2/8	5	5	Exchange Cove, AK	Wade J. Washke	Wade J. Washke	2004	10
110 4/8	112 6/8	18 5/8	18 1/8	15 6/8	4 6/8	4 5/8	4	4	Prince of Wales Island, AK	Cable Campbell	Cable Campbell	2004	11
109 2/8	113 6/8	15 6/8	15 7/8	14 2/8	4	4	5	5	Uganik Bay, AK	Harold S. Bomberger	Harold S. Bomberger	2005	12
107 4/8	112 5/8	18 1/8	17 1/8	14 4/8	3 7/8	3 7/8	5	5	Port Lyons, AK	Michael R. Franklin	Michael R. Franklin	2004	13
107 2/8	111 6/8	17 2/8	16 7/8	14 2/8	3 5/8	3 4/8	5	5	Uyak Bay, AK	Brian P. Swasey	Brian P. Swasey	2006	14
106 3/8	108 2/8	17 5/8	17 5/8	15 3/8	3 5/8	3 6/8	4	4	Larsen Bay, AK	Kelly D. Call	Kelly D. Call	2004	15
104 4/8	108 3/8	15 6/8	16	12 6/8	3 6/8	3 6/8	5	5	Deadman Bay, AK	Larry E. Sides, Jr.	Larry E. Sides, Jr.	2003	16
103 7/8	106 5/8	16 2/8	15 5/8	14 7/8	3 6/8	3 5/8	5	5	Uganik Passage, AK	Larry S. Hicks	Larry S. Hicks	2003	17
101 1/8	108 1/8	16 3/8	16 2/8	15 3/8	3 7/8	3 7/8	6	6	Kodiak Island, AK	David A. Garganta	David A. Garganta	2004	18
100 7/8	109 4/8	14 7/8	15	12 5/8	3 5/8	3 6/8	6	6	Prince of Wales Island, AK	James F. Baichtal	James F. Baichtal	2004	19
100 5/8	106 5/8	14 7/8	14 7/8	12 7/8	3 6/8	3 7/8	4	5	Sturgeon River, AK	Mick T. Waletzko	Mick T. Waletzko	2005	19
100 3/8	106 1/8	16 1/8	16 1/8	14 1/8	3 6/8	3 6/8	5	4	Lindenberg Pen., AK	Wade J. Washke	Wade J. Washke	2004	21
100 1/8	103 1/8	16 6/8	17 2/8	14 3/8	3 5/8	3 5/8	4	5	Deadman Bay, AK	Larry E. Sides, Jr.	Larry E. Sides, Jr.	2005	22

SITKA BLACKTAIL - NON-TYPICAL ANTLERS

Minimum Score 118

World's Record 134

Odocoileus hemionus sitkensis

Sitka blacktail deer includes trophies from coastal Alaska and the Queen Charlotte Islands of British Columbia.

Final Score	Gross Score	Length of Main Beam R.	L.	Inside Spread	Circumference at Smallest Place Between Burr & First Point R.	L.	Number of Points R.	L.	Locality	Hunter	Owner	Date Killed	Rank
124 2/8	129 3/8	18 3/8	16 6/8	15 4/8	3 6/8	3 6/8	6	7	Prince of Wales Island, AK	William C. Musser	William C. Musser	2005	1

TYPICAL SITKA BLACKTAIL
FINAL SCORE: 109-2/8
HUNTER: Harold S. Bomberger

TYPICAL SITKA BLACKTAIL
FINAL SCORE: 107-2/8
HUNTER: Brian P. Swasey

TYPICAL SITKA BLACKTAIL
FINAL SCORE: 100-7/8
HUNTER: James F. Baichtal

TYPICAL SITKA BLACKTAIL
FINAL SCORE: 100-7/8
HUNTER: Mick T. Waletzko

WHITETAIL DEER - TYPICAL ANTLERS

Minimum Score 160   *Odocoileus virginianus* and certain related subspecies   World's Record 213 5/8

Final Score	Gross Score	Length of Main Beam R	Length of Main Beam L	Inside Spread	Circumference at Smallest Place Between Burr & First Point R	L	Number of Points R	L	Locality	Hunter	Owner	Date Killed	Rank
201 1/8	209 7/8	29 6/8	29	24 1/8	5	5	6	5	Warren Co., OH	Bradley S. Jerman	Bradley S. Jerman	2004	1
198 3/8	220 1/8	26 7/8	26	19 4/8	4 7/8	4 7/8	7	7	Muskingum Co., OH	Timothy E. Reed	Timothy E. Reed	2004	2
196 3/8	201 5/8	25 7/8	26 1/8	23 1/8	5 4/8	5 4/8	5	5	Fulton Co., IL	Roger H. Mann	Roger H. Mann	2004	3
192 7/8	209 5/8	27 7/8	28 2/8	21 7/8	5	5 1/8	7	8	Marshall Co., MN	Richard Kasprowicz	T. Emanuelson & J. Kasprowicz	1973	4
192 5/8	199	30	30 3/8	23 1/8	5 1/8	5 3/8	5	5	Stark Co., IL	Rebecca Ratay	Rebecca Ratay	2003	5
192 1/8	203 4/8	27 1/8	26 6/8	19 7/8	5 3/8	5 2/8	6	5	El Paso Co., CO	Eddie L. Kinney	Eddie L. Kinney	2003	6
192	199 5/8	26	26 2/8	23	5 3/8	5 2/8	5	6	White Co., IN	Shaun M. Harvey	Shaun M. Harvey	2003	7
191 4/8	201 7/8	24 5/8	23 5/8	22 4/8	5 6/8	5 5/8	6	6	Hamilton Co., KS	Denis F. Geubelle	Denis F. Geubelle	2003	8
191 2/8	195 6/8	30 2/8	29 1/8	21 2/8	5 3/8	5 3/8	5	5	Trumbull Co., OH	Santo N. Fallo	Santo N. Fallo	2004	9
190 7/8	203 1/8	28 5/8	28 3/8	22 2/8	5 2/8	5	6	5	Cedar Co., NE	Picked Up	Harley L. Gowerly	1952	10
189 1/8	197 1/8	27	26 5/8	23 4/8	6 2/8	5 6/8	5	6	Shell River, MB	Jason R. Price	Jason R. Price	2003	11
189 1/8	197 5/8	26	24 7/8	20 7/8	4 6/8	4 5/8	6	6	Zavala Co., TX	Picked Up	Alberto Bailleres	2004	11
189	210 1/8	27 2/8	27 1/8	21 2/8	4 3/8	4 4/8	5	6	Pendleton Co., KY	Jason Newcomb	Jason Newcomb	2003	13
188 3/8	191	28 1/8	28 6/8	19 1/8	4 7/8	5	5	5	Macoupin Co., IL	Jess M. Gilpin	Jess M. Gilpin	2003	14
188 3/8	189 4/8	27 7/8	28 3/8	20 3/8	5 6/8	5 6/8	5	5	Penobscot Co., ME	Luther L. Tripp, Jr.	Luther L. Tripp, Jr.	2003	14
188 1/8	197 2/8	27 7/8	26 4/8	21 3/8	4 7/8	5	6	6	Nemaha Co., KS	Mark L. Heinen	Mark L. Heinen	2003	16
188	195 4/8	30	28 6/8	21 2/8	4 6/8	4 5/8	6	5	Washington Co., ME	Mr. Munson	Maine Antler Shed & Wildl. Mus.	PR 2006	17
187 7/8	219 3/8	29	28	20 5/8	5 3/8	5 2/8	6	7	White Earth Creek, AB	Alan L. Friend	Alan L. Friend	2004	18
187 6/8	190 6/8	27 4/8	27 4/8	21	4 7/8	4 7/8	5	5	Pike Co., IL	Mike C. Brown	Mike C. Brown	2004	19
187 3/8	202 7/8	28 3/8	27 3/8	20 3/8	4 5/8	4 4/8	7	6	Lewis Co., KY	Dale Mustard	Dale Mustard	2005	20
187 2/8	197 7/8	28 2/8	28 1/8	26 2/8	5 2/8	5 2/8	6	6	Johnson Co., MO	Richard A. Bruns	Richard A. Bruns	2003	21
187 2/8	195 6/8	29	28 5/8	21 4/8	5 2/8	5 2/8	5	5	Harvey Co., KS	Paula J. Wiggers	Paula J. Wiggers	2005	21
187 1/8	200	24 7/8	25 4/8	22 1/8	6 7/8	6 6/8	7	6	Gallatin Co., IL	Austin Perrone	Austin Perrone	2004	23
186 7/8	194 1/8	24 5/8	24 6/8	16 4/8	5 2/8	5 1/8	7	8	Lee Co., IA	Dan C. Enger	Dan C. Enger	2003	24
186 5/8	205	29 2/8	28 7/8	18 6/8	5 4/8	5 4/8	5	6	Holmes Co., OH	Kevin W. Grassbaugh	Kevin W. Grassbaugh	2004	25
186 4/8	194 2/8	30 4/8	31 2/8	23 5/8	5 4/8	5 4/8	6	6	Waukesha Co., WI	Mark Garlock	Mark Garlock	2003	26
186 4/8	192 2/8	26 1/8	25 3/8	20 6/8	5 1/8	5 1/8	6	6	Shoshone Co., ID	Mark A. Schilling	Mark A. Schilling	2005	26
186 1/8	194 4/8	28 5/8	28 6/8	23 2/8	5 3/8	5 3/8	6	5	Casey Co., KY	Noah Shirk, Jr.	Noah Shirk, Jr.	2003	28
185 6/8	191 7/8	27 2/8	26 6/8	22 2/8	5 3/8	5 2/8	5	5	Last Mountain Lake, SK	Kevin N. Lofgren	Kevin N. Lofgren	2003	29
185 4/8	205 2/8	28 7/8	27 2/8	20 5/8	5 4/8	5 4/8	7	7	Franklin Co., OH	Mark A. Scheel	Mark A. Scheel	2003	30
185 4/8	191 3/8	25 6/8	25 2/8	18 6/8	5 1/8	4 7/8	6	7	Lost Creek, AB	Ken R.D. Vickers	Ken R.D. Vickers	2004	30

Score	Main Beam R	Main Beam L	Inside Spread	Circ. R	Circ. L	Pts R	Pts L	Locality	Hunter	Owner	Date	Rank
185 4/8	26 4/8	26 3/8	20 4/8	4 6/8	5 1/8	7	6	Mercer Co., ND	Delton D. Schwarz	Delton D. Schwarz	2005	30
185 3/8	29 6/8	29 5/8	21 7/8	5 1/8	5 2/8	7	7	Nelson Co., KY	Joseph R. Wolf	Michael C. Parker	1961	33
185 3/8	25 5/8	25 5/8	18	4 4/8	4 4/8	6	7	Lincoln Co., MO	Norman R. Enloe	Norman R. Enloe	2003	33
185 3/8	29 4/8	28 5/8	24 4/8	5 6/8	5 5/8	5	6	Clark Co., KS	Cullen R. Spitzer	Cullen R. Spitzer	2004	33
185 3/8	27 5/8	27 1/8	23 4/8	4 3/8	4 4/8	6	7	Harper Co., KS	Robert G. Prickett	Robert G. Prickett	2005	33
185 1/8	29 6/8	27 6/8	19 6/8	6 2/8	6 3/8	5	8	Outagamie Co., WI	James W. Ernst	James W. Ernst	2005	37
185	26 5/8	26 2/8	21 6/8	5	5 1/8	7	6	Wayne Co., IA	Picked Up	Scott D. Lindsey	2000	38
184 3/8	29 5/8	28 3/8	21 5/8	5 5/8	5 5/8	9	7	Hemphill Co., TX	Tom W. Isaacs	Tom W. Isaacs	2003	39
184 1/8	28 7/8	28 6/8	24 7/8	5 1/8	4 7/8	6	6	Holmes Co., OH	Dale L. Mohler	Dale L. Mohler	2003	40
184 1/8	24 6/8	25	19 5/8	5 1/8	5 2/8	6	7	Sakwasew Lake, SK	Herb F. Siegele	Herb F. Siegele	2003	40
184 1/8	27 5/8	27 1/8	22 1/8	4 4/8	4 4/8	5	6	Monroe Co., WI	Donald H. Stieve	Donald H. Stieve	2003	40
184 1/8	28 2/8	28 3/8	17 7/8	5 6/8	5 6/8	5	6	Buffalo Co., WI	William C. Remington	William C. Remington	2005	40
184	25 7/8	24	25 2/8	5 5/8	5 5/8	6	5	Big Shell Lake, SK	Lana J. Kyliuk	Lana J. Kyliuk	2003	44
183 7/8	28 2/8	26 7/8	20 6/8	5 4/8	5 4/8	6	7	Greene Co., OH	Tim Mangan	Tim Mangan	2004	45
183 6/8	28	27 7/8	19 7/8	5 1/8	5 2/8	9	9	Benson Co., ND	James Krantz	James Krantz	2003	46
183 5/8	25 5/8	24 5/8	17 3/8	5 3/8	5 2/8	6	6	Pierce Co., ND	Dean A. Martin	Dean A. Martin	2003	47
183 4/8	25 5/8	24 5/8	17 4/8	4 4/8	5 7/8	6	8	Brown Co., KS	Robert L. Soden	Robert L. Soden	1991	48
183 4/8	26 6/8	25 3/8	21 5/8	6	5 6/8	5	7	Fulton Co., IL	Justin Foglesong	Justin Foglesong	2003	48
183 3/8	29 2/8	27 6/8	21 1/8	5 4/8	5 2/8	6	6	Turtle Lake, SK	Vince G. Halisky	Vince G. Halisky	2003	50
183 3/8	25	24 1/8	19 1/8	5 1/8	4 6/8	6	7	Bureau Co., IL	Paul Moon	Paul Moon	2003	50
183 3/8	27 2/8	27 1/8	17 5/8	4 6/8	5 5/8	7	6	Ripley Co., IN	Mark A. Bonnewell	Mark A. Bonnewell	2004	50
183 3/8	28 5/8	28 2/8	17 5/8	5 5/8	5 1/8	7	6	Stephenson Co., IL	Picked Up	William C. Scheider, Jr.	2006	50
183 2/8	26 6/8	27 1/8	21 4/8	5 2/8	4	6	5	Piatt Co., IL	Chad M. Gilbert	Chad M. Gilbert	2002	54
183 2/8	24 1/8	25 1/8	24	4	4 4/8	7	7	Van Buren Co., IA	R.J. & C.B. Livesay	R.J. & C.B. Livesay	2003	54
183 1/8	26 5/8	25 1/8	18 7/8	4 1/8	5 3/8	7	6	Henderson Co., KY	John Rutledge	John Rutledge	2003	56
183 1/8	28 5/8	29 3/8	22 6/8	5 4/8	5 1/8	6	6	Fish Lake, SK	Carson D. Hansen	Carson D. Hansen	2005	56
183	28 6/8	29	21 1/8	5 4/8	5 2/8	6	7	Russell Co., KY	Ricky D. Roy	Ricky D. Roy	2003	58
183	27 3/8	25 4/8	17 7/8	5 3/8	5 4/8	8	6	Champaign Co., OH	Dan Bigham	Dan Bigham	2004	58
183	27 4/8	25 5/8	19	5 3/8	4 6/8	7	5	Nemaha Co., KS	Jason Abitz	Jason Abitz	2005	58
182 4/8	26 2/8	26 2/8	18 3/8	5	4 4/8	7	6	Jersey Co., IL	Mike Ferguson	Mike Ferguson	2003	61
182 4/8	30 4/8	30	23 2/8	4 6/8	4 4/8	7	8	Oxford Co., ME	Clinton Bradbury	Clinton Bradbury	2004	61
182 4/8	27 1/8	25 4/8	18 6/8	4 4/8	5	5	5	Hamilton Co., OH	Robert P. Wood	Robert P. Wood	2004	61
182 3/8	25 1/8	25 3/8	20 3/8	5	5 6/8	8	7	Fayette Co., IA	Nick L. Soules	Nick L. Soules	2003	64
182 3/8	27 3/8	26 3/8	19 1/8	5 6/8	4 5/8	7	5	Pierce Co., WI	Jeremy M. Harshman	Jeremy M. Harshman	2005	64
182 2/8	28 1/8	26 3/8	22 6/8	4 5/8	4 6/8	5	5	Carlisle Co., KY	Chuck Edrington	Chuck Edrington	2003	66
182 2/8	26 5/8	26 2/8	21 4/8	4 6/8	5 3/8	6	6	Dimmit Co., TX	Stuart W. Stedman	Stuart W. Stedman	2004	66
182 2/8	27 4/8	27 4/8	19 2/8	5 3/8	5 7/8	6	6	Sullivan Co., IN	John M. Griswold	John M. Griswold	2005	66
182 1/8	27	27	21 3/8	5 7/8	5 4/8	5	6	La Salle Co., TX	Rene R. Barrientos	Rene R. Barrientos	2003	66
182 1/8	29 5/8	26 2/8	17 1/8	5 2/8	5	6	6	Woodford Co., IL	Jeff Jordan	Jeff Jordan	2004	69
182 1/8	27 2/8	31 2/8	21 5/8	5	5 3/8	5	5	Clay Co., IL	Timothy J. Williams	Timothy J. Williams	2004	69
182 1/8	26	27 5/8	21 5/8	5 3/8	5 1/8	6	6	Murray Lake, SK	Myron L. Dirksen	Myron L. Dirksen	2005	69
181 6/8	29 4/8	25 7/8	20 1/8	4 7/8	5 1/8	8	7	Scott Co., IA	Ivan Clark	Ivan Clark	1966	73

WHITETAIL DEER - TYPICAL ANTLERS

Odocoileus virginianus virginianus and certain related subspecies

Final Score	Gross Score	Length of Main Beam R.	L.	Inside Spread	Circumference at Smallest Place Between Burr & First Point R.	L.	Number of Points R.	L.	Locality	Hunter	Owner	Date Killed	Rank
181 6/8	189 4/8	30 2/8	29 6/8	19 3/8	4 5/8	4 6/8	6	5	Hillsborough Co., NH	Chuck Orleans	Chuck Orleans	2003	73
181 6/8	189	26 6/8	25	20	4 4/8	4 4/8	6	7	Adair Co., KY	Picked Up	Greg Wilson	2003	73
181 6/8	188 5/8	26 4/8	26 4/8	18 2/8	5 2/8	5	5	5	Nuevo Leon, MX	Ross E. Nutt	Ross E. Nutt	2004	73
181 4/8	190 4/8	26 3/8	25 3/8	17 3/8	5	4 7/8	7	6	La Salle Co., TX	Glenn Thurman	Glenn Thurman	2004	77
181 3/8	192 4/8	28 1/8	25 4/8	22 1/8	4 7/8	4 6/8	6	5	Fulton Co., IL	Edward G. Kruzan	Edward G. Kruzan	2004	78
181 3/8	188	26 3/8	26 7/8	19 5/8	4 7/8	4 7/8	7	6	Battle River, AB	Andreas Pagenkopf	Andreas Pagenkopf	2004	78
181 3/8	188 2/8	27 4/8	28 3/8	20 3/8	4 7/8	5 1/8	6	6	Taylor Co., IA	Brian E. Baker	Brian E. Baker	2005	78
181 2/8	190 5/8	25 2/8	25 3/8	18 3/8	5 1/8	5	6	6	Rusk Co., WI	Travis C. Loew	Travis C. Loew	2005	81
181 1/8	185 1/8	24	23 6/8	15 7/8	5 3/8	5 3/8	7	7	Webster Co., IA	Dave C. Hainzinger	Dave C. Hainzinger	2003	82
181 1/8	190 3/8	28 3/8	27 7/8	22 3/8	5 3/8	5 2/8	6	7	Brown Co., OH	Michael R. Olthaus	Michael R. Olthaus	2003	82
181 1/8	187 1/8	28 6/8	27 7/8	20 1/8	5 4/8	5 4/8	6	6	Price Co., WI	Mike J. Kosmer	Mike J. Kosmer	2005	82
181	203 5/8	25 4/8	25	23 4/8	5 3/8	5 5/8	8	6	Anderson Co., KS	Michael A. Irvin	Michael A. Irvin	2003	85
180 6/8	188 4/8	25 5/8	26	18 6/8	4 5/8	4 5/8	5	5	Chippewa Co., WI	Robert D. Ressemann	Robert D. Ressemann	2003	86
180 6/8	202 3/8	28 3/8	27	24 1/8	5 4/8	5 2/8	8	7	Martin Co., IN	Jon Sims	Picked Up	2003	86
180 6/8	187 7/8	27 5/8	29	21 2/8	5 2/8	5 1/8	5	5	Butler Co., KY	Mark S. Mulliniks	Mark S. Mulliniks	2004	86
180 6/8	208 7/8	24	24 3/8	22 2/8	4 4/8	4 5/8	7	9	Livingston Co., MO	Benjamin L. Sutton	Benjamin L. Sutton	2004	86
180 6/8	184 2/8	27 1/8	27 6/8	20 6/8	5 2/8	5 2/8	5	5	Cass Co., IL	James K. Deppe	James K. Deppe	2005	86
180 6/8	183 6/8	24 4/8	24 5/8	18 2/8	5 2/8	5 2/8	6	6	Randolph Co., IL	Albert J. Labukas, Jr.	Albert J. Labukas, Jr.	2005	86
180 4/8	192	25 7/8	24 4/8	19 1/8	4 6/8	5	5	7	Dooly Co., GA	Phillip T. Lewis	Phillip T. Lewis	2004	92
180 3/8	185 5/8	27	27 1/8	21 5/8	4 1/8	4 2/8	5	5	Greene Co., OH	Terry R. Pettit	Terry R. Pettit	2005	93
180 2/8	190 2/8	27 2/8	27 5/8	17 5/8	5 1/8	5 2/8	6	5	Livingston Co., KY	Bill Sutton	Bill Sutton	2003	94
180 2/8	184 4/8	26 2/8	25 6/8	16	4 1/8	4 2/8	6	6	Winona Co., MN	Mike S. Russeau	Mike S. Russeau	2004	94
180 2/8	185 4/8	23 1/8	25 1/8	23 2/8	4 5/8	4 4/8	6	6	Maverick Co., TX	Thomas D. Friedkin	Thomas D. Friedkin	2005	94
180 1/8	211 6/8	27 6/8	27 5/8	20 4/8	5 1/8	5 3/8	8	9	Butler Co., KY	Weldon DeWeese	Weldon DeWeese	2003	97
180 1/8	214 7/8	28 5/8	29 2/8	20 1/8	6 3/8	6 2/8	7	11	Martin Co., IN	Bobby V. Hardwick	Bobby V. Hardwick	2004	97
180 1/8	213 3/8	28	28 2/8	24 3/8	5 5/8	5 5/8	6	8	Greene Co., IL	Danne Zerow	Danne Zerow	2004	97
180	184 5/8	27 4/8	28 2/8	20 2/8	5	5 1/8	6	5	Hardin Co., IA	Ronald Cornwell	Ronald Cornwell	2003	100
180	182 5/8	32 1/8	31 5/8	24 2/8	5 1/8	5 1/8	4	4	Unknown	Unknown	Jeff Deck	PR 2003	100
180	189 7/8	25 7/8	26 6/8	17 6/8	4 3/8	4 4/8	5	5	Clayton Co., IA	Steven L. Lange	Steven L. Lange	2003	100
180	184 7/8	27 4/8	27 1/8	19 6/8	4 3/8	4 3/8	5	5	Frio Co., TX	Michael B. Smith	Michael B. Smith	2003	100
179 7/8	207 4/8	27 5/8	27 3/8	19 5/8	4 4/8	4 6/8	8	7	Edmonson Co., KY	W.B. Vincent	W.B. Vincent	1962	104
179 7/8	182 7/8	26 7/8	26 6/8	22 3/8	5 1/8	5 3/8	5	5	Reno Co., KS	Jeffrey C. Grippi	Jeffrey C. Grippi	2003	104
179 7/8	184 3/8	27 5/8	27 4/8	18 5/8	5 2/8	5 3/8	6	5	Warren Co., IA	Jason Henle	Jason Henle	2003	104

179 4/8	206 7/8	30 2/8	31	20 6/8	6 1/8	6 1/8	7	4	Mahoning Co., OH	Robert A. Haney	Wayne Williamson	1987	107
179 4/8	193	26 3/8	26 3/8	22 7/8	4 6/8	5 1/8	8	6	Adams Co., IL	Robert H. Belins	Robert H. Belins	1999	107
179 4/8	196 4/8	25 5/8	23 7/8	21 5/8	5 1/8	5 1/8	8	7	St. Clair Co., IL	Eric J. Gerfen	Eric J. Gerfen	2004	107
179 4/8	182 1/8	25 2/8	25 2/8	19 4/8	4 2/8	4 3/8	5	5	Knox Co., MO	Daniel B. Gerbes	Daniel B. Gerbes	2005	107
179 4/8	196 7/8	25 1/8	26 6/8	21 4/8	5 3/8	5 4/8	6	7	Jefferson Co., WI	Michael A. Mewis	Michael A. Mewis	2005	107
179 3/8	187 6/8	27	26 5/8	20 2/8	4 6/8	4 6/8	7	5	Lafayette Co., WI	David A. Carey	David A. Carey	2004	112
179 3/8	183	24 6/8	25 3/8	21 1/8	4 6/8	4 6/8	5	5	McLean Co., IL	Brian F. Devine	Brian F. Devine	2004	112
179 3/8	186 1/8	29 4/8	28 7/8	21 1/8	4 4/8	4 4/8	5	5	Coshocton Co., OH	Douglas C. Patterson	Douglas C. Patterson	2005	112
179 2/8	198 7/8	26 2/8	25 6/8	20 2/8	5	5 6/8	9	7	Clay Co., KS	Daton Hess	Daton Hess	2004	115
179 1/8	191	25 6/8	25 7/8	18 1/8	4 7/8	5	8	6	Harrison Co., IA	Ron Murray	Dorothy D. Murray	1998	116
179 1/8	192 7/8	27 6/8	26 3/8	20 7/8	5 5/8	5 5/8	8	5	Dunn Co., ND	John E. Bang	John E. Bang	2003	116
179	184 1/8	23 5/8	24 3/8	20 6/8	4 7/8	4 6/8	5	5	N. Saskatchewan River, SK	Ryan M. Haeusler	Ryan M. Haeusler	2003	118
179	185	26 3/8	25 4/8	18 4/8	4 4/8	4 4/8	6	5	Shelby Co., KY	Cliff G. Willoughby	Cliff G. Willoughby	2005	118
178 7/8	210 4/8	25 7/8	25 2/8	18 2/8	6	6	8	7	Brown Co., IL	Joshua Knight	Joshua Knight	2003	120
178 7/8	187 4/8	27 2/8	27 4/8	25	5	5	5	6	Houston Co., MN	David P. Bakkestuen	David P. Bakkestuen	2004	120
178 7/8	196 7/8	27 2/8	27 3/8	19 3/8	4 6/8	5	8	6	Fayette Co., IL	Jesse L. Rosenberger	Jesse L. Rosenberger	2004	120
178 7/8	191 5/8	27 4/8	27 3/8	17 2/8	4 6/8	4 5/8	6	7	Lucas Co., IA	Billy R. Green	Billy R. Green	2005	120
178 6/8	189 4/8	29 3/8	29 3/8	21 7/8	5 6/8	5 6/8	4	6	St. Louis Co., MO	Jim W. Winter	Jim W. Winter	2003	124
178 5/8	188 1/8	27	26 6/8	19 2/8	4 5/8	5 2/8	5	6	Caldwell Co., KY	Darren L. Ramey	Darren L. Ramey	2003	125
178 5/8	180 7/8	25 4/8	25 6/8	20 5/8	5 7/8	5 6/8	5	5	Crooked Creek, AB	Luke R. Viravec	Luke R. Viravec	2003	125
178 4/8	186	28 6/8	28 4/8	19	4 4/8	4 4/8	6	7	Jackson Co., MI	Paul L. Calvert	Paul L. Calvert	2003	127
178 4/8	183 6/8	26 4/8	26 5/8	24 4/8	4 2/8	4 2/8	6	5	Livingston Co., MO	Scott Fowler	Scott Fowler	2004	127
178 4/8	201 5/8	26 7/8	27 1/8	18 1/8	5 4/8	5 5/8	9	6	Lafayette Co., WI	Jeff C. Lien	Jeff C. Lien	2004	127
178 4/8	191 3/8	26	24 7/8	18 6/8	4 4/8	4 4/8	6	5	Carroll Co., IL	Jeffrey S. Reeder	Jeffrey S. Reeder	2005	127
178 3/8	190 1/8	26 7/8	26 2/8	22 4/8	4 2/8	4 2/8	5	7	Jim Lake, SK	Christopher P. McIntosh	Christopher P. McIntosh	2005	131
178 2/8	184 7/8	25 4/8	25 6/8	18 2/8	4 7/8	4 7/8	5	5	Porcupine Plain, SK	Donald V. Markese	Donald V. Markese	2003	132
178 2/8	182 6/8	22 6/8	23	16	4 3/8	4 3/8	6	6	Osage Co., MO	Robert R. Solomon	Robert R. Solomon	2004	132
178 1/8	195 5/8	29 1/8	28 2/8	19 3/8	5 4/8	5 4/8	6	6	Crittenden Co., KY	Floyd Carpenter	Floyd Carpenter	2004	134
178 1/8	182 7/8	26 6/8	25 5/8	19 7/8	5 4/8	5 2/8	5	5	Stoney Lake, SK	Robert Kopp	Robert Kopp	2004	134
178 1/8	198 1/8	27 7/8	27 6/8	25 7/8	5 5/8	5 5/8	7	8	Hardin Co., KY	Curtis L. Patton	Curtis L. Patton	2004	134
178	180 2/8	25 7/8	26 5/8	20 6/8	4 4/8	4 4/8	5	5	Lafayette Co., AR	Picked Up	C.E. Baker	1972	137
178	180	29 6/8	29 6/8	22 5/8	4 2/8	4 2/8	7	6	Butler Co., OH	Patrick M. Erb, Sr.	Patrick M. Erb, Sr.	2004	137
178	189 4/8	24 6/8	24 6/8	19 2/8	5 5/8	5 5/8	7	6	Pulaski Co., KY	Darrell Scruggs	Darrell Scruggs	2005	137
177 7/8	183 3/8	27 4/8	28	22 3/8	4 3/8	4 5/8	5	5	Franklin Co., IN	Zachary Placke	Zachary Placke	2003	140
177 7/8	183	26 4/8	26 2/8	19 7/8	5	5	6	6	Washtenaw Co., MI	Alan F. & Eva Schultz	Alan F. Schultz	2003	140
177 6/8	187 3/8	25 1/8	25 1/8	19 3/8	4 7/8	5 1/8	7	5	Namepi Creek, AB	Dwayne E. Kraychy	Dwayne E. Kraychy	1990	142
177 6/8	185 7/8	26 6/8	26 4/8	19 6/8	5 4/8	5 4/8	6	6	Madison Co., IA	Dan Golightly	Dan Golightly	2003	142
177 6/8	183 6/8	26 1/8	26 1/8	20 2/8	4 6/8	4 7/8	5	5	Dane Co., WI	Dean A. Carlson	Dean A. Carlson	2004	142
177 6/8	198 4/8	25 4/8	24 5/8	19 5/8	5 3/8	5 2/8	7	5	Gentry Co., MO	Chris I. Hunt	Chris I. Hunt	2004	142
177 6/8	182 7/8	24 7/8	25 5/8	20 6/8	5 6/8	5 7/8	5	5	Pope Co., IL	Troy K. Minemann	Troy K. Minemann	2004	142
177 6/8	181 1/8	25 6/8	25 6/8	18 6/8	5 7/8	5 7/8	5	5	Jefferson Co., WI	Ryan J. Ritacca	Ryan J. Ritacca	2004	142

WHITETAIL DEER - TYPICAL ANTLERS

Odocoileus virginianus virginianus and certain related subspecies

Final Score	Gross Score	Length of Main Beam		Inside Spread	Circumference at Smallest Place Between Burr & First Point		Number of Points		Locality	Hunter	Owner	Date Killed	Rank
		R.	L.		R.	L.	R.	L.					
177 6/8	185 7/8	25	24 6/8	21 5/8	4 4/8	4 5/8	5	7	Vermilion River, AB	Barton R. Barnett	Barton R. Barnett	2005	142
177 6/8	205 1/8	28 3/8	28 6/8	20 3/8	5 7/8	5 7/8	7	10	Warren Co., IN	Gerald A. Sheets	Gerald A. Sheets	2005	142
177 5/8	208 3/8	23 3/8	25	17 7/8	5 5/8	5 5/8	8	9	Woodford Co., IL	Paul Carapella	Paul Carapella	2003	150
177 5/8	187 4/8	25 1/8	25 2/8	17 3/8	4 7/8	4 7/8	6	5	Marion Co., KY	Jimmy Maupin	Jimmy Maupin	2003	150
177 5/8	193 1/8	27 5/8	28 3/8	18 4/8	5 4/8	5 4/8	7	6	Madison Co., IA	Dennis R. Kommes	Dennis R. Kommes	2004	150
177 4/8	192 5/8	25 4/8	25 5/8	18	5 2/8	5 1/8	6	6	Dearborn Co., IN	Wendell C. Whitaker	Wendell C. Whitaker	2003	153
177 4/8	182 3/8	26	27 2/8	20	4 7/8	4 6/8	6	6	Clarke Co., IA	Ted W. Miller	Ted W. Miller	2005	153
177 4/8	191 6/8	27 5/8	27 7/8	17 2/8	4 4/8	4 2/8	6	7	Marion Co., GA	Herschel B. Moore	Herschel B. Moore	2005	153
177 4/8	196	27 2/8	26 6/8	19 4/8	5 4/8	5 5/8	7	8	Pike Co., IL	Steve J. Slabe	Steve J. Slabe	2005	153
177 4/8	195 4/8	27 2/8	27 3/8	19 6/8	5	4 7/8	6	8	De Kalb Co., IN	Bradley A. Thurman	Bradley A. Thurman	2005	153
177 3/8	189	26 5/8	26 6/8	19	5 7/8	5 5/8	7	8	Neerlandia, AB	Charles T. Gibson	Charles T. Gibson	2003	158
177 3/8	185 5/8	28 7/8	27 7/8	19	4 2/8	4 2/8	6	5	Warren Co., IA	Charles W. Guhl	Charles W. Guhl	2003	158
177 3/8	207 7/8	27	24 7/8	20 7/8	4 4/8	4 4/8	6	9	Johnson Co., IL	Ronald R. Miller	Ronald R. Miller	2004	158
177 2/8	187 7/8	30	28 3/8	21 3/8	4 5/8	4 5/8	5	7	Hopkins Co., KY	Matthew E. Jones	Matthew E. Jones	2003	161
177 2/8	190 6/8	25	24 5/8	21 3/8	5 6/8	5 2/8	8	6	Carroll Co., IN	Patrick T. Leahy	Patrick T. Leahy	2003	161
177 2/8	191 4/8	25 6/8	26	13 6/8	5 4/8	5 5/8	6	6	Texas Co., MO	James T. Brentlinger	James T. Brentlinger	2004	161
177 2/8	187 4/8	28 1/8	26 5/8	20 4/8	4 7/8	4 7/8	6	5	Parke Co., IN	William H. Busse	William H. Busse	2004	161
177 2/8	181	25 3/8	25 3/8	17 4/8	5	4 6/8	6	6	Lewis Co., MO	Charles R. Sly	Charles R. Sly	2004	161
177 1/8	199 3/8	27 5/8	25 5/8	19 7/8	5 3/8	5 2/8	5	7	Burke Co., ND	Bill H. Hass	Bill H. Hass	1976	166
177 1/8	183 7/8	25	25 6/8	20 7/8	5 5/8	5 7/8	5	5	Sauk Co., WI	Kevin G. Alt	Kevin G. Alt	2003	166
177 1/8	200 1/8	26 7/8	28 3/8	21 3/8	4 6/8	4 6/8	6	6	Montgomery Co., MO	Jeff B. Eldringhoff	Jeff B. Eldringhoff	2003	166
177 1/8	194 4/8	21 5/8	25 3/8	17 5/8	5 2/8	5	7	7	Ohio Co., KY	Ernie D. Roach	Mary Roach	2003	166
177 1/8	185 2/8	24	24 1/8	19 3/8	4 2/8	4 2/8	7	5	Brooks Co., TX	Luke R. Corbett	Luke R. Corbett	2005	166
177 1/8	182 4/8	27 7/8	27 4/8	17 7/8	5 5/8	5 4/8	5	5	Hancock Co., KY	Kevin N. Lamar	Kevin N. Lamar	2005	166
177 1/8	180 2/8	25 6/8	24	18 7/8	4 6/8	4 7/8	5	5	Vernon Co., WI	Trent G. Strangstalien	Trent G. Strangstalien	2005	166
177 1/8	185 1/8	26 1/8	24 7/8	18 5/8	5 2/8	5 2/8	6	6	Otter Tail Co., MN	William J. Wagner	William J. Wagner	2006	166
177	193 3/8	28 5/8	29 4/8	20 3/8	4 6/8	4 6/8	8	8	Lewis Co., KY	Aaron R. Kegley	Aaron R. Kegley	2003	174
177	179 1/8	24 2/8	24 4/8	18 2/8	5 2/8	5 2/8	5	5	Fraser River, BC	Rick Roos	Rick Roos	2004	174
176 7/8	184	26 4/8	27 5/8	19 1/8	5 7/8	5 3/8	5	5	Fulton Co., IL	Gregory R Lingenfelter	Gregory R Lingenfelter	2001	176
176 7/8	195 2/8	27 2/8	26 6/8	20 3/8	5 2/8	5 2/8	5	5	Schuyler Co., IL	Rob Bartlett	Rob Bartlett	2003	176
176 7/8	180 5/8	26 1/8	25 2/8	17 1/8	4 6/8	4 6/8	5	5	Poweshiek Co., IA	Thomas W. Cirks	Thomas W. Cirks	2003	176
176 7/8	197 4/8	26 6/8	25 5/8	22 4/8	5 4/8	5 5/8	7	6	Wabamun Lake, AB	Chris J. Glionna	Chris J. Glionna	2003	176
176 7/8	183 2/8	23 4/8	25	17 3/8	5 2/8	5 1/8	6	5	Brooks Co., TX	Michael L. Owen	Michael L. Owen	2003	176

446

BOONE AND CROCKETT CLUB'S

Score								Locality	Hunter	Owner	Date	Rank
176 7/8	180 5/8	25 6/8	26 2/8	17 7/8	5 4/8	6	6	Greene Co., OH	Pete Scruggs	Pete Scruggs	2004	176
176 7/8	186 6/8	25 1/8	25 1/8	17 3/8	4 6/8	6	7	Adair Co., KY	Picked Up	Robert Sturgeon	2005	176
176 6/8	180 2/8	25 6/8	26 1/8	17 4/8	5	5	5	Last Mountain Lake, SK	Dana Morrison	Dana Morrison	1985	183
176 6/8	179 5/8	29 2/8	29 2/8	19 4/8	4 6/8	5	5	Rock Island Co., IL	Terry Barrett	Terry Barrett	2004	183
176 6/8	189 7/8	24 6/8	24 6/8	20	5 1/8	6	7	Kiskatinaw River, BC	Elinor C. Huntley	Elinor C. Huntley	2004	183
176 6/8	189	31 2/8	30 7/8	19 4/8	5 3/8	6	6	Dubuque Co., IA	Adam D. Young	Adam D. Young	2004	183
176 6/8	184 4/8	26 2/8	26 2/8	23 1/8	5 2/8	6	5	Trempealeau Co., WI	Robert J. Boberg	Robert J. Boberg	2005	188
176 5/8	182 1/8	25 6/8	25 6/8	18 4/8	4 1/8	7	6	Maverick Co., TX	Edward F. Marek	Edward F. Marek	2004	188
176 4/8	195 6/8	25	25	17 7/8	4 7/8	7	8	Jo Daviess Co., IL	Picked Up	Robert W. Heuerman	2001	189
176 4/8	194 3/8	26 4/8	26 4/8	20 1/8	5	8	7	Richland Co., IL	Kent Schulte	Kent Schulte	2002	189
176 4/8	184 3/8	24 7/8	24 7/8	22 2/8	5 2/8	5	5	St. Clair Co., IL	James J. Fournie	James J. Fournie	2003	189
176 4/8	200 6/8	24 3/8	24 3/8	19 1/8	4 7/8	6	9	McLeod Co., MN	Norman E. Gehrke	Norman E. Gehrke	2003	189
176 4/8	197 3/8	28 3/8	28 5/8	21 3/8	5 4/8	7	5	Cut Knife, SK	Thomas M. La Victoire	Thomas M. La Victoire	2003	189
176 4/8	182 6/8	26 6/8	27 7/8	16 2/8	4 3/8	5	5	Marion Co., MO	Geene A. Denish	Geene A. Denish	2004	189
176 4/8	185	24 2/8	24 1/8	24 1/8	4 2/8	6	7	Sled Lake, SK	Glenn E. Thompson	Glenn E. Thompson	2004	189
176 4/8	184 3/8	25 4/8	25 5/8	19 2/8	5 2/8	5	6	Casey Co., KY	E. Brad Calvert	E. Brad Calvert	2005	189
176 4/8	181	26 3/8	26 1/8	19 4/8	5	6	6	Jackson Co., KS	Kyle D. Holt	Kyle D. Holt	2005	189
176 4/8	189 6/8	25 7/8	26 1/8	23 4/8	5 6/8	7	6	Jefferson Co., WI	Keith H. Waldron	Keith H. Waldron	2005	189
176 3/8	179 4/8	25	25 3/8	20 3/8	5	5	5	McPherson Co., KS	Joey Beach	Joey Beach	2003	199
176 3/8	181 1/8	24 6/8	25 2/8	18 7/8	5 1/8	5	5	Assiniboine River, MB	John E. Major	John E. Major	2004	199
176 3/8	211 4/8	26 1/8	26	23 2/8	6	9	7	Peoria Co., IL	Troy Naylor	Troy Naylor	2004	199

TYPICAL WHITETAIL DEER
FINAL SCORE: 165-4/8
HUNTER: Quentin R. Smith

TYPICAL WHITETAIL DEER
FINAL SCORE: 165-7/8
HUNTER: Michel Paillard

TYPICAL WHITETAIL DEER
FINAL SCORE: 172-3/8
HUNTER: Phil W. Teinert

TYPICAL WHITETAIL DEER
FINAL SCORE: 161-1/8
HUNTER: Harold E. Turner, Jr.

WHITETAIL DEER - TYPICAL ANTLERS

Odocoileus virginianus virginianus and certain related subspecies

Final Score	Gross Score	Length of Main Beam R.	L.	Inside Spread	Circumference at Smallest Place Between Burr & First Point R.	L.	Number of Points R.	L.	Locality	Hunter	Owner	Date Killed	Rank
176 3/8	181 7/8	28 1/8	28 1/8	21	4	4 5/8	5	6	Fairfield Co., OH	D. Bruce Turley	D. Bruce Turley	2004	199
176 3/8	185 4/8	27	27	20 4/8	5 3/8	5 4/8	7	7	Wayne Co., KY	Michael Dobbs	Michael Dobbs	2006	199
176 2/8	193 5/8	25 2/8	26 4/8	21 2/8	5 3/8	5 1/8	5	5	Will Co., IL	Donald Yarnell	Donald Yarnell	2001	204
176 2/8	184 3/8	27	28	21 6/8	5	5 1/8	6	6	Comanche Co., KS	Thomas E. Baine	Thomas E. Baine	2003	204
176 2/8	180 3/8	24 4/8	24 3/8	22 2/8	5	4 7/8	5	5	Roseau Co., MN	Rodney J. Estling	Rodney J. Estling	2003	204
176 2/8	182 3/8	25	26	18	4 6/8	5	5	5	Saline Co., MO	Nick Huston	Nick Huston	2003	204
176 2/8	185 5/8	26 6/8	27 4/8	22	4 1/8	4 2/8	5	5	Essex Co., MA	Picked Up	Dean S. Romig	2003	204
176 2/8	182	26 4/8	25 4/8	18 6/8	4 7/8	4 7/8	6	6	Pine Co., MN	Jennifer Schneider	Jennifer Schneider	2003	204
176 2/8	178 4/8	26 5/8	27 2/8	17 4/8	4 5/8	4 5/8	5	5	Breckinridge Co., KY	Cary Kilgore	Cary Kilgore	2005	204
176 1/8	184 4/8	24 4/8	24 6/8	19	5	5 1/8	6	7	Petroleum Co., MT	William H. Lee, Jr.	William H. Lee, Jr.	2003	211
176 1/8	192 7/8	28	28 2/8	18 7/8	5 1/8	6 5/8	6	9	Rock Island Co., IL	Gary D. Hodge	Gary D. Hodge	2004	211
176 1/8	179 6/8	26 5/8	26 3/8	21 1/8	4 6/8	4 7/8	6	6	Carroll Co., OH	Donald A. Pontones	Donald A. Pontones	2004	211
176	184 3/8	28 2/8	27 4/8	22 3/8	4 4/8	4 4/8	6	5	Henry Co., KY	Ronnie L. Stephens, Jr.	Ronnie L. Stephens, Jr.	2003	214
176	189 2/8	24 6/8	24 5/8	18 4/8	5 1/8	5 2/8	7	6	Labette Co., KS	Michael S. Young	Michael S. Young	2003	214
176	182 2/8	25	26 3/8	17 2/8	4 4/8	4 5/8	5	6	Pierce Co., WI	Anthony W. Garner	Anthony W. Garner	2005	214
176	183	27 1/8	27 3/8	20	4 7/8	5	6	6	Monroe Co., WI	Douglas A. Scherf	Douglas A. Scherf	2005	214
175 7/8	181	27 1/8	26 1/8	19 3/8	4 3/8	4 4/8	5	5	Wayne Co., IL	Darrell L. Fickas	Darrell L. Fickas	2002	218
175 7/8	193 2/8	26 2/8	26 7/8	22 5/8	5 2/8	5 2/8	6	6	La Salle Co., TX	Rene R. Barrientos	Rene R. Barrientos	2003	218
175 7/8	186 7/8	24 6/8	24 6/8	16 2/8	4 6/8	4 6/8	6	7	Smoky Lake, AB	Brian G. Compo	Brian G. Compo	2004	218
175 7/8	177 5/8	27 6/8	27 3/8	22 5/8	4 7/8	4 7/8	5	5	Christian Co., KY	Fred M. Luttrell	Fred M. Luttrell	2004	218
175 7/8	183 5/8	26 3/8	24 2/8	20 3/8	5 3/8	5 3/8	6	6	Monmouth Co., NJ	James Porcelli	James Porcelli	2004	218
175 7/8	178 4/8	25 5/8	24 4/8	22 7/8	5	4 6/8	5	5	Armstrong Lake, AB	Vincent J. Sawchyn	Vincent J. Sawchyn	2004	218
175 7/8	202 1/8	26 3/8	27 1/8	19 7/8	4 6/8	4 6/8	7	7	Lafayette Co., WI	James J. Foecking, Jr.	James J. Foecking, Jr.	2005	218
175 6/8	184 4/8	26 3/8	26 5/8	22 4/8	5 3/8	5 4/8	5	6	Rush Co., IN	Picked Up	Ryan B. Miller	2001	225
175 6/8	178 2/8	27 3/8	26 6/8	18 4/8	4 6/8	4 6/8	5	5	Pike Co., OH	Jason Nathan	Jason Nathan	2004	225
175 6/8	182 7/8	25 6/8	26 4/8	21 6/8	5	5 1/8	6	6	Washburn Co., WI	Allen Spaeth	Allen Spaeth	2004	225
175 6/8	181 2/8	28	28	20 2/8	5 6/8	5 5/8	5	5	Kosciusko Co., IN	Chad Hartman	Chad Hartman	2005	225
175 6/8	186 3/8	27 1/8	27 2/8	21	5 2/8	5 1/8	6	6	Vermilion Bay, ON	Darrell R. VanPamel	Darrell R. VanPamel	2005	225
175 5/8	182	25 6/8	25 5/8	20 1/8	4 5/8	4 6/8	6	7	Sheboygan Co., WI	Bob W. Siech	Bob W. Siech	2002	230
175 5/8	180 7/8	26 4/8	26 1/8	17 5/8	4 3/8	4 3/8	5	5	Bayfield Co., WI	Jim Nieckula	Jim Nieckula	2003	230
175 5/8	177 3/8	24 1/8	24 2/8	19 3/8	5 2/8	5 1/8	5	5	Athabasca River, AB	Doug E. Owens	Doug E. Owens	2003	230
175 5/8	186 5/8	26 6/8	27 7/8	20 5/8	5	5	6	6	Webster Co., NE	Mark Nollette	Mark Nollette	2004	230
175 4/8	182 2/8	25 2/8	25 2/8	20	5 6/8	5 5/8	6	5	Warren Co., IL	Jim M. Ryan	Jim M. Ryan	2003	234

175 4/8	196 1/8	26 5/8	26 1/8	18	5 5/8	5 4/8	7	6	Prairie River, SK	Daryl Savage	Daryl Savage	2003	234
175 4/8	183 5/8	27 6/8	27	18 2/8	4 3/8	4 4/8	5	5	Jefferson Co., OH	Jason Woodward	Jason Woodward	2003	234
175 4/8	184 4/8	25 7/8	26	20 4/8	4 6/8	4 6/8	7	6	Rockingham Co., NH	Scot E. Chevalier	Scot E. Chevalier	2004	234
175 4/8	183 2/8	24 2/8	24 2/8	18 5/8	4 5/8	4 4/8	6	7	Reagan Co., TX	Tommy L. Hill, Jr.	Tommy L. Hill, Jr.	2004	234
175 4/8	186 5/8	25 7/8	26 2/8	15 6/8	5 1/8	5	7	6	Trempealeau Co., WI	Michael J. Krynicki	Michael J. Krynicki	2005	234
175 4/8	182 4/8	24 6/8	24 1/8	18	5	5	5	5	Scott Co., IA	Randy Templeton	Randy Templeton	2005	234
175 4/8	180 7/8	26 1/8	26 1/8	17 6/8	4 4/8	4 4/8	6	6	Hardeman Co., TX	Thomas E. Ward, Jr.	Thomas E. Ward, Jr.	2005	234
175 3/8	177 4/8	23 3/8	23 3/8	19 7/8	4 5/8	4 5/8	6	6	Door Co., WI	Adam C. LeBre	Adam C. LeBre	2003	242
175 3/8	182 2/8	29 3/8	29 6/8	19 1/8	4 6/8	4 6/8	5	6	Butler Co., KY	John S. Meyer	John S. Meyer	2003	242
175 3/8	188 6/8	27	27 7/8	19 3/8	5 1/8	5 1/8	6	6	Waterhen River, SK	Anthony W. Summitt	Anthony W. Summitt	2003	242
175 3/8	183 1/8	26	26 2/8	18 3/8	4 6/8	4 6/8	6	5	Ogle Co., IL	Rob Diehl	Rob Diehl	2004	242
175 2/8	194 1/8	28 1/8	27 5/8	19 3/8	4 7/8	4 7/8	6	7	Meade Co., KY	Ronald L. Biddle	Ronald L. Biddle	1989	246
175 2/8	187 7/8	25 3/8	25 6/8	16 6/8	5 1/8	5 1/8	7	6	Wayne Co., IN	Robert J. Morgan	Robert J. Morgan	2002	246
175 2/8	181 6/8	26 1/8	26 1/8	16 6/8	5	5	5	6	Lewis Co., MO	Marshall D. Morton	Marshall D. Morton	2004	246
175 2/8	185 7/8	25 1/8	23 5/8	17 4/8	4 6/8	4 6/8	5	6	Pierce Co., WI	Kenneth A. Harvey	Kenneth A. Harvey	2005	246
175 2/8	183 1/8	24 2/8	24 1/8	16 4/8	6	5 5/8	6	5	Lawrence Co., IL	Robert J. Ingram	Robert J. Ingram	2005	246
175 2/8	193 6/8	28	29	20 1/8	5 4/8	5 4/8	7	6	Wandering River, AB	Billy J. Starks	Billy J. Starks	2005	246
175 1/8	178 5/8	26 4/8	26 4/8	18 3/8	5 1/8	5 1/8	5	5	Rockingham Co., NH	Joseph Dunlap	Joseph Dunlap	2003	252
175 1/8	179 5/8	24 6/8	24 6/8	20 1/8	4 3/8	4 4/8	5	6	Handhill Lakes, AB	Murray Moench	Murray Moench	2003	252
175 1/8	199 5/8	25 1/8	24	18 4/8	4 7/8	4 7/8	9	10	Flathead Co., MT	Paul Persinger	Paul Persinger	2003	252
175 1/8	179 3/8	27	26 7/8	21 7/8	5	5 2/8	5	5	Edmonson Co., KY	Tony Sanders	Tony Sanders	2003	252
175 1/8	178 5/8	29 1/8	29 7/8	20 1/8	5 1/8	5 1/8	5	5	Vernon Co., WI	Robert D. Staley	Robert D. Staley	2003	252
175 1/8	184 2/8	26 6/8	27	17 6/8	4 7/8	4 7/8	6	5	Anderson Co., KS	Alan L. Rihner	Alan L. Rihner	2004	252
175 1/8	194 3/8	27 2/8	27 5/8	20 2/8	5 2/8	5 2/8	8	5	Greene Co., IL	Jerry L. Burns	Jerry L. Burns	2005	252
175 1/8	192 2/8	26 5/8	25	24 7/8	4 4/8	5	7	8	Maverick Co., TX	John A. Cardwell	John A. Cardwell	2005	252
175 1/8	186 1/8	31 4/8	29 6/8	27 3/8	5 6/8	5 6/8	5	4	Rusk Co., WI	Michael Joyner	Michael Joyner	2005	252
175	177 6/8	26 2/8	26 1/8	21	4 7/8	4 7/8	5	5	Juneau Co., WI	Jeffrey A. Potter	Jeffrey A. Potter	2003	261
175	193 4/8	25 1/8	25 1/8	17	4 4/8	4 4/8	7	6	Warren Co., MO	Brian Wagster	Brian Wagster	2003	261
175	188 6/8	27 4/8	26 3/8	18	4 4/8	4 4/8	6	6	Casey Co., KY	Michael L. Cooper	Michael L. Cooper	2004	261
175	188 6/8	25 6/8	25	17 6/8	4 6/8	4 3/8	7	7	Cass Co., MN	Bryan D. Clancy	Bryan D. Clancy	2005	261
175	176 6/8	27 1/8	27 2/8	19 6/8	4 3/8	5	5	5	Swift Current Creek, SK	Brian L. Dyck	Brian L. Dyck	2005	261
175	180 2/8	25 6/8	25 6/8	23 2/8	5	5	5	5	Madison Co., MS	Kyle F. Gordon	Kyle F. Gordon	2006	261
174 7/8	190 5/8	29 4/8	30	17 6/8	4 4/8	4 4/8	7	6	Hart Co., KY	Robert Hobbs	Roy J. Hobbs	1962	267
174 7/8	188 3/8	26	24 5/8	17 7/8	5 3/8	5 2/8	6	6	Dodge Co., NE	Kirk D. Brand	Kirk D. Brand	2003	267
174 7/8	177 3/8	28 7/8	28 6/8	19 5/8	5 2/8	5 2/8	5	5	Eau Claire Co., WI	T.P. & C.G. Gilbertson	T.P. & C.G. Gilbertson	2003	267
174 7/8	181	26 3/8	25 4/8	19 5/8	5 5/8	5 7/8	5	6	Randolph Co., MO	Dennis C. Squires	Dennis C. Squires	2003	267
174 7/8	184 1/8	24 2/8	24 2/8	19 3/8	5 3/8	5 2/8	6	5	Auburnton Creek, SK	Ron Webb	Ron Webb	2004	267
174 6/8	184 6/8	27 5/8	27 5/8	19 3/8	5	5	6	7	Pike Co., MO	Jim DeRousse	Jim DeRousse	2003	272
174 5/8	184 1/8	28 4/8	28 3/8	24	4 7/8	4 7/8	6	6	Coahuila, MX	Ignacio O'Higgins	Ignacio O'Higgins	2003	273
174 5/8	179 6/8	25 5/8	26 1/8	21 7/8	4 3/8	4 3/8	6	6	Ramsey Co., MN	Jim Tuerk	Jim Tuerk	2004	273
174 5/8	178 3/8	25 2/8	24 5/8	15 3/8	4 7/8	4 7/8	6	6	Lincoln Co., SD	Shana Van De Stroet	Shana Van De Stroet	2005	273
174 4/8	183 2/8	21 6/8	24 7/8	18 2/8	4 5/8	4 5/8	6	6	Jackson Co., IA	Gerald A. Knipfer	Gerald A. Knipfer	2003	276

WHITETAIL DEER - TYPICAL ANTLERS

Odocoileus virginianus virginianus and certain related subspecies

Final Score	Gross Score	Length of Main Beam R.	L.	Inside Spread	Circumference at Smallest Place Between Burr & First Point R.	L.	Number of Points R.	L.	Locality	Hunter	Owner	Date Killed	Rank
174 4/8	182 6/8	26 2/8	27 5/8	20 6/8	5 2/8	5	5	5	Keokuk Co., IA	Doug C. Sieren	Doug C. Sieren	2003	276
174 4/8	183 3/8	25 7/8	26	17 4/8	4 7/8	4 6/8	6	7	Callaway Co., MO	Dan R. Thomas	Dan R. Thomas	2003	276
174 4/8	182 7/8	25 4/8	25 6/8	18 6/8	5 2/8	5	6	5	Dimmit Co., TX	Dan Friedkin, Jr.	Dan Friedkin, Jr.	2004	276
174 4/8	176 7/8	28 4/8	27 6/8	22	4 6/8	4 6/8	5	5	Dickinson Co., KS	Larry S. Shankweiler	Larry S. Shankweiler	2005	276
174 3/8	181 2/8	29 2/8	29 5/8	19 5/8	5	5	5	6	Gallatin Co., IL	Scott G. Bosaw	Scott G. Bosaw	1999	281
174 3/8	179 6/8	24 4/8	24 3/8	22 1/8	4 4/8	4 4/8	6	5	Yuma Co., CO	Picked Up	Robert C. Phillips	2001	281
174 3/8	183 2/8	26 4/8	26 4/8	23 7/8	5 1/8	5	6	7	Carrot River, SK	Douglas H. Christianson	Douglas H. Christianson	2003	281
174 3/8	190 4/8	22 6/8	22 6/8	18 4/8	4 7/8	4 7/8	6	8	Leavenworth Co., KS	Charles L. Eibes	Charles L. Eibes	2003	281
174 3/8	190 7/8	24 3/8	24 7/8	21 2/8	5 6/8	6 3/8	8	6	Butler Co., OH	Mark Lagedrost	Mark Lagedrost	2004	281
174 3/8	188 6/8	29	27	18 7/8	5 2/8	5 3/8	6	6	Big Quill Lake, SK	Gary P. Tomchyshen	Gary P. Tomchyshen	2005	281
174 3/8	181 1/8	28	27 4/8	24 3/8	4 6/8	4 6/8	6	5	Prince George's Co., MD	Pat H. Henderson	Pat H. Henderson	2006	281
174 2/8	183 5/8	26 3/8	27 1/8	16 7/8	5 1/8	5	5	6	Mercer Co., IL	Tom C. Giarrante	Tom C. Giarrante	2002	288
174 2/8	183 4/8	27 6/8	27 3/8	21	4 6/8	4 6/8	7	5	Lake Co., OH	Jim Cecconi	Jim Cecconi	2004	288
174 2/8	182 5/8	28	28 5/8	22 5/8	5 6/8	5 4/8	6	5	Jo Daviess Co., IL	Thomas R. Dvorak	Thomas R. Dvorak	2004	288
174 2/8	187 5/8	26 6/8	27 2/8	20	5 3/8	5 3/8	5	6	Clark Co., IL	Max M. LeCrone	Max M. LeCrone	2005	288
174 1/8	201 6/8	29	28 3/8	21 7/8	4 7/8	4 6/8	8	6	Antelope Co., NE	Picked Up	Kenneth Pollock	1992	292
174 1/8	179 2/8	27 1/8	28 1/8	17 2/8	4 7/8	5	6	6	Orange Co., IN	Edgar Powell	Edgar Powell	1995	292
174 1/8	192 3/8	24 6/8	26	17 5/8	4	4 1/8	5	6	Ripley Co., IN	Aaron R. Allen	Aaron R. Allen	1997	292
174 1/8	178 1/8	25 1/8	25 6/8	20 5/8	5 5/8	5 5/8	6	5	Douglas Co., WI	Doug Anderson	Doug Anderson	2004	292
174 1/8	212 6/8	29 7/8	29 2/8	20 4/8	5 2/8	5 6/8	8	10	Macoupin Co., IL	Brian G. Orf	Brian G. Orf	2004	292
174 1/8	176 5/8	25 6/8	26	20 7/8	4 5/8	4 5/8	5	5	Zavala Co., TX	Bob Powell	Bob Powell	2004	292
174 1/8	178 5/8	26	26 3/8	18 1/8	4	4 2/8	6	6	Taylor Co., IA	Nathan P. Stiens	Nathan P. Stiens	2004	292
174 1/8	195 7/8	27 5/8	26 5/8	21 2/8	5 4/8	5 5/8	6	8	Greene Co., OH	Ted Terrell, Jr.	Ted Terrell, Jr.	2004	292
174 1/8	190 4/8	24 5/8	25 5/8	19 2/8	4 4/8	4 3/8	7	7	Mayes Co., OK	Chad R. Peters	Chad R. Peters	2005	292
174 1/8	204 6/8	25 6/8	26 6/8	18	4 7/8	5	7	9	Nose Creek, AB	Chris Popesco	Chris Popesco	2005	292
174	178 4/8	26	25 3/8	18 6/8	5 4/8	5 4/8	5	5	Woodford Co., KY	Michael L. Burleson	Michael L. Burleson	2003	302
174	181 1/8	25 3/8	25 3/8	22 2/8	4 7/8	4 7/8	6	6	Logan Co., KY	Kevin Sears	Kevin Sears	2003	302
174	176 5/8	25 6/8	26	18 4/8	4 6/8	4 6/8	6	5	Hampden Co., MA	Neil R. Bixby	Neil R. Bixby	2004	302
174	177 3/8	25 5/8	25 3/8	17 6/8	5 2/8	5 3/8	5	5	Meadow Lake, SK	Corbin R. Huxtable	Corbin R. Huxtable	2004	302
174	179 4/8	25 3/8	23 5/8	22	5	5	5	5	Pine River, BC	Alonzo E. Tricker	Alonzo E. Tricker	2004	302
174	180 6/8	27 2/8	27	19 3/8	5 3/8	5 2/8	6	5	Woodward Co., OK	Thomas D. Roedell	Thomas D. Roedell	2005	302
174	176 5/8	23 5/8	24 4/8	19 4/8	4 3/8	4 3/8	6	6	Pipestone Valley, SK	H. Haeusler & D.C. Sandgaard	Darren C. Sandgaard	2005	302
174	192 3/8	24 4/8	24 7/8	16 7/8	5 5/8	5 2/8	7	6	Calhoun Co., IL	Travis Simpson	Travis Simpson	2005	302

Score	Gross	R. Beam	L. Beam	Spread	R. Circ.	L. Circ.	R. Pts.	L. Pts.	Locality	Hunter	Owner	Date	Page
173 7/8	190 4/8	26 6/8	29	20 5/8	5 5/8	5 5/8	7	7	Buffalo Co., WI	Jeff N. Tirri	Jeff N. Tirri	2002	310
173 7/8	177 5/8	27 1/8	27 1/8	19 5/8	4 6/8	4 4/8	6	6	Delaware Co., OH	Jeff A. Daily	Jeff A. Daily	2003	310
173 7/8	183 4/8	27 4/8	27 3/8	20 3/8	4 4/8	4 4/8	6	5	Calhoun Co., SC	Oneal R. Hoffman	Oneal R. Hoffman	2003	310
173 7/8	176 3/8	26 5/8	26 3/8	21 3/8	4 6/8	4 6/8	5	5	Trempealeau Co., WI	Justin M. Heath	Justin M. Heath	2005	310
173 6/8	177 1/8	26	25 4/8	20 6/8	5 6/8	5 4/8	5	5	Crow Wing Co., MN	Melvin Falenschek	Melvin Falenschek	1947	314
173 6/8	176 5/8	25 1/8	24 3/8	19	4 6/8	4 6/8	5	5	Richland Co., WI	Greg Beighley	Greg Beighley	2003	314
173 6/8	188 5/8	26 2/8	26 7/8	21 1/8	4 6/8	4 6/8	7	6	Boyd Co., NE	Stanley J. McLaughlin	Stanley J. McLaughlin	2003	314
173 6/8	190 5/8	25 1/8	25	20 2/8	4 4/8	4 5/8	8	7	Jasper Co., IL	Tom Shelton	Tom Shelton	2003	314
173 6/8	179 6/8	26 4/8	26 6/8	18 2/8	5	5 2/8	5	5	Rockhaven, SK	Tom Hollman	Curtis P. Smiley	2003	314
173 6/8	177 3/8	29 3/8	29 1/8	21 6/8	5 1/8	5 2/8	5	5	Clinton Co., OH	James J. Day	James J. Day	2004	314
173 5/8	189 2/8	27 1/8	27	17 1/8	4 6/8	4 6/8	9	9	Bates Co., MO	Wayne Brown	Wayne Brown	1978	320
173 5/8	181 6/8	24 7/8	25 1/8	16 5/8	4	3 7/8	6	6	Washington Co., IL	Allen G. Albers	Allen G. Albers	2003	320
173 5/8	183 7/8	27 6/8	26 6/8	19 1/8	5 6/8	5 6/8	5	5	Pike Co., IL	Rickey D. Cleveland	Rickey D. Cleveland	2003	320
173 5/8	196 1/8	28 2/8	26 6/8	21	5 5/8	6	6	6	St. Louis Co., MN	Leroy Dobson	Leroy Dobson	2003	320
173 5/8	183 5/8	26 4/8	25 7/8	16 5/8	4 3/8	4 3/8	7	7	Wayne Co., IL	Matt Dust	Matt Dust	2004	320
173 5/8	180	25 2/8	25 2/8	20 5/8	5	5	6	6	Midnight Lake, SK	Joseph M. Harner	Joseph M. Harner	2004	320
173 5/8	177 4/8	24 4/8	25	15 7/8	5 5/8	5 1/8	5	5	Callaway Co., MO	Steve G. Peterson	Steve G. Peterson	2004	320
173 5/8	178 7/8	24 5/8	24 1/8	17 5/8	5 5/8	5 6/8	6	5	Jim Hogg Co., TX	Brian P. Austin	Brian P. Austin	2005	320
173 5/8	177 2/8	25 7/8	25 2/8	21 1/8	4 5/8	4 5/8	5	5	Buchanan Co., MO	Tony J. Mollus	Tony J. Mollus	2005	320
173 5/8	187 1/8	24 3/8	25 7/8	18 5/8	4 4/8	4 4/8	6	6	Franklin Co., ME	Unknown	Maine Antler Shed & PR Wildl. Mus.	2006	320
173 4/8	190 3/8	27 4/8	27 3/8	23 1/8	5 1/8	4 6/8	7	7	Huron Co., OH	David A. Fidler	David A. Fidler	2000	330
173 4/8	178 6/8	25 4/8	25 2/8	18 4/8	4 7/8	4 7/8	6	7	Knox Co., IL	Robert W. Crouse	Cabela's, Inc.	2002	330
173 4/8	176 4/8	24 5/8	24 6/8	22 6/8	5	5 2/8	5	5	Johnson Co., IL	Robert W. Dodson	Robert W. Dodson	2004	330
173 4/8	179 7/8	23 4/8	23 3/8	20 7/8	5 1/8	5 2/8	6	5	Echo Valley, SK	Alec Morrison	Alec Morrison	2004	330
173 4/8	189 7/8	29	29 2/8	24 7/8	5	5 1/8	6	6	Prince George Co., VA	Travis M. Powroznik	Travis M. Powroznik	2004	330
173 4/8	177 3/8	24 7/8	25 1/8	17	4 6/8	4 6/8	5	5	Butler Co., KS	Russell Thompson	Russell Thompson	2004	330
173 4/8	180	26 6/8	26 1/8	20	5 1/8	5 1/8	6	6	Montgomery Co., TN	Kyle R. Yates	Kyle R. Yates	2004	330
173 4/8	185 6/8	25 1/8	25 5/8	17	5	5	6	6	Kawagama Lake, ON	Joshua E. Morris	Joshua E. Morris	2005	330
173 3/8	190 7/8	25 2/8	25 7/8	15 3/8	5 3/8	5 4/8	6	6	Butler Co., KS	Cris Elinski	Cris Elinski	2003	338
173 3/8	187 2/8	24 2/8	24 2/8	20 1/8	4 3/8	4 3/8	7	7	Mouse Creek, AB	Todd A. Muenchrath	Todd A. Muenchrath	2003	338
173 3/8	184 1/8	26 1/8	25 7/8	17 6/8	5 4/8	5 4/8	6	5	Hancock Co., GA	Keith Thompson	Keith Thompson	2003	338
173 3/8	181 2/8	26 5/8	26	17 1/8	5 1/8	4 7/8	5	5	Waupaca Co., WI	Peter L. Radies	Peter L. Radies	2004	338
173 3/8	176 5/8	26 2/8	25 5/8	20 5/8	4 4/8	4 4/8	5	5	Waukesha Co., WI	Darin R. Zachow	Darin R. Zachow	2004	338
173 3/8	185 7/8	28	26 5/8	22 4/8	5 1/8	4 6/8	6	6	Guthrie Co., IA	Vernie W. Grasty	Vernie W. Grasty	2005	338
173 3/8	203 2/8	26 4/8	27	23 7/8	5 3/8	5 6/8	9	7	Macoupin Co., IL	Kerry L. Huff	Kerry L. Huff	2005	338
173 3/8	180 6/8	26 3/8	27 6/8	19 4/8	5 3/8	5 4/8	6	7	Richland Co., WI	Eric T. Janquart	Eric T. Janquart	2005	338
173 3/8	177 5/8	24 6/8	24 4/8	19 1/8	4 7/8	4 6/8	6	6	Maverick Co., TX	Donnie B. Seay	Donnie B. Seay	2005	338
173 3/8	186 2/8	24 7/8	24 2/8	20	5	4 7/8	7	7	Appanoose Co., IA	Tad D. Proudlove	Tad D. Proudlove	2006	338
173 2/8	193 5/8	26 4/8	26 4/8	21	4 2/8	4 2/8	6	6	Adolet Lake, IA	Allan N. Bogdan	Allan N. Bogdan	2003	348
173 2/8	183 1/8	27	26 4/8	21 2/8	5	4 7/8	6	6	Little Manitou Lake, SK	J. Hanson & C. Hanson	J. Hanson & C. Hanson	2003	348
173 2/8	187 5/8	27 6/8	27 4/8	21 2/8	5	5 2/8	5	7	Noble Co., OH	Julian S. Rich	Julian S. Rich	2003	348

WHITETAIL DEER - TYPICAL ANTLERS

Odocoileus virginianus virginianus and certain related subspecies

Final Score	Gross Score	Length of Main Beam R.	L.	Inside Spread	Circumference at Smallest Place Between Burr & First Point R.	L.	Number of Points R.	L.	Locality	Hunter	Owner	Date Killed	Rank
173 2/8	182 5/8	28	29	22 7/8	5 1/8	5 3/8	5	6	Crawford Co., WI	Charles E. Capesius	Charles E. Capesius	2004	348
173 2/8	180 3/8	28 3/8	28 5/8	20 6/8	5 4/8	5 3/8	6	5	Pine Co., MN	Ronald J. Drexl, Jr.	Ronald J. Drexl, Jr.	2004	348
173 2/8	183 4/8	27 3/8	27 1/8	19 6/8	5 1/8	5 1/8	5	4	Leech Lake, SK	Steven Yanyk	Steven Yanyk	2005	348
173 1/8	198 6/8	25 3/8	25 3/8	18 5/8	5 2/8	5	9	7	Butler Co., KY	Ken Wilson	Ken Wilson	2003	354
173 1/8	188 1/8	25 5/8	27 1/8	16 1/8	5 2/8	4 7/8	6	6	Morgan Co., CO	Dale Eberharter	Dale Eberharter	2004	354
173 1/8	181	27 5/8	27 3/8	20	5 2/8	5	6	6	Lake Co., SD	Roger Schrepel	Roger Schrepel	2004	354
173	184 7/8	27 6/8	26 4/8	19 5/8	5 1/8	5	6	5	Barron Co., WI	John Marzolf	John Marzolf	2003	357
173	177 2/8	25 3/8	26 1/8	21 2/8	4 5/8	4 5/8	5	5	Sussex Co., DE	Steven V. Cardano	Steven V. Cardano	2004	357
173	185	27 5/8	28 6/8	21 2/8	5 3/8	5 4/8	5	6	Grayson Co., KY	Joey England	Joey England	2004	357
173	179 3/8	24 5/8	23 2/8	18 6/8	4 7/8	4 6/8	5	5	Muscatine Co., IA	Ronald L. Henderson	Ronald L. Henderson	2005	357
173	182 7/8	25 6/8	25 3/8	22 3/8	5 3/8	5 5/8	6	5	Pierce Co., WI	Nathan T. Place	Nathan T. Place	2005	357
173	182 2/8	29 1/8	29 1/8	19	5 5/8	5 4/8	5	5	Pepin Co., WI	Picked Up	Sam Williams	2006	357
172 7/8	178 6/8	28 4/8	27 4/8	21 4/8	5	5	6	6	Moultrie Co., IL	David A. Boyer	David A. Boyer	2003	363
172 7/8	175 2/8	25 7/8	26 3/8	23 7/8	5 2/8	5 3/8	5	5	Beckham Co., OK	Frank M. Bullard	Frank M. Bullard	2003	363
172 7/8	196 7/8	25 7/8	25 4/8	21	5 6/8	5 4/8	8	5	Codette Lake, SK	Steve Clifford	Steve Clifford	2004	363
172 7/8	179 1/8	26 1/8	25 7/8	18 7/8	4 7/8	4 7/8	6	7	La Salle Co., TX	Clarence J. Kahlig	Clarence J. Kahlig	2004	363
172 7/8	204 2/8	26 2/8	25 4/8	19 7/8	5 4/8	5 4/8	9	6	Unknown	Unknown	Geoff Mahar	PR 2004	363
172 7/8	176 3/8	27 2/8	27 2/8	19 3/8	4 7/8	4 6/8	5	5	Warren Co., OH	Paul R. Sanwald	Paul R. Sanwald	2004	363
172 7/8	175 5/8	24 7/8	25 3/8	15 1/8	4 5/8	4 6/8	5	5	Clark Co., OH	Jason L. Stull	Jason L. Stull	2004	363
172 7/8	187 6/8	26 7/8	24 4/8	18 7/8	5 7/8	5 5/8	6	7	Brown Co., OH	Steven B. Conley	Steven B. Conley	2005	363
172 7/8	196 3/8	29 3/8	28 1/8	23 3/8	5 4/8	5 7/8	4	8	Harrison Co., MO	Tim J. Grassmid	Tim J. Grassmid	2005	363
172 7/8	176 5/8	25 3/8	25 1/8	21 1/8	4 6/8	4 7/8	6	6	Trempealeau Co., WI	Brian L. Hoesley	Brian L. Hoesley	2005	363
172 7/8	187 1/8	25	24 6/8	20 2/8	4 7/8	4 7/8	5	6	Carrot River, SK	Karl J. Lefever	Karl J. Lefever	2005	363
172 7/8	181 4/8	26 1/8	25 5/8	19 7/8	4 7/8	4 6/8	5	5	Portage Co., OH	Chris Farver	Chris Farver	2006	363
172 6/8	177 5/8	28 1/8	28 4/8	19 6/8	4 6/8	5	5	5	Callaway Co., MO	Brian M. Hughes	Brian M. Hughes	2002	375
172 6/8	189 1/8	25 3/8	25 2/8	17 6/8	5 4/8	5 4/8	6	7	Barber Co., KS	Michael Burden	Michael Burden	2004	375
172 6/8	185 1/8	26 7/8	25 7/8	18 7/8	5 2/8	5 3/8	6	8	Adams Co., WI	John P. Nawrot	John P. Nawrot	2004	375
172 6/8	190 2/8	27 6/8	27 5/8	19 3/8	5 5/8	5 6/8	6	6	Dubuque Co., IA	Daniel W. Reich, Sr.	Daniel W. Reich, Sr.	2005	375
172 6/8	186 2/8	26 3/8	26 2/8	19 5/8	4 7/8	5 2/8	6	5	Miami Co., IN	Matthew J. Stevens	Matthew J. Stevens	2005	375
172 5/8	176 3/8	25 1/8	24 7/8	20 7/8	5	5 2/8	5	5	Washington Co., IA	Bradley D. Balcar	Bradley D. Balcar	2003	380
172 5/8	176 3/8	25	25 4/8	16 7/8	5	5	5	5	Last Mountain Lake, SK	Jeff G. Brandt	Jeff G. Brandt	2003	380
172 5/8	185 2/8	28 3/8	26 4/8	21 3/8	4 6/8	4 5/8	6	5	Wheeler Co., TX	William P. Illig	William P. Illig	2003	380
172 5/8	179	25 1/8	24	18 7/8	5 4/8	5 5/8	5	5	Woodruff Co., AR	Charles L. Crafford	Charles L. Crafford	2004	380

Score		Main Beam R	Main Beam L	Inside Spread	Circ. R	Circ. L	Pts. R	Pts. L	Locality	Hunter	Owner	Date	Rank
172 5/8	182 6/8	25	25 3/8	22	4 6/8	4 6/8	6	6	Wapiti River, AB	Duane A. Hagman	Duane A. Hagman	2004	380
172 5/8	199	26 7/8	26 6/8	20 3/8	4 5/8	4 6/8	7	7	Greig Lake, SK	Arthur R. Bifulco III	Arthur R. Bifulco III	2005	380
172 5/8	198 6/8	29 6/8	30 2/8	19 6/8	5	5 1/8	7	7	Washington Co., MN	Craig A. Heininger	Craig A. Heininger	2005	380
172 4/8	184	27 4/8	26 4/8	22 7/8	5 1/8	5	6	6	Buffalo Co., WI	Donald Serum	Jerry Serum	1958	387
172 4/8	174 2/8	28	27 4/8	21	4 3/8	4 4/8	5	5	Rock Island Co., IL	Jeff Nesseler	Jeff Nesseler	2001	387
172 4/8	182 4/8	26 3/8	27	20 7/8	4 4/8	4 5/8	5	5	Maverick Co., TX	Joe B. Richter	Joe B. Richter	2003	387
172 4/8	197 6/8	27 5/8	26 7/8	18 3/8	4 7/8	4 7/8	7	7	Ottawa Co., OH	Dean E. Anderson	Dean E. Anderson	2004	387
172 4/8	176 7/8	25 5/8	25 1/8	19 6/8	4 3/8	4 4/8	5	6	N. Saskatchewan River, SK	Ivan W. Landego	Ivan W. Landego	2004	387
172 4/8	180 3/8	25 3/8	25 2/8	18 2/8	5 4/8	5 1/8	6	5	Warren Co., OH	John B. Luchini	John B. Luchini	2004	387
172 4/8	177 6/8	27 2/8	26 3/8	23 2/8	5 3/8	5 2/8	5	5	Des Moines Co., IA	Randy Templeton	Randy Templeton	2005	387
172 4/8	186 5/8	24 4/8	23 2/8	21 2/8	5 4/8	5 4/8	6	6	Pulaski Co., IL	David M. Foret	David M. Foret	2006	387
172 3/8	183 2/8	27	27 2/8	19 6/8	5 3/8	5 2/8	6	5	Chariton Co., MO	Phillip K. Krause	Phillip K. Krause	2002	395
172 3/8	177 4/8	28 2/8	27 3/8	22 1/8	5 6/8	5 6/8	5	4	McHenry Co., IL	George G. Gilpin, Jr.	George G. Gilpin, Jr.	2003	395
172 3/8	179 1/8	26 5/8	27 3/8	17 4/8	4 7/8	4 7/8	5	6	Pike Co., IL	Kevin L. Leahr	Kevin L. Leahr	2003	395
172 3/8	181 7/8	26 2/8	27 5/8	21 4/8	4 2/8	4 2/8	6	5	La Salle Co., TX	Phil W. Teinert	Phil W. Teinert	2003	395
172 3/8	178 2/8	28	26 2/8	19 3/8	4 3/8	4 2/8	5	5	Richland Co., WI	Ronald L. Jahr	Ronald L. Jahr	2005	395
172 2/8	178 4/8	25 5/8	25 1/8	21 2/8	4 7/8	4 7/8	6	5	Clare Co., MI	Don Wetherell	David S. Manges	1937	400
172 2/8	181 5/8	26	25	19 7/8	4 4/8	4 4/8	7	6	Linn Co., MO	Robert C. Head	Robert C. Head	2002	400
172 2/8	188 3/8	27 4/8	27 3/8	21 3/8	5	5 1/8	7	7	Maverick Co., TX	John A. Cardwell	John A. Cardwell	2003	400
172 2/8	174 3/8	25 4/8	25 5/8	14 6/8	4 7/8	5	5	5	Beaupre Creek, SK	Maurice A. Harvey	Maurice A. Harvey	2003	400

TYPICAL WHITETAIL DEER
FINAL SCORE: 161-3/8
HUNTER: Clemon R. Watts

TYPICAL WHITETAIL DEER
FINAL SCORE: 166-6/8
HUNTER: Ryan M. Elenbaas

TYPICAL WHITETAIL DEER
FINAL SCORE: 174-5/8
HUNTER: Ignacio O'Higgins

TYPICAL WHITETAIL DEER
FINAL SCORE: 178-5/8
HUNTER: Luke R. Viravec

WHITETAIL DEER - TYPICAL ANTLERS

Odocoileus virginianus virginianus and certain related subspecies

Final Score	Gross Score	Length of Main Beam R.	L.	Inside Spread	Circumference at Smallest Place Between Burr & First Point R.	L.	Number of Points R.	L.	Locality	Hunter	Owner	Date Killed	Rank
172 2/8	178 3/8	27 3/8	26	20 6/8	5 2/8	5 5/8	5	5	Maverick Co., TX	Thomas D. Friedkin	Thomas D. Friedkin	2004	400
172 2/8	181	25 3/8	25 3/8	20 6/8	4 6/8	4 4/8	5	5	Ford Co., KS	Agnes P. Gladden	Agnes P. Gladden	2004	400
172 2/8	181 6/8	26 1/8	26	18 4/8	4 7/8	4 7/8	5	6	Turtle Lake, SK	George J. Mehlrose III	George J. Mehlrose III	2005	400
172 1/8	181 4/8	25	23 6/8	16 1/8	4 3/8	4 4/8	6	7	Duval Co., TX	Michael E. Murray	Michael E. Murray	2003	407
172 1/8	177 4/8	23 3/8	22 6/8	16 3/8	4	4	6	6	Washington Co., KS	Scott B. Carpenter	Scott B. Carpenter	2004	407
172 1/8	177 2/8	27	25 6/8	19 7/8	4 2/8	4	5	6	Ringgold Co., IA	Kevin Hatch	Kevin Hatch	2004	407
172 1/8	177 7/8	26 3/8	25 7/8	21 7/8	5 1/8	5 4/8	5	5	Tawatinaw River, AB	Dwayne E. Kraychy	Dwayne E. Kraychy	2004	407
172 1/8	175 3/8	27	26 6/8	17 1/8	5 2/8	5	5	5	Miller Co., MO	Thomas F. Stockman	Thomas F. Stockman	2004	407
172 1/8	175 6/8	26 6/8	27 2/8	20 7/8	5	4 7/8	5	5	Monroe Co., AR	Coty K. Bones	Coty K. Bones	2005	407
172 1/8	176 5/8	26 5/8	26 2/8	17 7/8	4 6/8	4 6/8	6	6	Shawano Co., WI	Jack B. Nichols	Jack B. Nichols	2005	407
172 1/8	194 1/8	27 2/8	27 5/8	18 5/8	5 2/8	5 1/8	7	7	Worcester Co., MA	Paul A. Buccacio	Paul A. Buccacio	2006	407
172 1/8	180 1/8	27	27 3/8	24	5 2/8	5	6	5	Callaway Co., MO	T.J. Wallis	T.J. Wallis	2006	407
172	188	28 1/8	27	22 5/8	5 7/8	5 3/8	7	6	Folly Mt., NS	Dennis Lynds	Douglas J. Weatherbee	1998	416
172	184 6/8	26 1/8	26 5/8	19 7/8	4 7/8	4 6/8	6	6	Poinsett Co., AR	James G. McGwier	James G. McGwier	2003	416
172	188 2/8	29	29 6/8	17 1/8	4 6/8	4 6/8	7	7	Prince George's Co., MD	James Printz	James Printz	2003	416
172	176	24 3/8	25 5/8	19 6/8	4 6/8	4 5/8	5	5	Sauk Co., WI	Dennis F. Ellefson	Dennis F. Ellefson	2004	416
172	173 7/8	24 1/8	25	16 4/8	5	5 1/8	6	6	Pulaski Co., MO	Tim D. Foster	Tim D. Foster	2004	416
172	179 5/8	25 4/8	26 5/8	21 6/8	4 7/8	4 8/8	5	6	Sauk Co., WI	Richard L. Carver	Richard L. Carver	2005	416
171 7/8	183	25 3/8	25 3/8	21 4/8	4 4/8	4 2/8	6	5	Maverick Co., TX	Debra Friedkin	Debra Friedkin	2006	423
171 7/8	190 3/8	27 2/8	27 5/8	21 2/8	5 3/8	5	6	8	Webster Co., IA	Picked Up	Daniel Grossnickle	2003	423
171 7/8	176	25 1/8	26 1/8	21 7/8	4 6/8	4 6/8	6	5	Morrill Co., NE	Dennis Highby	Dennis Highby	2003	423
171 7/8	185	24 1/8	23 3/8	21 7/8	4 6/8	4 6/8	6	5	Monroe Co., MI	Michael P. Kiley	Michael P. Kiley	2003	423
171 7/8	180 3/8	26 3/8	25 7/8	18 4/8	4 7/8	4 7/8	7	8	Trigg Co., KY	Christine M. Abbott	Christine M. Abbott	2004	423
171 7/8	174 6/8	25 7/8	26	22	4 4/8	4 6/8	5	6	Lee Co., IA	Steve Kahl	Steve Kahl	2004	423
171 7/8	189 5/8	24 3/8	24 4/8	20 3/8	5 7/8	6	5	5	Henderson Co., KY	Nick Sandefur	Nick Sandefur	2005	423
171 6/8	176 7/8	27 2/8	26 7/8	18 7/8	4 6/8	4 7/8	8	6	Winnebago Co., WI	Zachary J. Stromske	Zachary J. Stromske	2005	431
171 6/8	180 7/8	25 4/8	26 3/8	21 3/8	4 7/8	4 7/8	6	5	Ashland Co., OH	Ryan D. Nickles	Ryan D. Nickles	2006	431
171 6/8	177 2/8	28 2/8	26 5/8	24 6/8	4 2/8	4 3/8	4	5	Logan Co., KY	Larry Walpole	John Walpole, Jr.	1977	431
171 6/8	185	27 7/8	27 7/8	23	4 4/8	4 6/8	5	4	Portage Co., OH	Michael R. Bedilion	Michael R. Bedilion	2003	431
171 6/8	174 5/8	26 4/8	26 4/8	21	5 2/8	5 3/8	7	7	Washington Co., OH	Thomas C. Farley	Thomas C. Farley	2003	431
171 6/8	188 1/8	26 1/8	26 2/8	19 4/8	5 3/8	5 2/8	5	5	Jackfish Lake, AB	Michael J. Horton	Michael J. Horton	2003	431
171 6/8	179 5/8	25 3/8	26 1/8	20 5/8	5	4 7/8	7	6	Maverick Co., TX	William A. Jordan, Jr.	William A. Jordan, Jr.	2003	431
171 6/8	179 5/8	24 5/8	25 3/8	17 4/8	5 1/8	5	6	6	Oakland Co., MI	Gary A. Libkuman	Gary A. Libkuman	2003	431

Score									Locality	Hunter	Owner	Date	Rank
171 6/8	190 5/8	28 1/8	28 1/8	22 3/8	5 1/8	5 2/8	7	6	Schuyler Co., IL	Joshua M. Phillips	Joshua M. Phillips	2003	431
171 6/8	175 2/8	25 4/8	24 4/8	19	5 7/8	5 7/8	5	5	Cass Co., MO	Cilby L. Rogers	Cilby L. Rogers	2003	431
171 6/8	184 6/8	21 6/8	23 5/8	20 6/8	4 4/8	4 4/8	9	6	Webb Co., TX	Dennis H. Eberhard	Dennis H. Eberhard	2004	431
171 6/8	176 6/8	26	26	15 4/8	4 7/8	5	5	6	McMullen Co., TX	Kirk M. Folsom	Kirk M. Folsom	2004	431
171 6/8	177	26 2/8	26 4/8	22 6/8	4 6/8	4 6/8	5	5	Nuevo Leon, MX	R. Steve Moore	R. Steve Moore	2004	431
171 6/8	196 5/8	27 2/8	27 7/8	24 3/8	5	5 1/8	7	7	Jo Daviess Co., IL	Martin E. Vrstal	Martin E. Vrstal	2005	431
171 6/8	194 4/8	26 6/8	26 7/8	17 2/8	5 5/8	5 3/8	9	7	Sawyer Co., WI	Ross A. Zietlow	Ross A. Zietlow	2005	431
171 5/8	192 3/8	26 6/8	26 6/8	23	4 7/8	4 6/8	5	5	Douglas Co., MN	Gary E. Zwieg	Gary E. Zwieg	1985	444
171 5/8	176	26 3/8	26 5/8	18 7/8	4 3/8	4 3/8	5	5	Shannon Co., MO	Picked Up	Scott D. Lindsey	2000	444
171 5/8	180 7/8	24 1/8	24 6/8	15 5/8	4 7/8	5	5	5	Sangamon Co., IL	Matt Strawn	Matt Strawn	2003	444
171 5/8	175 5/8	25 6/8	25 5/8	19 7/8	4 2/8	4 3/8	6	6	Webb Co., TX	John P. Meyer	John P. Meyer	2005	444
171 4/8	174 2/8	26 6/8	26 5/8	19 4/8	5 1/8	5 1/8	4	4	Hamilton Co., NY	Charles Carroll	Susan Farrell	PR 1940	448
171 4/8	175 1/8	26 6/8	27 6/8	20 2/8	5 3/8	5 2/8	6	4	Logan Co., KY	Don S. Houchens	Don S. Houchens	1969	448
171 4/8	182	28 2/8	28 4/8	20 6/8	5 5/8	5 3/8	6	6	Bredenbury, SK	Chris Evans	Chris Evans	2003	448
171 4/8	175	24 7/8	25	16	5 1/8	5 6/8	7	7	Wright Co., MO	D.E. Smith	D.E. Smith	2003	448
171 4/8	178 2/8	26 6/8	26 6/8	21 6/8	6	4 5/8	7	5	Humboldt Co., IA	Jerry B. Tokheim	Jerry B. Tokheim	2003	448
171 4/8	183	26 6/8	26 1/8	17 5/8	4 4/8	4 6/8	7	5	Guernsey Co., OH	Robert T. Fedorke, Jr.	Robert T. Fedorke, Jr.	2004	448
171 4/8	174 5/8	26 2/8	25 3/8	17 4/8	4 6/8	5	5	5	Powell Co., KY	Picked Up	KY Dept. Fish & Wildl.	2004	448
171 4/8	193 4/8	27 1/8	28 2/8	21 6/8	5 1/8	4 7/8	5	7	La Salle Co., TX	Rene R. Barrientos	Rene R. Barrientos	2005	448
171 3/8	179 5/8	28	26 6/8	20 7/8	5		5	5	Jefferson Co., AR	A.E. Crossett, Sr. & E.R. Simmons	Art E. Crossett, Jr.	1960	456
171 3/8	182 1/8	26 6/8	27 2/8	21 1/8	4 6/8	4 5/8	5	6	Sawyer Co., WI	Unknown	Ray T. Charles	1993	456
171 3/8	180	27	27	21 5/8	4 4/8	4 2/8	7	6	Adams Co., OH	John F. Hildebrand	John F. Hildebrand	2000	456
171 3/8	181 1/8	26 1/8	26 5/8	16 4/8	4 2/8	4 3/8	7	6	Fayette Co., KY	Larry A. White	Larry A. White	2000	456
171 3/8	186 4/8	27 5/8	26 1/8	17 4/8	4 5/8	5 2/8	7	7	Miami Co., IN	Bob A. Benzing	Bob A. Benzing	2003	456
171 3/8	182 2/8	26	23 6/8	17 3/8	5 2/8	4 7/8	6	5	Scott Co., IL	Cuyler S. Coleman	Cuyler S. Coleman	2003	456
171 3/8	178 3/8	26 7/8	25 4/8	23 7/8	4 7/8	4	6	7	Webb Co., TX	Tyler Russell	Tyler Russell	2003	456
171 3/8	182 7/8	25 4/8	25 2/8	23 3/8	4 2/8	5 1/8	6	6	Nisbet Plain, SK	Allen G. Prosser	Allen G. Prosser	2004	456
171 3/8	197 5/8	25 4/8	26 4/8	19 1/8	5 1/8	5 3/8	8	6	English River, ON	Albert G. Stella	Albert G. Stella	2005	456
171 2/8	174 4/8	24	23	16 4/8	5 3/8	5	5	5	Graham Co., KS	David C. Newton II	David C. Newton II	1999	465
171 2/8	184 7/8	25 2/8	24 1/8	19 4/8	5 1/8	5 1/8	7	7	Muriel Lake, AB	Jesse Rusty Flowers, Jr.	Jesse Rusty Flowers, Jr.	2003	465
171 2/8	174	24	24 4/8	18	4 6/8	5 1/8	6	5	Harding Co., SD	Chad M. Krempges	Chad M. Krempges	2003	465
171 2/8	181 5/8	25 1/8	24 1/8	18 2/8	5 5/8	4 6/8	6	5	Jackfish Lake, SK	William J. Sabatose	William J. Sabatose	2003	465
171 2/8	179	27 2/8	27 1/8	19 4/8	4 4/8	5 5/8	5	5	Juneau Co., WI	Tom Morris	Tom Morris	2004	465
171 2/8	179 2/8	28 2/8	28 2/8	20 4/8	4 6/8	4 5/8	5	5	St. Croix Co., WI	Clinton Schumacher	Clinton Schumacher	2004	465
171 2/8	184	25	25 1/8	21 1/8	5 4/8	5 4/8	5	5	Qu'Appelle River, SK	Evan R.J. Anderson	Evan R.J. Anderson	2005	465
171 2/8	184 4/8	26 5/8	27 2/8	17 3/8	5 1/8	5 2/8	6	6	Wabasha Co., MN	Eric G. Meyer	Eric G. Meyer	2005	465
171 1/8	180 1/8	24 6/8	25 6/8	25 4/8	5 2/8	5 2/8	6	8	White Co., IL	John McQueen	John McQueen	2002	473
171 1/8	177 3/8	26 5/8	25 4/8	21 3/8	4 7/8	4 7/8	5	7	Hopkins Co., KY	Jeremy A. Benson	Jeremy A. Benson	2003	473
171 1/8	191 7/8	30 5/8	27	22	5 4/8	5 2/8	7	6	Warren Co., IA	Mark Hunter	Mark Hunter	2003	473
171 1/8	186 4/8	28	28 6/8	24 6/8	5 2/8	5 1/8	6	6	Sauk Co., WI	Paul R. Voss	Paul R. Voss	2003	473
171 1/8	179 3/8	24 7/8	27 7/8	19 5/8	5	4 7/8	6	5	Porcupine Plain, SK	Robert Helland	Robert Helland	2004	473

WHITETAIL DEER - TYPICAL ANTLERS

Odocoileus virginianus virginianus and certain related subspecies

Final Score	Gross Score	Length of Main Beam R.	L.	Inside Spread	Circumference at Smallest Place Between Burr & First Point R.	L.	Number of Points R.	L.	Locality	Hunter	Owner	Date Killed	Rank
171 1/8	174 7/8	26 2/8	26 2/8	21 1/8	5 1/8	5 2/8	5	5	Montgomery Co., IL	Aaron R. Moore	Aaron R. Moore	2004	473
171 1/8	178 2/8	24 4/8	25 2/8	20 7/8	5 2/8	5 3/8	5	5	Menard Co., IL	Mike G. Staggs	Mike G. Staggs	2004	473
171 1/8	175 5/8	25	24 6/8	18 3/8	4 4/8	4 6/8	5	5	Outagamie Co., WI	Richard J. VerKuilen	Richard J. VerKuilen	2004	473
171 1/8	200	26 7/8	26 7/8	18 7/8	4 7/8	4 7/8	7	6	Dunn Co., WI	Israel A. Neumann	Israel A. Neumann	2005	473
171	179 6/8	23 4/8	23 3/8	15 7/8	5 5/8	5 6/8	7	7	Clay Co., IN	Daniel J. Corsaro	Daniel J. Corsaro	2003	482
171	182 1/8	26 2/8	26 6/8	19 6/8	4 7/8	5 2/8	6	6	Gregory Co., SD	James T. Thead	James T. Thead	2003	482
171	195 6/8	25 5/8	26 1/8	17 4/8	4 5/8	4 6/8	7	9	Allamakee Co., IA	Picked Up	Rodney W. Olson	2004	482
171	175	24 6/8	24 4/8	18 2/8	4 2/8	4 2/8	6	6	Fillmore Co., MN	Enos E. Hershberger	Enos E. Hershberger	2005	482
171	178 7/8	25 2/8	25 3/8	20	5 2/8	5	6	5	Edwards Co., IL	Jerry J. McVaigh	Jerry J. McVaigh	2005	482
171	177 4/8	26 6/8	26	23	4 6/8	4 6/8	6	5	Jim Hogg Co., TX	Harry C. Weil	Harry C. Weil	2005	482
170 7/8	177	27 5/8	27 5/8	21 4/8	4 4/8	4 5/8	5	6	Lorain Co., OH	Picked Up	Patrick J. Ives	2002	488
170 7/8	177 4/8	29 2/8	28 7/8	23 3/8	4 6/8	4 6/8	5	6	Trumbull Co., OH	Brady A. Riemenschneider	Brady A. Riemenschneider	2003	488
170 7/8	176 2/8	26 1/8	24 7/8	18 5/8	5 1/8	5 2/8	5	5	Highland Co., OH	Gerald A. Stewart	Gerald A. Stewart	2003	488
170 7/8	198 5/8	27 7/8	27 4/8	18 7/8	5	4 7/8	6	8	Hancock Co., IL	Jason B. Eland	Jason B. Eland	2004	488
170 7/8	178 6/8	26 1/8	27 2/8	16 5/8	4 6/8	5 1/8	5	6	Christian Co., KY	Jay R. Lee	Jay R. Lee	2004	488
170 7/8	179 1/8	27	26 5/8	18 3/8	4 7/8	4 4/8	5	5	Halifax Co., VA	Carl W. Younger	Carl W. Younger	2004	488
170 6/8	177 4/8	25 7/8	25 1/8	20	5 3/8	5 1/8	6	6	Morrison Co., MN	Robert A. Durant	Robert A. Durant	2003	494
170 6/8	180	25 7/8	25 5/8	19 1/8	5 2/8	5 3/8	7	7	Jones Co., IA	Mark Stahlberg	Mark Stahlberg	2003	494
170 6/8	178	25 2/8	26 2/8	22 1/8	4 6/8	4 6/8	6	5	Okmulgee Co., OK	Mike Throneberry	Mike Throneberry	2003	494
170 6/8	174 6/8	25 2/8	25 2/8	20 2/8	5 3/8	5 2/8	5	6	Fulton Co., IL	Michael C. Vaka	Michael C. Vaka	2003	494
170 6/8	176 1/8	27 2/8	25 7/8	23 6/8	5	5 4/8	5	5	Coshocton Co., OH	Steve T. Keirns	Steve T. Keirns	2004	494
170 6/8	181 7/8	28 4/8	28 6/8	19 2/8	4	3 7/8	6	6	Tipton Co., TN	Charles S. Treadwell III	Charles S. Treadwell III	2004	494
170 6/8	184 6/8	26 3/8	25 2/8	18 6/8	5 2/8	5 2/8	5	6	Paddle River, AB	Daryl L. Yagos	Daryl L. Yagos	2004	494
170 6/8	185 3/8	25 2/8	24	23 2/8	5	5 6/8	7	7	Waldsea Lake, SK	David R. Engele	David R. Engele	2005	494
170 6/8	175 1/8	27 2/8	26 5/8	20	4 5/8	4 6/8	5	5	Houston Co., MN	Picked Up	Doug A. Sanders	2005	494
170 5/8	176 2/8	25 5/8	25 3/8	19 7/8	6	6 2/8	5	5	Antelope Co., NE	Harlan D. Brandt	Harlan D. Brandt	1975	503
170 5/8	188	23	25	19 7/8	5 4/8	5 5/8	7	7	Dubuque Co., IA	Michael E. Culbertson	Michael E. Culbertson	2003	503
170 5/8	178 5/8	25 6/8	25 7/8	19 1/8	5 1/8	5 2/8	6	6	Hamilton Co., KS	Garry E. Fry	Garry E. Fry	2003	503
170 5/8	179	25 5/8	26	17 5/8	5 3/8	5 3/8	5	6	Walworth Co., WI	Jeff Hynous	Jeff Hynous	2003	503
170 5/8	188 1/8	27	26 4/8	20 1/8	6 1/8	5 7/8	6	6	Knox Co., MO	Bill A. Hamilton	Bill A. Hamilton	2004	503
170 5/8	178 3/8	27 7/8	27 6/8	18 4/8	5 6/8	5 3/8	6	5	Trempealeau Co., WI	Gregory Korpal	Gregory Korpal	2004	503
170 5/8	180	25 5/8	25 5/8	18 7/8	5 3/8	4 3/8	7	8	Maverick Co., TX	Larry J. Seydler	Larry J. Seydler	2004	503

Score	Gross Score	R. Main Beam	L. Main Beam	Inside Spread	R. Circ.	L. Circ.	R. Pts.	L. Pts.	Locality	By Whom Taken	Owner	Date	Page
170 5/8	176 5/8	25 2/8	25 4/8	20	5	4 6/8	5	6	Pine Co., MN	Gregory R. Kvasnicka	Gregory R. Kvasnicka	2005	503
170 4/8	172 2/8	25 4/8	25 4/8	18 6/8	4 3/8	4 2/8	5	5	Portage Co., OH	Daniel W. Kiser	Daniel W. Kiser	2003	511
170 4/8	177 7/8	25 1/8	22 5/8	19 2/8	4 5/8	4 6/8	6	5	Pennington Co., SD	Tom L. Kruger	Tom L. Kruger	2003	511
170 4/8	175 4/8	22 7/8	24 7/8	19	4 3/8	4 5/8	5	5	Carrot River, SK	Brent Freedman	Brent Freedman	2005	511
170 4/8	174 1/8	25 3/8	25	17 6/8	4	4 1/8	6	6	Lawrence Co., IN	Kevin W. Stailey	Kevin W. Stailey	2005	511
170 4/8	177 5/8	26 7/8	27 2/8	19 2/8	5 3/8	5 2/8	6	6	Mississippi Lake, ON	John G. Vanslette	John G. Vanslette	2005	511
170 3/8	181 5/8	26 5/8	26 1/8	22 5/8	4 6/8	4 4/8	5	5	Sorefoot Creek, SK	Steve Chaney	Willowbrook Wildlife Federation	1987	516
170 3/8	180 7/8	24	23 4/8	20 2/8	4 5/8	4 4/8	6	6	Sangamon Co., IL	Mike H. Shields	Mike H. Shields	2001	516
170 3/8	181 1/8	26 5/8	26 7/8	21 6/8	4 6/8	4 7/8	6	5	Lawrence Co., IN	Picked Up	William D. Hackney	2002	516
170 3/8	179 6/8	26 6/8	25 2/8	19 3/8	4 6/8	4 7/8	6	5	Benton Co., MO	Gary E. Brandes	Gary E. Brandes	2003	516
170 3/8	186 4/8	27 6/8	27 7/8	19 2/8	5 3/8	5 3/8	7	7	Cavalier Co., ND	Guy A. Johnson	Guy A. Johnson	2003	516
170 3/8	178 3/8	25 1/8	26 1/8	21 5/8	4 5/8	4 3/8	7	6	Grundy Co., IL	Matt W. Krull	Matt W. Krull	2003	516
170 3/8	173	24 6/8	24 5/8	21 1/8	5 1/8	5 2/8	6	5	McHenry Co., ND	Dan Leier	Dan Leier	2003	516
170 3/8	201 1/8	26 7/8	26 3/8	24 5/8	5 7/8	6	9	9	Otter Tail Co., MN	Merlyn D. Lokken	Merlyn D. Lokken	2003	516
170 3/8	173 5/8	28	26 3/8	19 3/8	4 1/8	4 1/8	5	5	Hancock Co., GA	Gary McMahan	Gary McMahan	2003	516
170 3/8	172 7/8	24 2/8	27 4/8	17 3/8	4 3/8	4 3/8	5	5	Oliver Co., ND	Mark A. Ogden	Mark A. Ogden	2003	516
170 3/8	184 1/8	25 5/8	24 4/8	23 3/8	4 3/8	5	6	6	La Salle Co., TX	Rene R. Barrientos	Rene R. Barrientos	2005	516
170 3/8	184 1/8	24 4/8	25	20 5/8	5 2/8	5 6/8	6	5	Fond du Lac Co., WI	Andrew M. Leonard	Andrew M. Leonard	2005	516
170 3/8	172 5/8	25 1/8	25 5/8	18 2/8	5 7/8	5 6/8	6	6	Stanley Co., SD	Mark D. Nuessle	Mark D. Nuessle	2005	516
170 3/8	177 2/8	24 6/8	25	18 1/8	4 4/8	4 3/8	7	6	Chip Lake, AB	Jonathan S. Ostermayer	Jonathan S. Ostermayer	2005	516
170 3/8	191 7/8	25 2/8	25 2/8	19 2/8	5 3/8	5 4/8	6	5	Guthrie Co., IA	Troy C. Sheeder	Troy C. Sheeder	2005	531
170 2/8	178 5/8	25 5/8	25	19 2/8	4 4/8	4 5/8	6	5	Jackson Co., IA	John E. Banowetz	John E. Banowetz	2003	531
170 2/8	181 4/8	26 2/8	27	21 1/8	5	5 1/8	6	6	Maverick Co., TX	Rex Dacus	Rex Dacus	2003	531
170 2/8	191 7/8	26 1/8	26	21	5	5 1/8	8	6	Garland Co., AR	Troy Graves	Troy Graves	2003	531
170 2/8	190 1/8	23 3/8	26	16	4 2/8	4 3/8	7	7	Dunn Co., WI	Les Kuesel	Les Kuesel	2003	531
170 2/8	172 4/8	24 4/8	24 6/8	17	5 2/8	5 3/8	5	5	Qu'Appelle River, SK	Kevin G. Lang	Kevin G. Lang	2003	531
170 2/8	173 6/8	24 3/8	24 6/8	20 4/8	4 6/8	4 5/8	5	5	Hancock Co., IL	Josh B. Gebhardt	Josh B. Gebhardt	2004	531
170 2/8	180	25 4/8	25	18 6/8	4 3/8	4 3/8	6	5	Edgar Co., IL	Joseph T. Hankins	Joseph T. Hankins	2004	531
170 2/8	182	26 1/8	23 6/8	18	4 7/8	4 7/8	6	6	Morrison Co., MN	Joe Kasper	Joe Kasper	2004	531
170 2/8	174	24	26 1/8	20	4 5/8	4 6/8	6	5	Bow River, AB	Gene Parent	Gene Parent	2004	531
170 2/8	184 1/8	26 3/8	25 6/8	16 6/8	5 1/8	5 3/8	7	7	Floyd Co., IN	Christopher C. Miller	Christopher C. Miller	2005	531
170 2/8	188 3/8	27	25 6/8	19 2/8	5 5/8	5 4/8	5	5	Nut Mt., SK	Andrew Murrison	Andrew Murrison	2005	531
170 2/8	179 5/8	27	27 3/8	19 4/8	6 3/8	6 2/8	5	5	Smith Co., TX	Clyde A. Weaver	Clyde A. Weaver	2005	531
170 1/8	177 1/8	26 5/8	27	19 4/8	4 5/8	4 5/8	5	5	Aroostook Co., ME	Kenneth T. Cheesman	Kenneth T. Cheesman	2001	543
170 1/8	187 6/8	27 4/8	27 4/8	20 7/8	4 4/8	4 4/8	7	7	Ross Co., OH	Jimmy J. McCleskey	Jimmy J. McCleskey	2001	543
170 1/8	176 5/8	26 2/8	26 2/8	18 1/8	4 2/8	4 2/8	6	5	Cumberland Co., ME	Thomas E. Dekutoski, Jr.	Thomas E. Dekutoski, Jr.	2003	543
170 1/8	173 3/8	24 5/8	24 4/8	18 1/8	5 3/8	5	5	5	Meigs Co., OH	Herbert C. Ervin	Herbert C. Ervin	2003	543
170 1/8	178 7/8	25 5/8	25 4/8	18 4/8	4 7/8	5 1/8	6	6	Lake of the Woods, ON	Mark Pentney	Mark Pentney	2003	543
170 1/8	195 2/8	23	24 1/8	20 2/8	4 2/8	4 5/8	8	7	Fremont Co., WY	Ben L. Wilkes	Ben L. Wilkes	2003	543
170 1/8	175 2/8	26 7/8	26	20 5/8	4 4/8	4 5/8	6	5	Goodwin Lake, AB	Leonard G. Burt	Leonard G. Burt	2004	543

WHITETAIL DEER - TYPICAL ANTLERS

Odocoileus virginianus virginianus and certain related subspecies

Final Score	Gross Score	Length of Main Beam R.	Length of Main Beam L.	Inside Spread	Circumference at Smallest Place Between Burr & First Point R.	L.	Number of Points R.	L.	Locality	Hunter	Owner	Date Killed	Rank
170 1/8	172 2/8	24 4/8	24	16 7/8	4 7/8	5	5	5	Mecklenburg Co., VA	Chad R. Coley	Chad R. Coley	2004	543
170 1/8	176 3/8	23 3/8	22 7/8	21 1/8	5 1/8	5 1/8	6	5	Emma Lake, SK	Michael L. Devaney	Michael L. Devaney	2004	543
170 1/8	174 6/8	22 4/8	23	20 3/8	5 5/8	5 5/8	6	6	Rock Co., WI	Matt J. Dilley	Matt J. Dilley	2004	543
170 1/8	173 2/8	27 3/8	27	20 7/8	4 7/8	4 6/8	6	5	Delaware Co., IA	Ian Goldsmith	Ian Goldsmith	2004	543
170 1/8	197 6/8	29 2/8	26 5/8	20 6/8	4 7/8	5	6	8	Greene Co., IN	Richard E. House	Richard E. House	2004	543
170 1/8	172 6/8	25 6/8	25 6/8	21 7/8	4 7/8	4 7/8	5	5	Marion Co., IA	Bruce A. Sanburn	Bruce A. Sanburn	2004	543
170 1/8	175 4/8	25 5/8	25 7/8	22 3/8	4 4/8	4 4/8	6	6	Allamakee Co., IA	Rodney A. Schlitter	Rodney A. Schlitter	2004	543
170 1/8	188 3/8	22 6/8	23 4/8	16	5 5/8	5 6/8	7	7	Cass Co., IL	Gregg A. Burrus	Gregg A. Burrus	2005	543
170 1/8	183	27 3/8	26 7/8	21 6/8	5 1/8	5 1/8	6	6	Harper Co., KS	Fred Newton	Fred Newton	2005	543
170 1/8	178 5/8	24 3/8	25	15 6/8	4 5/8	4 6/8	6	6	Souris River, MB	Brett R. Hermanson	Brett R. Hermanson	2006	543
170	175 3/8	26 5/8	25 2/8	23 1/8	4 7/8	4 7/8	6	6	Shelby Co., IL	Robert A. Coonce	Robert A. Coonce	1992	560
170	188 4/8	26 2/8	25 2/8	18 3/8	4 6/8	4 6/8	7	6	Nemaha Co., NE	Shawna A. Bennett	Shawna A. Bennett	2003	560
170	173 5/8	23 1/8	22 7/8	16 2/8	4 3/8	4 3/8	6	6	Duck Mt., SK	Ian D. Fleming	Ian D. Fleming	2003	560
170	172 4/8	24 7/8	25 3/8	16 4/8	5	4 7/8	5	5	Waupaca Co., WI	Richard A. Hedtke	Richard A. Hedtke	2003	560
170	173 4/8	24 4/8	24 4/8	16 2/8	4 1/8	4 1/8	5	5	Stutsman Co., ND	Lee E. Garrett	Lee E. Garrett	2004	560
170	192 6/8	25 4/8	25 5/8	23 6/8	6	6	8	7	Marion Co., KS	Jeremy D. Husong	Jeremy D. Husong	2004	560
170	175 4/8	24 6/8	25 4/8	22 6/8	4 6/8	4 7/8	5	5	Vernon Co., WI	Robert Oliver	Robert Oliver	2004	560
170	185 3/8	28 2/8	25 5/8	21 1/8	4 5/8	4 6/8	6	6	Charles Co., MD	Lawrence C. Parsley	Lawrence C. Parsley	2004	560
170	187 4/8	25 5/8	24	20 4/8	6 1/8	6	5	5	Peoria Co., IL	David B. Voorhees	David B. Voorhees	2005	560
169 7/8	176 7/8	25 4/8	26 1/8	17	4 5/8	4 6/8	5	6	Spencer Co., IN	Brennan Chandler	Brennan Chandler	2004	569
169 6/8	181 6/8	25 5/8	25 2/8	20 5/8	4 3/8	4 2/8	7	6	Medina Co., OH	Sean E. Reusch	Sean E. Reusch	2003	570
169 6/8	184 3/8	27 7/8	27 7/8	21 1/8	5 1/8	4 7/8	7	4	Kent Co., MI	Thomas A. Heald	Thomas A. Heald	2005	570
169 5/8	175 3/8	24 2/8	23 5/8	20 7/8	5	5 1/8	7	5	Miami Co., KS	Charles M. Brink	Charles M. Brink	2001	572
169 5/8	176 2/8	24 6/8	25 1/8	19 1/8	4 3/8	5	5	5	Henry Co., IL	Michael R. Nordstrom	Michael R. Nordstrom	2005	572
169 4/8	177	24 7/8	24 3/8	21	4 7/8	4 7/8	5	5	Vermilion Co., IL	Ronald Huls	Ronald Huls	2003	574
169 4/8	177 5/8	25 7/8	26 3/8	18	3 5/8	3 6/8	6	6	Dougherty Co., GA	Phillip E. Webb	Phillip E. Webb	2004	574
169 3/8	178 1/8	25 2/8	26 4/8	21 1/8	4 4/8	4 5/8	7	6	Jefferson Co., NE	Carol A. Schwisow	Carol A. Schwisow	2004	576
169 3/8	179	25 7/8	26 2/8	17 5/8	5 6/8	5 7/8	5	6	Thayer Co., NE	Brent L. Nelson	Brent L. Nelson	2005	576
169 2/8	184	26 7/8	25 6/8	20 6/8	4 5/8	4 4/8	5	5	Idaho Co., ID	Jeremy L. Badertscher	Jeremy L. Badertscher	1992	578
169 2/8	177 6/8	26 4/8	26 6/8	18 5/8	4 2/8	4 1/8	6	6	Richland Co., WI	Kevin A. Stagman	Kevin A. Stagman	2002	578
169 2/8	172	24	23 1/8	17 6/8	5	5	5	5	Clayton Co., IA	Steven V. Hansel	Steven V. Hansel	2004	578
169 1/8	172 5/8	26 7/8	27	20 1/8	4 3/8	4 2/8	5	5	Dodge Co., GA	Tony D. McCranie	Tony D. McCranie	2005	581
169 1/8	177 4/8	25 7/8	26 1/8	19 5/8	4 7/8	5 4/8	6	6	Nestor Falls, ON	Norman E. Morrison	Norman E. Morrison	2006	581

169	179 3/8	24 2/8	25 3/8	17 4/8	5 2/8	5 1/8	6	5	Seminole Co., OK	Steve P. West	Steve P. West	2003	583
169	184 1/8	28 3/8	27 5/8	18 1/8	4 6/8	4 5/8	4	6	Lafayette Co., WI	Jesse T. Burris	Tom Burris	2004	583
169	171 1/8	23 6/8	23 6/8	17 6/8	5	5 1/8	5	5	Buffalo Co., WI	Ronald J. Jilot	Ronald J. Jilot	2004	583
169	191 6/8	27 2/8	27 2/8	19 3/8	5 5/8	5 7/8	7	7	Van Buren Co., MI	Larry A. Jones	Larry A. Jones	2004	583
169	178 4/8	25	26	20 1/8	5	5	6	5	Clearwater Co., MN	Dennis A. Dicks	Dennis A. Dicks	2005	583
169	187	25 6/8	26 5/8	17 2/8	4 5/8	5	5	6	Dane Co., WI	Benjamin S. Mussehl	Benjamin S. Mussehl	2005	583
168 7/8	173 7/8	26	26 3/8	19 6/8	4 7/8	4 4/8	5	6	Clearwater Co., ID	Arthur H. Baker	Arthur H. Baker	1997	589
168 7/8	172 1/8	23	23	19 1/8	4 6/8	4 5/8	5	5	Greene Co., VA	Dexter A. Eppard	Dexter A. Eppard	2004	589
168 7/8	181 3/8	26 6/8	26 6/8	17 7/8	4 5/8	6 2/8	5	6	Noble Co., OH	Brian D. Ferguson	Brian D. Ferguson	2004	589
168 6/8	173	24 4/8	24 4/8	20 2/8	5 6/8	4 5/8	4	4	Spencer Co., KY	Gene E. Nethery	Gene E. Nethery	1970	592
168 6/8	180 6/8	25 4/8	25 4/8	18 4/8	4 4/8	4 4/8	5	5	Fleming Co., KY	Austin N. Ball	Austin N. Ball	2003	592
168 6/8	171 7/8	26 5/8	26 5/8	18 4/8	4 5/8	4 5/8	4	4	Pike Co., OH	Denver J. McMillion	Denver J. McMillion	2003	592
168 6/8	189 7/8	27 7/8	27 7/8	16 6/8	4 4/8	4 5/8	4	4	Hardin Co., KY	Eddie Miller	Eddie Miller	2003	592
168 6/8	193	27 6/8	27 6/8	22	5 3/8	5 3/8	7	7	Rock Island Co., IL	Rob Mindock	Rob Mindock	2003	592
168 6/8	174 6/8	24 3/8	25 2/8	19	5 1/8	5 3/8	6	5	Pope Co., MN	Nash C. Anderson	Nash C. Anderson	2004	592
168 4/8	176 3/8	24 4/8	24	17 7/8	5	4 7/8	5	5	Taylor Co., IA	Scott R. Groholski	Scott R. Groholski	2003	598
168 4/8	179 6/8	25 3/8	24 1/8	18 7/8	5 1/8	5 1/8	6	7	Allegheny Co., PA	Ronald F. Novak	Ronald F. Novak	2003	598
168 4/8	174 5/8	26 2/8	25 4/8	18	4 7/8	4 7/8	7	6	Hardin Co., KY	Tommy Huff	Tommy Huff	2004	598
168 4/8	176	25 2/8	26	19	4 6/8	4 4/8	5	6	Chester Co., PA	Jack A. Horosky	Jack A. Horosky	2005	598
168 3/8	173 4/8	26 3/8	26 3/8	20 3/8	4 5/8	4 3/8	5	6	Buffalo Co., WI	Shawn Dupee	Shawn Dupee	2003	602
168 3/8	174 1/8	26 2/8	25 3/8	20 1/8	4 4/8	4 3/8	5	5	Adams Co., OH	Jeff R. Osborne	Jeff R. Osborne	2003	602
168 3/8	198	24 2/8	24 2/8	16 4/8	4 4/8	4 6/8	5	5	Fairfield Co., OH	Kirk H. Smith	Kirk H. Smith	2003	602
168 3/8	171 2/8	27	26 5/8	19 7/8	4 7/8	4 5/8	7	7	Grant Co., WI	Kurt M. Haines	Kurt M. Haines	2004	602
168 3/8	174 1/8	25 4/8	25 2/8	17 3/8	4 3/8	4 4/8	5	6	Jefferson Co., KY	Christopher C. Parrott	Christopher C. Parrott	2004	602
168 3/8	173 2/8	25 1/8	26 1/8	19 3/8	4 2/8	4 3/8	5	5	Harding Co., SD	Brian S. Cook	Brian S. Cook	2005	602
168 3/8	179 4/8	25 2/8	25 2/8	18 1/8	4 5/8	4 2/8	5	6	Talbot Co., MD	J. Richard Jablin	J. Richard Jablin	2005	602
168 2/8	173 6/8	26 3/8	25 6/8	17 6/8	4 4/8	4 6/8	6	6	Pepin Co., WI	Tim Stajkowski	Tim Stajkowski	2004	609
168 2/8	172 1/8	24 5/8	23 7/8	19	4 5/8	4 4/8	5	6	Polk Co., WI	Kyle Louis	Kyle Louis	2005	609
168 1/8	178 6/8	24 4/8	24	18 3/8	4 6/8	4 5/8	7	5	Logan Co., KY	William S. McCarley II	William S. McCarley II	1995	611
168 1/8	184 5/8	23 3/8	24 2/8	18 7/8	5 2/8	4 6/8	6	6	Sauk Co., WI	David M. Greene	David M. Greene	2003	611
168 1/8	180 7/8	27	25 6/8	18 7/8	4 6/8	5 3/8	8	6	Vigo Co., IN	Jonathan F. Pounds	Jonathan F. Pounds	2003	611
168 1/8	180 5/8	27 5/8	27 7/8	18 7/8	5 6/8	4 4/8	5	5	Fayette Co., KY	Benjamin S. Ramsey	Benjamin S. Ramsey	2003	611
168 1/8	182	25 6/8	27 1/8	16 1/8	5 1/8	4 4/8	5	5	Adams Co., IN	Chad Sprunger	Chad Sprunger	2003	611
168	174 2/8	27 7/8	26	24	4 3/8	5 6/8	5	6	Geauga Co., OH	Steven J. Dillworth	Steven J. Dillworth	2003	616
168	183 3/8	25 1/8	22 7/8	22 7/8	5 2/8	5 1/8	6	5	Hollow Lake, AB	Tadeusz J. Kaczynski	Tadeusz J. Kaczynski	2004	616
168	186 7/8	26	25 2/8	16 2/8	5 2/8	4 5/8	7	7	Edmonson Co., KY	Jason Massey	Jason Massey	2004	616
168	177 6/8	23 2/8	20 4/8	20 4/8	4 3/8	4 6/8	7	6	Muhlenberg Co., KY	Tim W. McCoy	Tim W. McCoy	2004	616
168	178 6/8	27 2/8	22 2/8	22 2/8	4 4/8	4 4/8	6	5	Macoupin Co., IL	Thomas L. Hill	Thomas L. Hill	2005	616
168	181 6/8	26 3/8	23 7/8	23 7/8	5 7/8	4 4/8	6	5	Qu'Appelle River, SK	Chris Repski	Chris Repski	2005	616
168	170 3/8	26 1/8	26	17 4/8	5 3/8	5 3/8	4	4	Strawberry Lakes, SK	Christopher Thompson	Christopher Thompson	2005	616
167 6/8	176 4/8	24 5/8	25 5/8	17 6/8	5 3/8	5 5/8	5	6	Shelby Co., IL	Eugene D. Wooters	Eugene D. Wooters	2005	616
167 6/8	173 4/8	24 7/8	25 1/8	17	4 2/8	3 7/8	6	6	Carter Co., MO	Linda J. Taylor	Linda J. Taylor	2003	624

WHITETAIL DEER - TYPICAL ANTLERS

Odocoileus virginianus virginianus and certain related subspecies

Final Score	Gross Score	Length of Main Beam R.	L.	Inside Spread	Circumference at Smallest Place Between Burr & First Point R.	L.	Number of Points R.	L.	Locality	Hunter	Owner	Date Killed	Rank
167 6/8	175 3/8	24 7/8	25 6/8	18 2/8	5 1/8	4 7/8	6	5	Oconto Co., WI	Adam Firgens	Adam Firgens	2004	624
167 5/8	171 1/8	26 5/8	26 3/8	22 5/8	4 7/8	5	5	5	Lawrence Co., IN	Charles R. George	Charles R. George	1989	626
167 5/8	172 7/8	23 7/8	24 5/8	17 7/8	4 1/8	4 2/8	6	6	Iowa Co., IA	Matthew J. Brunssen	Matthew J. Brunssen	2003	626
167 5/8	188 2/8	26	25 5/8	17 6/8	5 4/8	5 4/8	7	6	Webster Co., NE	Scott A. Olsen	Scott A. Olsen	2003	626
167 5/8	178 6/8	24 6/8	25 4/8	18 2/8	4 3/8	4 3/8	8	6	Coahuila, MX	Jimmy Watson	Jimmy Watson	2003	626
167 5/8	171 2/8	24 7/8	25	18 3/8	5 2/8	5 1/8	6	6	Trigg Co., KY	James L. Bayer, Jr.	James L. Bayer, Jr.	2004	626
167 5/8	187 2/8	26	25 4/8	19 5/8	5	5 2/8	6	5	Crooked Lake, SK	Stuart V. Cairns	Stuart V. Cairns	2004	626
167 5/8	188 7/8	25 3/8	26 1/8	19 3/8	4 7/8	4 6/8	6	8	Adams Co., IL	Matthew W. Hinkamper	Matthew W. Hinkamper	2004	626
167 5/8	179 7/8	28 6/8	28 2/8	23 6/8	4 3/8	4 2/8	5	6	Wicomico Co., MD	John Heaphy	John Heaphy	2005	626
167 4/8	176 7/8	23	23 1/8	16 6/8	4 2/8	4 2/8	7	6	Brooks Co., TX	John R. Rea	John R. Rea	2004	634
167 3/8	172	29	27 4/8	23 1/8	5 1/8	5 2/8	5	5	Dore Lake, SK	Robert L. Allen	Robert L. Allen	2003	635
167 3/8	184 4/8	26 2/8	24 1/8	21	4 7/8	4 7/8	7	7	Dunn Co., WI	Jeff Lake	Jeff Lake	2003	635
167 3/8	187 4/8	26 5/8	27	21	5 3/8	5 3/8	7	5	McLean Co., IL	Michael Slown	Michael Slown	2003	635
167 3/8	178 5/8	24 6/8	24 4/8	20 1/8	5 4/8	5 2/8	5	6	Union Co., NM	Bret Dillon	B. Dillon, D. Dillon, & D. Lettis	2004	635
167 3/8	172 5/8	30 3/8	31 2/8	20 3/8	5	5	4	5	Ohio Co., KY	Jeremy Allen	Jeremy Allen	2005	635
167 3/8	171 7/8	27 1/8	26 7/8	22 3/8	4 6/8	4 5/8	5	4	Buffalo Co., WI	Kyle A. Danzinger	Kyle A. Danzinger	2005	635
167 3/8	169 2/8	27 1/8	28	20 5/8	4 1/8	4 1/8	5	5	Washington Co., KS	Brian W. McCoy	Brian W. McCoy	2005	635
167 3/8	174 4/8	24 6/8	24 5/8	18 7/8	4 4/8	4 4/8	6	7	Richland Co., WI	Ron W. Wontor	Ron W. Wontor	2005	643
167 2/8	181 5/8	24 3/8	24 5/8	17	5 2/8	5 1/8	5	6	Jersey Co., IL	Antonio E. Malone	Antonio E. Malone	2003	643
167 2/8	174 2/8	25 3/8	23 7/8	20 4/8	5 3/8	5 4/8	6	5	Kiskatinaw River, BC	Craig Bahm	Craig Bahm	2004	643
167 2/8	196 2/8	26 4/8	27 3/8	19	4 4/8	4 4/8	6	9	Marshall Co., IN	Peggy Gantz	Peggy Gantz	2004	643
167 2/8	181 5/8	29 2/8	28 2/8	22 6/8	5 4/8	5 3/8	6	7	Ashtabula Co., OH	Mark R. Johnson	Mark R. Johnson	2004	643
167 2/8	180 3/8	27 2/8	26	25 2/8	5 1/8	5 1/8	5	6	Brown Co., IL	John Steele	John Steele	2004	643
167 2/8	181 3/8	23	23 6/8	21 7/8	4 4/8	4 4/8	7	6	Edwards Co., IL	James M. Baker	James M. Baker	2005	643
167 2/8	182 7/8	25 1/8	24 4/8	21 5/8	4 5/8	4 7/8	5	6	Gasconade Co., MO	Aaron Coen	Aaron Coen	2005	643
167 2/8	189 1/8	23 5/8	23	18	5 4/8	5 4/8	7	8	Le Flore Co., OK	Robert D. Keylon	Robert D. Keylon	2005	643
167 2/8	173 2/8	26 4/8	26 5/8	16 2/8	4 6/8	4 6/8	5	5	Elk Co., KS	Steve A. Webb, Jr.	Steve A. Webb, Jr.	2005	643
167 1/8	173 5/8	23 7/8	22 2/8	19 7/8	5 3/8	5 3/8	5	5	Big River, SK	Picked Up	Donald E. Avers	2000	652
167 1/8	176 4/8	25 4/8	25 6/8	20	4 1/8	4 1/8	7	5	Coos Co., NH	Gerard J. Perreault	Gerard J. Perreault	2003	652
167 1/8	176 1/8	27 3/8	25 4/8	18 5/8	4 4/8	4 4/8	6	5	Dooly Co., GA	Jeff Caswell	Jeff Caswell	2004	652
167 1/8	182 6/8	25 4/8	25 4/8	26 7/8	5 1/8	5 2/8	7	6	Pike Co., MO	Bobby G. Garner	Bobby G. Garner	2004	652
167 1/8	174 5/8	29	29	20 5/8	5 1/8	5	5	5	Houston Co., MN	Jeff J. Novak	Jeff J. Novak	2004	652

Score							Points		Location	Hunter	Owner	Date	No.
167 1/8	185 3/8	24 4/8	25	20 3/8	5 2/8	4 7/8	7	6	Jefferson Co., OH	Jeffrey T. Shimon	Jeffrey T. Shimon	2004	652
167 1/8	173 2/8	26 1/8	25 5/8	20 4/8	4 4/8	4 3/8	6	5	Cattaraugus Co., NY	Mitchell S. Baxter	Mitchell S. Baxter	2005	652
167 1/8	189 6/8	26 3/8	29 3/8	22	5 7/8	5 5/8	7	5	Sauk Co., WI	Bradley T. Breunig	Bradley T. Breunig	2005	652
167 1/8	170 6/8	24 2/8	25 7/8	16 3/8	4 5/8	5	5	5	Mission Lake, SK	James Kelly	James Kelly	2005	652
167 1/8	192 6/8	25 4/8	25	19 6/8	5 1/8	5	6	6	Okanagan Lake, BC	Dianne Schilling	Dianne Schilling	2005	652
167	172 4/8	25 3/8	25	19 6/8	5 1/8	5	5	5	La Porte Co., IN	Earl H. Ward	Earl H. Ward	1989	662
167	178 6/8	26	25 1/8	18 1/8	4 4/8	4 4/8	7	7	Christian Co., IL	Luigi Belcastro	Luigi Belcastro	2003	662
167	188	28 3/8	26 1/8	17 5/8	4 5/8	4 7/8	7	8	Jackson Co., IA	Marvin Good	Marvin Good	2003	662
167	172 5/8	27 2/8	25 5/8	19 6/8	4	4	5	5	Allegan Co., MI	Kevin R. Leith	Kevin R. Leith	2003	662
167	178 1/8	25	24 3/8	20	5 2/8	5 2/8	5	5	Issaquena Co., MS	William C. McGee, Jr.	William C. McGee, Jr.	2003	662
167	186 3/8	27 2/8	27	22 5/8	5 4/8	5 3/8	6	7	Buffalo Co., WI	Justin W. Poehnelt	Justin W. Poehnelt	2003	662
167	188 7/8	27 2/8	26 2/8	17 3/8	4 4/8	4 5/8	7	7	Lawrence Co., IN	Jeff Ralph	Jeff Ralph	2003	662
167	172 1/8	24 4/8	24 1/8	19	4 7/8	5	5	5	Metcalfe Co., KY	A. Leroy Smith	A. Leroy Smith	2003	662
167	190 4/8	27 1/8	26 4/8	18 1/8	5 4/8	4 7/8	7	5	Hamilton Co., OH	Gregory W. Morgan	Gregory W. Morgan	2004	662
167	176 7/8	27 4/8	26 4/8	18 2/8	4 5/8	4 2/8	7	6	Bleckley Co., GA	Chad Peterson	Chad Peterson	2004	662
166 7/8	187 1/8	25 5/8	25 4/8	20 3/8	5 6/8	5 6/8	7	6	Carroll Co., OH	Todd S. Brooks	Todd S. Brooks	2001	672
166 7/8	173 3/8	24 1/8	23 5/8	17 5/8	4 7/8	5	6	6	Pierce Co., WI	Sheldon Johnson	Sheldon Johnson	2001	672
166 7/8	173 4/8	25 1/8	24 2/8	18 7/8	4 7/8	5 1/8	6	6	Owen Co., IN	J.C. Linville	J.C. Linville	2004	672
166 7/8	197 4/8	28 1/8	29	23 5/8	6 3/8	6 2/8	7	7	Livingston Co., IL	Joseph M. Wolf	Joseph M. Wolf	2005	672
166 6/8	178 3/8	26 4/8	26 4/8	21 4/8	4 4/8	4 4/8	6	6	La Crosse Co., WI	Barbara E. Hale	Sean P. Hale	2003	676
166 6/8	172 3/8	27	25 7/8	15 2/8	4 5/8	4 4/8	5	5	Crittenden Co., KY	Jared L. Belt	Jared L. Belt	2004	676

TYPICAL WHITETAIL DEER
FINAL SCORE: 162-1/8
HUNTER: Sam Fett

TYPICAL WHITETAIL DEER
FINAL SCORE: 163-3/8
HUNTER: Mark S. Rader

TYPICAL WHITETAIL DEER
FINAL SCORE: 196-6/8*
HUNTER: Justin L. Metzner

TYPICAL WHITETAIL DEER
FINAL SCORE: 182-1/8
HUNTER: Jeff Jordan

WHITETAIL DEER - TYPICAL ANTLERS

Odocoileus virginianus virginianus and certain related subspecies

Final Score	Gross Score	Length of Main Beam R.	L.	Inside Spread	Circumference at Smallest Place Between Burr & First Point R.	L.	Number of Points R.	L.	Locality	Hunter	Owner	Date Killed	Rank
166 6/8	171 6/8	26 1/8	25 1/8	16 2/8	4 7/8	4 7/8	5	6	Kandiyohi Co., MN	Wade H. Johnson	Wade H. Johnson	2004	676
166 6/8	169 3/8	23 6/8	23 6/8	17 6/8	5 2/8	5 3/8	5	5	Park Co., MT	Ben Webb	Ben Webb	2004	676
166 6/8	194	25	25 4/8	20 7/8	5 2/8	4 7/8	8	6	Fulton Co., IL	Ryan M. Elenbaas	Ryan M. Elenbaas	2005	676
166 6/8	170	25 6/8	26 1/8	21 6/8	4 2/8	4 2/8	5	5	Noble Co., IN	Jason Lutter	Jason Lutter	2005	676
166 6/8	182 7/8	24 6/8	25 6/8	18 6/8	6 3/8	6 1/8	6	5	Union Co., IL	Michael E. Newell, Jr.	Michael E. Newell, Jr.	2005	676
166 6/8	174 3/8	27 6/8	28 1/8	20 4/8	4 7/8	5	4	4	Mercer Co., IL	Roger D. Secymore	Roger D. Secymore	2005	676
166 5/8	170 7/8	28 1/8	26 6/8	23 5/8	5 2/8	5 1/8	4	4	Jackson Co., IA	Robert E. Henning	Robert E. Henning	1974	684
166 5/8	173	24 7/8	24 4/8	16 6/8	4 6/8	4 6/8	6	7	Adams Co., IL	Ray Madison	Ray Madison	1999	684
166 5/8	169 7/8	22 5/8	22 6/8	19 1/8	5 1/8	5 1/8	5	5	Franklin Co., IL	Scott A. Carr	Scott A. Carr	2004	684
166 4/8	179 3/8	23 4/8	24	17 4/8	5 5/8	5 1/8	5	5	Daviess Co., MO	Raymond Harves	Raymond Harves	1995	687
166 4/8	181 4/8	24 6/8	24 2/8	17 6/8	5 1/8	5	6	6	Good Spirit Lake, SK	Grant Frederickson	Grant Frederickson	2003	687
166 4/8	172 1/8	22 3/8	23	18	5 3/8	5 5/8	7	6	Olmsted Co., MN	Brian P. Schmoll	Brian P. Schmoll	2003	687
166 4/8	171 6/8	26 5/8	26 3/8	17 6/8	4 6/8	4 7/8	5	5	Yazoo Co., MS	Randy Taylor	Randy Taylor	2003	687
166 4/8	181 1/8	25 7/8	26	19 2/8	4 3/8	4 4/8	5	7	Putnam Co., MO	Neil E. Lowe	Neil E. Lowe	2004	687
166 4/8	194	21 7/8	22 1/8	16 6/8	4 2/8	4 3/8	7	8	Maverick Co., TX	Michael F. Biry	Michael F. Biry	2005	687
166 4/8	171	24 4/8	24 6/8	17 6/8	5 2/8	5 3/8	5	5	Hamilton Co., IL	Todd Oliver	Todd Oliver	2005	687
166 4/8	195 5/8	24 2/8	23 4/8	17 6/8	5	5 1/8	10	5	Neosho Co., KS	John A. Yarber	John A. Yarber	2005	687
166 3/8	179 3/8	22 7/8	22 5/8	15 7/8	4 2/8	4 2/8	6	7	Chautauqua Co., KS	James M. Stevens	James M. Stevens	2002	695
166 3/8	170 7/8	24 1/8	24 3/8	16 7/8	4 6/8	4 7/8	6	6	Rock Co., WI	Jamie L. Eldred	Jamie L. Eldred	2004	695
166 3/8	170 2/8	25 2/8	26 1/8	21 5/8	5 1/8	5 2/8	5	5	Dodge Co., WI	Ted J. Gorgan	Ted J. Gorgan	2005	695
166 2/8	177 1/8	27	26	19 1/8	5 5/8	5 6/8	5	5	Knox Co., IN	Sean McCarty	Sean McCarty	2000	698
166 2/8	172 3/8	27 7/8	27 2/8	21 2/8	4 7/8	5	5	5	Waupaca Co., WI	Russell E. Olson	Russell E. Olson	2000	698
166 2/8	172	24 2/8	24 6/8	19 4/8	4 6/8	4 7/8	5	5	Waupaca Co., WI	Bruce Learman	Bruce Learman	2004	698
166 2/8	171 4/8	26 1/8	26 5/8	24 2/8	5 4/8	5 4/8	5	5	Jefferson Co., IA	Andrew Rogers	Andrew Rogers	2004	698
166 2/8	170 4/8	25 1/8	25 7/8	18 2/8	5 2/8	5 3/8	5	5	Hubbard Co., MN	Christopher M. Haley	Christopher M. Haley	2005	698
166 1/8	176 7/8	25 5/8	25 1/8	18 7/8	5 4/8	5 4/8	6	6	Hamlin Co., SD	Bohn L. Peterson	Bohn L. Peterson	1967	703
166 1/8	171 1/8	25 7/8	26 1/8	17 1/8	4 4/8	4 2/8	6	6	Carroll Co., KY	Roger Ogburn	Roger Ogburn	1988	703
166 1/8	175 4/8	26 2/8	25 4/8	19 2/8	4 7/8	5 1/8	6	6	Randolph Co., IL	J.L. Hargis	J.L. Hargis	1991	703
166 1/8	168 7/8	25 5/8	25 5/8	18 5/8	4 5/8	4 3/8	5	5	Harrison Co., KY	Julie Fryman	Julie Fryman	2002	703
166 1/8	173	24 4/8	24	16 2/8	4 2/8	4 2/8	6	6	Prairie Co., MT	Charles V. Long, Jr.	Charles V. Long, Jr.	2003	703
166 1/8	174 4/8	23 6/8	23 2/8	19 2/8	5 6/8	6	6	6	Van Buren Co., IA	Michael S. Mahurin	Michael S. Mahurin	2003	703
166 1/8	175 1/8	23 4/8	24 6/8	19 7/8	4 2/8	4 2/8	6	6	Wilbarger Co., TX	Bonnie Jean Thomas	Bonnie Jean Thomas	2004	703
166 1/8	169 5/8	24 4/8	24	18 1/8	5 1/8	5 1/8	6	6	Livingston Co., MO	Ramey B. Webb	Ramey B. Webb	2004	703

The two small film-strip/photo icons appear in the top margin over two of the columns.

Score	Gross Score	R. Main Beam	L. Main Beam	Inside Spread	R. Circ.	L. Circ.	R. Pts.	L. Pts.	Locality	Hunter	Owner	Date	Page
166 1/8	195 5/8	26 6/8	26 5/8	19 3/8	5 6/8	6	6	5	Edgar Co., IL	Robert F. Calvert	Robert F. Calvert	2005	703
166	172 2/8	24 6/8	23 4/8	18	6 1/8	6 2/8	5	5	Union Co., IA	Patrick Alexander, Jr.	Patrick Alexander, Jr.	2002	712
166	182 6/8	27 5/8	28 3/8	21	4 6/8	4 5/8	5	8	Winona Co., MN	Brendan P. Christenson	Brendan P. Christenson	2003	712
166	171 6/8	24 2/8	23 7/8	18 4/8	5 1/8	5	6	5	Turtle Lake, SK	Walter S. McDonald	Walter S. McDonald	2003	712
166	174 1/8	27 5/8	28 1/8	18 2/8	4 6/8	4 6/8	6	5	Montgomery Co., TN	David L. Reece	David L. Reece	2004	712
166	190 3/8	26 6/8	26 6/8	19 4/8	5 5/8	5 4/8	8	8	Stearns Co., MN	Steven A. Ritter	Steven A. Ritter	2005	712
166	167 7/8	26 5/8	26 3/8	17 6/8	4 3/8	4 4/8	5	5	Fulton Co., NY	Mark A. Young, Sr.	Mark A. Young, Sr.	2005	712
165 7/8	170 1/8	27 7/8	27	21 7/8	4 7/8	4 6/8	4	4	Dane Co., WI	Duane R. Johnson	Duane R. Johnson	2003	718
165 7/8	173 4/8	22	22 7/8	17	5	5	7	7	Osage Co., OK	Terry L. Peckham-LaVier	Terry L. Peckham-LaVier	2003	718
165 7/8	174	26 6/8	24 6/8	19 1/8	5 4/8	5 4/8	5	5	Aroostook Co., ME	Michel Paillard	Michel Paillard	2004	718
165 7/8	173 7/8	27 7/8	26 7/8	21 5/8	5 1/8	5 2/8	6	6	Barren Co., KY	Ronnie Garmon	Ronnie Garmon	2005	718
165 6/8	176 1/8	24 4/8	24 2/8	17	4 6/8	4 4/8	5	5	Calhoun Co., IL	Tim P. Friedel	Tim P. Friedel	2003	722
165 6/8	170 7/8	25	23 3/8	20	5 6/8	5 5/8	5	5	Schuyler Co., IL	Mark A. Edwards	Mark A. Edwards	2004	722
165 6/8	171 1/8	24 5/8	24	17	5 2/8	5 4/8	6	6	Harrison Co., IN	Curtis L. Bussabarger	Curtis L. Bussabarger	2005	722
165 6/8	181 7/8	25 1/8	24 3/8	20 3/8	5 4/8	5 4/8	7	7	Medina Co., OH	Timothy L. Copperman	Timothy L. Copperman	2005	722
165 6/8	178 2/8	27	26 4/8	23 1/8	5 1/8	5 1/8	6	6	Dauphin Co., PA	Scott A. Cisney	Scott A. Cisney	2005	726
165 5/8	179 1/8	24 4/8	24 4/8	20 6/8	6	6	7	7	Pratt Co., KS	Kent L. Goyen	Kent L. Goyen	2005	726
165 5/8	168 6/8	26 6/8	26 1/8	19 6/8	4 4/8	4 4/8	5	5	Buffalo Co., WI	Mike Kilness	Mike Kilness	2003	728
165 5/8	179	25 1/8	26 3/8	22 6/8	5 5/8	5 3/8	6	6	Summit Co., OH	Gregory Maczko	Gregory Maczko	2004	728
165 5/8	172 7/8	27 7/8	24 7/8	19 7/8	5 6/8	5 4/8	5	5	Trigg Co., KY	Mike E. Thomas	Mike E. Thomas	2004	728
165 4/8	169 1/8	24 3/8	29 1/8	20 6/8	5 1/8	5	5	5	Lincoln Co., CO	Quentin R. Smith	Quentin R. Smith	2006	728
165 4/8	170 1/8	26 5/8	24	17 7/8	5 3/8	5 3/8	6	6	Oconto Co., WI	Ronald Thomson	Ronald Thomson	1998	732
165 4/8	175 5/8	24 6/8	25 6/8	18 2/8	5	5	6	5	Buffalo Co., WI	Jeff Brunn	Jeff Brunn	2003	732
165 4/8	189 6/8	23 2/8	26 1/8	16 5/8	5 3/8	5 3/8	7	7	Dane Co., WI	Jack Northrop	Jack Northrop	2004	732
165 4/8	172 1/8	25	23 3/8	21 7/8	4 7/8	5	5	5	Marathon Co., WI	Chad J. Curtis	Chad J. Curtis	2005	732
165 3/8	174 4/8	26 1/8	25	16 5/8	5 1/8	5 1/8	6	6	Marquette Co., WI	Richard L. Larson, Jr.	Richard L. Larson, Jr.	2005	732
165 3/8	170 2/8	23 7/8	25 7/8	17 7/8	5 2/8	5 2/8	6	5	Richland Co., WI	Bill F. McCann	Bill F. McCann	2005	732
165 3/8	177	25 4/8	23 6/8	17 7/8	4	4	5	5	McPherson Co., KS	Bryan D. Zerger	Bryan D. Zerger	1995	738
165 3/8	168 1/8	25 5/8	26	18 6/8	4 3/8	4 3/8	4	4	Muskingum Co., OH	Jeff R. Berry	Jeff R. Berry	2002	738
165 3/8	169 1/8	24 1/8	24 2/8	20 4/8	5 2/8	5 4/8	5	5	Jo Daviess Co., IL	Bradley J. Bauer	Bradley J. Bauer	2004	738
165 3/8	168 7/8	22 6/8	23 1/8	19 2/8	4 1/8	4 1/8	5	5	Rosebud Co., MT	Mark Beaudin	Mark Beaudin	2004	738
165 2/8	178 2/8	26 2/8	26 2/8	16	4 2/8	4 2/8	5	5	Dubuque Co., IA	Matthew J. Breiner	Matthew J. Breiner	2004	738
165 2/8	178	24 6/8	24 1/8	20 1/8	5 2/8	5 2/8	6	5	Clearwater Co., MN	Gary D. Fultz	Gary D. Fultz	2005	738
165 2/8	173 5/8	24 1/8	24 6/8	18 3/8	5 1/8	5 4/8	6	5	Penobscot Co., ME	Duane B. Furge	Duane B. Furge	2005	738
165 2/8	174 6/8	25 5/8	24 1/8	18 3/8	4 6/8	4 7/8	5	5	Stokes Co., NC	Greg J. Robertson	Greg J. Robertson	2003	745
165 2/8	172 7/8	28 4/8	26 7/8	19 3/8	4 2/8	4 2/8	5	5	Pontotoc Co., MS	Ross Brown	Ross Brown	2004	745
165 1/8	167 1/8	28 6/8	27	18 1/8	4 7/8	4 7/8	5	5	Turtle Lake, SK	Peter J. Iglesias	Peter J. Iglesias	2005	745
165 1/8	168 6/8	25	28	18 1/8	4 1/8	4 1/8	5	5	Morrison Co., MN	Dennis A. Fischer	Dennis A. Fischer	2005	748
165 1/8	171 3/8	25 4/8	24 3/8	19	5 1/8	5	5	5	Pope Co., MN	Mark A. Herr	Mark A. Herr	2003	748
165	176 3/8	21 7/8	25	16 3/8	6 5/8	6 3/8	6	6	Vernon Co., WI	Gerald Schumacher	Gerald Schumacher	2003	748
165	169 6/8	25 4/8	24 5/8	20 4/8	5 2/8	5 2/8	5	5	Cherokee Co., KS	Mickey P. Zahn	Mickey P. Zahn	2003	748

WHITETAIL DEER - TYPICAL ANTLERS

Odocoileus virginianus virginianus and certain related subspecies

Final Score	Gross Score	Length of Main Beam R.	Length of Main Beam L.	Inside Spread	Circ. at Smallest Place Between Burr & First Point R.	Circ. at Smallest Place Between Burr & First Point L.	Number of Points R.	Number of Points L.	Locality	Hunter	Owner	Date Killed	Rank
165	175 6/8	25 4/8	24 2/8	18 5/8	4 6/8	4 5/8	5	6	Otter Tail Co., MN	Miles L. Nelson	Miles L. Nelson	2004	748
165	189 2/8	26 2/8	26 4/8	19 4/8	5	5	7	7	Peoria Co., IL	Andy Szewczyk	Andy Szewczyk	2004	748
165	202 2/8	25	25	21 2/8	5 4/8	5 4/8	8	8	Hancock Co., IL	Donna J. Cook	Donna J. Cook	2005	748
165	169	24 4/8	25 3/8	17 4/8	5	5	6	6	Concho Co., TX	Kenneth R. Pearson	Kenneth R. Pearson	2005	748
165	171	24 7/8	25 4/8	19	5 4/8	5 3/8	5	5	Arkansas Co., AR	Lance A. Stroh	Lance A. Stroh	2005	748
164 7/8	179	25 3/8	24	19 3/8	5 2/8	5 1/8	7	7	Pike Co., IL	William V. Riggs IV	William V. Riggs IV	2003	757
164 7/8	172 1/8	23	23 2/8	16 4/8	4 6/8	4 6/8	6	6	Ness Co., KS	Tavis D. Rogers	Tavis D. Rogers	2003	757
164 7/8	176 6/8	26 3/8	27 4/8	18 4/8	5	5 1/8	7	5	Kersley, BC	Andy Quamme	Andy Quamme	2004	757
164 7/8	172 3/8	25 5/8	25 3/8	17 4/8	4 7/8	5	5	5	Phillips Co., KS	Michael J. Fazende	Michael J. Fazende	2005	757
164 7/8	174 2/8	27	28	19 5/8	5 2/8	5	6	6	Putnam Co., IN	Gary D. Hanley	Gary D. Hanley	2005	757
164 6/8	172	23 4/8	23 6/8	22 6/8	4 6/8	5	5	5	Labette Co., KS	Justin C. Willems	Justin C. Willems	2002	762
164 6/8	173 2/8	23 6/8	23 1/8	17 2/8	5 1/8	5 1/8	6	6	Jackson Co., IA	B.J. Eiben	B.J. Eiben	2003	762
164 6/8	185 5/8	25 6/8	24 2/8	19 7/8	5 3/8	5 6/8	8	7	Eau Claire Co., WI	Brian S. Williamsen	Brian S. Williamsen	2004	762
164 5/8	182 7/8	25 7/8	26 2/8	17 3/8	5 2/8	5 1/8	8	5	Otter Tail Co., MN	Jerry L. Judson	Jerry L. Judson	1989	765
164 5/8	185 2/8	25 5/8	25 2/8	16 7/8	4 3/8	4 6/8	7	6	Greene Co., IL	Webb L. Cunningham	Webb L. Cunningham	2001	765
164 5/8	172 2/8	22 4/8	23 2/8	19 1/8	5 4/8	5 4/8	5	6	Harrison Co., IA	M. Scott Ghan	M. Scott Ghan	2003	765
164 5/8	176 7/8	25 4/8	24 5/8	20 1/8	5 5/8	5 6/8	7	5	Republic Co., KS	Steven J. McManaman	Steven J. McManaman	2003	765
164 5/8	177	25 6/8	25 5/8	20 7/8	5 1/8	5 2/8	5	7	Cold Lake, SK	Robert D. Riether	Robert D. Riether	2003	765
164 5/8	175 2/8	26 6/8	27 2/8	23 7/8	5	5 1/8	5	6	Dunn Co., WI	David Waterhouse	David Waterhouse	2003	765
164 5/8	171 1/8	25 6/8	24 7/8	18 5/8	4 5/8	4 3/8	5	6	Trempealeau Co., WI	Steve J. Brady	Steve J. Brady	2004	765
164 5/8	170 6/8	23 6/8	24	17 3/8	6 5/8	6 6/8	5	6	Lancaster Co., NE	Corinna Vokoun	Corinna Vokoun	2004	765
164 5/8	183 1/8	26	24 5/8	22 6/8	5 5/8	5 3/8	7	6	Meade Co., KS	Brady S. Wiens	Brady S. Wiens	2004	765
164 5/8	170 7/8	27 5/8	26 4/8	20 7/8	5 3/8	5	5	5	Douglas Co., MN	Jeff S. McPhail	Jeff S. McPhail	2005	765
164 5/8	167 1/8	25 7/8	26 1/8	16 5/8	4 2/8	4 1/8	5	5	Goodhue Co., MN	Picked Up	Michael J. Neknez	2005	765
164 4/8	174 7/8	25 4/8	22 5/8	20	5	4 5/8	6	6	Lake Co., MT	Lee Manicke	Lee Manicke	1990	776
164 4/8	167	26 1/8	26 4/8	17 2/8	5 4/8	5 3/8	5	5	Logan Co., KY	David Motsinger	David Motsinger	1994	776
164 4/8	176 2/8	26 6/8	27 1/8	19 6/8	4 7/8	4 7/8	6	6	Perry Co., IL	Brian J. Huck	Brian J. Huck	2003	776
164 4/8	178 5/8	27 7/8	27 6/8	21 7/8	5	4 6/8	6	6	Hart Co., KY	Reggie McCubbin	Reggie McCubbin	2003	776
164 4/8	171 4/8	23 7/8	23 4/8	18	4 5/8	4 4/8	6	6	Weyakwin Lake, SK	Andy Milam	Andy Milam	2003	776
164 4/8	176 1/8	23 4/8	22 7/8	14 5/8	4 3/8	4 4/8	7	7	Uvalde Co., TX	Gary G. Patterson	Gary G. Patterson	2004	776
164 4/8	182 6/8	24 6/8	24 1/8	21 5/8	4 5/8	4 5/8	6	8	Dodge Co., WI	Jerome M. Schwartz	Jerome M. Schwartz	2004	776
164 4/8	178 6/8	26 4/8	27 3/8	18 2/8	4 5/8	4 7/8	6	6	Buffalo Co., WI	Hunter Folkedahl	Hunter Folkedahl	2005	776
164 4/8	188 2/8	26 5/8	27 7/8	17 7/8	6 1/8	6 1/8	7	5	Warren Co., IN	Tim Wadkins	Tim Wadkins	2005	776

164 3/8	170 7/8	26 2/8	16 3/8	5	5	5	6	Niagara Co., NY	Mark S. Irlbacher	Mark S. Irlbacher	2002	785
164 3/8	170 1/8	23 2/8	18 5/8	5	5	5	5	Hamilton Co., KS	William J. Ciccone	William J. Ciccone	2003	785
164 3/8	189	26 2/8	18 2/8	4 7/8	4 6/8	6	6	Monroe Co., WI	Richard L. Guy	Richard L. Guy	2003	785
164 3/8	170 2/8	25 7/8	18 3/8	5 1/8	5	5	5	Horsehead Creek, SK	F. Ritchie McQueeney	F. Ritchie McQueeney	2004	785
164 3/8	174 3/8	25 3/8	22 5/8	5 2/8	5	5	5	Dubuque Co., IA	Jim M. Thiltgen	Jim M. Thiltgen	2005	785
164 2/8	169 6/8	24 1/8	16 4/8	6	5 6/8	5	6	Caldwell Co., MO	Robert Knudson	Robert Knudson	1995	790
164 2/8	179	26	22 7/8	5 2/8	5 2/8	5	6	Reno Co., KS	Jamie M. Conlee	Jamie M. Conlee	2003	790
164 2/8	181 1/8	22 1/8	17 3/8	5 1/8	5	7	7	Tom Green Co., TX	Byron L. Hendrix	Byron L. Hendrix	2003	790
164 2/8	168 5/8	23 4/8	15 6/8	4 6/8	4 6/8	5	5	Cherokee Co., KS	Ira D. Corbitt	Ira D. Corbitt	2004	790
164 2/8	172 2/8	25 3/8	24	5	4 6/8	5	5	Warren Co., MO	Cody Hammel	Cody Hammel	2004	790
164 2/8	170 4/8	25 4/8	17 6/8	4 6/8	4 4/8	6	6	Butler Co., KY	Dale Nash	Dale Nash	2004	790
164 2/8	177 1/8	25	17	4 5/8	4 5/8	6	6	Oswego Co., NY	Donald Davenport	Donald Davenport	2005	790
164 2/8	171 2/8	24 6/8	18 4/8	5 4/8	6	7	5	Monroe Co., MO	Julie C. Neer	Julie C. Neer	2005	790
164 2/8	168 3/8	26 1/8	17 2/8	4 6/8	4 6/8	5	5	Waushara Co., WI	Thomas G. Tuchscherer	Thomas G. Tuchscherer	2006	790
164 1/8	182 4/8	25	20 5/8	4 7/8	4 6/8	5	5	Grayson Co., KY	Denny Baxter	Denny Baxter	2004	799
164 1/8	176 2/8	23 5/8	18	4 4/8	4 4/8	7	7	Johnson Co., NE	Brett P. Bock	Brett P. Bock	2004	799
164 1/8	174 5/8	23 4/8	17 2/8	4 6/8	4 4/8	7	7	Nemaha Co., NE	Ken J. Hatten	Ken J. Hatten	2004	799
164 1/8	175 2/8	26	21 1/8	5 4/8	5 4/8	5	5	Sauk Co., WI	Bernard W. Quinlan	Bernard W. Quinlan	2004	799
164	168 1/8	26 2/8	17	4 2/8	4 2/8	6	6	Lake of the Rivers, SK	Peter Coleman	Peter Coleman	2003	803
164	173 3/8	26 6/8	19 6/8	3 6/8	4	6	5	Rockingham Co., NC	Douglas R. Jones, Sr.	Douglas R. Jones, Sr.	2003	803
164	169 3/8	24 6/8	23 4/8	4 4/8	4 4/8	5	6	Cass Co., MN	Ethan R. Rudbeck	Ethan R. Rudbeck	2003	803
164	169 5/8	27 2/8	20	4 2/8	4 3/8	5	5	Lunenburg Co., VA	Major G. Ball	Major G. Ball	2004	803
164	181 2/8	25 3/8	16 7/8	4 7/8	4 6/8	9	8	Leslie Co., KY	Tyler M. Kilburn	Tyler M. Kilburn	2006	803
163 7/8	167 2/8	28 4/8	20 7/8	4 6/8	4 4/8	5	5	Gregory Co., SD	Steve V. Day	Steve V. Day	2004	808
163 7/8	171 2/8	25 4/8	17 1/8	4 4/8	4 5/8	5	6	Calumet Co., WI	Brett T. Wilkens	Brett T. Wilkens	2004	808
163 7/8	178 5/8	22 5/8	19 2/8	5 3/8	5 3/8	7	8	Jones Co., IA	Douglas P. Stoll	Douglas P. Stoll	2006	808
163 6/8	167 5/8	25 3/8	18	4 1/8	4 2/8	6	6	Essex Co., NY	Margaret H. Smith	Margaret H. Smith	1945	811
163 6/8	166 7/8	22 3/8	20 2/8	4 6/8	4 7/8	6	5	Whiteside Co., IL	Shawn C. Ryan	Shawn C. Ryan	2002	811
163 6/8	176 4/8	28 3/8	21 4/8	4 7/8	5	5	5	Hampshire Co., MA	Ken Carpenter	Ken Carpenter	2003	811
163 6/8	172 2/8	25 4/8	18	4 6/8	4 6/8	6	6	Wayne Co., IA	Andy C. Decker	Andy C. Decker	2003	811
163 6/8	178 5/8	24 5/8	17 5/8	4 5/8	4 5/8	6	8	Adams Co., OH	Paul Phillips	Paul Phillips	2003	811
163 6/8	168 4/8	25 3/8	20	4 2/8	4 2/8	5	5	Guernsey Co., OH	Phillip E. Sherman	Phillip E. Sherman	2003	811
163 6/8	178 1/8	26 3/8	16 4/8	5 4/8	5 4/8	7	6	Harlan Co., KY	Glenn Helton, Jr.	Glenn Helton, Jr.	2004	811
163 6/8	167 7/8	25 6/8	19 2/8	4 3/8	4 3/8	5	5	Buffalo Co., WI	Roland Hermundson	Roland Hermundson	2004	811
163 6/8	170 7/8	25 3/8	19 4/8	4 2/8	4 2/8	6	6	Outagamie Co., WI	Jim K. Knoke	Jim K. Knoke	2004	811
163 6/8	175 5/8	27	19	4 7/8	4 7/8	5	5	Wicomico Co., MD	Louis E. Stanovich	Louis E. Stanovich	2004	811
163 6/8	183	25	18 1/8	5	5	6	6	Madison Co., IL	Ronald A. Buente	Ronald A. Buente	2005	811
163 6/8	168	28 3/8	21	5 6/8	5 7/8	4	4	Fayette Co., KY	Danny G. Jones	Danny G. Jones	2005	811
163 5/8	173 4/8	24 1/8	15 7/8	5 4/8	5 2/8	6	7	Randolph Co., IL	Delbert L. Wall	Delbert L. Wall	2003	823
163 5/8	168 1/8	24 4/8	19 5/8	4 7/8	4 7/8	5	5	Green Co., WI	Christopher A. Isely	Christopher A. Isely	2004	823
163 5/8	175 5/8	22 6/8	17 7/8	4 6/8	4 6/8	6	6	Nodaway Co., MO	Adam Weldon	Adam Weldon	2004	823
163 4/8	182 5/8	23 5/8	19 4/8	5 1/8	4 7/8	7	6	Cook Co., MN	C. Frenchy Goodboe	Florence L. Wold	1955	826

WHITETAIL DEER - TYPICAL ANTLERS

Odocoileus virginianus virginianus and certain related subspecies

Final Score	Gross Score	Length of Main Beam R.	L.	Inside Spread	Circumference at Smallest Place Between Burr & First Point R.	L.	Number of Points R.	L.	Locality	Hunter	Owner	Date Killed	Rank
163 4/8	166 3/8	26	26	21 2/8	5 2/8	5 1/8	4	4	Washington Co., IA	Larry Blum	Larry Blum	2002	826
163 4/8	180 7/8	25 6/8	24 5/8	19	4 1/8	4 2/8	7	6	Boone Co., MO	Leon P. Slate	Leon P. Slate	2003	826
163 4/8	172 3/8	23 5/8	23 2/8	17 2/8	4 3/8	4 2/8	7	6	Shawano Co., WI	Richard A. Giese	Richard A. Giese	2004	826
163 4/8	190 1/8	25 6/8	25 6/8	21	5 4/8	5 2/8	8	9	Marshall Co., IN	James A. Hampson	James A. Hampson	2004	826
163 4/8	171 3/8	24 4/8	24 4/8	17	5	5	5	6	Oneida Co., WI	Ryan M. Kocian	Ryan M. Kocian	2005	826
163 4/8	175	24 6/8	24 5/8	17 5/8	5	5 2/8	6	5	Vinton Co., OH	James E. Paris, Sr.	James E. Paris, Sr.	2005	826
163 3/8	184	27 6/8	26	28 5/8	5 3/8	5 2/8	7	6	Switzerland Co., IN	John A. Mays	John A. Mays	2002	833
163 3/8	172 1/8	25 2/8	24 6/8	17 3/8	5 6/8	5 5/8	7	5	Crawford Co., WI	Jon A. Mageland	Jon A. Mageland	2003	833
163 3/8	171 7/8	24 7/8	24 6/8	20 2/8	4 4/8	4 3/8	6	6	Cross Co., AR	Steven D. Jones	Steven D. Jones	2004	833
163 3/8	177 1/8	28 3/8	27 7/8	21 4/8	4 7/8	4 7/8	6	8	Cheyenne Co., KS	Rodney A. Lindsten	Rodney A. Lindsten	2004	833
163 3/8	189	26 4/8	26 6/8	16 2/8	5	5 2/8	5	9	Turner Co., GA	Stacy Keen	Stacy Keen	2005	833
163 3/8	174 6/8	26 2/8	28 2/8	19 1/8	4 7/8	5	6	7	Dougherty Co., GA	James C. Lawson	James C. Lawson	2005	833
163 3/8	176	22	22 2/8	16 6/8	5 4/8	5 5/8	6	8	Pine River, BC	Marty C. Loring	Marty C. Loring	2005	833
163 3/8	191 6/8	27 3/8	28 6/8	20 5/8	5 4/8	5 2/8	5	9	Gentry Co., MO	Kevin B. Martin	Kevin B. Martin	2005	833
163 3/8	167 7/8	27 4/8	26	20 7/8	4 7/8	4 7/8	5	5	Moore Co., NC	Michael B. Morris	Michael B. Morris	2005	833
163 3/8	169 4/8	25 7/8	26 6/8	21 3/8	4 7/8	4 7/8	5	4	Ashland Co., OH	Mark S. Rader	Mark S. Rader	2005	833
163 2/8	178 2/8	24 2/8	24 5/8	19 5/8	5 1/8	5 2/8	6	6	Goodhue Co., MN	Loren Brusehaver	Loren Brusehaver	1960	843
163 2/8	167 5/8	22	21 4/8	17 2/8	4 4/8	4 4/8	6	6	Williamson Co., IL	William R. Abernathy	William R. Abernathy	1996	843
163 2/8	188 6/8	26 7/8	28 2/8	23 7/8	4 4/8	4 4/8	6	8	St. Louis Co., MN	Christian Kopp	Christian Kopp	1998	843
163 2/8	178 4/8	24	24 2/8	18 2/8	5	5	7	8	Bollinger Co., MO	Ronnie Eftink	Ronnie Eftink	2004	843
163 2/8	179 2/8	26 3/8	26 1/8	20 5/8	4 5/8	4 6/8	7	8	Clark Co., KS	Mark A. Meadors	Mark A. Meadors	2004	843
163 2/8	166 2/8	26 5/8	26 2/8	19	5 4/8	5 3/8	5	5	Ashland Co., OH	Jon A. Byers	Jon A. Byers	2005	843
163 2/8	171 7/8	24 6/8	23	17 4/8	5	4 6/8	6	5	Coahoma Co., MS	Melvin W. Woods, Jr.	Melvin W. Woods, Jr.	2005	843
163 1/8	165 2/8	28 2/8	27 7/8	20 7/8	5 6/8	5 6/8	4	4	Worcester Co., MA	G. Robert Eden	G. Robert Eden	2002	850
163 1/8	183 2/8	23 2/8	24	20 2/8	5 5/8	5 2/8	9	7	Sauk Co., WI	William Hellenbrand	William Hellenbrand	2002	850
163 1/8	176 1/8	23 1/8	23 1/8	18 1/8	4 7/8	4 4/8	5	6	Grant Co., WI	Steve M. Traudt	Steve M. Traudt	2002	850
163 1/8	182	25 1/8	24 7/8	18 5/8	5 6/8	6 1/8	6	6	Waupaca Co., WI	Rosemary Bazile	Rosemary Bazile	2003	850
163 1/8	172	25 6/8	26 1/8	17 6/8	5 1/8	5 2/8	6	5	Knox Co., MO	Randy G. Craig	Randy G. Craig	2003	850
163 1/8	165 3/8	26 6/8	27 1/8	20 5/8	4 4/8	4 4/8	6	5	Schuyler Co., MO	Gene F. Kampe	Gene F. Kampe	2003	850
163 1/8	170 1/8	25 4/8	26 4/8	17 5/8	5 1/8	5 3/8	5	6	Greenwood Co., KS	Cedric V. Hunter, Jr.	Cedric V. Hunter, Jr.	2004	850
163 1/8	167 2/8	28	27 1/8	20 1/8	4 5/8	4 6/8	6	6	Hopkins Co., KY	Kelly N. Smith	Kelly N. Smith	2004	850
163 1/8	181 6/8	23 6/8	23 7/8	18 5/8	4 5/8	4 5/8	6	5	Harper Co., OK	John A. Spears	John A. Spears	2004	850
163 1/8	164 5/8	24 1/8	23 7/8	20 3/8	4 1/8	4 1/8	5	5	Tama Co., IA	Bryan Valline	Bryan Valline	2004	850

									Locality	Hunter	Owner	Date	Rank
163 1/8	20 6/8	21 7/8	167	18 7/8	5 5/8	5 5/8	5	5	Adams Co., IL	Timothy D. Walmsley	Timothy D. Walmsley	2004	850
163 1/8	27	27 4/8	167	16 3/8	5 1/8	5 1/8	5	5	Miami Co., OH	Ralph J. Bateman	Ralph J. Bateman	2005	850
163 1/8	25 6/8	28 3/8	169 1/8	19 1/8	5 1/8	4 6/8	5	5	Linn Co., IA	James V. Miller	James V. Miller	2005	850
163 1/8	25 5/8	26 3/8	169 7/8	21 1/8	4 5/8	4 6/8	6	5	Fairfield Co., OH	Joshua F. Poston	Joshua F. Poston	2005	850
163 1/8	23 4/8	23 7/8	165	19 1/8	4 5/8	4 4/8	5	5	Brown Co., WI	Don M. Vanden Avond	Don M. Vanden Avond	2005	850
163	23 6/8	23 5/8	167 3/8	20	4 7/8	4 6/8	6	6	Itasca Co., MN	Wayne Erickson	Wayne Erickson	1964	865
163	26 5/8	27 2/8	182	18 4/8	4 5/8	4 2/8	6	6	Barton Co., MO	Dustin L. Chasteen	Dustin L. Chasteen	2004	865
163	25 7/8	25 5/8	164 4/8	17 2/8	5	5	4	6	Jones Co., IA	Kevin Muehlenkamp	Kevin Muehlenkamp	2004	865
163	26	26 6/8	165 6/8	22 6/8	5 4/8	5 4/8	4	4	Breckinridge Co., KY	David C. Paul	David C. Paul	2004	865
163	24 6/8	23 3/8	172 7/8	20 6/8	5 2/8	5 6/8	7	4	Furnas Co., NE	Douglas B. Garey	Douglas B. Garey	2005	865
163	28 1/8	27 4/8	169 2/8	23 4/8	4 7/8	5 2/8	5	6	Piscataquis Co., ME	John P. Turgeon	John P. Turgeon	2005	865
162 7/8	25 4/8	25 1/8	167 6/8	20 1/8	5	4 4/8	5	4	Bienville Parish, LA	Bill Ogletree	W. Timothy Ogletree	1962	871
162 7/8	25 1/8	24 4/8	165 2/8	16 5/8	4 1/8	4	5	5	Walworth Co., WI	Robert Chelminiak	Robert Chelminiak	2003	871
162 7/8	25 1/8	25 4/8	167 4/8	15 7/8	4 4/8	4 6/8	5	5	Chippewa Co., WI	Delbert H. Helland	Delbert H. Helland	2003	871
162 7/8	23 7/8	23 6/8	167 6/8	18 5/8	5 2/8	5 2/8	5	5	La Porte Co., IN	Tony M. Sikora	Tony M. Sikora	2003	871
162 7/8	24 4/8	24 1/8	166 1/8	15 5/8	5 4/8	5	5	5	Allamakee Co., IA	Todd Lapel	Todd Lapel	2004	871
162 7/8	23 6/8	23 2/8	193 5/8	21 3/8	4 2/8	4 3/8	7	7	Randolph Co., MO	Greg D. McCluskey	Greg D. McCluskey	2004	871
162 7/8	23 3/8	23 4/8	178 1/8	19 6/8	4 5/8	4 6/8	6	6	Lee Co., IL	Charles W. Rehor	Charles W. Rehor	2004	871
162 7/8	25 6/8	26 4/8	176 4/8	19 6/8	5	5	6	6	High Prairie, AB	Glenn E. Thompson	Glenn E. Thompson	2000	871
162 6/8	24 7/8	25 6/8	180	16 4/8	6	6 2/8	5	6	Otter Lake, SK	Gordon D. Mitchell	Gordon D. Mitchell	2003	879
162 6/8	27 5/8	28 6/8	173 7/8	21	4 2/8	4 2/8	6	7	Taylor Co., WV	Michael T. Heldreth	Michael T. Heldreth	2003	879
162 6/8	25 5/8	25 2/8	166 5/8	21 2/8	4 5/8	4 5/8	5	5	Lafayette Co., MO	Picked Up	Steve Schreiman	2004	879
162 6/8	25 1/8	25 6/8	168 3/8	17 4/8	4 1/8	4 1/8	5	5	Jefferson Co., IN	James D. Mullins	James D. Mullins	2004	879
162 6/8	24 4/8	24 5/8	186 7/8	22 5/8	4 7/8	4 7/8	6	7	Rock Co., WI	Lyle C. Yaun	Lyle C. Yaun	2005	879
162 6/8	25 4/8	26	170 6/8	20 2/8	4 2/8	4 2/8	6	5	Breckinridge Co., KY	Jack Hayden	Jack Hayden	2005	879
162 6/8	24 4/8	24 6/8	168 5/8	17 4/8	5 3/8	5 4/8	4	4	Price Co., WI	Richard J. Pohlod	Richard J. Pohlod	2005	879
162 5/8	25 7/8	26 3/8	168 2/8	18 2/8	4 4/8	4 4/8	6	6	Kosciusko Co., IN	Rodney C. Spurlin	Rodney C. Spurlin	2000	879
162 5/8	26 2/8	27 5/8	172 7/8	18 7/8	4 3/8	4 4/8	5	6	Clark Co., MO	Kenny Dunn	Kenny Dunn	2003	887
162 5/8	26 1/8	25 1/8	175 5/8	16 6/8	5 3/8	5 3/8	6	7	Johnson Co., NE	Lavon D. Beethe	Lavon D. Beethe	2005	887
162 5/8	25 3/8	25 5/8	169 4/8	16 3/8	5 2/8	5 2/8	5	5	Ashtabula Co., OH	Daniel J. Feke	Daniel J. Feke	2000	887
162 4/8	29 6/8	30 4/8	167 3/8	27 6/8	5 1/8	5 3/8	4	4	Mt. Yamaska, QC	Andre Beaudry	Andre Beaudry	2003	890
162 4/8	26 3/8	26 2/8	179 7/8	18 3/8	5	4 6/8	6	6	Ulster Co., NY	Eric Foose	Eric Foose	2003	890
162 4/8	26 6/8	26 6/8	176 7/8	22	4 7/8	4 6/8	6	6	Grayson Co., KY	Picked Up	Martin Meredith	2004	890
162 4/8	25 1/8	25	182 4/8	20 7/8	4 6/8	4 1/8	8	7	Adams Co., MS	Keith Boykin	Keith Boykin	2003	890
162 4/8	27	27 1/8	170	20 2/8	4 1/8	4	5	6	Martin Co., IN	James A. Schoen	James A. Schoen	2004	890
162 4/8	26 2/8	26 2/8	177 1/8	19 4/8	4 7/8	5	6	5	Winnebago Co., WI	Adam R. Stanek	Adam R. Stanek	2005	890
162 3/8	24 4/8	24 6/8	167 5/8	20 7/8	4 6/8	4 6/8	5	5	Perry Co., TN	Guy Adkins	Judy Adkins	1983	896
162 3/8	24 6/8	24 1/8	169 4/8	18 2/8	4 7/8	4 6/8	6	5	Sully Co., SD	Tim J. Stampe	Tim J. Stampe	1993	896
162 3/8	24 1/8	24 1/8	166	17 7/8	5 1/8	5	5	5	Monroe Co., MO	Joseph T. Gilliam	Joseph T. Gilliam	2004	896
162 3/8	25 7/8	25 7/8	171	15 1/8	4 7/8	4 6/8	6	6	Ohio Co., KY	Ben Groves	Ben Groves	2004	896
162 3/8	25 6/8	25 3/8	175 6/8	17 5/8	5 1/8	5 2/8	7	7	Laurens Co., GA	Jeff B. Hall	Jeff B. Hall	2004	896
162 3/8	27 7/8	27 1/8	173 7/8	19 2/8	5 2/8	5 3/8	5	5	Shawnee Co., KS	Michael J. Kruger	Michael J. Kruger	2004	896

WHITETAIL DEER - TYPICAL ANTLERS

Odocoileus virginianus virginianus and certain related subspecies

Final Score	Gross Score	Length of Main Beam R.	L.	Inside Spread	Circumference at Smallest Place Between Burr & First Point R.	L.	Number of Points R.	L.	Locality	Hunter	Owner	Date Killed	Rank
162 3/8	193 5/8	26 1/8	26 6/8	17	5 3/8	5	8	8	Harrison Co., MO	Matthew S. Graham	Matthew S. Graham	2005	896
162 3/8	168 4/8	25 6/8	25 4/8	19 7/8	4 4/8	4 3/8	6	5	Orange Co., IN	Picked Up	Mark A. Verble	2005	896
162 3/8	174	24 4/8	24 5/8	19 4/8	5 4/8	5 5/8	5	6	Wabasha Co., MN	Christian G. Ratz	Christian G. Ratz	2006	896
162 2/8	181 7/8	25 2/8	25	18 2/8	4 4/8	4 3/8	8	6	Lake of the Woods, ON	Bill Dawson	Bill Dawson	2000	905
162 2/8	185 2/8	24 6/8	25 1/8	21 6/8	5 5/8	5 6/8	6	6	Brookings Co., SD	Todd Goodfellow	Todd Goodfellow	2003	905
162 2/8	176	25	23 7/8	16 3/8	4 7/8	4 6/8	5	5	Saunders Co., NE	David M. Lorenzen	David M. Lorenzen	2003	905
162 2/8	166	24 1/8	25 2/8	20 2/8	5 3/8	5 4/8	5	7	Fisher River, MB	Guy J. Murphy	Guy J. Murphy	2003	905
162 2/8	183 4/8	26 1/8	25 6/8	21 1/8	5 3/8	5 4/8	6	5	Breckinridge Co., KY	Larry Severs	Larry Severs	2003	905
162 2/8	166 1/8	26 1/8	26	21	4 3/8	4 2/8	6	8	Richland Co., OH	Derrick D. Fair	Derrick D. Fair	2004	905
162 2/8	183 1/8	24 1/8	23 4/8	16 7/8	5 1/8	4 7/8	7	5	Jones Co., SD	Crystal Fosheim	Crystal Fosheim	2004	905
162 2/8	169 3/8	25 5/8	25 7/8	18 4/8	4 5/8	4 5/8	5	7	Grant Co., WI	Bradley R. Hellenbrand	Bradley R. Hellenbrand	2004	905
162 2/8	173 3/8	24 4/8	24 7/8	17 4/8	5 6/8	5 6/8	6	6	Woodbury Co., IA	Jason W. Hempey	Jason W. Hempey	2004	905
162 2/8	169 1/8	24 7/8	25 6/8	18 7/8	4 6/8	4 5/8	6	5	Page Co., VA	Michael S. Turner	Michael S. Turner	2004	905
162 2/8	178 3/8	24	24 1/8	19 4/8	5	4 6/8	8	6	Little Sand Lake, ON	Peter Marcinuk	Peter Marcinuk	2005	905
162 2/8	165 5/8	23 1/8	23 3/8	18	4 7/8	4 5/8	5	5	Ingham Co., MI	Mark D. McCrackin	Mark D. McCrackin	2005	905
162 2/8	184 2/8	27 7/8	29	21 1/8	4 4/8	4 7/8	7	8	Green Lake Co., WI	Matthew J. Reilly	Matthew J. Reilly	2005	905
162 2/8	167	24 5/8	24 3/8	15 6/8	4 4/8	4 6/8	5	6	Washtenaw Co., MI	Shawn R. Spilak	Shawn R. Spilak	2005	905
162 1/8	173 1/8	25 5/8	25 7/8	25 7/8	4 2/8	4 2/8	5	6	Wilbarger Co., TX	Ed K. Burdett	Ed K. Burdett	2003	919
162 1/8	170 1/8	23 5/8	23 6/8	16 4/8	5 2/8	5 1/8	6	5	Marathon Co., WI	Joseph A. Staszak	Joseph A. Staszak	2003	919
162 1/8	169 2/8	25 1/8	27 1/8	24 1/8	4 5/8	4 7/8	5	5	Harvey Co., KS	John Wiebe	John Wiebe	2003	919
162 1/8	181 2/8	24 6/8	25 1/8	23 4/8	4 4/8	4 2/8	8	7	Winnebago Co., WI	Jari Boyce	Jari Boyce	2004	919
162 1/8	186 5/8	27 6/8	26 7/8	16 1/8	5	5	6	8	Spencer Co., KY	Darrel Falin	Darrel Falin	2004	919
162 1/8	169 7/8	24 5/8	24 5/8	15 2/8	4 7/8	5	6	6	Putnam Co., MO	Tony M. Freeman	Tony M. Freeman	2004	919
162 1/8	166 1/8	23 5/8	22 5/8	15 5/8	4 2/8	4 4/8	6	6	Van Buren Co., IA	Mike Raue	Mike Raue	2004	919
162 1/8	171	26 2/8	25 5/8	19 2/8	5 1/8	5 1/8	5	6	Grand Forks Co., ND	Gregory A. Stoik	Gregory A. Stoik	2004	919
162 1/8	176 1/8	25 3/8	25 5/8	20 1/8	4 4/8	4 5/8	6	7	Barber Co., KS	Jeffery C. Wilson	Jeffery C. Wilson	2004	919
162 1/8	166	23 7/8	24 4/8	20 1/8	5 7/8	5 5/8	5	5	Otter Tail Co., MN	Sam Fett	Sam Fett	2005	919
162 1/8	166 1/8	23 5/8	24	18 3/8	5	5 2/8	5	5	Wood Co., WI	Nathaniel M. Krueger	Nathaniel M. Krueger	2005	919
162 1/8	167 3/8	22 7/8	22 6/8	17 7/8	4 6/8	4 6/8	5	6	Harrison Co., MO	Donald W. Martine	Donald W. Martine	2005	919
162 1/8	180 1/8	24 5/8	25 1/8	18 7/8	4 5/8	4 5/8	6	5	La Salle Co., TX	Weldon L. Nichols	Weldon L. Nichols	2006	919
162	174	25 1/8	25 3/8	18 2/8	4 4/8	4 5/8	6	7	Carroll Co., NH	David M. Greene	David M. Greene	2002	932
162	165 6/8	22 3/8	23 2/8	17 2/8	4 5/8	4 5/8	5	5	Webster Co., KY	Larry E. Daub	Larry E. Daub	2003	932
162	172	25 6/8	26 2/8	19 3/8	5 6/8	5 6/8	5	4	Monona Co., IA	Kevin Goslar	Kevin Goslar	2003	932

Score	Gross	R. Beam	L. Beam	Inside Spread	Circ. R	Circ. L	Pts. R	Pts. L	Hunter	Owner	Locality	Rank	Date
162	183 1/8	24	24 5/8	16 7/8	5 2/8	5 2/8	8	8	Ralph Whitsell	Ralph Whitsell	Howell Co., MO	932	2003
162	173 5/8	23 2/8	24 3/8	19 1/8	4 1/8	3 7/8	7	6	Ronald G. Moen	Ronald G. Moen	Little Trout Lake, ON	932	2004
162	169 3/8	23 2/8	23 4/8	24 5/8	5 1/8	5 2/8	5	6	Gregory Walsh	Gregory Walsh	Tuscarawas Co., OH	932	2004
162	170 4/8	26 6/8	26 7/8	22 4/8	4 6/8	4 5/8	6	5	Jeramie D. Pluemer	Jeramie D. Pluemer	Grant Co., WI	932	2005
162	166 5/8	23 2/8	23 7/8	16 6/8	4	4 2/8	5	6	Bob J. Wells	Bob J. Wells	Marshall Co., MN	932	2005
162	170 1/8	25 3/8	24 1/8	16 2/8	4 1/8	4 1/8	6	5	Randy R. Wilson	Randy R. Wilson	Dawson Co., NE	932	2005
161 7/8	164 5/8	23 2/8	24 2/8	16 5/8	4	4 1/8	5	5	Joseph D. Kleczynski	Joseph D. Kleczynski	Porcupine Plain, SK	941	2003
161 7/8	176 2/8	25 3/8	24 7/8	19 7/8	4 7/8	5	5	4	Picked Up	Ron Dennison	Knox Co., ME	941	2004
161 7/8	171 2/8	26	25 2/8	18	4 4/8	4 4/8	5	6	Picked Up	Roy J. Maul	Morgan Co., IL	941	2004
161 7/8	171 5/8	25 6/8	26	17 5/8	5 6/8	5 6/8	6	6	Charles E. Riehn	Charles E. Riehn	Butler Co., KY	941	2004
161 7/8	177 6/8	24	23 7/8	22 5/8	4 6/8	4 1/8	7	6	Joe M. Hilliard	Joe M. Hilliard	Kleberg Co., TX	941	2005
161 6/8	163 7/8	25 1/8	25 1/8	17 6/8	4 1/8	5	5	6	Steve French	Steve French	Edmonson Co., KY	946	1993
161 6/8	177 1/8	23 4/8	24 7/8	18 2/8	5	5 3/8	6	4	Ramsay Simmons III	Ramsay Simmons III	Two Hills, AB	946	2001
161 6/8	164	25 7/8	23 5/8	18 6/8	5 3/8	4 7/8	4	7	Todd D. Day	Todd D. Day	Marion Co., IN	946	2003
161 6/8	182 4/8	23 4/8	23 5/8	16	4 7/8	4 5/8	8	6	Jeffrey J. Roloff	Jeffrey J. Roloff	Macon Co., MO	946	2003
161 6/8	171 3/8	27 5/8	27 6/8	20 2/8	4 5/8	4 5/8	6	5	Daniel J. Tomon	Daniel J. Tomon	Coshocton Co., OH	946	2003
161 6/8	165 4/8	25	25	19 4/8	4 5/8	5 1/8	5	5	Dan Van Zeeland	Dan Van Zeeland	Outagamie Co., WI	946	2003
161 6/8	166 2/8	23 5/8	23 7/8	17 4/8	5 1/8	4 6/8	5	6	Harold D. Sylvester, Jr.	Harold D. Sylvester, Jr.	Lenawee Co., MI	946	2004
161 6/8	166 6/8	25 7/8	25 4/8	18 2/8	4 6/8	4 5/8	5	5	Tony White	Tony White	Grayson Co., KY	946	2004
161 5/8	180 6/8	23 6/8	22 5/8	16	4 5/8	4 1/8	5	6	Clint M. Daniels	Clint M. Daniels	Grundy Co., MO	954	2004
161 5/8	172 2/8	23 6/8	23 6/8	16 1/8	4 1/8	4 4/8	6	7	Glenn A. Hendon	Glenn A. Hendon	Livingston Co., KY	954	1990
161 5/8	169 7/8	23 2/8	23 2/8	15 5/8	4 3/8	4 7/8	7	5	John Oldham	John Oldham	Graves Co., KY	954	2003
161 5/8	165 1/8	24 5/8	24 7/8	16 3/8	5	5 2/8	5	7	Stephen Davis	Stephen Davis	Laurel Co., KY	954	2003
161 5/8	179 5/8	27 2/8	26 7/8	19 1/8	5 2/8	4 5/8	7	5	Allan H. Toms	Allan H. Toms	Frederick Co., MD	954	2004
161 5/8	175 5/8	26 2/8	25 6/8	19	4 4/8	5 4/8	5	6	Matthew W. Trevis	Matthew W. Trevis	Carlton Co., MN	954	2004
161 5/8	172 7/8	25	25	18 5/8	5 7/8	5 7/8	7	5	Shawn P. Wilson	Shawn P. Wilson	Parke Co., IN	954	2004
161 5/8	165 7/8	25 4/8	25 4/8	18 5/8	4 6/8	4 6/8	7	6	Jim C. Hinrichs	Jim C. Hinrichs	Trempealeau Co., WI	954	2004
161 5/8	189 1/8	27 1/8	27 1/8	20	4 7/8	4 7/8	6	5	John Christofferson	Ronald K. Ramerth	Minnesota	954	2005
161 4/8	188 1/8	26 3/8	26 3/8	21 4/8	5 1/8	5 1/8	5	6	Jeff Payne	Jeff Payne	Morris Co., KS	962	1955
161 4/8	163 4/8	27 2/8	27 2/8	22 4/8	5 2/8	5 2/8	7	9	Picked Up	MN Dept. Nat. Res.	Aitkin Co., MN	962	2000
161 4/8	164 7/8	23 1/8	23 1/8	23 1/8	4 6/8	4 6/8	8	4	Michael K. Campbell	Michael K. Campbell	Baca Co., CO	962	2002
161 4/8	165 7/8	24	24	19 2/8	4 5/8	4 5/8	4	5	Gary Cormican	Gary Cormican	Dunn Co., WI	962	2003
161 4/8	183 4/8	25 5/8	25 5/8	19 1/8	4 6/8	4 6/8	5	5	Brad Guralski	Brad Guralski	Marathon Co., WI	962	2003
161 4/8	167 3/8	22 1/8	22 1/8	15 4/8	5	5	7	7	Jonathan R. Koelling	Jonathan R. Koelling	Gentry Co., MO	962	2003
161 4/8	168	22 2/8	22 2/8	19	5	5	6	6	Jeffrey A. Ehmi	Jeffrey A. Ehmi	Wells Co., ND	962	2004
161 4/8	186 1/8	27 3/8	27 3/8	19 7/8	5 1/8	5 1/8	5	6	Noel D. Eltzroth	Noel D. Eltzroth	Huntington Co., IN	962	2004
161 4/8	168 3/8	24 4/8	24 4/8	18 4/8	4 5/8	4 5/8	6	5	Peter J. Gould	Peter J. Gould	Battle River, SK	962	2004
161 4/8	170 1/8	24 7/8	24 7/8	19	4 4/8	4 5/8	5	5	Mitchell D. Simon	Mitchell D. Simon	Morgan Co., MO	962	2004
161 4/8	168	26 1/8	26 1/8	17 4/8	4 2/8	4 2/8	5	4	Roger F. Baylor	Roger F. Baylor	Dubuque Co., IA	962	2005
161 4/8	168 2/8	27 5/8	27 5/8	21	3 4/8	3 7/8	6	5	Karen N. Harpole	Karen N. Harpole	Dimmit Co., TX	962	2005
161 4/8	167 4/8	24	24	17 1/8	5 2/8	5 2/8	5	6	James B. Rogers II	James B. Rogers II	Jackfish Lake, SK	962	2005
161 3/8	178 7/8	26 1/8	24 5/8	18 4/8	4 2/8	4 2/8	6	6	Ray Madison	Ray Madison	Adams Co., IL	976	1993

WHITETAIL DEER - TYPICAL ANTLERS

Odocoileus virginianus virginianus and certain related subspecies

Final Score	Gross Score	Length of Main Beam R.	L.	Inside Spread	Circumference at Smallest Place Between Burr & First Point R.	L.	Number of Points R.	L.	Locality	Hunter	Owner	Date Killed	Rank
161 3/8	172 7/8	22 5/8	22 6/8	16 6/8	4 1/8	4 3/8	7	7	Nez Perce Co., ID	Jack S. Snider	Jack S. Snider	2000	976
161 3/8	174 7/8	25 2/8	24 6/8	19 3/8	5 4/8	5 4/8	6	6	Ottawa Co., KS	Timmy W. Evans	Timmy W. Evans	2003	976
161 3/8	166 3/8	23 6/8	25 3/8	20 5/8	4 5/8	4 5/8	5	4	Brown Co., IL	Greg C. Flynn	Greg C. Flynn	2003	976
161 3/8	194 2/8	26 1/8	28	21 5/8	5 4/8	5 5/8	7	8	Licking Co., OH	Kim Laymon	Kim Laymon	2003	976
161 3/8	166 1/8	24	25	18 7/8	4 7/8	4 7/8	5	5	Chippewa Co., WI	Trenton T. Sweeney	Trenton T. Sweeney	2003	976
161 3/8	180 1/8	25 2/8	25 5/8	21 6/8	5 3/8	5 3/8	6	6	Pulaski Co., IN	Brian L. Kunce	Brian L. Kunce	2004	976
161 3/8	186	29 6/8	27 6/8	20	5	5 3/8	7	6	Perry Co., KY	James C. Oakes	James C. Oakes	2004	976
161 3/8	168 5/8	26	26 3/8	17 6/8	4 7/8	4 6/8	6	5	Henderson Co., IL	Clemon R. Watts	Clemon R. Watts	2004	976
161 3/8	163 1/8	26 5/8	25 5/8	18 3/8	4 2/8	4 2/8	5	5	Turner Co., GA	Travis L. Hobby	Travis L. Hobby	2005	976
161 2/8	167 1/8	26 1/8	24 2/8	16 6/8	4 5/8	4 4/8	5	5	Marquette Co., WI	Richard H. Bondowski	Richard H. Bondowski	2002	986
161 2/8	168 1/8	27 5/8	28	20 1/8	5 1/8	5	4	5	Clinton Co., IL	Doug Spihlmann	Doug Spihlmann	2002	986
161 2/8	173 6/8	24 7/8	25 2/8	19 1/8	5 1/8	5 1/8	6	6	Pike Co., OH	Roy Craig	Roy Craig	2003	986
161 2/8	169	26 2/8	25 2/8	19 4/8	4 5/8	4 5/8	5	5	Noble Co., IN	Frank A. Kimmell	Frank A. Kimmell	2003	986
161 2/8	170 5/8	23 6/8	23 2/8	27 7/8	4 4/8	4 2/8	6	5	Marshall Co., IN	Cody W. Leed	Cody W. Leed	2003	986
161 2/8	166 7/8	23 7/8	24 2/8	19 4/8	4 7/8	5 2/8	5	5	Peace River, AB	David L. Witt	David L. Witt	2005	986
161 1/8	166 1/8	24 5/8	23 7/8	19 5/8	4 2/8	4 2/8	5	5	Union Co., IA	Guillermo Garcia	Guillermo Garcia	2002	992
161 1/8	163 7/8	26 2/8	26 7/8	21 3/8	4 3/8	4 3/8	5	5	Delaware Co., IA	Dwayne Frommelt	Dwayne Frommelt	2004	992
161 1/8	174 2/8	24 2/8	25 3/8	19 3/8	5 6/8	5 5/8	5	5	McHenry Co., IL	Tim A. Reeves	Tim A. Reeves	2004	992
161 1/8	169	22 4/8	23 2/8	16 7/8	4 3/8	4 3/8	6	6	Coahuila, MX	Harold E. Turner, Jr.	Harold E. Turner, Jr.	2004	992
161 1/8	175 2/8	21 4/8	24 2/8	19 1/8	5	5	6	7	Ballard Co., KY	Brett Wilson	Brett Wilson	2004	992
161 1/8	171 6/8	29	29 6/8	21	5 1/8	5 2/8	6	5	Whitley Co., IN	Brandt Barnett	Brandt Barnett	2005	992
161	176 4/8	25 3/8	25 6/8	19 2/8	4 4/8	4 2/8	8	5	Rugby Lake, ON	Thomas S. Dyer	Thomas S. Dyer	2003	998
161	169 2/8	26 4/8	25 4/8	20 1/8	4 6/8	4 7/8	6	6	Ashtabula Co., OH	Anthony Giannell	Anthony Giannell	2003	998
161	165	24 3/8	24 7/8	20	4 7/8	4 7/8	5	4	Scott Co., KS	Darin J. Hoover	Darin J. Hoover	2003	998
161	172 7/8	26 4/8	27 3/8	20 2/8	5	5	6	4	McLean Co., IL	Steve Musselman	Steve Musselman	2003	998
161	175 7/8	25 6/8	25 4/8	17 6/8	4 7/8	4 7/8	6	8	Douglas Co., WI	Jeffrey D. Waters	Jeffrey D. Waters	2003	998
161	173 5/8	25 2/8	25 7/8	19	5 2/8	5 2/8	7	7	Ashtabula Co., OH	Herbert G. Locy III	Herbert G. Locy III	2004	998
161	165 4/8	24 2/8	25 3/8	17 6/8	3 5/8	3 7/8	5	5	Pepin Co., WI	Brent E. King	Brent E. King	2005	998
161	173 4/8	26 3/8	27 1/8	20 3/8	4 5/8	4 3/8	5	7	Shawano Co., WI	Brenda M. Malueg	Brenda M. Malueg	2005	998
160 7/8	172 3/8	26	25 6/8	16 7/8	5	5 2/8	7	5	Turner Co., GA	Wayne Barber	Wayne Barber	2003	1,006
160 7/8	170 5/8	23 2/8	24 5/8	19 3/8	5 3/8	4 6/8	6	6	Adams Co., IL	Christian L. Sanders	Christian L. Sanders	2003	1,006
160 7/8	168 1/8	25	25 4/8	18 7/8	5 2/8	5 1/8	5	5	Metcalfe Co., KY	Brian Sharp	Brian Sharp	2003	1,006
160 7/8	176	24	23 7/8	19 6/8	5 3/8	5 3/8	7	6	White Fox, SK	William J. Feher	William J. Feher	2005	1,006

Score	Gross Score	Length of Main Beam R.	Length of Main Beam L.	Inside Spread	Circumference R.	Circumference L.	Points R.	Points L.	Owner	Locality	Hunter	Date Killed	Rank
160 7/8	176 7/8	23 6/8	23 4/8	19 4/8	5 5/8	5 4/8	6	7	Tyler J. Hicks	Floyd Co., IA	Tyler J. Hicks	2005	1,006
160 6/8	162 6/8	23 4/8	23 3/8	16 6/8	4 2/8	4 3/8	5	5	Edward Conley	Greenup Co., KY	Edward Conley	1992	1,011
160 6/8	178 1/8	23 3/8	23 6/8	14 7/8	4 1/8	4 3/8	8	5	Ken O. Mitchell	Pike Co., MO	Ken O. Mitchell	2000	1,011
160 6/8	173 1/8	25 7/8	26 2/8	17	4 7/8	4 7/8	6	5	Tony S. Korfhage	Jefferson Co., KY	Tony S. Korfhage	2002	1,011
160 6/8	169 7/8	26 5/8	25 7/8	21	4 4/8	4 2/8	5	5	Curtis A. Berry	Erie Co., OH	Curtis A. Berry	2003	1,011
160 6/8	169 7/8	24 1/8	25 2/8	15 4/8	4 3/8	4 3/8	5	5	Brian Stanley	Shoshone Co., ID	Brian Stanley	2003	1,011
160 6/8	167	23 6/8	24 1/8	18 4/8	4 4/8	4 5/8	5	5	Cody J. Merk	Rock Co., WI	Cody J. Merk	2004	1,011
160 6/8	169 3/8	24 6/8	29	22 6/8	5 2/8	4 7/8	4	4	Bruce Sigler	Lewis Co., MO	Bruce Sigler	2004	1,011
160 6/8	162 6/8	24 4/8	24 3/8	15 4/8	4 5/8	4 6/8	5	5	Christopher M. Severino	Pickerel Lake, ON	Christopher M. Severino	2005	1,011
160 5/8	162 6/8	24 4/8	24 7/8	20 3/8	4 3/8	4 4/8	5	5	William O. Allender	Powder River Co., MT	William O. Allender	1972	1,019
160 5/8	166	23 5/8	24 1/8	16 3/8	4 6/8	4 5/8	6	6	Picked Up	Chisago Co., MN	Laverne J. Gilbertson	2000	1,019
160 5/8	190 1/8	25 3/8	25 1/8	18 7/8	5 7/8	5 4/8	6	9	Philip R. Morris	Houston Co., MN	Philip R. Morris	2003	1,019
160 5/8	168	27 6/8	27 4/8	24 1/8	4 5/8	4 4/8	5	6	Jed A. Brown	Webb Co., TX	Jed A. Brown	2004	1,019
160 5/8	165 5/8	27	26 3/8	21 3/8	4 4/8	4 4/8	5	5	James M. Duncan, Sr.	Polk Co., WI	James M. Duncan, Sr.	2004	1,019
160 5/8	168 6/8	25 1/8	25 2/8	20 7/8	5 3/8	5 3/8	6	5	Brian J. Holloway	Sauk Co., WI	Brian J. Holloway	2004	1,019
160 5/8	164 3/8	25 2/8	25 6/8	19 7/8	4 3/8	4 4/8	5	5	Raymond J. Sheredy	Indiana Co., PA	Raymond J. Sheredy	2004	1,019
160 5/8	167 5/8	24 7/8	25	17 1/8	5 1/8	5	6	6	Mark L. Bettis, Jr.	Morrison Co., MN	Mark L. Bettis, Jr.	2005	1,019
160 5/8	167 2/8	25 2/8	25 1/8	20 4/8	4 3/8	4 4/8	5	6	Thersa L. Crosby	Woodson Co., KS	Thersa L. Crosby	2006	1,019
160 4/8	176 7/8	24 4/8	25 7/8	17 5/8	5 1/8	5	8	5	Virginia L. Ploof	Itasca Co., MN	Dianne Payment	1959	1,028
160 4/8	166 7/8	26 2/8	26 7/8	18 6/8	4 2/8	4 4/8	5	5	Tom A. Grover	Schuyler Co., IL	Tom A. Grover	1991	1,028
160 4/8	184 4/8	24 5/8	23 5/8	20 4/8	4 7/8	5	5	6	Thaddeus J. Lauer	Greene Co., IL	Thaddeus J. Lauer	2003	1,028

TYPICAL WHITETAIL DEER
FINAL SCORE: 161-2/8
HUNTER: Cody W. Leed

TYPICAL WHITETAIL DEER
FINAL SCORE: 167
HUNTER: Justin W. Poehnelt

TYPICAL WHITETAIL DEER
FINAL SCORE: 173-7/8
HUNTER: Justin M. Heath

TYPICAL WHITETAIL DEER
FINAL SCORE: 160
HUNTER: Jesse J. Derr

WHITETAIL DEER - TYPICAL ANTLERS

Odocoileus virginianus virginianus and certain related subspecies

Final Score	Gross Score	Length of Main Beam R.	L.	Inside Spread	Circumference at Smallest Place Between Burr & First Point R.	L.	Number of Points R.	L.	Locality	Hunter	Owner	Date Killed	Rank
160 4/8	175 6/8	25 6/8	25 2/8	20 2/8	4 4/8	4 5/8	6	6	Johnson Co., MO	William R. Snyder	William R. Snyder	2003	1,028
160 4/8	163 2/8	24 6/8	24 5/8	17 4/8	4 4/8	4 6/8	4	4	New Haven Co., CT	Picked Up	Matt B. Ellis	2004	1,028
160 4/8	168 7/8	24 3/8	23 4/8	16 4/8	4 7/8	5	7	5	Otoe Co., NE	Harrison C. Kreifels	Harrison C. Kreifels	2004	1,028
160 4/8	167 3/8	25 3/8	25 6/8	19 2/8	4 6/8	4 6/8	5	5	Gage Co., NE	Brian D. Toalson	Brian D. Toalson	2004	1,028
160 4/8	163 6/8	25 4/8	25 4/8	21 4/8	4 5/8	5 2/8	5	5	Dearborn Co., IN	Gregory M. Gavin	Gregory M. Gavin	2005	1,028
160 4/8	174 3/8	25 3/8	26 5/8	18 7/8	5 3/8	5 2/8	6	5	Jo Daviess Co., IL	Eric W. Siese	Eric W. Siese	2005	1,028
160 3/8	169 6/8	27 1/8	27 3/8	18 2/8	5	4 7/8	5	5	Whiteside Co., IL	Jamie L. Dietz	Jamie L. Dietz	2003	1,037
160 3/8	167 5/8	25	26 3/8	19 3/8	4 6/8	4 6/8	5	5	Anoka Co., MN	Picked Up	Laverne J. Gilbertson	2003	1,037
160 3/8	163 5/8	25 6/8	26	19 3/8	5	5 1/8	5	5	Hartford Co., CT	Steven L. Glode	Steven L. Glode	2003	1,037
160 3/8	180	26	26	19	4 3/8	4 2/8	7	6	Callaway Co., MO	Mario Kriete	Mario Kriete	2003	1,037
160 3/8	164	27 5/8	27 7/8	21 3/8	5 2/8	5 1/8	5	5	Jefferson Co., KY	John Murphy	John Murphy	2003	1,037
160 3/8	166 7/8	25	24	19 1/8	5 3/8	5 1/8	5	5	Keokuk Co., IA	Eric J. Stein	Eric J. Stein	2003	1,037
160 3/8	165 2/8	24 6/8	24 5/8	17 7/8	4 6/8	4 7/8	5	5	Dodge Co., NE	Ralph N. Swanson	Ralph N. Swanson	2003	1,037
160 3/8	178 4/8	28 7/8	28 4/8	20 2/8	5 5/8	5 3/8	6	6	Logan Co., KY	J. David Fields	J. David Fields	2004	1,037
160 3/8	179	25 1/8	25 4/8	19 4/8	4 6/8	4 5/8	8	5	Stevens Co., WA	Richard E. Johanson	Richard E. Johanson	2004	1,037
160 3/8	169 2/8	22 6/8	24 3/8	18 3/8	3 7/8	4 1/8	6	5	Stewart Co., TN	Mickey Lehman	Mickey Lehman	2004	1,037
160 3/8	170 2/8	25	25	16 7/8	5 3/8	5	6	6	Kay Co., OK	Larry E. McPeak	Larry E. McPeak	2004	1,037
160 2/8	167 6/8	25 4/8	26 1/8	18 7/8	4 3/8	4 4/8	5	6	Turtle Lake, SK	John T. Barber	John T. Barber	2005	1,051
160 2/8	169 3/8	25 5/8	24 1/8	18 7/8	5 5/8	5 5/8	6	5	Sheep River, AB	Jerry W. Legere	Jerry W. Legere	2005	1,051
160 2/8	167 2/8	25 7/8	24 4/8	17 7/8	5 4/8	5 2/8	5	5	Morgan Co., CO	Steven A. Manos	Steven A. Manos	2005	1,051
160 2/8	170 6/8	25 7/8	27 4/8	20 5/8	5 1/8	5 2/8	7	5	Yuma Co., CO	Axel A. Lindsten	Rodney A. Lindsten	1992	1,051
160 2/8	170 5/8	26 4/8	24 5/8	19 6/8	4 7/8	5	6	5	Cooper Co., MO	Trevor G. Cunningham	Trevor G. Cunningham	2003	1,051
160 2/8	168 3/8	23 5/8	24 3/8	15 3/8	4 3/8	4 3/8	5	6	Floyd Co., IN	Dennis Mayfield	Dennis Mayfield	2003	1,051
160 2/8	166 1/8	25 4/8	25 2/8	19 2/8	4 4/8	4 4/8	5	5	Morgan Co., OH	Brandon S. Burton	Brandon S. Burton	2004	1,051
160 1/8	176 7/8	25 1/8	25 6/8	17 3/8	4 6/8	4 6/8	6	6	Henry Co., KY	Donald Harrison	Donald Harrison	2004	1,058
160 1/8	169 5/8	25 6/8	25 6/8	21	4 6/8	4 7/8	5	4	Clayton Co., IA	Glenn Pauly	Glenn Pauly	2004	1,058
160 1/8	168	23 1/8	23 3/8	17 6/8	4 6/8	4 5/8	7	7	Caldwell Co., KY	Ken Carson	Ken Carson	2005	1,058
160 1/8	174 7/8	27 1/8	26 2/8	18 6/8	5 5/8	5 5/8	6	6	Oneida Co., WI	Arlo Lundberg, Sr.	Ray T. Charles	1972	1,058
160 1/8	180 4/8	23	23	18 3/8	5 7/8	5 7/8	7	6	Rich Lake, AB	Thomas E. Linton	Thomas E. Linton	2001	1,058
160 1/8	175 2/8	24 4/8	24 5/8	15 7/8	4 6/8	5	9	6	Houston Co., GA	Eddie Watson	Eddie Watson	2002	1,058
160 1/8	170 4/8	25 4/8	25 6/8	18 7/8	5 3/8	5 3/8	5	5	Holmes Co., OH	Randy Childers	Randy Childers	2003	1,058
160 1/8	178 6/8	25	24 4/8	18 3/8	4 1/8	4	7	7	Zavala Co., TX	Josh C. Fox	Josh C. Fox	2003	1,058
160 1/8	162 6/8	22	21 6/8	17 5/8	4 2/8	4 3/8	5	5	Trempealeau Co., WI	Nick Fredrixon	Nick Fredrixon	2003	1,058

Score					Points		Locality	Hunter	Owner	Date	Rank
160 1/8	25 6/8	25 7/8	17 4/8	5 2/8	7	7	Belmont Co., OH	Tom Gardner	Tom Gardner	2003	1,058
160 1/8	24 6/8	23 3/8	19 5/8	4 2/8	5	5	Pierce Co., WI	Cory Haglund	Cory Haglund	2003	1,058
160 1/8	25 7/8	26	18 5/8	4 4/8	5	6	Henry Co., KY	Dustin Hamilton	Dustin Hamilton	2003	1,058
160 1/8	25 6/8	25 6/8	23 6/8	6	6	5	Leaf Lake, SK	Daniel Harnois	Daniel Harnois	2003	1,058
160 1/8	25 3/8	24 5/8	16 3/8	4 7/8	6	6	Union Co., IA	Mickey W. Hellickson	Mickey W. Hellickson	2003	1,058
160 1/8	25 3/8	25	17 1/8	5 2/8	5	5	Trempealeau Co., WI	Cory M. Hestekin	Cory M. Hestekin	2003	1,058
160 1/8	23 2/8	24 1/8	18 1/8	3 6/8	5	5	Osage Co., MO	Shay Abel	Shay Abel	2004	1,058
160 1/8	24 2/8	22 3/8	16 3/8	4	5	5	Johnson Co., NE	Dale H. Baker	Dale H. Baker	2004	1,058
160 1/8	24 3/8	23 7/8	18 6/8	4 3/8	8	8	Loudoun Co., VA	Mark T. Cullinane	Mark T. Cullinane	2004	1,058
160 1/8	24 6/8	24 2/8	18 4/8	4 6/8	5	6	Whitley Co., KY	Anthony Lawson	Anthony Lawson	2004	1,058
160	25 6/8	26 1/8	18 4/8	5 2/8	8	8	Muhlenberg Co., KY	Chris Bumps	Chris Bumps	2003	1,074
160	26	25 5/8	20 3/8	4 6/8	6	8	Otter Lake, SK	Gordon D. Mitchell	Gordon D. Mitchell	2003	1,074
160	25 4/8	23 5/8	20 2/8	5 1/8	5	5	Rusk Co., WI	Justin Sather	Justin Sather	2003	1,074
160	27	27 6/8	19 3/8	5 4/8	6	4	McPherson Co., KS	Charles A. Fenstermaker	Charles A. Fenstermaker	2004	1,074
160	24 3/8	25 3/8	18 6/8	5 1/8	6	6	Lake Co., IN	Andrew M. Fox	Andrew M. Fox	2004	1,074
160	25 5/8	26	22 2/8	4 7/8	6	6	Rawlins Co., KS	Edward D. Porubsky	Edward D. Porubsky	2004	1,074
160	23 7/8	23 5/8	17 6/8	4 2/8	5	5	Todd Co., SD	Patrick J. Sposato	Patrick J. Sposato	2004	1,074
160	24 2/8	26	17	4 5/8	6	7	Hancock Co., ME	Jesse J. Derr	Jesse J. Derr	2005	1,074
160	23 6/8	24 1/8	22 3/8	4 3/8	6	5	Dorchester Co., MD	James P. Heisey, Jr.	James P. Heisey, Jr.	2005	1,074
160	21 1/8	24 2/8	17 4/8	3 6/8	6	6	Northampton Co., NC	Joseph E. Sawyer	Joseph E. Sawyer	2005	1,074
200 1/8*	26 3/8	26 5/8	18 7/8	4 7/8	7	7	Otauwau River, AB	Eugene I. Kurinka	Eugene I. Kurinka	2005	
198 3/8*	26	25 2/8	21 7/8	4 6/8	6	6	Good Spirit Lake, SK	Blaine D. Kreps	Blaine D. Kreps	2005	
196 6/8*	29 6/8	27 6/8	19 5/8	5	5	7	Adams Co., OH	Justin L. Metzner	Justin L. Metzner	2006	

* Final score subject to revision by additional verifying measurements.

Minimum Score 185   *Odocoileus virginianus virginianus* and certain related subspecies   World's Record 333 7/8

Final Score	Gross Score	Length of Main Beam R.	L.	Inside Spread	Circumference at Smallest Place Between Burr & First Point R.	L.	Number of Points R.	L.	Locality	Hunter	Owner	Date Killed	Rank
295 3/8	304 4/8	21 6/8	24 5/8	18 4/8	6 5/8	6 6/8	25	22	McDonough Co., IL	Scott R. Dexter	Scott R. Dexter	2004	1
295 3/8	304 7/8	30 2/8	29	25 1/8	5 4/8	5 7/8	18	17	Adams Co., OH	Jonathan R. Schmucker	Jonathan R. Schmucker	2006	1
267 1/8	283 4/8	25 7/8	27 4/8	18 2/8	6 4/8	7	16	21	Mason Co., IL	David H. Jones	David H. Jones	2003	3
256 3/8	260 4/8	25 5/8	25 7/8	20 5/8	6 1/8	6 2/8	12	10	Marshall Co., IL	Steve Wallis	Steve Wallis	2004	4
253 1/8	260 6/8	30 1/8	27 3/8	20 4/8	5 4/8	5 4/8	8	18	Buchanan Co., IA	Brian Andrews	Brian Andrews	2003	5
251 6/8	256 6/8	26	27	21	4 4/8	4 6/8	16	11	Clark Co., IL	Kenneth D. Shumaker	Kenneth D. Shumaker	2005	6
250 5/8	265 2/8	22 6/8	28 3/8	20 3/8	6 3/8	7 4/8	11	17	Switzerland Co., IN	Zoltan Dobsa	Cabela's, Inc.	1977	7
249 3/8	256 5/8	22 1/8	22 1/8	19	4 4/8	4 3/8	17	16	Trigg Co., KY	Dann T. Hughes	Dann T. Hughes	2005	8
248	254 1/8	22 1/8	22 4/8	17 4/8	6 2/8	5 4/8	20	13	Osborne Co., KS	Picked Up	Rich E. Bouchey	2005	9
247 4/8	256 7/8	27 2/8	26	18 5/8	5 6/8	6	12	17	Carroll Co., OH	Marlon S. Hale	Marlon S. Hale	2005	10
245	260	28 6/8	28 6/8	21 7/8	5 6/8	5 7/8	14	12	Washington Co., KS	John A. Payne	John A. Payne	2003	11
243 4/8	264 3/8	22 2/8	24 2/8	20 7/8	5 7/8	5 6/8	18	15	Harrison Co., IA	Tim S. Waldron	Tim S. Waldron	2005	12
243	249 4/8	18 6/8	21	12 7/8	5 4/8	5 5/8	18	17	Pike Co., IL	Harry J. Kinowski III	Harry J. Kinowski III	2004	13
242 7/8	247 1/8	25 2/8	24 4/8	18 1/8	6 1/8	5 4/8	13	11	Douglas Co., KS	Ira A. Faust	Ira A. Faust	2002	14
240 3/8	244 4/8	17	17 4/8	18 5/8	4 6/8	4 5/8	10	19	Hughes Co., OK	David L. Lambert	David L. Lambert	2003	15
240	255 7/8	31 6/8	30 3/8	21 5/8	5 4/8	5 6/8	17	13	Waldo Co., ME	Raymond Pooler	Maine Antler Shed & Wildl. Mus.	1960	16
237 6/8	242 4/8	27 2/8	27	24 1/8	6 1/8	5 4/8	10	10	Platte Co., MO	Alan F. Kane	Alan F. Kane	2005	17
237 2/8	251 5/8	22 5/8	25 1/8	22 4/8	6	5 5/8	17	15	Turtle Lake, SK	Max D. Bru	Cabela's, Inc.	2001	18
236 6/8	248 3/8	23	25 2/8	15	5 3/8	4 7/8	17	12	Brokenhead River, MB	Richard J. Gobeil	Richard J. Gobeil	2003	19
236 1/8	241	25 2/8	25 1/8	17	5 4/8	5 7/8	14	13	Shellbrook, SK	Michael J. Tanchuk	Michael J. Tanchuk	2004	20
235	238 6/8	27 5/8	28 2/8	24 6/8	5 2/8	5	13	8	Hancock Co., ME	Picked Up	Bruce A. Damon	2003	21
234 7/8	249 4/8	26 7/8	25	22 4/8	6 7/8	7 2/8	8	15	Jersey Co., IL	Chad Goetten	Chad Goetten	2003	22
234 3/8	246	27 6/8	26 5/8	18	6 6/8	6	9	13	Vernon Co., MO	David T. Sparks	David T. Sparks	2004	23
234 2/8	245 5/8	28 4/8	28	19	6 7/8	7	12	11	Decatur Co., IN	Jack E. Keihn	Jack E. Keihn	2005	24
233 2/8	238 7/8	27 3/8	27 4/8	18 6/8	6 2/8	6	11	11	Woodson Co., KS	Randy Clarke	Cabela's, Inc.	2004	25
233 1/8	240 6/8	27 6/8	26 4/8	19 6/8	4 7/8	5	12	10	Allamakee Co., IA	Harvey Dirks	Harvey Dirks	2003	26
232 4/8	251	28 5/8	23 2/8	22 1/8	5 7/8	6 7/8	12	18	Jackson Co., KY	Gregory L. Wilson	Gregory L. Wilson	2005	27
231 7/8	242 1/8	18 6/8	16 2/8	16 7/8	5 5/8	5 1/8	14	15	Carter Co., OK	C. Steve Risinger	C. Steve Risinger	2005	28
231 4/8	238 3/8	30	29 5/8	22 3/8	5 3/8	5 2/8	6	9	Scioto Co., OH	Roger D. Lewis	Roger D. Lewis	2003	29
230 6/8	236 4/8	25 6/8	29	20 2/8	4 6/8	4 6/8	10	10	Pettis Co., MO	Charles R. DeWitt	Charles R. DeWitt	2003	30
230	240 4/8	27 2/8	27 3/8	21 7/8	5 5/8	5 4/8	11	11	Vernon Co., WI	Lee Johnston	Lee Johnston	2005	31
229 6/8	235 7/8	23 4/8	24	14 2/8	6	6 4/8	11	13	Pike Co., IL	Kory M. McAllister	Kory M. McAllister	2004	32

Score	Main Beam	Main Beam	Inside Spread	Circ.	Circ.	Points	Points	Locality	Hunter	Owner	Date	Photo
229 2/8	29	29	17 5/8	6 4/8	6 3/8	16	11	Crawford Co., KS	Dennis D. Jameson	Cabela's, Inc.	2003	33
229 2/8	24 6/8	25	18 6/8	6 6/8	7 2/8	12	11	Buffalo Co., WI	Brian G. Stenseth	Brian G. Stenseth	2004	33
229 2/8	23	21 5/8	16 6/8	5 5/8	5 1/8	17	11	McLean Co., IL	Brent F. Van Hoveln	Brent F. Van Hoveln	2005	33
227 7/8	26 3/8	23 4/8	19 1/8	5 3/8	4 6/8	13	15	West Prairie River, AB	Charles J. Dube	Charles J. Dube	2005	36
227 3/8	29 7/8	28 2/8	22 2/8	5 6/8	5 6/8	13	14	Oliver Co., ND	Robert Schmitt	Robert Schmitt	2003	37
227 3/8	25 6/8	25	20 5/8	5 3/8	5 3/8	12	12	Collingsworth Co., TX	H. Hunt Allred	H. Hunt Allred	2004	37
226 7/8	27 4/8	26 6/8	20	5 1/8	5 2/8	14	14	Adams Co., IL	Steven L. DeWitt	Steven L. DeWitt	2006	39
226 6/8	22 2/8	22 2/8	15 2/8	5 4/8	5 2/8	13	11	Neosho Co., KS	W. Kirk Keller	W. Kirk Keller	2005	40
226 5/8	27 6/8	22 4/8	25	5 1/8	5 4/8	9	11	Otter Tail Co., MN	Brandon Bernu	Brandon Bernu	2005	41
226 4/8	22 5/8	22 4/8	20 4/8	5 4/8	5	13	16	Peace River, AB	Ronald F. Clous	Ronald F. Clous	2005	42
226 4/8	21	21 6/8	21	6 5/8	6 5/8	15	15	Clay Co., TX	Sherman G. Wyman	Sherman G. Wyman	2005	42
226 1/8	28 7/8	28 5/8	18 3/8	4 5/8	4 5/8	14	15	Hart Co., KY	Picked Up	Jerry T. Johnson	2005	44
225 7/8	26 6/8	26 6/8	19	5 3/8	5 3/8	16	11	Van Buren Co., IA	William K. Pfaff	William K. Pfaff	2003	45
225 7/8	26 1/8	26	16	5 1/8	4 7/8	10	11	Hillsdale Co., MI	Aaron M. Davis	Aaron M. Davis	2004	45
225 6/8	26 6/8	26	25 6/8	5 4/8	5 5/8	15	10	Scioto Co., OH	Virgil L. Laxton	Virgil L. Laxton	2004	47
225 2/8	28 5/8	26 5/8	16 2/8	5 2/8	5 4/8	12	12	Penobscot Co., ME	Unknown	Maine Antler Shed & Wildl. Mus.	PR 2004	48
225	23 4/8	23 5/8	19 6/8	6 1/8	6 1/8	15	9	Kandiyohi Co., MN	Bradley Karl	Bradley Karl	2004	49
225	23 7/8	24 4/8	20 7/8	5 3/8	5 3/8	11	11	Monroe Co., IL	Russ W. Nobbe	Russ W. Nobbe	2005	49
224 7/8	22 6/8	24 5/8	16 7/8	5 7/8	5 4/8	12	12	Buffalo Co., WI	Paul Hofer	Paul Hofer	2003	51
224 7/8	26 5/8	26 2/8	18 2/8	5	5	10	16	Sedgwick Co., KS	Terry L. Alsup	Terry L. Alsup	2004	51
224 3/8	24 1/8	24 1/8	19 4/8	5 2/8	5 2/8	13	12	Lenore Lake, SK	Jody Vedress	Jody Vedress	2004	53
224 3/8	21 2/8	23	20 6/8	4 5/8	4 5/8	15	17	Cape Girardeau Co., MO	Lynn Yount	Lynn Yount	2005	53
224 2/8	25 2/8	24 1/8	18 1/8	4 7/8	4 7/8	13	13	St. Louis Co., MN	Peter Privett	Peter Privett	2004	55
224 2/8	19 5/8	20 5/8	17 5/8	4	4	15	11	McLennan Co., TX	Picked Up	Cynthia S. Parongao	2005	55
224 1/8	29 1/8	29 1/8	25 6/8	6 2/8	5 7/8	6	14	Des Moines Co., IA	Steve Coates	Steve Coates	2003	57
224 1/8	26 3/8	26 3/8	21	6 5/8	6	8	11	La Salle Co., IL	John Jeffries	John Jeffries	2003	57
223 5/8	25 3/8	25 3/8	22	6	6	8	11	Jefferson Co., MO	Eugene Gill	Eugene Gill	2004	59
223 3/8	26 6/8	26 1/8	26 1/8	5 1/8	6	14	7	Saline Co., KS	Clyde K. Keen	Clyde K. Keen	2003	60
223 1/8	25 7/8	25 7/8	19 1/8	5 1/8	4 7/8	10	13	Washington Co., AR	Richard L. Little	Richard L. Little	2004	61
223 1/8	24 1/8	24 1/8	25 2/8	5 4/8	5	15	10	Red River Parish, LA	Todd M. Tracy	Todd M. Tracy	2005	61
223	29	29	21 1/8	5 4/8	5 4/8	12	10	Lancaster Co., NE	Jeffrey A. Moody	Jeffrey A. Moody	2003	63
222 7/8	21 6/8	21 6/8	22 6/8	4 7/8	4 6/8	10	9	Van Buren Co., IA	Gene Wensel	Gene Wensel	2004	64
222 3/8	26 6/8	26 6/8	21 2/8	4 4/8	4 6/8	10	12	Linn Co., IA	Travis R. Hanf	Travis R. Hanf	2003	65
222 3/8	23 1/8	23 2/8	20 4/8	5 4/8	5 4/8	11	10	Thickwood Hills, SK	Richard Harder	Richard Harder	2005	65
222 2/8	28 6/8	28 6/8	17 2/8	5 7/8	6 1/8	9	10	Vermilion Co., IL	Jeffrey R. Kepling	Jeffrey R. Kepling	2004	67
222 2/8	23 6/8	24 5/8	20 3/8	4 7/8	4 5/8	15	9	Ramsey Co., MN	Debra J. Luzinski	Debra J. Luzinski	2006	67
221 7/8	26	26	17 3/8	6 3/8	6 3/8	11	11	Adams Co., IL	Picked Up	Victor Rowley	2006	69
221 6/8	27	27 5/8	21	6 2/8	6 2/8	12	10	Shelby Co., IL	Marvin L. Binnion	Marvin L. Binnion	2001	70
221 4/8	23 2/8	25	21 1/8	6	5 2/8	11	11	Winneshiek Co., IA	Brian K. LaRue	Brian K. LaRue	2005	71
221 3/8	28 1/8	28 7/8	28 7/8	6 7/8	6 2/8	10	12	Washington Co., NE	Clint T. Barnes	Clint T. Barnes	2005	72
220 7/8	27 3/8	26 6/8	18 2/8	5 1/8	5 3/8	11	10	Osceola Co., IA	Troy J. Vandehoef	Troy J. Vandehoef	2005	73

Odocoileus virginianus virginianus and certain related subspecies

Final Score	Gross Score	Length of Main Beam		Inside Spread	Circumference at Smallest Place Between Burr & First Point		Number of Points		Locality	Hunter	Owner	Date Killed	Rank
		R.	L.		R.	L.	R.	L.					
220 6/8	227 4/8	19 6/8	19 2/8	15 6/8	6 5/8	7	13	12	Clinton Co., IN	Picked Up	Warren G. Leonard	2004	74
220 2/8	229 4/8	27 1/8	26 3/8	20 3/8	6 3/8	6 4/8	12	12	Martin Co., IN	David G. Brasseur	David G. Brasseur	2004	75
220	227	25 7/8	26 5/8	18 4/8	4 7/8	4 6/8	9	8	Clay Co., KS	Jeffrey W. Severson	Jeffrey W. Severson	2004	76
219 7/8	223 7/8	25	24 1/8	18	5 2/8	5 3/8	10	10	Henderson Co., IL	Mark Loving	Mark Loving	2004	77
219 6/8	231	26 3/8	24	18 2/8	5 6/8	7 1/8	11	11	Adams Co., IL	Eric Peters	Eric Peters	2003	78
219 6/8	224 2/8	25 4/8	27	19 5/8	5 7/8	5 6/8	12	12	Hocking Co., OH	Aaron J. Ireland	Aaron J. Ireland	2004	78
219 5/8	224 1/8	25 2/8	25	15 1/8	5 6/8	5 5/8	14	13	Wadena Co., MN	Rick Schoenrock	Rick Schoenrock	2003	80
219 5/8	227	24 3/8	25 4/8	22	4 6/8	4 6/8	12	11	Guernsey Co., OH	Tim R. King	Tim R. King	2005	80
219 4/8	237 7/8	29 2/8	27	18 6/8	5 1/8	5 2/8	10	11	Mahnomen Co., MN	Jesse Wolbeck	Jesse Wolbeck	2003	82
219 4/8	236 1/8	23 3/8	25 6/8	21 1/8	6	5 1/8	12	8	Saskatchewan	Unknown	Lynn G. Duckworth PR	2004	82
219 3/8	222 2/8	27	27 5/8	23 5/8	5 4/8	5 4/8	10	4	Fremont Co., CO	Lucas T. Hays	Lucas T. Hays	2003	84
218 5/8	231 5/8	27 1/8	24 2/8	22 7/8	5 6/8	5 6/8	12	9	McLean Co., IL	Josh Roop	Josh Roop	2005	85
218 4/8	228 6/8	24 5/8	26 4/8	23 5/8	6 4/8	5 4/8	8	11	Pike Co., IL	Scott Jones	Scott Jones	2004	86
218 4/8	224	26 2/8	26 5/8	19 5/8	5 1/8	5 2/8	10	9	Bureau Co., IL	Daniel C. Larson	Daniel C. Larson	2005	86
218 2/8	227 3/8	27 6/8	29 7/8	20 3/8	5 5/8	5 7/8	10	8	Monroe Co., IA	Kevin Halbmaier	Kevin Halbmaier	2003	88
218 2/8	227 1/8	27 4/8	27	19 3/8	5 7/8	5 4/8	9	9	Blindman River, AB	Mike McRee	Mike McRee	2004	88
218 2/8	229 7/8	27 2/8	24 7/8	20 5/8	7 3/8	7 3/8	11	12	Wicomico Co., MD	M. Carroll Huston, Jr.	M. Carroll Huston, Jr.	2005	88
217 7/8	222 3/8	23 6/8	23 5/8	26 6/8	6 4/8	6 3/8	11	7	Wayne Co., IL	Dustin D. Toombs	Dustin D. Toombs	2003	91
217 7/8	229 4/8	27 2/8	26 6/8	19 7/8	6 1/8	5 7/8	10	14	Monona Co., IA	Jason L. McDonald	Jason L. McDonald	2005	91
217 6/8	229 4/8	26 4/8	26 1/8	19 2/8	7 4/8	6 7/8	12	11	Marshall Co., IA	Jeffrey T. Manzer	Jeffrey T. Manzer	2003	93
217 5/8	227 7/8	24 5/8	23 4/8	14 7/8	5 6/8	6 2/8	10	14	Putnam Co., MO	Terry W. Tucker	Terry W. Tucker	2005	94
217 4/8	226	26 3/8	25 4/8	20	5 1/8	5 2/8	11	9	Fayette Co., IL	Clement Lilly	Clement Lilly	1966	95
217 1/8	230 5/8	22 2/8	21 6/8	11 7/8	5 4/8	5 4/8	17	13	Ottawa Co., KS	John H. West	John H. West	2004	96
216 7/8	230 2/8	27 5/8	26 6/8	20 1/8	5 1/8	5 4/8	10	11	Pope Co., MN	Morten Olson	Clyde Olson	1963	97
216 6/8	221 7/8	26 3/8	25 3/8	18 7/8	6	6 1/8	10	9	Morgan Co., IL	Dustin Molohon	Dustin Molohon	2003	98
216 3/8	220 6/8	29 2/8	29 2/8	22 2/8	5 3/8	5 3/8	6	9	Waukesha Co., WI	David W. Klermund	David W. Klermund	2003	99
216 3/8	232 7/8	23 6/8	20 2/8	17 7/8	6 6/8	7 5/8	15	14	Kootenai Co., ID	Joseph S. LaPlante	Joseph S. LaPlante	2005	99
216 2/8	221 4/8	26 6/8	25 3/8	21	4 4/8	4 6/8	8	11	Birch River, MB	Klaas Koop	Daryn Eakin	1969	101
216 2/8	224 1/8	27 5/8	26 1/8	18 6/8	4 4/8	4 5/8	11	9	Adair Co., KY	Picked Up	Gerry Wethington	1998	101
216 1/8	224 5/8	27 4/8	26 6/8	16 4/8	6	6	16	16	Gage Co., NE	Steve C. Behrens	Steve C. Behrens	2005	103
215 5/8	225	20 4/8	22 3/8	15 2/8	6 2/8	4 5/8	15	8	Zavala Co., TX	Larry H. Wilkey	Larry H. Wilkey	2005	104
215 3/8	221 1/8	26 1/8	25 3/8	17 7/8	5 6/8	5 4/8	13	14	Woods Co., OK	Buster Burton	Buster Burton	2003	105
215 3/8	228 1/8	26 2/8	24 2/8	20 3/8	5	4 6/8	12	11	Lewis Co., MO	Jill L. Brocksmith	Jill L. Brocksmith	2005	105

Score	Gross Score	R. Beam	L. Beam	Inside Spread	R. Circ.	L. Circ.	R. Pts.	L. Pts.	Locality	Hunter	Owner	Date	Rank
215 2/8	217 5/8	25 3/8	25 2/8	19 6/8	4 6/8	4 6/8	12	10	Grayson Co., KY	Bobby Edrington	Bobby Edrington	2004	107
215 2/8	226 1/8	25 7/8	25 2/8	19	5 6/8	5 3/8	11	13	Mayes Co., OK	Carl R. Scott	Carl R. Scott	2004	107
214 7/8	223 1/8	27 5/8	27 3/8	21 7/8	5 3/8	5 1/8	8	9	Atascosa Co., TX	Marty L. Griffith	Marty L. Griffith	2005	109
214 7/8	223	25 5/8	28 1/8	21 6/8	5 6/8	6	8	11	Clinton Co., IA	Darrel H. Ploog	Darrel H. Ploog	2005	109
214 6/8	224 3/8	24 3/8	24 2/8	18 4/8	5 4/8	5 5/8	11	9	Pawnee Co., NE	Chris Kramer	Cabela's, Inc.	2003	111
214 4/8	220 3/8	26 4/8	27 4/8	25 3/8	6 2/8	6 3/8	9	12	Pike Co., IL	John M. Thomas	John M. Thomas	2004	112
214 1/8	223 2/8	23 5/8	23 1/8	16 1/8	4 5/8	4 7/8	11	12	Douglas Co., WI	Larry Kline	Larry Kline	2004	113
212 6/8	219 2/8	26	25 4/8	18 2/8	5 6/8	5 6/8	11	7	Clark Co., IN	Picked Up	Cabela's, Inc.	2003	114
212 6/8	218 1/8	24 1/8	24 4/8	19 2/8	5 6/8	6 6/8	17	13	Garfield Co., OK	David Foltz	David Foltz	2004	114
212 5/8	216	25 6/8	25 4/8	18 3/8	5 1/8	5 3/8	11	12	Noble Co., IN	Lyman Holbrook	Lyman Holbrook	2003	116
212 5/8	223 7/8	23 5/8	23 6/8	20 1/8	5 3/8	5 4/8	8	11	Pontotoc Co., MS	Stephen G. McBrayer	Stephen G. McBrayer	2005	116
212 4/8	220 7/8	25 1/8	23 5/8	17 4/8	4 6/8	5	15	11	Lincoln Co., OK	Donald Townsend	Donald Townsend	2004	118
212 4/8	216	25 6/8	24 5/8	14 4/8	5 4/8	5 4/8	9	5	Good Spirit Lake, SK	Picked Up	Ian Thomas	2005	118
212 3/8	219 5/8	24 6/8	24 6/8	21 1/8	5 2/8	5 2/8	13	15	Greene Co., IL	Jim Leitner	Jim Leitner	2004	120
212 2/8	230 6/8	26 7/8	23 6/8	18 3/8	6 5/8	7 1/8	12	13	Stanton Co., NE	Jack J. Grevson	Jack J. Grevson	1962	121
212 1/8	218 4/8	25 2/8	26 3/8	16 1/8	4 7/8	5	10	8	Last Mountain Lake, SK	R. Douglas Kelln	R. Douglas Kelln	2003	122
212 1/8	221 3/8	25 2/8	24 3/8	17 2/8	5 2/8	6	13	11	Lafayette Co., MO	Picked Up	Wendell R. Schmidt	2004	122
212	218 5/8	25 4/8	27 1/8	25 3/8	4 5/8	4 4/8	9	8	Dodge Co., WI	John R. Hoey	John R. Hoey	1955	124
212	220 7/8	27 7/8	28 1/8	18 7/8	5 4/8	5 4/8	7	7	Macoupin Co., IL	Brett Herbeck	Brett Herbeck	2004	124
211 7/8	222 6/8	27 4/8	27 4/8	22 6/8	5 1/8	5 2/8	9	8	Grundy Co., MO	Johnny C. Norris	Johnny C. Norris	2005	126
211 6/8	222 2/8	26 1/8	27 3/8	—	5 5/8	5 5/8	11	10	Pettis Co., MO	Marvin E. Shull	Marvin E. Shull	2000	127

NON-TYPICAL WHITETAIL DEER
FINAL SCORE: 204-4/8
HUNTER: William B. Manning

NON-TYPICAL WHITETAIL DEER
FINAL SCORE: 189
HUNTER: Mitchell Price

NON-TYPICAL WHITETAIL DEER
FINAL SCORE: 229-2/8
HUNTER: Brian G. Stenseth

NON-TYPICAL WHITETAIL DEER
FINAL SCORE: 190-2/8
HUNTER: Charles F. French

WHITETAIL DEER - NON-TYPICAL ANTLERS

Odocoileus virginianus virginianus and certain related subspecies

Final Score	Gross Score	Length of Main Beam R.	L.	Inside Spread	Circumference at Smallest Place Between Burr & First Point R.	L.	Number of Points R.	L.	Locality	Hunter	Owner	Date Killed	Rank
211 5/8	220 7/8	23 4/8	24 2/8	16 2/8	5 7/8	6 3/8	13	12	Adams Co., IL	Picked Up	Bill Oakman	2005	128
211 3/8	215 6/8	29 7/8	29 1/8	18 2/8	5	4 6/8	11	6	Ashland Co., OH	Jon A. Byers	Jon A. Byers	2003	129
211 2/8	215 3/8	25	25 6/8	18	3 7/8	4	8	6	Allamakee Co., IA	Jason J. Johnson	Jason J. Johnson	2003	130
211 1/8	218 3/8	26 1/8	25 7/8	16 3/8	6	6 1/8	11	12	McHenry Co., IL	Chadd W. Hartwig	Chadd W. Hartwig	2003	131
210 6/8	217 6/8	27 6/8	28 7/8	19 6/8	4 6/8	4 7/8	8	9	Harvey Co., KS	Rudolf Hiebert, Jr.	Rudolf Hiebert, Jr.	2003	132
210 3/8	227	23	24 3/8	18 4/8	5 2/8	5 3/8	9	15	Madison Co., IA	Lucas W. Dudney	Lucas W. Dudney	2005	133
210 3/8	214 7/8	29 6/8	29 3/8	23 5/8	6 1/8	6	8	8	Holmes Co., OH	Picked Up	Douglas L. Mills	2006	133
210 2/8	214 3/8	24 2/8	25 1/8	17 6/8	5 6/8	5 5/8	10	11	Henry Co., MO	Roger McKinley	Roger McKinley	2004	135
210 2/8	213 7/8	25 5/8	25 4/8	19 7/8	5 2/8	5 3/8	8	12	Decatur Co., KS	Shannon D. Bird	Shannon D. Bird	2005	135
210	225 4/8	25 6/8	27 6/8	19 7/8	6 5/8	6 4/8	10	8	Barron Co., WI	Jeffrey P. Crotteau	Jeffrey P. Crotteau	2005	137
209 7/8	216 1/8	28 2/8	28 6/8	17 4/8	5 6/8	5 6/8	8	8	St. Louis Co., MN	Ben Teeno Sibinski	Dale Sibinski	1957	138
209 7/8	214	27 4/8	27 6/8	22	5	5	10	10	Grayson Co., KY	Pat Croghan	Pat Croghan	1987	138
209 7/8	223 4/8	24 5/8	25 4/8	17 2/8	4 6/8	4 6/8	11	11	Columbia Co., WI	Eric Eichline	Eric Eichline	2003	138
209 7/8	216 7/8	25 1/8	26 3/8	18 2/8	5 6/8	5 3/8	8	11	Calumet Co., WI	Picked Up	James Hagenow	2004	138
209 6/8	219 4/8	27 2/8	27 3/8	20 5/8	5 1/8	5 2/8	8	9	Hancock Co., IL	Brian D. Gaines	Brian D. Gaines	2005	142
209 5/8	222 6/8	26 1/8	27 1/8	23 7/8	5 1/8	5 3/8	14	8	Green Lake Co., WI	Ervin O. Miller	Ervin O. Miller	2004	143
209 4/8	220 5/8	23 2/8	23 4/8	18 5/8	6 5/8	6 3/8	10	12	Dubuque Co., IA	Luke R. Hoerner	Luke R. Hoerner	2006	144
209 4/8	214 1/8	25 4/8	25 5/8	21 5/8	4 6/8	5	8	8	Unknown	Unknown	Maine Antler Shed & PR Wildl. Mus.	2006	144
209 2/8	216	26 2/8	28 5/8	19 2/8	5 1/8	5 1/8	13	7	Swift Current, SK	Howie F. Ellis	Howie F. Ellis	2003	146
209 1/8	224 7/8	25 4/8	27 4/8	15 6/8	7 6/8	5 6/8	11	10	Lee Co., IL	Matthew W. Ganz	Matthew W. Ganz	2005	147
209	217 5/8	26	25 4/8	17	5 2/8	5 2/8	8	12	Washburn Co., WI	Matthew T. Bray	Matthew T. Bray	2003	148
209	216 1/8	25 4/8	25 1/8	19 5/8	6 5/8	6 5/8	13	11	Erie Co., OH	Arnold G. Hamilton	Arnold G. Hamilton	2003	148
208 6/8	216 1/8	24 3/8	24 4/8	16 1/8	4 7/8	4 3/8	12	11	Benton Co., IA	Richard F. Zerba	Richard F. Zerba	2005	150
208 5/8	211 4/8	28 5/8	29 2/8	23 1/8	5 4/8	5 4/8	8	5	Warren Co., IA	Randy Holland	Randy Holland	2003	151
208 4/8	217 7/8	25 4/8	26 1/8	18	4 7/8	5 2/8	9	8	Floyd Co., VA	Leslie E. Hall	Leslie E. Hall	2005	152
208 4/8	218 6/8	17 3/8	21 3/8	14 4/8	5 6/8	6 2/8	14	13	Sussex Co., DE	Keith H. Lee	Keith H. Lee	2005	152
208 2/8	215 1/8	23 4/8	25	23 4/8	6	6 5/8	6	11	Meeting Lake, SK	Garry Weran	Garry Weran	2003	154
208 2/8	215 1/8	23 2/8	22	16 4/8	5 3/8	6 2/8	11	9	Pike Co., IL	Brian K. Dobbins	Brian K. Dobbins	2005	154
208 2/8	216 2/8	28 4/8	28 5/8	21 6/8	6 4/8	6 2/8	8	9	Lincoln Co., MO	Rick D. Jameson	Rick D. Jameson	2005	154
208 1/8	210 7/8	27 2/8	26 7/8	18 3/8	5	5	10	9	Carter Co., KY	David L. Jessie	David L. Jessie	2003	157
208 1/8	216 3/8	29 2/8	30 1/8	22 6/8	5 1/8	5	11	5	N. Saskatchewan River, AB	Steven W. Ostrander	Steven W. Ostrander	2006	157

Score								Locality	Owner	Hunter	Date	Rank
208	220 1/8	25 7/8	23 1/8	16 1/8	6 2/8	12	8	Barton Co., KS	Marvin C. Sessler	Marvin C. Sessler	2004	159
207 7/8	218 5/8	27 4/8	28 4/8	21 1/8	4 6/8	9	10	St. Joseph Co., IN	James L. Stone	IN Dept. Nat. Res.	2002	160
207 7/8	215 4/8	28 3/8	28 3/8	22	5	10	6	Muscatine Co., IA	Matt Garvin	Matt Garvin	2003	160
207 7/8	214 3/8	24 6/8	25 5/8	21 1/8	4 7/8	10	8	St. Clair Co., IL	Tyler J. Middendorf	Tyler J. Middendorf	2004	160
207 7/8	209 5/8	25 6/8	24 7/8	19 7/8	5 2/8	8	9	Last Mountain Lake, SK	Dana Morrison	Dana Morrison	2005	160
207 7/8	213 5/8	25 2/8	25	20	5 1/8	8	11	Vernon Co., WI	Bradley J. Spaulding	Bradley J. Spaulding	2005	160
207 5/8	217 1/8	28 4/8	28 1/8	19 4/8	5 6/8	10	9	Barren Co., KY	Dale Fancher	Dale Fancher	2004	165
207 4/8	211	22 7/8	24	20 3/8	5 1/8	7	9	Boone Co., IA	Wayne E. Nelson	Wayne E. Nelson	2004	166
207 2/8	214 6/8	25 2/8	24 6/8	18	5 2/8	7	11	Moultrie Co., IL	Don R. Higgins	Don R. Higgins	2004	167
207 1/8	218 5/8	28	28	22 1/8	5 2/8	10	7	Macon Co., IL	Shannon Babb	Shannon Babb	2004	168
207 1/8	213 7/8	26	25 7/8	21 4/8	5 4/8	10	8	Wayne Co., IL	Brandon K.W. Caudle	Brandon K.W. Caudle	2005	168
207	219 3/8	26	25 4/8	18 5/8	5 2/8	11	8	Neely Lake, SK	Ken W. Hayworth	Ken W. Hayworth	2004	170
206 6/8	218 6/8	25 6/8	25 7/8	19 5/8	5 4/8	13	9	Greene Co., OH	Robert M. Gerleman	Cabela's, Inc.	2003	171
206 6/8	215	25 7/8	25 4/8	18 3/8	5 3/8	8	9	Zavala Co., TX	Alberto Bailleres	Alberto Bailleres	2006	171
206 3/8	214 3/8	27 5/8	28 4/8	21 4/8	5 1/8	13	9	Clinton Co., OH	Mike Warnock	Mike Warnock	2003	173
206 3/8	211 5/8	27	28	18 3/8	5 7/8	10	9	Greene Co., IL	Randy A. Varble	Randy A. Varble	2004	174
206 3/8	212 3/8	24 2/8	24 1/8	15 5/8	5 2/8	9	14	Lucas Co., IA	Steven E. Lutz	Steven E. Lutz	2005	174
206 2/8	216 3/8	27 5/8	26 5/8	20 6/8	6 1/8	7	10	Lancaster Co., NE	Robert P. Findley	Robert P. Findley	2005	176
206 1/8	216 7/8	29 4/8	30	25 2/8	5 3/8	9	9	Monroe Co., IA	Donald Mason	Donald Mason	2003	177
206 1/8	211 3/8	27 2/8	27 1/8	19 7/8	4 6/8	10	11	Noble Co., IN	Shane T. Silver	Shane T. Silver	2004	177
206	226	22 4/8	26 5/8	16 4/8	5 5/8	11	11	Warren Co., MO	Robert L. Reese	Robert L. Reese	2006	179
205 6/8	207 6/8	25	24 4/8	19	4 7/8	9	10	Love Co., OK	Nolan L. Hester, Jr.	Nolan L. Hester, Jr.	2003	180
205 6/8	216 4/8	23 7/8	22	16 4/8	5 4/8	11	12	Todd Co., MN	Glenn E. Pesta	Glenn E. Pesta	2003	180
205 6/8	218 6/8	22	23 3/8	18 7/8	6 2/8	9	10	Monroe Co., IA	Brandon Williams	Brandon Williams	2003	180
205 5/8	211 3/8	25 4/8	24 6/8	14 2/8	5	11	11	Shawano Co., WI	Brenda L. Tauferner	Brenda L. Tauferner	2004	183
205 4/8	214 7/8	22 3/8	25 3/8	18 2/8	5 4/8	8	6	Pine River, BC	Brogan Didier	Brogan Didier	2004	184
205 4/8	211 3/8	27 7/8	28 1/8	18 2/8	5 1/8	9	13	Grant Co., WI	Charles R. Wright	Charles R. Wright	2005	184
205 3/8	212 1/8	28 5/8	29 2/8	24 7/8	7 4/8	8	11	Penobscot Co., ME	Picked Up	Toby L. Montgomery	2004	186
205 2/8	216 7/8	24 4/8	25 4/8	20 3/8	5 5/8	12	11	Marshall Co., MN	Unknown	Greg Hestekind	PR 1970	187
205 2/8	216 3/8	24 5/8	25 1/8	22 2/8	5 1/8	10	9	Calhoun Co., IL	Bobby R. Woods	Bobby R. Woods	2001	187
205 2/8	217 6/8	24 4/8	21 7/8	18 1/8	5 4/8	6	17	Scott Co., IL	John H. Fryman	John H. Fryman	2003	187
205 1/8	209 2/8	22 6/8	23	14 6/8	5 3/8	14	10	Montague Co., TX	Don E. Haley	Don E. Haley	2003	190
205 1/8	215 2/8	26	26	16 7/8	4 6/8	7	8	Oldman Lake, AB	Charles Hann	Charles Hann	2003	190
204 7/8	208 5/8	25 2/8	25 6/8	18 4/8	4 6/8	10	9	Warren Co., MO	Gary Eschbach	Gary Eschbach	2003	192
204 7/8	209 3/8	27 5/8	27 5/8	22 5/8	5 5/8	10	12	Vermilion Co., IL	Philip Batroni	Philip Batroni	2004	192
204 7/8	212 2/8	26 3/8	25	19 4/8	5 7/8	12	9	Marion Co., KS	Darren W. Anderson	Darren W. Anderson	2005	192
204 7/8	211 6/8	24 2/8	24 1/8	22	5 3/8	9	12	Outagamie Co., WI	Randy L. Kabble	Randy L. Kabble	2005	192
204 5/8	219 2/8	27 6/8	28 1/8	22 6/8	5 6/8	11	7	Knox Co., IL	Brent T. Lindsey	Brent T. Lindsey	2005	196
204 5/8	209 7/8	25 6/8	26 4/8	16 6/8	4 7/8	8	11	Jefferson Co., OH	Geary A. Bennington, Sr.	Geary A. Bennington, Sr.	2006	196
204 4/8	210 6/8	24	24 4/8	18 2/8	5 6/8	9	9	N. Battleford, SK	William B. Manning	William B. Manning	2003	198
204 4/8	211 1/8	23 6/8	23	21 1/8	5 3/8	9	11	Rush Co., IN	Picked Up	William R. Miller	2003	198

WHITETAIL DEER - NON-TYPICAL ANTLERS

Odocoileus virginianus virginianus and certain related subspecies

Final Score	Gross Score	Length of Main Beam R.	L.	Inside Spread	Circumference at Smallest Place Between Burr & First Point R.	L.	Number of Points R.	L.	Locality	Hunter	Owner	Date Killed	Rank
204 4/8	251 4/8	26	25 4/8	18 4/8	4 7/8	4 7/8	8	8	Vermilion Co., IL	John T. Little	John T. Little	2005	198
204 3/8	207 6/8	27 2/8	27 1/8	19 1/8	6 1/8	6 2/8	10	9	Adams Co., OH	Stephen M. Rohling	Stephen M. Rohling	2002	201
204 3/8	208 7/8	25 2/8	25 4/8	17 3/8	6 2/8	6 1/8	11	9	Roseau Co., MN	Patrick F. Lorenson	Patrick F. Lorenson	2003	201
204 3/8	210 6/8	25 7/8	26 2/8	22 6/8	5 6/8	5 5/8	8	9	Smoky Lake, AB	Bradley H. Williamson	Bradley H. Williamson	2005	201
204 2/8	208 5/8	25 6/8	26	15	5 1/8	5 1/8	10	8	Chippewa Co., WI	Unknown	Terry Rouleau	1960	204
204 2/8	208 6/8	30	29 1/8	22 5/8	5 6/8	5 6/8	7	7	Morrow Co., OH	Lonnie J. Brake	Lonnie J. Brake	2003	204
204 2/8	211 1/8	26 3/8	25 3/8	21 2/8	5 4/8	5 4/8	7	11	Dubuque Co., IA	Mark A. Meyers	Mark A. Meyers	2003	204
204 1/8	223 3/8	24 3/8	25	21	5 3/8	5 2/8	14	7	Butler Co., OH	Heather M. Martin	Heather M. Martin	2003	207
204 1/8	209 5/8	24	23 1/8	18 5/8	5 7/8	5 3/8	7	10	Ingham Co., MI	Dustin W. Hotchkin	Dustin W. Hotchkin	2003	207
204	206 3/8	25 2/8	25 5/8	20 5/8	4 5/8	4 7/8	6	8	Cuyahoga Co., OH	James J. Gazso	James J. Gazso	2004	209
203 7/8	211 5/8	25 4/8	25 7/8	19 2/8	5 5/8	5 5/8	10	9	Lincoln Co., MO	Calvin L. Slaughter, Jr.	Calvin L. Slaughter, Jr.	2005	210
203 6/8	208 7/8	24 5/8	24 7/8	19 2/8	5 2/8	5	9	9	Carrot River, SK	Chancy C. Branning	Chancy C. Branning	2003	211
203 6/8	212 4/8	24 5/8	23 2/8	21 4/8	5	4 7/8	9	11	Marshall Co., IL	Clyde Winkler	Clyde Winkler	2005	211
203 5/8	213 4/8	26 2/8	25 6/8	17 3/8	5 4/8	5 1/8	10	13	Benton Co., IA	Rick D. Gibson	Rick D. Gibson	2004	213
203 5/8	210 7/8	26	25 5/8	19	6	6	9	12	Pike Co., IL	Chester L. Conner	Chester L. Conner	2005	213
203 3/8	211	26 2/8	26 6/8	14 6/8	5 4/8	5 1/8	12	11	White Co., IL	Scott A. Emery	Scott A. Emery	2001	215
203 3/8	226 5/8	20 4/8	25 5/8	16 6/8	10 4/8	6 7/8	14	11	Chase Co., KS	Stephen J. Stivaly	Stephen J. Stivaly	2003	215
203 2/8	207 7/8	27 4/8	28 4/8	20 3/8	4 7/8	4 7/8	9	7	Saline Co., MO	Donald G. Wilson	Donald G. Wilson	2005	217
203 1/8	206 4/8	27 3/8	27	20 4/8	5 1/8	5	8	7	Jennings Co., IN	Thomas J. Burchell	Thomas J. Burchell	2003	218
203 1/8	208 2/8	24 7/8	26 6/8	23	5	5 2/8	9	8	Fulton Co., IL	David K. Altig	David K. Altig	2005	218
203 1/8	226 3/8	22 2/8	28 3/8	12	6 6/8	6 3/8	16	9	Warren Co., IA	Tim C. Deskin	Tim C. Deskin	2006	218
203	209 7/8	25 2/8	25 5/8	17 4/8	5	5 2/8	9	8	Clearwater Co., MN	Darin K. Beckstrand	Darin K. Beckstrand	2003	221
202 7/8	210 5/8	25 3/8	26 2/8	20 7/8	5 6/8	5 6/8	8	11	Rice Co., KS	Michael E. Mode	Michael E. Mode	2005	222
202 7/8	212	25 1/8	26 3/8	20 6/8	5 7/8	5 5/8	10	8	Henry Co., IN	Randy Spence	Randy Spence	2005	222
202 6/8	207 5/8	29	28 5/8	21 4/8	4 6/8	4 5/8	5	9	Kittson Co., MN	Scott W. Field	Scott W. Field	2003	224
202 6/8	207 2/8	24 3/8	25	21 3/8	5 2/8	4 7/8	11	7	McClain Co., OK	Mike L. Meeks	Mike L. Meeks	2003	224
202 5/8	209	26 2/8	26 7/8	16 6/8	4 7/8	5 1/8	8	9	Beaver River, SK	Aivars O. Berkis	Aivars O. Berkis	2003	226
202 5/8	218 6/8	28 4/8	27 1/8	21 5/8	5 1/8	5 5/8	10	17	Randolph Co., IL	Bill Murray	Bill Murray	2003	226
202 5/8	210 5/8	27 2/8	27 1/8	19 3/8	5 5/8	5 2/8	8	6	Richland Co., OH	G. Douglas Mitchell	G. Douglas Mitchell	2004	226
202 5/8	208	25 3/8	25 2/8	19	5 4/8	5 4/8	12	7	Cass Co., IL	Jason Rhoton	Jason Rhoton	2005	226
202 4/8	206 7/8	27	27 4/8	21 3/8	6 2/8	6 2/8	11	6	Van Wert Co., OH	James C. Bettinger	James C. Bettinger	2003	230
202 4/8	211 3/8	28 4/8	29 2/8	21 2/8	5 4/8	5 5/8	9	9	Franklin Co., KY	Dale S. Southworth	Dale S. Southworth	2003	230
202 4/8	208	23 6/8	23 2/8	16 3/8	4 5/8	4 5/8	9	10	Fickle Lake, AB	Lee O. Nickerson	Lee O. Nickerson	2004	230

Score							Pts	Locality	Pts			Year	Rank
202 3/8	24 2/8	25	213 4/8	18 4/8	5 2/8	5 3/8	9	Lawrence Co., IL	10	Troy Dickens	Troy Dickens	2003	233
202 3/8	25 7/8	27 5/8	210 2/8	17 1/8	5 5/8	5 4/8	9	Sussex Co., DE	8	Jeffrey K. Foskey	Jeffrey K. Foskey	2003	233
202 2/8	25 4/8	26 6/8	207 7/8	15 5/8	5 1/8	5	12	Becker Co., MN	7	Clarence Clark, Jr.	Clarence Clark, Jr.	2003	235
201 7/8	24 6/8	22	213 5/8	15 6/8	5 2/8	5	13	Tate Co., MS	10	Bobby Smith	Bobby Smith	1993	236
202 1/8	24 2/8	25 7/8	206 1/8	20	5 4/8	5 1/8	8	Delaware Co., IN	8	Charles H. Harvey	Charles H. Harvey	2004	236
202	28 6/8	28 7/8	214 6/8	23 4/8	5 2/8	5 5/8	8	Jackson Co., MO	7	Sterling D. Mathis	Sterling D. Mathis	2003	238
202	28 6/8	28	211 5/8	22	5 5/8	5 4/8	7	Tippecanoe Co., IN	9	Sam D. Brooks II	Sam D. Brooks II	2005	238
202	24 4/8	24 3/8	210 3/8	16 5/8	5 6/8	5 6/8	14	Washington Co., IL	10	Phillip A. Carrico	Phillip A. Carrico	2005	238
201 7/8	27 5/8	23 1/8	210 4/8	18 6/8	5	5 1/8	8	Whitley Co., KY	5	Richie Bledsoe	Richie Bledsoe	1986	241
201 7/8	22	22 1/8	206 4/8	20 4/8	5 5/8	5 5/8	11	Davis Co., IA	11	Kevin J. Scott	Kevin J. Scott	2003	241
201 7/8	27 5/8	27 6/8	207 5/8	21 3/8	5 6/8	5 5/8	11	Dodge Co., WI	10	Timothy Foulk	Timothy Foulk	2004	241
201 7/8	26 5/8	25 1/8	210 2/8	21 3/8	5 2/8	4 7/8	7	Clark Co., IL	7	Troy Biddle	Troy Biddle	2005	241
201 6/8	23 2/8	23 3/8	204 2/8	17 6/8	5 1/8	5 4/8	10	Barber Co., KS	10	Justin K. Bridges	Justin K. Bridges	2001	245
201 6/8	24 4/8	24 3/8	206 3/8	19 4/8	5 1/8	5 3/8	9	Clayton Co., IA	11	John A. Barnes	John A. Barnes	2003	245
201 6/8	24 7/8	25	205 7/8	19 4/8	5	5	7	Steepbank Lake, AB	8	Robert J. Kruger	Robert J. Kruger	2003	245
201 6/8	29	30	207 5/8	20 7/8	5 5/8	5 5/8	11	Jackson Co., IA	7	Joey I. Nachtman	Joey I. Nachtman	2004	245
201 5/8	28 6/8	29	205 3/8	19 1/8	4 7/8	4 7/8	8	Jackson Co., IA	9	Dennis Stecklein	Dennis Stecklein	2004	245
201 5/8	26 5/8	26 4/8	204 4/8	21 7/8	5 2/8	5 1/8	9	Osborne Co., KS	9	Matthew W. Long	Matthew W. Long	2004	250
201 5/8	27 5/8	26 7/8	207 5/8	20 4/8	5 1/8	5 1/8	12	McLean Co., IL	9	Kevin J. Stieghorst	Kevin J. Stieghorst	2004	250
201 4/8	26 3/8	26	210 2/8	20 3/8	5 6/8	6 1/8	14	Aitkin Co., MN	12	Matthew J. Finlayson	Matthew J. Finlayson	2005	250
201 4/8	26 2/8	27	207 2/8	16 7/8	6	5 7/8	12	Macon Co., MO	10	Tanner A. Brundage	Tanner A. Brundage	2003	253
201 3/8	28 4/8	27 3/8	209 4/8	20 5/8	5 2/8	5 4/8	7	Red Lake Co., MN	7	Patrick C. Herold	Jackie Tatur	1955	254
201 2/8	24 1/8	24 1/8	212 6/8	21 4/8	7 3/8	4 7/8	13	Jackson Co., IA	6	Mark A. Henfrey	Mark A. Henfrey	2005	255
201 1/8	24 4/8	24 4/8	206 4/8	17 6/8	5 6/8	5 6/8	7	Washington Co., WI	8	Duane D. Radder	Duane D. Radder	2003	256
201 1/8	28 1/8	28 1/8	206	19 4/8	4 5/8	4 6/8	6	Schuyler Co., IL	6	Michael Nichols	Michael Nichols	2004	256
201 1/8	25 3/8	25 4/8	208 3/8	24 4/8	5 7/8	5 7/8	8	Grundy Co., IL	8	Earl L. Immormino	Earl L. Immormino	2005	256
201	22 7/8	23 7/8	203 7/8	18 2/8	6	6	9	Mabel Lake, BC	8	Ben Holland	Jerry Reinhardt	2003	259
201	28	31 6/8	210 5/8	20 5/8	5 2/8	5 3/8	7	Norfolk Co., MA	8	Picked Up	Jeff Draper	2004	259
200 7/8	28 1/8	28 1/8	207 1/8	22 2/8	5 4/8	5 3/8	10	Jackson Co., IA	7	Garry Connell	Garry Connell	2005	261
200 6/8	28 2/8	27 6/8	205 7/8	18 2/8	4 6/8	4 5/8	6	Monroe Co., IA	6	Jason Vickerman	Jason Vickerman	2004	262
200 5/8	24 6/8	22 4/8	216 2/8	19 5/8	4 4/8	5	12	Portage Co., OH	12	Roswell Spooner	Roswell Spooner	2003	263
200 5/8	24 5/8	28 1/8	208 1/8	14 7/8	8 4/8	9	8	Johnson Co., IA	8	Michael L. Bauwens	Michael L. Bauwens	2004	263
200 5/8	26 7/8	27 4/8	207 4/8	18 6/8	5 7/8	6 3/8	7	Delaware Co., OH	12	Shawn D. Gaines	Shawn D. Gaines	2005	263
200 4/8	22 2/8	21 4/8	204 6/8	15 7/8	5 6/8	6	8	The Pas, MB	12	Chris D. Alyea	Chris D. Alyea	2003	266
200 4/8	24 3/8	24 6/8	203 1/8	19 3/8	5 1/8	5	11	Newton Co., AR	11	Kylan McCutcheon	Kylan McCutcheon	2004	266
200 4/8	27	27	206 7/8	18 1/8	5 2/8	5 3/8	12	Morgan Co., IL	9	Mark L. Hopkins	Mark L. Hopkins	2005	266
200 3/8	26 7/8	27 3/8	205 3/8	22 2/8	5 6/8	5 6/8	7	Guernsey Co., OH	10	Robert T. Fedorke, Jr.	Picked Up	1994	269
200 3/8	25 7/8	27 6/8	210 7/8	19 7/8	6 3/8	6 1/8	10	Saddle Hills, AB	10	Jared C. Wild	Jared C. Wild	2004	269
200 2/8	24	24	210 3/8	21	6	5 5/8	8	Morgan Co., MO	8	Daren K. Williams	Daren K. Williams	2003	271
200 2/8	28 4/8	28 4/8	206 7/8	21 2/8	5 1/8	5 4/8	8	Columbia Co., WI	7	Darren Mitchell	Darren Mitchell	2004	271
200 2/8	26 5/8	26	208 3/8	17 4/8	5 4/8	5 1/8	9	Dodge Co., WI	8	Anthony Strobel	Picked Up	2004	271
200 1/8	27 2/8	27 2/8	212 1/8	20 4/8	6	6	7	Sangamon Co., IL	10	Dan G. Hupp	Dan G. Hupp	2004	274

Odocoileus virginianus virginianus and certain related subspecies

Final Score	Gross Score	Length of Main Beam R.	Length of Main Beam L.	Inside Spread	Circumference at Smallest Place Between Burr & First Point R.	Circumference at Smallest Place Between Burr & First Point L.	Number of Points R.	Number of Points L.	Locality	Hunter	Owner	Date Killed	Rank
200 1/8	211 6/8	26 2/8	26 4/8	18 5/8	5 5/8	5 4/8	9	9	Lucas Co., IA	David Piatz	David Piatz	2004	274
200	210 5/8	26 6/8	27 7/8	19 5/8	5 7/8	5 5/8	10	10	Henry Co., IL	Fred G. Murphy, Sr.	Fred G. Murphy, Sr.	2004	276
200	206 5/8	27 5/8	27 5/8	20 6/8	6 2/8	6 2/8	9	7	Du Page Co., IL	Picked Up	Richard L. Reindl	2006	276
199 6/8	205	24 2/8	25 1/8	17 5/8	5	5	8	9	Greenup Co., KY	Edward Conley	Edward Conley	1986	278
199 6/8	213 6/8	27 3/8	27 4/8	20	4 7/8	4 7/8	7	8	Todd Co., MN	Richard E. Baum	Richard E. Baum	2003	278
199 6/8	205 2/8	23 6/8	23 5/8	18 1/8	5 7/8	5 6/8	12	13	Carroll Co., OH	Eddie E. Mayle	Eddie E. Mayle	2003	278
199 6/8	208 4/8	29 5/8	28 6/8	22 1/8	4 3/8	4 3/8	9	9	Cuyahoga Co., OH	John R. Stofan	John R. Stofan	2004	282
199 5/8	206 4/8	22 3/8	22 5/8	17 2/8	5	4 6/8	13	9	Hempstead Co., AR	Nathan Driver	Nathan Driver	2002	282
199 5/8	205 2/8	19 2/8	19 7/8	18 2/8	6 6/8	7	16	10	Lee Co., IA	Dan C. Enger	Dan C. Enger	2003	282
199 5/8	202	23 2/8	23	18 5/8	4 4/8	4 4/8	12	9	Carrot River, SK	James D. Hoover	James D. Hoover	2005	282
199 5/8	208 6/8	21 4/8	23 4/8	18 1/8	5 3/8	5 1/8	9	9	Grand Prairie, AB	Bill Friesen	Bill Friesen	2006	282
199 4/8	214 4/8	26 3/8	27	21 7/8	5 5/8	6	8	10	Jefferson Co., IL	James A. Hart	James A. Hart	2004	286
199 4/8	206 1/8	24 6/8	26	17 6/8	5	5	8	6	Mellette Co., SD	Steven P. Peterson	Steven P. Peterson	2004	286
199 4/8	206 7/8	26 7/8	25 7/8	17 6/8	5 3/8	5 2/8	8	9	Wabasha Co., MN	Adam Moyer	Adam Moyer	2005	286
199 3/8	212 4/8	22 3/8	23 3/8	17	4 2/8	4 2/8	9	11	Holmes Co., MS	John E. Hays	John E. Hays III	1976	289
199 3/8	207 1/8	25 2/8	21 4/8	18 6/8	4 6/8	4 6/8	9	8	Nodaway Co., MO	James Marriott	Cabela's, Inc.	2003	289
199 3/8	203 3/8	25 6/8	27	18 2/8	5 2/8	5 2/8	10	9	Harrison Co., IN	Joseph C. Kuerzi, Jr.	Joseph C. Kuerzi, Jr.	2003	289
199 3/8	204 5/8	24 2/8	23 6/8	18 3/8	4 6/8	4 6/8	10	7	Maverick Co., TX	Brian C. Harrison	Brian C. Harrison	2004	289
199 3/8	204 2/8	25 3/8	25 4/8	18 3/8	5 3/8	5 3/8	9	12	Itasca Co., MN	Jack Trenberth	Jack Trenberth	2004	289
199 2/8	203 1/8	22 2/8	22 2/8	17 5/8	4 2/8	4 4/8	8	9	Unknown	Unknown	Anthony B. Schwab	1930	294
199 2/8	203 7/8	27 4/8	27 5/8	18 5/8	5	5	8	9	Scotland Co., MO	Joan M. Kriesmann	Joan M. Kriesmann	2003	294
199 2/8	205 5/8	26 2/8	26 2/8	19 1/8	5	5 1/8	9	9	Graves Co., KY	Ike Murphy	Ike Murphy	2003	294
199 2/8	203 3/8	25 7/8	26 6/8	17 2/8	5 7/8	5 6/8	8	8	Pheasant Creek, SK	Aron C. Hershmiller	Aron C. Hershmiller	2005	294
199 2/8	208 3/8	27 2/8	24 7/8	16 7/8	5	4 6/8	8	11	Owen Co., IN	Henry E. Miller	Henry E. Miller	2005	294
199 1/8	207 4/8	28 3/8	26 7/8	18 5/8	5 4/8	5 5/8	8	9	Shelby Co., IL	Sam Perry	Sam Perry	2003	299
199 1/8	224 7/8	26	24 7/8	15 4/8	7 1/8	9	12	18	Sumner Co., KS	Richard J. Becker	Richard J. Becker	2005	299
198 7/8	202	25 6/8	24 7/8	20 2/8	5 7/8	6 4/8	6	9	Decatur Co., IA	David C. Fuller	David C. Fuller	2003	301
198 7/8	202 4/8	27 6/8	27 6/8	20 7/8	4 4/8	4 4/8	9	9	Licking Co., OH	Henry R. Jackson, Jr.	Henry R. Jackson, Jr.	2003	301
198 7/8	210 6/8	22 5/8	25 4/8	20 1/8	5 1/8	5 2/8	10	7	Barron Co., WI	Jay R. Woelffer	Jay R. Woelffer	2003	301
198 7/8	201 2/8	25 5/8	24 4/8	19 1/8	4 7/8	4 7/8	8	10	Natrona Co., WY	Mark J. Stoeger	Mark J. Stoeger	2004	301
198 6/8	203 3/8	24 1/8	24 2/8	19	5 4/8	5 6/8	8	7	Grand Forks Co., ND	Philip M. Gratton	Jeffrey P. Gratton	1955	305
198 6/8	206 7/8	26 7/8	25 6/8	19 6/8	4 6/8	4 5/8	9	9	Otter Lake, SK	Thomas E. Glass	Thomas E. Glass	2001	305
198 6/8	210 6/8	28	28	15 4/8	5 7/8	5 6/8	8	11	Menard Co., IL	Ronald J. Wadsworth	Ronald J. Wadsworth	2004	305

Score	Gross Score	Main Beam R	Main Beam L	Inside Spread	Circ. R	Circ. L	Points R	Points L	Locality	Hunter	Owner	Date	Rank
198 5/8	209 6/8	26 7/8	24 4/8	19 6/8	4 7/8	5	12	13	Harrison Co., IN	Edward Kramer	Edward Kramer	2003	308
198 4/8	203 7/8	23 3/8	23 4/8	16	4 6/8	4 6/8	12	9	Steuben Co., NY	Rex D. Taft	Rex D. Taft	2005	309
198 4/8	208 4/8	27 3/8	27 1/8	19 4/8	5	5 2/8	11	6	Ross Co., OH	Nicole R. Wolf	Nicole R. Wolf	2005	309
198 3/8	202 7/8	24 3/8	24	18 1/8	5 1/8	4 5/8	7	6	Loudoun Co., VA	Allen F. Woodward	Allen F. Woodward	1984	311
198 3/8	205 1/8	28 2/8	30 1/8	20	5 2/8	5	8	9	Pike Co., OH	Lenny J. Downs	Lenny J. Downs	1999	311
198 3/8	202 5/8	24 7/8	22 5/8	17	6 1/8	6	10	10	Delaware Co., OH	Larry M. Longshore	Larry M. Longshore	2003	311
198 3/8	206	23 3/8	22 7/8	19 4/8	5 3/8	5 4/8	18	16	Butler Co., KS	Caiden Bump	Caiden Bump	2004	311
198 3/8	209 3/8	25 7/8	26 2/8	22 2/8	7 2/8	6 1/8	10	7	De Witt Co., IL	Leslie W. Day	Leslie W. Day	2004	311
198 3/8	207 2/8	29 1/8	28 7/8	21 5/8	4 6/8	4 5/8	6	7	Adams Co., IL	Brent Nebe	Brent Nebe	2004	311
198 2/8	202 1/8	24 4/8	26 1/8	18 3/8	5 1/8	5	10	8	Marion Co., IA	Ryan D. Buffington	Ryan D. Buffington	2003	317
198 2/8	207 6/8	25 1/8	26 5/8	18 6/8	6 2/8	5 7/8	12	8	Abrey Lake, SK	Kevin J. Gartner	Kevin J. Gartner	2003	317
198 2/8	202 2/8	26	27 7/8	21 3/8	4 7/8	5 1/8	8	8	Maverick Co., TX	T.J. duPerier	T.J. duPerier	2004	317
198 1/8	203 4/8	26 3/8	25 7/8	22 7/8	5	4 7/8	8	8	Wisconsin	Unknown	Scott Halama	PR 1970	320
198 1/8	202 7/8	23 2/8	23 3/8	19 3/8	5 3/8	5 3/8	9	8	De Kalb Co., IL	John Georgean	John Georgean	2003	320
198 1/8	204	27 7/8	27 1/8	22 4/8	5 6/8	5 6/8	12	11	Schuyler Co., IL	Steve S. Hamilton	Steve S. Hamilton	2004	320
198	202 7/8	24 3/8	18	18	4 5/8	4 7/8	10	9	Dubois Co., IN	Scott J. Fromme	Scott J. Fromme	2000	323
198	207 5/8	25 7/8	24 5/8	19 4/8	4 7/8	4 6/8	12	7	Polk Co., WI	Nicholas J. Shaffar	Nicholas J. Shaffar	2005	323
197 6/8	208 5/8	27 7/8	27 7/8	18 5/8	6 2/8	6	12	7	Licking Co., OH	Picked Up	Rosanna J. Grunewald	2004	325
197 6/8	220 4/8	28 4/8	25 6/8	21 2/8	4 7/8	6	5	12	Pike Co., IL	Picked Up	Jimmy Wand	2005	325
197 5/8	204 7/8	24 4/8	25 4/8	19 3/8	5 3/8	9 2/8	7	5	Fox Creek, AB	Irvin M. Bignell	Irvin M. Bignell	2004	327
197 4/8	213 1/8	25 6/8	24 5/8	21 4/8	6 2/8	7 6/8	10	8	Jasper Co., IL	Michael Mulvey	Michael Mulvey	2005	328

NON-TYPICAL WHITETAIL DEER
FINAL SCORE: 189-4/8
HUNTER: Marilyn L. Winters

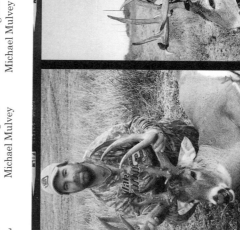

NON-TYPICAL WHITETAIL DEER
FINAL SCORE: 192-6/8
HUNTER: Ron Mason

NON-TYPICAL WHITETAIL DEER
FINAL SCORE: 195-1/8
HUNTER: James A. Rogers, Jr.

NON-TYPICAL WHITETAIL DEER
FINAL SCORE: 190-5/8
HUNTER: Jerry A. Ripp, Jr.

WHITETAIL DEER - NON-TYPICAL ANTLERS

Odocoileus virginianus virginianus and certain related subspecies

Final Score	Gross Score	Length of Main Beam R.	L.	Inside Spread	Circumference at Smallest Place Between Burr & First Point R.	L.	Number of Points R.	L.	Locality	Hunter	Owner	Date Killed	Rank
197 4/8	207 6/8	25 2/8	26 1/8	16 2/8	5 5/8	5 4/8	6	5	Crittenden Co., KY	Sean Shuecraft	Sean Shuecraft	2005	328
197 3/8	209 5/8	25	24 7/8	18 2/8	5 3/8	5 3/8	9	13	Morgan Co., MO	Leon Patten	Leon Patten	2003	330
197 3/8	201	26 1/8	26	19	4 3/8	4 2/8	8	7	Monroe Co., WI	Fred Amacher	Fred Amacher	2004	330
197 2/8	203 4/8	24	24 2/8	20 2/8	5 5/8	6 1/8	9	13	Linn Co., MO	Eric Meyer	Eric Meyer	2004	332
197 1/8	201 6/8	28 7/8	27 5/8	21 6/8	4 3/8	4 7/8	6	9	Warren Co., MO	Jerry Tonioli	Jerry Tonioli	1971	333
197 1/8	206 3/8	27	26 7/8	20	5 2/8	4 7/8	9	10	Hollow Lake, AB	Tadeusz J. Kaczynski	Tadeusz J. Kaczynski	2002	333
197 1/8	200 1/8	24 7/8	24 7/8	19 2/8	5	4 7/8	9	8	Guthrie Co., IA	Gary W. Young	Gary W. Young	2004	333
197	207 2/8	27 4/8	28	18	4 3/8	4 4/8	9	6	Montgomery Co., PA	Christian H. Jones	Christian H. Jones	2004	336
197	205 2/8	27 1/8	26 6/8	21 3/8	4 7/8	5 3/8	8	7	Kent Co., DE	Robert P. Reeves, Jr.	Robert P. Reeves, Jr.	2004	336
197	200	25 4/8	25	20 2/8	5 5/8	5 5/8	10	8	Mahaska Co., IA	Larry G. Vander Linden	Larry G. Vander Linden	2004	336
197	205 2/8	29 2/8	26 7/8	21 6/8	6	6 1/8	8	9	Crawford Co., WI	Gary L. Birkholz	Gary L. Birkholz	2005	336
197	203 7/8	24 4/8	23 1/8	22 3/8	4 4/8	4 4/8	7	7	Kearny Co., KS	Gary L. Shumate	Gary L. Shumate	2005	336
197	202 6/8	27 7/8	25 6/8	19 3/8	5 4/8	5 6/8	5	9	Adams Co., MS	Patrick R. Cenac	Patrick R. Cenac	2006	336
196 7/8	201 7/8	26 4/8	26 4/8	21 6/8	5 6/8	5 5/8	9	9	Itasca Co., MN	Clyde Sucher	Ray Davidson	1928	342
196 7/8	209 3/8	28	30	27 3/8	5 5/8	5 1/8	10	9	Pratt Co., KS	Kelley G. Murphy	Kelley G. Murphy	2001	342
196 7/8	208	26 4/8	29 2/8	22 1/8	4 6/8	4 7/8	9	8	Morrow Co., OH	Clyde E. Robinson	Clyde E. Robinson	2003	342
196 7/8	209 7/8	23 7/8	24 3/8	16 4/8	6 6/8	6 7/8	11	11	Jefferson Co., IA	Lloyd D. Manor	Lloyd D. Manor	2005	342
196 7/8	201 5/8	26 4/8	27 4/8	15 4/8	5 4/8	5 4/8	8	7	Hardin Co., KY	Jamie Sadler	Jamie Sadler	2005	342
196 6/8	200 5/8	26 2/8	26 4/8	19 5/8	6	5 7/8	6	8	Kittson Co., MN	T.K. Sylvester	T.K. Sylvester	1960	347
196 6/8	205 7/8	24 2/8	23 2/8	25 7/8	4 6/8	7 7/8	9	12	Okfuskee Co., OK	David W. Day	David W. Day	2003	347
196 6/8	207 7/8	25 1/8	26 4/8	18 2/8	5 2/8	5 3/8	6	11	Crawford Co., IL	Scott Schackmann	Scott Schackmann	2003	347
196 6/8	203	24 3/8	25 4/8	18 6/8	5 2/8	5 4/8	8	7	Putnam Co., MO	David A. Brown	David A. Brown	2004	347
196 6/8	202 3/8	25 2/8	24 7/8	19 5/8	4 5/8	4 4/8	8	8	Nez Perce Co., ID	Jack S. Snider	Jack S. Snider	2004	347
196 6/8	202 2/8	25 2/8	24 1/8	17 6/8	6 4/8	6	8	8	Fayette Co., IL	Walter L. Evans	Walter L. Evans	2005	347
196 5/8	206 6/8	29 3/8	28 4/8	23 6/8	5 5/8	5 2/8	8	7	Licking Co., OH	Stephen E. Esker	Stephen E. Esker	1994	353
196 5/8	202 7/8	25 4/8	25 4/8	22 5/8	4 6/8	4 6/8	8	6	Schuyler Co., IL	Justin D. Ketterman	Justin D. Ketterman	2004	353
196 5/8	206 6/8	17 6/8	19 6/8	16 2/8	4 6/8	3 7/8	16	17	Lincoln Co., OK	Waylon L. Johnson	Waylon L. Johnson	2005	353
196 5/8	207 1/8	24 6/8	19 3/8	23 1/8	5 2/8	5 2/8	7	11	Caroline Co., MD	Charles H. Pitts, Jr.	Charles H. Pitts, Jr.	2005	353
196 5/8	211 1/8	25 5/8	26 4/8	20 1/8	6 3/8	6	10	8	Adams Co., IL	Picked Up	Michael E. Stark	2005	353
196 5/8	206 5/8	28 2/8	26 6/8	18 2/8	5 3/8	5 6/8	8	7	Tuscarawas Co., OH	Troy A. Wrather	Troy A. Wrather	2005	353
196 4/8	208 2/8	25 5/8	23 4/8	22 7/8	6 2/8	6 4/8	6	10	Island Lake, AB	Colin Crumb	Colin Crumb	2003	359
196 4/8	202	25 5/8	26	20 3/8	5 2/8	5 2/8	7	7	Waushara Co., WI	Scott Reis	Scott Reis	2003	359
196 4/8	201 7/8	24 7/8	26	21 7/8	4 7/8	5 1/8	9	11	Menard Co., TX	Allan J. Rasmussen, Jr.	Allan J. Rasmussen, Jr.	2004	359

Score	Gross Score	Main Beam R.	Main Beam L.	Inside Spread	Circ. R.	Circ. L.	Points R.	Points L.	Locality	Owner	Hunter	Date Killed	Rank
196 4/8	198 3/8	24 7/8	24 6/8	18 5/8	4 5/8	4 6/8	8	6	Eau Claire Co., WI	Dave R. Stevens	Dave R. Stevens	2004	359
196 4/8	201 4/8	26 7/8	28 2/8	21 7/8	5 5/8	5 5/8	8	9	Polk Co., IA	Michael G. Fairchild	Michael G. Fairchild	2005	359
196 4/8	208 2/8	24	25 2/8	18 6/8	4 6/8	4	10	7	Livingston Co., MO	Aaron J. Ragsdale	Aaron J. Ragsdale	2005	359
196 4/8	209 1/8	29 5/8	25 1/8	26 1/8	5 1/8	5 4/8	8	12	Fentress Co., TN	Joshua I. Young	Joshua I. Young	2005	359
196 3/8	201 4/8	27	25 5/8	22	5	4 7/8	8	7	Keokuk Co., IA	Patrick J. Hammes	Patrick J. Hammes	2002	366
196 3/8	201 2/8	26 7/8	27 1/8	18 5/8	5	5 2/8	8	9	Appanoose Co., IA	Shannon P. Seddon	Shannon P. Seddon	2004	366
196 3/8	203 3/8	22 7/8	22 7/8	17 7/8	4 6/8	5	9	10	Thurston Co., NE	Brian G. Loofe	Brian G. Loofe	2005	366
196 2/8	212 6/8	25 6/8	23 7/8	14 2/8	5 1/8	5	9	10	Audrain Co., MO	John Grillo	John Grillo	2004	369
196 2/8	200 2/8	25 1/8	25	21 6/8	5 2/8	5 1/8	9	8	Crittenden Co., AR	Tasker R. Alexander	Tasker R. Alexander	2005	369
196 1/8	202 1/8	25 2/8	25 2/8	18 2/8	5 2/8	5 3/8	9	7	Clay Co., IL	Craig A. Petersen	Craig A. Petersen	2003	371
196 1/8	204 6/8	28 5/8	27 5/8	18 3/8	5	5	9	8	Owen Co., KY	Stephen M. Goins	Stephen M. Goins	2004	371
196 1/8	204 4/8	24 3/8	24 4/8	15 6/8	4 7/8	4 7/8	10	13	Casey Co., KY	Lester Roy	Lester Roy	2005	371
196 1/8	203 3/8	25 1/8	24	20 3/8	5 7/8	5 4/8	10	8	Putnam Co., IN	Kenny Short	Kenny Short	2005	371
196	205 1/8	28 1/8	28 3/8	20 3/8	5 5/8	5 4/8	9	10	Koochiching Co., MN	MN DNR - Enforcement	Picked Up	2002	375
196	202 6/8	25 5/8	25	19 5/8	4 4/8	4 4/8	8	11	Coles Co., IL	John Bailey	John Bailey	2004	375
196	201 1/8	28	27 4/8	18 5/8	4 6/8	4 6/8	10	9	Henry Co., MO	Shelby W. Scott	Shelby W. Scott	2004	375
196	201 1/8	25 5/8	25 2/8	18	5 1/8	5	7	9	White Fox River, SK	Steve Dobko	Steve Dobko	2005	375
196	199 5/8	24 2/8	25 6/8	19 2/8	4 7/8	4 7/8	8	8	Rat Lake, AB	Clem R. Gascon	Clem R. Gascon	2005	375
196	199 3/8	26 1/8	27	22 7/8	5	5	9	6	Maverick Co., TX	Robert M. Monroe	Robert M. Monroe	2003	375
195 7/8	200 1/8	25	25 1/8	17 2/8	6	5 4/8	9	12	Bates Co., MO	Christopher R. Farmer	Christopher R. Farmer	2005	381
195 7/8	204 1/8	25	23 5/8	17 5/8	4 4/8	4 5/8	9	11	Woodford Co., IL	Marc S. Anthony	Marc S. Anthony	2005	381
195 7/8	201 2/8	25 3/8	26	22	6 3/8	6 3/8	15	15	Wayne Co., OH	Gary L. Fowler	Gary L. Fowler	2005	381
195 7/8	204 3/8	26 5/8	23 2/8	20 7/8	5 4/8	5 5/8	8	8	Gallia Co., OH	Roy D. Wynn	Roy D. Wynn	2005	381
195 6/8	205 2/8	19 2/8	20 2/8	17 6/8	4 6/8	4 6/8	10	13	Garvin Co., OK	Travis Bagwell	Travis Bagwell	2003	385
195 6/8	204 1/8	28 1/8	28 1/8	18	4	4	8	7	Monroe Co., IN	Dave R. Holmes	Dave R. Holmes	2003	385
195 6/8	201 2/8	26 6/8	28 2/8	16 6/8	4 7/8	4 4/8	7	9	Sawyer Co., WI	Gary A. Schmoldt	Gary A. Schmoldt	2005	385
195 5/8	203 6/8	23 5/8	25 7/8	16 1/8	4 3/8	4 6/8	10	13	Jackfish Lake, AB	Eli C. Saunders	Eli C. Saunders	2002	388
195 5/8	201 3/8	23	23	16 2/8	4 7/8	4 6/8	9	12	Stevens Co., WA	Barry E. Tindal	Barry E. Tindal	2004	388
195 5/8	203 3/8	23 3/8	23 3/8	18 2/8	4 7/8	5 5/8	7	8	Dunns Valley, ON	Patrick J. Newell	Patrick J. Newell	2005	388
195 4/8	210 7/8	27 2/8	27 2/8	18 1/8	5 2/8	5	10	5	Fulton Co., IL	Randy D. Strode	Randy D. Strode	2004	391
195 4/8	199 1/8	27 5/8	26 5/8	22 4/8	4 7/8	5	7	9	Clayton Co., IA	Burt Blair	Burt Blair	2005	391
195 4/8	199 7/8	26	25 3/8	22 4/8	5 3/8	5 3/8	7	9	Trigg Co., KY	Morgan Booth	Morgan Booth	2005	391
195 4/8	201 1/8	29 1/8	26 2/8	18	5 4/8	5 4/8	8	9	Dodge Co., WI	Lisa M. Braun	Lisa M. Braun	2005	391
195 4/8	203 6/8	28 2/8	28	21 4/8	5 1/8	5 1/8	10	9	Grand Forks Co., ND	Jeff Gratton	Jeff Gratton	2005	391
195 4/8	205 2/8	24 3/8	25 2/8	17 3/8	5 6/8	5 4/8	10	9	Kankakee Co., IL	Todd R. Olson	Todd R. Olson	2005	391
195 4/8	200 7/8	24 2/8	24 6/8	18 5/8	5 1/8	5 1/8	5	5	Fulton Co., IN	Tony L. Runkle	Tony L. Runkle	2005	391
195 4/8	201	22 5/8	23 2/8	17 2/8	6 2/8	6 4/8	5	10	Van Buren Co., IA	Kaley D. Fleig	Kaley D. Fleig	2005	391
195 3/8	202 2/8	27 2/8	23 2/8	25 3/8	4 7/8	4 7/8	11	9	Shelby Co., OH	Phil Schulze	Phil Schulze	2003	398
195 3/8	199 7/8	26 5/8	27 7/8	19 4/8	4 6/8	4 6/8	8	9	Lorain Co., OH	Eric Feron	Eric Feron	2003	398
195 3/8	203 6/8	25 3/8	26 4/8	18 5/8	6	6	7	9	Washtenaw Co., MI	Michael A. Marcum	Michael A. Marcum	2004	398
195 3/8	208	25 5/8	26 4/8	19 6/8	5 7/8	5 7/8	7	7				2003	398
195 2/8	197 5/8	27 2/8	26 7/8	21 7/8	4 7/8	4 7/8	11	11	Dutchess Co., NY	Scott W. Soterion	Scott W. Soterion	2003	402
195 2/8	205 2/8	24 7/8	26	19 7/8	5 1/8	5 2/8	9	8	Todd Co., MN	D.J. & L. Strobel	David J. Strobel	2004	402

WHITETAIL DEER - NON-TYPICAL ANTLERS

Odocoileus virginianus virginianus and certain related subspecies

Final Score	Gross Score	Length of Main Beam R.	L.	Inside Spread	Circumference at Smallest Place Between Burr & First Point R.	L.	Number of Points R.	L.	Locality	Hunter	Owner	Date Killed	Rank
195 6/8	200 6/8	24 3/8	24 1/8	21	6 3/8	6 1/8	7	9	Olmsted Co., MN	Mark Wegman	Mark Wegman	2004	402
195 2/8	209 1/8	24	26 5/8	18 6/8	6	5 4/8	11	10	Chautauqua Co., KS	Peter D. Dimick	Peter D. Dimick	2005	402
195 2/8	199 5/8	27 1/8	26 6/8	21 2/8	5 5/8	5 3/8	6	6	Greene Co., IN	Thomas L. Egnew	Thomas L. Egnew	2005	402
195 2/8	202 3/8	23 2/8	24	18 1/8	4 6/8	4 6/8	8	9	Jones Co., IA	Jason A. Hasler	Jason A. Hasler	2005	402
195 2/8	199 4/8	26 3/8	25 5/8	19 2/8	5 6/8	5 7/8	9	7	Richland Co., WI	James Torrez	James Torrez	2005	402
195 2/8	204 5/8	26 1/8	26	18 3/8	6 2/8	5 6/8	9	10	Burke Co., ND	Jeff Bohl	Jeff Bohl	2006	402
195 1/8	198 3/8	24 4/8	22 7/8	21 1/8	7	7 4/8	8	9	Atchison Co., MO	Gary O. Pfeil	Gary O. Pfeil	2003	410
195 1/8	200 5/8	29 6/8	28 5/8	20 7/8	5 2/8	5 2/8	6	7	Brightsand Lake, SK	Richard Womble	Richard Womble	2003	410
195 1/8	203 4/8	26 5/8	26 3/8	18 1/8	5 7/8	5 4/8	9	7	Hemphill Co., TX	Lynn Guthrie	Lynn Guthrie	2005	410
195 1/8	199 7/8	24	24 5/8	19 1/8	4 6/8	4 6/8	11	10	Montgomery Co., IN	James A. Rogers, Jr.	James A. Rogers, Jr.	2005	410
195	198 4/8	25 4/8	24 5/8	19 2/8	5 4/8	5 6/8	6	6	Todd Co., MN	William R. Heldman	Annette Heldman	1976	414
195	207 1/8	27 4/8	26 7/8	18 2/8	5 6/8	5 5/8	10	9	Lewis Co., KY	Ray McMillan	Ray McMillan	2003	414
195	219 3/8	29 5/8	23 7/8	19 1/8	6 5/8	6 6/8	10	9	Parke Co., IN	Brian K. Berrisford	Brian K. Berrisford	2004	414
195	201 7/8	22 7/8	23 6/8	17 3/8	5 3/8	5 4/8	9	7	Milam Co., TX	Chris R. Glaser	Chris R. Glaser	2004	414
195	200 6/8	24 3/8	24	18	4 7/8	5 1/8	8	7	Putnam Co., IN	Scott C. Marsteller	Scott C. Marsteller	2004	414
195	205 3/8	26 7/8	25 6/8	21 7/8	5 2/8	5 4/8	9	8	Stephenson Co., IL	James E. Farmer	James E. Farmer	2005	414
194 7/8	203	23	24 2/8	13 2/8	6 1/8	6 1/8	7	8	Henderson Co., IL	Lindsay R. Wilkins	Lindsay R. Wilkins	2003	420
194 6/8	202 1/8	24 4/8	24	18 5/8	5 4/8	5 5/8	7	7	Putnam Co., MO	Emily A. McQueen	Emily A. McQueen	2003	421
194 5/8	204 1/8	22 5/8	22	17 4/8	5	5	9	11	Itasca Co., MN	Arthur Derfler	Arthur Derfler	1964	422
194 5/8	199 4/8	24 3/8	25 1/8	19 1/8	5 5/8	5 4/8	8	10	Martin Co., IN	James W. Pellam	James W. Pellam	2002	422
194 5/8	200 3/8	23	24 7/8	16 4/8	5	5 1/8	9	10	Ottawa Co., KS	Leland G. Kindall	Leland G. Kindall	2003	422
194 4/8	202 1/8	26 5/8	26 5/8	19 6/8	4 6/8	5 2/8	10	9	Butler Co., KY	Kevin J. Phelps	Kevin J. Phelps	2005	425
194 3/8	199 7/8	24	24	19	5 6/8	5 7/8	9	10	Morrison Co., MN	John Boeder	John Boeder	2003	426
194 3/8	203	22 5/8	25 2/8	19 6/8	5 3/8	5 2/8	11	9	Parke Co., IN	Fred Prewitt, Sr.	Fred Prewitt, Sr.	2005	426
194	203 3/8	25 3/8	25 5/8	22 1/8	6 3/8	6	12	9	Fentress Co., TN	David L. Smith	David L. Smith	2003	428
194	201	27 2/8	27 1/8	17 6/8	4 6/8	4 5/8	7	7	Jersey Co., IL	William Dailey	William Dailey	2005	428
193 7/8	199 3/8	25 4/8	24	19 4/8	6 1/8	5 6/8	9	7	Parke Co., IN	Michael E. Fisher	Michael E. Fisher	2005	430
193 6/8	199 5/8	26	27 1/8	18 1/8	4 7/8	4 6/8	8	9	Benton Co., MO	Picked Up	Larry Davis	2002	431
193 6/8	196 2/8	25	25	18 7/8	5 2/8	5 3/8	9	9	Kalamazoo Co., MI	Robert B. Frantz	Robert B. Frantz	2005	431
193 5/8	197 3/8	26 2/8	25 4/8	19 4/8	4 7/8	4 6/8	9	8	Dane Co., WI	Eric Hanson	Eric Hanson	2004	433
193 5/8	203 5/8	26 1/8	25 4/8	20	6	6 2/8	10	6	Montgomery Co., KY	Bobby G. Crowe	Bobby G. Crowe	2005	433
193 4/8	202 2/8	24 7/8	25 7/8	19 1/8	5 5/8	5 3/8	10	8	La Salle Co., IL	Robert M. Baldin	Robert M. Baldin	2005	435
193 4/8	201 7/8	28 5/8	27 4/8	19 3/8	5 2/8	5 2/8	6	7	Perth Co., ON	Dan Thomson	Dan Thomson	2005	435

									Locality	Hunter	Owner	Date	Rank
193 4/8	206	23 6/8	25 1/8	19	5 4/8	5 7/8	8	11	Douglas Co., MN	Steve A. Wendland	Steve A. Wendland	2005	435
193 3/8	206 2/8	24 3/8	23 6/8	15 4/8	5 7/8	6 5/8	11	11	White Earth Creek, AB	Douglas J. Doshewnek	Douglas J. Doshewnek	2004	438
193 3/8	198 4/8	28 3/8	26 6/8	23 5/8	5 4/8	5	8	10	Starke Co., IN	Paul R. Zerbee	Paul R. Zerbee	2004	438
193 2/8	203 6/8	24 6/8	26	23	5 3/8	5 2/8	8	8	Crawford Co., IL	Jackson Jenkins	Jackson Jenkins	2003	440
193 2/8	202 2/8	27 4/8	25	18 5/8	5 5/8	5 5/8	10	9	Crawford Co., OH	Martin Jones	Martin Jones	2003	440
193 2/8	204 3/8	27 3/8	25 4/8	19	5 4/8	5 4/8	7	8	Noble Co., IN	Chris Addison	Chris Addison	2004	440
193	200 6/8	23	27	16	4 6/8	4 4/8	10	7	Nuckolls Co., NE	Tim S. Brewster	Tim S. Brewster	2004	443
193	197 3/8	26 2/8	22 4/8	20	6 6/8	6 6/8	9	11	Jackson Co., WI	Joey Arneson	Joey Arneson	2005	443
193	199 2/8	23 2/8	23 2/8	19 6/8	4 4/8	4 4/8	12	11	Sauk Co., WI	Justin Walker	Justin Walker	2005	443
192 7/8	196 6/8	23 4/8	24	19	4 6/8	4 6/8	8	10	Buck Lake, AB	Charles T. Fleenor	Charles T. Fleenor	2003	446
192 7/8	202 5/8	24 6/8	25 7/8	17	5 7/8	6 1/8	8	10	Reno Co., KS	Joe D. Hilley	Joe D. Hilley	2003	446
192 7/8	200 3/8	26 2/8	27 2/8	23 5/8	5 4/8	5 7/8	7	7	Highland Co., OH	Stephen F. Blaut	Stephen F. Blaut	2004	446
192 7/8	202 2/8	26 1/8	22	22	4 6/8	4 3/8	10	8	Parke Co., IN	Michael S. Jones	Michael S. Jones	2005	446
192 6/8	199 7/8	21 5/8	25 2/8	17 2/8	7	6 7/8	11	11	Pike Co., IL	Ron Mason	Ron Mason	2004	450
192 6/8	199	28 3/8	27 4/8	21 3/8	5 7/8	5 7/8	8	8	Darke Co., OH	Carol E. Christian	Carol E. Christian	2005	450
192 6/8	201 6/8	24 6/8	23 4/8	23 4/8	4 4/8	4 3/8	9	8	Ontario Co., NY	Andy Hall	Andy Hall	2005	450
192 5/8	203 6/8	26 7/8	21	21	5 4/8	5 2/8	10	14	Lorain Co., OH	Jason Schwartz	Jason Schwartz	2003	453
192 4/8	197 4/8	22 4/8	22 7/8	19 1/8	5	5 5/8	11	11	Wabasha Co., MN	Dennis C. Foster	Dennis C. Foster	2003	454
192 4/8	196 5/8	25 2/8	26 6/8	18 5/8	5 2/8	5 2/8	7	6	Juneau Co., WI	Michael J. Krivitz	Michael J. Krivitz	2005	454
192 4/8	201 3/8	24 3/8	25 4/8	15	5 7/8	5 7/8	14	8	Warren Co., KY	Paul Campbell	Paul Campbell	2006	454
192 3/8	198 3/8	27 4/8	27 2/8	18 1/8	5 4/8	5 4/8	9	7	Logan Co., KY	Eric Stamps	Eric Stamps	1983	457
192 3/8	199	26	26 3/8	17	4 7/8	4 5/8	8	7	Madison Co., IA	Drew Love	Mike Love	2003	457
192 3/8	199 4/8	26 3/8	24 7/8	21 1/8	5 2/8	4 6/8	12	12	Garfield Co., OK	Jay Sweetwood	Jay Sweetwood	2005	457
192 3/8	198	24 7/8	25 6/8	18 2/8	4 6/8	4 7/8	8	9	Estill Co., KY	Kenny Tucker	Kenny Tucker	2003	457
192	198	22 5/8	24 6/8	18 6/8	5 1/8	5 4/8	7	10	Allen Co., IN	Wayne Leazier, Jr.	Wayne Leazier, Jr.	2005	462
192	203 6/8	27 6/8	27	20 1/8	5 6/8	5 2/8	9	6	Casey Co., KY	John P. Phillippe	John P. Phillippe	2003	462
191 7/8	198 1/8	24 3/8	23 6/8	18 2/8	5	5	8	9	Knox Co., IL	Kirk D. Vollmer	Kirk D. Vollmer	2004	462
191 7/8	199 1/8	24 6/8	24 2/8	17 3/8	5 2/8	5 2/8	8	11	Buchanan Co., IA	Kevin J. Peterson	Kevin J. Peterson	2005	465
191 7/8	201 3/8	26	24 3/8	17 7/8	4 4/8	4 4/8	9	9	Flotten Lake, SK	Dennis Seamanik	Dennis Seamanik	2003	465
191 6/8	196 6/8	26 6/8	26 1/8	23	4 6/8	4 7/8	7	6	Clarke Co., IA	Brian Hennefeld	Brian Hennefeld	2004	465
191 6/8	197 3/8	26 3/8	24 4/8	18 2/8	4 5/8	4 5/8	6	9	Maverick Co., TX	Frank J. Tilicek III	Frank J. Tilicek III	2004	468
191 5/8	193 6/8	24 4/8	22 3/8	16 2/8	5 4/8	5 4/8	8	11	Grayson Co., KY	Carl S. Decker, Jr.	Carl S. Decker, Jr.	2003	468
191 5/8	200 1/8	23 4/8	23 4/8	16	6 1/8	6 6/8	9	10	Kiskatinaw River, BC	Clifford Patterson	Clifford Patterson	2005	470
191 4/8	195 2/8	25	28 4/8	18 6/8	5 2/8	5 2/8	7	8	Calhoun Co., MI	Daniel B. Farmer	Daniel B. Farmer	2005	470
191 4/8	202 2/8	24 2/8	28 2/8	19 3/8	6 1/8	6 1/8	7	8	Barton Co., KS	Mark E. Johnson	Mark E. Johnson	2005	470
191 4/8	196	24 4/8	21 3/8	18 6/8	5 6/8	5 3/8	10	14	Hastings Co., ON	Tony J. Soikie	Tony J. Soikie	2005	473
191 4/8	206 6/8	26 4/8	25 2/8	20 1/8	5 3/8	4 6/8	7	7	Westmoreland Co., PA	Regis J. Rosborough	Regis J. Rosborough	2004	473
191 4/8	195 3/8	24 1/8	24 7/8	14 5/8	4 6/8	4 6/8	11	12	Hidalgo Co., TX	Cullen R. Looney	Cullen R. Looney	2005	475
191 3/8	196 1/8	26 1/8	24 7/8	18 2/8	5 4/8	5 2/8	11	8	Valley Co., NE	Shane M. Arduser	Shane M. Arduser	2003	475
191 3/8	197 1/8	23 4/8	22 3/8	17 5/8	5 3/8	5 4/8	9	7	Owen Co., IN	Jeremy R. Feltner	Jeremy R. Feltner	2005	477
191 2/8	201 1/8	28 2/8	28 4/8	17 3/8	6 2/8	6 1/8	8	8	Hart Co., KY	Randall Bentley	Randall Bentley	2004	477
191 2/8	199 2/8	24 4/8	24 4/8	16 3/8	5 1/8	4 6/8	9	8	Alexander Co., IL	Gary A. Slusher	Gary A. Slusher	2004	477

Odocoileus virginianus virginianus and certain related subspecies

Final Score	Gross Score	Length of Main Beam R.	Length of Main Beam L.	Inside Spread	Circumference at Smallest Place Between Burr & First Point R.	L.	Number of Points R.	L.	Locality	Hunter	Owner	Date Killed	Rank
191 4/8	193 6/8	21 7/8	22 4/8	23 7/8	4	4	10	10	Tate Co., MS	Jody W. Freeman	Jody W. Freeman	2005	477
191 3/8	195 2/8	25 1/8	25 4/8	19 7/8	6 2/8	6 2/8	8	7	Trimble Co., KY	Kenneth Boehnlein	Kenneth Boehnlein	2003	480
191 1/8	195 3/8	25 3/8	24 1/8	18 5/8	6	5 6/8	8	8	Iowa Co., WI	Jim A. Conner	Jim A. Conner	2003	481
191	200 6/8	25 1/8	20 6/8	18 6/8	5 4/8	5 6/8	8	10	Sedgwick Co., KS	Vol D. Jordan	Vol D. Jordan	2003	482
191	195 6/8	20 7/8	20 6/8	16 2/8	5 6/8	5 7/8	10	8	Osage Co., KS	Carl R. Metter	Carl R. Metter	2005	482
190 7/8	199	23 6/8	24 4/8	15 3/8	6 3/8	6 5/8	9	9	Jackson Co., MI	Ryan M. Mains	Ryan M. Mains	2003	484
190 6/8	197 5/8	24 5/8	24 7/8	18 1/8	5	5 2/8	9	10	Owsley Co., KY	Donald M. Price	Donald M. Price	2003	485
190 5/8	196 6/8	27 5/8	27	22 6/8	5 7/8	5 7/8	7	7	Columbia Co., WI	Jerry A. Ripp, Jr.	Jerry A. Ripp, Jr.	2005	486
190 5/8	200 4/8	19 2/8	22 7/8	22 6/8	4 7/8	4 5/8	9	8	Butler Co., KS	James M. Vaught	James M. Vaught	2005	486
190 4/8	197 4/8	27 3/8	25 5/8	18 2/8	5 7/8	5 5/8	7	12	Fentress Co., TN	Ted R. Harvey	Ted R. Harvey	2000	488
190 4/8	201 4/8	20 1/8	21 3/8	22	4 7/8	5 1/8	11	13	Warren Co., IA	Kelly Grandstaff	Kelly Grandstaff	2003	488
190 4/8	198 4/8	26 2/8	25 6/8	19 5/8	4 7/8	4 6/8	11	8	Motley Co., TX	Mark D. Purcell II	Mark D. Purcell II	2004	488
190 4/8	201 4/8	26 7/8	25 7/8	18 3/8	5 1/8	5 2/8	8	8	Will Co., IL	Lee R. Wollenberg	Lee R. Wollenberg	2005	488
190 3/8	199 2/8	22 2/8	24 5/8	15 3/8	7 1/8	7 1/8	10	12	Parke Co., IN	Michael V. Fowler	Michael V. Fowler	2004	492
190 2/8	194 5/8	28 2/8	26 7/8	17 7/8	5 2/8	5 2/8	8	8	St. Louis Co., MO	John I. Lasley	John I. Lasley	2004	493
190 2/8	198 3/8	24 4/8	23 5/8	16 7/8	5 3/8	5 4/8	7	7	Battle River, AB	Charles F. French	Charles F. French	2005	493
190 1/8	194 6/8	27 1/8	27 6/8	16 4/8	4 5/8	4 5/8	11	11	Clay Co., KY	Shannon L. Collins	Shannon L. Collins	2004	495
190 1/8	200 3/8	26	25 6/8	22 4/8	5 6/8	6	7	7	Ohio Co., KY	Mark L. Simmons	Mark L. Simmons	2004	495
190	197	26 6/8	26 4/8	19 4/8	5 6/8	5 5/8	10	9	Logan Co., CO	Ed T. Gorman	Ed T. Gorman	2005	495
190	198 3/8	23 3/8	25 6/8	19 7/8	6 4/8	6 4/8	6	6	Hardin Co., KY	John T. Davis, Jr.	John T. Davis, Jr.	2003	498
189 7/8	198 4/8	24 7/8	26	19 4/8	5	5	10	9	Clark Co., IL	Michael G. Nuxoll	Michael G. Nuxoll	2002	499
189 7/8	193 2/8	23	23 1/8	18 2/8	3 7/8	3 6/8	8	7	Walworth Co., WI	Picked Up	Duane C. Dorn	2003	499
189 7/8	194 4/8	27 1/8	26 5/8	19 2/8	5	5 1/8	7	8	Wyoming Co., NY	Samuel D. Thaw	Samuel D. Thaw	2004	499
189 6/8	192 5/8	27	27 1/8	19 5/8	4 5/8	4 3/8	9	8	Hardin Co., KY	Ronnie D. Peters	Ronnie D. Peters	2003	502
189 6/8	195 4/8	26 4/8	26 2/8	21	4 2/8	4 2/8	8	9	Lewis Co., KY	Brandon L. Kamer	Brandon L. Kamer	2004	502
189 5/8	195 7/8	26 6/8	26 4/8	17 4/8	4 4/8	4 4/8	10	10	Spokane Co., WA	Michael S. Davis	Michael S. Davis	2005	504
189 5/8	195 1/8	25 7/8	25 4/8	19 1/8	6 1/8	5 4/8	12	8	Beaverlodge River, AB	Bruno L. Graw	Bruno L. Graw	2005	504
189 4/8	227 2/8	12 4/8	25 7/8	15	6 1/8	5	10	7	Livingston Co., MO	Steve Hall	Kyle H. Hibner	2001	506
189 4/8	194 3/8	26 2/8	26 1/8	15 3/8	4 3/8	4 3/8	8	11	Maverick Co., TX	Marilyn L. Winters	Marilyn L. Winters	2004	506
189 4/8	195	25 6/8	25 7/8	21 3/8	4 4/8	4 5/8	9	9	Forest Co., PA	James C. Riggle	James C. Riggle	2005	506
189 3/8	194	26	25 1/8	19	6	5 4/8	10	9	Webster Co., MO	A. Kelso Currie II	A. Kelso Currie II	2003	509
189 3/8	193 6/8	27 1/8	26 6/8	24 6/8	5	5	6	6	Jo Daviess Co., IL	Curtis A. Cook	Curtis A. Cook	2005	509
189 3/8	199 3/8	24 1/8	24 7/8	18 6/8	5 5/8	5 2/8	10	8	Harrison Co., IA	Anthony J. Fitzmaurice	Anthony J. Fitzmaurice	2005	509

Length of Main Beam R	L	Inside Spread	Circumference R	L	Points R	L	Locality	Hunter	Owner	Date Killed	Rank
25 4/8	25 2/8	17 5/8	5	5	8	9	Christian Co., KY	Mark D. Jenkins	Mark D. Jenkins	2005	509
25 1/8	25 4/8	14 3/8	5 5/8	5 5/8	7	8	Crittenden Co., KY	Robert S. Millsaps	Robert S. Millsaps	2005	509
28 5/8	28 7/8	20 1/8	4 3/8	4 3/8	7	7	Isanti Co., MN	James C. Herbst	James C. Herbst	2003	514
28	27 1/8	19 6/8	5 5/8	5 4/8	5	7	Winneshiek Co., IA	Gerald Folstad	Gerald Folstad	2004	514
25 6/8	25 4/8	20 5/8	5	4 7/8	7	6	Worcester Co., MA	Robert D. Heyes	Robert D. Heyes	2004	514
25 5/8	25 3/8	17 4/8	5 1/8	5	10	9	Warren Co., KY	Kimberly Hester	Kimberly Hester	2005	517
25 4/8	26	15 4/8	6 4/8	6 3/8	5	10	Juneau Co., WI	Morgan L. Wolfrum	Morgan L. Wolfrum	2005	517
24 1/8	26 4/8	23 2/8	5 5/8	5 4/8	6	7	Cowley Co., KS	Joe D. Carder	Joe D. Carder	2003	519
24 7/8	24 6/8	19 4/8	8	5 5/8	11	11	Belmont Co., OH	Mitchell Price	Mitchell Price	2004	519
20 6/8	25 5/8	20	5 6/8	6	8	11	Unknown	Unknown	Jay A. Kasten	PR 2006	519
25 3/8	25 5/8	19 1/8	5 7/8	6 1/8	8	7	Winnebago Co., WI	Ken E. Markofski	Ken E. Markofski	2003	522
26	24 4/8	20 3/8	5 4/8	5 2/8	7	7	Rock Co., WI	Cory Mielke	Cory Mielke	2004	522
27	27 2/8	18 1/8	4 6/8	4 6/8	8	8	Lincoln Co., KY	Nelson J. Kramer	Nelson J. Kramer	1999	524
27	27 4/8	16 5/8	7 5/8	7 5/8	9	10	Cherokee Co., KS	Picked Up	Joshua H. Fiscus	2005	524
24 1/8	23 4/8	19 1/8	5 4/8	5 4/8	8	9	Williams Co., OH	Sherman P. Baker II	Sherman P. Baker II	2004	526
23 4/8	25 2/8	18 1/8	5	4 7/8	6	6	Barron Co., WI	Ricky C. Reichert	Ricky C. Reichert	2005	526
26 7/8	26 6/8	16 5/8	4 3/8	4 4/8	9	9	Itasca Co., MN	Jeffrey K. Kirk	Jeffrey K. Kirk	2004	528
25 1/8	24 6/8	19 4/8	4 6/8	4 7/8	10	9	Lincoln Co., NE	Bruce A. Meyer	Bruce A. Meyer	2005	528
26 6/8	25 6/8	18 1/8	4 7/8	4 7/8	12	12	Reynolds Co., MO	Jim Johnson	Jim Johnson	2004	530
25 2/8	26 4/8	24	5 3/8	5 3/8	10	10	Williams Co., OH	Craig A. Wagner	Craig A. Wagner	2004	530
27	24 7/8	21 7/8	5 1/8	5 1/8	10	10	New Castle Co., DE	Allan E. Boleslawski	Allan E. Boleslawski	2005	530
23 6/8	24 3/8	21 7/8	5 5/8	5 5/8	7	8	Dawson Co., NE	Tyson Sarratt	Tyson Sarratt	2005	530
28	30 1/8	20 2/8	5 1/8	5 1/8	8	10	Kendall Co., IL	Lawrence M. Madrigal	Lawrence M. Madrigal	2003	534
26 5/8	27 1/8	16 6/8	5 4/8	5 4/8	10	6	Ford Co., IL	Jeremiah Brandon	Jeremiah Brandon	2004	534
25 2/8	23 6/8	18 1/8	5 3/8	4 6/8	6	8	Wells Co., IN	Zane Gearheart	Zane Gearheart	2003	536
24 7/8	23	15 5/8	7 5/8	7 5/8	11	6	Kansas	Picked Up	B&C National Collection	PR 2004	536
23 1/8	27	21 4/8	5 1/8	5 1/8	8	8	Dodge Co., WI	Ken Strahota, Jr.	Ken Strahota, Jr.	2003	538
26 4/8	26 4/8	21 3/8	6 4/8	6 2/8	6	7	Buffalo Co., WI	Robert J. Alexejun	Robert J. Alexejun	2004	539
27 2/8	25 7/8	18 2/8	5 2/8	5 2/8	7	8	Clark Co., IL	Steven B. Parr	Steven B. Parr	2005	539
24 7/8	23 6/8	16	4 3/8	4 3/8	7	7	Meadow Lake, SK	William Rohan	William Rohan	2005	539
23 2/8	22 2/8	19	5	5	7	6	Clark Co., IN	Andrew Mason	Andrew Mason	1994	542
28 2/8	25 3/8	19 4/8	5 1/8	5 1/8	8	8	Clark Co., SD	Lloyd Kamegieter	Lloyd Kamegieter	2004	542
21 6/8	23 1/8	17 3/8	5 6/8	5 6/8	9	9	De Kalb Co., IN	Adam O'Connor	Adam O'Connor	2004	542
26 2/8	26 2/8	18 1/8	4 7/8	4 7/8	8	7	Todd Co., MN	Paul A. Heinen	Paul A. Heinen	2005	542
26 6/8	26 6/8	20	4 7/8	5	8	9	St. Louis Co., MN	Peter J. Norick	Peter J. Norick	2005	542
24 6/8	24 6/8	22 6/8	5	4 6/8	9	10	Anderson Co., SC	Delton Roe	Delton Roe	2004	547
23 4/8	23 4/8	15 3/8	4 3/8	4 3/8	9	7	Stoddard Co., MO	Jeffrey L. Hale	Jeffrey L. Hale	2005	547
25 4/8	27	18 5/8	4 4/8	4 4/8	9	8	Ohio Co., KY	Picked Up	Travis M. Camp	1999	549
27	25 6/8	19	5 1/8	5 1/8	9	7	Dubois Co., IN	James A. Voges	James A. Voges	2004	549
24 6/8	25 6/8	20 1/8	5 4/8	5 4/8	9	9	Moniteau Co., MO	Craig A. Ash	Craig A. Ash	2005	549
25 4/8	25 3/8	19 2/8	4 2/8	4 2/8	7	7	Geauga Co., OH	David T. Majka	David T. Majka	2003	552

WHITETAIL DEER - NON-TYPICAL ANTLERS

Odocoileus virginianus virginianus and certain related subspecies

Final Score	Gross Score	Length of Main Beam R	L	Inside Spread	Circumference at Smallest Place Between Burr & First Point R	L	Number of Points R	L	Locality	Hunter	Owner	Date Killed	Rank
186 6/8	195	25 2/8	26 4/8	21	4 2/8	4 4/8	7	6	Maverick Co., TX	Steve E. Holloway	Steve E. Holloway	2003	553
186 6/8	194 2/8	23 4/8	24 3/8	17 2/8	5 4/8	5 4/8	7	7	McDonough Co., IL	Jack Laverdiere	Jack Laverdiere	2003	553
186 6/8	193	27 7/8	27 2/8	18 2/8	6 3/8	6 3/8	5	8	Fayette Co., IA	Joseph Schmitz	Joseph Schmitz	2004	553
186 5/8	195 1/8	24 4/8	24 3/8	16 6/8	5 5/8	5 3/8	9	10	Comanche Co., OK	Brian J. Roberts	Brian J. Roberts	2004	556
186 4/8	192 3/8	22 3/8	24 6/8	14 7/8	4 4/8	4 3/8	10	7	Montgomery Co., IL	Brett Goldsmith	Brett Goldsmith	2003	557
186 4/8	194 4/8	24 1/8	25 2/8	19 6/8	4 7/8	4 6/8	10	8	Whitesand River, SK	Curtis M. Melnechenko	Curtis M. Melnechenko	2004	557
186 4/8	191	23 7/8	23 5/8	17 1/8	4 7/8	4 7/8	9	9	Brown Co., IL	Kevin E. Wort	Kevin E. Wort	2005	557
186 3/8	193 4/8	21 1/8	21 3/8	15 4/8	4 6/8	4 6/8	11	9	Wells Co., ND	Dustin L. Willey	Dustin L. Willey	2003	560
186 3/8	193 6/8	26 3/8	27 4/8	20	5	4 6/8	6	6	Knox Co., NE	Larrene O. Hibbs	Larrene O. Hibbs	2004	560
186 3/8	188	26 2/8	26	18 7/8	4 5/8	4 5/8	10	8	Marathon Co., WI	Marjorie A. Ostrowski	Marjorie A. Ostrowski	2004	560
186 3/8	190 4/8	26 6/8	26 2/8	18 3/8	4 7/8	5	7	7	Waupaca Co., WI	Larry S. Young	Larry S. Young	2005	560
186 2/8	192 1/8	26 3/8	26 7/8	18 2/8	5 5/8	5 7/8	7	9	Douglas Co., WI	Mark P. Haan	Mark P. Haan	2005	564
186 1/8	198 1/8	24 2/8	25 1/8	21 5/8	6 5/8	6 3/8	7	9	Adams Co., IL	James J. Trutwin	James J. Trutwin	2003	565
186 1/8	194 4/8	26 5/8	27 4/8	21 6/8	5 2/8	5 3/8	9	8	Washington Co., WI	Steven J. Biksadski	Steven J. Biksadski	2005	565
186 1/8	194 5/8	25 5/8	25 2/8	20 4/8	5 5/8	5 7/8	8	8	Clinton Co., OH	Scott A. Bradley	Scott A. Bradley	2005	565
186 1/8	196 7/8	24 4/8	25 2/8	19 3/8	5 4/8	6 2/8	6	10	Franklin Co., MA	Mary May Pratt	Mary May Pratt	2005	565
186 1/8	190 2/8	26 2/8	25	19 1/8	5 1/8	5 1/8	8	8	Mills Co., IA	Randy M. Wendt	Randy M. Wendt	2005	565
186	187 5/8	26 4/8	26 1/8	18 6/8	5 3/8	5 3/8	7	7	Pike Co., MO	Richard W. Braun, Jr.	Richard W. Braun, Jr.	2004	570
186	190 7/8	26 5/8	25 2/8	20 3/8	5 7/8	6 2/8	7	8	Racine Co., WI	Andrew D. Delimat, Jr.	Andrew D. Delimat, Jr.	2004	570
186	191 5/8	21 6/8	21 5/8	16 3/8	5 7/8	6 2/8	12	8	Kent Co., MI	Drew Doornbos	Drew Doornbos	2004	570
186	195 1/8	25 4/8	26 5/8	27	5 6/8	6	6	8	Crawford Co., KS	David W. Strukel	David W. Strukel	2005	570
185 7/8	193 7/8	25 4/8	24 3/8	23 2/8	4 6/8	4 6/8	8	6	Crawford Co., WI	Aaron J. Richter	Aaron J. Richter	2003	574
185 7/8	193 7/8	22 4/8	23 1/8	15 4/8	4 4/8	4 3/8	9	9	Callaway Co., MO	Tim P. Payne	Tim P. Payne	2004	574
185 7/8	195 5/8	22 7/8	23 7/8	12 7/8	6 3/8	8 5/8	9	15	Morgan Co., GA	J. Lamar Banks, Jr.	J. Lamar Banks, Jr.	2005	574
185 7/8	197 4/8	24 7/8	26 4/8	20	4 6/8	4 5/8	7	9	Warren Co., OH	Michael A. Krumnauer	Michael A. Krumnauer	2005	574
185 7/8	210 3/8	24 1/8	26 1/8	20 4/8	5 5/8	6	8	9	Hendricks Co., IN	Ted W. Lorts	Ted W. Lorts	2005	574
185 6/8	195 6/8	25 1/8	25 2/8	19 4/8	4 6/8	4 2/8	13	10	Pickaway Co., OH	Rick L. Richards	Rick L. Richards	2002	579
185 6/8	203 5/8	19	21 4/8	16 3/8	7 1/8	6 5/8	9	11	Bledsoe Co., TN	Jerry Daniel	Jerry Daniel	2003	579
185 4/8	194 4/8	28 2/8	27 6/8	19 1/8	5	5 2/8	9	9	St. Louis Co., MN	Olaf A. Ness	Olaf A. Ness	1966	581
185 4/8	194 5/8	26 6/8	26 3/8	19 1/8	6 1/8	5 5/8	9	6	Van Buren Co., IA	Paul A. Craver	Paul A. Craver	2005	581
185 4/8	197 5/8	25 2/8	26 1/8	20	4 4/8	4 5/8	8	8	Richland Co., WI	Dwain E. Werch	Dwain E. Werch	2005	581
185 3/8	190 3/8	24 5/8	26 1/8	21 4/8	4 6/8	4 6/8	6	8	Kingman Co., KS	Kenny S. Kautzer	Kenny S. Kautzer	2004	584
185 3/8	190 2/8	24 2/8	23 1/8	15 5/8	4 4/8	4 4/8	7	7	Todd Co., MN	Kathleen R. Shamp	Kathleen R. Shamp	2005	584

Score									Locality	Hunter	Date	Rank
185 2/8	194 2/8	25 3/8	27 6/8	19	4 2/8	4 3/8	9	7	Breckinridge Co., KY	Billy H. Brooks	1984	586
185 2/8	188 7/8	26	25 2/8	16 6/8	5	5	9	8	Lyon Co., KS	Mark E. DeWitt	2003	586
185 1/8	190 5/8	26	25 4/8	19	4 2/8	4 1/8	10	6	Pelican Lake, MB	Dorothy C. Dawson	1972	588
185 1/8	195 3/8	24 2/8	25 2/8	17	5 3/8	5 3/8	6	7	Heard Co., GA	Dan Attaway	1976	588
185 1/8	187 3/8	25 1/8	25 4/8	19 4/8	4 4/8	4 4/8	7	8	Hopkins Co., KY	Russell O. Holloman	1999	588
185 1/8	189 2/8	25 3/8	26 5/8	18 4/8	4 2/8	4 2/8	8	7	Oconto Co., WI	Dawn M. Janousky	2003	588
185 1/8	192 6/8	22 7/8	25 6/8	20 3/8	5	5	9	7	Carlisle Co., KY	Ray Ledet	2003	588
185 1/8	192 1/8	23 1/8	22 2/8	16 4/8	5 1/8	5 2/8	12	11	Jasper Co., IN	John M. Babe	2005	588
185 1/8	190	24 7/8	24 4/8	20 5/8	5 1/8	5	8	10	Richland Co., ND	Jeff L. Johnson	2005	588
185 1/8	191 1/8	19 3/8	20 3/8	17 6/8	4 5/8	4 7/8	13	11	Webster Co., KY	Shon Wright	2002	595
185	185	27 4/8	25 7/8	20 4/8	4	4 1/8	8	9	Knox Co., IL	Gary Sampson	2003	595
185	204 6/8	25 3/8	24 2/8	20 2/8	4 4/8	4 3/8	8	8	Waushara Co., WI	Kevin D. Fenske	2004	595
185	193 1/8	23	25	23 5/8	5 1/8	5 3/8	11	7	Bonner Co., ID	Steve D. Spletstoser	2004	595
185	190 4/8	25 5/8	27 3/8	27 1/8	4 7/8	4 7/8	7	11	Webb Co., TX	James N. Gallagher, Jr.	2005	595
255 6/8*	270	26 7/8	24 4/8	17 2/8	6 7/8	6 3/8	14	16	Leavenworth Co., KS	Ronald H. Ewert, Jr.	2004	595

* Final score subject to revision by additional verifying measurements.

NON-TYPICAL WHITETAIL DEER
FINAL SCORE: 267-1/8
HUNTER: David H. Jones

NON-TYPICAL WHITETAIL DEER
FINAL SCORE: 188-7/8
HUNTER: Cory Mielke

NON-TYPICAL WHITETAIL DEER
FINAL SCORE: 223-3/8
HUNTER: Clyde K. Keen

NON-TYPICAL WHITETAIL DEER
FINAL SCORE: 234-7/8
HUNTER: Chad Goetten

COUES' WHITETAIL DEER - TYPICAL ANTLERS

Odocoileus virginianus couesi

Minimum Score 100 — World's Record 144 1/8

Final Score	Gross Score	Length of Main Beam R.	L.	Inside Spread	Circ. at Smallest Place Between Burr & First Point R.	L.	No. of Points R.	L.	Locality	Hunter	Owner	Date Killed	Rank
122 4/8	124 1/8	19 3/8	19	18 2/8	4 3/8	4 3/8	4	4	Sonora, MX	Terry C. Hickson	Terry C. Hickson	2005	1
120 2/8	122 3/8	18 3/8	18	15 2/8	4 4/8	4 4/8	4	4	Pima Co., AZ	Eric C. Rhicard	Eric C. Rhicard	2006	2
120 1/8	126 7/8	18 4/8	18 7/8	17 3/8	4	4	4	5	Pima Co., AZ	William P. Mattausch, Jr.	William P. Mattausch, Jr.	2006	3
119 5/8	127 6/8	18 3/8	18 5/8	13 7/8	4 6/8	4 4/8	6	5	Sonora, MX	Scott A. Limmer	Scott A. Limmer	2006	4
119 1/8	121 4/8	19 2/8	18 4/8	14 5/8	4	4 1/8	5	5	Pima Co., AZ	Picked Up	Jesse M. Branger	2004	5
117 4/8	119 5/8	18 7/8	19 2/8	16	4	4	4	4	Pima Co., AZ	Hubert R. Sipe	Hubert R. Sipe	1980	6
115 6/8	121 2/8	19 6/8	20 4/8	15 6/8	3 7/8	3 6/8	5	4	Santa Cruz Co., AZ	Tim Case	Tim Case	1995	7
115 2/8	117 7/8	16 5/8	16 7/8	14 6/8	4 2/8	4 2/8	4	4	Hidalgo Co., NM	Patrick H. Lyons	Patrick H. Lyons	2005	8
115 1/8	119	18	17 1/8	13 1/8	4 1/8	4 2/8	4	4	Sonora, MX	Jack W. Moore	Jack W. Moore	2004	9
114 2/8	116	17 7/8	17 5/8	17 4/8	3 7/8	4	4	4	Pima Co., AZ	Michael B. Stearns	Michael B. Stearns	2004	10
113 7/8	118 1/8	18 1/8	18 5/8	14 6/8	4	4	4	5	Sonora, MX	Darr A. Colburn	Darr A. Colburn	2005	11
113	123 3/8	18 7/8	18 2/8	13 2/8	3 6/8	3 6/8	5	7	Sonora, MX	James A. Reynolds	James A. Reynolds	2003	12
112 7/8	120 2/8	19 4/8	17 1/8	16 5/8	3 6/8	3 7/8	4	4	Pima Co., AZ	Mark Hardy	Mark Hardy	2003	13
112 5/8	116 6/8	16 2/8	16 4/8	10 7/8	4 2/8	4 2/8	5	5	Sonora, MX	Jefre R. Bugni	Jefre R. Bugni	2005	14
112 2/8	113 7/8	18	17 2/8	13 2/8	4 2/8	4 2/8	4	4	Sonora, MX	Scott A. Limmer	Scott A. Limmer	2004	15
112 1/8	119 5/8	19 7/8	18 4/8	14 3/8	3 7/8	4 1/8	4	4	Sonora, MX	Grady L. Miller	Grady L. Miller	2005	16
112	117 6/8	17	16 6/8	15	3	3	4	5	Santa Cruz Co., AZ	Larry J. Osborne	Larry J. Osborne	2003	17
111 7/8	115 5/8	18 2/8	18 2/8	15 2/8	4 7/8	4 6/8	5	4	Sonora, MX	Michael L. Braegelmann	Michael L. Braegelmann	2003	18
111 7/8	113 3/8	19 3/8	19 1/8	12 7/8	3 5/8	3 5/8	4	4	Pima Co., AZ	Gabriel Ruiz	Gabriel Ruiz	2003	18
111 6/8	122	20 4/8	20 2/8	14 2/8	4 2/8	4 1/8	4	6	Sonora, MX	Picked Up	Ricardo A. Andrade	1987	20
111	113 6/8	17 4/8	17 2/8	13	4	4	4	4	Pima Co., AZ	John P. Maclatchie	John P. Maclatchie	2004	21
110 7/8	117 5/8	19 4/8	18 2/8	13 5/8	4 1/8	4 1/8	5	4	Pima Co., AZ	Andrew J. Pacheco	Andrew J. Pacheco	2005	22
110 3/8	112	18 2/8	17 7/8	14 7/8	3 5/8	3 6/8	4	4	Sonora, MX	Wade C. McElwain	Wade C. McElwain	1999	23
110 2/8	114 7/8	17 5/8	15 5/8	15 4/8	4 2/8	4 2/8	4	4	Gila Co., AZ	Darrell D. Robinette	Darrell D. Robinette	2004	24
110 1/8	112 3/8	17 3/8	17 2/8	13 7/8	3 5/8	3 6/8	4	4	Pima Co., AZ	Todd A. Steagall	Todd A. Steagall	2002	25
110	113 4/8	18	17 5/8	12 4/8	3 6/8	3 5/8	4	4	Cochise Co., AZ	Lawson Barrett	Lawson Barrett	2003	26
109 2/8	116	19 2/8	18 4/8	16 4/8	3 7/8	3 7/8	4	5	Gila Co., AZ	John R. Mayfield	John R. Mayfield	2004	27
108 2/8	116 5/8	17 2/8	17 5/8	13 6/8	3 7/8	3 6/8	5	5	Sonora, MX	Hubert R. Kennedy	Hubert R. Kennedy	2006	28
107 4/8	118 3/8	19 3/8	18 7/8	14 1/8	4	4	5	4	Santa Cruz Co., AZ	Danny L. Howard	Danny L. Howard	1991	29
107 4/8	110	17	17	14	4 6/8	4 4/8	4	4	Cochise Co., AZ	Dorothy C. Dolan	Dorothy C. Dolan	2004	29
107 2/8	110 4/8	17 3/8	16 6/8	13 4/8	4	4	4	4	Sonora, MX	Clint Mayeur	Clint Mayeur	2006	31
107	115 5/8	17 4/8	17 4/8	13	4	4	6	5	Sonora, MX	Mick J. McFadden	Mick J. McFadden	2006	32

106 7/8	111	16 3/8	16	11 3/8	4 1/8	3 7/8	5	6	Sonora, MX	Mark D. Sipe	2002	33
105 7/8	108 3/8	17 5/8	17 6/8	14 3/8	3 7/8	3 6/8	4	4	Sierra Co., NM	David A. Widby	2005	34
105 5/8	119 6/8	18 1/8	14 7/8	14	3 7/8	3 7/8	6	6	Chihuahua, MX	Kelly E. McLean	2004	35
105 5/8	110 6/8	17 7/8	16 7/8	12 1/8	4 4/8	4 6/8	5	4	Sonora, MX	John R. Garr	2005	35
105	111 7/8	18 1/8	17 2/8	12	3 6/8	3 7/8	5	4	Grant Co., NM	James O. Piles	2003	37
105	109 1/8	16 3/8	16 2/8	14 4/8	3 7/8	3 6/8	5	5	Greenlee Co., AZ	Chase L. Caldwell	2005	37
104 2/8	114 7/8	17 6/8	15 4/8	10 4/8	3 6/8	3 6/8	7	5	Cochise Co., AZ	Lawson Barrett	2000	39
104	112	17	16 5/8	13	4 3/8	4 4/8	4	5	Sonora, MX	Jay R. Bollinger	2006	40
103 4/8	105 2/8	17 3/8	15 7/8	16 4/8	3 7/8	3 7/8	4	4	Sonora, MX	Eric D. Stanosheck	2005	41
103 4/8	107 5/8	16 6/8	15 7/8	14	3 4/8	3 4/8	4	4	Gila Co., AZ	Rod A. Pinkett	2006	41
103 3/8	105 7/8	15 7/8	15 5/8	11 5/8	3 5/8	3 6/8	4	4	Sonora, MX	Jack Reneau	2005	43
103 2/8	105 4/8	17	16 6/8	14 4/8	3 4/8	3 4/8	4	4	Sonora, MX	Mathew B. Dominy	2005	44
103 1/8	105 4/8	17 5/8	17 3/8	15 7/8	3 6/8	3 6/8	4	4	Gila Co., AZ	Jeff S. Eagar	2004	45
102 2/8	104 3/8	16	15 6/8	13 6/8	3 6/8	4	4	6	Sonora, MX	Norton E. Miller	1964	46
100	105 6/8	16 3/8	16 2/8	15 4/8	4 1/8	3 5/8	5	4	Pima Co., AZ	Keith D. Riefkohl	2005	47
100	104 4/8	17	16 2/8	15 5/8	4	4	4	5	Sonora, MX	Linda K. Sipe	2005	47
130 2/8*	133 7/8	22 3/8	22 3/8	18 2/8	4	3 6/8	4	4	Sonora, MX	Neil G. Sutherland II	2004	
124 6/8*	130 1/8	20	20 7/8	14 6/8	5 3/8	5 2/8	4	4	Cochise Co., AZ	Daniel J. Filleman	2004	
120 1/8*	125 7/8	18 7/8	19	15 6/8	4 2/8	4 2/8	4	5	Sonora, MX	John O. Cook III	2006	

* Final score subject to revision by additional verifying measurements.

TYPICAL COUES' WHITETAIL
FINAL SCORE: 112-2/8
HUNTER: Scott A. Limmer

TYPICAL COUES' WHITETAIL
FINAL SCORE: 103-3/8
HUNTER: Jack Reneau

TYPICAL COUES' WHITETAIL
FINAL SCORE: 115-1/8
HUNTER: Jack W. Moore

TYPICAL COUES' WHITETAIL
FINAL SCORE: 103-2/8
HUNTER: Mathew B. Dominy

COUES' WHITETAIL DEER - NON-TYPICAL ANTLERS

Odocoileus virginianus couesi

Minimum Score 105

World's Record 196 $^2/_8$

Final Score	Gross Score	Length of Main Beam R.	L.	Inside Spread	Circumference at Smallest Place Between Burr & First Point R.	L.	Number of Points R.	L.	Locality	Hunter	Owner	Date Killed	Rank
134 $^4/_8$	137 $^5/_8$	19 $^6/_8$	20 $^3/_8$	15 $^6/_8$	4 $^1/_8$	4	6	7	Sonora, MX	James Schacherl	James Schacherl	2005	1
134 $^1/_8$	141 $^4/_8$	17 $^4/_8$	18 $^7/_8$	13 $^3/_8$	4 $^4/_8$	4 $^3/_8$	11	7	Sonora, MX	Picked Up	Ricardo A. Andrade	2000	2
121	124 $^6/_8$	17 $^6/_8$	17 $^7/_8$	13 $^5/_8$	4 $^1/_8$	4 $^2/_8$	6	7	Sonora, MX	James G. Petersen	James G. Petersen	2006	3
111 $^6/_8$	123 $^5/_8$	17 $^6/_8$	15	12 $^1/_8$	3 $^7/_8$	3 $^6/_8$	4	6	Sonora, MX	Keith D. Riefkohl	Keith D. Riefkohl	2005	4
111 $^1/_8$	117 $^2/_8$	17 $^7/_8$	19 $^2/_8$	10 $^6/_8$	3 $^4/_8$	3 $^4/_8$	5	8	Sonora, MX	Michael C. Ballew	Michael C. Ballew	2003	5
108 $^3/_8$	112 $^4/_8$	17 $^6/_8$	18	13 $^1/_8$	3 $^6/_8$	3 $^5/_8$	7	4	Sonora, MX	William H. Wrye, Jr.	William H. Wrye, Jr.	2006	6
137 $^2/_8$*	140 $^6/_8$	20 $^7/_8$	19 $^6/_8$	15 $^6/_8$	4	4 $^1/_8$	6	7	Sonora, MX	Robert A. Carothers	Robert A. Carothers	2005	
127 $^4/_8$*	132 $^5/_8$	18	18	13 $^5/_8$	3 $^5/_8$	3 $^5/_8$	6	6	Sonora, MX	Gary A. Denton	Gary A. Denton	2005	

* Final score subject to revision by additional verifying measurements.

TYPICAL COUES' WHITETAIL
FINAL SCORE: 105-5/8
HUNTER: John R. Garr

TYPICAL COUES' WHITETAIL
FINAL SCORE: 110-2/8
HUNTER: Darrell D. Robinette

NON-TYPICAL COUES' WHITETAIL
FINAL SCORE: 111-1/8
HUNTER: Michael C. Ballew

NON-TYPICAL COUES' WHITETAIL
FINAL SCORE: 137-2/8*
HUNTER: Robert A. Carothers

CANADA MOOSE

Alces alces americana and Alces alces andersoni

Minimum Score 185

World's Record 242

Canada moose includes trophies from Newfoundland and Canada (except for Yukon Territory and Northwest Territories), Maine, Minnesota, New Hampshire, North Dakota, and Vermont.

Final Score	Gross Score	Greatest Spread	Length of Palm		Width of Palm		Circumference of Beam at Smallest Place		Number of Normal Points		Locality	Hunter	Owner	Date Killed	Rank
			R.	L.	R.	L.	R.	L.	R.	L.					
227 6/8	233 2/8	59 2/8	45	46	18	16 5/8	7 5/8	7 6/8	15	18	Kawdy Mt., BC	Frank A. Hanks	Frank A. Hanks	2004	1
220 2/8	225 5/8	68 2/8	38 7/8	38 4/8	18 4/8	16 4/8	8	8	16	13	Somerset Co., ME	D. Toma & J. Toma	Maine Antler Shed & Wildl. Mus.	1988	2
216 2/8	220 3/8	61	46 1/8	48 6/8	14 2/8	14 4/8	7 2/8	7 4/8	11	10	Lake Co., MN	D.C. Rengo & J.C. Rengo	Dennis C. Rengo	2006	3
216 1/8	225 7/8	63 7/8	45 6/8	44 2/8	14 6/8	17 6/8	6 5/8	6 7/8	11	14	Aroostook Co., ME	Chris T. Smith	Cabela's, Inc.	2005	4
211 6/8	216 1/8	61 2/8	37 4/8	38 6/8	13 4/8	14 4/8	7 6/8	7 7/8	17	17	Aroostook Co., ME	Dale J. O'Leary	Dale J. O'Leary	2004	5
211 3/8	214 5/8	64 3/8	39 4/8	42	12 4/8	13 2/8	7 4/8	7 4/8	14	14	Stupart Lake, MB	Ronald V. Flatgard	Ronald V. Flatgard	2006	6
211 1/8	215 7/8	56 5/8	44 5/8	42 3/8	16 6/8	17 2/8	7 1/8	7 1/8	13	11	Teslin River, BC	Ken R. Schultz	Ken R. Schultz	2005	7
210 7/8	215 6/8	61 5/8	41 5/8	41	14 3/8	18 3/8	8 2/8	8 4/8	11	11	Otter Lake, BC	Robert Tibbo	Robert Tibbo	2003	8
210 1/8	217	52 7/8	45 1/8	46	14 2/8	14 2/8	7 6/8	7 6/8	12	16	Camp Island, BC	James S. Henderson	James S. Henderson	2003	9
209 4/8	212 6/8	61 4/8	44	43 1/8	13	12 6/8	7 2/8	7 1/8	11	13	Jennings River, BC	Douglas A. Rehbein	Douglas A. Rehbein	2004	10
207 7/8	213 3/8	55 5/8	41 3/8	43 6/8	14 2/8	15 2/8	7 4/8	7 5/8	13	15	Telegraph Creek, BC	Pamela Lathrop	Pamela Lathrop	2005	11
206 5/8	214	56 3/8	47 6/8	43 4/8	12 6/8	10 6/8	8	7 7/8	14	13	Kawdy Plateau, BC	Larry L. Dearking	Larry L. Dearking	2005	12
206 1/8	208 5/8	68 5/8	35 7/8	37 7/8	13 1/8	13 4/8	7 6/8	7 7/8	12	12	Lac Carriere, QC	Howard E. Taylor	M. Peck, Jr. & B.T. Peck	1948	13
205 5/8	210	65 1/8	42	38 6/8	12 6/8	11 5/8	7 7/8	7 7/8	12	12	Clifton Lake, MB	Steve B. Vihnanek	Steve B. Vihnanek	2005	14
203 6/8	208 3/8	57 4/8	40 6/8	41 7/8	13 4/8	13	7 3/8	7 3/8	15	12	Unexpected Lake, ON	Lenard B. Krolyk	Lenard B. Krolyk	2003	15
203 6/8	206 6/8	54 4/8	41 6/8	42	16 1/8	15 5/8	7 4/8	7 2/8	12	10	Kawdy Mt., BC	Jim Lowry	Jim Lowry	2003	15
203 2/8	206 6/8	63 2/8	34 1/8	35 1/8	15	14 4/8	7 3/8	7 3/8	16	14	Gataga River, BC	Dan J. Cisewski	Dan J. Cisewski	2004	17
203 2/8	210 7/8	58 2/8	44	39 4/8	11 6/8	12 7/8	8 2/8	8 2/8	13	15	Chuchinka Creek, BC	Jerry J. Claflin	Jerry J. Claflin	2004	17
203 2/8	207 6/8	59 4/8	43 1/8	40 6/8	14	13	7 2/8	7 1/8	11	12	Kawdy Mt., BC	Wade L. Hanks	Wade L. Hanks	2004	17
203 1/8	208 3/8	62 5/8	36 3/8	34 4/8	20	19 5/8	7 1/8	7 1/8	12	9	Spatzizi Plateau, BC	Roger H. Jensen	Roger H. Jensen	2005	20
203	207 5/8	57 2/8	42 4/8	44 5/8	14 3/8	13 7/8	7 4/8	7 4/8	11	9	Camp Island Lake, BC	Steven M. Low	Steven M. Low	2003	21
203	206	56	44 7/8	44 3/8	12	14 3/8	7 2/8	7 2/8	10	10	Dease Lake, BC	John McClay	John McClay	2005	21
202 2/8	202 7/8	59 2/8	39 3/8	39 3/8	12 5/8	13 2/8	7 4/8	7 4/8	12	12	Stikine River, BC	David S. Marek	David S. Marek	1998	23
201 7/8	207 7/8	59 5/8	36 6/8	35	17 1/8	14 2/8	6 7/8	7 1/8	15	16	Franklin Co., ME	Picked Up	Toby L. Montgomery	2005	24
201 1/8	203 6/8	51 7/8	40 4/8	40 5/8	14 4/8	13	7 1/8	7 1/8	15	14	Manitoba	Picked Up	John E. Major	1953	25
200 3/8	206 4/8	56 7/8	41	43 7/8	12 5/8	13 6/8	7 1/8	7 2/8	11	13	Warren Lake, ON	Gary D. Benson	Gary D. Benson	2003	26
200 2/8	207 1/8	47	43 4/8	47 4/8	12 2/8	13 1/8	7 2/8	7 7/8	13	15	Bowron River, BC	Walter H. Paetkau	Walter H. Paetkau	2005	27

Score	Greatest Spread	Width of Palm R	Width of Palm L	Length of Palm R	Length of Palm L	Circ. Beam R	Circ. Beam L	Points R	Points L	Locality	Hunter	Owner	Date Killed	Rank
199 2/8	60 2/8	41 5/8	42 7/8	14	16 3/8	7 7/8	8	7	9	Marsh Creek, AB	Otto W. Hellum	Otto W. Hellum	2005	28
199	201 6/8	49 6/8	45 3/8	12 4/8	13 7/8	7 6/8	7 6/8	9	10	McGregor River, BC	Larry C. Adey	Rose Adey	2004	29
198 5/8	200 3/8	59 5/8	39 7/8	14 2/8	12 5/8	7 1/8	7 1/8	10	10	Liege River, AB	Bernie G. Belland	Bernie G. Belland	2005	30
198 4/8	205 3/8	52	43 6/8	14 7/8	13 2/8	7 3/8	7 4/8	14	13	Telegraph Creek, BC	John C. Marsh	John C. Marsh	2004	31
198 2/8	201	61 4/8	36	13 3/8	13 1/8	7 4/8	7 2/8	13	12	Cook Co., MN	Michael Withers	Michael Withers	2003	32
198 2/8	205 1/8	53	41 5/8	13 2/8	15 5/8	7 5/8	8 2/8	14	12	Cody Lake, BC	Kenneth R. Womack	Kenneth R. Womack	2005	32
198	203 1/8	58 4/8	39 1/8	15 4/8	13	8 2/8	8 2/8	12	10	Coos Co., NH	Daniel R. Cushing	Daniel R. Cushing	2004	34
197 7/8	200 5/8	54 5/8	36 6/8	13 3/8	14 4/8	7 4/8	7 5/8	14	15	Moodie Lake, BC	Mitchell Stauner	Mitchell Stauner	2005	35
197 5/8	199 2/8	54 3/8	37 2/8	13 2/8	12 1/8	7 2/8	7 1/8	13	13	Anvil Mt., BC	Randy L. Mendenhall	Randy L. Mendenhall	2004	36
197 4/8	204 1/8	59 2/8	39 6/8	13 1/8	11 2/8	6 7/8	7	13	13	Level Mt. Range, BC	Michael J. Sondeno	Michael J. Sondeno	2003	37
197 3/8	203 2/8	48 1/8	38	16 4/8	19 5/8	7 7/8	7 7/8	9	11	Kechika River, BC	Bryan K. Martin	Bryan K. Martin	2005	38
197 3/8	212	63 5/8	42	15	13 1/8	7 6/8	7 7/8	14	14	Rainbow Lake, AB	Brian D. Nielson	Brian D. Nielson	2005	38
196 6/8	203 2/8	58	37 4/8	13	15 2/8	7 4/8	7 4/8	9	10	Coal River, BC	Jim Shockey	Jim Shockey	2003	40
196 3/8	198 6/8	48 7/8	43 1/8	15	14 5/8	7 3/8	7 3/8	15	13	Kechika River, BC	Trevor D. Ellingson	Trevor D. Ellingson	2005	41
196 1/8	203 6/8	59 3/8	38 6/8	12 3/8	11 1/8	7 2/8	7 3/8	14	11	Piscataquis Co., ME	L.L. Levesque & K. Pierce	Lonnie L. Levesque	2006	42
195 6/8	202 4/8	50 6/8	42 2/8	15 2/8	14 4/8	6 6/8	6 6/8	11	15	Babine Lake, BC	Thomas Vaida	Thomas Vaida	2004	43
195 4/8	197 4/8	53 6/8	38 7/8	13 2/8	14	6 6/8	6 7/8	12	13	Little Dease Lake, BC	Bill Mace	Bill Mace	2004	44
195 2/8	198 7/8	55 4/8	39 6/8	12 6/8	11 5/8	7 4/8	7 4/8	13	11	Big Valley, AB	Katherina D. Butterwick	Katherina D. Butterwick	2005	45
195 2/8	206 1/8	59 2/8	41 5/8	15 4/8	11 6/8	7 5/8	7 6/8	14	11	Diefenbaker Lake, SK	Kathy Bennett	Kathy Bennett	2006	45

CANADA MOOSE
FINAL SCORE: 188-2/8
HUNTER: Dale Hislop

CANADA MOOSE
FINAL SCORE: 197-3/8
HUNTER: Bryan K. Martin

CANADA MOOSE
FINAL SCORE: 197-7/8
HUNTER: Mitchell Stauner

CANADA MOOSE
FINAL SCORE: 192-5/8
HUNTER: Larry K. Fulton

CANADA MOOSE

Alces alces americana and *Alces alces andersoni*

Final Score	Gross Score	Greatest Spread	Length of Palm R	L	Width of Palm R	L	Circumference of Beam at Smallest Place R	L	Number of Normal Points R	L	Locality	Hunter	Owner	Date Killed	Rank
$195^{1/8}$	$197^{5/8}$	$57^{1/8}$	$36^{7/8}$	$37^{6/8}$	14	$15^{4/8}$	$7^{2/8}$	$7^{1/8}$	11	11	Billard Lake, MB	Walter N. Fett	Walter N. Fett	2005	47
195	$200^{2/8}$	56	$40^{6/8}$	$41^{1/8}$	$12^{3/8}$	$13^{3/8}$	$7^{4/8}$	$7^{3/8}$	9	13	Scoop Lake, BC	Dave V. Bell	Dave V. Bell	2003	48
195	$201^{6/8}$	$55^{4/8}$	$34^{3/8}$	$37^{1/8}$	$15^{3/8}$	$13^{3/8}$	8	$7^{7/8}$	14	16	Washington Co., ME	Dennis J. McHugh, Sr.	Dennis J. McHugh, Sr.	2005	48
$194^{4/8}$	$200^{7/8}$	$56^{4/8}$	$38^{1/8}$	$38^{2/8}$	$12^{6/8}$	$12^{5/8}$	$6^{3/8}$	$6^{2/8}$	13	15	Battle River, AB	Gary Kenna	Gary Kenna	2003	50
$194^{4/8}$	$196^{4/8}$	60	$38^{1/8}$	$36^{2/8}$	$12^{4/8}$	$12^{4/8}$	$7^{4/8}$	$7^{5/8}$	11	11	Josephine Creek, BC	Thomas W. Krenn	Thomas W. Krenn	2004	50
$194^{2/8}$	$196^{1/8}$	57	$40^{5/8}$	40	12	$12^{2/8}$	$6^{5/8}$	$6^{5/8}$	11	10	Toad River, BC	Steve Hornady	Steve Hornady	2004	52
$194^{1/8}$	$196^{7/8}$	$63^{7/8}$	39	$40^{4/8}$	$10^{1/8}$	$11^{2/8}$	$7^{1/8}$	7	9	9	Dry Lake, BC	Carean Goss	Carean Goss	2003	53
$193^{6/8}$	$200^{6/8}$	$61^{7/8}$	$36^{1/8}$	$35^{7/8}$	$17^{2/8}$	$13^{4/8}$	$7^{1/8}$	7	11	10	Essex Co., VT	David F. Werner	David F. Werner	2004	54
$193^{2/8}$	198	$55^{6/8}$	$43^{6/8}$	$39^{4/8}$	$13^{2/8}$	$13^{1/8}$	$7^{4/8}$	$7^{1/8}$	9	9	Melgard Lake, BC	Mark A. Glow	Mark A. Glow	2005	55
$192^{5/8}$	$196^{2/8}$	$61^{7/8}$	$37^{3/8}$	$38^{4/8}$	$13^{6/8}$	$12^{3/8}$	$7^{5/8}$	$7^{6/8}$	8	9	Tatshenshini River, BC	Larry K. Fulton	Larry K. Fulton	2004	56
$192^{2/8}$	$196^{5/8}$	$55^{2/8}$	$35^{5/8}$	$35^{1/8}$	$12^{6/8}$	$13^{5/8}$	$7^{1/8}$	$7^{1/8}$	14	15	Buffalo River, AB	Dennis Elverud	Dennis Elverud	2005	57
$192^{1/8}$	$194^{7/8}$	$62^{1/8}$	38	39	$9^{5/8}$	$10^{2/8}$	$7^{4/8}$	$7^{3/8}$	10	11	Wernham Lake, MB	Matt J. Rohl	Matt J. Rohl	2004	58
192	$195^{3/8}$	54	$36^{2/8}$	$36^{1/8}$	$15^{4/8}$	$12^{2/8}$	$7^{5/8}$	$7^{5/8}$	13	13	Blue River, BC	Len H. Guldman	Len H. Guldman	2004	59
$191^{6/8}$	$196^{1/8}$	$60^{2/8}$	$36^{2/8}$	$36^{6/8}$	10	$11^{6/8}$	7	$7^{1/8}$	13	13	Williston Lake, BC	Kathy S. Haldorson	Kathy S. Haldorson	2005	60
$191^{3/8}$	$192^{6/8}$	$65^{7/8}$	$32^{7/8}$	$32^{3/8}$	$12^{6/8}$	$13^{4/8}$	$7^{6/8}$	$7^{5/8}$	10	10	Entwine Lake, ON	Bernhard A. Ellingson	Bernhard A. Ellingson	2005	61
$191^{2/8}$	$198^{3/8}$	$57^{6/8}$	$36^{4/8}$	$39^{2/8}$	$13^{7/8}$	$14^{2/8}$	$7^{3/8}$	$7^{3/8}$	9	13	Kelsall River, BC	Robert T. Henson	Robert T. Henson	2003	62
$191^{1/8}$	$191^{7/8}$	59	$38^{3/8}$	$38^{3/8}$	$12^{5/8}$	$13^{1/8}$	$7^{2/8}$	$7^{1/8}$	8	8	Whiteclay Lake, ON	John E. Herbst	John E. Herbst	2005	62
191	193	$55^{2/8}$	$37^{4/8}$	$37^{1/8}$	$12^{7/8}$	$12^{4/8}$	$7^{1/8}$	$7^{2/8}$	11	12	Makomesut Lake, ON	Brent J. Larson	Brent J. Larson	2003	64
191	$199^{7/8}$	49	$36^{6/8}$	$42^{1/8}$	$13^{1/8}$	$14^{4/8}$	$7^{1/8}$	$7^{2/8}$	14	16	Rabbit River, BC	Edward J. Urlacher	Edward J. Urlacher	2005	64
$190^{7/8}$	$202^{2/8}$	$59^{3/8}$	$36^{4/8}$	$44^{3/8}$	11	$13^{1/8}$	$7^{2/8}$	$7^{2/8}$	11	12	Aroostook Co., ME	Peter H. Fiori, Sr.	Michael J. Fiori	2004	66
$190^{7/8}$	$193^{5/8}$	$55^{7/8}$	$34^{6/8}$	$34^{4/8}$	$14^{3/8}$	14	$7^{5/8}$	8	13	11	Camp Lake, BC	Tyler R. Joy	Tyler R. Joy	2004	66
$189^{7/8}$	197	$58^{3/8}$	$41^{3/8}$	40	$9^{6/8}$	13	$8^{1/8}$	$7^{4/8}$	11	9	Terrace Bay, ON	Samuel H. Schmidt	Samuel H. Schmidt	2005	68
$189^{6/8}$	$191^{1/8}$	$52^{4/8}$	$35^{5/8}$	$35^{5/8}$	$13^{2/8}$	12	7	$7^{1/8}$	14	14	Beaver Head Lake, MB	James P. Winski	James P. Winski	2003	69
$189^{5/8}$	$195^{7/8}$	$56^{3/8}$	$38^{2/8}$	$41^{3/8}$	$12^{3/8}$	$12^{3/8}$	7	$7^{2/8}$	9	10	Ospika River, BC	Mark A. Wayne	Mark A. Wayne	2003	70
$189^{2/8}$	$193^{5/8}$	$58^{6/8}$	$35^{5/8}$	$35^{3/8}$	$10^{4/8}$	$12^{2/8}$	$7^{3/8}$	$7^{6/8}$	12	14	Peace River, AB	Justin Severance	Justin Severance	2001	71
$189^{2/8}$	$203^{5/8}$	$60^{4/8}$	$32^{1/8}$	$42^{7/8}$	$14^{3/8}$	$14^{7/8}$	$7^{7/8}$	8	10	13	Cook Co., MN	David E. Zieroth	David E. Zieroth	2005	71
189	$194^{1/8}$	$54^{6/8}$	40	$38^{7/8}$	11	$12^{6/8}$	$6^{2/8}$	$6^{4/8}$	11	13	Teslin River, BC	John R. Garr	John R. Garr	2005	73
$188^{7/8}$	$194^{5/8}$	$58^{7/8}$	$35^{4/8}$	38	$12^{6/8}$	$11^{7/8}$	$7^{5/8}$	8	10	12	Somerset Co., ME	Brenda S. Markee	Brenda S. Markee	2003	74
$188^{2/8}$	$191^{6/8}$	$55^{6/8}$	$38^{2/8}$	$38^{1/8}$	$12^{2/8}$	$12^{4/8}$	7	$6^{7/8}$	9	12	Graham River, BC	Dale Hislop	Dale Hislop	2006	75
$188^{2/8}$	$191^{1/8}$	$53^{2/8}$	$37^{4/8}$	$38^{6/8}$	$12^{2/8}$	$11^{6/8}$	$7^{2/8}$	$7^{3/8}$	12	11	Duffield Creek, BC	Tyson L. Miller	Tyson L. Miller	2006	75
$188^{1/8}$	$188^{3/8}$	$49^{1/8}$	37	37	$13^{2/8}$	$13^{4/8}$	$7^{2/8}$	$7^{2/8}$	12	12	Lac des Milles Lac, ON	Allen D. Clark	Allen D. Clark	2003	77
188	$192^{3/8}$	52	$35^{2/8}$	$37^{3/8}$	$16^{4/8}$	$15^{6/8}$	$7^{4/8}$	7	11	10	Washington Co., ME	Jeffrey C. Gallant	Jeffrey C. Gallant	2003	78
$187^{6/8}$	$191^{6/8}$	$45^{6/8}$	$41^{3/8}$	$39^{4/8}$	$14^{6/8}$	$15^{7/8}$	$6^{6/8}$	$6^{6/8}$	11	10	Pickle Lake, ON	Dennis Ellis	Dennis Ellis	2005	79

187 5/8	198 4/8	63 7/8	33 6/8	36 6/8	13 3/8	13 7/8	7 5/8	7 2/8	10	9	Somerset Co., ME	Edmund J. Lemaire	Edmund J. Lemaire	2005	80
187 4/8	189 7/8	55 6/8	35 5/8	36 2/8	12 6/8	12	7 2/8	7 2/8	12	11	Piscataquis Co., ME	Jeremy Cupero	Jeremy Cupero	1995	81
187 2/8	194 5/8	61 2/8	36 6/8	37 2/8	13 5/8	11	7 4/8	7 2/8	12	8	Somerset Co., ME	Ellen M. Bubier	Ellen M. Bubier	2004	82
187 1/8	192 7/8	56 7/8	31 7/8	35	15	16 4/8	7 3/8	7 2/8	12	11	Pigeon River, MB	Erik C. Thienpondt	Erik C. Thienpondt	2005	83
186 5/8	193 5/8	59 3/8	36 4/8	33 1/8	12 2/8	12 6/8	7 3/8	7 2/8	14	11	North Knife Lake, MB	Terry Radsick	Terry Radsick	2005	84
186 3/8	193 7/8	57 3/8	36 7/8	39 5/8	10 2/8	12 3/8	6 3/8	7	13	11	Telegraph Creek, BC	Jason M. Marsh	Jason M. Marsh	2004	85
186 2/8	187 6/8	51 4/8	38 2/8	37 3/8	11 4/8	11	8	8 1/8	11	11	Somerset Co., ME	Lawrence E. Ingham	Lawrence E. Ingham	2005	86
186	198 1/8	54 4/8	37 5/8	42	15	11 7/8	7 6/8	8 3/8	11	9	Gataga River, BC	Jim Zuge	Jim Zuge	2004	87
186	192 5/8	62	36 2/8	41 1/8	13 5/8	14 3/8	7 1/8	7 1/8	5	6	Sandridge Lake, ON	Michael J. Staelgrave	Michael J. Staelgrave	2006	87
185 6/8	194 2/8	55 6/8	38	43 2/8	10 3/8	10 1/8	6 7/8	6 7/8	10	13	Kitchener Lake, BC	Nate K. Jensen	Nate K. Jensen	2005	89
185 5/8	190 7/8	54 5/8	36 1/8	38 6/8	11 2/8	12 2/8	7 1/8	7 6/8	11	12	Mercutio Lake, ON	Jim L. Gianladis	Jim L. Gianladis	2003	90
185 3/8	191 2/8	62 3/8	37 1/8	32 4/8	11 4/8	12 6/8	8 4/8	8 4/8	9	9	Coos Co., NH	Gerald R. Lund	Gerald R. Lund	1993	91
185 3/8	195 2/8	55 1/8	40	35 3/8	15	13 1/8	7 5/8	8	12	9	Coos Co., NH	David B. Gagnier	David B. Gagnier	2005	91
185	193 5/8	54 6/8	34 2/8	37 3/8	14 3/8	13 1/8	7 2/8	7 4/8	11	13	Sydney Lake, ON	Dale E. Roethemeyer	Dale E. Roethemeyer	1993	93
225 *	230	62 6/8	47 1/8	46 1/8	14	15 7/8	8 1/8	8	13	15	Cassiar Mts., BC	Mark K. Jackson	Mark K. Jackson	2004	
214 7/8*	219 5/8	69 5/8	40	40 5/8	17 3/8	15 3/8	7 2/8	7 3/8	12	10	Black Mt., NS	Douglas J. Weatherbee	Douglas J. Weatherbee	2004	
213 2/8*	215	54 2/8	44	43 7/8	16 1/8	15 4/8	7 1/8	7 1/8	14	13	Liard River, BC	Patrick R. Rice	Patrick R. Rice	2003	
213 2/8*	226 6/8	61 2/8	44	47	14	18 2/8	8	8 2/8	10	16	Coos Co., NH	T. Dube & L. Dube	T. Dube & L. Dube	2005	

* Final score subject to revision by additional verifying measurements.

ALASKA-YUKON MOOSE
FINAL SCORE: 235-1/8
HUNTER: Dale A. Boorsma

ALASKA-YUKON MOOSE
FINAL SCORE: 217
HUNTER: Gregory A. Bode

ALASKA-YUKON MOOSE
FINAL SCORE: 211-3/8
HUNTER: Nicholas A. Unrein

ALASKA-YUKON MOOSE

Alces alces gigas

Minimum Score 210

World's Record 261 5/8

Alaska-Yukon moose includes trophies from Alaska, Yukon Territory, and Northwest Territories.

Final Score	Gross Score	Greatest Spread	Length of Palm R	Length of Palm L	Width of Palm R	Width of Palm L	Circ. of Beam R	Circ. of Beam L	Points R	Points L	Locality	Hunter	Owner	Date Killed	Rank
254 5/8	258 5/8	70 7/8	46 4/8	48 2/8	22 2/8	23 1/8	8 1/8	8 4/8	15	16	Kvichak River, AK	Franz Kohlroser	Franz Kohlroser	2005	1
244	253 7/8	75 2/8	45 1/8	47 1/8	20 6/8	18	8 2/8	8 3/8	15	14	Pingston Creek, AK	Jerry D. Whisenhunt	Jerry D. Whisenhunt	2004	2
236 4/8	239 7/8	66 4/8	44 4/8	44 4/8	17 4/8	17 5/8	8 4/8	8 6/8	15	16	Selawik River, AK	Bruce G. Mountain	Bruce G. Mountain	2005	3
236	248 6/8	74	52 2/8	48 5/8	17 5/8	14 5/8	8 6/8	8 7/8	12	12	Kilbuck Mts., AK	Eric R. Arnette	Eric R. Arnette	2004	4
236	241 3/8	69	50 2/8	49 4/8	15 6/8	17 2/8	7 7/8	7 6/8	12	11	King Salmon River, AK	Grady J. Colby	Grady J. Colby	2004	5
235 7/8	240 5/8	64 1/8	53 3/8	51 7/8	14	17 1/8	9	9 1/8	11	11	Gana River, NT	Matthew H. Smith	Matthew H. Smith	2006	6
235 4/8	239 6/8	75 4/8	41 2/8	42 4/8	18 6/8	20 6/8	7	7	14	13	Susitna River, AK	Mathew R. Edmondson	Mathew R. Edmondson	2004	7
235 1/8	240 4/8	69 1/8	47 4/8	47 5/8	15 7/8	14 6/8	7 6/8	7 7/8	17	13	Kaiyuh Mts., AK	Dale A. Boorsma	Dale A. Boorsma	2005	8
234 6/8	239 1/8	67 2/8	45 6/8	49 5/8	17	16 4/8	7 4/8	7 4/8	14	14	Nisling River, YT	Scott A. Boettcher	Scott A. Boettcher	2005	9
234 6/8	240 4/8	66	47 3/8	47 1/8	17	17 1/8	7 5/8	7 2/8	18	13	Chilikadrotna River, AK	Daniel E. Kenney	Daniel E. Kenney	2005	9
234 2/8	236 1/8	77 6/8	46 1/8	45 7/8	14 2/8	12 6/8	7 5/8	7 6/8	12	12	Big Mt., AK	Scott N. McLean	Scott N. McLean	2005	11
232 6/8	234 6/8	65 2/8	47 4/8	46 6/8	15 4/8	14 4/8	7 6/8	7 4/8	15	15	Boulder Creek, AK	Robert L. Aukeman	Robert L. Aukeman	2002	12
231 7/8	235 2/8	64 3/8	49	48 2/8	14 1/8	14 6/8	7 3/8	7 3/8	16	14	Lake Clark, AK	Mike D. Stegewans	Mike D. Stegewans	1998	13
229 1/8	233	63 1/8	50 2/8	47 6/8	15 2/8	15	7 3/8	7 2/8	13	14	Mother Goose Lake, AK	Thomas E. Monacelli	Thomas E. Monacelli	2005	14
229	233 3/8	70 6/8	46 6/8	47 1/8	14 4/8	15 3/8	7 3/8	7 4/8	11	12	Cinder River, AK	Dwayne E. Heikes	Dwayne E. Heikes	2006	15
228 5/8	234 4/8	67 1/8	47 3/8	43	16 6/8	17 2/8	7	7	15	14	Springway Creek, AK	Robert N. Toman	Robert N. Toman	1995	16
228 2/8	237 6/8	63 4/8	50 2/8	46 4/8	17 5/8	17	7 3/8	7 4/8	12	15	Minto Lakes, AK	C.W. Mahlen, Jr., & C.W. Mahlen IV	Charles W. Mahlen IV	2005	17
227 5/8	234 2/8	62 1/8	45 4/8	43 2/8	19 2/8	18	7 4/8	7 5/8	17	14	Pickerel Lake, AK	Michael J. Macauley	Michael J. Macauley	2004	18
225 7/8	232 5/8	70 3/8	39 5/8	40 2/8	15 4/8	18 2/8	6 5/8	7	16	19	Alaska Range, AK	Dennis C. Grimm	Dennis C. Grimm	2004	19
225 5/8	228 5/8	63 7/8	46 4/8	47 3/8	15 4/8	14 3/8	8	8	12	13	MacMillan River, YT	Kevin Cresci	Kevin Cresci	2003	20
225 4/8	230	63	47 4/8	48	12 4/8	14 4/8	8 2/8	8 2/8	13	15	Noatak River, AK	George A. Cook III	George A. Cook III	2004	21
225 3/8	233 4/8	67 1/8	46 4/8	46 5/8	14 6/8	17 6/8	7 3/8	7 3/8	11	14	Kokrine Hills, AK	Bruce A. Gaugler	Bruce A. Gaugler	2001	22
225 2/8	230 6/8	68 6/8	40 4/8	43	15 4/8	16	8 2/8	8 6/8	14	16	Mountain River, NT	George A. Pickel	George A. Pickel	2004	23
225 2/8	230 3/8	68	47 6/8	50 2/8	14 7/8	13 4/8	7 3/8	7 5/8	10	11	Koyukuk River, AK	Jack W. Jaynes	Jack W. Jaynes	2005	23
225 2/8	231 2/8	74 2/8	43	42 4/8	13 3/8	15 6/8	8 5/8	8 6/8	11	14	King Salmon River, AK	Gregory A. Zurn	Gregory A. Zurn	2006	23
224 7/8	230 4/8	68 7/8	44	45 2/8	16 2/8	16 5/8	7 2/8	7 2/8	11	13	Nuyakuk River, AK	Byron Lamb	Byron Lamb	2004	26
224 7/8	235 6/8	69 7/8	45 1/8	41	19 2/8	17 4/8	8	8	13	12	Iowithla River, AK	Allen N. Gilliland	Allen N. Gilliland	2006	26
224 5/8	228 5/8	66 1/8	45 7/8	45 6/8	13 3/8	16 1/8	8 2/8	8 1/8	12	13	Hess River, YT	Jim Shockey	Jim Shockey	2003	28
224 1/8	226 1/8	63 7/8	47 7/8	47	14 4/8	15 4/8	7 5/8	7 5/8	11	11	Red Paint Creek, AK	Colin Onaka	Colin Onaka	2003	29

Score	Gross Score									Locality	Hunter	Owner	Date	Rank
223 7/8*	226 7/8	51 1/8	54 7/8	53	15 2/8	15 2/8	8 1/8	8 2/8	10 / 11	Cinder River, AK	Frank J. Fazzio, Jr.	Frank J. Fazzio, Jr.	2004	30
223 6/8	229	63	44 1/8	45 5/8	17 2/8	14 4/8	7 6/8	7 6/8	14 / 15	Nenana Mt., AK	David W. Boone	David W. Boone	2004	31
220 6/8	229 4/8	61 6/8	46 2/8	44 4/8	12 6/8	14 4/8	8 2/8	8 4/8	14 / 19	Bonnet Plume River, YT	Jeffery K. Van Wart, Sr.	Jeffery K. Van Wart, Sr.	2003	32
220 6/8	235 6/8	71	43 4/8	43 6/8	14 5/8	14	7 7/8	8	12 / 16	Huslia River, AK	Ryan Schiermeier	Ryan Schiermeier	2006	32
218 6/8	221	71 2/8	43 1/8	44	13	14 3/8	7 5/8	7 5/8	10 / 10	King Salmon River, AK	Glenn R. Koch	Glenn R. Koch	2002	34
218 3/8	228 6/8	63 3/8	44 6/8	42 5/8	19	14	8 1/8	7 7/8	16 / 13	Nonvianuk River, AK	Richard J. Jacob	Richard J. Jacob	2001	35
218 3/8	219 7/8	65 1/8	41 5/8	41 2/8	15 3/8	14 2/8	7 1/8	7 1/8	14 / 14	Mulchatna River, AK	James W. Kelley III	James W. Kelley III	2003	35
217	221 6/8	57 4/8	42 6/8	42 4/8	15 4/8	18	7 2/8	7 2/8	15 / 15	Selawik Hills, AK	Gregory A. Bode	Gregory A. Bode	2005	37
216	220 6/8	65	40 4/8	40 7/8	15 5/8	14 3/8	7 6/8	7 5/8	13 / 16	Big Creek, AK	Byron Whitney	Byron Whitney	2004	38
215 7/8	221 3/8	69 7/8	43 2/8	46	13 2/8	13 6/8	7 4/8	7 6/8	9 / 11	Nusagagak River, AK	Greg F. Down	Greg F. Down	2003	39
215 6/8	219 3/8	65 6/8	42 4/8	42 2/8	12 2/8	12 4/8	7 1/8	7	14 / 15	Stephan Lake, AK	Jake D. Jefferson	Jake D. Jefferson	2002	40
215 6/8	217 7/8	58	44 6/8	43 6/8	14	13 7/8	8 2/8	8 2/8	13 / 14	MacMillan River, YT	John S. Bell	John S. Bell	2003	40
215 5/8	221 5/8	67 1/8	44 7/8	41 1/8	12 6/8	11 5/8	7 4/8	7 4/8	14 / 15	Caribou Mt., AK	James L. Wontor	James L. Wontor	1986	42
215	218 1/8	64 4/8	44	44	11 7/8	11 7/8	7 3/8	7 5/8	12 / 14	Hoholitna River, AK	Jeffrey Jesionowski	Jeffrey Jesionowski	2005	43
215	223 1/8	64 6/8	39 3/8	41 4/8	17 4/8	16 4/8	8 2/8	8 2/8	12 / 13	Huslia River, AK	Bert L. Gordon	Bert L. Gordon	2006	43
214 6/8	218 2/8	65 6/8	42	45 2/8	15 4/8	15 2/8	7 2/8	7 2/8	10 / 10	Koyukuk River, AK	Craig R. Stevens	Craig R. Stevens	2002	45
214 6/8	217 3/8	65	44 1/8	44 3/8	14 2/8	14 5/8	7 4/8	7 4/8	9 / 11	Logging Cabin Creek, AK	Dennis M. Carey	Dennis M. Carey	2005	45
214 4/8	225 3/8	69 2/8	37 6/8	42	16 2/8	17 6/8	8 2/8	8 1/8	11 / 14	Kvichak River, AK	Anthony M. Ferrito	Anthony M. Ferrito	2006	47
213 7/8	219 2/8	63 1/8	43 6/8	45	12 2/8	12 1/8	7 4/8	7 4/8	12 / 16	Nowitna River, AK	George E. Dantin III	George E. Dantin III	2004	48
213 7/8	223 4/8	66 3/8	44 4/8	40 6/8	13 4/8	15 2/8	10 5/8	8 4/8	11 / 13	Tsiu River, AK	Bruce Brock	Bruce Brock	2006	48
212 4/8	221 1/8	58 4/8	43 4/8	43 7/8	14 6/8	15 7/8	7 2/8	7 3/8	12 / 17	Salcha River, AK	John R. Coulter	John R. Coulter	2005	50
212	226 4/8	71 4/8	37	45 1/8	12 7/8	16 2/8	8 3/8	8 3/8	12 / 15	Melozitna River, AK	Joseph Barrus	Joseph Barrus	2002	51
211 3/8	216 5/8	64 5/8	39 4/8	39 1/8	12 7/8	13 4/8	8 7/8	9 1/8	13 / 15	Mystery Creek, AK	Nicholas A. Unrein	Nicholas A. Unrein	2005	52
211 2/8	217 4/8	58	42 6/8	45 2/8	17 6/8	16	7 3/8	7 3/8	11 / 11	Tagagawik River, AK	Lyle C. Heger	Lyle C. Heger	2004	53
211	216 5/8	61 2/8	44 4/8	41 4/8	15 4/8	14	7 3/8	7 4/8	13 / 12	Bear Lake, AK	Paula K. Barry	Paula K. Barry	2005	54
210 6/8	212 5/8	61 2/8	44 4/8	43 3/8	15 6/8	15 2/8	7 3/8	7 1/8	9 / 9	Koyuk River, AK	Glenn M. Smith	Glenn M. Smith	2004	55
210 3/8	214 7/8	68 1/8	40 6/8	41 4/8	14 6/8	16 2/8	7 1/8	7 3/8	9 / 9	Koyuk River, AK	Gerald K. Kusar	Gerald K. Kusar	2004	56
210 1/8	220	59 5/8	43 5/8	41 4/8	13 7/8	18 5/8	7 7/8	7 7/8	12 / 15	Koyukuk River, AK	Eddie D. Rathie	Eddie D. Rathie	2004	57
210	214	61 6/8	42 6/8	41 4/8	15 4/8	13 7/8	7 7/8	7 6/8	11 / 12	King Salmon River, AK	Robert G. Blanke	Robert G. Blanke	2004	58
255 4/8*	257 7/8	76 2/8	52 1/8	52 3/8	17 4/8	18 3/8	8	8 2/8	13 / 13	Anvik River, AK	Jack F. Nelsen	Jack F. Nelsen	2004	
240 1/8*	248 7/8	64 5/8	48	44 1/8	23 1/8	22 1/8	8 4/8	9 3/8	16 / 13	Tagagawik River, AK	Charles S. Winters	Charles S. Winters	2006	
238 1/8*	244 6/8	65 1/8	47 7/8	52 1/8	18 1/8	18 2/8	8	8 2/8	13 / 13	Mount Gillis, YT	Peter C. Nalos	Peter C. Nalos	2004	

* Final score subject to revision by additional verifying measurements.

SHIRAS MOOSE

Alces alces shirasi

Minimum Score 140

World's Record 205 4/8

Shiras moose includes trophies taken in Colorado, Idaho, Montana, Utah, Washington, and Wyoming.

Final Score	Gross Score	Greatest Spread	Length of Palm R.	L.	Width of Palm R.	L.	Circumference of Beam at Smallest Place R.	L.	Number of Normal Points R.	L.	Locality	Hunter	Owner	Date Killed	Rank
187 1/8	190 7/8	59 5/8	38 6/8	40 3/8	11 4/8	12 4/8	6 4/8	6 5/8	7	8	Shoshone Co., ID	Chad Hammons	Chad Hammons	2005	1
183 6/8	184 2/8	54 6/8	33 3/8	33 5/8	12	12 2/8	6 1/8	6 1/8	13	13	Stevens Co., WA	Marc W. Babiar	Marc W. Babiar	2005	2
182 3/8	184 6/8	56 3/8	33 6/8	32 5/8	12 6/8	12 7/8	6 6/8	6 5/8	11	12	Eagle Co., CO	John T. Stafford, Jr.	Cabela's, Inc.	2005	3
181 2/8	184	51	36 2/8	34	13	13 2/8	7 1/8	7 3/8	11	11	Flathead Co., MT	Robert P. Barnaby	Robert P. Barnaby	2004	4
180 4/8	185 5/8	57 2/8	34 1/8	36 1/8	11 4/8	11 4/8	6 4/8	6 5/8	11	10	Benewah Co., ID	Ronald L. Moore	Ronald L. Moore	2005	5
179 6/8	183 3/8	56	34 3/8	35 4/8	14 4/8	13	6 4/8	6 4/8	9	8	Flathead Co., MT	David B. Armstrong	David B. Armstrong	2006	6
179 1/8	180 3/8	49 7/8	32 4/8	33 4/8	14 4/8	14 2/8	6 7/8	6 7/8	11	11	Idaho Co., ID	Eldon H. Campbell	Eldon H. Campbell	2005	7
177 4/8	182 2/8	51 2/8	36 5/8	34 2/8	11 5/8	11 2/8	6 5/8	6 5/8	13	11	Weber Co., UT	Dennis Jeppsen	Dennis Jeppsen	2004	8
177	179 7/8	45 4/8	33 4/8	35 3/8	12 5/8	11 5/8	6 5/8	6 5/8	14	14	Larimer Co., CO	John D. Borrego	John D. Borrego	2005	9
176 6/8	177 3/8	54 6/8	37 7/8	37 6/8	9 4/8	9 1/8	6 2/8	6 1/8	8	8	Flathead Co., MT	Kenneth D. Kysar	Kenneth D. Kysar	2003	10
176 3/8	178	46 3/8	35 1/8	35	12	12 2/8	7	7 2/8	12	11	Jackson Co., CO	Scott M. Hushbeck	Scott M. Hushbeck	2006	11
176 2/8	182	50	37 6/8	38	9 4/8	11 6/8	6 7/8	7 1/8	9	12	Pend Oreille Co., WA	Leroy Cooper	Leroy Cooper	2004	12
176 1/8	183 2/8	44 3/8	36	32 3/8	14 1/8	14	6 4/8	6 7/8	13	16	Beaverhead Co., MT	Robert C. Griffin	Robert C. Griffin	2005	13
175 5/8	182 1/8	55 1/8	37 4/8	38	10 6/8	12 5/8	6 4/8	6 5/8	6	8	Clearwater Co., ID	Alvin G. Cary	Alvin G. Cary	2005	14
175 2/8	177 5/8	46	32 6/8	33 4/8	12 6/8	12 2/8	6 5/8	6 6/8	14	13	Bingham Co., ID	Jay L. Merritt	Jay L. Merritt	1997	15
174 3/8	178 3/8	49 5/8	36 6/8	36 2/8	13 4/8	12 1/8	7 1/8	7	9	7	Larimer Co., CO	Thomas P. Grainger	Thomas P. Grainger	2006	16
174	176 4/8	44 4/8	34	35	12 4/8	12	6 6/8	7	13	12	Teton Co., WY	Louie M. Anderson	Louie M. Anderson	2004	17
174	180 1/8	50	36 7/8	38 5/8	11 3/8	11	6 5/8	6 5/8	10	12	Stevens Co., WA	Ed Nordby	Ed Nordby	2004	17
173 5/8	176	46 1/8	32 2/8	34 2/8	12 1/8	11 7/8	6 3/8	6 4/8	12	12	Idaho Co., ID	Susan M. Roach	Vernon F. Roach	2004	19
172 7/8	179 4/8	46 7/8	37 4/8	35 7/8	12 2/8	14 6/8	6 4/8	6 1/8	9	10	Beaverhead Co., MT	Darrel S. Johnson	Darrel S. Johnson	2004	20
172 2/8	180 4/8	43 4/8	37	35 6/8	11 3/8	13 1/8	6 6/8	7	10	12	Summit Co., UT	Bruce D. Chinberg	Bruce D. Chinberg	2005	21
171 3/8	175 6/8	49 1/8	33 2/8	37 3/8	11 2/8	14 2/8	6 3/8	6 3/8	11	15	Idaho Co., ID	Ronald L. Miller	Cabela's, Inc.	1987	22
170 1/8	173 4/8	53 1/8	36 2/8	34 5/8	12 4/8	12 2/8	6 5/8	6 5/8	9	9	Glacier Co., MT	Larry L. Kieft	Larry L. Kieft	2006	23
169 7/8	174	48 5/8	37	34 5/8	9 4/8	8 7/8	7	7 1/8	8	9	Utah Co., UT	Brent L. Skidmore	Brent L. Skidmore	2006	24
169 6/8	171 3/8	49 4/8	32 2/8	32	12 1/8	9 6/8	7	7	11	10	Teton Co., WY	John G. Hill	John G. Hill	2003	25
168 4/8	174 6/8	44 2/8	36 1/8	32 4/8	12 2/8	11 7/8	6 3/8	6 2/8	10	11	Stevens Co., WA	Jeff McKeen	Jeff McKeen	2004	26
168 4/8	169 3/8	49 2/8	33 1/8	33 1/8	11 3/8	14 6/8	6 4/8	6 3/8	11	9	Ravalli Co., MT	Chester W. Southwell	Chester W. Southwell	2004	26
168 2/8	172 1/8	50 2/8	36 4/8	37 4/8	9 4/8	12 2/8	6 1/8	6 1/8	9	9	Spokane Co., WA	David W. Bridges	David W. Bridges	2003	28
168	172 5/8	55 2/8	30 1/8	31 2/8	9 3/8	8 4/8	7	7 7/8	7	8	Albany Co., WY	Torrey S. Powers	Torrey S. Powers	2004	29
167 7/8	171 6/8	47 7/8	36 7/8	37 4/8	9 7/8	11 7/8	6 7/8	6 7/8	10	11	Beaverhead Co., MT	Mark Krpan	Mark Krpan	2004	30
167 4/8	171 7/8	47 4/8	34 6/8	32 5/8	10	12 2/8	6 3/8	6 3/8	8	11	Missoula Co., MT	Tony Hage	Tony Hage	2004	31

166 4/8	170 3/8	48	35 1/8	34 6/8	12 5/8	10 1/8	6 3/8	6 3/8	8	9	Jason D. Keim	Pend Oreille Co., WA	Jason D. Keim	2005	32
166 1/8	168 5/8	42 5/8	33 5/8	34 1/8	11 5/8	10 7/8	6 2/8	6 4/8	12	11	Rita M. Schall	Madison Co., ID	Rita M. Schall	2004	33
165 4/8	166 4/8	47 6/8	31 4/8	31 6/8	10 4/8	11 2/8	6 7/8	6 7/8	10	10	Glen A. Anderson	Teton Co., WY	Glen A. Anderson	2004	34
165	170 6/8	42 6/8	33	36 4/8	12	11 6/8	6 7/8	6 7/8	10	10	Daniel R. Rentz	Sublette Co., WY	Daniel R. Rentz	2004	35
164 6/8	168	44	33 2/8	33	10 3/8	11 2/8	7	7	10	12	Daniel J. Pearson	Madison Co., ID	Daniel J. Pearson	2006	36
164	169 4/8	57	32 5/8	30 1/8	10	10 6/8	6 5/8	6 3/8	7	9	Boyd R. Olson	Shoshone Co., ID	Boyd R. Olson	2004	37
162 6/8	167 5/8	43 6/8	32 1/8	35 4/8	10 5/8	12	5 6/8	5 7/8	11	11	C. Duane Kikendall	Bonner Co., ID	C. Duane Kikendall	2005	38
162 4/8	167	40 6/8	35 6/8	33 3/8	12	12	6 5/8	6 4/8	9	11	Laird S. Ayers	Lincoln Co., MT	Laird S. Ayers	2004	39
162 2/8	168 6/8	51 4/8	29 4/8	31 1/8	13	11 3/8	6 6/8	6 4/8	8	11	Steve Darst	Shoshone Co., ID	Steve Darst	2005	40
162 2/8	166 6/8	51 2/8	32 1/8	29 5/8	9 1/8	10 7/8	6 6/8	7	10	10	Shawn D. Christenson	Carbon Co., WY	Shawn D. Christenson	2006	40
162	168 5/8	53 4/8	27 4/8	32	11 5/8	11 4/8	6 2/8	6 2/8	9	11	Jim Shockey	Weber Co., UT	Jim Shockey	1999	42
161 7/8	167 4/8	46 3/8	32 1/8	29 4/8	12 7/8	12	6 2/8	6 3/8	10	12	Kolton Brewer	Summit Co., UT	Kolton Brewer	2006	43
161 5/8	171	47 1/8	31 1/8	33 7/8	11 4/8	12 7/8	6 5/8	6 7/8	8	13	Dwight K. Neilson	Summit Co., UT	Dwight K. Neilson	2005	44
161 4/8	166 1/8	49 4/8	33 5/8	34 5/8	8 5/8	10 2/8	6 2/8	6 2/8	8	8	Derek Wiench	Clearwater Co., ID	Derek Wiench	2003	45
161 4/8	164 1/8	47 4/8	30 7/8	32	10 6/8	10 4/8	5 5/8	5 7/8	11	10	Jay A. Morine	Flathead Co., MT	Jay A. Morine	2006	45
161 3/8	169 6/8	40 3/8	33 2/8	36 1/8	11 2/8	12 5/8	6 1/8	6	10	14	Jon P. Miller	Morgan Co., UT	Jon P. Miller	2004	47
161	164 1/8	43 4/8	31 6/8	31 1/8	12 3/8	11	6 5/8	6 5/8	10	11	B. Jay Perry	Lincoln Co., MT	B. Jay Perry	2006	48
160 7/8	165 1/8	45 1/8	32 4/8	34 1/8	9 2/8	9 6/8	6 2/8	6 1/8	9	12	Verle L. Barrow	Cache Co., UT	Verle L. Barrow	2003	49
160	163 6/8	44 4/8	31 2/8	30	12 2/8	11	7	6 6/8	10	11	Doug C. Weinrich	Mineral Co., CO	Doug C. Weinrich	2004	50
159 6/8	164 7/8	44	32 2/8	34	10 4/8	8 1/8	6 4/8	6 4/8	11	12	Dell R. Hogy	Grand Co., CO	Dell R. Hogy	2003	51
159 6/8	164 6/8	53	29 6/8	32 3/8	10 2/8	10 1/8	6 4/8	5 4/8	10	8	Kevin Kennedy	Pend Oreille Co., WA	Kevin Kennedy	2005	51

SHIRAS MOOSE
FINAL SCORE: 177
HUNTER: John D. Borrego

SHIRAS MOOSE
FINAL SCORE: 157
HUNTER: Mark L. Dunham

SHIRAS MOOSE
FINAL SCORE: 149-4/8
HUNTER: Elane M. Burkhalter

SHIRAS MOOSE
FINAL SCORE: 170-1/8
HUNTER: Larry L. Kieft

SHIRAS MOOSE

Alces alces shirasi

Final Score	Gross Score	Greatest Spread	Length of Palm		Width of Palm		Circumference of Beam at Smallest Place		Number of Normal Points		Locality	Hunter	Owner	Date Killed	Rank
			R.	L.	R.	L.	R.	L.	R.	L.					
159 5/8	163 5/8	48 7/8	30 1/8	31 4/8	11 1/8	10 4/8	5 5/8	5 6/8	9	11	Weber Co., UT	Michael H. Rose	Michael H. Rose	2006	53
159 4/8	163	46 6/8	30	32	10 3/8	11 6/8	6 1/8	6	10	10	Sweetwater Co., WY	John E. Draycott	John E. Draycott	2000	54
159 2/8	160 1/8	45 6/8	30 2/8	30 4/8	10 6/8	10 2/8	6 2/8	6 3/8	10	10	Boundary Co., ID	J. Scott Way	J. Scott Way	2003	55
158 7/8	167 6/8	47 1/8	38 2/8	32 5/8	9 2/8	10 3/8	7	7 1/8	7	9	Larimer Co., CO	Scott P. Wilson	Scott P. Wilson	2006	56
158 5/8	163 3/8	46 5/8	29 4/8	27	11 7/8	11 5/8	6 3/8	6 3/8	13	11	Weber Co., UT	Jeff E. Bartholomew	Jeff E. Bartholomew	2005	57
157 4/8	158 2/8	39 2/8	31 2/8	30 5/8	11 4/8	11 4/8	6	6 1/8	11	11	Lincoln Co., WY	George Deavor	George Deavor	1988	58
157 4/8	161 5/8	46 2/8	31 5/8	30 4/8	9 3/8	12 3/8	5 6/8	5 6/8	10	10	Cache Co., UT	Deon L. Johnson	Deon L. Johnson	2004	58
157 3/8	158 4/8	36 3/8	32 1/8	31 2/8	10 5/8	10 7/8	6 5/8	6 5/8	12	12	Summit Co., UT	David J. Maynarich	David J. Maynarich	2004	60
157 2/8	165	50	35 1/8	34	8 3/8	9	6 2/8	6 2/8	5	11	Uinta Co., WY	Donald P. Chase	Donald P. Chase	2005	61
157 1/8	160 4/8	45 7/8	29 5/8	30 7/8	10	10 3/8	6	6 6/8	10	11	Boundary Co., ID	Richard M. Penn	Richard M. Penn	2005	62
157	159 2/8	47 6/8	27 5/8	27 6/8	12 5/8	10 5/8	6 3/8	6 4/8	10	10	Summit Co., UT	Mike T. Schneider	Mike T. Schneider	2004	63
157	166 5/8	44 6/8	32 3/8	30 3/8	12 6/8	10 2/8	6 5/8	6 4/8	10	11	Teton Co., WY	Steven P. Boero	Steven P. Boero	2005	63
157	163 7/8	45	36	30 2/8	11 5/8	11 4/8	6 2/8	6 2/8	8	9	Idaho Co., ID	Tammy L. Frost	Tammy L. Frost	2005	63
157	160 6/8	47	30 5/8	27 3/8	10	10 1/8	6 5/8	7	11	11	Weber Co., UT	Mark L. Dunham	Mark L. Dunham	2006	63
156 6/8	158 2/8	38 6/8	32 5/8	31 6/8	9 4/8	9	7 2/8	7 3/8	11	11	Big Horn Co., WY	Jeff A. Schweighart	Jeff A. Schweighart	2004	67
156 2/8	162	49 2/8	28 2/8	31 1/8	9 2/8	11 1/8	6	6	10	11	Shoshone Co., ID	Larry D. Frisbie	Larry D. Frisbie	2004	68
156 2/8	158 7/8	42 6/8	31	32 6/8	10	9 3/8	6 5/8	6 3/8	10	10	Stevens Co., WA	Tod Xiongxtoyed	Tod Xiongxtoyed	2004	68
155 7/8	160 2/8	46 5/8	32	28 1/8	10 2/8	10 5/8	6 3/8	6 2/8	10	10	Jackson Co., CO	Charles R. Rupp	Charles R. Rupp	1998	70
155 6/8	161 5/8	44 4/8	30 1/8	28 2/8	12 7/8	13 5/8	6 4/8	6 6/8	8	11	Park Co., WY	Marty D. Moeding	Marty D. Moeding	2004	71
155 6/8	159 6/8	43 2/8	28 2/8	30 6/8	12 1/8	11 5/8	6 3/8	6 3/8	10	11	Rich Co., UT	Marty Halpern	Marty Halpern	2005	71
155 5/8	159 2/8	47 1/8	31 2/8	29 4/8	9 1/8	9 5/8	7	6 5/8	9	10	Jackson Co., CO	Kirk S. Anderson	Kirk S. Anderson	2004	73
155 2/8	159 6/8	52 4/8	30 5/8	28	10	9 1/8	6 2/8	6 2/8	9	8	Park Co., MT	Stephen A. Sommerfeld	Stephen A. Sommerfeld	2001	74
155	161 4/8	50	28	31 5/8	11 5/8	8 6/8	6 6/8	6 6/8	9	9	Salt Lake Co., UT	Gary T. Albert	Gary T. Albert	2004	75
155	166 7/8	46 6/8	31	39 6/8	9 4/8	11 3/8	6 5/8	6 7/8	7	8	Pend Oreille Co., WA	Steve L. Smith	Steve L. Smith	2004	75
154 6/8	159 5/8	50	29 3/8	32	8 4/8	9 6/8	5 4/8	5 4/8	9	10	Jefferson Co., MT	Al Martini	Al Martini	2004	77
154 5/8	158 5/8	48 1/8	29 7/8	30	9 1/8	10	6 2/8	6 2/8	11	8	Pend Oreille Co., WA	Bernie L. Nelson	Bernie L. Nelson	2005	78
154	156 3/8	55	30 4/8	29 3/8	6 4/8	7 6/8	6 5/8	6 5/8	7	7	Carbon Co., WY	Rex A. Morgan	Rex A. Morgan	2006	79
153 2/8	158	45 6/8	29 3/8	31 7/8	9 2/8	10 1/8	6 1/8	6 1/8	9	10	Uinta Co., WY	Glen O. Hallows	Glen O. Hallows	2005	80
152 4/8	154 5/8	39 6/8	31 3/8	31 5/8	10 3/8	9 4/8	6 4/8	6 4/8	9	10	Missoula Co., MT	Bridger D. Stratford	Bridger D. Stratford	2005	81
152 2/8	155 7/8	40 6/8	33	32	10 5/8	9	6 6/8	6 6/8	9	8	Teton Co., WY	Lloyd L. Wilson III	Lloyd L. Wilson III	2003	82
151 3/8	153 4/8	45 7/8	31 6/8	31 7/8	8 2/8	7 3/8	6 6/8	6 5/8	7	8	Sheridan Co., WY	Troy Carnes	Troy Carnes	2003	83
151 2/8	152 6/8	45 2/8	27 6/8	27 4/8	9 4/8	10 4/8	6 2/8	6	10	10	Teton Co., WY	Jake L. Phillips	Jake L. Phillips	2003	84

Final Score											Locality	Owner	Hunter	Date	No.
149 4/8*	153 7/8	43 4/8	28 2/8	27 4/8	9 5/8	12 1/8	6	5 7/8	11	10	Flathead Co., MT	James Matthews	James Matthews	2003	85
149 4/8	154 4/8	42 6/8	32 3/8	30 7/8	10	10 4/8	6 4/8	6 4/8	6	9	Carbon Co., WY	Elane M. Burkhalter	Elane M. Burkhalter	2004	85
149 2/8	156 3/8	40 6/8	37 1/8	34 2/8	12 4/8	9 4/8	5 6/8	5 4/8	5	6	Beaverhead Co., MT	Blake Nelson	Blake Nelson	2004	87
148 4/8	158	49 6/8	32 2/8	26 6/8	9 1/8	10	6 5/8	6 4/8	10	7	Lincoln Co., MT	Robert Hanneman	Robert Hanneman	2004	88
148	154 6/8	38 2/8	28	30 4/8	12 6/8	10 4/8	6 3/8	6 3/8	10	12	Park Co., WY	Dan S. Webber	Dan S. Webber	2006	89
147 7/8	154 6/8	42 7/8	31 1/8	29 6/8	11 3/8	7 7/8	6 7/8	6 7/8	10	8	Sublette Co., WY	George R. Skaggs	George R. Skaggs	2005	90
147 6/8	151 5/8	47	29 5/8	30 2/8	8 6/8	9 6/8	5	5 2/8	7	9	Teton Co., WY	Larry S. Hicks	Larry S. Hicks	1995	91
147 3/8	158 5/8	44 1/8	34 4/8	28 7/8	9	12 3/8	5 6/8	6	10	8	Jackson Co., CO	Terrane A. Whitecotton	Terrane A. Whitecotton	2005	92
147 2/8	148 5/8	44	26 2/8	27 1/8	10	10 1/8	5 6/8	5 3/8	10	10	Bannock Co., ID	Jerry McIntosh	Jerry McIntosh	2004	93
146 6/8	155 6/8	49 2/8	34 4/8	30 4/8	6 4/8	7 1/8	6 5/8	6 2/8	8	6	Pend Oreille Co., WA	Daren A. Bateman	Daren A. Bateman	2004	94
146 4/8	148 4/8	40 4/8	26 6/8	26 4/8	11 1/8	9 4/8	6 1/8	6	11	11	Sublette Co., WY	Kurt W. Krech	Kurt W. Krech	2005	95
146	149	44 2/8	31 4/8	30 4/8	8 4/8	6 6/8	5 7/8	5 5/8	8	8	Teton Co., WY	Brent Z. Wilkes	Brent Z. Wilkes	2004	96
145 1/8	148 5/8	53 1/8	25 7/8	24 4/8	9 2/8	8 1/8	5 3/8	5 3/8	9	9	Sublette Co., WY	Leon S. Phillips	Leon S. Phillips	2005	97
144 7/8	150	39 5/8	29 3/8	27 4/8	9 3/8	10 7/8	6 6/8	7 4/8	10	9	Sheridan Co., WY	Clay Beard	Clay Beard	2005	98
144 5/8	147 5/8	48 1/8	24 1/8	22 3/8	10 7/8	11 1/8	7	7	9	9	Hinsdale Co., CO	Edward R. Smith	Edward R. Smith	2005	99
144 2/8	147	37	29 2/8	29 2/8	11	11	6 2/8	6 3/8	9	9	Sublette Co., WY	Joseph A. DiPasqua	Joseph A. DiPasqua	2005	100
143 4/8	147 5/8	35 2/8	33	31	8	8	6 2/8	6 2/8	11	9	Lincoln Co., WY	Margaret Deavor	Margaret Deavor	1980	101
143 4/8	144 5/8	45 2/8	31	27 2/8	9	9	6	5 7/8	8	9	Summit Co., CO	William J. McEwen	William J. McEwen	2006	101
143 1/8	147 7/8	43 3/8	26 2/8	31 4/8	6 7/8	6 7/8	5 7/8	6 1/8	8	8	Pend Oreille Co., WA	Blane Crawford	Blane Crawford	2003	103
143 1/8	146 6/8	46 5/8	31 1/8	29	7 4/8	7 3/8	5 7/8	5 7/8	8	7	Bonner Co., ID	Daniel W. Taylor	Daniel W. Taylor	2003	103
142 5/8	146 5/8	46 1/8	28 4/8	27 4/8	6 5/8	7	6 1/8	6 1/8	9	8	Spokane Co., WA	Richard L. Lapinski, Sr	Richard L. Lapinski, Sr	2004	105
142 4/8	146 7/8	40 4/8	28 7/8	28	9 6/8	10 1/8	6 3/8	6 2/8	7	10	Granite Co., MT	Vince Van Witbeck	Vince Van Witbeck	2005	106
142 2/8	149 3/8	34 2/8	33	30	10 5/8	9 4/8	7	7	9	8	Sheridan Co., WY	Scott E. Sullivan	Scott E. Sullivan	1990	107
142	144 1/8	47 2/8	26 2/8	28	7 1/8	7 2/8	6 2/8	6	8	8	Wasatch Co., UT	Dennis L. Howell	Dennis L. Howell	2004	108
141	144 1/8	41 2/8	29 3/8	30 2/8	8 7/8	7 5/8	5 7/8	5 7/8	7	8	Jackson Co., CO	Terrance S. Marcum	Terrance S. Marcum	2004	109
141	143 1/8	44	24 2/8	22 6/8	10 3/8	9 7/8	5 7/8	6	10	9	Weber Co., UT	Rick M. Winn	Rick M. Winn	2004	109
140 6/8	142 2/8	48	24 7/8	27 4/8	7 2/8	7 4/8	5 7/8	5 7/8	6	7	Pend Oreille Co., WA	Daniel J. Jonassen	Daniel J. Jonassen	2004	111
140 2/8	142	41	24 6/8	25 7/8	12 5/8	13 1/8	5 2/8	5 3/8	7	7	Bear Lake Co., ID	Jay Thompson	Jay Thompson	2002	112
140 2/8	141 7/8	40	27 1/8	28 4/8	9 3/8	9 3/8	5 5/8	5 5/8	8	8	Wasatch Co., UT	Keldon A. Paxman	Keldon A. Paxman	2003	112
140 2/8	146 1/8	39 6/8	26 4/8	27 4/8	9 4/8	11	6 2/8	6 2/8	8	8	Lincoln Co., MT	Michael F. Shepard	Michael F. Shepard	2004	112
140 2/8	142 7/8	42 2/8	24 7/8	26 4/8	10 5/8	10 7/8	5 4/8	5 6/8	9	11	Teton Co., WY	Jason M. Marsh	Jason M. Marsh	2006	112
140	147 5/8	45 2/8	29	26	9 2/8	10	5 7/8	5 7/8	6	8	Gallatin Co., MT	Lucas J. Steffenson	Picked Up	2004	116
199 6/8*	205	60	42 5/8	39	13 5/8	13 2/8	6 7/8	6 5/8	11	12	Glacier Co., MT	Polite H. Pepion	Polite H. Pepion	2003	
182 2/8*	187 3/8	56 2/8	38 1/8	36 4/8	11 2/8	12 6/8	7 2/8	7 2/8	10	8	Fremont Co., ID	Kevin D. Hall	Kevin D. Hall	2000	
181 1/8*	185 3/8	54 6/8	33 6/8	35 5/8	10 3/8	11 2/8	7 2/8	7 3/8	13	12	Glacier Co., MT	Kory McGavin	Kory McGavin	2005	

* Final score subject to revision by additional verifying measurements.

MOUNTAIN CARIBOU

Rangifer tarandus caribou

Minimum Score 360

World's Record 453

Mountain caribou includes trophies from Alberta, British Columbia, southern Yukon Territory, and the Mackenzie Mountains of Northwest Territories.

Final Score	Gross Score	Length of Main Beam R.	L.	Inside Spread	Circ. at Smallest Place Between Brow and Bez Points R.	L.	Length of Brow Points R.	L.	Width of Brow Points R.	L.	No. of Points R.	L.	Locality	Hunter	Owner	Date Killed	Rank
437 6/8	445 5/8	42 2/8	44 6/8	40 2/8	7 4/8	7 4/8	13 7/8	13 5/8	10 1/8	4 1/8	18	18	Tucho Lake, BC	William F. Nye	William F. Nye	2004	1
427 1/8	452 6/8	45 6/8	43 6/8	36 2/8	7 4/8	7 3/8	18 7/8	18 3/8	14 7/8	13 4/8	19	21	Russell Range, YT	John S. Bell	John S. Bell	2005	2
418 3/8	439 3/8	50 6/8	53 5/8	27 5/8	6 6/8	6 6/8	7 7/8	15 7/8	1/8	13 1/8	15	18	Mackenzie Mts., NT	William J. Smith	William J. Smith	2004	3
417 7/8	427 5/8	46 4/8	45 4/8	41 4/8	6 3/8	6 7/8	17 3/8	18	12 3/8	13 3/8	18	16	Mackenzie Mts., NT	F. Dave Zanetell, Jr.	F. Dave Zanetell, Jr.	2006	4
417 4/8	436 5/8	49 1/8	48 5/8	40	5 6/8	5 7/8	20 6/8	19 5/8	15 4/8	6 7/8	17	16	Mountain River, NT	Stephen Lamb	Stephen Lamb	2004	5
417 2/8	429 6/8	53 4/8	51 2/8	36 3/8	5 7/8	5 6/8	19 1/8	21 1/8	10 7/8	9	12	12	Aishihik Lake, YT	Michael V. Scott	Michael V. Scott	2004	6
411 4/8	422	46 4/8	45 4/8	37 1/8	5 6/8	5 7/8	19 2/8	19	12 5/8	4 4/8	16	14	Redstone River, NT	Frank L. Stukel	Frank L. Stukel	2003	7
409 3/8	428 6/8	46 3/8	47 2/8	38 2/8	5 7/8	6 2/8	19 7/8	16 1/8	16	9 5/8	23	14	Mackenzie Mts., NT	Joseph C. Arakas	Joseph C. Arakas	2002	8
409 2/8	418 4/8	45 5/8	45 1/8	27 1/8	5 4/8	5 4/8	16	16 3/8	13	12	22	25	Mackenzie Mts., NT	James L. Price	James L. Price	2006	9
408 5/8	426	45 5/8	45	33 2/8	7 2/8	7	9 2/8	16 6/8	1/8	10 4/8	12	12	Tootsee Lake, BC	Randall M. Schellenberg	Randall M. Schellenberg	2004	10
406 5/8	436 6/8	41 1/8	42 3/8	36 1/8	8 6/8	7 7/8	2	9 6/8	1/8	1/8	18	21	Tsenaglode Lake, BC	Justin R. Edwards	Justin R. Edwards	2004	11
406 5/8	411 3/8	48 2/8	47 6/8	41 5/8	7	7	16 1/8	13 1/8	11 6/8	2 4/8	22	21	Drury Lake, YT	Robert C. Lott, Jr.	Robert C. Lott, Jr.	2005	11
404 7/8	417 5/8	51 4/8	48	45 7/8	5 5/8	5 5/8	5/8	19 4/8	1/8	16 6/8	16	20	Fire Lake, YT	Douglas A. Bleyenburg	Douglas A. Bleyenburg	2005	13
404 3/8	415 2/8	44 6/8	43 1/8	39 1/8	7 2/8	7 4/8	3 2/8	16	1/8	13 1/8	18	21	Mackenzie Mts., NT	Rick W. Duff	Rick W. Duff	2005	14
403 5/8	413 4/8	49 1/8	49 6/8	40 6/8	7 2/8	7	14	4 3/8	8 3/8	1/8	17	17	Klappan River, BC	G.A. Lyon	Richard J. Christoforo	1921	15
402 2/8	417 3/8	42 2/8	39 4/8	31	6 2/8	6 1/8	15	16 7/8	11	12 5/8	27	26	Mackenzie Mts., NT	Robert E. Vlach, Jr.	Robert E. Vlach, Jr.	2006	16
401 3/8	416 3/8	51 4/8	52 1/8	40 7/8	6 1/8	6 3/8	18 6/8	17 2/8	2	12 6/8	10	19	Aishihik Lake, YT	Jennifer Mervyn	Jennifer Mervyn	2002	17
401 2/8	412 6/8	46 1/8	47 7/8	37 6/8	6 7/8	7	23 4/8	18	18 1/8	1/8	22	12	Josephine Creek, BC	Timothy J. Koll	Timothy J. Koll	2004	18
400 2/8	417 3/8	50 2/8	46 2/8	35 6/8	6	6 4/8	18	15 6/8	7	11 4/8	14	14	Gana River, NT	Jason R. Pierson	Jason R. Pierson	2006	19
399 4/8	412 3/8	46 7/8	48 1/8	40 7/8	7 6/8	7 6/8	15 2/8	16 3/8	12 2/8	12 2/8	14	18	Gana River, NT	John C. Marsh	John C. Marsh	2006	20
396 3/8	405 4/8	49 4/8	49 4/8	36	6 7/8	6 5/8	17 4/8	20 2/8	3 1/8	11 2/8	12	17	Little Rancheria River, BC	Kent D. Petovello	Kent D. Petovello	2006	21
393 6/8	404 2/8	52	52 6/8	32 5/8	6	6 1/8	9 4/8	20 7/8	1/8	16 5/8	12	19	Mackenzie Mts., NT	Andrew Pedroncelli	Andrew Pedroncelli	2005	22
392 5/8	402 4/8	43	46	39 3/8	6 3/8	6 4/8	5 7/8	21 1/8	1/8	18 5/8	12	24	Dick Lake, BC	Mike Bingen	Mike Bingen	2004	23
391 5/8	400	46 7/8	47 6/8	47 6/8	5 2/8	5 3/8	17	17	10 7/8		14	16	Ash Lake, BC	Andy Miller	Andy Miller	2005	24
390 1/8	407 6/8	48 6/8	54 7/8	31 1/8	7 3/8	7 4/8	21 5/8	23	11 6/8	3 7/8	14	16	Ruby Range, YT	Mary C. Scott	Mary C. Scott	2005	25
389 1/8	402	54 6/8	54 4/8	40 4/8	8	7 2/8	3 1/8	19 1/8	1/8	13	10	15	Aishihik Lake, YT	Larry I. Fliehs	Larry I. Fliehs	2006	26
388 1/8	400 2/8	49 7/8	50 3/8	32 1/8	5 6/8	5 6/8	18	16 5/8	11	10 5/8	21	20	Mackenzie Mts., NT	Raymond H. Osgood	Raymond H. Osgood	2006	27
386 4/8	404	41	45 4/8	35 2/8	6 1/8	6 4/8	14	16 3/8	5 7/8	9 2/8	12	14	Pelly Mts., YT	Todd Bader	Todd Bader	2004	28
380 3/8	386 7/8	44 2/8	45 3/8	34 6/8	6	6 1/8	18 4/8	3 5/8	1/8	15 1/8	13	18	Mountain River, NT	George A. Pickel	George A. Pickel	2004	29

Score													Locality	Owner	Hunter	Date	Rank
379⁷/₈	394⁴/₈	39⁶/₈	40⁵/₈	36³/₈	9⁷/₈	6⁷/₈	12³/₈	14¹/₈	5	5⁶/₈	16	19	Anahim Lake, BC	Hunter C.E. Swift	Hunter C.E. Swift	2003	30
379¹/₈	395	42²/₈	43³/₈	29⁵/₈	8⁵/₈	8¹/₈	14¹/₈	13²/₈	3⁷/₈	8⁶/₈	23	19	Natla River, NT	Scott W. Wilkinson	Scott W. Wilkinson	2005	31
378⁷/₈	395⁷/₈	47⁵/₈	48	31	6²/₈	6²/₈	16⁶/₈	9⁴/₈	11⁴/₈	¹/₈	18	17	Stikine River, BC	David Hall	David Hall	2005	32
378¹/₈	391	47²/₈	48⁷/₈	44²/₈	6	5⁷/₈	15⁵/₈		11⁴/₈		15	13	McClure Lake, NT	Frederick P. Deverse	Frederick P. Deverse	2005	33
374¹/₈	388³/₈	45⁵/₈	46	32²/₈	6	5⁷/₈	19³/₈		13⁵/₈		7	13	Isaac Creek, YT	Terrance S. Marcum	Terrance S. Marcum	2004	34
373³/₈	382⁷/₈	43³/₈	46⁴/₈	36⁷/₈	5⁷/₈	6	8¹/₈	16⁶/₈	¹/₈	13³/₈	12	15	Klappan River, BC	G.A. Lyon	Richard J. Christoforo	1921	35
372⁷/₈	380²/₈	51³/₈	50¹/₈	32¹/₈	6³/₈	6²/₈	14⁵/₈	10²/₈	7¹/₈	¹/₈	15	14	McClure Lake, NT	Lee M. Wahlund	Lee M. Wahlund	2004	36
371⁷/₈	386⁶/₈	44²/₈	47²/₈	42³/₈	6²/₈	6²/₈	17¹/₈	3⁴/₈	11²/₈	¹/₈	14	14	Twitya River, NT	Derek Forsbloom	Mike Skrove	2006	37
369⁴/₈	386²/₈	46⁷/₈	45⁷/₈	45²/₈	7²/₈	6⁵/₈	2²/₈	15⁵/₈	¹/₈	10⁷/₈	16	15	Gana River, NT	Matthew H. Smith	Matthew H. Smith	2006	38
366⁶/₈	384⁷/₈	48³/₈	45⁷/₈	34⁷/₈	6³/₈	6¹/₈	17⁶/₈	16		10¹/₈	16	9	Spinel Lake, BC	Edwin A. Johnston	Edwin A. Johnston	2006	39
366¹/₈	373⁴/₈	44¹/₈	43³/₈	35⁶/₈	7⁴/₈	7	16⁶/₈	8⁶/₈	12⁴/₈	¹/₈	20	14	Gana River, NT	Jason M. Marsh	Jason M. Marsh	2006	40
365⁷/₈	392⁶/₈	50¹/₈	47⁶/₈	37⁶/₈	6⁷/₈	7	9⁵/₈	18²/₈	¹/₈	12⁷/₈	14	13	Dudidontu River, BC	David G. Grandbois	David G. Grandbois	2005	41
365	376¹/₈	43¹/₈	42	38²/₈	9²/₈	7⁷/₈	15²/₈	14¹/₈		8²/₈	17	17	Josephine Creek, BC	Gary E. Janssen	Gary E. Janssen	2004	42
365	373²/₈	47¹/₈	45²/₈	34⁴/₈	6¹/₈	6²/₈	14	15⁵/₈		7	14	13	Bug Lake, BC	Carl J. Wohlfert	Carl J. Wohlfert	2002	43
364¹/₈	386⁶/₈	37⁴/₈	38²/₈	34³/₈	7⁷/₈	7¹/₈	14⁴/₈	12²/₈		¹/₈	16	14	Mt. Dent, BC	Picked Up	Michelle A. Marchand	2004	44
362⁷/₈	373²/₈	41⁷/₈	31⁷/₈	42	5⁶/₈	5⁵/₈	3²/₈	19⁴/₈	¹/₈	16⁴/₈	20	25	Mackenzie Mts., NT	Carla Pierson	Carla Pierson	2006	45
362¹/₈	417⁷/₈	42	36⁴/₈	36⁴/₈	5⁷/₈	5⁸/₈	13⁴/₈	17⁶/₈	1³/₈	13¹/₈	17	22	Aishihik Lake, YT	Leonard R. Beecher	Leonard R. Beecher	2003	46
442¹/₈*	450¹/₈	52⁵/₈	52⁴/₈	44⁶/₈	5⁶/₈	5⁴/₈	23	21⁴/₈	15⁶/₈	2³/₈	19	17	Canyon Lake, YT	Valerie Drummond	Valerie Drummond	2003	
433¹/₈*	457⁷/₈	46⁷/₈	48⁷/₈	35⁵/₈	6³/₈	6⁴/₈	12⁷/₈	18⁴/₈	¹/₈	11⁴/₈	15	17	Anvil Range, YT	Robert Sorensen	Robert Sorensen	2005	
419¹/₈*	437⁶/₈	49³/₈	46²/₈	33¹/₈	6⁶/₈	6⁸/₈	23²/₈	23²/₈	4⁴/₈	17	15		Prospector Mt., YT	Steven K. Hennig	Steven K. Hennig	2006	

* Final score subject to revision by additional verifying measurements.

MOUNTAIN CARIBOU
FINAL SCORE: 400-2/8
HUNTER: Jason R. Pierson

MOUNTAIN CARIBOU
FINAL SCORE: 409-2/8
HUNTER: James L. Price

MOUNTAIN CARIBOU
FINAL SCORE: 388-1/8
HUNTER: Raymond H. Osgood

MOUNTAIN CARIBOU
FINAL SCORE: 365
HUNTER: Gary E. Janssen

WOODLAND CARIBOU

Rangifer tarandus caribou

World's Record 419 5/8

Minimum Score 265

Woodland caribou includes trophies from Nova Scotia, New Brunswick, and Newfoundland.

Final Score	Gross Score	Length of Main Beam R	L	Inside Spread	Circumference at Smallest Place Between Brow and Bez Points R	L	Length of Brow Points R	L	Width of Brow Points R	L	Number of Points R	L	Locality	Hunter	Owner	Date Killed	Rank
384 2/8	400	39 2/8	39 1/8	39 3/8	5 6/8	6 5/8	14 1/8	18 4/8	10 2/8	17 3/8	16	19	Sam's Pond, NL	James H. Holt	James H. Holt	2005	1
353 2/8	361 1/8	41 5/8	40 7/8	40 1/8	6	5 5/8	15 1/8	16 3/8	11 5/8	14 4/8	15	17	Northern Pen., NL	Dale L. Hardy	Dale L. Hardy	2000	2
340 5/8	354 5/8	49 3/8	49 4/8	37 1/8	5 4/8	5 4/8	15 5/8	17 7/8	14 7/8	18 7/8	10	14	Sam's Pond, NL	Scott A. Trujillo	Scott A. Trujillo	2006	3
335 5/8	349 3/8	37 5/8	40 5/8	33 6/8	5 2/8	5 5/8	17 3/8	9 5/8	12 2/8	1/8	18	12	Dolland Pond, NL	Larry A. Welchlen	Larry A. Welchlen	2005	4
325 2/8	341 2/8	43 6/8	43 5/8	33 1/8	5 6/8	5 6/8	15 5/8	15 7/8	11 2/8	11 1/8	13	13	Deer Lake, NL	Stephen J. Della Bella	Stephen J. Della Bella	2005	5
323 4/8	329 3/8	41 6/8	41 2/8	27 5/8	5 1/8	5 1/8	16 1/8	18	1/8	16 3/8	10	15	Daniels Harbour, NL	Daniel R.J. DeHaan	Daniel R.J. DeHaan	2001	6
323 2/8	330	44 2/8	46	37 1/8	5 5/8	5 5/8	2	18 5/8	1/8	16 3/8	15	22	Middle Ridge Pond, NL	Lee M. Stabe	Lee M. Stabe	2005	7
321 3/8	333 5/8	33 3/8	32 7/8	27 6/8	5 3/8	5	14 6/8	17 3/8	13	12 6/8	20	16	Long Pond, NL	Jeffrey Stine	Jeffrey Stine	2003	8
320 4/8	327 3/8	38 3/8	40 5/8	28 4/8	5 1/8	5	17	17 4/8	14 6/8	5 4/8	18	14	Portland Creek, NL	Gale H. Mills	Gale H. Mills	2004	9
315 5/8	323 6/8	37 7/8	38 3/8	34	5 3/8	5 3/8	8 2/8	18 5/8	1 6/8	16	14	18	Middle Ridge Pond, NL	Jay R. Wolfenden	Jay R. Wolfenden	2004	10
314 6/8	325 7/8	37 6/8	36 4/8	31 1/8	5 3/8	5 2/8	16	16 1/8	13	14 2/8	15	16	Blue Pond, NL	Ralph E. Borton	Ralph E. Borton	2004	11
309 7/8	324 3/8	37 2/8	35 3/8	33 7/8	5 1/8	5 1/8	15 6/8	15 4/8	12 4/8	13 2/8	16	16	Taylor Brook, NL	David Bosscher	David Bosscher	2001	12
308 7/8	322 1/8	43 6/8	42 7/8	34 3/8	5 2/8	5 5/8	10 5/8	14 2/8	1/8	9	9	13	Mount Peyton, NL	Jim Shockey	Jim Shockey	1999	13
307	313 5/8	45 5/8	46	31 3/8	5 5/8	5 6/8	13 6/8	9 4/8	10	1/8	12	13	Romaine River, NL	Glenn E. Thompson	Glenn E. Thompson	1993	14
304 7/8	310	35	36 4/8	33 4/8	5 1/8	5 5/8	14 1/8	14 2/8	8 5/8	10 3/8	12	15	Portland Creek, NL	Susan A. Smith	Susan A. Smith	2005	15
301 7/8	316 4/8	38 7/8	39 3/8	37 1/8	5	4 7/8	14	13 3/8	9	1/8	15	12	Middle Pond, NL	Raymond L. Meyers	Raymond L. Meyers	1994	16
300 6/8	314	42 6/8	45 2/8	40 1/8	4 5/8	5	17 1/8	16 1/8	5 4/8	9 3/8	9	10	Great Gull Lake, NL	Myron D. Maker	Myron D. Maker	2003	17
298 4/8	309 3/8	46	44 4/8	29 3/8	5 7/8	6	16 1/8	16 2/8	1/8	13 1/8	12	18	Gander Lake, NL	Robert M. Bingman	Robert M. Bingman	2005	18
297 5/8	302 6/8	36 6/8	36 4/8	29 6/8	4 6/8	5	13 3/8	14 3/8	9	10 7/8	14	14	Grand Lake, NL	Michael L. Ellingson	Michael L. Ellingson	2003	19
296 3/8	306 4/8	34 5/8	32 6/8	27 1/8	5 7/8	5 7/8	9 6/8	17 1/8	5	16 7/8	14	15	Sam's Pond, NL	James E. Herren	James E. Herren	2004	20
296 1/8	310 4/8	37	37	30 4/8	5	5 7/8	14 1/8	13 4/8	9 4/8	12 4/8	17	16	Deer Lake, NL	Joseph L. LaNou	Joseph L. LaNou	2005	21
293 1/8	305 4/8	38	39 2/8	31 2/8	5 1/8	5 1/8	15 4/8	13 2/8	10 3/8	4 4/8	18	10	Meelpaeg Lake, NL	Mark A. Gons	Mark A. Gons	2004	22
292	300 5/8	37	37 4/8	26	5	5 4/8	17 1/8	16 5/8	13 3/8	14 5/8	20	18	Parson's Pond, NL	Richard J. Caro	Richard J. Caro	2005	23
291 7/8	304 6/8	35 7/8	36 6/8	29 5/8	4 5/8	4 7/8	4	15 5/8	1/8	11 2/8	11	19	Tom Rose's Pond, NL	A.C. Smid	A.C. Smid	2005	24
291	300 7/8	35 2/8	35 3/8	20 2/8	5 2/8	5 7/8	15	15 5/8	10 2/8	9 3/8	14	12	Ten Mile Lake, NL	Chris L. Gillespie	Chris L. Gillespie	2004	25
290 7/8	304 3/8	37 6/8	39 3/8	25	5 1/8	5 5/8	5 2/8	12 6/8	1	12 1/8	15	22	Conne River, NL	Joel E. Noel	Joel E. Noel	2005	26
289 6/8	304 2/8	35 4/8	34 2/8	22 7/8	5 1/8	5 5/8	13 7/8	14 5/8	9 7/8	12 4/8	16	16	Deer Lake, NL	Steven J. Manty	Steven J. Manty	2005	27
288 4/8	296 5/8	35 6/8	35 5/8	22 7/8	4 5/8	4 6/8	17 7/8	16 6/8	6 1/8	14 3/8	14	15	Dolland Pond, NL	Larry A. Welchlen	Larry A. Welchlen	2005	28

287 4/8	306 4/8	37	39 5/8	29 1/8	5 1/8	5 4/8	15 3/8	11 4/8	14 1/8	1 3/8	13	11	Middle Ridge, NL	Kirk D. Petersen	Kirk D. Petersen	2004	29
284 1/8	294 1/8	33 4/8	36 3/8	23	5 5/8	5 6/8	18 6/8	16 2/8	15 4/8	1 7/8	15	10	Mount Peyton, NL	Daniel P. Hiatt	Daniel P. Hiatt	2004	30
273 5/8	286	39 7/8	38	31 7/8	5 2/8	5 2/8	2 1/8	13 5/8	1/8	10 7/8	11	12	Middle Ridge Pond, NL	John H. Gilliland	John H. Gilliland	2004	31
271 4/8	278 5/8	37 7/8	38	25 1/8	4 7/8	5 2/8	14	15 3/8	1/8	12 3/8	13	17	Northern Pen., NL	Richard W. Cherry	Richard W. Cherry	2003	32
270 1/8	293 7/8	43	44 2/8	26 6/8	6 3/8	5 4/8	13 7/8	9 5/8	10 4/8	1/8	17	11	Mount Peyton, NL	Keith M. Nowell	Keith M. Nowell	2000	33
266 3/8	270 5/8	35	35 2/8	30 6/8	5	5	13 6/8	4 1/8	11 5/8	1/8	14	11	Grey River, NL	James M. Makris	James M. Makris	2004	34

WOODLAND CARIBOU
FINAL SCORE: 290-7/8
HUNTER: Joel E. Noel

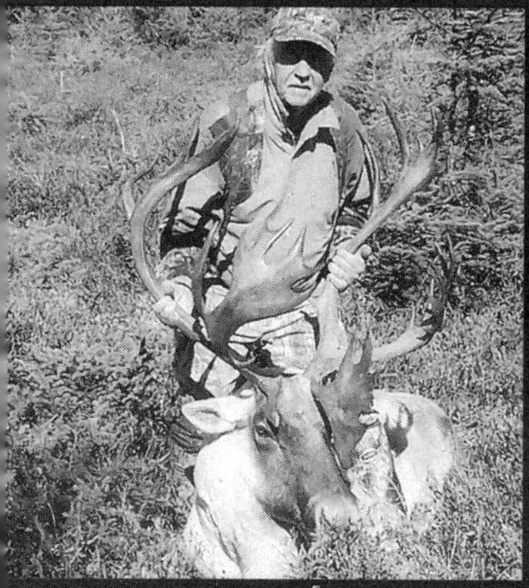

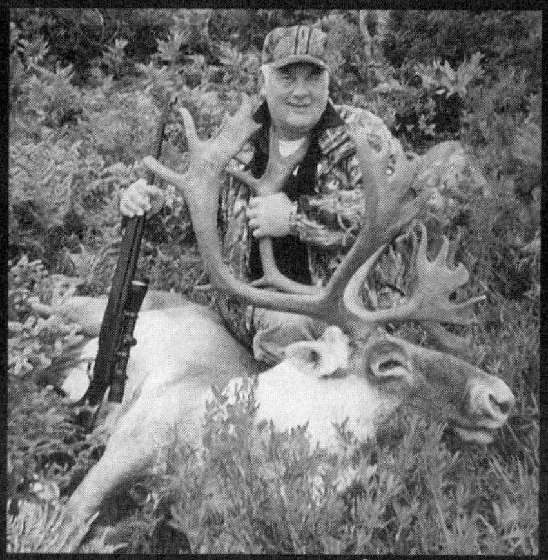

MOUNTAIN CARIBOU
FINAL SCORE: 289-6/8
HUNTER: Steven J. Manty

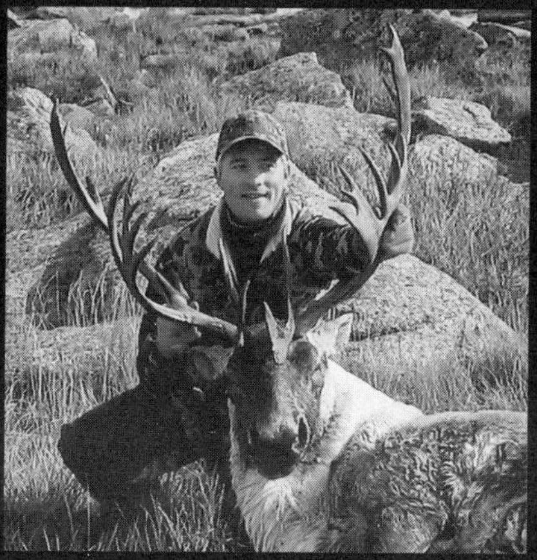

MOUNTAIN CARIBOU
FINAL SCORE: 297-5/8
HUNTER: Michael L. Ellingson

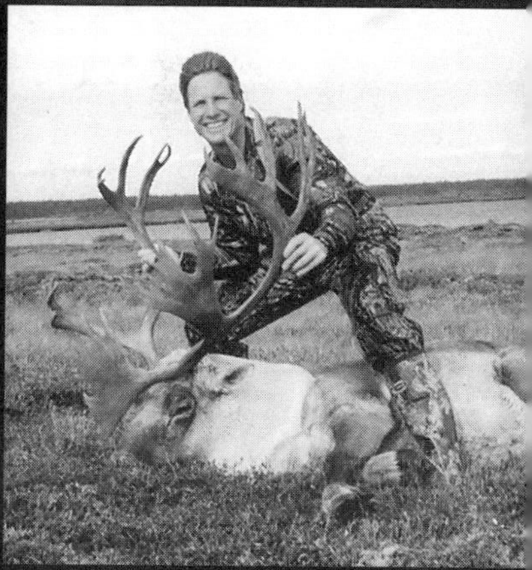

WOODLAND CARIBOU
FINAL SCORE: 291-7/8
HUNTER: A.C. Smid

BARREN GROUND CARIBOU

Rangifer tarandus granti

Minimum Score 375

World's Record 477

Barren ground caribou includes trophies from Alaska and northern Yukon Territory.

Final Score	Gross Score	Length of Main Beam R.	L.	Inside Spread	Circumference at Smallest Place Between Brow and Bez Points R.	L.	Length of Brow Points R.	L.	Width of Brow Points R.	L.	Number of Points R.	L.	Locality	Hunter	Owner	Date Killed	Rank
444 4/8	456 4/8	62 4/8	60 6/8	52 5/8	5 6/8	5 4/8	20 5/8	15 2/8	16 7/8	9 5/8	16	20	Alaska Pen., AK	Joseph H. Johnson	Cabela's, Inc.	1976	1
404	414	57	55 7/8	46 4/8	5 4/8	5 5/8	17 6/8	19 1/8	13 1/8	11 6/8	22	21	Unimak Island, AK	Anthony Cocozzo	Anthony Cocozzo	2002	2
401 6/8	413 2/8	50 2/8	49 1/8	39 4/8	5 5/8	5 5/8	19	18	5 6/8	13	16	16	Nelchina River, AK	Mark J. Bly	Mark J. Bly	2006	3
401	412 5/8	53 1/8	53 4/8	40 6/8	6 7/8	6 2/8	2 6/8	17 1/8	1/8	14 2/8	16	21	Ogilvie Mts., YT	Maurice Bower	Maurice Bower	2003	4
400	408	45	43 4/8	34 2/8	5 3/8	5 3/8	20 7/8	17	11 6/8	9 5/8	24	21	Adak Island, AK	Grant E. Carlson	Grant E. Carlson	2005	5
393 1/8	409 2/8	53	49 4/8	32 4/8	5 3/8	5 3/8	12 3/8	21 2/8	1/8	17 1/8	16	18	Mulchatna River, AK	William R. Bulawa	William R. Bulawa	1998	6
388	398 4/8	44 7/8	44 2/8	36 2/8	6	6	4 1/8	15 1/8	1/8	12 3/8	13	17	Bonnet Plume River, YT	Larry D. Hancock	Larry D. Hancock	2003	7
385 2/8	400 5/8	47 5/8	49 2/8	43 3/8	6	6	15	7 3/8	11 4/8	3	21	20	Adak Island, AK	Thomas M. Taylor	Thomas M. Taylor	2006	8
380 2/8	394 5/8	50 2/8	49 1/8	34 2/8	7	8 3/8	10 5/8	14 7/8	1/8	11 5/8	11	19	Kenai Mts., AK	John K. Frederikson	John K. Frederikson	2006	9
380	392 7/8	43	40 5/8	25 3/8	5 6/8	5 4/8	7 4/8	17	1/8	14 4/8	11	23	Adak Island, AK	Mark R. Wagner	Mark R. Wagner	2005	10
378 4/8	403 6/8	52 7/8	56 7/8	49 3/8	4 7/8	4 7/8	15 3/8	20 3/8	7 6/8	10 5/8	16	16	Cathedral Valley, AK	Thomas V. Arnim	Thomas V. Arnim	2003	11
378	394 7/8	51 4/8	49 4/8	41	6	6 3/8	1	17 2/8	1/8	11 5/8	15	23	Unimak Island, AK	Marvin R. Selke	Marvin R. Selke	2004	12
377 5/8	395 3/8	32 7/8	42 6/8	34 5/8	7 5/8	7 1/8	15 2/8	2 5/8	6 2/8	7/8	16	12	Adak Island, AK	Harry D. Nelson	Harry D. Nelson	2005	13
377 3/8	389	51 4/8	50 6/8	39 2/8	6 2/8	5 4/8	19 7/8	20 2/8	1/8	9 7/8	15	19	Mulchatna River, AK	Charles E. Hendrix	Charles E. Hendrix	1995	14
438 1/8*	447 7/8	53 7/8	53 7/8	49 1/8	5 7/8	5 7/8	18 1/8	19	8 5/8	7	17	18	Gillett Pass, AK	Ernest A. Dahman	Ernest A. Dahman	1965	
427 7/8*	450 5/8	47 6/8	51 4/8	41 1/8	7 1/8	7 3/8	18 1/8	4 2/8	8 4/8	1/8	25	16	Adak Island, AK	Brian P. Reynolds	Brian P. Reynolds	2003	
417 1/8*	431 6/8	46 2/8	41	38 6/8	6 1/8	6 1/8	20 3/8	20 4/8	14 6/8	15	17	18	Bonnet Plume Lake, YT	Paul W. DeMinck	Paul W. DeMinck	2005	
416 6/8*	433 7/8	49 1/8	49 4/8	33 1/8	4 7/8	5 7/8	19 7/8	20	15 4/8	5 3/8	17	13	Shagak Bay, AK	Aaron K. Dahlstrom	Aaron K. Dahlstrom	2003	
404 1/8*	413	56 4/8	57	51 6/8	5 7/8	5 6/8	19 2/8	6 4/8	12 2/8	1/8	23	14	Unimak Island, AK	Lee I. Branch	Lee I. Branch	2004	

* Final score subject to revision by additional verifying measurements.

BARREN GROUND CARIBOU
FINAL SCORE: 417-1/8*
HUNTER: Paul W. DeMinck

BARREN GROUND CARIBOU
FINAL SCORE: 380
HUNTER: Mark R. Wagner

BARREN GROUND CARIBOU
FINAL SCORE: 404
HUNTER: Anthony Cocozzo

CENTRAL CANADA BARREN GROUND CARIBOU

Minimum Score 345   *Rangifer tarandus groenlandicus*   World's Record 433 4/8

Central Canada barren ground caribou occur on Baffin Island and the mainland of Northwest Territories, with geographic boundaries of the Mackenzie River to the west; the north edge of the continent to the north (excluding any islands except Baffin Island); Hudson Bay to the east; and the southern boundary of Northwest Territories to the south. The boundary also includes the northwest corner of Manitoba north of the south limit of township 87 and west of the Little Churchill River, Churchill River, and Hudson Bay.

Final Score	Gross Score	Length of Main Beam R.	L.	Inside Spread	Circ. Smallest Place Between Brow and Bez Points R.	L.	Length of Brow Points R.	L.	Width of Brow Points R.	L.	Number of Points R.	L.	Locality	Hunter	Owner	Date Killed	Rank
406 2/8	415 4/8	55 2/8	54 4/8	38 5/8	6 2/8	6	15 5/8	16	8 5/8	14 1/8	15	15	Bekere Lake, NT	Robert F. Fairchild	Robert F. Fairchild	2005	1
392 2/8	410 4/8	45 3/8	44 7/8	27 6/8	6 4/8	5 6/8	18 6/8	17	14 2/8	11 4/8	20	17	Bekere Lake, NT	Robert F. Fairchild	Robert F. Fairchild	2005	2
382 3/8	399	52 3/8	53	41 6/8	5 2/8	4 7/8	5 7/8	18 6/8	3 3/8	15 1/8	12	15	Point Lake, NT	N. Guy Eastman	N. Guy Eastman	2002	3
379 4/8	388 2/8	50 5/8	50 3/8	28 3/8	7	7 3/8	16 7/8	15 6/8	9 6/8	11 4/8	21	19	Humpy Lake, NT	Matthew G. Jones	Matthew G. Jones	1999	4
376 1/8	386 7/8	48	51	34 2/8	5 4/8	5 4/8	17 1/8	16 6/8	4	11 6/8	19	18	Bekere Lake, NT	Edwin A. Johnston	Edwin A. Johnston	2003	5
376 1/8	383 7/8	48 2/8	48 4/8	34 1/8	4 6/8	4 5/8	16 2/8	13 4/8	13 5/8	3 5/8	24	17	Glover Lake, MB	Art Rempel	Art Rempel	2003	5
375 6/8	384	47	46 7/8	38	7 2/8	6 4/8	12 7/8	13 1/8	4 5/8	7 7/8	20	20	Artillery Lake, NT	Glenn A. Miller	Glenn A. Miller	2003	7
375 5/8	387	53 4/8	50 2/8	25 4/8	5 3/8	5 2/8	12 4/8	14 1/8	7 2/8	11 6/8	17	24	Rendez-vous Lake, NT	Robert Morgan	Robert Morgan	2005	8
373 1/8	379	47 1/8	46 7/8	25 2/8	5 2/8	5 2/8	17 5/8	21 2/8	5 6/8	15 2/8	15	14	Courageous Lake, NT	Allan N. McNay	Allan N. McNay	2004	9
370 4/8	378 4/8	52 7/8	52 7/8	35 4/8	4 5/8	4 5/8	15 4/8	14 3/8	10 3/8	3 4/8	16	14	Egenolf Lake, MB	Daniel J. Smith	Daniel J. Smith	2003	10
366 6/8	378 5/8	52 2/8	54	40 2/8	5 4/8	5 3/8	17 1/8	6	13 4/8	1/8	16	13	Bekere Lake, NT	Eric Nysse	Eric Nysse	2004	11
365 6/8	373 3/8	50 2/8	49 7/8	42 5/8	5	5	17 5/8	13 6/8	10 6/8	8	22	18	Lac de Gras, NT	Keith M. Nowell	Keith M. Nowell	2002	12
364 5/8	376 5/8	52 4/8	49 4/8	42 6/8	6 2/8	6 5/8	3 4/8	18 6/8	1/8	8 6/8	11	13	Courageous Lake, NT	Unknown	Robert H. Turturro	1954	13
364 4/8	383 6/8	52	55 5/8	33 5/8	5 5/8	6	7 5/8	23 1/8	1/8	16 4/8	12	18	Rendez-vous Lake, NT	Robert Morgan	Robert Morgan	2005	14
364 2/8	377 7/8	42	41	34 3/8	4 4/8	4 1/8	14 4/8	15 7/8	11 3/8	13 5/8	19	18	Nejanilini Lake, MB	Robert Andjelic	Robert Andjelic	2004	15
363 3/8	379 4/8	47 1/8	47 6/8	31 7/8	5 3/8	5 6/8	14 5/8	14	9 2/8	10 5/8	16	16	Bekere Lake, NT	Richard W. Gilbert	Richard W. Gilbert	2003	16
362 3/8	377 5/8	40 5/8	38 6/8	30 7/8	7 6/8	6 7/8	16	14	12 3/8	4 1/8	27	20	Granet Lake, NT	Jim Shockey	Jim Shockey	2001	17
361 6/8	369 5/8	52 4/8	51	33 6/8	5 2/8	5 2/8	18 7/8	11	14 4/8	1/8	17	13	Granet Lake, NT	Jim Shockey	Jim Shockey	2001	18
361 3/8	368	54 4/8	54	38 2/8	5 4/8	5 1/8	18 3/8	18	14 2/8	4	13	12	Humpy Lake, NT	Michael Richardson	Michael Richardson	2003	19
361 2/8	373	50 2/8	51 4/8	24 7/8	5 5/8	6	13 5/8	16 1/8	8 6/8	7 5/8	21	21	Nejanilini Lake, MB	Donald L. Pannell	Donald L. Pannell	2004	20
361 1/8	380 2/8	50 3/8	51 1/8	28 2/8	5 1/8	5 4/8	21 6/8	5 7/8	18 1/8	1/8	23	13	Courageous Lake, NT	Allan N. McNay	Allan N. McNay	2005	21
360 4/8	371 5/8	56 3/8	57 1/8	38	4 4/8	4 5/8	14 2/8	16 1/8	6	8 5/8	9	14	Noname Lake, MB	Edwin H. Starke, Jr.	Edwin H. Starke, Jr.	2003	22

359 5/8	368 5/8	48	48 3/8	28 7/8	5 5/8	6	18 6/8	16 1/8	6	11 3/8	11	12	Bekere Lake, NT	Richard W. Gilbert	2003	23
357 4/8	363 1/8	51 4/8	51 7/8	33 1/8	5 2/8	5 2/8	16 4/8	4 4/8	13 2/8	1/8	19	14	Egenolf Lake, MB	Daniel J. Smith	2003	24
357 1/8	369 4/8	52 7/8	53 1/8	37	4 5/8	4 4/8	19 4/8	5	16 2/8	1/8	19	12	Point Lake, NT	Blair C. Rumble	1999	25
350 5/8	362 3/8	49 2/8	47 2/8	28 2/8	5 2/8	5	15	16	12 4/8	12 5/8	13	16	Obstruction Rapids, NT	Gerald E. Rightmyer	2003	26
346 7/8	354 6/8	40 6/8	42	18 3/8	4 1/8	4 1/8	1 4/8	17	15 1/8	1/8	26	16	Humpy Lake, NT	Dan S. Muchow	2005	27
345 4/8	358 4/8	50	49 4/8	26 2/8	6 4/8	5 5/8	3	17 1/8	1/8	14	15	25	Rendez-vous Lake, NT	Martin R. Riedner	2002	28
398 7/8*	408 5/8	51 1/8	49 6/8	37 1/8	5 3/8	5 3/8	19 4/8	16 4/8	14 1/8	1/8	21	17	Bekere Lake, NT	Eric Nysse	2004	
379 5/8*	396 4/8	48 5/8	48 4/8	24 3/8	5 1/8	5 6/8	24 3/8	18 6/8	17 4/8	12 3/8	25	15	Courageous Lake, NT	James B. Tiessen	2004	

* Final score subject to revision by additional verifying measurements.

CENTRAL CANADA
BARREN GROUND CARIBOU
FINAL SCORE: 346-7/8
HUNTER: Dan S. Muchow

CENTRAL CANADA
BARREN GROUND CARIBOU
FINAL SCORE: 361-1/8
HUNTER: Allan N. McNay

QUEBEC-LABRADOR
CARIBOU
FINAL SCORE: 372-3/8
HUNTER: Remo R. Pizzagalli

QUEBEC-LABRADOR
CARIBOU
FINAL SCORE: 385-5/8
HUNTER: Steven S. Bruggeman

QUEBEC-LABRADOR CARIBOU

Rangifer tarandus

Minimum Score 365

World's Record 474 6/8

Quebec-Labrador caribou includes trophies from Quebec and Labrador.

Final Score	Gross Score	Length of Main Beam R.	L.	Inside Spread	Circumference at Smallest Place Between Brow and Bez Points R.	L.	Length of Brow Points R.	L.	Width of Brow Points R.	L.	Number of Points R.	L.	Locality	Hunter	Owner	Date Killed	Rank
424 2/8	438 6/8	53 4/8	51 4/8	45 6/8	5 2/8	5 2/8	18 6/8	17 3/8	12 3/8	11	24	22	Clearwater Lake, QC	Woody Groves	Woody Groves	2005	1
423 4/8	436 3/8	53 1/8	53 6/8	46 1/8	5 3/8	5 3/8	17 4/8	16 5/8	9 3/8	9 3/8	21	20	Lac a L'Eau-Claire, QC	Stewart N. Shaft	Stewart N. Shaft	2005	2
413 6/8	423 5/8	45 5/8	48 1/8	40 5/8	6 3/8	6 4/8	20 4/8	20 5/8	16 6/8	14	22	21	Minto Lake, QC	Gordon G. Swenson	Gordon G. Swenson	2005	3
411 1/8	441 3/8	50 6/8	47 1/8	45	5 7/8	6	20 5/8	20 4/8	15 4/8	17	21	19	Lac a L'Eau-Claire, QC	Stewart N. Shaft	Stewart N. Shaft	2005	4
407 4/8	422	53	50	43 2/8	5 7/8	5 5/8	16 4/8	17 3/8	6 5/8	12	29	23	Clearwater Lake, QC	Mark A. Wayne	Mark A. Wayne	2005	5
406 5/8	414 7/8	48 5/8	49	39 2/8	5 4/8	4 6/8	17 3/8	18 7/8	14 2/8	14 3/8	19	19	Messin Lake, QC	Christopher Duddy	Christopher Duddy	2005	6
404 4/8	414 4/8	49 2/8	46 3/8	46 6/8	5 2/8	5	20 5/8	17 1/8	11 6/8	12 4/8	22	16	Clearwater Lake, QC	George D. Hurry	George D. Hurry	2006	7
404 1/8	423 3/8	45 5/8	48 2/8	45 5/8	5 6/8	5 6/8	6 2/8	16 7/8	1/8	13 4/8	23	29	Nastapoka River, QC	Don E. Eason	Don E. Eason	2005	8
404	415 3/8	43 4/8	42 7/8	45 6/8	5 3/8	5 3/8	17 2/8	17 5/8	12 3/8	13	22	24	Innu Lake, NL	Randy L. Hermann	Randy L. Hermann	2006	9
403 4/8	410 3/8	42 5/8	40 7/8	42 7/8	5 4/8	5 4/8	17 3/8	18 4/8	12 6/8	10 4/8	22	20	Ptarmigan Creek, QC	Michael D. Hendrickson	Michael D. Hendrickson	2005	10
402 3/8	427 2/8	46 3/8	46 3/8	39	4 7/8	5 1/8	20	19 6/8	16 2/8	16 3/8	23	16	Lake Desbergeres, QC	Brett A. Jones	Brett A. Jones	2004	11
399 2/8	406	48 2/8	48 1/8	44 6/8	4 3/8	4 3/8	22 7/8	22 7/8	10 5/8	18 3/8	19	22	George River, QC	Michael Fede	Michael Fede	2006	12
395 3/8	409 3/8	49 5/8	46 7/8	33 3/8	4 7/8	5	21 5/8	20 4/8	18 2/8	13 3/8	24	24	Bobby Lake, QC	David V. Hofer	David V. Hofer	2005	13
390 7/8	396 2/8	48 3/8	48 4/8	40 3/8	5 3/8	5 1/8	15 4/8	16 3/8	11 3/8	7 6/8	13	13	Clearwater Lake, QC	Michael G. Maben	Michael G. Maben	2005	14
390 1/8	402 7/8	47 7/8	49 1/8	37 7/8	4 7/8	5	20	18 1/8	16 2/8	15 7/8	23	23	Clearwater Lake, QC	Steven S. Bruggeman	Steven S. Bruggeman	2005	15
388 3/8	406 1/8	50 6/8	52 4/8	46 4/8	4 6/8	4 6/8	16 2/8	17 5/8	10	5	22	18	Leaf River, QC	Keith A. McCray	Keith A. McCray	2005	16
387 6/8	398 6/8	62 1/8	60 7/8	53 7/8	5 3/8	5 3/8	10	17 6/8	11 6/8	1/8	13	15	Delay River, QC	Roy M. Goodwin	Roy M. Goodwin	1987	17
387 4/8	405	43 5/8	46 2/8	51 2/8	5 1/8	5 6/8	15 1/8	18 4/8	10 4/8	1/8	17	15	Mollet Lake, QC	Ronald C. Miller	Ronald C. Miller	2005	18
387	396 6/8	47 6/8	48 1/8	40	5 2/8	5	16	17 6/8	14 4/8	3	15	17	Minto Lake, QC	Gregory G. Kass	Gregory G. Kass	2006	19
386 7/8	399 4/8	43 5/8	44 5/8	39 6/8	4 7/8	4 7/8	15 4/8	18 4/8	14 3/8	15	22	22	Lake Tasiataq, QC	Thomas J. Greenia	Thomas J. Greenia	2005	20
386 3/8	402 3/8	50	51	37 2/8	5 1/8	5 2/8	15 6/8	17 3/8	9 7/8	12 3/8	22	16	Leaf River, QC	Gary L. Hilliard	Gary L. Hilliard	2005	21
386	416 4/8	48 1/8	42 7/8	41 5/8	4 6/8	4 5/8	20 2/8	12 4/8	18 6/8	5 1/8	28	27	Lake Irene, QC	Robert L. St. Onge	Robert L. St. Onge	2005	22
385 5/8	405 4/8	41	40 6/8	38 5/8	5	5 2/8	16 6/8	16 2/8	1 3/8	10 5/8	17	20	Clearwater Lake, QC	Steven S. Bruggeman	Steven S. Bruggeman	2005	23
384 6/8	395 2/8	48 5/8	50	44 6/8	5 1/8	5 1/8	14 2/8	16 3/8	12	12 7/8	13	17	Lac Retty, QC	Douglas Manthey	Douglas Manthey	2003	24
383 4/8	397 6/8	49 2/8	52 4/8	42 2/8	5 7/8	4 7/8	19 3/8	10	15 4/8	1/8	17	14	Ptarmigan Lake, QC	Arnold A. Patterson	Arnold A. Patterson	2004	25
382 4/8	393 7/8	48 6/8	48 5/8	50 6/8	5 2/8	5 2/8	16 4/8	15 2/8	9 3/8	4 5/8	15	15	Mollet Lake, QC	Lance E. White	Lance E. White	2005	26
382 2/8	399 3/8	54 5/8	50 3/8	44	5 4/8	5 2/8	19 6/8	17 7/8	15 4/8	1/8	23	18	Kakiattukallak Lake, QC	Daniel A. Scott	Daniel A. Scott	2005	27

Score	M1	M2	M3	M4	M5	M6	M7	M8	R	L	Locality	Owner	Hunter	Date	Rank
381 4/8	50	50 6/8	40 7/8	5 7/8	5 6/8	16 4/8	9 5/8	11 6/8	15	15	Minto Lake, QC	Lawrence R. Cox	Lawrence R. Cox	2006	28
381 3/8	47 2/8	47 2/8	28 2/8	4 5/8	4 6/8	20 1/8	13	14 6/8	17	25	Lefebvre River, QC	Guillermo Ramirez	Guillermo Ramirez	2005	29
380 4/8	50 3/8	48 1/8	47 3/8	5	5 1/8	18 6/8	18 3/8	1/8	18	17	Lake Desbergeres, QC	Eugene R. Blair	Eugene R. Blair	2005	30
380 3/8	51 5/8	48 7/8	38 4/8	5 2/8	5 6/8	13 2/8	14 7/8	1/8	18	13	Fontisson Lake, QC	David S. Sanders	David S. Sanders	2004	31
380 1/8	55 5/8	53	27 7/8	5 1/8	5 2/8	17 5/8	13 7/8	13 4/8	20	17	Caniapiscau River, QC	Brian E. Galligan	Brian E. Galligan	1989	32
380 1/8	39 5/8	41 4/8	34 1/8	5 2/8	5 2/8	17	13 1/8	15 1/8	26	27	Lac Cramolet, QC	LeRoy J. Swain	LeRoy J. Swain	2006	32
380	49 2/8	49	40 5/8	5 4/8	5 1/8	16 6/8	15 7/8	9 7/8	29	23	Lake Lafleur, QC	Allen Blanke	Allen Blanke	2003	34
380	47 2/8	43 7/8	44 1/8	4 5/8	5	15	9 4/8	11 7/8	20	20	Lake Elsie, QC	Ron L. Gallman	Ron L. Gallman	2004	34
380	54 1/8	54 2/8	38 2/8	5 4/8	5 6/8	16	2 5/8	11	20	17	Caniapiscau River, QC	Roy A. Muir	Roy A. Muir	2005	34
377 3/8	50 4/8	49	38 4/8	4 3/8	4 3/8	20 3/8	13 2/8	17 5/8	23	17	Lake Ribero, QC	Michael A. Baronyak	Michael A. Baronyak	2004	37
377	51 7/8	50 2/8	44	5 5/8	4 7/8	14 1/8	15 1/8	9 2/8	15	18	Mollet Lake, QC	Robert M. Anderson	Robert M. Anderson	2004	38
376 6/8	46 4/8	47	37 7/8	5 1/8	5 2/8	16 3/8	14 4/8	13 4/8	25	28	Lake Merville, QC	Robert W. Thomas	Robert W. Thomas	2003	39
376 3/8	53 3/8	51 6/8	46 6/8	5	5	7	18 7/8	15 5/8	17	17	Normand Lake, QC	Jim Shockey	Jim Shockey	1999	40
376 3/8	46 4/8	47 4/8	37 7/8	4 3/8	4 3/8	18 3/8	16 2/8	12 4/8	17	19	Martha Lake, QC	Brett W. Schultz	Brett W. Schultz	2005	40
375 5/8	50 4/8	49 5/8	35 6/8	5 1/8	5 1/8	16	16 3/8	7 6/8	20	20	Lefebvre River, QC	Guillermo Ramirez	Guillermo Ramirez	2005	42
375 5/8	50 5/8	48 7/8	46 3/8	5 5/8	5 2/8	13 1/8	14 5/8	6 5/8	18	14	Tasiataq Lake, QC	Michael W. Sherman	Michael W. Sherman	2006	42
375 2/8	47	47 1/8	43 7/8	4 6/8	4 7/8	14 4/8	5 3/8	1/8	21	19	Caniapiscau River, QC	Charles T. Muir	Charles T. Muir	2005	44
375 2/8	48 1/8	48 2/8	37 2/8	6 3/8	5 7/8	17 3/8	12	1/8	21	15	Lac a L'Eau-Claire, QC	Mark A. Wayne	Mark A. Wayne	2005	44
374 7/8	54 3/8	54 5/8	44 1/8	5 5/8	5 5/8	21 5/8	4	18 4/8	14	22	Pons River, QC	Raymond W. Swope	Raymond W. Swope	2006	46
374 2/8	42 2/8	41 6/8	39 1/8	5 2/8	5 2/8	4	16 4/8	14 6/8	19	28	Lake Lagus, QC	B. Hall Bridgforth	B. Hall Bridgforth	2005	47
373 3/8	49 3/8	52	40 5/8	5	4 6/8	17 4/8	18 3/8	12 7/8	22	16	Lac Lachaine, QC	Marc D. Johnson	Marc D. Johnson	2003	48
372 4/8	49 3/8	56 6/8	46 1/8	5 4/8	5 1/8	18 7/8	15 1/8	6 3/8	13	11	Minto Lake, QC	Ralph G. DiMartino, Sr.	Ralph G. DiMartino, Sr.	2005	49
372 3/8	43 2/8	45 6/8	44 6/8	4 6/8	4 7/8	18 5/8	16 2/8	10 4/8	15	17	La Grande River, QC	Remo R. Pizzagalli	Remo R. Pizzagalli	2005	50
370 7/8	44 2/8	48 6/8	41 3/8	5 4/8	5 1/8	16 1/8	14 2/8	8 3/8	21	18	Snow Lake, QC	John P. Turgeon	John P. Turgeon	2005	51
370	50 4/8	50 6/8	50 1/8	4 5/8	4 7/8	21 5/8	18 3/8	11 7/8	15	13	Leaf River, QC	Shawn R. Andres	Shawn R. Andres	2006	52
369 6/8	47 5/8	42 5/8	42	5	5 1/8	16	15 2/8	12 2/8	22	16	Pons River, QC	Lester G. Elwood	Lester G. Elwood	2002	53
369	48 5/8	48 6/8	38 5/8	4 6/8	4 6/8	17	11 6/8	11 6/8	16	17	Leaf River, QC	Jason R. Helton	Jason R. Helton	2005	53
368 1/8	46 4/8	46 2/8	35 4/8	5	4 7/8	14 7/8	9	13 3/8	17	20	Cow Lake, NL	Stephen R. Bowers	Stephen R. Bowers	2006	55
368 1/8	48 3/8	46 6/8	37	5	4 6/8	16 1/8	14 1/8	8 1/8	18	18	Messin Lake, QC	Jonathan S. Becker	Jonathan S. Becker	2005	56
367 7/8	44 6/8	44 5/8	46 3/8	4 6/8	5 4/8	16 3/8	1 2/8	11 4/8	19	14	Nulhaluk Lake, QC	James N. Watson	James N. Watson	2005	57
367 1/8	46 3/8	40	48 2/8	4 7/8	5	17 1/8	14 7/8	9 5/8	19	15	Bull Lake, QC	Donald L. Strickler	Donald L. Strickler	2003	58
366	40	41 7/8	38 1/8	5 3/8	5 2/8	15	18	1 3/8	17	18	Jobert Lake, QC	Carl W. Peterson	Carl W. Peterson	2003	
418 4/8* 429	55 5/8	55 7/8	48	5 1/8	5	17 7/8	19 6/8	12	15	16	Schefferville, QC	Narciso Gregori	Narciso Gregori	1979	59

* Final score subject to revision by additional verifying measurements.

PRONGHORN

Antilocapra americana americana and related subspecies

Minimum Score 80 · World's Record 95

Final Score	Gross Score	Length of horn R.	L.	Circumference of Base R.	L.	Circumference at Third Quarter R.	L.	Inside Spread	Tip to Tip Spread	Length of Prong R.	L.	Locality	Hunter	Owner	Date Killed	Rank
91	91 6/8	15 2/8	15 3/8	7 3/8	7 3/8	3 3/8	3 4/8	10 3/8	6 1/8	6 6/8	6 4/8	Carbon Co., UT	Rick D. Ullery	Rick D. Ullery	2003	1
91	91 7/8	16 5/8	16 2/8	6 7/8	6 7/8	3 7/8	3 5/8	11 2/8	8 2/8	6 3/8	6 3/8	Lincoln Co., NM	Dan E. Fox	Dan E. Fox	2006	1
90 6/8	91 2/8	17 3/8	17 4/8	6 5/8	6 6/8	3 6/8	3 6/8	8 2/8	2	5 5/8	5 5/8	Yavapai Co., AZ	Wayne W. Webber	Wayne W. Webber	2004	3
90 4/8	91 5/8	19	18 7/8	6 2/8	6 3/8	2 4/8	2 5/8	11 7/8	11 6/8	6 7/8	7 4/8	Grant Co., ND	Francis J. Dobitz	Cabela's, Inc.	2005	4
90 2/8	91 2/8	17 2/8	18 7/8	7	7	3 2/8	3 1/8	7 6/8	3 3/8	6 6/8	6 2/8	Coconino Co., AZ	Jimmy J. Liautaud	Jimmy J. Liautaud	2005	5
89 4/8	90 1/8	16 2/8	16 1/8	7 3/8	7 2/8	3 2/8	3 1/8	8 7/8	3 4/8	7	6 2/8	Carbon Co., WY	Donald E. Perrien	Donald E. Perrien	2005	6
89 2/8	90 1/8	17	16 7/8	7	7	3	2 7/8	11 2/8	4 1/8	6 6/8	7	Perkins Co., SD	Heath W. Larson	Heath W. Larson	2003	7
89 2/8	91 5/8	17 5/8	16 7/8	6 6/8	6 5/8	3	2 6/8	14 4/8	12 6/8	7 4/8	6 5/8	Socorro Co., NM	David J. Chavez	David J. Chavez	2006	7
88 6/8	91 1/8	15 5/8	16 2/8	7 2/8	7 5/8	2 6/8	3	8 7/8	5 3/8	7 2/8	8 1/8	Lake Co., OR	Larry Conn	Larry Conn	2003	9
88 6/8	89 7/8	16 7/8	16 7/8	6 5/8	6 4/8	3 2/8	3	8 6/8	2 6/8	6 2/8	6 6/8	Lincoln Co., NM	Curtis J. Babler	Curtis J. Babler	2005	9
88 6/8	90	17	17 2/8	7 2/8	7 1/8	2 7/8	2 7/8	10 5/8	7	5 3/8	6	Natrona Co., WY	Mickey A. Anderson, Jr.	Mickey A. Anderson, Jr.	2006	9
88 4/8	88 7/8	17 2/8	17 2/8	7 3/8	7 1/8	2 6/8	2 6/8	9 2/8	4	6 1/8	6 1/8	Carbon Co., WY	Hillary J. Condit	Hillary J. Condit	2004	12
88 2/8	88 5/8	15 7/8	15 6/8	7 1/8	7 2/8	2 7/8	2 7/8	11 5/8	8 3/8	6 5/8	6 5/8	Carbon Co., WY	Bobby D. Raines	Bobby D. Raines	2005	13
88 2/8	89 3/8	16	15 4/8	6 7/8	6 7/8	3 6/8	3 6/8	8 1/8	5 7/8	5 7/8	5 6/8	Lincoln Co., NM	Paul E. Wollenman	Paul E. Wollenman	2005	13
88 2/8	90 2/8	16 1/8	15 1/8	7 1/8	7 5/8	3 5/8	3 5/8	9 4/8	5 5/8	6 2/8	6 1/8	Lincoln Co., NM	Justin D. Fox	Justin D. Fox	2006	13
88 2/8	90 5/8	16 2/8	16 4/8	6 7/8	7	4 1/8	3 4/8	14 2/8	10 5/8	6 2/8	6	Yavapai Co., AZ	Eric S. Gardner	Eric S. Gardner	2006	13
88	89 4/8	16 5/8	17 1/8	6 6/8	6 6/8	2 4/8	2 5/8	5 1/8	6 1/8	7	6 3/8	Modoc Co., CA	Todd W. Keys	Todd W. Keys	2003	17
88	88 6/8	16	15 7/8	7 2/8	7 2/8	3	3	11 4/8	7 6/8	6 3/8	6	Platte Co., WY	Joseph A. DiPasqua	Joseph A. DiPasqua	2004	17
87 6/8	88 3/8	15 2/8	15 2/8	7 2/8	7 2/8	2 7/8	2 6/8	11 1/8	7 7/8	6 7/8	6 4/8	Fallon Co., MT	Lonnie R. Gorder	Lonnie R. Gorder	2004	19
87 6/8	89 5/8	17	16 1/8	7 2/8	7 2/8	2 6/8	2 6/8	16	13	6	6 6/8	Mora Co., NM	Becke Medlin	Becke Medlin	2004	19
87 6/8	88 3/8	17	16 5/8	6 3/8	6 2/8	2 6/8	2 6/8	13 1/8	8 1/8	6 5/8	6 5/8	Carbon Co., WY	Jason H. Weber	Jason H. Weber	2006	19
87 4/8	88 7/8	17 1/8	16 5/8	7 4/8	7 3/8	2 7/8	2 6/8	11	7 2/8	5 5/8	6 1/8	Carbon Co., WY	Edwin L. Nunn	Edwin L. Nunn	2004	22
87 4/8	88 6/8	16 6/8	16 6/8	7	7 1/8	2 5/8	2 7/8	11 1/8	8 1/8	6 4/8	6	Torrance Co., NM	Randy D. Vander Meulen	Randy D. Vander Meulen	2004	22
87 2/8	87 5/8	16 5/8	16 5/8	7 1/8	7	3	3	10 1/8	4	5 5/8	5 4/8	Apache Co., AZ	Carl W. Daily	Cabela's, Inc.	2004	24
87 2/8	88	14 6/8	14 6/8	6 5/8	6 6/8	4	4	12 3/8	10 7/8	5 7/8	5 7/8	Mohave Co., AZ	Dan J. Helm	Dan J. Helm	2004	24
87 2/8	87 6/8	15 6/8	15 6/8	6 4/8	6 3/8	3 6/8	3 5/8	10 5/8	6 2/8	6	6 1/8	Coconino Co., AZ	Terry L. Herndon	Terry L. Herndon	2004	24
87 2/8	88 4/8	16 2/8	16 1/8	7 4/8	7 4/8	3 3/8	3 2/8	12	12	5 5/8	5 6/8	Carbon Co., WY	John G. Carnes	John G. Carnes	2006	24
87 2/8	88 1/8	16 6/8	17 1/8	6 5/8	6 4/8	2 2/8	2 3/8	9 1/8	2 2/8	7 1/8	6 7/8	Mora Co., NM	Frank P. Carozza	Frank P. Carozza	2006	24
87	87 4/8	17	17 1/8	6 3/8	6 4/8	3 2/8	3 3/8	6 5/8	4 2/8	5 6/8	5 7/8	Socorro Co., NM	John J. Lazzeroni	John J. Lazzeroni	2003	29
87	88 4/8	17 4/8	17 7/8	6 6/8	6 5/8	2 7/8	3 1/8	10 2/8	5 5/8	5	5 1/8	Yavapai Co., AZ	Richard J. Fleury, Jr.	Richard J. Fleury, Jr.	2004	29
87	87 2/8	15 5/8	15 5/8	7	7	3 1/8	3 2/8	6 5/8	2 6/8	6 1/8	6 2/8	Sweetwater Co., WY	Jerry D. Dye	Jerry D. Dye	2005	29

Score											Locality	Hunter	Owner	Date	Rank
87	87 4/8	16	16 1/8	6 3/8	6 3/8	3 4/8	3 4/8	9 3/8	3 6/8	6 2/8	Socorro Co., NM	Robert D. Griego	Robert D. Griego	2005	29
87	87 5/8	15 7/8	16	7 1/8	7 2/8	2 7/8	2 7/8	6	5 3/8	6 4/8	Carbon Co., WY	Dylan R. Snodgrass	Dylan R. Snodgrass	2005	29
87	87 3/8	16 3/8	16 2/8	7 2/8	7 2/8	2 6/8	2 6/8	10 3/8	5 2/8	5 3/8	Carbon Co., WY	Brandon J. Hushbeck	Brandon J. Hushbeck	2006	29
86 6/8	88 1/8	17	16 6/8	6 4/8	6 4/8	3 1/8	3 1/8	8 7/8	3 4/8	5 5/8	Lincoln Co., NM	William J. Barnett	William J. Barnett	2005	35
86 6/8	87 4/8	15 3/8	15 1/8	7 3/8	7 3/8	3 2/8	3 2/8	13	9 6/8	5 5/8	Fremont Co., WY	Kelly H. Dolph	Kelly H. Dolph	2005	35
86 4/8	87 6/8	15 4/8	15 7/8	6 7/8	6 7/8	3 3/8	3 3/8	13 5/8	11 4/8	6 5/8	Socorro Co., NM	Ronald Van Voorhis	Ronald Van Voorhis	2003	37
86 4/8	87 3/8	16	16	6 6/8	6 6/8	3	3	8 6/8	3 2/8	6 2/8	Mora Co., NM	Len H. Guldman	Len H. Guldman	2004	37
86 4/8	87 1/8	17 6/8	17 6/8	6 5/8	6 5/8	3 4/8	3 4/8	9 5/8	6 6/8	6	Coconino Co., AZ	Lawrence M. Kochevar	Lawrence M. Kochevar	2005	37
86 4/8	88	15 7/8	15 6/8	6 2/8	6 2/8	3 1/8	3 1/8	18 6/8	6 6/8	6 2/8	Carbon Co., WY	Travis R. Risner	Travis R. Risner	2005	37
86 4/8	87 5/8	15 5/8	15 7/8	7 4/8	7 4/8	2 6/8	2 6/8	10 3/8	5 4/8	6 3/8	Graham Co., AZ	Dale Hislop	Dale Hislop	2006	37
86 2/8	87 7/8	15	15 6/8	6 6/8	6 6/8	3 2/8	3 2/8	10 5/8	5 4/8	7 2/8	Malheur Co., OR	Ethan A. Banducci	Ethan A. Banducci	2003	42
86 2/8	86 7/8	15 7/8	15 7/8	7 3/8	7 3/8	2 2/8	2 2/8	13 4/8	8	5 3/8	Cibola Co., NM	John Gisi	John Gisi	2003	42
86 2/8	88	18 3/8	18	6 5/8	6 5/8	3 3/8	3 3/8	10	8 4/8	5 5/8	Hudspeth Co., TX	Jerome O. Chapman	Jerome O. Chapman	2004	42
86 2/8	86 5/8	16 3/8	16 5/8	7 1/8	7 1/8	2 4/8	2 4/8	8 3/8	5 7/8	6	Washoe Co., NV	Timothy H. Humes	Timothy H. Humes	2005	42
86 2/8	87 2/8	17 1/8	17 1/8	6 3/8	6 3/8	2 6/8	2 6/8	7 1/8	2 4/8	6 1/8	Humboldt Co., NV	William J. Ricci	William J. Ricci	2005	42
86 2/8	87 2/8	15	15	8	8	3	3	10 6/8	6 6/8	6 4/8	Carbon Co., WY	Suzanne Kawaters	Suzanne Kawaters	2006	42
86	87 1/8	17 3/8	17 6/8	6 4/8	6 4/8	2 6/8	2 6/8	11 5/8	7 2/8	6	Sweetwater Co., WY	Jack E. Risner	Jack E. Risner	2006	42
86	86 5/8	16 4/8	16 6/8	5 7/8	5 7/8	2 7/8	2 7/8	9 1/8	5 4/8	7 7/8	Milk River, AB	Keith R. Heppler	Keith R. Heppler	2003	49
86	86 6/8	15 7/8	15 6/8	6 5/8	6 5/8	3 1/8	3 1/8	11 3/8	10 1/8	6 6/8	Jackson Co., CO	Denis R. McClure	Denis R. McClure	2003	49
86	88 1/8	17 5/8	17 7/8	6 6/8	6 6/8	3	3	16 4/8	17 4/8	6 5/8	Modoc Co., CA	Joe E. Dutton	Joe E. Dutton	2004	49
86	86 1/8	16	16 1/8	6 4/8	6 4/8	3	3	10 4/8	8	5 5/8	Harding Co., NM	Chad A. Waligura	Chad A. Waligura	2005	49
85 6/8	86 3/8	16 6/8	16 6/8	7	7	3 1/8	3 1/8	10 3/8	7 3/8	5 5/8	Socorro Co., NM	Douglas J. Aikin	Douglas J. Aikin	2006	49
85 6/8	86 4/8	16	16	6 6/8	6 6/8	2 6/8	2 6/8	8 4/8	4 2/8	5	Socorro Co., NM	Gilbert T. Adams III	Gilbert T. Adams III	2001	54
85 6/8	86 4/8	15 7/8	15 6/8	6 6/8	6 6/8	3 2/8	3 2/8	8	4 4/8	5 4/8	Fremont Co., WY	John K. Metzler	John K. Metzler	2003	54
85 6/8	86 4/8	17 5/8	17 7/8	6 7/8	6 7/8	3 1/8	3 1/8	8 7/8	5/8	4 7/8	Perkins Co., SD	Aaron B. Ambur	Aaron B. Ambur	2004	54
85 6/8	86 5/8	16	16 1/8	6 7/8	6 7/8	2 7/8	2 7/8	10 5/8	7 6/8	5 4/8	Natrona Co., WY	Alfred J. Gemrich	Alfred J. Gemrich	2004	54
85 6/8	86	14 5/8	14 6/8	7	7	2 4/8	2 4/8	9 1/8	5 7/8	6 4/8	Lincoln Co., NM	Jimmy J. Liautaud	Jimmy J. Liautaud	2004	54
85 6/8	86 6/8	17	17	6 2/8	6 2/8	3 4/8	3 4/8	8 4/8	4	5 7/8	Washoe Co., NV	Patricia A. Lowery	Patricia A. Lowery	2004	54
85 6/8	86 3/8	16	16	6 4/8	6 4/8	2 7/8	2 7/8	13 7/8	11 2/8	6	Socorro Co., NM	John Teeter	John Teeter	2004	54
85 6/8	86	15 2/8	15 4/8	6 4/8	6 4/8	3 1/8	3 1/8	6 6/8	0 6/8	6 4/8	Emery Co., UT	Denny Austad	Denny Austad	2006	54
85 6/8	86 2/8	14 5/8	14 5/8	7 5/8	7 5/8	2 5/8	2 5/8	12 7/8	9 4/8	6 2/8	Carbon Co., WY	Miguel Martinez	Miguel Martinez	2006	54
85 4/8	86 2/8	16	15 7/8	7 4/8	7 4/8	2 6/8	2 6/8	10 2/8	7 1/8	5 6/8	Sweetwater Co., WY	Unknown	D.R. & J. Harrow	PR 1980	54
85 4/8	86 1/8	15 6/8	16	7 4/8	7 4/8	2 6/8	2 6/8	11	4 7/8	7	Rosebud Co., MT	Shane P. Schulze	Shane P. Schulze	2003	63
85 4/8	86 4/8	16 5/8	16 5/8	6 2/8	6 2/8	2 5/8	2 5/8	7 3/8	3 2/8	6 1/8	Lincoln Co., NM	Kent M. Sams	Kent M. Sams	2004	63
85 4/8	86 5/8	15 4/8	15 4/8	7 4/8	7 4/8	3 1/8	3 1/8	16 6/8	15 7/8	5 4/8	Natrona Co., WY	Peter J. Burke	Peter J. Burke	2005	63
85 4/8	86 2/8	17 3/8	17 3/8	7 2/8	7 2/8	3	3	10 7/8	7 1/8	5 5/8	Coconino Co., AZ	Norman P. Don	Norman P. Don	2005	63
85 4/8	86 3/8	16 3/8	16 3/8	6 7/8	6 7/8	2 5/8	2 5/8	8 5/8	1 2/8	6	Lea Co., NM	Randy L. Hughes	Randy L. Hughes	2005	63
85 4/8	85 6/8	14	14 2/8	7 5/8	7 5/8	2 7/8	2 7/8	11 6/8	9 5/8	5	Fremont Co., WY	Karl K. Kukuchka	Karl K. Kukuchka	2005	63
85 2/8	85 6/8	16 3/8	16 3/8	6 3/8	6 3/8	3	3	15	10 1/8	5 5/8	Emery Co., UT	Mel L. Helm	Mel L. Helm	2002	70
85 2/8	85 6/8	15 3/8	15 5/8	7	7	2 3/8	2 3/8	10 7/8	8 3/8	6 5/8	Fremont Co., WY	Daniel G. Horath	Daniel G. Horath	2004	70
85 2/8	86	17	16 7/8	6 6/8	6 6/8	2 4/8	2 4/8	10 3/8	5 2/8	5 1/8	Pershing Co., NV	John Sarvis	John Sarvis	2004	70
85 2/8	86	16 3/8	16 2/8	7 1/8	7 1/8	2 5/8	2 5/8	7	2 1/8	5 7/8	Carbon Co., WY	William R. Chandler	William R. Chandler	2005	70

PRONGHORN

Antilocapra americana americana and related subspecies

Final Score	Gross Score	Length of horn R	L	Circumference of Base R	L	Circumference at Third Quarter R	L	Inside Spread	Tip to Tip Spread	Length of Prong R	L	Locality	Hunter	Owner	Date Killed	Rank
85 2/8	86 6/8	14 1/8	14	6 7/8	6 6/8	3 3/8	3 3/8	10 3/8	9	5 7/8	5	Crook Co., WY	Cleveland B. Holloway	Cleveland B. Holloway	2005	70
85 2/8	86 1/8	16 2/8	16 4/8	6 4/8	6 4/8	3 3/8	2 7/8	10 1/8	8	6 3/8	6	Natrona Co., WY	Mike R. Bailey	Mike R. Bailey	2006	70
85 2/8	85 6/8	15	15	7 3/8	7 1/8	3	2 7/8	13	11	6 1/8	6 1/8	Carbon Co., WY	Neil Q. Carrico	Neil Q. Carrico	2006	70
85 2/8	86 2/8	15	14 7/8	8	8	3 3/8	3 2/8	8 1/8	3 5/8	5 5/8	6 1/8	Jackson Co., SD	Nicholas J. Patterson	Nicholas J. Patterson	2006	70
85 2/8	86	16	16 1/8	6 4/8	6 3/8	3	3	10 3/8	5 6/8	6	6	Natrona Co., WY	Constantine C. Prodromakis	Constantine C. Prodromakis	2006	70
85	86 2/8	16	15 7/8	6	6 1/8	3 2/8	3 2/8	12 4/8	9 7/8	6 4/8	6	Catron Co., NM	Douglas C. Heiner	Douglas C. Heiner	2003	79
85	86 1/8	17 2/8	17 6/8	6 4/8	6 4/8	2 5/8	2 7/8	14	11 2/8	5 6/8	5 5/8	Lincoln Co., WY	Waylon S. Cornia	Waylon S. Cornia	2004	79
85	86 3/8	16 6/8	16 7/8	6 4/8	6 4/8	2 6/8	3 1/8	8 4/8	2 7/8	5 7/8	5 4/8	Campbell Co., WY	Tony D. Haag	Tony D. Haag	2004	79
85	85 3/8	15 3/8	15 3/8	6 6/8	6 6/8	3	3 1/8	7 7/8	5	5 3/8	5 3/8	Natrona Co., WY	Kayla L. Morrison	Kayla L. Morrison	2004	79
85	85 6/8	16 6/8	16 7/8	7	7 1/8	2 4/8	2 5/8	7 3/8	2	6	6 2/8	Pershing Co., NV	Stanley H. Brown, Jr.	Stanley H. Brown, Jr.	2005	79
85	86 6/8	17 1/8	16 5/8	6 3/8	6 3/8	2 6/8	2 6/8	21 7/8	19 6/8	5 5/8	6 3/8	Grant Co., NM	Mike E. Dean	Mike E. Dean	2005	79
85	85 4/8	16 1/8	16 2/8	6 1/8	6 1/8	3	3 1/8	9 6/8	5 6/8	6 1/8	6 1/8	Mora Co., NM	Lyle C. Foster	Lyle C. Foster	2005	79
85	85 6/8	15 3/8	15 1/8	7 3/8	7 2/8	3 1/8	3	12 1/8	11 7/8	6 1/8	6 1/8	Sheridan Co., WY	Garry Reese	Garry Reese	2005	79
85	86 1/8	16 2/8	16 7/8	6 5/8	6 4/8	2 6/8	2 5/8	9 3/8	4 3/8	6 6/8	6 5/8	Jones Co., SD	Steven J. Tatum	Steven J. Tatum	2005	79
85	86 3/8	16	16 4/8	6 3/8	6 4/8	3 1/8	3 2/8	10 6/8	6 6/8	5 6/8	5 4/8	Catron Co., NM	M. Frederick Zink	M. Frederick Zink	2005	79
85	85 7/8	18	17 7/8	6 3/8	6 5/8	2 6/8	2 6/8	8 2/8	3	5 3/8	5 3/8	Cimarron Co., OK	Todd W. Bradley	Todd W. Bradley	2006	79
85	86 1/8	17 2/8	17 2/8	6 2/8	6 2/8	3	2 6/8	15	12 2/8	6 4/8	6 2/8	Yavapai Co., AZ	Mark D. Thomson	Mark D. Thomson	2006	79
84 6/8	87 2/8	16 6/8	15 7/8	7 3/8	7 3/8	2 6/8	2 4/8	5 2/8	3 7/8	5 3/8	6	Humboldt Co., NV	Ian O. Muceus	Ian O. Muceus	2003	91
84 6/8	85 5/8	15 7/8	16	7 1/8	6 7/8	2 6/8	2 6/8	10 3/8	6 5/8	6	5 5/8	Carbon Co., WY	Francis J. Cuneo, Jr.	Francis J. Cuneo, Jr.	2004	91
84 6/8	85 5/8	15	15 2/8	7 3/8	7 3/8	2 7/8	2 6/8	9 1/8	5 4/8	6 2/8	6 4/8	Carbon Co., WY	David R. Harrow	David R. Harrow	2004	91
84 6/8	85 7/8	15 3/8	15 4/8	6 7/8	6 6/8	3	3	10	5 4/8	6 1/8	5 4/8	Lassen Co., CA	Mike D. Lindsey	Mike D. Lindsey	2004	91
84 6/8	85 3/8	15 5/8	15 4/8	7 6/8	7 4/8	2 2/8	2 4/8	10 1/8	6 2/8	5 7/8	5 7/8	Carbon Co., WY	Jared J. Mason	Jared J. Mason	2004	91
84 6/8	86 5/8	17 6/8	17 6/8	7 2/8	7 1/8	2 5/8	2 4/8	9 2/8	4 3/8	5 1/8	4 5/8	Hot Springs Co., WY	Derek K. Nichols	Derek K. Nichols	2004	91
84 6/8	85 1/8	15 2/8	15 2/8	7	7	2 7/8	3	11 1/8	6 5/8	5 5/8	5 6/8	Cochran Co., TX	Dianne Peden	Dianne Peden	2004	91
84 6/8	86 2/8	15 5/8	15 5/8	6 5/8	6 5/8	2 6/8	2 7/8	10 1/8	7 2/8	6 5/8	7	Lincoln Co., NM	John F. Babler	John F. Babler	2005	91
84 6/8	86 7/8	17 1/8	16 7/8	6 6/8	6 5/8	2 7/8	3	9 6/8	5	5 4/8	5	Emery Co., UT	Alan L. Girod	Alan L. Girod	2005	91
84 6/8	85 4/8	15	15 2/8	7	7	2 7/8	3	7 5/8	3 4/8	6 1/8	5 7/8	Carbon Co., WY	Scott M. Hushbeck	Scott M. Hushbeck	2005	91
84 6/8	87 4/8	16 5/8	16 2/8	6 7/8	6 4/8	2 5/8	2 6/8	12	3 4/8	5 5/8	6 2/8	Moffat Co., CO	Jason P. Kastendieck	Jason P. Kastendieck	2005	91
84 6/8	84 7/8	17 4/8	17 4/8	6 1/8	6 1/8	2 4/8	2 4/8	11 5/8	5 2/8	6	6	Elko Co., NV	Tamara L. Mariluch	Tamara L. Mariluch	2005	91
84 6/8	85 4/8	17 3/8	17 3/8	6 6/8	6 5/8	2 6/8	2 6/8	11 5/8	7	4 6/8	5	Hudspeth Co., TX	Daniel H. McBride	Daniel H. McBride	2005	91
84 6/8	86 2/8	14 5/8	14 6/8	6 5/8	6 3/8	3 1/8	3 3/8	11 2/8	10 2/8	5 7/8	6 2/8	Colfax Co., NM	Tracy L. Tomlin	Tracy L. Tomlin	2005	91
84 6/8	85 4/8	16 5/8	16 6/8	6 7/8	6 7/8	2 3/8	2 5/8	9 3/8	3 4/8	5 7/8	5 5/8	Colfax Co., NM	Robert D. Jones	Robert D. Jones	2006	91

Score												Locality	By Whom Killed	Owner	Date Killed	Rank
84 4/8	85 7/8	16 4/8	16 3/8	10 1/8	2 3/8	2 3/8	6 4/8	6 4/8	4 6/8	7 2/8	6 2/8	Washoe Co., NV	Louis G. Damonte, Jr.	Louis G. Damonte, Jr.	2001	106
84 4/8	85	15 2/8	15 2/8	9	3 4/8	3 4/8	6 6/8	7	4 5/8	5 1/8	5 2/8	Apache Co., AZ	Steven H. Brower	Steven H. Brower	2004	106
84 4/8	84 6/8	16 1/8	16 2/8	9 5/8	2 5/8	2 6/8	6 4/8	6 4/8	4	6	6	Campbell Co., WY	Gerald L. Frey, Jr.	Gerald L. Frey, Jr.	2005	106
84 4/8	85	15 3/8	15 1/8	9 7/8	2 4/8	2 4/8	7 3/8	6 4/8	5	6 1/8	6 2/8	Owyhee Co., ID	Randy W. Haight	Randy W. Haight	2005	106
84 4/8	85	16 2/8	16 1/8	10 5/8	3	3	6 3/8	7 3/8	5 1/8	5 7/8	5 6/8	Billings Co., ND	Lyndon L. Mertz	Lyndon L. Mertz	2005	106
84 4/8	85	14 2/8	14 2/8	8 6/8	3	3	7 4/8	7 4/8	7 5/8	5 6/8	5 5/8	Carbon Co., WY	Jason L. Snell	Jason L. Snell	2005	106
84 4/8	85	14 5/8	14 4/8	11 4/8	3	3 1/8	7 3/8	7 3/8	9	5 5/8	5 6/8	Carbon Co., WY	Timothy W. Stanosheck	Timothy W. Stanosheck	2005	106
84 7/8	84 7/8	15 1/8	15 1/8	13 1/8	2 7/8	3 1/8	7	7	8 7/8	5 2/8	5 2/8	Colfax Co., NM	Tracy L. Tomlin	Tracy L. Tomlin	2006	106
84 4/8	86 2/8	15 4/8	16 5/8	10 6/8	3 3/8	3 2/8	6 5/8	6 4/8	9 3/8	6	6 1/8	Moffat Co., CO	John C. Vanko	John C. Vanko	2006	106
84 2/8	86 1/8	15 7/8	15 4/8	12 3/8	2 5/8	2 6/8	7 1/8	6 7/8	7	6 6/8	6	Sweetwater Co., WY	Rod H. Mathill	Rod H. Mathill	1981	115
84 2/8	85 1/8	17 1/8	17	8 7/8	2 5/8	2 6/8	6 4/8	6 3/8	2 7/8	5 6/8	6	Lincoln Co., NM	Robert Churchwell	Robert Churchwell	1998	115
84 2/8	85	18 1/8	18	17	2 3/8	2 2/8	6 3/8	6 2/8	13 7/8	5 4/8	5 2/8	Harney Co., OR	Bill Croxen	Bill Croxen	2003	115
84 2/8	84 5/8	16 4/8	16 5/8	14 4/8	2 7/8	2 7/8	6 5/8	6 5/8	12 3/8	5	5 1/8	Washoe Co., NV	Michael J. Ellena	Michael J. Ellena	2004	115
84 2/8	85 4/8	17 5/8	17 1/8	8 6/8	2 3/8	2 4/8	6 2/8	6 3/8	4	5 6/8	6	Lincoln Co., NM	Don H. Grimes	Don H. Grimes	2005	115
84 2/8	85 2/8	17	16 6/8	11 4/8	2 6/8	3	6 6/8	6 6/8	5 6/8	5	5 2/8	Brewster Co., TX	Arthur G. Rivera	Arthur G. Rivera	2005	115
84 2/8	84 5/8	16 7/8	16 6/8	12 2/8	2 5/8	2 5/8	6 4/8	6 4/8	6 4/8	5 6/8	5 2/8	Humboldt Co., NV	L. Alan Forman	L. Alan Forman	2006	115
84 2/8	85 2/8	18 2/8	18 2/8	12 7/8	2 4/8	2 4/8	6 1/8	6 1/8	8 4/8	5 3/8	5 2/8	Humboldt Co., NV	Nick Perchetti	Nick Perchetti	2006	115
84 2/8	86	16	16	8 6/8	2 7/8	2 6/8	6 5/8	6 5/8	3 2/8	6 6/8	5 7/8	Humboldt Co., NV	Kathy Putvain	Kathy Putvain	2006	115
84 2/8	85 7/8	16 5/8	16 3/8	17	2 5/8	2 5/8	6 5/8	6 5/8	15	5 2/8	6 1/8	Lipscomb Co., TX	Joe E. Wimpee	Joe E. Wimpee	2006	115
84	84 4/8	16 4/8	16 4/8	9 3/8	2 4/8	2 4/8	6 1/8	6 1/8	5 5/8	6 1/8	6 1/8	Butte Co., ID	Kirk Drussel	Paul E. Harrell	1940	125

PRONGHORN
FINAL SCORE: 82-2/8
HUNTER: Dan E. McBride

PRONGHORN
FINAL SCORE: 86-2/8
HUNTER: Timothy H. Humes

PRONGHORN
FINAL SCORE: 80
HUNTER: Barry D. Miller

PRONGHORN
FINAL SCORE: 85-6/8
HUNTER: Aaron B. Ambur

PRONGHORN

Antilocapra americana americana and related subspecies

Final Score	Gross Score	Length of horn R.	L.	Circumference of Base R.	L.	Circumference at Third Quarter R.	L.	Inside Spread	Tip to Tip Spread	Length of Prong R.	L.	Locality	Hunter	Owner	Date Killed	Rank
84	85 1/8	14 4/8	14 4/8	7 4/8	7 2/8	2 7/8	2 6/8	6 7/8	4 7/8	6 1/8	6 4/8	Carbon Co., WY	Kerry G. Keane	Kerry G. Keane	2003	125
84	85 7/8	16 7/8	16 4/8	6 5/8	6 2/8	3	2 7/8	12 6/8	9 7/8	6 2/8	5 4/8	Petroleum Co., MT	Daniel T. Locati	Daniel T. Locati	2003	125
84	85 2/8	16	15 4/8	7 7/8	7 6/8	2 6/8	2 7/8	13	11 7/8	4 5/8	4 4/8	Colfax Co., NM	Dan E. McBride	Dan E. McBride	2004	125
84	84 6/8	16 4/8	16 3/8	7	7	2 6/8	2 5/8	9 2/8	4 5/8	5 4/8	5 6/8	Lake Co., OR	Jerad L. Mitchell	Jerad L. Mitchell	2004	125
84	85	16 6/8	16 5/8	7	6 6/8	3	3	8	2 1/8	5 1/8	4 6/8	Custer Co., CO	Rickey N. Nicholson	Rickey N. Nicholson	2004	125
84	84 5/8	15 4/8	15 4/8	6 5/8	6 5/8	2 7/8	2 6/8	11 1/8	9 1/8	6 1/8	6 1/8	Fremont Co., WY	Jeffrey D. Borges	Jeffrey D. Borges	2005	125
84	84 4/8	16	16	6 5/8	6 7/8	2 5/8	2 5/8	11 5/8	9 1/8	6 2/8	6 2/8	Fremont Co., WY	Will R. Coleman	Will R. Coleman	2005	125
84	84 3/8	16	16	6 7/8	6 7/8	2 4/8	2 5/8	12 5/8	7 6/8	5 7/8	5 5/8	Jackson Co., CO	Tomme L. Gold	Tomme L. Gold	2005	125
84	84 3/8	14 1/8	14 2/8	7 2/8	7 2/8	2 4/8	2 4/8	8 2/8	3 3/8	7 1/8	7 3/8	Baker Co., OR	James N. Grove	James N. Grove	2005	125
84	85 2/8	15 5/8	15 6/8	6 7/8	6 6/8	3 5/8	3 2/8	10 1/8	8 5/8	5 6/8	5 3/8	Carbon Co., WY	Larry S. Hicks	Larry S. Hicks	2005	125
84	84 6/8	16 4/8	16 4/8	6 5/8	6 6/8	3 2/8	3 1/8	6 6/8	8 5/8	5 1/8	5 4/8	Rosebud Co., MT	Matthew W. Howard	Matthew W. Howard	2005	125
84	85	15 6/8	15 4/8	7 3/8	7 2/8	2 6/8	2 6/8	11 2/8	9	5 5/8	5 2/8	Natrona Co., WY	Shawn L. Wagner	Shawn L. Wagner	2005	125
84	84 5/8	15 5/8	15 5/8	7	6 7/8	3 1/8	3 1/8	11 3/8	8 2/8	5 6/8	5 5/8	Carbon Co., WY	J. Mike Clegg	J. Mike Clegg	2006	125
84	84 5/8	16 1/8	16	7	7	3	2 7/8	11	6 4/8	5 3/8	5 2/8	Natrona Co., WY	Lee D. Geisser	Lee D. Geisser	2006	125
84	84 1/8	14 7/8	15	6 4/8	6 4/8	2 4/8	2 4/8	11 6/8	9 1/8	6 4/8	6 4/8	Carbon Co., WY	Larry S. Hicks	Larry S. Hicks	2006	125
83 6/8	84 7/8	14 7/8	15	7 2/8	7 1/8	2 7/8	2 6/8	16 2/8	14 1/8	5 7/8	6 1/8	Washoe Co., NV	James F. Anderson	James F. Anderson	2003	141
83 6/8	84 5/8	18	17 5/8	6 4/8	6 4/8	2 6/8	2 6/8	9 2/8	3 4/8	4 4/8	4 6/8	Torrance Co., NM	Joanne Crigler	Joanne Crigler	2004	141
83 6/8	84 6/8	16	15 5/8	7 3/8	7 2/8	3 1/8	3 1/8	9 4/8	5	5 2/8	5 3/8	Colfax Co., NM	Charles LaPorte	Charles LaPorte	2004	141
83 6/8	85 3/8	16	16 7/8	6 4/8	6 4/8	2 3/8	2 4/8	7 2/8	3 2/8	6 4/8	7	Colfax Co., NM	Charlie A. Schlosser	Charlie A. Schlosser	2004	141
83 6/8	85 3/8	15 1/8	15	7	6 7/8	2 4/8	2 4/8	9 4/8	4 4/8	7 4/8	6 3/8	Blaine Co., ID	Ralph Appa	Ralph Appa	2005	141
83 6/8	84 2/8	16 4/8	16 4/8	6 4/8	6 4/8	2 6/8	2 6/8	9 6/8	4 3/8	6 1/8	5 5/8	Pershing Co., NV	Chad D. Bliss	Chad D. Bliss	2005	141
83 6/8	84 2/8	15 4/8	15 6/8	7	7	2 5/8	2 5/8	9 2/8	5 3/8	5 7/8	5 6/8	Rosebud Co., MT	Jim E. Bolender	Jim E. Bolender	2005	141
83 6/8	84 3/8	16 1/8	16	6 5/8	6 4/8	2 4/8	2 4/8	10	4 6/8	6 4/8	6 4/8	Perkins Co., SD	Jeffrey M. Drexler	Jeffrey M. Drexler	2005	141
83 6/8	84 2/8	16 1/8	16	6 5/8	6 5/8	2 5/8	2 6/8	10 5/8	7 2/8	5 5/8	5 5/8	Billings Co., ND	Shawn W. Kukowski	Shawn W. Kukowski	2005	141
83 6/8	84 3/8	14 6/8	14 6/8	7	6 7/8	3 3/8	3 2/8	9 7/8	7 5/8	5 3/8	5 4/8	Lea Co., NM	Douglas E. Kyle, Jr.	Douglas E. Kyle, Jr.	2005	141
83 6/8	84 1/8	16 2/8	16 2/8	6 1/8	6 2/8	3 3/8	3 2/8	9	3 1/8	5 4/8	5 3/8	Socorro Co., NM	James G. Petersen	James G. Petersen	2005	141
83 6/8	86 5/8	15 2/8	17 3/8	6 4/8	6 4/8	3 3/8	3 1/8	11 2/8	8 4/8	6 3/8	6 2/8	Socorro Co., NM	Justin N. Trail	Justin N. Trail	2005	141
83 6/8	84 7/8	17	16 4/8	6 2/8	6 2/8	3 1/8	2 6/8	12 4/8	7 7/8	5 4/8	5 4/8	Albany Co., WY	Donny J. Robbins	Donny J. Robbins	2006	141
83 4/8	84 5/8	15 3/8	15 3/8	6 2/8	6 3/8	2 6/8	2 6/8	7 3/8	5	6 2/8	7	Sweetwater Co., WY	Kenneth L. West	Kenneth L. West	2004	154
83 4/8	84 3/8	15 5/8	15 5/8	5 7/8	5 7/8	2 6/8	2 5/8	9 7/8	5 1/8	7 3/8	7 2/8	Rosebud Co., MT	Laurel R. Doney	Laurel R. Doney	2005	154
83 4/8	84 2/8	16 6/8	16 6/8	6 4/8	6 4/8	2 6/8	2 6/8	8 7/8	3 2/8	5 3/8	4 7/8	Catron Co., NM	Dale Hislop	Dale Hislop	2005	154
83 4/8	84	17	16 7/8	6 3/8	6 4/8	2 7/8	3	13 1/8	8 7/8	4 2/8	4 1/8	Hudspeth Co., TX	William G. Kyle	William G. Kyle	2005	154
83 4/8	83 7/8	17 1/8	17 2/8	6 5/8	6 5/8	2 3/8	2 3/8	16 5/8	12 3/8	5 1/8	5	Washoe Co., NV	Kevin Retterath	Kevin Retterath	2005	154

Score											Name	Locality	Date	Rank
83 4/8	84	16 1/8	16 4/8	6 4/8	6 4/8	2 4/8	2 4/8	12 3/8	7 6/8	5 7/8	Shawn L. Wagner	Carbon Co., WY	2006	154
83 4/8	84 7/8	15 3/8	15 7/8	6 6/8	6 6/8	2 4/8	2 6/8	12 2/8	8 4/8	6 4/8	Jason D. Winters	Lincoln Co., NM	2006	154
83 2/8	84 6/8	15 4/8	15 2/8	6 6/8	6 4/8	2 6/8	2 6/8	11 6/8	10 5/8	5 6/8	Gary Hubbell	Jackson Co., CO	2003	161
83 2/8	84 3/8	16	16 2/8	7 1/8	7 2/8	2 4/8	2 4/8	9 5/8	5 4/8	5	Nathan S. Miller	Fremont Co., WY	2003	161
83 2/8	84 6/8	15 1/8	15 6/8	6 3/8	6 2/8	3 4/8	3 4/8	17 7/8	14 5/8	5 2/8	Sam T. Scaling	Quay Co., NM	2003	161
83 2/8	84 3/8	17 3/8	17	6 1/8	6 1/8	3 6/8	3 6/8	7	1 2/8	5 4/8	Justen M. Anderson	Otero Co., NM	2004	161
83 2/8	84 2/8	15 5/8	15 4/8	6 7/8	5 7/8	2 6/8	2 7/8	8 6/8	5	6 4/8	Miles Fedinec	Moffat Co., CO	2004	161
83 2/8	84 6/8	16 1/8	16 3/8	6	6 6/8	2 5/8	2 6/8	10 3/8	6 6/8	5 6/8	Matthew D. McGuire	Lincoln Co., NM	2004	161
83 2/8	84 2/8	15	15 1/8	6 5/8	6	2 5/8	2 7/8	12 2/8	5 5/8	6	Elliott E. Stancik	Hudspeth Co., TX	2004	161
83 2/8	84	15 6/8	16	7	6 5/8	3 1/8	3	9 7/8	5 4/8	4 4/8	Marc L. Bartoskewitz	Hudspeth Co., TX	2005	161
83 2/8	83 5/8	12 7/8	13	8 2/8	7	3 4/8	3 4/8	7 4/8	4 4/8	5 3/8	Rodney S. Cook	Moffat Co., CO	2005	161
83 2/8	86 3/8	15 7/8	15 6/8	6	6	3 1/8	3 2/8	12 4/8	5 6/8	5 4/8	Grant E. Crutchley	Eureka Co., NV	2005	161
83 2/8	83 6/8	15 5/8	15 6/8	6 7/8	6	2 7/8	2 7/8	13 1/8	8 6/8	5 4/8	David G. Paullin	Campbell Co., WY	2005	161
83 2/8	83 6/8	17 1/8	17 1/8	6 4/8	7	2 7/8	2 7/8	11 1/8	9 2/8	5 1/8	James S. Torland	Harney Co., OR	2005	161
83 2/8	83 6/8	16 7/8	16 5/8	6 1/8	6 5/8	2 5/8	2 5/8	12 7/8	6 4/8	5 2/8	Larry M. Wright	Mora Co., NM	2005	161
83 2/8	84 1/8	16 4/8	16 4/8	6 4/8	6 1/8	2 6/8	2 6/8	8 7/8	9 4/8	5 6/8	James D. Knight	Colfax Co., NM	2006	161
83 2/8	84 1/8	16 2/8	16 2/8	6 7/8	6 4/8	2 5/8	2 5/8	12 4/8	3	5 4/8	Shane A. Mathill	Carbon Co., WY	2006	161
83 2/8	83 1/8	16 6/8	17	6 2/8	6 5/8	2 6/8	2 7/8	7 3/8	9 4/8	5 2/8	Daniel H. McBride	Catron Co., NM	2006	161
83	83 1/8	16 7/8	16 7/8	5 7/8	5 7/8	2 6/8	2 7/8	8 6/8	3 5/8	5 5/8	Jasen R. Landsberger	Billings Co., ND	2003	177
83	84 2/8	16	16	6 2/8	6 1/8	3	3	9 3/8	4 4/8	6 3/8	Lori P. Baugher	Apache Co., AZ	2004	177
83	83 6/8	15 5/8	15 6/8	6 2/8	6	2 4/8	2 4/8	9 7/8	6 6/8	6 7/8	Danny Betancourt	Elko Co., NV	2004	177

PRONGHORN
FINAL SCORE: 82-2/8
HUNTER: David R. Brimager

PRONGHORN
FINAL SCORE: 87-6/8
HUNTER: Jason H. Weber

PRONGHORN
FINAL SCORE: 90-2/8
HUNTER: Jimmy J. Liautaud

PRONGHORN
FINAL SCORE: 83-6/8
HUNTER: Joanne Crigler

PRONGHORN

Antilocapra americana americana and related subspecies

Final Score	Gross Score	Length of horn R.	L.	Circumference of Base R.	L.	Circumference at Third Quarter R.	L.	Inside Spread	Tip to Tip Spread	Length of Prong R.	L.	Locality	Hunter	Owner	Date Killed	Rank
83	84	15 5/8	15 4/8	6 3/8	6 2/8	2 5/8	2 4/8	8 1/8	4	6 6/8	6 4/8	Sweetwater Co., WY	Stephen D. Lynn	Stephen D. Lynn	2004	177
83	85 6/8	14 3/8	15 2/8	7 1/8	7 2/8	3	3 2/8	11	7 3/8	5 1/8	5 2/8	Apache Co., AZ	Bethena C. Pugh	Bethena C. Pugh	2004	177
83	84	16	15 6/8	7	7	2 3/8	2 3/8	10 1/8	6 1/8	5 4/8	5 2/8	Natrona Co., WY	Mark G. Tanner	Mark G. Tanner	2004	177
83	83 3/8	15 5/8	15 5/8	6 6/8	6 6/8	2 6/8	2 6/8	10 7/8	7 4/8	5 6/8	5 4/8	Sheridan Co., WY	William E. Walters	William E. Walters	2004	177
83	83 6/8	14 4/8	14 6/8	6 6/8	6 6/8	3	3	10 2/8	7 6/8	5 5/8	5 7/8	Carbon Co., WY	Lowell L. Hawthorne	Lowell L. Hawthorne	2005	177
83	85	15	16 2/8	6 4/8	6 4/8	3	3	10	7	6 6/8	6 1/8	Otero Co., NM	Michael S. Rex	Michael S. Rex	2005	177
83	84 2/8	17	16 5/8	6 4/8	6 4/8	3 2/8	2 6/8	9 5/8	6 5/8	5 2/8	5 2/8	Hamilton Co., KS	Kenneth L. Roybal	Kenneth L. Roybal	2005	177
83	84 7/8	14 5/8	15 6/8	6 5/8	6 4/8	3 2/8	3 1/8	9 3/8	6	6 5/8	6 1/8	Moffat Co., CO	John C. Vanko	John C. Vanko	2005	177
83	83 5/8	16 4/8	16 5/8	6 4/8	6 4/8	2 4/8	2 5/8	10 2/8	4 6/8	5 2/8	5 3/8	Weld Co., CO	Clint A. DePorter	Clint A. DePorter	2006	177
83	84 1/8	15 3/8	15 7/8	6 5/8	6 4/8	2 4/8	2 4/8	13	10 5/8	6 2/8	6 4/8	Fremont Co., WY	Dan Steffenhagen	Dan Steffenhagen	2006	177
82 6/8	83 6/8	16 4/8	16 2/8	6 3/8	6 5/8	2 4/8	2 4/8	10	5 6/8	6 1/8	5 6/8	Custer Co., MT	Steve Brett	Steve Brett	2003	190
82 6/8	85 1/8	15 1/8	15 6/8	6 4/8	6 4/8	2 2/8	2 4/8	10 6/8	6 2/8	4 4/8	5 3/8	Albany Co., WY	Charles D. Mullins	Charles D. Mullins	2003	190
82 6/8	84 5/8	15 2/8	16 2/8	7	6 7/8	2 7/8	2 6/8	12 4/8	10 7/8	6 2/8	5 6/8	Perkins Co., SD	Tyler J. Dutton	Tyler J. Dutton	2004	190
82 6/8	83 1/8	14 6/8	14 6/8	6 2/8	6 2/8	2 7/8	2 7/8	10 3/8	7 7/8	6 3/8	6 5/8	Natrona Co., WY	Roger D. Foutz	Roger D. Foutz	2004	190
82 6/8	83 3/8	16 2/8	16 1/8	6	6	3	3	9 1/8	5 1/8	5 6/8	5 4/8	Colfax Co., NM	Wyatt E. McGuire	Wyatt E. McGuire	2004	190
82 6/8	83 3/8	15 2/8	15	7 1/8	7	2 5/8	2 5/8	9	7 3/8	5 3/8	5 3/8	Carbon Co., WY	Marvin F. Papke	Marvin F. Papke	2004	190
82 6/8	84 3/8	16 1/8	16 3/8	7 2/8	7 1/8	2 4/8	2 3/8	13 5/8	10 1/8	5 5/8	6 2/8	Washoe Co., NV	Gabriel A. Pincolini	Gabriel A. Pincolini	2004	190
82 6/8	83 4/8	15 3/8	15 3/8	6	6	3	3	10 6/8	5 4/8	6 3/8	6 3/8	Luna Co., NM	Lee Frudden	Lee Frudden	2005	190
82 6/8	84 1/8	14 2/8	15	7 4/8	7 4/8	2 6/8	2 6/8	12 7/8	10 4/8	5 4/8	5 1/8	Sweetwater Co., WY	Amanda K. Serres	Amanda K. Serres	2005	190
82 6/8	83 3/8	14 5/8	14 4/8	7 2/8	7 3/8	2 7/8	2 7/8	9 7/8	4 4/8	5 6/8	5 4/8	Carbon Co., WY	David H. Vieira, Jr.	David H. Vieira, Jr.	2005	190
82 6/8	83 4/8	17 1/8	16 7/8	6 1/8	5 7/8	2 7/8	2 7/8	14 4/8	9 7/8	5 1/8	5 2/8	Lincoln Co., NM	Neal W. Ackerly	Neal W. Ackerly	2006	190
82 6/8	83 2/8	14 7/8	15 1/8	6 5/8	6 4/8	2 5/8	2 5/8	12 5/8	8 4/8	6 2/8	6 3/8	Carbon Co., WY	James H. Cordonier, Sr.	James H. Cordonier, Sr.	2006	190
82 6/8	83 1/8	15 1/8	15 1/8	7	7	3	3	9 2/8	4 7/8	5 4/8	5 5/8	Moffat Co., CO	Kirk L. Phillips	Kirk L. Phillips	2006	190
82 4/8	83 2/8	16	15 3/8	6 5/8	6 6/8	2 6/8	2 6/8	11 2/8	8 2/8	5 5/8	5 5/8	Hudspeth Co., TX	Doyle D. Rollins	Doyle D. Rollins	2002	203
82 4/8	85	16 1/8	16 1/8	7 2/8	7 3/8	2 7/8	2 7/8	7 5/8	4 4/8	6 4/8	4 3/8	Cherry Co., NE	Darren R. Strizek	Darren R. Strizek	2003	203
82 4/8	83 2/8	16 3/8	16 1/8	6 5/8	6 6/8	2 5/8	2 4/8	7 1/8	2 1/8	5 4/8	5 4/8	Carbon Co., WY	Robert J. Anderson	Robert J. Anderson	2004	203
82 4/8	83 4/8	15 7/8	16 2/8	6 7/8	7	2 3/8	2 3/8	12 2/8	9 6/8	5 7/8	6 2/8	Natrona Co., WY	Justin R. Frick	Justin R. Frick	2004	203
82 4/8	83 2/8	15 4/8	15 3/8	6 7/8	6 5/8	2 7/8	2 7/8	10 2/8	5 6/8	5 3/8	5 5/8	Carter Co., MT	Scott H. Geston	Scott H. Geston	2004	203
82 4/8	83 5/8	16	16 1/8	6 5/8	6 3/8	2 4/8	2 5/8	12 1/8	9 4/8	6 1/8	5 6/8	Pershing Co., NV	Dean Henderson	Dean Henderson	2004	203
82 4/8	83 1/8	15 6/8	15 7/8	6 6/8	6 6/8	2 6/8	2 7/8	11 6/8	8 4/8	5 2/8	5	Johnson Co., WY	Cynthia J. McCombs	Cynthia J. McCombs	2004	203
82 4/8	83 5/8	14 2/8	14 2/8	7	6 7/8	2 6/8	2 6/8	9 3/8	5 3/8	6 6/8	6 2/8	Carbon Co., WY	Robert F. Richmond	Robert F. Richmond	2004	203
82 4/8	83 4/8	16 4/8	16 4/8	6 5/8	6 4/8	2 6/8	2 5/8	12 3/8	6 3/8	6	5 6/8	Humboldt Co., NV	Elwin A. Robison	Elwin A. Robison	2004	203

Rank	Score	Gross	Length R	Length L	Circ. Base R	Circ. Base L	Circ. 3rd R	Circ. 3rd L	Inside Spread	Tip to Tip	Prong R	Prong L	Locality	Hunter	Owner	Date Killed
203	82 4/8	83 6/8	15 5/8	16	6 7/8	6 7/8	2 4/8	2 4/8	12 4/8	8 1/8	5 3/8	5 5/8	Perkins Co., SD	Daniel F. Sehr	Daniel F. Sehr	2004
203	82 4/8	83 4/8	15 1/8	15 2/8	6 5/8	6 5/8	2 7/8	2 7/8	10 4/8	8 3/8	4 6/8	5 3/8	Campbell Co., WY	Vincent M. Stephan	Vincent M. Stephan	2004
203	82 4/8	83 6/8	15 6/8	15 3/8	6 6/8	6 6/8	2 4/8	2 4/8	13	9 7/8	6	5 3/8	Carbon Co., WY	Charles B. Black	Charles B. Black	2005
203	82 4/8	84 1/8	17 1/8	16 5/8	6 1/8	6	2 5/8	3	10	5	5 5/8	6 4/8	Catron Co., NM	David J. Grossenbach	David J. Grossenbach	2005
203	82 4/8	83 3/8	14 2/8	14 2/8	6 7/8	6 7/8	3	2 7/8	11	8 2/8	6 2/8	5 6/8	Box Elder Co., UT	David R. Harrow	David R. Harrow	2005
203	82 4/8	82 6/8	13 6/8	13 6/8	7 4/8	7 4/8	2 7/8	2 7/8	7 3/8	6 7/8	5 6/8	5 6/8	Carbon Co., WY	Jared J. Mason	Jared J. Mason	2005
203	82 4/8	82 4/8	15	15	6 3/8	6 3/8	2 7/8	2 7/8	11 1/8	7 4/8	6	6	Lincoln Co., NM	Russell A. Reed	Russell A. Reed	2005
203	82 4/8	83 4/8	16	15 6/8	7 3/8	7 3/8	2 7/8	2 5/8	11	6 7/8	5 2/8	5 2/8	Humboldt Co., NV	Duane F. Butler	Duane F. Butler	2006
203	82 4/8	83 3/8	15 4/8	15 3/8	6 6/8	6 6/8	2 4/8	2 5/8	12 2/8	11 3/8	5	5 4/8	Hudspeth Co., TX	William S. Pickett III	William S. Pickett III	2006
203	82 4/8	83 7/8	16 3/8	16 5/8	6 7/8	6 7/8	3	3	9 2/8	6 6/8	5 6/8	6	Carbon Co., WY	Danny D. Robinett	Danny D. Robinett	2006
222	82 2/8	82 7/8	16 3/8	16 2/8	5 7/8	5 7/8	2 5/8	2 6/8	10 2/8	6 2/8	4 2/8	4 2/8	Mora Co., NM	David P. McBrayer	David P. McBrayer	1992
222	82 2/8	83 7/8	16 4/8	17	6 4/8	6 4/8	2 4/8	2 4/8	11 4/8	8 2/8	5	5	Hudspeth Co., TX	Ralph W. Donaho	Ralph W. Donaho	2003
222	82 2/8	83	14 6/8	15	6 7/8	6 6/8	3 1/8	3 1/8	9 5/8	8	5 5/8	5 4/8	Socorro Co., NM	Todd A. Romsa	Todd A. Romsa	2003
222	82 2/8	83 2/8	14 6/8	14 6/8	6 7/8	6 7/8	2 6/8	2 6/8	15 7/8	12 3/8	4 6/8	4 2/8	Socorro Co., NM	Greg B. Buck	Greg B. Buck	2004
222	82 2/8	82 7/8	16 1/8	16	7 1/8	7 2/8	2 2/8	2 2/8	12 7/8	16 4/8	5 6/8	5 6/8	Sublette Co., WY	Robert D. Hammer	Robert D. Hammer	2004
222	82 2/8	84 3/8	16 6/8	16 1/8	7	7	2 6/8	2 6/8	11 7/8	8 2/8	5 4/8	5 5/8	Carbon Co., WY	Dan E. McBride	Dan E. McBride	2004
222	82 2/8	84	14 3/8	13 7/8	6 4/8	6 6/8	3	3	12	7	5 4/8	6 4/8	Colfax Co., NM	Kyra L. Weisdorfer	Kyra L. Weisdorfer	2004
222	82 2/8	83	16 1/8	16 3/8	6 5/8	6 6/8	2 6/8	2 6/8	8 3/8	2 1/8	5 4/8	5 4/8	Powder River Co., MT	Dale M. Berger	Dale M. Berger	2005
222	82 2/8	83 1/8	15 5/8	15 7/8	6 3/8	6 2/8	2 6/8	2 5/8	7 7/8	4 1/8	5 7/8	5 5/8	Meade Co., SD	Kerry D. Bowman	Kerry D. Bowman	2005
222	82 2/8	82 3/8	15 4/8	15 4/8	6 2/8	6 2/8	3 3/8	3 3/8	10 4/8	6 4/8	5 4/8	5 4/8	Sweetwater Co., WY	Len H. Guldman	Len H. Guldman	2005
222	82 2/8	83 1/8	15 4/8	15 5/8	7 3/8	7 4/8	2 5/8	2 7/8	9 7/8	6 4/8	5	5 2/8	Carter Co., MT	Todd L. Kanavel	Todd L. Kanavel	2005
222	82 2/8	83 7/8	16 4/8	16 5/8	6 3/8	6 5/8	2 5/8	2 6/8	10	5 1/8	6	7	Uinta Co., WY	Jeremy D. Matthews	Jeremy D. Matthews	2005
222	82 2/8	82 6/8	15 7/8	16	7	7	2 7/8	2 4/8	8	2 6/8	4 2/8	4 3/8	Presidio Co., TX	Heath A. Sisk	Heath A. Sisk	2005
222	82 2/8	83 3/8	16 4/8	16 1/8	7	7	2 4/8	2 4/8	10 1/8	5 2/8	5 1/8	5 1/8	Quay Co., NM	Scott D. Watkins	Scott D. Watkins	2005
222	82 2/8	83 2/8	16	15 7/8	7	7 1/8	2 5/8	2 5/8	11 1/8	10 1/8	5 6/8	5 5/8	Carbon Co., WY	Gregory W. Young	Gregory W. Young	2005
222	82 2/8	82 5/8	15 1/8	15	6 2/8	7 1/8	2 4/8	2 4/8	10 1/8	7 4/8	5 4/8	5 4/8	Lincoln Co., WY	Darrell G. Alder	Darrell G. Alder	2006
222	82 2/8	82 5/8	15 4/8	15 4/8	6 3/8	6 3/8	2 6/8	2 4/8	9 1/8	5	6 1/8	6 1/8	Hudspeth Co., TX	David R. Brimager	David R. Brimager	2006
222	82 2/8	83 5/8	16	15 3/8	7	7	2 4/8	2 6/8	12 2/8	9 1/8	5 5/8	5 4/8	Carbon Co., WY	Patrick T. Stanosheck	Patrick T. Stanosheck	2006
242	82	84 5/8	16 2/8	17 4/8	6 1/8	7 4/8	2 5/8	2 6/8	12	9 7/8	6	5 4/8	Lincoln Co., NM	Lori A. Winters	Lori A. Winters	2006
242	82	83 1/8	14 7/8	14 4/8	7 3/8	7 3/8	3 1/8	3 1/8	8 5/8	6 4/8	6	5 4/8	Carbon Co., WY	Gregory W. Young	Gregory W. Young	2006
242	82	83 2/8	15 6/8	15 7/8	6 4/8	6 4/8	2 6/8	2 4/8	10 2/8	14	5 4/8	5 7/8	Albany Co., WY	Lewis Porter	Lewis Porter	2006
242	82	82 5/8	15 3/8	15 3/8	7 1/8	7 1/8	2 7/8	2 3/8	5	10 7/8	5 2/8	5 3/8	Coconino Co., AZ	James Rinehart	James Rinehart	PR 1960
242	82	82 7/8	15 7/8	15 5/8	6 5/8	6 5/8	2 7/8	2 6/8	9 2/8	5	4 7/8	4 7/8	Sublette Co., WY	Mathew B. Dominy	Mathew B. Dominy	2000
242	82	82 6/8	15 2/8	15 1/8	6 6/8	6 6/8	2 4/8	3	12 7/8	9 4/8	4 5/8	4 7/8	Torrance Co., NM	Jeff A. Brown	Jeff A. Brown	2001
242	82	82 4/8	15 2/8	15 6/8	7 5/8	7 1/8	3 2/8	2 4/8	10 3/8	9 4/8	5	4 7/8	Lincoln Co., CO	Steve W. Brown	Steve W. Brown	2003
242	82	82 4/8	16	15 5/8	6 1/8	6 2/8	2 4/8	2 4/8	10 6/8	3 5/8	4 7/8	5	Niobrara Co., WY	Meridee Burgess	Meridee Burgess	2003
242	82	83 4/8	15 5/8	15 5/8	6 1/8	6 2/8	3 1/8	3	7 4/8	6	6 1/8	6	Socorro Co., NM	Rodney Damm	Rodney Damm	2003
242	82	83	14 3/8	14 3/8	7 4/8	7 1/8	2 6/8	2 5/8	11	8 4/8	4 6/8	4 3/8	Colfax Co., NM	Craig T. Huff	Craig T. Huff	2003
242	82	83 3/8	15	14 3/8	7 3/8	7 2/8	2 4/8	2 4/8	12 4/8	8 4/8	5 6/8	4 6/8	Elko Co., NV	Charles LaPorte	Charles LaPorte	2003
242	82	83 2/8	16	15	6 1/8	6 1/8	2 6/8	2 4/8	12 4/8	8 4/8	5 6/8	6	Grant Co., NM	Joe R. Bennett	Joe R. Bennett	2004
242	82	83 5/8	16 5/8	16 5/8	6 3/8	6 1/8	2 7/8	2 6/8	17 6/8	14	5 7/8	5 7/8	Fremont Co., WY	Thomas P. Grainger	Thomas P. Grainger	2004
242	82	82 1/8	14 4/8	14 3/8	7	7	3 1/8	3 1/8	10 5/8	10	5	5	Fremont Co., WY	Keith D. Harrow	Keith D. Harrow	2004

PRONGHORN

Antilocapra americana americana and related subspecies

Final Score	Gross Score	Length of horn R.	L.	Circumference of Base R.	L.	Circumference at Third Quarter R.	L.	Inside Spread	Tip to Tip Spread	Length of Prong R.	L.	Locality	Hunter	Owner	Date Killed	Rank
82	82³/₈	15²/₈	15¹/₈	6⁶/₈	6⁶/₈	2⁶/₈	2⁶/₈	7⁷/₈	7	5³/₈	5³/₈	Carbon Co., WY	Bert Herrera	Bert Herrera	2004	242
82	82⁶/₈	16	16²/₈	6³/₈	6⁴/₈	3	3¹/₈	10³/₈	10⁴/₈	4⁷/₈	4⁷/₈	Hudspeth Co., TX	Gerald P. McBride	Gerald P. McBride	2004	242
82	82⁵/₈	16⁴/₈	16	6²/₈	6²/₈	2³/₈	2³/₈	8⁴/₈	4⁶/₈	6	6	Pershing Co., NV	Jesse D. Norcutt	Jesse D. Norcutt	2004	242
82	82⁵/₈	15	15²/₈	6³/₈	6³/₈	2⁷/₈	2⁶/₈	12⁵/₈	10⁵/₈	6²/₈	6²/₈	Carbon Co., WY	William S. Pickett III	William S. Pickett III	2004	242
82	82⁶/₈	14⁶/₈	15	6⁵/₈	6⁶/₈	2⁷/₈	2⁷/₈	11	6⁶/₈	5⁵/₈	5⁷/₈	Sweetwater Co., WY	Miles Searle	Miles Searle	2004	242
82	82⁷/₈	15²/₈	15³/₈	6⁷/₈	6⁶/₈	2⁵/₈	2⁷/₈	8	3⁴/₈	5⁷/₈	6¹/₈	Carbon Co., WY	Charlie G. Staser	Charlie G. Staser	2004	242
82	82²/₈	17⁶/₈	17⁵/₈	6	6	2⁶/₈	2⁶/₈	9³/₈	3⁴/₈	4⁶/₈	4⁶/₈	Lincoln Co., NM	Richard M. Young, Jr.	Richard M. Young, Jr.	2004	242
82	82²/₈	16	16	6	6	2⁷/₈	2⁷/₈	12⁶/₈	12³/₈	5⁴/₈	5⁵/₈	Custer Co., MT	Rob Arnaud	Rob Arnaud	2005	242
82	82⁵/₈	15⁴/₈	15⁴/₈	6⁶/₈	6⁷/₈	2⁴/₈	2⁵/₈	12²/₈	8²/₈	5⁷/₈	6²/₈	Campbell Co., WY	Mark H.A. Bolding	Mark H.A. Bolding	2005	242
82	83¹/₈	16⁵/₈	16³/₈	6⁴/₈	6⁵/₈	2⁵/₈	2⁵/₈	7¹/₈	2⁷/₈	5⁴/₈	5⁷/₈	Lassen Co., CA	Jeffrey B. Buck	Jeffrey B. Buck	2005	242
82	82⁷/₈	16	15⁷/₈	6⁶/₈	6⁷/₈	2⁶/₈	2⁷/₈	8⁶/₈	4³/₈	5³/₈	5⁴/₈	Sweetwater Co., WY	Andrew Day	Andrew Day	2005	242
82	82⁷/₈	15⁷/₈	15⁷/₈	6⁷/₈	6⁶/₈	2⁷/₈	3²/₈	9⁶/₈	3⁷/₈	4⁷/₈	4⁵/₈	Humboldt Co., NV	Keith D. Harrow	Keith D. Harrow	2005	242
82	83³/₈	15⁴/₈	16	6⁴/₈	6⁴/₈	2⁴/₈	2⁶/₈	12⁵/₈	9³/₈	6²/₈	6	Sweetwater Co., WY	Kathy A. Hawley	Kathy A. Hawley	2005	242
82	83	14⁵/₈	14	7²/₈	7¹/₈	2⁵/₈	2⁵/₈	13⁵/₈	11⁶/₈	5⁵/₈	5⁵/₈	Natrona Co., WY	Chad A. Lewis	Chad A. Lewis	2005	242
82	83⁷/₈	17	17³/₈	6⁶/₈	7²/₈	2⁶/₈	2⁶/₈	15¹/₈	13³/₈	4⁵/₈	5³/₈	Navajo Co., AZ	Darrel M. Lippert	Darrel M. Lippert	2005	242
82	82⁵/₈	16³/₈	16²/₈	5⁷/₈	5⁷/₈	2⁶/₈	2⁶/₈	12³/₈	8³/₈	5³/₈	5²/₈	Catron Co., NM	Harry R. Martz, Jr.	Harry R. Martz, Jr.	2005	242
82	82³/₈	16¹/₈	16³/₈	6⁴/₈	6⁴/₈	2⁷/₈	3	11²/₈	10³/₈	4⁶/₈	4⁶/₈	Carbon Co., WY	Garland E. Sawyers	Garland E. Sawyers	2005	242
82	82⁶/₈	16⁴/₈	16¹/₈	6³/₈	6²/₈	2³/₈	2³/₈	20⁶/₈	21⁶/₈	5¹/₈	5¹/₈	Lincoln Co., NM	Michael J. Van Der Sanden	Michael J. Van Der Sanden	2005	242
82	82²/₈	16⁶/₈	16⁷/₈	6⁴/₈	6⁴/₈	2⁶/₈	2⁶/₈	10³/₈	5	5	4⁷/₈	Lincoln Co., NM	Curt L. Dinges	Curt L. Dinges	2006	242
82	82⁷/₈	15	14⁷/₈	7⁴/₈	7⁴/₈	2⁶/₈	2⁶/₈	8²/₈	3⁶/₈	5⁶/₈	5⁶/₈	Campbell Co., WY	Edward A. Lemaster	Edward A. Lemaster	2006	242
82	83⁶/₈	14⁷/₈	15⁴/₈	6⁴/₈	6³/₈	3¹/₈	2⁷/₈	10⁴/₈	8⁶/₈	6²/₈	5⁶/₈	Johnson Co., WY	J. Scott McIlvoy	J. Scott McIlvoy	2006	242
82	83⁷/₈	15⁵/₈	15⁷/₈	6⁵/₈	6⁵/₈	2⁴/₈	2⁶/₈	14³/₈	11	6¹/₈	5¹/₈	Great Sand Hills, SK	Kelsey M. Seidle	Kelsey M. Seidle	2006	242
82	84	14⁴/₈	14¹/₈	7⁶/₈	7⁶/₈	2⁴/₈	2⁵/₈	11	8	5³/₈	5⁶/₈	Carbon Co., WY	Timothy W. Stanosheck	Timothy W. Stanosheck	2006	242
81⁶/₈	82⁶/₈	15⁷/₈	15⁶/₈	6⁴/₈	6²/₈	2⁶/₈	2⁶/₈	8⁷/₈	7¹/₈	5⁵/₈	5⁵/₈	Fremont Co., WY	Greg E. Fuechsel	Greg E. Fuechsel	2004	276
81⁶/₈	83⁶/₈	15⁷/₈	16¹/₈	7	7	3³/₈	2⁵/₈	9⁵/₈	8⁵/₈	5²/₈	5	Socorro Co., NM	Keith D. Harrow	Keith D. Harrow	2004	276
81⁶/₈	82³/₈	16⁵/₈	16³/₈	6⁶/₈	6⁶/₈	2⁶/₈	3¹/₈	13	9⁶/₈	4⁷/₈	5	Socorro Co., NM	Bryan A. Kinsey	Bryan A. Kinsey	2004	276
81⁶/₈	82	14⁶/₈	14⁶/₈	6⁵/₈	6⁴/₈	2⁶/₈	2⁶/₈	10	6⁴/₈	6²/₈	6³/₈	Garfield Co., MT	Delmar H. Lemons	Delmar H. Lemons	2004	276
81⁶/₈	82¹/₈	15²/₈	15³/₈	6⁶/₈	6⁶/₈	2³/₈	2⁴/₈	11⁷/₈	7⁴/₈	6³/₈	6³/₈	Perkins Co., SD	Matthew M. Wipf	Matthew M. Wipf	2004	276
81⁶/₈	82¹/₈	14⁷/₈	14⁷/₈	6⁴/₈	6⁴/₈	2⁷/₈	2⁷/₈	11	8⁴/₈	5¹/₈	5	Colfax Co., NM	Darren A. Cross	Darren A. Cross	2005	276
81⁶/₈	82⁴/₈	15⁵/₈	15⁷/₈	6⁶/₈	6⁶/₈	2⁷/₈	3	12	10⁴/₈	5⁶/₈	6	Custer Co., CO	Craig D. Stuart	Craig D. Stuart	2005	276

81 6/8	82 5/8	16 3/8	16 4/8	6 2/8	2 4/8	9 5/8	5 5/8	George A. Baldonado	Torrance Co., NM	2006	276
81 6/8	82	16	15 7/8	6 6/8	2 4/8	10 4/8	5 4/8	Paul J. Courpet	Lassen Co., CA	2006	276
81 6/8	82 1/8	16 3/8	16 1/8	6 3/8	2 5/8	8 2/8	5 3/8	Scott B. Nelson	Washoe Co., NV	2006	276
81 4/8	82 3/8	17	16 4/8	6 4/8	2 5/8	9 2/8	5 1/8	Charles R. Scoggins	Lincoln Co., NM	2003	286
81 4/8	82 6/8	16 2/8	16	7	2 4/8	9 5/8	4 7/8	David A. Barno	Harney Co., OR	2004	286
81 4/8	83 2/8	16 3/8	17	6 7/8	2 3/8	8 6/8	5 2/8	Peter H. Johnson	Jackson Co., CO	2004	286
81 4/8	82 1/8	15 7/8	15 6/8	6 2/8	2 5/8	10 6/8	4 6/8	Robert E. Likens	Elbert Co., CO	2004	286
81 4/8	83 1/8	14 6/8	14 4/8	7	2 6/8	8 4/8	5 5/8	Rickey D. Loock	Sioux Co., NE	2004	286
81 4/8	82 1/8	15 1/8	15	6 7/8	3	9 2/8	6 1/8	J. Mike Clegg	Carbon Co., WY	2005	286
81 4/8	82 2/8	15 3/8	15 3/8	6 3/8	2 5/8	12 1/8	6	Robert D. Jones	Colfax Co., NM	2005	286
81 4/8	82 5/8	15 3/8	15 3/8	6 5/8	2 7/8	13 3/8	4 6/8	Remo R. Pizzagalli	Grant Co., NM	2005	286
81 4/8	83 5/8	14 7/8	14 7/8	6 6/8	2 6/8	10 4/8	6 1/8	Bruce J. Pranger	Perkins Co., SD	2005	286
81 4/8	82 2/8	16 4/8	16 1/8	7 4/8	2 3/8	11 7/8	4 4/8	Scott L. Allen	Malheur Co., OR	2006	286
81 4/8	82 2/8	15 7/8	16	6 4/8	2 4/8	9 3/8	5 6/8	Andy P. Johnson	Uinta Co., WY	2006	286
81 2/8	81 6/8	15 5/8	15 5/8	6 6/8	2 5/8	10 5/8	5 5/8	Jeff Ensor	Converse Co., WY	2000	297
81 2/8	82 4/8	16	16 4/8	6 6/8	2 6/8	13 7/8	5	Sherry E. Buck	Socorro Co., NM	2003	297
81 2/8	82 1/8	16 4/8	16 1/8	6 2/8	2 6/8	10 7/8	5 3/8	Larissa J. Thompson	Rosebud Co., MT	2003	297
81 2/8	81 5/8	15 2/8	15 5/8	6 5/8	2 4/8	7 6/8	5 7/8	Lori A. Campbell	Lincoln Co., WY	2004	297
81 2/8	82 6/8	15 6/8	15 5/8	6 7/8	2 5/8	8	5 5/8	Pamela S. Coburn	Carbon Co., UT	2004	297
81 2/8	83 1/8	16 3/8	17 6/8	5 6/8	2 3/8	14 2/8	5 4/8	Justin J. Del Re	Catron Co., NM	2004	297
81 2/8	81 7/8	15 4/8	15 5/8	6 5/8	2 6/8	9 4/8	5 2/8	Austin W. Patzer	Carbon Co., WY	2004	297

PRONGHORN
FINAL SCORE: 82
HUNTER: Joe R. Bennett

PRONGHORN
FINAL SCORE: 85
HUNTER: Lyle C. Foster

PRONGHORN
FINAL SCORE: 84-2/8
HUNTER: Joe E. Wimpee

PRONGHORN
FINAL SCORE: 80-4/8
HUNTER: Joel D. Harris

PRONGHORN

Antilocapra americana americana and related subspecies

Final Score	Gross Score	Length of horn R.	L.	Circumference of Base R.	L.	Circumference at Third Quarter R.	L.	Tip to Tip Spread	Inside Spread	Length of Prong R.	L.	Locality	Hunter	Owner	Date Killed	Rank
81 2/8	82 3/8	15 6/8	15 5/8	6 4/8	6 3/8	2 4/8	2 5/8	9 7/8	12 4/8	6 4/8	5 7/8	Park Co., CO	David H. Reekers, Jr.	David H. Reekers, Jr.	2004	297
81 2/8	82 2/8	16 4/8	16 5/8	6	5 7/8	2 5/8	2 4/8	7 5/8	12	6	6	Lake Co., OR	Mary A. Wood	Mary A. Wood	2004	297
81 2/8	82 7/8	17 4/8	17 1/8	6 3/8	6 2/8	2 4/8	2 4/8	2	7	5 3/8	4 6/8	Harding Co., NM	Jules L. Farmer	Jules L. Farmer	2005	297
81 2/8	81 6/8	16 1/8	16	6 4/8	6 3/8	2 4/8	2 4/8	5 6/8	9 6/8	5 7/8	5 7/8	Fremont Co., WY	Dale Hislop	Dale Hislop	2005	297
81 2/8	81 7/8	14 7/8	14 6/8	6 4/8	6 4/8	3	2 7/8	6 7/8	10 3/8	5	5	Carbon Co., WY	Rip P. Miller	Rip P. Miller	2005	297
81 2/8	83 2/8	14 6/8	14 4/8	6	5 6/8	2 4/8	2 6/8	3 4/8	9 2/8	8 4/8	7 4/8	Humboldt Co., NV	Jeff M. Snyder	Jeff M. Snyder	2005	297
81 2/8	82 2/8	13 7/8	14 1/8	7	6 6/8	3	3	8 6/8	11 1/8	5 5/8	5 3/8	Weld Co., CO	David L. Birdsall	David L. Birdsall	2006	297
81 2/8	82 3/8	14 6/8	14 6/8	6 5/8	6 3/8	2 4/8	3	10 5/8	13 2/8	6	5 5/8	Fremont Co., WY	Gerald R. Gold	Gerald R. Gold	2006	297
81 2/8	83	16 3/8	15 7/8	6 3/8	6 2/8	3 1/8	3	3 2/8	7 7/8	5 4/8	5 3/8	Jones Co., SD	Clayton D. Miller	Clayton D. Miller	2006	297
81 2/8	81 6/8	15 1/8	15 2/8	6 4/8	6 4/8	2 4/8	2 5/8	8	12 2/8	5 6/8	5 6/8	Carbon Co., WY	Eric D. Stanosheck	Eric D. Stanosheck	2006	297
81	81 6/8	16 3/8	16 4/8	6 2/8	6	3	3	5 5/8	10 1/8	5 2/8	5 2/8	Washoe Co., NV	Ken Cassas	Ken Cassas	2003	314
81	81 4/8	16 3/8	16 4/8	6 5/8	6 5/8	2 5/8	2 6/8	6 4/8	11 4/8	4	4 1/8	Coconino Co., AZ	John P. Clark	John P. Clark	2003	314
81	82	14 4/8	14 5/8	7 2/8	7 1/8	2 6/8	2 6/8	6 5/8	10 1/8	5	5 5/8	Washoe Co., NV	Beth A. Bridges	Beth A. Bridges	2004	314
81	81 5/8	15 4/8	15 2/8	6 4/8	6 4/8	2 5/8	2 6/8	8 6/8	11 4/8	5	5	Carbon Co., WY	Danette L. Perrien	Danette L. Perrien	2004	314
81	83 1/8	14	15 3/8	7 3/8	7 2/8	2 6/8	2 7/8	4 6/8	8 7/8	5 4/8	5 7/8	Humboldt Co., NV	Duane F. Butler	Duane F. Butler	2005	314
81	81 6/8	14 5/8	14 5/8	7 2/8	7 2/8	2 6/8	2 6/8	8 5/8	12 3/8	5 3/8	5	Powder River Co., MT	Bernard Crane	Jack H. Crane	2005	314
81	81 6/8	16 1/8	15 7/8	6 5/8	6 6/8	2 4/8	2 6/8	4 3/8	9	5 2/8	5 3/8	Carbon Co., WY	Michael J. Eckert	Michael J. Eckert	2005	314
81	81 3/8	15	14 6/8	6 6/8	6 6/8	2 6/8	2 6/8	11 6/8	14 4/8	5 7/8	5 7/8	Perkins Co., SD	Michael J. Erhart	Michael J. Erhart	2005	314
81	81 1/8	15 1/8	15 1/8	6 4/8	6 4/8	2 6/8	2 6/8	6 5/8	11 5/8	5 7/8	5 7/8	Lincoln Co., CO	Brandon D. McCullough	Brandon D. McCullough	2005	314
81	82	15 7/8	15 7/8	6	5 7/8	3	2 7/8	2 6/8	7 5/8	5 4/8	5 4/8	Carbon Co., WY	Robert F. Richmond	Robert F. Richmond	2005	314
81	81 2/8	15 6/8	15 6/8	6 3/8	6 2/8	2 5/8	2 5/8	3 5/8	8 5/8	5 3/8	5 3/8	Sweetwater Co., WY	William J. Swartz, Jr.	William J. Swartz, Jr.	2005	314
81	82	15 1/8	15	7 2/8	7 1/8	3	3	5 2/8	8 5/8	5	4 4/8	Humboldt Co., NV	Keith D. Harrow	Keith D. Harrow	2006	314
81	83	15	15	7 6/8	7 6/8	2 4/8	2 1/8	7 6/8	11	4 5/8	5 2/8	Carbon Co., WY	Michael H. Ryder	Michael H. Ryder	2006	314
80 6/8	81 5/8	16	16 3/8	6 6/8	6 4/8	2 6/8	2 6/8	5 7/8	9 2/8	5 1/8	5 2/8	Fremont Co., WY	Michael T. Berthod	Michael T. Berthod	2003	327
80 6/8	82	16 2/8	16	6 4/8	6 4/8	2 7/8	2 5/8	6 2/8	11	4 7/8	5 2/8	Phillips Co., MT	Tom Schumacher	Kevin L. Salsbery	2003	327
80 6/8	82 2/8	16	15 3/8	6 2/8	6 3/8	2 4/8	2 4/8	12 2/8	13 1/8	6	6 2/8	Washakie Co., WY	Mark I. Walker	Mark I. Walker	2003	327
80 6/8	81 2/8	15 6/8	16	6 3/8	6 2/8	2 6/8	2 6/8	7 5/8	9 5/8	5 3/8	5 3/8	El Paso Co., CO	Dennis K. Hess	Dennis K. Hess	2004	327
80 6/8	82 3/8	15 2/8	15 4/8	6 7/8	6 7/8	2 7/8	2 7/8	4 1/8	9	5 4/8	4 4/8	Colfax Co., NM	Robert D. Jones	Robert D. Jones	2004	327
80 6/8	81 2/8	14 6/8	14 6/8	6 4/8	6 3/8	2 7/8	2 7/8	6 4/8	9 6/8	5	4 1/8	Uinta Co., WY	Gary D. Whited	Gary D. Whited	2004	327
80 6/8	82 7/8	15	15 7/8	7	7	2 7/8	2 7/8	12 4/8	16 3/8	5 6/8	5 6/8	Hudspeth Co., TX	Donald W. Buckner	Donald W. Buckner	2005	327
80 6/8	81 5/8	16 7/8	16 5/8	5 7/8	6	3	3	8 7/8	12 6/8	4 6/8	4 6/8	Hudspeth Co., TX	John D. Clader	John D. Clader	2005	327

Score	Gross Score	Length of Horn R	Length of Horn L	Circ. of Base R	Circ. of Base L	Circ. 3rd Qtr R	Circ. 3rd Qtr L	Length of Prong R	Length of Prong L	Tip to Tip Spread	Inside Spread	Locality	Hunter	Owner	Date Killed	Rank
80 6/8	82 1/8	14	14 4/8	6 6/8	6 6/8	2 4/8	2 6/8	6	6 3/8	6 6/8	11 3/8	Phillips Co., MT	Kaylee J. Olson	Kaylee J. Olson	2005	327
80 6/8	82 1/8	15 3/8	15 5/8	7	7	2 4/8	2 6/8	5 6/8	5 1/8	8 2/8	11 2/8	Carbon Co., WY	Jimmy E. Roberts	Jimmy E. Roberts	2005	327
80 6/8	82 1/8	17 2/8	16 4/8	5 6/8	5 6/8	2 5/8	2 5/8	5 5/8	5 2/8	2 1/8	7 2/8	Lassen Co., CA	Jim G. Sims	Jim G. Sims	2005	327
80 6/8	81 6/8	15 3/8	15 4/8	6 2/8	6 1/8	2 7/8	2 6/8	6	6 2/8	2 5/8	7 3/8	Albany Co., WY	Allen O. Brandt	Allen O. Brandt	2006	327
80 6/8	82	15 3/8	15 5/8	6 6/8	6 7/8	2 4/8	2 6/8	5 7/8	5 3/8	4 7/8	8 7/8	Grand Co., CO	Kameal J. Clark	Kameal J. Clark	2006	327
80 6/8	82 2/8	15 3/8	15 5/8	6 2/8	6 1/8	2 5/8	2 6/8	5 4/8	4 3/8	6 4/8	10	Albany Co., WY	Lance M. Gatlin	Lance M. Gatlin	2006	327
80 6/8	81 5/8	16 1/8	16 2/8	6	6	2 7/8	3	5 1/8	4 2/8	5 1/8	10 3/8	Natrona Co., WY	John G. LaLonde	John G. LaLonde	2006	327
80 4/8	81 3/8	14 6/8	14 4/8	6 6/8	6 6/8	2 4/8	2 3/8	5 3/8	6 3/8	9 4/8	13 2/8	Blaine Co., MT	Joel D. Sullivan	Joel D. Sullivan	2003	342
80 4/8	81 3/8	14 4/8	14 6/8	6 4/8	6 4/8	3	3	4 5/8	5 3/8	10 2/8	12 3/8	Natrona Co., WY	Tom L. Swartz	Tom L. Swartz	2003	342
80 4/8	80 7/8	14 7/8	15 2/8	6 6/8	6 5/8	3	3	5 3/8	5 3/8	12 3/8	11 5/8	Cibola Co., NM	Robert M. Aikin	Robert M. Aikin	2004	342
80 4/8	81 6/8	14 7/8	14 4/8	6 6/8	6 4/8	2 7/8	2 7/8	6 5/8	6 5/8	11 5/8	9	Rio Grande Co., CO	Robert Crask	Robert Crask	2004	342
80 4/8	82 2/8	13 2/8	12 7/8	7 1/8	7	2 4/8	2 6/8	6 5/8	6	5 2/8	10 7/8	Fremont Co., WY	Steve D. Krier	Steve D. Krier	2004	342
80 4/8	82 2/8	15 6/8	15 5/8	6 4/8	6 5/8	2 2/8	2 3/8	5 7/8	5 5/8	10 7/8	9 3/8	Carbon Co., WY	Valerie A. Mason	Valerie A. Mason	2004	342
80 4/8	81 1/8	15 2/8	15 4/8	6 5/8	6 4/8	2 4/8	2 5/8	5 4/8	5 7/8	5 2/8	9	Natrona Co., WY	Gary Nehring	Gary Nehring	2004	342
80 4/8	81 1/8	15	15	6 4/8	6 4/8	2 4/8	2 6/8	5 2/8	5 2/8	6 3/8	8 5/8	Blaine Co., ID	Scott J. Scifres	Scott J. Scifres	2004	342
80 4/8	82 3/8	14 2/8	14 7/8	6 4/8	6 4/8	2 7/8	2 6/8	6 3/8	6 3/8	3 1/8	9 3/8	Campbell Co., WY	Joel D. Harris	Joel D. Harris	2005	342
80 4/8	81 2/8	15	15 5/8	6 4/8	6 4/8	2 7/8	2 7/8	5	5 2/8	5	12 2/8	Carbon Co., WY	Pat P. Jaure	Pat P. Jaure	2005	342
80 4/8	81 1/8	15 4/8	15 5/8	6 4/8	6 4/8	3	3	5 3/8	5	9 2/8	11 4/8	Bigstick Lake, SK	Kevin J. Paslawski	Kevin J. Paslawski	2005	342
80 4/8	81	16 5/8	16 4/8	5 7/8	6	2 3/8	2 4/8	4 7/8	5 2/8	7 5/8	13 2/8	Lake Co., OR	Pamela M. Uebler	Pamela M. Uebler	2005	342
80 4/8	81 1/8	14 2/8	14 1/8	7	7	2 6/8	2 6/8	5 3/8	4 6/8	7 7/8	10 1/8	Carbon Co., WY	Tom P. Entinger	Tom P. Entinger	2006	342
80 4/8	81 1/8	15	15	6 3/8	6 3/8	2 7/8	2 6/8	5 1/8	6	7 1/8	7 6/8	Humboldt Co., NV	Scott L. George	Scott L. George	2006	342
80 4/8	81 6/8	17 2/8	17 1/8	6 5/8	6 4/8	2 4/8	2 4/8	5 4/8	4 3/8	3	10 2/8	Baker Co., OR	Byron J. Henry	Byron J. Henry	2006	342
80 4/8	81 4/8	15 4/8	15 3/8	6 1/8	6 1/8	2 6/8	2 6/8	4 3/8	5 3/8	3 7/8	8 2/8	Custer Co., CO	John M. Lamb	John M. Lamb	2006	342
80 4/8	80 5/8	15 4/8	15 5/8	6 3/8	6 3/8	3	3 4/8	5 3/8	5 5/8	5	10 6/8	Union Co., NM	Mark Sanders	Mark Sanders	2006	342
80 2/8	81	16 5/8	15 6/8	6 2/8	6 2/8	3 4/8	3 4/8	5 4/8	5 7/8	5 3/8	9 3/8	Valley Co., MT	Don L. Elletson	Don L. Elletson	1978	359
80 2/8	82 1/8	17	17 1/8	6 1/8	6 1/8	3	2 7/8	5 6/8	4	2 7/8	10 5/8	Yavapai Co., AZ	Thomas E. Butler	Thomas E. Butler	2000	359
80 2/8	81	16	15 6/8	6 4/8	6 5/8	2 7/8	3	4 3/8	4 6/8	5 4/8	9 3/8	Union Co., NM	Myra E. Lowery	Myra E. Lowery	2002	359
80 2/8	81	15 4/8	15 3/8	6 3/8	6 3/8	2 4/8	2 6/8	4 6/8	5 1/8	8 3/8	16 3/8	Mora Co., NM	Kenneth L. Ebbens	Kenneth L. Ebbens	2003	359
80 2/8	80 6/8	16 5/8	16 5/8	6	5 7/8	3	2 6/8	5 2/8	4 6/8	14	13 7/8	Grant Co., NM	Lanny S. Rominger	Lanny S. Rominger	2003	359
80 2/8	81	14	14	6 3/8	6 4/8	2 6/8	3	4 4/8	4 4/8	11 6/8	11 6/8	Brewster Co., TX	Larry A. Yahnian	Larry A. Yahnian	2004	359
80 2/8	81 4/8	14 7/8	14 7/8	6 4/8	6 3/8	2 6/8	2 4/8	4 3/8	5 3/8	9	8 5/8	Carbon Co., WY	Larry S. Hicks	Larry S. Hicks	2004	359
80 2/8	81 3/8	14 7/8	14 7/8	6 1/8	6	3	3	5 2/8	4 6/8	6 3/8	10 5/8	Washoe Co., NV	Lynn C. Jasmine	Lynn C. Jasmine	2004	359
80 2/8	80 5/8	15 6/8	15 6/8	6 7/8	6 3/8	2 6/8	2 4/8	4 5/8	4 6/8	4 6/8	10 2/8	Carbon Co., UT	Debbie Lofley	Debbie Lofley	2004	359
80 2/8	82 1/8	15 4/8	15 2/8	6 4/8	6 4/8	3	2 6/8	5 6/8	4 6/8	8 5/8	12	Lincoln Co., NM	Donald E. Perrien	Donald E. Perrien	2004	359
80 2/8	81	15	15 4/8	6 4/8	6 7/8	2 4/8	3	5 3/8	5 7/8	6 2/8	9	Converse Co., WY	Norman L. Thurston, Jr.	Norman L. Thurston, Jr.	2004	359
80 2/8	80 4/8	15 1/8	15 1/8	6 4/8	6 4/8	2 5/8	2 5/8	4 7/8	5 1/8	6 1/8	8 5/8	Slope Co., ND	Craig A. Wendt	Craig A. Wendt	2004	359
80 2/8	80 5/8	16 6/8	16 5/8	5 6/8	5 6/8	2 5/8	2 5/8	5 2/8	5 3/8	9 1/8	13	Catron Co., NM	Shelley L. Hall	Shelley L. Hall	2005	359
80 2/8	80 7/8	14 6/8	14 6/8	6 3/8	6 3/8	3 1/8	2 7/8	5 4/8	5 5/8	4 6/8	9 3/8	Blaine Co., MT	Glenn A. Perry	Glenn A. Perry	2005	359
80 2/8	81 2/8	15 3/8	15 6/8	6 4/8	6 4/8	3 1/8	2 7/8	5	5 1/8	3 6/8	8	Sweetwater Co., WY	Duane F. Butler	Duane F. Butler	2006	359
80 2/8	81	16 7/8	16 5/8	6 4/8	6 4/8	2 4/8	2 4/8	4 6/8	5 1/8	6	12	Carbon Co., WY	Desiree N. Cragoe	Desiree N. Cragoe	2006	359
80 2/8	80 6/8	14 7/8	14 7/8	6 4/8	6 4/8	2 2/8	2 3/8	5 7/8	5 6/8	3	7 3/8	Baker Co., OR	Scott W. Green	Scott W. Green	2006	359

Final Score	Gross Score	Length of horn R.	L.	Circumference of Base R.	L.	Circumference at Third Quarter R.	L.	Inside Spread	Tip to Tip Spread	Length of Prong R.	L.	Locality	Hunter	Owner	Date Killed	Rank
80 2/8	82	15 5/8	15 1/8	6 4/8	6 2/8	2 6/8	2 5/8	11 1/8	5 6/8	5 1/8	4 5/8	Iron Co., UT	Rulon C. Jones	Rulon C. Jones	2006	359
80 2/8	81 3/8	17	16 5/8	6 1/8	6	2 5/8	2 3/8	15 5/8	10 7/8	5 3/8	5 4/8	Apache Co., AZ	Linda K. Sipe	Linda K. Sipe	2006	359
80 2/8	81 5/8	16 6/8	16 4/8	6	6	3 1/8	2 7/8	10 2/8	5 1/8	4 6/8	4 1/8	Guadalupe Co., NM	Rick A. Urban	Rick A. Urban	2006	359
80	80 6/8	14 2/8	14 2/8	6 4/8	6 4/8	2 5/8	2 4/8	8 1/8	4 4/8	5 4/8	6	Carbon Co., WY	Gerald A. Steele	Gerald A. Steele	2002	379
80	81	14 6/8	14 6/8	6 4/8	6 1/8	3	3	10 2/8	6 4/8	5 6/8	5 4/8	Sweetwater Co., WY	Stephen F. Bennett, Sr.	Stephen F. Bennett, Sr.	2003	379
80	80 4/8	15 5/8	15 6/8	6 1/8	6 2/8	2 4/8	2 4/8	14 5/8	11 2/8	5 3/8	5 2/8	Grant Co., NM	Mike Goodart	Mike Goodart	2003	379
80	81 4/8	15 2/8	14 7/8	6 1/8	6 3/8	2 5/8	2 4/8	12 3/8	9	5 5/8	5 4/8	Sierra Co., NM	Joe M. Keathley	Joe M. Keathley	2003	379
80	80 7/8	14 6/8	15	6 3/8	6 4/8	2 6/8	2 7/8	13 1/8	9 6/8	5 1/8	5 1/8	Humboldt Co., NV	Richard E. Krajewski	Richard E. Krajewski	2003	379
80	81 3/8	16	16	6 4/8	6 4/8	2 6/8	2 7/8	10 5/8	4 7/8	5 5/8	4 5/8	Sweetwater Co., WY	Nicole L. Peterson	Nicole L. Peterson	2003	379
80	80 4/8	16	15 7/8	6 2/8	6 2/8	2 4/8	2 4/8	11 3/8	8	4 7/8	5	Washoe Co., NV	Gregory J. Shutt	Gregory J. Shutt	2003	379
80	80 7/8	15 2/8	15 1/8	6 4/8	6 3/8	2 5/8	2 5/8	9 2/8	4	5 6/8	5 4/8	Elko Co., NV	Jesse L. Hellwinkel	Jesse L. Hellwinkel	2004	379
80	81 5/8	14 1/8	14 4/8	7 5/8	7 4/8	3 4/8	3 4/8	6 4/8	2	3 2/8	4 1/8	Campbell Co., WY	Gregg C. Homola	Gregg C. Homola	2004	379
80	80 3/8	15 1/8	15 1/8	6 4/8	6 3/8	2 5/8	2 4/8	10 4/8	6 1/8	6	5 7/8	Garden Co., NE	Marvin C. Larabee, Jr.	Marvin C. Larabee, Jr.	2004	379
80	81 3/8	14 3/8	14 5/8	7 1/8	7 1/8	2 6/8	2 7/8	7 5/8	4 2/8	4 5/8	5 2/8	Campbell Co., WY	Scott Paulin	Scott Paulin	2004	379
80	81 1/8	14 7/8	15 3/8	6 5/8	6 6/8	2 4/8	2 6/8	10 6/8	7 3/8	5 6/8	5 6/8	Weston Co., WY	Tim L. Vernon	Tim L. Vernon	2004	379
80	80 6/8	15 7/8	16	6 4/8	6 5/8	2 3/8	2 2/8	12 3/8	8	4 6/8	4 7/8	Harney Co., OR	Michael D. Wilson	Michael D. Wilson	2004	379
80	81	16 5/8	16 5/8	6 4/8	6 3/8	2 4/8	2 4/8	8	2 2/8	5 3/8	4 6/8	Conejos Co., CO	Eric H. Boley	Eric H. Boley	2005	379
80	81	15 2/8	15 1/8	6 3/8	6 2/8	3 1/8	2 7/8	14 3/8	11 7/8	5 1/8	5	Sherman Co., KS	Larry W. Crouse	Larry W. Crouse	2005	379
80	80 7/8	15 5/8	15	7 1/8	7 1/8	2 4/8	2 4/8	6 4/8	6 8/8	4 5/8	4 6/8	Humboldt Co., NV	David R. Hoid	David R. Hoid	2005	379
80	80 1/8	15 2/8	15 2/8	6 7/8	6 7/8	2 2/8	2 2/8	12	7 4/8	5 2/8	5 3/8	Washoe Co., NV	Bowen S. Kindred	Bowen S. Kindred	2005	379
80	80 6/8	14 6/8	14 4/8	6 2/8	6 1/8	2 6/8	2 6/8	11 1/8	8 6/8	6 3/8	6 3/8	Saguache Co., CO	Douglas E. Pittman	Douglas E. Pittman	2005	379
80	80 2/8	16 2/8	16 4/8	6 1/8	6 1/8	2 5/8	2 5/8	17 1/8	14	5 4/8	5 4/8	Johnson Co., WY	Maurice R. Johnson	Maurice R. Johnson	2006	379
80	80 1/8	14	14	7	7	2 5/8	2 5/8	10 5/8	8 3/8	5 5/8	5 4/8	S. Saskatchewan River, SK	Susan J. Malone	Susan J. Malone	2006	379
80	80 4/8	15 5/8	15 5/8	5 6/8	5 5/8	3 1/8	3 1/8	11 2/8	7 7/8	4 6/8	5		Barry D. Miller	Barry D. Miller	2006	379
80	81	15	16	5 7/8	5 7/8	3 2/8	3 2/8	13 2/8	13 3/8	5 5/8	5 5/8	Campbell Co., WY	Michael L. Oakley	Michael L. Oakley	2006	379
80	80 1/8	15 1/8	15	7 1/8	7 1/8	2 4/8	2 4/8	10 2/8	8 2/8	4 4/8	4 4/8	Carbon Co., WY	Duwayne Statzer	Duwayne Statzer	2006	379
80	81	16 3/8	16 3/8	6 2/8	6 1/8	2 5/8	2 5/8	13 3/8	11 6/8	5 1/8	5 2/8	Harding Co., SD	Dennis A. Wilaby	Dennis A. Wilaby	2006	379
94 2/8*	95	16 5/8	16 4/8	7 6/8	7 5/8	3 7/8	3 7/8	10 2/8	4 5/8	6 5/8	6 1/8	Yavapai Co., AZ	Denny Austad	Denny Austad	2006	
94 *	96 7/8	17 7/8	17	7 2/8	7 3/8	3 5/8	3 4/8	8 1/8	5 1/8	7	5 7/8	Coconino Co., AZ	Patrick Brewer	Patrick Brewer	2003	
94 *	95 2/8	16 2/8	16 2/8	7 2/8	7 3/8	4	4	11	6 6/8	7 1/8	6 3/8	Yavapai Co., AZ	Wayne W. Webber	Wayne W. Webber	2004	
94 *	94 3/8	17 2/8	17 1/8	7 2/8	7 3/8	3	3	15	13 5/8	7 5/8	7 5/8	Washoe Co., NV	Sam S. Jaksick, Jr.	Sam S. Jaksick, Jr.	2006	
91 1/8*	92 1/8	16 6/8	16 5/8	7 6/8	7 6/8	3 1/8	3 1/8	10 4/8	5	6 1/8	6 3/8	Lake Co., OR	Rick D. Ullery	Rick D. Ullery	2004	

* Final score subject to revision by additional verifying measurements.

PRONGHORN
FINAL SCORE: 80-2/8
HUNTER: Desiree N. Cragoe

PRONGHORN
FINAL SCORE: 80-6/8
HUNTER: Donald W. Buckner

PRONGHORN
FINAL SCORE: 82-4/8
HUNTER: Charles B. Black

PRONGHORN
FINAL SCORE: 85
HUNTER: Mike E. Dean

BISON

Minimum Score 115

Bison bison bison and *Bison bison athabascae*

World's Record 136 4/8

Trophies are acceptable only from states and provinces that recognize bison as a wild and free-ranging game animal and for which a hunting license and/or big game tag is required for hunting.

Final Score	Gross Score	Length of horn R.	L.	Circumference of Base R.	L.	Circumference at Third Quarter R.	L.	Greatest Spread	Tip to Tip Spread	Locality	Hunter	Owner	Date Killed	Rank
130 4/8	131 4/8	20 7/8	21 1/8	14 7/8	15 2/8	6 5/8	6 4/8	33 6/8	28 2/8	Custer Co., SD	Jeffrey S. Shoaf	Jeffrey S. Shoaf	2006	1
130 2/8	130 7/8	22	22 2/8	16 1/8	15 6/8	5 4/8	5 4/8	33 4/8	26 4/8	Custer Co., SD	Mark D. Farnam	Mark D. Farnam	2004	2
127 6/8	129 1/8	18 3/8	17 7/8	15 6/8	16	7	7 4/8	34 4/8	31 2/8	Custer Co., SD	Bronko A. Terkovich	Bronko A. Terkovich	2005	3
127 2/8	128 7/8	17 2/8	17	14 2/8	13 4/8	9 6/8	9 4/8	31 4/8	28 7/8	Teton Co., WY	Alex Hoover	Alex Hoover	2005	4
125 6/8	128	18 5/8	18 1/8	14 5/8	14 4/8	7 6/8	7 5/8	32 7/8	27 1/8	Custer Co., SD	Stephen M. Van Poucke	Stephen M. Van Poucke	2005	5
124 6/8	126 3/8	18	17 4/8	15 4/8	16	6 5/8	6 2/8	30 2/8	24 3/8	Park Co., MT	Charles R. Clough	Charles R. Clough	2006	6
124 2/8	124 2/8	20	20	15 6/8	15 6/8	5 1/8	5 1/8	30	25 4/8	Moraine Lake, YT	Leonard R. Beecher	Leonard R. Beecher	2005	7
124	126 4/8	14 7/8	15 2/8	14 2/8	14 2/8	8 4/8	8 7/8	28 1/8	25 1/8	Davis Co., UT	Travis D. Pehrson	Travis D. Pehrson	2005	8
122 6/8	123 7/8	17 4/8	17	13 2/8	13 1/8	8 1/8	8	28 7/8	24 6/8	Teton Co., WY	Tom R. Wadley	Tom R. Wadley	2003	9
122 6/8	123 4/8	17 5/8	17 6/8	14 2/8	14 3/8	6 4/8	6 6/8	33	27 4/8	Teton Co., WY	Scott A. Buschelman	Scott A. Buschelman	2005	9
122 6/8	123 6/8	18 2/8	18 7/8	16	16	5 2/8	5 3/8	28 7/8	20 6/8	Grand Co., UT	Robert C. Chapoose, Jr.	Robert C. Chapoose, Jr.	2005	9
122 2/8	123 6/8	19	18 7/8	13 7/8	13 7/8	6 2/8	6 2/8	30 3/8	24 1/8	Garfield Co., UT	Robert K. Turner	Robert K. Turner	2004	12
121 7/8	122 5/8	18 3/8	18 3/8	14 6/8	14 6/8	6	5 5/8	26 7/8	19 6/8	Pink Mt., BC	Tom Foss	Tom Foss	2003	13
121 7/8	122 3/8	18 2/8	18 2/8	14 7/8	15	5 5/8	5 6/8	27 7/8	22 1/8	Garfield Co., UT	R. Kendal Oldroyd	R. Kendal Oldroyd	2003	13
121 4/8	121 7/8	17 6/8	18 2/8	14 5/8	14 6/8	6 4/8	6 4/8	29	27 6/8	Custer Co., SD	Paul A. Lautner	Paul A. Lautner	2005	15
121 2/8	121 7/8	18 4/8	19 3/8	14 6/8	14 6/8	6 3/8	5 6/8	31 7/8	28 3/8	Custer Co., SD	Luke A. Terkovich	Luke A. Terkovich	2005	15
121 2/8	123 1/8	20 5/8	19 7/8	14 2/8	14 1/8	5 6/8	5 2/8	33 1/8	24 3/8	Custer Co., SD	David R. Lautner	David R. Lautner	2003	17
120 4/8	121 7/8	18 2/8	17 1/8	14 1/8	14 3/8	6 6/8	6 6/8	28 7/8	19 1/8	Custer Co., SD	Scott R. Gold	Scott R. Gold	2003	18
120 2/8	121 6/8	19	19 1/8	14 3/8	14 4/8	6 4/8	6	28 6/8	20 5/8	Aishihik River, YT	Tony J. Grabowski	Tony J. Grabowski	2005	18
120 2/8	121 1/8	16 5/8	17 2/8	15 3/8	15 7/8	5 6/8	5 6/8	27 3/8	26 1/8	Aishihik Lake, YT	Jim Shockey	Jim Shockey	1998	20
120	119 4/8	16 7/8	18 4/8	13 2/8	13 3/8	7 4/8	7 4/8	29 6/8	24	Teton Co., WY	Allen Pehringer	Allen Pehringer	2004	21
118 4/8	120 6/8	19 4/8	18 2/8	13 3/8	13 5/8	5 4/8	6	31 1/8	23 7/8	Teton Co., WY	Jim T. Sessions	Jim T. Sessions	2005	22
118	118	18	18 1/8	13 6/8	13 6/8	6	5 6/8	29 6/8	24	Custer Co., SD	Gordon R. Bush	Gordon R. Bush	2003	23
117 2/8	118 5/8	18 7/8	18 1/8	13 6/8	13 4/8	6 6/8	6 4/8	29 4/8	23 7/8	Custer Co., SD	Timothy J. Koll	Timothy J. Koll	2005	24
117	120	20 4/8	18 7/8	14 2/8	14	5 6/8	5	31 2/8	22 7/8	Custer Co., SD	Dan S. Muchow	Dan S. Muchow	2004	25
116 4/8	116 6/8	17 3/8	17 3/8	14 5/8	14 5/8	5 7/8	5 6/8	26 4/8	26	Teton Co., WY	Jason A. Swanson	Jason A. Swanson	2004	26
115 4/8	116 7/8	17 2/8	18 3/8	13 3/8	13 3/8	6 1/8	6 2/8	28 2/8	19 4/8	Custer Co., SD	Shamus M. McCarthy	Shamus M. McCarthy	2000	27
115 4/8	116 1/8	18 3/8	18 3/8	13 6/8	13 6/8	4 7/8	5	26 6/8	20 2/8	Garfield Co., UT	Kelly Christiansen	Kelly Christiansen	2003	27
115 2/8	118 4/8	17 7/8	18 6/8	14 6/8	14 7/8	4 2/8	5 2/8	28 6/8	22 6/8	Aishihik Lake, YT	Tim Mervyn	Tim Mervyn	2004	29
115	116 2/8	17	17 7/8	12 6/8	13	6 7/8	7 2/8	26 6/8	19 1/8	Teton Co., WY	Jay B. Myers	Jay B. Myers	2002	30

115	115 7/8	17	17 3/8	13	13	6 4/8	6 7/8	28 4/8	24 3/8	Teton Co., WY	Brent Z. Wilkes	Brent Z. Wilkes	2004
132 *	133 1/8	18 4/8	19	16	16 2/8	6 7/8	7	30 6/8	25 5/8	Custer Co., SD	John F. Babler	John F. Babler	2004
128 2/8*	129 2/8	21 1/8	21 5/8	14 6/8	14 6/8	6 2/8	6	31 5/8	22 5/8	Gladstone Lakes, YT	Peter J. Bringsli	Kurt Bringsli	2002

* Final score subject to revision by additional verifying measurements.

BISON
FINAL SCORE: 132*
HUNTER: John F. Babler

BISON
FINAL SCORE: 120-2/8
HUNTER: Tony J. Grabowski

BISON
FINAL SCORE: 122-6/8
HUNTER: Robert C. Chapoose, Jr.

BISON
FINAL SCORE: 117
HUNTER: Timothy J. Koll

ROCKY MOUNTAIN GOAT

Oreamnos americanus americanus and related subspecies

Minimum Score 47

World's Record 56 6/8

Final Score	Gross Score	Length of horn R.	Length of horn L.	Circumference of Base R.	Circumference of Base L.	Circumference at Third Quarter R.	Circumference at Third Quarter L.	Greatest Spread	Tip to Tip Spread	Locality	Hunter	Owner	Date Killed	Rank
54 4/8	54 4/8	11 2/8	11 2/8	5 6/8	5 6/8	1 6/8	1 6/8	9	8 3/8	Revillagigedo Island, AK	Edward E. Toribio	Edward E. Toribio	2004	1
54 2/8	54 4/8	9 5/8	9 4/8	6 3/8	6 3/8	2 1/8	2 1/8	7 4/8	7 2/8	Duchesne Co., UT	Craig L. Rippen	Craig L. Rippen	2006	2
53 4/8	53 5/8	10 4/8	10 4/8	5 6/8	5 7/8	2	2	7 7/8	6 6/8	Kalum Lake, BC	Daryl K. Schultz	Daryl K. Schultz	2005	3
53 4/8	53 4/8	10 6/8	10 5/8	6	6	2	2	7 4/8	7 2/8	Kitwanga River, BC	Robert A. Burlone	Robert A. Burlone	2005	4
53 2/8	53 2/8	10 3/8	10 5/8	5 7/8	5 7/8	1 7/8	1 7/8	7 6/8	7 5/8	Chilkat Pen., AK	Aaron E. Woodrow	Aaron E. Woodrow	2001	5
53	53	10	10	6	6	2	2	6 5/8	6	Foch Lake, BC	Peter Giangiulio	Peter Giangiulio	2005	5
53	53 7/8	10 7/8	11 4/8	5 5/8	5 5/8	1 7/8	1 7/8	7 4/8	6 3/8	Foch Lake, BC	Joseph B. Arnett	Joseph B. Arnett	2006	5
53	53 4/8	11 2/8	11 1/8	5 5/8	5 5/8	2	1 7/8	8 3/8	7 1/8	Kalum Lake, BC	Shad M. Wheeler	Shad M. Wheeler	2006	5
52 6/8	52 7/8	10	10	6 1/8	6 1/8	1 7/8	1 7/8	7 2/8	6 7/8	Skeena River, BC	Allen V. Bolen	Allen V. Bolen	2005	9
52 6/8	53 4/8	10 6/8	11	5 6/8	5 7/8	1 7/8	1 7/8	8 1/8	7 6/8	Baker Co., OR	Matthew J. Waite	Matthew J. Waite	2006	9
52 4/8	52 5/8	10 4/8	10 5/8	5 6/8	5 6/8	2 1/8	2 1/8	6 7/8	5 3/8	Cleveland Pen., AK	Clifford L. Adamson	Clifford L. Adamson	1980	11
52 4/8	52 6/8	10	9 7/8	5 6/8	5 6/8	2	2	6 6/8	4 6/8	Rudyerd Bay, AK	Greg A. Jennen	Greg A. Jennen	2005	11
52 2/8	52 4/8	10 5/8	10 5/8	5 4/8	5 5/8	2	2	6 5/8	5 5/8	Elko Co., NV	Jerry R. Gomez	Jerry R. Gomez	2003	13
52 2/8	52 3/8	10 4/8	10 4/8	5 7/8	6	1 7/8	1 7/8	8	7 3/8	Blue River, BC	James Glaicar	James Glaicar	2006	13
52 2/8	53 5/8	10 2/8	11 3/8	6	6	2 2/8	2	7	6 2/8	Mirror Lake, AK	James K. Nordmark	James K. Nordmark	2006	13
52	52 3/8	10 3/8	10 5/8	6	6	1 6/8	1 6/8	7 7/8	7 3/8	Moose Creek, BC	Kenneth M. Warlick	Kenneth M. Warlick	2003	16
52	52 1/8	10 1/8	10 1/8	5 5/8	5 5/8	2 1/8	2 1/8	9	9	Tanzilla River, BC	Robert E. Reedy, Jr.	Robert E. Reedy, Jr.	2004	16
51 6/8	53	10 4/8	9 6/8	6	6 1/8	2	2	6 4/8	6	Granby River, BC	Blair D. Soars	Blair D. Soars	2004	18
51 6/8	51 7/8	10 3/8	10 3/8	5 6/8	5 6/8	2	2	8 2/8	7 3/8	Nanika Lake, BC	Gary Crawford	Gary Crawford	2005	18
51 6/8	51 7/8	9 1/8	9 2/8	6 2/8	6 2/8	2	2	6 5/8	6 2/8	Morice River, BC	David Novak	David Novak	2005	18
51 4/8	51 7/8	10 4/8	10 5/8	6 1/8	5 7/8	2	2	7 2/8	7	Sargent Icefield, AK	Thomas S. Hundley	Thomas S. Hundley	1979	21
51 4/8	51 4/8	9 5/8	9 5/8	5 7/8	5 7/8	2	2	7 3/8	6 7/8	Dease Lake, BC	Kenneth G. Bergfeld	Kenneth G. Bergfeld	2003	21
51 4/8	51 5/8	10 4/8	10 5/8	5 7/8	5 7/8	1 7/8	1 7/8	7 6/8	6 7/8	Chismore Creek, BC	Jerry L. Harbottle	Jerry L. Harbottle	2003	21
51 4/8	51 7/8	11 4/8	11 3/8	5 1/8	5 2/8	1 7/8	1 7/8	8	6 6/8	Horn Cliffs, AK	Fred W. Williams	Fred W. Williams	2004	21
51 2/8	51 7/8	10	10 2/8	6 1/8	6 1/8	1 7/8	1 7/8	7 1/8	5 7/8	Beaver River, BC	Robert P. Braubach	Robert P. Braubach	2006	26
51	51 4/8	9 3/8	9 3/8	5 7/8	5 7/8	1 7/8	1 7/8	7	6 4/8	Klastline River, BC	David R. Hatten	David R. Hatten	2005	27
51	51 5/8	9 5/8	9 2/8	5 7/8	5 7/8	1 7/8	1 7/8	8 1/8	7 2/8	Kelsall River, BC	Robert T. Henson	Robert T. Henson	2003	27
51	51 1/8	9 7/8	10	5 6/8	5 6/8	2 1/8	2 1/8	6 3/8	6	Khutzeymateen River, BC	Mark Reagan	Mark Reagan	2004	27
51	51 4/8	10 1/8	10 2/8	5 5/8	5 4/8	2	2	8 6/8	8 3/8	Zymoetz River, BC	Chad D. Ridley	Chad D. Ridley	2004	27
51	51 4/8	9 7/8	10 1/8	5 7/8	6	1 7/8	1 7/8	7 5/8	7 2/8	Falls River, BC	Joseph R. Russo	Joseph R. Russo	2004	27
51	51 3/8	10 2/8	10 2/8	5 7/8	5 6/8	1 6/8	2	7 2/8	6 2/8	Elko Co., NV	David H. Edwards	David H. Edwards	2005	27

Score									Locality			Date	Rank
50 6/8	51 2/8	10 5/8	10 5/8	5 7/8	5 5/8	1 6/8	7 4/8	1 6/8	Spatsizi River, BC	Brian R. Biewer	Brian R. Biewer	2004	32
50 6/8	51 1/8	10 1/8	10 1/8	5 6/8	5 6/8	2	7 5/8	2	Atlin Lake, BC	Boyd L. Mothe, Jr.	Boyd L. Mothe, Jr.	2004	32
50 6/8	51 1/8	9 7/8	9 7/8	5 7/8	5 6/8	2 1/8	6 4/8	2 1/8	Stikine River, BC	Chris S. Swain	Chris S. Swain	2005	32
50 4/8	50 5/8	10 1/8	10	5 7/8	5 7/8	1 6/8	7 1/8	1 6/8	Summit Co., CO	Robert C. Davis	Robert C. Davis	2003	35
50 4/8	50 6/8	9 5/8	9 6/8	5 6/8	5 5/8	2	7 7/8	2	Clore River, BC	Jason M. Wall	Jason M. Wall	2005	35
50 2/8	50 2/8	9 7/8	9 7/8	5 7/8	5 7/8	2	6	2	Mt. McLeod, BC	Rodney Worth	Frank Kantor	1986	37
50 2/8	50 3/8	9 6/8	9 6/8	5 5/8	5 5/8	2	8 4/8	2	Chilko Lake, BC	Everett W. Barber	Everett W. Barber	2003	37
50 2/8	50 3/8	9 6/8	9 6/8	5 5/8	5 5/8	2	6 6/8	2	Swan Lake, AK	John C. Burick	John C. Burick	2004	37
50 2/8	50 3/8	10 3/8	10 2/8	5 5/8	5 5/8	1 7/8	6 6/8	1 7/8	Elko Co., NV	Christopher R. Stack	Christopher R. Stack	2004	37
50 2/8	50 2/8	9 6/8	9 5/8	5 4/8	5 4/8	2	7	2	Kodiak Island, AK	Roger L. Valley	Roger L. Valley	2004	37
50 2/8	50 6/8	9 1/8	9 1/8	5 7/8	5 7/8	2	7 3/8	2	Cape Yakataga, AK	Jeremy K. Warren	Jeremy K. Warren	2004	37
50 2/8	50 7/8	9 5/8	9 5/8	5 6/8	5 6/8	2 1/8	7 4/8	2 1/8	Weber Co., UT	Michael K. Christensen	Michael K. Christensen	2005	37
50	50 7/8	10 2/8	9 4/8	5 6/8	5 6/8	1 7/8	5 4/8	1 7/8	Elko Co., NV	Kevin J. Hull	Kevin J. Hull	2003	44
50	50 7/8	9 7/8	9 7/8	6	6	2	6 2/8	2	Zymoetz River, BC	Doug J. Kroeker	Doug J. Kroeker	2003	44
50	50 2/8	9 4/8	9 5/8	5 5/8	5 5/8	1 7/8	6 4/8	1 7/8	Utah Co., UT	Kenneth L. Allen	Kenneth L. Allen	2004	44
50	50 3/8	10 2/8	10 3/8	5 4/8	5 4/8	1 6/8	7	1 6/8	Park Co., CO	Scott T. Ross	Scott T. Ross	2004	44
50	50 2/8	10	9 7/8	5 7/8	5 7/8	1 7/8	7 2/8	1 7/8	Hugh Smith Lake, AK	Michael C. Snapp	Michael C. Snapp	2004	44
50	51 1/8	10 2/8	10	5 4/8	5 4/8	2	8	1 6/8	Columbia Glacier, AK	Alfred L. Wynn	Alfred L. Wynn	2004	44
50	50 4/8	9 3/8	9 4/8	5 5/8	5 7/8	1 6/8	6	1 7/8	Utah Co., UT	John R. Karren	John R. Karren	2005	44
50	50 1/8	9 6/8	9 6/8	6	6	1 6/8	6 5/8	1 6/8	Brewer Creek, BC	Yvan A. Kathriner	Yvan A. Kathriner	2005	44
50	50	10 1/8	10 1/8	5 5/8	5 5/8	1 6/8	6 6/8	1 6/8	Monashee Mts., BC	Loren E. Kohnen	Loren E. Kohnen	2005	44

ROCKY MOUNTAIN GOAT
FINAL SCORE: 47
HUNTER: Arthur J. Panicco

ROCKY MOUNTAIN GOAT
FINAL SCORE: 50
HUNTER: Christopher O. Wells

ROCKY MOUNTAIN GOAT
FINAL SCORE: 51-4/8
HUNTER: Robert P. Braubach

ROCKY MOUNTAIN GOAT
FINAL SCORE: 47-2/8
HUNTER: Raymond W. Swope

ROCKY MOUNTAIN GOAT

Oreamnos americanus americanus and related subspecies

Final Score	Gross Score	Length of horn R.	L.	Circumference of Base R.	L.	Circumference at Third Quarter R.	L.	Greatest Spread	Tip to Tip Spread	Locality	Hunter	Owner	Date Killed	Rank
50	50 3/8	10	9 6/8	5 4/8	5 4/8	1 7/8	1 7/8	7 7/8	7 2/8	Prince William Sound, AK	William E. Stevens	William E. Stevens	2006	44
50	50 3/8	10 5/8	10 4/8	5 5/8	5 6/8	1 6/8	1 6/8	6 1/8	5 2/8	Flathead River, BC	Christopher O. Wells	Christopher O. Wells	2006	44
49 6/8	50 1/8	9 7/8	9 6/8	5 4/8	5 5/8	2	2	8 5/8	8	Lang Creek, BC	Matthew H. Cadden	Matthew H. Cadden	2005	55
49 6/8	50 3/8	10 1/8	9 4/8	6	6	1 7/8	1 7/8	7 7/8	7 7/8	Gallatin Co., MT	Chad D. Moody	Chad D. Moody	2005	55
49 4/8	50	9 6/8	9 7/8	5 4/8	5 5/8	1 7/8	1 7/8	6 6/8	6	Eddontenajon Lake, BC	Greg Shuttleworth	Greg Shuttleworth	2004	57
49 4/8	49 6/8	10 1/8	10	5 4/8	5 4/8	1 6/8	1 6/8	6 4/8	6 2/8	Lachmach Lake, BC	David J. Einarson	David J. Einarson	2005	57
49 2/8	50	10 4/8	9 7/8	5 6/8	5 6/8	1 6/8	1 6/8	8 1/8	7 7/8	Baker Co., OR	John E. Benson	John E. Benson	2005	59
49 2/8	50	10 1/8	9 5/8	5 5/8	5 5/8	1 7/8	1 7/8	7 5/8	7	Quash Creek, BC	Gary C. Sessions	Gary C. Sessions	2005	59
49 2/8	49 6/8	10	9 7/8	5 4/8	5 4/8	1 6/8	1 7/8	7 2/8	6 6/8	Knik Glacier, AK	Jack L. Morey, Jr.	Jack L. Morey, Jr.	2006	59
49	49 1/8	9 4/8	9 5/8	5 6/8	5 6/8	1 7/8	1 7/8	5 7/8	5 4/8	Findlay Creek, BC	David P. McBrayer	David P. McBrayer	1991	62
49	49	9 5/8	9 4/8	5 5/8	5 5/8	1 7/8	1 7/8	6 7/8	5 7/8	Spatsizi Plateau, BC	Ray E. Dukes	Ray E. Dukes	1993	63
48 6/8	49 1/8	9 2/8	9 1/8	5 4/8	5 5/8	2	2	7 4/8	7 2/8	Taku River, BC	Michael G. Adams	Michael G. Adams	2003	63
48 6/8	49 2/8	9 6/8	10 1/8	5 4/8	5 4/8	1 6/8	1 6/8	6 6/8	6 3/8	Judith Basin Co., MT	Robert M. Downey	Robert M. Downey	2005	63
48 6/8	49 5/8	10	9 2/8	5 5/8	5 5/8	1 7/8	1 7/8	6 6/8	6 1/8	Wallowa Co., OR	W. Wayne York	W. Wayne York	2005	63
48 6/8	49 2/8	10 2/8	10	5 3/8	5 4/8	1 6/8	1 6/8	6 7/8	6 2/8	Kuldo Lake, BC	Rick Dunkerley	Rick Dunkerley	2006	63
48 4/8	48 7/8	9 5/8	9 7/8	5 2/8	5 2/8	1 7/8	1 7/8	7 6/8	7 3/8	Tsiu River, AK	Philip M. Ripepi	Philip M. Ripepi	2003	68
48 4/8	49 1/8	9 2/8	9 2/8	5 4/8	5 4/8	1 6/8	1 6/8	6 6/8	6 5/8	Elko Co., NV	Douglas A. Hooper	Douglas A. Hooper	2004	68
48 4/8	49 1/8	9 7/8	9 2/8	5 6/8	5 6/8	1 6/8	1 6/8	8	7 4/8	Quash Creek, BC	Byron Whitney	Byron Whitney	2005	68
48 4/8	48 5/8	9 2/8	9 2/8	5 5/8	5 4/8	1 7/8	1 7/8	5 6/8	5 4/8	Elko Co., NV	L. Alan Forman	L. Alan Forman	2006	68
48 2/8	49 1/8	10	9 4/8	5 6/8	5 4/8	1 7/8	1 7/8	8 6/8	8 4/8	Bug Lake, BC	C. Craig Kirby	C. Craig Kirby	2003	72
48 2/8	49 4/8	10 6/8	10	5	5	1 6/8	1 6/8	7 5/8	6 6/8	Patterson River, AK	Christine Medalen	Christine Medalen	2003	72
48	48 3/8	10 4/8	10 4/8	5 1/8	5 1/8	1 5/8	1 6/8	7 4/8	6 1/8	Tracy Arm, AK	Bruce S. Ivey	Bruce S. Ivey	2005	72
48	48 1/8	9 4/8	9 5/8	5 4/8	5 4/8	1 6/8	1 6/8	6 4/8	6 3/8	Carbon Co., MT	Shawn M. Mains	Shawn M. Mains	2003	75
48	48 3/8	9 6/8	9 7/8	5 4/8	5 4/8	1 7/8	1 6/8	7 4/8	7	Sicintine Lake, BC	Sid E. Lewis	Sid E. Lewis	2004	75
47 6/8	48 6/8	10	9 5/8	5 2/8	5 2/8	1 7/8	1 6/8	7 4/8	7 1/8	Spatsizi River, BC	Paul R. Esch	Paul R. Esch	2002	77
47 6/8	48 1/8	9 3/8	9 2/8	5 2/8	5 2/8	1 6/8	1 6/8	5 4/8	4 7/8	Foch Lake, BC	Norman C. Montano	Norman C. Montano	2006	77
47 4/8	47 6/8	9 4/8	9 4/8	5 2/8	5 2/8	1 6/8	1 5/8	6 4/8	6 4/8	Elko Co., NV	Jerry W. Lowery	Jerry W. Lowery	2002	79
47 4/8	47 5/8	9 5/8	9 6/8	5 2/8	5 2/8	1 6/8	1 6/8	5 3/8	4 3/8	Leduc Lake, AK	Charles R. Reed	Charles R. Reed	2003	79
47 4/8	47 5/8	9	9	5 4/8	5 4/8	2	2	5 3/8	4 3/8	Chelan Co., WA	Richard A. Gutzwiler	Richard A. Gutzwiler	2004	79
47 4/8	47 6/8	9 3/8	9 3/8	5 3/8	5 4/8	1 6/8	1 6/8	7 1/8	6 7/8	Beaver Co., UT	Gary A. Durfee	Gary A. Durfee	2005	79
48	48	9 1/8	9 2/8	5 4/8	5 5/8	1 7/8	1 7/8	6 6/8	6	Tsetia Creek, BC	A.C. Smid	A.C. Smid	2006	79

										Owner	Hunter	Locality	Date	Rank
47 4/8	47 5/8	9 4/8	9 4/8	5 3/8	5 3/8	1 7/8	1 7/8	8	7 6/8	Lowell T. Stevens III	Lowell T. Stevens III	Prince William Sound, AK	2006	79
47 2/8	47 7/8	9 6/8	10 1/8	5 4/8	5 4/8	1 5/8	1 6/8	6 3/8	5 6/8	Rod Boyer	Rod Boyer	Moonlit Creek, BC	2006	85
47 2/8	47 6/8	9 2/8	9 6/8	5 4/8	5 4/8	1 6/8	1 6/8	8 1/8	8	Raymond W. Swope	Raymond W. Swope	Colony Glacier, AK	2006	85
47	47	9 6/8	9 6/8	5 2/8	5 2/8	1 6/8	1 6/8	6 4/8	5 5/8	Gregory L. Solseth	Gregory L. Solseth	Clear Creek Co., CO	2002	87
47	47 2/8	10	9 7/8	5 1/8	5 2/8	1 4/8	1 4/8	6 6/8	5 7/8	Rick A. Carter	Rick A. Carter	Sanders Co., MT	2003	87
47	47 2/8	9 7/8	9 7/8	5 3/8	5 3/8	1 5/8	1 5/8	6 2/8	5 4/8	Gary Root	Gary Root	Teton Co., MT	2004	87
47	47 5/8	10 3/8	10 1/8	5 2/8	5 1/8	1 5/8	1 5/8	7 3/8	7 2/8	Arthur J. Panicco	Arthur J. Panicco	Park Co., CO	2005	87
47	47 2/8	10 1/8	10	5 2/8	5 2/8	1 4/8	1 4/8	6 7/8	6 2/8	Mick T. Waletzko	Mick T. Waletzko	Lincoln Co., MT	2005	87
47	47 5/8	9 1/8	9 3/8	5 4/8	5 4/8	1 5/8	1 5/8	6 3/8	5 5/8	Lance D. Gorley	Lance D. Gorley	Wallowa Co., OR	2006	87
54 4/8*	54 7/8	11 2/8	11 1/8	6	6	2	1 7/8	7 7/8	6 6/8	Jerry Den Boer	Jerry Den Boer	Tanzilla River, BC	2004	87

* Final score subject to revision by additional verifying measurements.

ROCKY MOUNTAIN GOAT
FINAL SCORE: 48
HUNTER: Sid E. Lewis

ROCKY MOUNTAIN GOAT
FINAL SCORE: 49-4/8
HUNTER: Greg Shuttleworth

ROCKY MOUNTAIN GOAT
FINAL SCORE: 50
HUNTER: Yvan A. Kathriner

ROCKY MOUNTAIN GOAT
FINAL SCORE: 51-4/8
HUNTER: Jerry L. Harbottle

MUSK OX

Ovibos moschatus moschatus and certain related subspecies

Minimum Score 105

New World's Record 129 (tie)

Final Score	Gross Score	Length of Horn R.	L.	Width of Boss R.	L.	Circumference at Third Quarter R.	L.	Greatest Spread	Tip to Tip Spread	Locality	Hunter	Owner	Date Killed	Rank
129	131	28 2/8	28 6/8	12 1/8	11 3/8	5 7/8	6 3/8	31 4/8	30 4/8	Coppermine River, NU	Jim Shockey	Jim Shockey	2006	1
128 6/8	130 4/8	29 4/8	30 4/8	11 1/8	10 7/8	6 2/8	6	27 1/8	25 4/8	Kugluktuk, NU	Tony L. Spriggs	Tony L. Spriggs	2004	2
128 2/8	129 3/8	31 5/8	31 7/8	10 4/8	10 4/8	5 5/8	6	29 6/8	29	Coppermine River, NU	Jim Shockey	Jim Shockey	2006	3
123 6/8	124 5/8	29 2/8	29 2/8	10 4/8	10 2/8	6 2/8	5 7/8	28 1/8	25 7/8	Kugluktuk, NU	Ben F. Carter III	Ben F. Carter III	2004	4
122 2/8	127 7/8	28 5/8	27	10 7/8	10 5/8	6 7/8	5 6/8	32 4/8	32 4/8	Coppermine River, NU	Jim Shockey	Jim Shockey	1997	5
122	123 4/8	27 2/8	27 6/8	10 7/8	10 6/8	6 3/8	6 2/8	29 1/8	28 6/8	Kugluktuk, NU	Jess M. Forton	Jess M. Forton	2004	6
122	126 2/8	30 3/8	28	10 6/8	11	5 6/8	4 7/8	30 4/8	29 7/8	Kugluktuk, NU	Vincent T. Ciaburri	Vincent T. Ciaburri	2006	6
121	123 4/8	29 5/8	30 3/8	11	11	5 1/8	6 1/8	29 4/8	28	Kugluktuk, NU	Jack Feightner	Jack Feightner	2005	8
119	123 3/8	27 5/8	29 2/8	9 4/8	9 3/8	6 4/8	6 6/8	26 2/8	26	Baker Lake, NU	Picked Up	Cabela's, Inc.	2005	9
117 4/8	119 2/8	27 1/8	26 3/8	10	10 1/8	5 2/8	5 1/8	25 3/8	23	Granet Lake, NT	Jim Shockey	Jim Shockey	2001	10
117	118 5/8	27 6/8	28 3/8	10	10	5 2/8	5 5/8	29	28 5/8	Kugluktuk, NU	James E. Schmid	James E. Schmid	2005	11
116	120 1/8	27 1/8	28 5/8	10 2/8	9 6/8	4 7/8	5 5/8	30 6/8	30 4/8	Dease Arm, NT	Michaux Nash, Jr.	Michaux Nash, Jr.	2003	12
115 6/8	115 6/8	26 2/8	26 2/8	9 1/8	9 2/8	5 7/8	5 7/8	28 1/8	27	Melbourne Island, NU	Keith M. Nowell	Keith M. Nowell	2006	13
115	118 1/8	27 7/8	26 6/8	10 4/8	10 3/8	5 4/8	5 3/8	26 7/8	23 7/8	Kugluktuk, NU	Patrick C. Allen	Patrick C. Allen	2005	14
114 4/8	117	27	28 4/8	10 2/8	10 2/8	5	5 3/8	29 2/8	28 6/8	Asiak River, NU	David W. Baxter	David W. Baxter	2004	15
114 2/8	114 7/8	26 4/8	26 5/8	9 4/8	9 7/8	5 3/8	5 3/8	26 2/8	22 5/8	Anderson River, NT	William F. Kneer, Jr.	William F. Kneer, Jr.	2004	16
113 4/8	114 4/8	25 6/8	25 2/8	10 3/8	10 2/8	5 5/8	5 4/8	28	27 4/8	Cambridge Bay, NU	Picked Up	Blake A. Klema	2005	17
113	115 1/8	26 4/8	27 5/8	10 4/8	10 4/8	4 5/8	5 1/8	26 3/8	24 2/8	Anderson River, NT	Don K. Graham	Don K. Graham	2003	18
113	114 4/8	24 6/8	25 2/8	10	9 6/8	5 6/8	6	29 1/8	28 4/8	Scented Grass Hills, NT	Troy E. Major II	Troy E. Major II	2004	18
113	114 4/8	28 1/8	27 3/8	9	9	5 7/8	5 4/8	28 1/8	26 7/8	Kugluktuk, NU	Vincent T. Ciaburri	Vincent T. Ciaburri	2006	18
112 4/8	116 2/8	27	25 5/8	9 5/8	10 3/8	6	5 4/8	28	27 3/8	Ellice River, NU	Michael D. Fain	Michael D. Fain	2003	21
111 6/8	113	27 1/8	26 3/8	9 3/8	9 4/8	5 2/8	5 3/8	28 4/8	27 3/8	Ellice River, NU	Vaughn Wright	Vaughn Wright	2004	22
111	112 1/8	27 7/8	28 5/8	9 4/8	9 3/8	4 3/8	4 3/8	25 4/8	20 5/8	Horton River, NT	Steven Gauvin	Steven Gauvin	2006	23
110 6/8	113 6/8	26 2/8	28 1/8	9 4/8	9 4/8	5	5 1/8	29 7/8	29 5/8	Gjoa Haven, NU	Picked Up	Jim Niven	2004	24
110	111 7/8	27 1/8	26 3/8	9 2/8	9 4/8	5 3/8	5 1/8	31 2/8	31 2/8	Aylmer Lake, NT	William J. McKee	William J. McKee	2004	25
108 6/8	109 4/8	26	26 2/8	8 3/8	8 2/8	5 6/8	5 1/8	25 6/8	25 4/8	Sinuk River, AK	Todd Lovell	Todd Lovell	2004	26
108 4/8	108 7/8	25	25 2/8	8 4/8	8 3/8	5 4/8	5 5/8	26	25 4/8	Kougarok River, AK	Mark W. Smith	Mark W. Smith	2005	27
108	109 4/8	26 4/8	26	8 5/8	8 5/8	5 1/8	4 7/8	28 1/8	27 6/8	Shishmaref, AK	Richard H. Dykema	Richard H. Dykema	2006	28
107 2/8	108 5/8	25 2/8	26 1/8	8 5/8	8 4/8	5 2/8	5 3/8	25	24 2/8	Nunivak Island, AK	Curtis E. Stoner	Curtis E. Stoner	2005	29

Score		Length of Horn R	Length of Horn L	Width of Boss R	Width of Boss L	Width at Third Quarter R	Width at Third Quarter L	Greatest Spread	Locality	Owner	By Whom Killed	Date	Page
107	111	25⁴/₈	27¹/₈	9¹/₈	9²/₈	5⁵/₈	4⁵/₈	26⁴/₈	Coyote Creek, AK	Mark W. Kelso	Mark W. Kelso	2003	30
106²/₈	110¹/₈	27²/₈	27¹/₈	9⁶/₈	9³/₈	4⁴/₈	5²/₈	26⁶/₈	Ellice River, NU	Ronald J. Bartels	Ronald J. Bartels	2004	31
106²/₈	109⁴/₈	27³/₈	26⁶/₈	8⁵/₈	8⁵/₈	4⁵/₈	5³/₈	26²/₈	Nunivak Island, AK	Winifred B. Kessler	Winifred B. Kessler	2005	31
106	107³/₈	25⁵/₈	26⁶/₈	7⁴/₈	7⁴/₈	5²/₈	5	26²/₈	Nelson Island, AK	Martin L. Smith	Martin L. Smith	2003	33
105⁶/₈	106⁴/₈	26	27⁶/₈	7⁷/₈	8	5	4⁶/₈	27¹/₈	Lisburne Hills, AK	James D. Unrein	Picked Up	1993	34
105²/₈	107⁷/₈	25⁶/₈	27⁴/₈	8²/₈	8	5	5⁵/₈	27²/₈	Sadlerochit River, AK	Aaron Agiak	Aaron Agiak	1986	35
105³/₈	106³/₈	26²/₈	24⁴/₈	9⁴/₈	9⁶/₈	5	4⁴/₈	22⁷/₈	Wellington Bay, NU	Bernie Smits	Bernie Smits	2004	35
105²/₈	107⁴/₈	25³/₈	29³/₈	9⁴/₈	9	5	5⁴/₈	28¹/₈	Umingmaktok, NU	Robert D. Hancock, Jr.	Robert D. Hancock, Jr.	2005	35
105	108⁴/₈	25⁴/₈	25¹/₈	9¹/₈	9¹/₈	4⁴/₈	5¹/₈	21¹/₈	Rendez-vous Lake, NT	Don Coffman	Don Coffman	2003	38
105	106⁶/₈	26²/₈	27⁴/₈	9¹/₈	9¹/₈	4⁷/₈	4⁵/₈	26⁶/₈	Nunivak Island, AK	Dan Alzheimer	Dan Alzheimer	2004	38
105	105⁵/₈	25²/₈	25¹/₈	8³/₈	8³/₈	5¹/₈	5	24⁴/₈	Nunivak Island, AK	Douglas Baily	Douglas Baily	2005	38
105	107¹/₈	26	24³/₈	8⁷/₈	9	4⁵/₈	5	21	Anderson River, NT	Bryan J. Westcott	Bryan J. Westcott	2006	38

MUSK OX
FINAL SCORE: 106-2/8
HUNTER: Winifred B. Kessler

MUSK OX
FINAL SCORE: 107
HUNTER: Mark W. Kelso

MUSK OX
FINAL SCORE: 112-4/8
HUNTER: Michael D. Fain

MUSK OX
FINAL SCORE: 105
HUNTER: Dan Alzheimer

BIGHORN SHEEP

Ovis canadensis canadensis and certain related subspecies

Minimum Score 175 World's Record 208 3/8

Final Score	Gross Score	Length of horn R.	Length of horn L.	Circumference of Base R.	Circumference of Base L.	Circumference at Third Quarter R.	Circumference at Third Quarter L.	Greatest Spread	Tip to Tip Spread	Locality	Hunter	Owner	Date Killed	Rank
199	199 4/8	41 2/8	40 4/8	17 5/8	17 3/8	9 4/8	9 3/8	25	18 3/8	Fergus Co., MT	Robert E. Seelye	Robert E. Seelye	2004	1
198 3/8	199 4/8	43 5/8	44 4/8	17 1/8	17 2/8	8	8 6/8	23 4/8	23 3/8	Blaine Co., MT	Stephen C. Morrical	Stephen C. Morrical	2006	2
197 1/8	197 3/8	41 4/8	40 7/8	16 1/8	16	10 5/8	10 6/8	22 4/8	16 4/8	Ewin Creek, BC	Steven S. Bruggeman	Steven S. Bruggeman	2004	3
196 7/8	197 5/8	41 5/8	41 4/8	16 3/8	16 3/8	10 4/8	10 2/8	23 1/8	21 7/8	Blaine Co., MT	Daniel R. Spicher	Daniel R. Spicher	2006	4
196 4/8	196 6/8	43	42 6/8	16 4/8	16 4/8	9 2/8	9 2/8	21	18 6/8	Grave Lake, BC	Mark C. Medcalf	Mark C. Medcalf	2004	5
196	196 4/8	40 4/8	40 2/8	16	16 1/8	10 7/8	10 6/8	22 2/8	16 4/8	Fording River, BC	Stephen J. Halko	Stephen J. Halko	2004	6
195 7/8	195 7/8	41	43 3/8	15 5/8	15 6/8	10	10 2/8	22 5/8	20 7/8	Luscar Mt., AB	Trevor C. Nahayowski	Trevor C. Nahayowski	2005	7
194 4/8	195 6/8	42 6/8	41 2/8	16 2/8	16 1/8	9 7/8	9 3/8	22	20 7/8	Sanders Co., MT	Kelly B. McAllister	Kelly B. McAllister	2006	8
193 1/8	193 7/8	45 5/8	40 4/8	16	16 1/8	8 4/8	9 1/8	27	27 2/8	Fergus Co., MT	Eldon L. Buckner	Eldon L. Buckner	2006	9
192 4/8	193 2/8	41 1/8	41 1/8	15 2/8	15 2/8	11 3/8	11	22 3/8	17 7/8	Gregg River, AB	Rodney W.J. Dziadyk	Rodney W.J. Dziadyk	2000	10
190 7/8	191 2/8	38 3/8	38 6/8	17	17	9 5/8	9 3/8	20 2/8	19 6/8	Fergus Co., MT	Jason Redfield	Jason Redfield	2004	11
190 6/8	191 6/8	39 4/8	43 2/8	15 2/8	15 4/8	9 7/8	10 2/8	21	21	Fergus Co., MT	Kelly D. Brandt	Kelly D. Brandt	2003	12
190 6/8	190 7/8	40 2/8	40	16 6/8	16 6/8	8 7/8	8 7/8	24 7/8	21 7/8	Blaine Co., MT	Carrie R. Shockley	Carrie R. Shockley	2005	12
190 5/8	191	38 3/8	38 4/8	17 7/8	17 7/8	9 2/8	9 2/8	26 3/8	24 5/8	Elko Co., NV	Jesse E. Ferrer	Jesse E. Ferrer	2006	14
190 4/8	190 6/8	44 3/8	43 5/8	14 4/8	14 4/8	9	9 1/8	27	26 4/8	Sanders Co., MT	George B. Mercer	George B. Mercer	2005	15
190 3/8	191 1/8	39 4/8	39 3/8	15 7/8	15 7/8	9 6/8	10 2/8	22 2/8	15 3/8	Ewin Creek, BC	Ralf Martini	Ralf Martini	2004	16
190 3/8	191 6/8	40	39 7/8	16	16 1/8	9 7/8	9 7/8	23	22 5/8	Baker Co., OR	Richard V. Oleson	Richard V. Oleson	2004	16
189 4/8	190 5/8	40 3/8	40 3/8	16	16 1/8	10 2/8	9 4/8	23	23	Elko Co., NV	Jerry H. Lazzari	Jerry H. Lazzari	2004	18
188 7/8	189 2/8	40 3/8	40 2/8	15 1/8	15	10 6/8	10 6/8	21 1/8	19 6/8	Red Deer River, AB	Picked Up	Sally Fairbank	1988	19
188 5/8	189 1/8	39 1/8	38 6/8	16 3/8	16 3/8	9 2/8	9 5/8	24	21 2/8	Nez Perce Co., ID	Justin M. Armstrong	Justin M. Armstrong	2003	20
188 5/8	190 1/8	40 4/8	40 1/8	17	16 7/8	8 6/8	7 5/8	23 1/8	20 5/8	Chouteau Co., MT	Forrest L. Kerns	Forrest L. Kerns	2005	20
188 4/8	188 6/8	43 3/8	42 7/8	14 3/8	14 3/8	9	9	24	24	Baker Co., OR	Russell A. Young	Russell A. Young	2005	22
188 2/8	188 4/8	39 7/8	39 3/8	15 4/8	15 4/8	10 1/8	10 2/8	21 7/8	18 6/8	Luscar Mt., AB	Picked Up	AB Fish & Wildlife	2003	23
188 2/8	188 7/8	39 3/8	39 5/8	14 7/8	15	11 4/8	11 6/8	19 7/8	15 7/8	Cadomin Creek, AB	Kevin D. Kopas	Kevin D. Kopas	2004	23
188 2/8	188 7/8	39 2/8	42 2/8	16 1/8	16 3/8	8 4/8	8 3/8	26	26	Deer Lodge Co., MT	Tom L. Reilly	Tom L. Reilly	2005	23
188	188 7/8	37 3/8	40 3/8	15 4/8	15 5/8	10 3/8	10 1/8	24 1/8	19 3/8	Taos Co., NM	Thomas J. Hufnagel	Thomas J. Hufnagel	2005	26
187 7/8	187 7/8	38 7/8	39 6/8	14 7/8	14 7/8	11 3/8	11	22 4/8	19 3/8	Sanders Co., MT	Martin A. Brower	Martin A. Brower	2004	27
187 3/8	189 2/8	38 6/8	40	16 7/8	16 5/8	8 2/8	9 1/8	20 3/8	20 1/8	Fergus Co., MT	Jason M. Matzinger	Jason M. Matzinger	2006	28
187 2/8	187 6/8	41 2/8	42	15 5/8	15 5/8	8 5/8	9 1/8	24 2/8	20 3/8	Missoula Co., MT	Scott A. Wolff	Scott A. Wolff	2006	29
186 7/8	187 3/8	43 4/8	43 7/8	14 5/8	14 5/8	8 2/8	8 2/8	23 5/8	23 5/8	Columbia Co., WA	Randy R. Pittman	Randy R. Pittman	2005	30
186 6/8	187 2/8	40	39 4/8	15 7/8	15 7/8	9 4/8	9 3/8	23 4/8	22 7/8	Baker Co., OR	Mark V. Christman	Mark V. Christman	2005	31
186 5/8	187	37	40 3/8	16	16	9 6/8	9 4/8	24 5/8	24	Fergus Co., MT	Randolph J. Tuhy	Randolph J. Tuhy	2003	32
186 2/8	187 2/8	37 3/8	38 7/8	16 1/8	16	9 2/8	9 6/8	25	17 7/8	Gunnison Co., CO	Danny J. Meyring	Danny J. Meyring	2005	33

Score										Locality	Owner	Hunter	Date	Rank
186 1/8	187 2/8	38 2/8	40 3/8	15 1/8	15 2/8	10	10 3/8	18 2/8	21 5/8	Baker Co., OR	Edward H. Elms	Edward H. Elms	2005	34
185 7/8	186	36 4/8	35 5/8	16 4/8	16 3/8	10	10	15	23 1/8	Las Animas Co., CO	Charles I. Kelly	Charles I. Kelly	2005	35
185 7/8	186 5/8	41 5/8	40 6/8	15 4/8	15 4/8	8 3/8	8 7/8	22 2/8	22 4/8	Blaine Co., MT	Marc P. DeLong	Marc P. DeLong	2006	35
185 6/8	187 3/8	37 1/8	43 3/8	15 4/8	15 4/8	9 3/8	8 6/8	24 6/8	25 3/8	Granite Co., MT	David Tingley	David Tingley	2004	37
185 6/8	186 5/8	40	40 6/8	15 2/8	15 5/8	9	9 4/8	20 4/8	23 1/8	Ravalli Co., MT	William B. Martin	William B. Martin	2006	37
185 5/8	186 5/8	39 5/8	39 2/8	16	15 2/8	9 1/8	8 4/8	17 2/8	18 2/8	Granite Co., MT	Matthew P. Seidel	Matthew P. Seidel	2005	39
185 3/8	185 7/8	35 3/8	36 6/8	15 6/8	15 7/8	10 6/8	11	20 4/8	21 7/8	Granite Co., MT	Picked Up	Granite Co. Mus. & Cultural Center	2005	40
185 2/8	185 4/8	40 1/8	40 1/8	15	15	9 3/8	9 5/8	22 4/8	22 5/8	Lemhi Co., ID	Ed W. Rochnowski	Ed W. Rochnowski	2005	41
185 2/8	185 4/8	38	37 4/8	16 1/8	16 2/8	9 4/8	9 4/8	19 6/8	23 6/8	Fergus Co., MT	Kenneth A. Madsen, Jr.	Kenneth A. Madsen, Jr.	2006	41
185 1/8	185 6/8	38 2/8	40 1/8	15 3/8	15 5/8	9 3/8	9 4/8	19 1/8	20 2/8	Lewis & Clark Co., MT	John J. McCarthy	John J. McCarthy	2003	43
185	185 4/8	39 3/8	42 3/8	16	16	8	8	27	29 5/8	Granite Co., MT	Hugh D. Jones	Hugh D. Jones	2005	44
184 7/8	185 4/8	38	37 5/8	16 4/8	16 4/8	8 5/8	8 6/8	17 3/8	23 5/8	Gunnison Co., CO	Frederick R. Saltus, Jr.	Frederick R. Saltus, Jr.	2004	45
184 7/8	186 2/8	36 2/8	36 1/8	16	16 2/8	10 3/8	10 7/8	20 3/8	21 4/8	Chouteau Co., MT	William J. Hoving	W.J. & S. Hoving	2006	45
184 5/8	185	37	39 1/8	15	15 1/8	10 1/8	10 1/8	17 1/8	22 5/8	Huerfano Co., CO	Picked Up	Daniel J. Larkin III	2005	47
184 2/8	184 5/8	38 4/8	39	15 1/8	15	9 7/8	9 5/8	21	21 4/8	Gilliam Co., OR	Frank R. LaRoche	Frank R. LaRoche	2004	48
184 1/8	186 2/8	41 3/8	43	13 4/8	14 4/8	9 5/8	9 2/8	20 2/8	21 4/8	Wallowa Co., OR	Picked Up	OR Dept. of Fish & Wildlife	2004	49
184 1/8	184 5/8	40 2/8	41 7/8	15 2/8	15 3/8	8 2/8	8 4/8	23 6/8	25 1/8	Powell Co., MT	Richard P. Truzzolino	Richard P. Truzzolino	2004	49
184 1/8	184 7/8	41	36 3/8	16 4/8	16 3/8	8	8 1/8	23	23 1/8	Ravalli Co., MT	Forest E. Hayes	Forest E. Hayes	2005	49
184	184 6/8	36 1/8	37 5/8	15 5/8	15 6/8	10 3/8	10 4/8	18	21	Blaine Co., MT	Benjamin C. Erickson	Benjamin C. Erickson	2004	52
183 7/8	184 5/8	40 4/8	40 7/8	15	15 2/8	8 2/8	8 3/8	22	22	Ravalli Co., MT	Greg T. McFadden	Greg T. McFadden	2004	53
183 7/8	184 3/8	40 2/8	40 3/8	16	16	8 2/8	8	23 3/8	23 5/8	Deer Lodge Co., MT	Donna L. Morgan	Donna L. Morgan	2004	53
183 7/8	184 1/8	39 4/8	38 1/8	17	17	8 1/8	8	20	22 1/8	Silver Bow Co., MT	Allen R. Ormesher	Allen R. Ormesher	2004	53
183 6/8	184	39	37 2/8	14 7/8	15	10 4/8	10 3/8	18 1/8	21 2/8	Luscar Mt., AB	Brett T. Layden	Brett T. Layden	2005	56
183 6/8	184 2/8	41 1/8	39 5/8	15 2/8	15 4/8	8 4/8	8 2/8	21	24 1/8	Ravalli Co., MT	Gary K. Nehring	Gary K. Nehring	2006	56
183 6/8	183 7/8	37	37 6/8	15 4/8	15 6/8	10 1/8	10 1/8	20	21 2/8	Blaine Co., MT	Dixie L. Selting	Dixie L. Selting	2006	56
183 5/8	184	38 6/8	38 5/8	16 3/8	16 1/8	9 3/8	9 5/8	22 4/8	22 4/8	Opal Range, AB	Brian A. Hauck	Brian A. Hauck	2004	59
183 5/8	184 3/8	37 1/8	37 2/8	15 5/8	15 2/8	10	10	23 2/8	25	Elko Co., NV	Michael E. Gilbert	Michael E. Gilbert	2006	59
183 5/8	183 5/8	38 1/8	38	14 6/8	14 6/8	10 2/8	10 1/8	22	22	Blaine Co., MT	Thomas E. Tyre, Jr.	Thomas E. Tyre, Jr.	2006	59
183 3/8	184 1/8	40 5/8	39 4/8	16	16 1/8	8	7 5/8	16	18 6/8	Ewin Creek, BC	Ted Monfee	Ted Monfee	2004	62
183 3/8	184 1/8	38 6/8	40 3/8	15 6/8	15 6/8	8 4/8	8 4/8	22 7/8	23 2/8	Sanders Co., MT	Grant G. Grisak	Grant G. Grisak	2005	62
183 3/8	183 6/8	40 2/8	39 3/8	15 4/8	15 4/8	8 2/8	8 4/8	18 4/8	19 4/8	Deer Lodge Co., MT	Lloyd C. Hettick	Lloyd C. Hettick	2005	62
183 2/8	183 6/8	39 4/8	39 6/8	16 3/8	16 1/8	8 5/8	8 5/8	21	22 6/8	Elko Co., NV	Paul J. Harris	Paul J. Harris	2004	65
183 1/8	183 4/8	38 5/8	38 5/8	14 6/8	14 6/8	10 1/8	10 2/8	16 6/8	21 2/8	Taos Co., NM	Tim Westall	Tim Westall	2003	66
183	183 2/8	39 1/8	39 1/8	15 2/8	15 1/8	9	9 1/8	18 2/8	20 6/8	Fergus Co., MT	Thomas L. Teague	Thomas L. Teague	2002	67
183	183 7/8	37 4/8	39	15 4/8	15 2/8	9 7/8	10	22 5/8	24 2/8	Fergus Co., MT	Shawn R. Andres	Shawn R. Andres	2004	67
183	185 5/8	38 2/8	41 6/8	15 6/8	15 6/8	8 7/8	9 7/8	18 4/8	22 3/8	Baker Co., OR	Matt C. Pettet	Matt C. Pettet	2006	67
183	183 2/8	36 7/8	36 3/8	15 5/8	15 4/8	10 1/8	10 1/8	16 7/8	20 4/8	Park Co., CO	Josh R. Wojciehoski	Josh R. Wojciehoski	2006	67
182 7/8	183 5/8	39 6/8	39 1/8	17	17 1/8	7 1/8	7	20 7/8	22 4/8	Sheep Mt., BC	Sam A. Medcalf	Sam A. Medcalf	2004	71
182 6/8	183 3/8	39 6/8	37 4/8	14 7/8	14 7/8	10 1/8	9 7/8	21	24 1/8	Powell Co., MT	Erik M. Ogren	Erik M. Ogren	2005	72

BIGHORN SHEEP

Ovis canadensis canadensis and certain related subspecies

Final Score	Gross Score	Length of horn R.	Length of horn L.	Circumference of Base R.	Circumference of Base L.	Circumference at Third Quarter R.	Circumference at Third Quarter L.	Greatest Spread	Tip to Tip Spread	Locality	Hunter	Owner	Date Killed	Rank
182 6/8	184 3/8	37 6/8	39 6/8	15 2/8	15 2/8	8 6/8	9 3/8	23 5/8	18 4/8	Gunnison Co., CO	Lance C. Ready	Lance C. Ready	2005	72
182 6/8	182 7/8	35 5/8	36 2/8	15 5/8	15 5/8	10 4/8	10 3/8	21 2/8	19 6/8	Ravalli Co., MT	Chris R. Troupe	Chris R. Troupe	2005	72
182 5/8	182 7/8	39 5/8	38 2/8	14 6/8	14 6/8	9 3/8	9 1/8	23 2/8	15 7/8	Crowsnest Pass, AB	Otto Hagglund	Karl J. Hagglund	PR 1930	75
182 4/8	183 1/8	40 2/8	40 4/8	15 6/8	15 5/8	7 6/8	7 6/8	25 3/8	25 1/8	Fergus Co., MT	George R. Poertner	George R. Poertner	2004	76
182 2/8	183 6/8	39 4/8	38	15 6/8	15 5/8	9 4/8	8 6/8	20 2/8	20 2/8	Sanders Co., MT	Mabel A. Flanagan	Mabel A. Flanagan	2003	77
182 2/8	184 4/8	38 4/8	39 2/8	15 1/8	15 4/8	9 7/8	9	21 4/8	20 2/8	Sanders Co., MT	Arthur R. Schauer	Arthur R. Schauer	2004	77
182 2/8	182 7/8	37	40	15 6/8	15 6/8	8 6/8	8 2/8	23 4/8	22 4/8	Blaine Co., MT	Lucinda L. Layne	Lucinda L. Layne	2004	77
182 2/8	183 1/8	38 3/8	38 5/8	14 3/8	14 4/8	10 5/8	10 2/8	20 1/8	16 4/8	Cadomin, AB	Jill P. Frederick	Jill P. Frederick	2005	77
182 2/8	183 2/8	36	36	15 7/8	15 7/8	10 5/8	10 2/8	23 2/8	21 3/8	Blaine Co., MT	Gary D. Troester	Gary D. Troester	2005	77
182 2/8	182 4/8	42 4/8	41 4/8	15 4/8	15 5/8	7	7	25 2/8	25 2/8	Beaverhead Co., MT	Robert D. Hartwell	Robert D. Hartwell	2006	77
182 1/8	182 5/8	38	39 3/8	14 5/8	14 6/8	9 6/8	10	21	20 4/8	Lewis & Clark Co., MT	Jason Brandenburger	Jason Brandenburger	2003	83
182 1/8	182 6/8	37 2/8	37 7/8	14 4/8	14 5/8	11	10 7/8	21 1/8	18 5/8	Granite Co., MT	Kevin V. Burns	Kevin V. Burns	2003	83
182 1/8	182 3/8	38 5/8	41 4/8	15	15 1/8	8 2/8	8 1/8	23 5/8	23 3/8	Missoula Co., MT	Ty Cavanaugh	Ty Cavanaugh	2003	83
182 1/8	182 6/8	41 1/8	40 6/8	14 3/8	14 2/8	9 4/8	9 2/8	21 4/8	19	Ravalli Co., MT	Johnny Bush	Johnny Bush	2005	83
182 1/8	182 6/8	39 2/8	41 3/8	15 2/8	15 1/8	8 5/8	8 5/8	24	24	Granite Co., MT	Bill Gaynor	Bill Gaynor	2006	83
182	182 5/8	39	38	15 4/8	15 5/8	8 6/8	8 6/8	24 4/8	23 4/8	Sanders Co., MT	Mike G. Phelan	Mike G. Phelan	2003	88
182	182 2/8	41	40 2/8	14	14	9 3/8	9 3/8	22 2/8	17 2/8	Fremont Co., WY	Jim P. Collins, Jr.	Jim P. Collins, Jr.	2004	88
181 7/8	182 3/8	39 6/8	40 3/8	15 2/8	15 2/8	8 1/8	8 3/8	25 7/8	25 4/8	Granite Co., MT	Roland H. Smathers, Jr.	Roland H. Smathers, Jr.	1997	90
181 4/8	182 4/8	37 6/8	37 6/8	14 6/8	14 7/8	10 3/8	10 1/8	22 1/8	20 5/8	Gilliam Co., OR	Picked Up	OR Dept. of Fish & Wildlife	2002	91
181 4/8	182	39 4/8	39	15	15 1/8	9	8 6/8	20 1/8	17	Canal Flats, BC	Ken R. Schultz	Ken R. Schultz	2006	91
181 1/8	182	38 7/8	37 7/8	15	15 1/8	9 1/8	8 5/8	22 3/8	15 4/8	Nez Perce Co., ID	Mike A. Carpinito	Mike A. Carpinito	2006	93
181 1/8	181 4/8	39 4/8	37 5/8	15 4/8	15 4/8	9 4/8	9 2/8	26 3/8	25 7/8	Missoula Co., MT	Robert R. Coffman, Jr.	Robert R. Coffman, Jr.	2006	94
180 7/8	181 1/8	36 2/8	36 3/8	16	16	8 7/8	8 7/8	22 4/8	21 5/8	Gilliam Co., OR	Scott C. Cooke	Scott C. Cooke	2004	95
180 7/8	181 2/8	38 3/8	36 6/8	15 1/8	15 1/8	9 5/8	9 4/8	21 6/8	19 4/8	Sanders Co., MT	Martin Desapio	Martin Desapio	2004	95
180 7/8	181	42 4/8	42 3/8	15 4/8	15 4/8	7	7	28	28	Lewis & Clark Co., MT	Robert A. Bartram	Robert A. Bartram	2005	95
181 4/8	181 1/8	39 3/8	38 6/8	14 4/8	14 5/8	9 4/8	9 2/8	22 2/8	16 2/8	Dawes Co., NE	Joe Glover, Jr.	Joe Glover, Jr.	2005	95
180 6/8	182 2/8	40 2/8	37	15 1/8	15 2/8	9 3/8	8 5/8	21 4/8	20 4/8	Sanders Co., MT	Greg L. McGuire	Greg L. McGuire	2004	99
180 5/8	180 7/8	35 5/8	34 6/8	16 4/8	16 5/8	8 7/8	8 7/8	24 1/8	17 6/8	Emery Co., UT	Robert T. Etzel	Robert T. Etzel	2004	100
180 5/8	181 4/8	34 7/8	36 4/8	16	16	9 2/8	9 7/8	17 3/8	16 5/8	Huerfano Co., CO	Wade D. Shults	Wade D. Shults	2004	100
180 4/8	180 4/8	38 2/8	39 2/8	14 1/8	14 1/8	10 1/8	10 1/8	21 5/8	18 3/8	Mora Co., NM	Kevin Fox	Kevin Fox	2004	102

Final Score	Gross	Length R	Length L	Base Circ. R	Base Circ. L	3rd Qtr. R	3rd Qtr. L	Greatest Spread	Tip to Tip	Locality	Hunter	Owner	Date	Rank
180 4/8	182 6/8	37 2/8	34 6/8	16	15 6/8	10 2/8	9 2/8	22 1/8	21	Blaine Co., MT	Harold G. Huston	Harold G. Huston	2004	102
180 4/8	182	34 1/8	33 5/8	16 3/8	16 7/8	10 3/8	11 2/8	22 5/8	17 1/8	Teller Co., CO	Merlynn K. Jones	Merlynn K. Jones	2006	102
180 3/8	181 1/8	39 1/8	39 2/8	15 4/8	15 4/8	8 4/8	8	27 5/8	26 7/8	Granite Co., MT	John C. O'Toole	John C. O'Toole	2004	105
180 3/8	181 1/8	35 5/8	36	16 1/8	15 5/8	9 3/8	9 3/8	21 7/8	20 6/8	Gilliam Co., OR	Picked Up	OR Dept. of Fish & Wildlife	2004	105
180 3/8	180 6/8	36 4/8	35 5/8	15 3/8	15 3/8	10	10 2/8	24 6/8	24	Deer Lodge Co., MT	Paul W. Teagle	Paul W. Teagle	2005	105
180 3/8	180 5/8	35 7/8	37 6/8	15 4/8	15 4/8	9 4/8	9 4/8	21 4/8	20 6/8	Granite Co., MT	Christopher J. Houle	Christopher J. Houle	2006	105
180 2/8	181 6/8	38 7/8	37 1/8	15 7/8	15 7/8	9 5/8	8 7/8	19 7/8	17 2/8	Sanders Co., MT	Kirk D. Pederson	Kirk D. Pederson	2005	109
180 2/8	180 4/8	39 7/8	39 7/8	15 6/8	15 7/8	7 6/8	7 6/8	24 6/8	25	Deer Lodge Co., MT	Jacob M. Koelzer	Jacob M. Koelzer	2006	109
180	180 6/8	40 5/8	40 5/8	14 1/8	14 1/8	9	9	21 4/8	18 5/8	Ravalli Co., MT	Todd C. Earp	Todd C. Earp	2003	111
180	180 5/8	38 4/8	39	16	9	8 5/8	7 7/8	22 4/8	21 5/8	Granite Co., MT	Ben Van Alstine	Ben Van Alstine	2004	111
180	180 6/8	38 4/8	38 6/8	15 6/8	15 6/8	8 5/8	8 5/8	25	25	Missoula Co., MT	Stan M. Billingsley	Stan M. Billingsley	2005	111
180	180 6/8	38 4/8	39 2/8	15 1/8	15	8 6/8	9 1/8	20 4/8	17 6/8	Deer Lodge Co., MT	Debra J. Acebedo	Debra J. Acebedo	2006	111
180	181 7/8	38 6/8	38	14 7/8	14 7/8	10 2/8	9 5/8	21 1/8	18 1/8	Lake Co., MT	Picked Up	Jane Whiting	2006	111
179 4/8	179 6/8	36 7/8	39 1/8	15 3/8	10 2/8	8 4/8	8 4/8	22 2/8	19 5/8	Blaine Co., MT	Austin M. Small	Austin M. Small	2003	116
179 3/8	182	36 5/8	38 2/8	16 1/8	15 3/8	7 6/8	7 6/8	24 7/8	24 2/8	Sanders Co., MT	Keith R. Balfourd	Keith R. Balfourd	2004	117
179 3/8	179 5/8	40	40 3/8	15	16 1/8	7 4/8	7 3/8	23	15 2/8	Elk Valley, BC	Ronny Bohrmann	Ronny Bohrmann	2004	117
179 3/8	180	37 2/8	37 5/8	15	15 4/8	10 1/8	10 2/8	21	17	San Miguel Co., NM	Lane J. Kinney	Lane J. Kinney	2004	117
179 1/8	180	39 2/8	38 5/8	15 4/8	14 6/8	8 1/8	7 6/8	23 4/8	23 3/8	Sanders Co., MT	Anthony J. McDonnell	Anthony J. McDonnell	2004	120
179 1/8	180 3/8	40 4/8	37 3/8	16	15 6/8	7 2/8	7 6/8	25 5/8	25 4/8	Ravalli Co., MT	Jerome C. Kahler	Jerome C. Kahler	2005	120
179	181	38 1/8	37 1/8	14 6/8	14 4/8	10 5/8	9 7/8	24 1/8	20 2/8	Ravalli Co., MT	Brad Walker	Brad Walker	2004	122

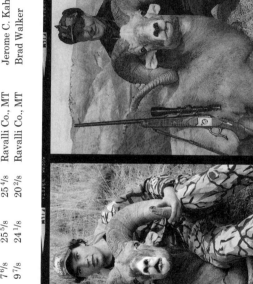

BIGHORN SHEEP
FINAL SCORE: 178-5/8
HUNTER: Daniel F. Wand

BIGHORN SHEEP
FINAL SCORE: 182-6/8
HUNTER: Erik M. Ogren

BIGHORN SHEEP
FINAL SCORE: 193-1/8
HUNTER: Eldon L. Buckner

BIGHORN SHEEP
FINAL SCORE: 180-7/8
HUNTER: Scott C. Cooke

BIGHORN SHEEP

Ovis canadensis canadensis and certain related subspecies

Final Score	Gross Score	Length of horn R.	L.	Circumference of Base R.	L.	Circumference at Third Quarter R.	L.	Greatest Spread	Tip to Tip Spread	Locality	Hunter	Owner	Date Killed	Rank
179	179²/₈	35²/₈	35⁴/₈	15⁷/₈	16	9⁴/₈	9⁴/₈	22	19⁶/₈	Sanders Co., MT	Steven R. Martin	Steven R. Martin	2005	122
178⁷/₈	179⁵/₈	37²/₈	37¹/₈	15⁷/₈	15⁶/₈	9³/₈	9¹/₈	20⁷/₈	15	Granite Co., MT	Scott J. Waletzko	Scott J. Waletzko	2003	124
178⁵/₈	178⁷/₈	36⁷/₈	35⁶/₈	16	16	8³/₈	8³/₈	23⁷/₈	13⁴/₈	Hinsdale Co., CO	Daniel F. Wand	Daniel F. Wand	2005	125
178²/₈	178⁶/₈	42	38²/₈	15	15	7⁶/₈	7⁴/₈	22⁶/₈	17⁶/₈	Dawes Co., NE	Steve W. Furley	Steve W. Furley	2003	126
178¹/₈	178⁷/₈	39²/₈	38⁵/₈	16²/₈	16²/₈	6²/₈	6⁶/₈	29⁶/₈	29⁵/₈	Sanders Co., MT	John C. Dovey	John C. Dovey	2005	127
178¹/₈	179⁵/₈	38⁷/₈	36⁶/₈	15³/₈	15⁴/₈	8²/₈	8⁶/₈	20	19²/₈	Mineral Co., MT	Nathan L. Kauffman	Nathan L. Kauffman	2006	127
177⁵/₈	178⁷/₈	38⁷/₈	34⁴/₈	16⁶/₈	16⁵/₈	8	7⁶/₈	22⁷/₈	22³/₈	Granite Co., MT	Richard J. Hoffman	Richard J. Hoffman	2005	129
177³/₈	177⁷/₈	35	36³/₈	15	15	10³/₈	10¹/₈	20	18⁷/₈	Granite Co., MT	Trent Nielsen	Trent Nielsen	2004	130
176⁶/₈	177⁴/₈	36⁷/₈	37⁷/₈	14¹/₈	14⁴/₈	10¹/₈	9⁶/₈	21⁴/₈	21	Lewis & Clark Co., MT	Daniel L. Rossmiller	Daniel L. Rossmiller	2005	131
176⁴/₈	177	38³/₈	38⁷/₈	14³/₈	14³/₈	9	8⁶/₈	21³/₈	18⁴/₈	Teton Co., MT	David S. Lorash	David S. Lorash	2003	132
176⁴/₈	177²/₈	37⁵/₈	34³/₈	14⁷/₈	14⁵/₈	10²/₈	10	21³/₈	20⁴/₈	Sherman Co., OR	Michael S. Bohna	Michael S. Bohna	2004	132
176³/₈	176⁶/₈	38⁶/₈	36³/₈	14⁵/₈	14⁶/₈	8⁷/₈	8⁷/₈	23	21¹/₈	Lewis & Clark Co., MT	Delmar E. Hayden	Delmar E. Hayden	2005	134
176	176³/₈	40⁶/₈	37⁶/₈	15	15	7⁶/₈	8	22	21	Sanders Co., MT	Robert H. Berreth	Robert H. Berreth	2004	135
176	176⁴/₈	37⁶/₈	38⁶/₈	13⁴/₈	13⁴/₈	10²/₈	10²/₈	21⁴/₈	16⁶/₈	Santa Fe Co., NM	Mike P. Felten	Mike P. Felten	2006	135
175⁷/₈	176¹/₈	38²/₈	37⁷/₈	16⁷/₈	16⁷/₈	6⁶/₈	6⁶/₈	22⁴/₈	22⁴/₈	S. Castle River, AB	Ginger A. Holladay	Ginger A. Holladay	2004	137
175⁶/₈	176¹/₈	38²/₈	39⁶/₈	13³/₈	13³/₈	9³/₈	9⁴/₈	20¹/₈	18	Missoula Co., MT	Darcy J. Brunett	Darcy J. Brunett	2003	138
175³/₈	176³/₈	33⁶/₈	34⁷/₈	14⁶/₈	14⁷/₈	9⁷/₈	10⁴/₈	23⁶/₈	20¹/₈	Park Co., CO	Tom Colander	Tom Colander	2004	139
175³/₈	175⁴/₈	37²/₈	38⁵/₈	14³/₈	14⁴/₈	8²/₈	8²/₈	22³/₈	19	Park Co., WY	Paul D. Ringler	Paul D. Ringler	2006	139
175²/₈	175⁷/₈	36⁴/₈	37	15²/₈	15⁵/₈	8⁵/₈	8⁴/₈	22¹/₈	19⁴/₈	Elko Co., NV	Les W. Boni	Les W. Boni	2005	141
175	175³/₈	36²/₈	35⁶/₈	14⁶/₈	14⁷/₈	9⁶/₈	9⁴/₈	22²/₈	16²/₈	Teton Co., MT	Dan Oakland	Dan Oakland	2003	142
184⁴/₈*	198⁷/₈	41⁵/₈	43¹/₈	16³/₈	16⁴/₈	10⁷/₈	10⁶/₈	24³/₈	19¹/₈	Taos Co., NM	B. Neal Ainsworth, Jr.	B. Neal Ainsworth, Jr.	2005	
197²/₈*	198	40⁵/₈	41³/₈	16¹/₈	16²/₈	11²/₈	11³/₈	20⁶/₈	20⁶/₈	Ewin Creek, BC	David P. Rivers	David P. Rivers	2003	

* Final score subject to revision by additional verifying measurements.

DESERT SHEEP
FINAL SCORE: 174-6/8
HUNTER: Kevin D. Peterson

DESERT SHEEP
FINAL SCORE: 178-6/8
HUNTER: Brenton L. Scott

DESERT SHEEP
FINAL SCORE: 169-7/8
HUNTER: Skylar J. Hansen

BIGHORN SHEEP
FINAL SCORE: 186-1/8
HUNTER: Edward H. Elms

DESERT SHEEP

Ovis canadensis nelsoni and certain related subspecies

Minimum Score 165

World's Record 205 $^1/_8$

Final Score	Gross Score	Length of horn R.	Length of horn L.	Circumference of Base R.	Circumference of Base L.	Circumference at Third Quarter R.	Circumference at Third Quarter L.	Greatest Spread	Tip to Tip Spread	Locality	Hunter	Owner	Date Killed	Rank
$188^2/_8$	$188^5/_8$	$37^4/_8$	$38^4/_8$	$17^1/_8$	17	$8^7/_8$	$8^7/_8$	22	$18^4/_8$	Hidalgo Co., NM	Russell A. Young	Russell A. Young	2006	1
$185^2/_8$	$186^2/_8$	$38^4/_8$	$37^6/_8$	16	$16^2/_8$	$9^2/_8$	$9^1/_8$	$20^4/_8$	17	Sonora, MX	K. Michael Ingram	K. Michael Ingram	2005	2
$183^5/_8$	$183^5/_8$	$36^6/_8$	$36^3/_8$	$15^6/_8$	$15^6/_8$	10	10	$24^6/_8$	$24^4/_8$	Brewster Co., TX	Terry J. Fricks	Terry J. Fricks	2005	3
$182^6/_8$	$185^5/_8$	$36^6/_8$	$39^5/_8$	$15^4/_8$	$15^2/_8$	$9^2/_8$	$10^6/_8$	17	$17^7/_8$	Hidalgo Co., NM	Thomas D. Friedkin	Thomas D. Friedkin	2005	4
182	$184^6/_8$	$40^1/_8$	$41^7/_8$	14	$13^4/_8$	$11^1/_8$	$10^6/_8$	$24^1/_8$	$23^3/_8$	Riverside Co., CA	Picked Up	Craig Smithson	1973	5
$181^7/_8$	182	$36^4/_8$	$36^1/_8$	$16^3/_8$	$16^3/_8$	$9^3/_8$	$9^4/_8$	$22^4/_8$	$21^6/_8$	Baja Calif. Sur, MX	James G. Petersen	James G. Petersen	2005	6
$181^5/_8$	$182^2/_8$	$39^5/_8$	$37^2/_8$	$15^5/_8$	$15^4/_8$	9	$8^4/_8$	$23^2/_8$	$23^2/_8$	Pinal Co., AZ	Tammy J. Ulmer	Tammy J. Ulmer	2003	7
180	$180^2/_8$	$36^2/_8$	$39^2/_8$	$15^5/_8$	$15^4/_8$	$8^5/_8$	$8^4/_8$	$23^2/_8$	$23^7/_8$	Brewster Co., TX	Glenn Thurman	Glenn Thurman	2004	8
180	$180^7/_8$	$35^2/_8$	$35^6/_8$	$16^4/_8$	$16^3/_8$	$9^2/_8$	$9^5/_8$	$22^1/_8$	$21^2/_8$	Mohave Co., AZ	Lorin J. Wilkin	Lorin J. Wilkin	2004	8
$179^5/_8$	$181^7/_8$	39	$38^7/_8$	$14^7/_8$	$14^6/_8$	$10^2/_8$	10	$23^1/_8$	$18^5/_8$	Tiburon Island, MX	Russell A. Young	Russell A. Young	2005	10
$178^6/_8$	181	$38^1/_8$	$36^5/_8$	$15^2/_8$	$15^2/_8$	$10^2/_8$	$9^2/_8$	$22^5/_8$	20	Hidalgo Co., NM	Brenton L. Scott	Brenton L. Scott	2004	11
$178^1/_8$	$179^4/_8$	$37^7/_8$	$36^6/_8$	$15^4/_8$	$15^4/_8$	$9^2/_8$	$8^4/_8$	$21^5/_8$	$16^4/_8$	Tiburon Island, MX	Alfred E. Baldwin	Alfred E. Baldwin	2002	12
$176^4/_8$	$176^6/_8$	$38^7/_8$	$39^3/_8$	$13^7/_8$	$13^7/_8$	$8^3/_8$	$8^4/_8$	$26^2/_8$	$25^7/_8$	Brewster Co., TX	Picked Up	TX Parks & Wildlife Dept.	2006	13
$176^3/_8$	$176^7/_8$	37	$37^3/_8$	$14^5/_8$	$14^4/_8$	$9^4/_8$	$9^4/_8$	$21^7/_8$	$18^3/_8$	La Paz Co., AZ	Garth Carter	Garth Carter	2003	14
176	$176^6/_8$	$34^6/_8$	$36^6/_8$	$15^5/_8$	$15^6/_8$	$8^7/_8$	$9^2/_8$	$22^6/_8$	$19^7/_8$	Clark Co., NV	L. Victor Clark	L. Victor Clark	2005	15
175	177	$37^3/_8$	$35^5/_8$	$16^2/_8$	$16^3/_8$	$8^1/_8$	$8^2/_8$	$18^1/_8$	$18^1/_8$	Baja Calif. Sur, MX	David M. Merkel	David M. Merkel	2005	16
$174^6/_8$	175	$37^4/_8$	37	15	15	$9^2/_8$	$9^1/_8$	$20^4/_8$	14	Hidalgo Co., NM	Kevin D. Peterson	Kevin D. Peterson	2005	17
$174^5/_8$	$175^3/_8$	$37^1/_8$	$38^6/_8$	$15^2/_8$	$15^3/_8$	$7^4/_8$	8	$21^2/_8$	21	Baja Calif., MX	Derek A. Burdeny	Derek A. Burdeny	2004	18
$174^5/_8$	$174^7/_8$	$35^3/_8$	36	$15^2/_8$	$15^2/_8$	$8^7/_8$	$8^6/_8$	19	$18^4/_8$	San Bernardino Co., CA	Wayne S. Close	Wayne S. Close	2005	18
$174^5/_8$	$175^5/_8$	$36^4/_8$	$37^5/_8$	$14^5/_8$	$14^5/_8$	$9^4/_8$	$9^7/_8$	27	27	Clark Co., NV	Jelindo A. Tiberti III	Jelindo A. Tiberti III	2005	18
$174^1/_8$	$174^1/_8$	37	$35^7/_8$	$14^1/_8$	$14^1/_8$	$9^7/_8$	$9^7/_8$	$25^2/_8$	$25^2/_8$	Nye Co., NV	Brent D. Haliwell	Brent D. Haliwell	2003	21
$174^4/_8$	$174^4/_8$	$36^2/_8$	$36^4/_8$	$15^1/_8$	$15^1/_8$	$9^2/_8$	$8^7/_8$	$20^6/_8$	$20^1/_8$	Baja Calif. Sur, MX	Ricky M. Davis	Ricky M. Davis	2005	22
$173^5/_8$	$173^6/_8$	$34^6/_8$	$34^1/_8$	$15^7/_8$	16	$8^6/_8$	$8^6/_8$	$21^4/_8$	$19^1/_8$	Maricopa Co., AZ	Michael A. Ronning	Michael A. Ronning	2005	23
$173^3/_8$	$174^2/_8$	$34^4/_8$	$35^5/_8$	$14^3/_8$	$14^4/_8$	$8^6/_8$	$9^7/_8$	22	21	Nye Co., NV	Picked Up	Michael S. Perchetti	2003	24
$173^1/_8$	$173^3/_8$	38	$36^1/_8$	$14^3/_8$	$14^3/_8$	9	9	$22^4/_8$	$21^4/_8$	Clark Co., NV	T.R. White	T.R. White	2005	25
$172^3/_8$	173	$33^5/_8$	$36^6/_8$	$15^4/_8$	$15^2/_8$	$9^5/_8$	$9^4/_8$	$20^5/_8$	$20^5/_8$	Mohave Co., AZ	Gabriel M. Lopez, Jr.	Gabriel M. Lopez, Jr.	2005	26
172	$172^7/_8$	$38^4/_8$	38	$13^1/_8$	$13^4/_8$	$9^3/_8$	$9^2/_8$	$19^5/_8$	$18^5/_8$	Tiburon Island, MX	Steven S. Bruggeman	Steven S. Bruggeman	2003	27
172	$172^1/_8$	$36^6/_8$	35	$14^6/_8$	$14^6/_8$	$9^1/_8$	$9^1/_8$	$20^3/_8$	$18^6/_8$	Nye Co., NV	Stephen Lattin	Stephen Lattin	2004	27
$171^6/_8$	$172^2/_8$	$34^4/_8$	$34^2/_8$	15	$15^1/_8$	$9^2/_8$	9	$22^2/_8$	$21^6/_8$	Nye Co., NV	Robert J. Lekumberry	Robert J. Lekumberry	2003	29
$171^5/_8$	$172^1/_8$	$33^7/_8$	32	$15^5/_8$	$15^4/_8$	$9^3/_8$	$9^1/_8$	$24^2/_8$	$23^3/_8$	Nye Co., NV	LeRoy A. Perks, Jr.	LeRoy A. Perks, Jr.	2003	30
171	$171^3/_8$	36	$35^4/_8$	$14^7/_8$	$14^7/_8$	$8^6/_8$	$8^4/_8$	$25^4/_8$	$24^4/_8$	Churchill Co., NV	Brent D. Seline	Brent D. Seline	2003	31
171	$172^4/_8$	35	$36^4/_8$	$14^6/_8$	$15^1/_8$	$9^4/_8$	$8^6/_8$	$21^2/_8$	$16^2/_8$	Tiburon Island, MX	John McCall	John McCall	2004	31

171	172 2/8	35 1/8	36 7/8	15	15 1/8	8 4/8	8	21 7/8	19 2/8	Maricopa Co., AZ	Jerry R. Tyrrell	Jerry R. Tyrrell	2004	31
170 4/8	171 2/8	36 4/8	36 6/8	14 7/8	14 6/8	8 2/8	8 3/8	21 3/8	21 2/8	La Paz Co., AZ	Donald R. Cradic	Donald R. Cradic	2003	34
170 3/8	170 6/8	34 5/8	34	15 1/8	15 1/8	9 5/8	9 3/8	21 4/8	17 6/8	San Bernardino Co., CA	Brian H. Davis	Brian H. Davis	2006	35
170 1/8	170 6/8	39 4/8	43 3/8	14 3/8	14 3/8	5 7/8	6 1/8	28 2/8	28 2/8	Carmen Island, MX	B. Neal Ainsworth, Jr.	B. Neal Ainsworth, Jr.	2005	36
170 1/8	170 6/8	35 4/8	34 5/8	15 2/8	15 1/8	8 3/8	8	22 4/8	21 6/8	Nye Co., NV	Ryan Polish	Ryan Polish	2005	36
170	170 4/8	33 5/8	34 3/8	14 6/8	14 4/8	9 1/8	9 2/8	22	19	La Paz Co., AZ	Wayne K. Gunnell	Wayne K. Gunnell	2004	38
170	170 5/8	34 6/8	35	15 2/8	15	8 2/8	8 4/8	22 4/8	22	Clark Co., NV	John K. Hillenbrand	John K. Hillenbrand	2004	38
169 7/8	170 6/8	38	38 1/8	13 3/8	13 4/8	9 6/8	9 3/8	21 1/8	20	Clark Co., NV	Skylar J. Hansen	Skylar J. Hansen	2005	40
169 7/8	171 1/8	33 4/8	33 5/8	15 2/8	15 5/8	8 4/8	8 7/8	24 4/8	23 7/8	Brewster Co., TX	Randy R. Pittman	Randy R. Pittman	2005	40
169 6/8	170 2/8	34 2/8	33 6/8	15 2/8	15 2/8	8 2/8	8 4/8	21 1/8	19 5/8	Clark Co., NV	Tom A. Walkley	Tom A. Walkley	2004	42
169 4/8	170 2/8	35 4/8	35	13 7/8	13 7/8	9 6/8	9 5/8	21 1/8	18	Sonora, MX	Charles I. Kelly	Charles I. Kelly	2005	43
169 3/8	169 6/8	34 4/8	35 3/8	14 4/8	14 4/8	8 4/8	8 3/8	26 7/8	26 4/8	Mineral Co., NV	William Stinson	William Stinson	2003	44
169 1/8	169 6/8	35	36 1/8	14 5/8	14 5/8	9	8 7/8	20 5/8	20	San Bernardino Co., CA	Edward V. Anderson	Edward V. Anderson	2003	45
169 1/8	169 4/8	35 2/8	35 4/8	14 3/8	14 3/8	8 4/8	8 3/8	20 6/8	18 7/8	La Paz Co., AZ	Dale E. Toweill	Dale E. Toweill	2005	45
168 6/8	169 4/8	34 7/8	35 1/8	16 1/8	16 5/8	7 1/8	7 2/8	17 1/8	17 1/8	Sonora, MX	Dale K. Marrou	Dale K. Marrou	2005	47
168 6/8	170 2/8	35 5/8	33 5/8	14 4/8	14 3/8	9 2/8	8 6/8	18 2/8	18 2/8	Carmen Island, MX	Richard G. Bailey	Richard G. Bailey	2006	47
168 5/8	169 4/8	35 3/8	35 4/8	14 3/8	14 4/8	9 2/8	9 2/8	23 4/8	22 7/8	Clark Co., NV	Ron L. Fagg	Ron L. Fagg	2003	49
168 4/8	169 4/8	36 4/8	37	13 6/8	13 6/8	9 4/8	9 2/8	24 4/8	23 6/8	Clark Co., NV	Martha H. Heckman	Martha H. Heckman	2005	50
168 3/8	170 1/8	37 2/8	32 5/8	15 1/8	15 3/8	8 3/8	7 3/8	23	22 6/8	Washington Co., UT	Shawn A. Labrum	Shawn A. Labrum	2003	51
168 3/8	169 4/8	34 7/8	34	15 3/8	15 6/8	8 3/8	8 2/8	19	15	Baja Calif., MX	Randall K. Rauschmier	Randall K. Rauschmier	2004	51
168 3/8	169 1/8	33 4/8	32 5/8	14 3/8	14 3/8	9 5/8	9	24 1/8	24 1/8	Hudspeth Co., TX	William M. Wheless IV	William M. Wheless IV	2005	51
168 2/8	169 2/8	33 4/8	34 2/8	14 7/8	14 3/8	9 3/8	9 5/8	23 5/8	23 1/8	Clark Co., NV	John Reed	John Reed	2004	54
168 2/8	170 3/8	31 7/8	34 7/8	14 5/8	14 7/8	9 1/8	10 1/8	23 4/8	22 4/8	Maricopa Co., AZ	Amber J. Richardson	Amber J. Richardson	2004	54
168 1/8	168 7/8	34 2/8	31 3/8	14 7/8	14 7/8	9 7/8	9 3/8	23 4/8	23 4/8	Clark Co., NV	Henry Thornhill	Henry Thornhill	2003	56
168	168 3/8	34 2/8	35 2/8	15 3/8	15 4/8	7 7/8	8	23 2/8	23 2/8	San Bernardino Co., CA	James C. Hankla	James C. Hankla	2003	57
168	168 5/8	35 5/8	36 1/8	13 3/8	13 4/8	9 6/8	9 6/8	20 5/8	19 3/8	Nye Co., NV	John V. Zenz	John V. Zenz	2004	57
167 5/8	167 5/8	35 1/8	35 6/8	13 6/8	13 4/8	9	9	17	17 2/8	Baja Calif., MX	William C. Foose	William C. Foose	2004	59
167 3/8	167 3/8	34 6/8	35 4/8	15 1/8	15 1/8	7 3/8	7 3/8	22 5/8	22 2/8	Mohave Co., AZ	Rick Farthing	Picked Up	1972	60
167 2/8	167 2/8	35 6/8	36 4/8	14 3/8	14 3/8	7 6/8	7 6/8	19 4/8	16 1/8	Sonora, MX	Ronald C. Miller	Ronald C. Miller	1999	60
167 1/8	168 1/8	36 4/8	34 5/8	14 1/8	14 4/8	8 1/8	8 1/8	20 4/8	20 4/8	Clark Co., NV	Richard W. Howell	Richard W. Howell	2003	62
167 1/8	167 3/8	36 5/8	33 6/8	13 7/8	14 1/8	8	8	23 3/8	23	Brewster Co., TX	Ronald W. Marsh	Ronald W. Marsh	2005	62
166 7/8	166 7/8	33 5/8	36 4/8	14	13 7/8	8 3/8	8 4/8	25 4/8	24 4/8	Mohave Co., AZ	Efren G. Ruiz	Efren G. Ruiz	2004	64
166 3/8	166 7/8	34 4/8	33 4/8	14 2/8	14 3/8	9 3/8	9 1/8	28 1/8	27 3/8	Nye Co., NV	Gary H. Wilcox, Jr.	Gary H. Wilcox, Jr.	2004	65
166 2/8	166 4/8	32 7/8	31 7/8	14 3/8	14 3/8	9 4/8	9 5/8	21 7/8	21 6/8	Maricopa Co., AZ	Jim G. Winjum	Jim G. Winjum	2004	65
166 2/8	167 3/8	34	34 6/8	13 7/8	13 7/8	10 3/8	10 3/8	19 5/8	18 5/8	Clark Co., NV	Rafael Betancourt III	Rafael Betancourt III	2005	65
165 7/8	166 5/8	34 1/8	34 4/8	14 6/8	15	7 5/8	7 8/8	25 5/8	24 5/8	Churchill Co., NV	Lance Lemaire	Lance Lemaire	2003	68
165 4/8	166 6/8	35 3/8	36 1/8	14 2/8	14 1/8	7 7/8	7 7/8	19	17 7/8	Yuma Co., AZ	Dennis H. Moss	Dennis H. Moss	2004	69
183 6/8*	184 4/8	37 3/8	39 3/8	15 7/8	16	9 1/8	9 3/8	20 4/8	18 6/8	Baja Calif. Sur, MX	Troy D. Vest	Troy D. Vest	2006	57

* Final score subject to revision by additional verifying measurements.

DALL'S SHEEP

Ovis dalli dalli and *Ovis dalli kenaiensis*

Minimum Score 160   World's Record 189 6/8

Final Score	Gross Score	Length of horn R.	L.	Circumference of Base R.	L.	Circumference at Third Quarter R.	L.	Greatest Spread	Tip to Tip Spread	Locality	Hunter	Owner	Date Killed	Rank
178 4/8	178 6/8	43 4/8	43 4/8	14 5/8	14 4/8	6 5/8	6 4/8	28 4/8	28 4/8	Mackenzie Mts., NT	Cody A. Miller	Cody A. Miller	2005	1
173 4/8	173 6/8	43 3/8	43 1/8	13 6/8	13 6/8	5 7/8	5 6/8	24 7/8	24 6/8	Chugach Mts., AK	Nick J. Duncan	Nick J. Duncan	2006	2
173 3/8	173 4/8	41 7/8	42 4/8	14	14	6	6 1/8	23 6/8	23 5/8	Alaska Range, AK	Cynthia Cassell	Cynthia Cassell	2004	3
171 7/8	172 6/8	38 1/8	40	15	14 7/8	6 6/8	7	26 6/8	26 2/8	Chugach Mts., AK	James G. Petersen	James G. Petersen	2004	4
171 5/8	171 7/8	42 4/8	42 5/8	14 1/8	14 1/8	5 7/8	5 7/8	25 1/8	25	Tazlina Glacier, AK	Jake W. Staser	Jake W. Staser	2005	5
171 2/8	171 3/8	42 2/8	41 2/8	14	14	6 1/8	6 1/8	31 7/8	31 7/8	Mackenzie Mts., NT	Terry R. Hansen	Terry R. Hansen	2005	6
171	171 1/8	42	42 2/8	14 3/8	14 3/8	5 4/8	5 4/8	30 5/8	30 5/8	Mackenzie Mts., AK	John J. Goddard	John J. Goddard	2004	7
171	171 5/8	42	42	13 4/8	13 5/8	6 4/8	6 6/8	25 2/8	25 2/8	Sheenjek River, AK	Joseph A. Benson III	Joseph A. Benson III	2006	7
170 1/8	170 1/8	42 4/8	42 3/8	13	13	6 1/8	6 1/8	27 2/8	27 2/8	Godlin River, NT	Thomas L. Teague	Thomas L. Teague	2003	9
169 4/8	169 5/8	42	42	13	13 1/8	6 5/8	6 5/8	26 5/8	26 5/8	Bonnet Plume River, YT	Don W. Ledbetter	Don W. Ledbetter	2005	10
169	169 2/8	40 5/8	39 3/8	14 2/8	14 2/8	6	6	24 2/8	24 1/8	Ruby Range, YT	Dave Turchanski	Dave Turchanski	2006	11
168 4/8	168 6/8	43	42 6/8	13 5/8	13 5/8	5 4/8	5 3/8	32 6/8	32 5/8	Chugach Mts., AK	Merle J. Uscola	Merle J. Uscola	2005	12
167 6/8	168 1/8	41 2/8	42	13 3/8	13 3/8	5 5/8	5 6/8	27 4/8	27 2/8	Mackenzie Mts., NT	Timothy H. Humes	Timothy H. Humes	2006	13
167 5/8	168 1/8	39 3/8	40 2/8	13 6/8	13 5/8	6 4/8	6 5/8	22 7/8	22 5/8	Mackenzie Mts., NT	Robert G. Spencer	Robert G. Spencer	2005	14
167 3/8	167 3/8	40 6/8	38 7/8	14 2/8	14 2/8	5 6/8	6	27 4/8	27 4/8	Chugach Mts., AK	Joseph C. Cerwonka	Joseph C. Cerwonka	1963	15
167 3/8	168 3/8	40 5/8	40 4/8	13 5/8	14 3/8	6 1/8	6 1/8	28 7/8	28 4/8	Chugach Mts., AK	William H. Bunting	William H. Bunting	2005	15
166 5/8	167 5/8	39 6/8	39 3/8	14	14 1/8	6	6 1/8	23 7/8	23 6/8	Twin Lakes, AK	Bryan L. McGregor	Bryan L. McGregor	2005	17
166 4/8	167 3/8	39 7/8	38 5/8	15	14 6/8	5 6/8	5 6/8	25	25	Devilhole Creek, YT	Dan Du Bose	Dan Du Bose	2006	18
166 3/8	167	40 1/8	40 2/8	14	14 2/8	5 5/8	5 5/8	25 3/8	25 2/8	Chugach Mts., AK	Derek R. Harbula	Derek R. Harbula	2003	19
166 3/8	167 1/8	40 3/8	37 6/8	13 6/8	13 6/8	7 1/8	6 7/8	24	24	Rock Candy Creek, AK	Wayne G. Wilson	Wayne G. Wilson	2004	19
166 3/8	167	38 2/8	41 5/8	14 2/8	14 2/8	6 5/8	6 4/8	25 6/8	25 6/8	Chitina River, AK	Jerrell F. Coburn	Jerrell F. Coburn	2006	19
166 3/8	167 7/8	35 7/8	40	14 2/8	15 2/8	6 4/8	6 5/8	22	21 6/8	Mackenzie Mts., NT	William Osuchowski	William Osuchowski	2006	19
166 2/8	166 3/8	38	40 2/8	13 4/8	13 4/8	6 6/8	6 6/8	21	20 7/8	Brooks Range, AK	Vance M. Julian	Vance M. Julian	2002	23
165 6/8	166	39	39	14	14 2/8	6 2/8	6 2/8	27 7/8	27 7/8	Mackenzie Mts., NT	Milton Schultz, Jr.	Milton Schultz, Jr.	2005	24
165 5/8	165 7/8	40 2/8	40 5/8	13 4/8	13 5/8	5 5/8	5 5/8	26 1/8	26	Ogilvie Mts., YT	Doris Twichell	Doris Twichell	2005	25
165 4/8	165 5/8	39 2/8	37	14	14	6 2/8	6 2/8	24	24	Tatonduk River, YT	J.H. Rhea	J.H. Rhea	2006	26
165 2/8	165 4/8	41 6/8	41 6/8	13	13	5 4/8	5 4/8	25 6/8	25 6/8	Tok River, AK	Scott M. Buckingham	Scott M. Buckingham	2005	27
165	165 3/8	41	38	13 4/8	13 3/8	6 4/8	6 6/8	19 6/8	19 4/8	Chugach Mts., AK	L. Victor Clark	L. Victor Clark	2005	28
165	165 3/8	40	40	13 6/8	13 7/8	5 4/8	5 3/8	22 4/8	22 3/8	Alaska Range, AK	Peter L. Malecha	Peter L. Malecha	2005	28
164 6/8	165 2/8	40	40 2/8	14	14	6	5 7/8	23 5/8	23 5/8	Arctic Red River, NT	Sidney P. Groll	Sidney P. Groll	2006	30
164 5/8	165	38 7/8	40	13 7/8	13 7/8	6 1/8	5 7/8	25 3/8	24 6/8	Redstone River, NT	Carl Sporer	Carl Sporer	2004	31

Score	Score									Locality	Hunter	Owner	Date	Rank
164³/₈	165	40³/₈	39²/₈	12⁴/₈	12⁴/₈	7⁵/₈	7²/₈	24²/₈	24²/₈	Hart River, YT	William C. Foose	William C. Foose	2005	32
163⁵/₈	164⁴/₈	36⁵/₈	36⁶/₈	13⁶/₈	14	6⁷/₈	7¹/₈	21⁷/₈	21¹/₈	Chugach Mts., AK	Lance A. Kronberger	Lance A. Kronberger	2005	33
163²/₈	163⁴/₈	40²/₈	39⁶/₈	13⁴/₈	13⁴/₈	5⁶/₈	5⁶/₈	29²/₈	29²/₈	Old Woman Creek, AK	John M. Hanner	John M. Hanner	2003	34
163¹/₈	163²/₈	39⁶/₈	39⁷/₈	13⁶/₈	13⁵/₈	5⁶/₈	5⁶/₈	26²/₈	26¹/₈	Tanana Hills, AK	Scott M. Luber	Scott M. Luber	2004	35
163	163⁶/₈	40¹/₈	39³/₈	13⁶/₈	13⁴/₈	5⁴/₈	5³/₈	26⁶/₈	26⁴/₈	Aishihik Lake, YT	Larry N. Puckett	Larry N. Puckett	2005	36
163	163	38²/₈	39	13⁵/₈	13⁶/₈	5⁶/₈	5⁶/₈	25²/₈	25²/₈	Ruby Range, YT	Kelly Wiebe	Kelly Wiebe	2005	36
162⁵/₈	163⁴/₈	41¹/₈	40⁶/₈	13³/₈	13¹/₈	5³/₈	5²/₈	30²/₈	30²/₈	Kongakut River, AK	Frederick R. Kloos	Frederick R. Kloos	2004	38
162³/₈	163¹/₈	38⁵/₈	39⁶/₈	13⁵/₈	13⁴/₈	5⁷/₈	5⁷/₈	24⁴/₈	24²/₈	Keele River, NT	Fitzhugh K. Peters	Fitzhugh K. Peters	2002	39
162²/₈	163⁶/₈	39⁴/₈	39²/₈	15	14¹/₈	5⁶/₈	5⁶/₈	26	26	Moraine Lake, YT	John Beecher	John Beecher	2006	40
162²/₈	162⁴/₈	39⁴/₈	40	12⁶/₈	12⁶/₈	6⁴/₈	6²/₈	25⁶/₈	25⁶/₈	Bonnet Plume River, YT	Michael D. Moore	Michael D. Moore	2006	40
161³/₈	161⁵/₈	38⁴/₈	39³/₈	13³/₈	13³/₈	5⁷/₈	5⁷/₈	27³/₈	27	Talkeetna Mts., AK	Stanley J. Schmidt	Stanley J. Schmidt	2003	42
161²/₈	161⁴/₈	37⁴/₈	37	12²/₈	12¹/₈	8¹/₈	8	22²/₈	22²/₈	Baird Mts., AK	Dwight H. Kramer	Dwight H. Kramer	1976	43
161¹/₈	162²/₈	41²/₈	37⁷/₈	13⁶/₈	13⁴/₈	5³/₈	5⁷/₈	38⁵/₈	38³/₈	White River, YT	Stephen F. Cotta	Stephen F. Cotta	2006	44
160⁷/₈	161⁴/₈	41⁷/₈	41⁶/₈	12⁴/₈	12⁵/₈	5	5³/₈	30⁴/₈	30²/₈	Primrose River, YT	Jeffrey T. Shaffer	William Piper	1974	45
160⁷/₈	161³/₈	36	39⁷/₈	14	13⁷/₈	5⁷/₈	5⁶/₈	24⁷/₈	24⁷/₈	Liard Range, NT	Edward S. Jankowski	Edward S. Jankowski	2004	45
160⁷/₈	160⁷/₈	36	36³/₈	14	14	6	6	25⁴/₈	25⁴/₈	Chugach Mts., AK	David R. Lautner	David R. Lautner	2005	45
160³/₈	160⁶/₈	40⁴/₈	39⁷/₈	13¹/₈	13¹/₈	5³/₈	5⁴/₈	23⁶/₈	23⁶/₈	Sifton Range, YT	Fred M. Pannunzio	Fred M. Pannunzio	2005	48
160¹/₈	160⁶/₈	36¹/₈	38²/₈	13⁶/₈	13⁵/₈	6	6	21⁷/₈	21⁷/₈	Arctic Red River, NT	Craig P. Mitton	Craig P. Mitton	2005	49
173⁶/₈*	174²/₈	40⁶/₈	40⁴/₈	15	15	6⁷/₈	6⁶/₈	23⁴/₈	23⁵/₈	Chugach Mts., AK	Edward S. Halstead	Edward S. Halstead	2003	
173⁴/₈*	174²/₈	40²/₈	40²/₈	14⁴/₈	14⁵/₈	6¹/₈	6¹/₈	26⁶/₈	27	Chugach Mts., AK	Aaron Kelly	Aaron Kelly	2004	

* Final score subject to revision by additional verifying measurements.

STONE'S SHEEP

Ovis dalli stonei

Minimum Score 165

World's Record 196 6/8

Final Score	Gross Score	Length of horn R.	L.	Circumference of Base R.	L.	Circumference at Third Quarter R.	L.	Greatest Spread	Tip to Tip Spread	Locality	Hunter	Owner	Date Killed	Rank
179 5/8	180 1/8	42 7/8	43	15	15	6 4/8	6 2/8	22 6/8	22 4/8	Hook Lake, BC	Jelindo A. Tiberti II	Jelindo A. Tiberti II	2005	1
171 2/8	173 1/8	41 6/8	42 4/8	13 6/8	13 6/8	6 1/8	7 4/8	25 1/8	25 1/8	Turnagain River, BC	John Colby	Daniel S. Werbe	1967	2
171	171 3/8	43 5/8	43 3/8	13 4/8	13 5/8	5 5/8	5 5/8	26 4/8	26 4/8	Kechika Range, BC	Rick E. Hilgersom	Rick E. Hilgersom	2004	3
170 6/8	171 2/8	41 7/8	44 7/8	13 6/8	13 6/8	5 4/8	5 5/8	24 7/8	24 5/8	Eight Mile Creek, BC	Thomas E. Lester	Thomas E. Lester	2006	4
170 2/8	170 6/8	40 1/8	40 3/8	14 6/8	14 6/8	5 5/8	5 4/8	25 7/8	25 5/8	McDonald Creek, BC	Bruce Radford	Bruce Radford	2003	5
168 1/8	168 4/8	40 3/8	40 4/8	13 7/8	13 6/8	6	6	25	24 7/8	Lapie Lake, BC	Patrick L. Kirsch	Patrick L. Kirsch	2004	6
173 5/8*	174	39 1/8	38 6/8	15 1/8	15 1/8	6 6/8	6 5/8	23 2/8	23	Muncho Lake, BC	Charles P. Pinjuv	Charles P. Pinjuv	2004	
172 3/8*	172 6/8	42 7/8	43 2/8	14 2/8	14 1/8	6 2/8	6 1/8	27 4/8	27 4/8	Toad River, BC	Jeffrey K. Chaulk	Jeffrey K. Chaulk	2004	
171 5/8*	171 6/8	42 1/8	39 4/8	14 2/8	14 2/8	6 1/8	6 1/8	24 4/8	24 3/8	Braid Creek, BC	James G. Petersen	James G. Petersen	2005	
171 2/8*	171 7/8	42	37	14 2/8	14 4/8	7	6 6/8	24 6/8	23 7/8	Muncho Lake, BC	Matt A. Meyer	Matt A. Meyer	2005	

* Final score subject to revision by additional verifying measurements.

DALL'S SHEEP
FINAL SCORE: 162-3/8
HUNTER: Fitzhugh K. Peters

DALL'S SHEEP
FINAL SCORE: 166-3/8
HUNTER: Jerrell F. Coburn

STONE'S SHEEP
FINAL SCORE: 172-3/8*
HUNTER: Jeffrey K. Chaulk

DALL'S SHEEP
FINAL SCORE: 165-5/8
HUNTER: Doris Twichell

OFFICIAL SCORE CHARTS FOR NORTH AMERICAN BIG GAME TROPHIES

250 Station Drive
Missoula, MT 59801
(406) 542-1888

BOONE AND CROCKETT CLUB®
OFFICIAL SCORING SYSTEM FOR NORTH AMERICAN BIG GAME TROPHIES

BEAR

	MINIMUM SCORES		KIND OF BEAR (check one)
	AWARDS	ALL-TIME	
black bear	20	21	☐ black bear
grizzly bear	23	24	☑ grizzly
Alaska brown bear	26	28	☐ Alaska brown bear
polar bear	27	27	☐ polar

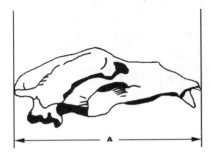

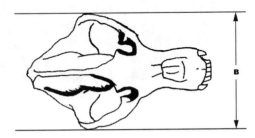

SEE OTHER SIDE FOR INSTRUCTIONS	MEASUREMENTS
A. Greatest Length Without Lower Jaw	17 4/16
B. Greatest Width	10 9/16
FINAL SCORE	27 13/16

Exact Locality Where Killed: **Big River (Lone Mt.), Alaska**

Date Killed: **1976** Hunter: **Picked Up**

Trophy Owner: **Gordon E. Scott** Telephone #:

Trophy Owner's Address:

Trophy Owner's E-mail: Guide's Name:

Remarks: (Mention Any Abnormalities or Unique Qualities)

I, _____ **Alan Jubenville** _____, certify that I have measured this trophy on **01/15/2003**
PRINT NAME MM/DD/YYYYY

at _**Fairbanks, AK**_____
STREET ADDRESS CITY STATE/PROVINCE

and that these measurements and data are, to the best of my knowledge and belief, made in accordance with the instructions given.

Witness: _____ Signature: _____ I.D. Number ☐☐☐☐
B&C OFFICIAL MEASURER

INSTRUCTIONS FOR MEASURING BEAR

Measurements are taken with calipers or by using parallel perpendiculars, to the nearest **one-sixteenth** of an inch, without reduction of fractions. Official measurements cannot be taken until the skull has air dried for at least 60 days after the animal was killed. All adhering flesh, membrane and cartilage must be completely removed **before** official measurements are taken.

  A. Greatest Length is measured between perpendiculars parallel to the long axis of the skull, without the lower jaw and excluding malformations.

  B. Greatest Width is measured between perpendiculars at right angles to the long axis.

ENTRY AFFIDAVIT FOR ALL HUNTER-TAKEN TROPHIES

For the purpose of entry into the Boone and Crockett Club's® records, North American big game harvested by the use of the following methods or under the following conditions are ineligible:

   I. Spotting or herding game from the air, followed by landing in its vicinity for the purpose of pursuit and shooting;
   II. Herding or chasing with the aid of any motorized equipment;
   III. Use of electronic communication devices to guide hunters to game, artificial lighting, electronic light intensifying devices (night vision optics), sights with built-in electronic range-finding capabilities, thermal imaging equipment, electronic game calls or cameras/timers/motion tracking devices that transmit images and other information to the hunter;
   IV. Confined by artificial barriers, including escape-proof fenced enclosures;
   V. Transplanted for the purpose of commercial shooting;
   VI. By the use of traps or pharmaceuticals;
   VII. While swimming, helpless in deep snow, or helpless in any other natural or artificial medium;
   VIII. On another hunter's license;
   IX. Not in full compliance with the game laws or regulations of the federal government or of any state, province, territory, or tribal council on reservations or tribal lands;

Please answer the following questions:

Were dogs used in conjunction with the pursuit and harvest of this animal?
    ☐ Yes   ☐ No

If the answer to the above question is yes, answer the following statements:

    1. I was present on the hunt at the times the dogs were released to pursue this animal.
       ☐ True ☐ False

    2. If electronic collars were attached to any of the dogs, receivers were not used to harvest this animal.
       ☐ True ☐ False

To the best of my knowledge the answers to the above statements are true. If the answer to either #1 or #2 above is false, please explain on a separate sheet.

I certify that the trophy scored on this chart was not taken in violation of the conditions listed above. In signing this statement, I understand that if the information provided on this entry is found to be misrepresented or fraudulent in any respect, it will not be accepted into the Awards Program and 1) all of my prior entries are subject to deletion from future editions of **Records of North American Big Game** 2) future entries may not be accepted.

FAIR CHASE, as defined by the Boone and Crockett Club®, is the ethical, sportsmanlike and lawful pursuit and taking of any free-ranging wild, native North American big game animal in a manner that does not give the hun̲t̲e̲r̲ ̲ ̲ ̲ ̲ ̲ ̲age over such game animals.

The Boone and Crockett Club® may exclude the entry of any animal that it deem̲ ̲ ̲ ̲ ̲ ̲ ̲ ̲ ̲ ̲cal manner or under conditions deemed inappropriate by the Club.

Date: _____ Signature of Hunter: _____
                                                 (SI̲ ̲PUBLIC.)

Date: _____ Signature of Notary or

Records of
North American
Big Game

250 Station Drive
Missoula, MT 59801
(406) 542-1888

BOONE AND CROCKETT CLUB®
OFFICIAL SCORING SYSTEM FOR NORTH AMERICAN BIG GAME TROPHIES
COUGAR AND JAGUAR

	MINIMUM SCORES		KIND OF CAT (check one)
	AWARDS	ALL-TIME	■ cougar
cougar	14 - 8/16	15	☐ jaguar
jaguar	14 - 8/16	14 - 8/16	

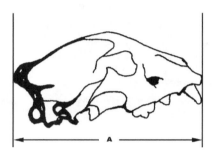
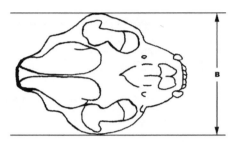

SEE OTHER SIDE FOR INSTRUCTIONS	MEASUREMENTS
A. Greatest Length Without Lower Jaw	9 8/16
B. Greatest Width	6 10/16
FINAL SCORE	16 2/16

Exact Locality Where Killed: **Sundance Lake, Alberta**

Date Killed: **12/1/2005**   Hunter: **Joseph Gore, Jr.**

Trophy Owner: **Same**   Telephone #:

Trophy Owner's Address:

Trophy Owner's E-mail: Guide's Name:

Remarks: (Mention Any Abnormalities or Unique Qualities)

I, _____**David Paplawski**_____ , certify that I have measured this trophy on ___**2/2/2006**___
          PRINT NAME   MM/DD/YYYYY

at _**Calgary, Alberta**_____
    STREET ADDRESS   CITY   STATE/PROVINCE

and that these measurements and data are, to the best of my knowledge and belief, made in accordance with the instructions given.

Witness: _____   Signature: _____   I.D. Number ☐☐☐☐
                                                              B&C OFFICIAL MEASURER

COPYRIGHT © 2006 BY BOONE AND CROCKETT CLUB®

INSTRUCTIONS FOR MEASURING COUGAR AND JAGUAR

Measurements are taken with calipers or by using parallel perpendiculars, to the nearest **one-sixteenth** of an inch, without reduction of fractions. Official measurements cannot be taken until the skull has air dried for at least 60 days after the animal was killed. All adhering flesh, membrane and cartilage must be completely removed **before** official measurements are taken.

- **A. Greatest Length** is measured between perpendiculars parallel to the long axis of the skull, without the lower jaw and excluding malformations.
- **B. Greatest Width** is measured between perpendiculars at right angles to the long axis.

ENTRY AFFIDAVIT FOR ALL HUNTER-TAKEN TROPHIES

For the purpose of entry into the Boone and Crockett Club's® records, North American big game harvested by the use of the following methods or under the following conditions are ineligible:

- I. Spotting or herding game from the air, followed by landing in its vicinity for the purpose of pursuit and shooting;
- II. Herding or chasing with the aid of any motorized equipment;
- III. Use of electronic communication devices to guide hunters to game, artificial lighting, electronic light intensifying devices (night vision optics), sights with built-in electronic range-finding capabilities, thermal imaging equipment, electronic game calls or cameras/timers/motion tracking devices that transmit images and other information to the hunter;
- IV. Confined by artificial barriers, including escape-proof fenced enclosures;
- V. Transplanted for the purpose of commercial shooting;
- VI. By the use of traps or pharmaceuticals;
- VII. While swimming, helpless in deep snow, or helpless in any other natural or artificial medium;
- VIII. On another hunter's license;
- IX. Not in full compliance with the game laws or regulations of the federal government or of any state, province, territory, or tribal council on reservations or tribal lands;

Please answer the following questions:

Were dogs used in conjunction with the pursuit and harvest of this animal?
☐ Yes   ☐ No

If the answer to the above question is yes, answer the following statements:

1. I was present on the hunt at the times the dogs were released to pursue this animal.
   ☐ True ☐ False

2. If electronic collars were attached to any of the dogs, receivers were not used to harvest this animal.
   ☐ True ☐ False

To the best of my knowledge the answers to the above statements are true. If the answer to either #1 or #2 above is false, please explain on a separate sheet.

I certify that the trophy scored on this chart was not taken in violation of the conditions listed above. In signing this statement, I understand that if the information provided on this entry is found to be misrepresented or fraudulent in any respect, it will not be accepted into the Awards Program and 1) all of my prior entries are subject to deletion from future editions of **Records of North American Big Game** 2) future entries may not be accepted.

FAIR CHASE, as defined by the Boone and Crockett Club®, is the ethical, sportsmanlike and lawful pursuit and taking of any free-ranging wild, native North American big game animal in a manner that does not give the hunter an improper advantage over such game animals.

The Boone and Crockett C̶ entry of any animal that it deems to have been taken in an unethical manner or under conditions dee̶

Date

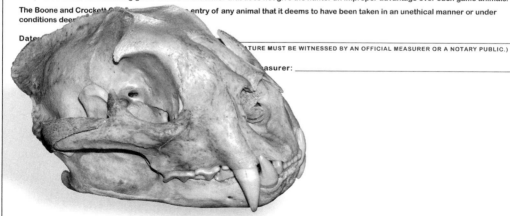

(̶ATURE MUST BE WITNESSED BY AN OFFICIAL MEASURER OR A NOTARY PUBLIC.)

̶asurer: _____

250 Station Drive
Missoula, MT 59801
(406) 542-1888

BOONE AND CROCKETT CLUB®
OFFICIAL SCORING SYSTEM FOR NORTH AMERICAN BIG GAME TROPHIES

WALRUS

KIND OF WALRUS (check one)

☐ Atlantic
■ Pacific

	MINIMUM SCORES	
	AWARDS	ALL-TIME
Atlantic	95	95
Pacific	100	100

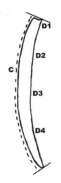

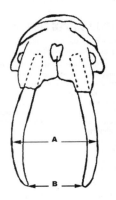

SEE OTHER SIDE FOR INSTRUCTIONS		COLUMN 1	COLUMN 2	COLUMN 3
A. Greatest Spread (If possible)	8 4/8	Right Tusk	Left Tusk	Difference
B. Tip to Tip Spread (If possible)	5/8			
C. Entire Length of Loose Tusk		32 7/8	33 4/8	5/8
D-1. Circumference of Base		7 2/8	7 3/8	1/8
D-2. Circumference at First Quarter	Location of First Quarter Circumference: 8 3/8	7 6/8	7 7/8	1/8
D-3. Circumference at Second Quarter	Location of Second Quarter Circumference: 16 6/8	6 5/8	6 6/8	1/8
D-4. Circumference at Third Quarter	Location of Third Quarter Circumference: 25 1/8	5 2/8	5 2/8	
	TOTALS	59 6/8	60 6/8	1

ADD	Column 1	59 6/8	Exact Locality Where Killed: **Cape Nome, AK**
	Column 2	60 6/8	Date Killed: 9/7/2003 Hunter: **Picked Up**
	Subtotal	120 4/8	Trophy Owner: **M. Wayne Carey** Telephone #:
SUBTRACT Column 3		1	Trophy Owner's Address:
FINAL SCORE		119 4/8	Trophy Owner's E-mail: Guide's Name:
			Remarks: (Mention Any Abnormalities or Unique Qualities)

I, **Rudy Drobnick** _____, certify that I have measured this trophy on **11/18/2003**
       PRINT NAME   MM/DD/YYYY

at **Salt Lake, Utah** _____
       STREET ADDRESS   CITY   STATE/PROVINCE

and that these measurements and data are, to the best of my knowledge and belief, made in accordance with the instructions given.

Witness: _____ Signature: _____ I.D. Number [ ][ ][ ][ ]
                                                              B&C OFFICIAL MEASURER

COPYRIGHT © 2006 BY BOONE AND CROCKETT CLUB®

INSTRUCTIONS FOR MEASURING WALRUS

All measurements must be made with a 1/4-inch wide flexible steel tape to the nearest one-eighth of an inch. Enter fractional figures in eighths, without reduction. Tusks **should** be removed from mounted specimens for measuring. Official measurements cannot be taken until tusks have air dried for at least 60 days after the animal was killed.

- **A. Greatest spread** is measured between perpendiculars at a right angle to the center line of the skull. **Greatest spread does not add into the final score.**
- **B. Tip to Tip Spread** is measured between tips of tusks. **Tip to tip spread does not add into the final score.**
- **C. Entire Length of Loose Tusk** is measured over outer curve from a point in line with the greatest projecting edge of the base to a point in line with tip.
- **D-1. Circumference of Base** is measured at a right angle to axis of tusk. **Do not** follow irregular edge of tusk; the line of measurement must be entirely on tusk material.
- **D-2-3-4. Divide length** of longer tusk by four. Starting at base, mark **both** tusks at these quarters (even though the other tusk is shorter) and measure circumferences at these marks.

ENTRY AFFIDAVIT FOR ALL HUNTER-TAKEN TROPHIES

For the purpose of entry into the Boone and Crockett Club's® records, North American big game harvested by the use of the following methods or under the following conditions are ineligible:

- I. Spotting or herding game from the air, followed by landing in its vicinity for the purpose of pursuit and shooting;
- II. Herding or chasing with the aid of any motorized equipment;
- III. Use of electronic communication devices to guide hunters to game, artificial lighting, electronic light intensifying devices (night vision optics), sights with built-in electronic range-finding capabilities, thermal imaging equipment, electronic ̲ ̲ ̲ ̲ or cameras/timers/motion tracking devices that transmit images and other information to the hunter;
- IV. Confined by artificial barriers, including escape-proof fenced enclosures;
- V. Transplanted for the purpose of commercial shooting;
- VI. By the use of traps or pharmaceuticals;
- VII. While swimming, helpless in deep snow, or helpless in any other natural or artificial medium;
- VIII. On another hunter's license;
- IX. Not in full compliance with the game laws or regulations of the federal government or of any state, ̲ ̲ ̲ ̲ ̲ tribal council on reservations or tribal lands;

I certify that the trophy scored on this chart was not taken in violation of the conditions listed above. In sig̲ ̲ ̲ ̲ ng ̲ ̲ ̲ ̲ understand that if the information provided on this entry is found to be misrepresented or fraudulent in any respect, it w̲ ̲ ̲ ̲ a ̲ ̲ ̲ to the Awards Program and 1) all of my prior entries are subject to deletion from future editions of **Records of N ̲ ̲ ̲ ̲ ̲ Game** 2) future entries may not be accepted.

FAIR CHASE, as defined by the Boone and Crockett Club®, is the ethical, sportsmanlike and lawful pursuit ̲ ̲ ng ̲ ̲ ̲ e-ranging wild, native North American big game animal in a manner that does not give the hunter an improper advan ̲ ̲ ̲ er s ̲ ̲ ̲ animals.

The Boone and Crockett Club® may exclude the entry of any animal that it deems to have been taken in an ̲ ̲ ̲ al m ̲ ̲ ̲ under conditions deemed inappropriate by the Club.

Date:_____ Signature of Hunter:_____
(SIGNATURE MUST BE WITNESSED BY AN OFFICIAL ̲ ̲ ̲ ER OR ̲ ̲ ̲ Y PUBLIC.)

Date:_____ Signature of Notary or Official Measurer: _____

Records of
North American
Big Game

250 Station Drive
Missoula, MT 59801
(406) 542-1888

BOONE AND CROCKETT CLUB

OFFICIAL SCORING SYSTEM FOR NORTH AMERICAN BIG GAME TROPHIES

TYPICAL AMERICAN ELK (WAPITI)

MINIMUM SCORES	
AWARDS	ALL-TIME
360	375

Detail of Point Measurement

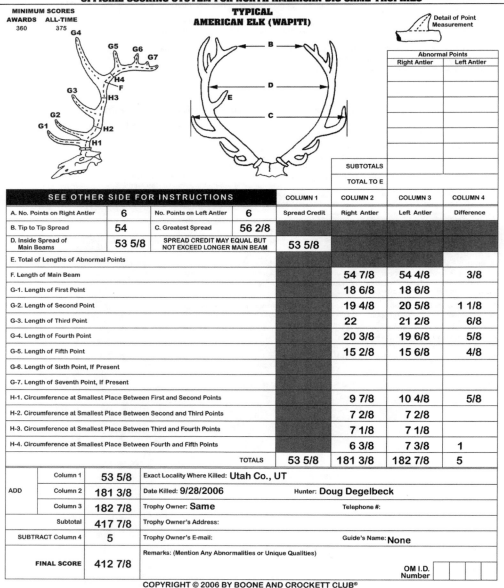

Abnormal Points	
Right Antler	Left Antler

					COLUMN 1	COLUMN 2	COLUMN 3	COLUMN 4
SEE OTHER SIDE FOR INSTRUCTIONS					Spread Credit	Right Antler	Left Antler	Difference
A. No. Points on Right Antler	6	No. Points on Left Antler	6					
B. Tip to Tip Spread	54	C. Greatest Spread	56 2/8					
D. Inside Spread of Main Beams	53 5/8	SPREAD CREDIT MAY EQUAL BUT NOT EXCEED LONGER MAIN BEAM		53 5/8				
E. Total of Lengths of Abnormal Points								
F. Length of Main Beam						54 7/8	54 4/8	3/8
G-1. Length of First Point						18 6/8	18 6/8	
G-2. Length of Second Point						19 4/8	20 5/8	1 1/8
G-3. Length of Third Point						22	21 2/8	6/8
G-4. Length of Fourth Point						20 3/8	19 6/8	5/8
G-5. Length of Fifth Point						15 2/8	15 6/8	4/8
G-6. Length of Sixth Point, If Present								
G-7. Length of Seventh Point, If Present								
H-1. Circumference at Smallest Place Between First and Second Points						9 7/8	10 4/8	5/8
H-2. Circumference at Smallest Place Between Second and Third Points						7 2/8	7 2/8	
H-3. Circumference at Smallest Place Between Third and Fourth Points						7 1/8	7 1/8	
H-4. Circumference at Smallest Place Between Fourth and Fifth Points						6 3/8	7 3/8	1
				TOTALS	53 5/8	181 3/8	182 7/8	5

ADD	Column 1	53 5/8	Exact Locality Where Killed: Utah Co., UT
	Column 2	181 3/8	Date Killed: 9/28/2006 Hunter: **Doug Degelbeck**
	Column 3	182 7/8	Trophy Owner: **Same** Telephone #:
	Subtotal	417 7/8	Trophy Owner's Address:
SUBTRACT Column 4		5	Trophy Owner's E-mail: Guide's Name: **None**
FINAL SCORE		412 7/8	Remarks: (Mention Any Abnormalities or Unique Qualities)

OM I.D. Number

COPYRIGHT © 2006 BY BOONE AND CROCKETT CLUB®

I, _____ Kenny E. Leo _____, certify that I have measured this trophy on _____ 12/4/2006 _____
PRINT NAME   MM/DD/YYYYY

at _____ Price, UT _____
STREET ADDRESS   CITY   STATE/PROVINCE

and that these measurements and data are, to the best of my knowledge and belief, made in accordance with the instructions given.

Witness: _____ Signature: _____ I.D. Number [ ][ ][ ][ ]
B&C OFFICIAL MEASURER

INSTRUCTIONS FOR MEASURING TYPICAL AMERICAN ELK (WAPITI)

All measurements must be made with a 1/4-inch wide flexible steel tape to the nearest one-eighth of an inch. (Note: A flexible steel cable can be used to measure points and main beams only.) Enter fractional figures in eighths, without reduction. Official measurements cannot be taken until the antlers have air dried for at least 60 days after the animal was killed.

A. Number of Points on Each Antler: To be counted a point, the projection must be at least one inch long, with length exceeding width at one inch or more of length. All points are measured from tip of point to nearest edge of beam as illustrated. Beam tip is counted as a point but not measured as a point. **Point totals do not add into the final score.**

B. Tip to Tip Spread is measured between tips of main beams. **Tip to tip spread does not add into the final score.**

C. Greatest Spread is measured between perpendiculars at a right angle to the center line of the skull at widest part, whether across main beams or points. **Greatest spread does not add into the final score.**

D. Inside Spread of Main Beams is measured at a right angle to the center line of the skull at widest point between main beams. Enter this measurement again as the Spread Credit if it is less than or equal to the length of the longer main beam; if greater, enter longer main beam length for Spread Credit.

E. Total of Lengths of all Abnormal Points: Abnormal Points are those non-typical in location (such as points originating from a point or from bottom or sides of main beam) or pattern (extra points, not generally paired). Measure in usual manner and record in appropriate blanks.

F. Length of Main Beam is measured from the center of the lowest outside edge of burr over the outer side to the most distant point of the main beam. The point of beginning is that point on the burr where the center line along the outer side of the beam intersects the burr, then following generally the line of the illustration.

G-1-2-3-4-5-6-7. Length of Normal Points: Normal points project from the top or front of the main beam in the general pattern illustrated. They are measured from nearest edge of main beam over outer curve to tip. Lay the tape along the outer curve of the beam so that the top edge of the tape coincides with the top edge of the beam on both sides of point to determine the base line for point measurement. Record point length in appropriate blanks.

H-1-2-3-4. Circumferences are taken as detailed in illustration for each measurement.

ENTRY AFFIDAVIT FOR ALL HUNTER-TAKEN TROPHIES

For the purpose of entry into the Boone and Crockett Club's® records, North American big game harvested by the use of the following methods or under the following conditions are ineligible:

I.   Spotting or herding game from the air, followed by landing in its vicinity for the purpose of pursuit and shooting;

II.   Herding or chasing with the aid of any motorized equipment;

III.   Use of electronic communication devices to guide hunters to game, artificial lighting, electronic light intensifying devices (night vision optics), sights with built-in electronic range-finding capabilities, thermal imaging equipment, electronic game calls or cameras/timers/motion tracking devices that transmit images and other information to the hunter;

IV.   Confined by artificial barriers, including escape-proof fenced enclosures;

V.   Transplanted for the purpose of commercial shooting;

VI.   By the use of traps or pharmaceuticals;

VII.   While swimming, helpless in deep snow, or helpless in any other natural or artificial medium;

VIII.   On another hunter's license;

IX.   Not in full compliance with the game laws or regulations of the federal government, or any state, province, territory, or tribal council on reservations or tribal lands;

I certify that the trophy scored on this chart was not taken in violation of the conditions listed above. In signing this statement, I understand that if the information provided on this entry is found to be misrepresented or fraudulent in any way, it will not be accepted into the Awards Program and 1) all of my prior entries are subject to deletion from future editions of Records of North American Big Game and 2) future entries may not be accepted.

FAIR CHASE, as defined by the Boone and Crockett Club®, is the ethical, sportsmanlike and lawful pursuit and taking of any free-ranging wild, native North American big game animal in a manner that does not give the hunter an improper advantage over such animals.

The Boone and Crockett Club® may exclude the entry of any animal that it deems to have been taken under conditions deemed inappropriate by the Club.

Date: _____ Signature of Hunter: _____
(SIGNATURE MUST BE WITNESSED BY AN OFFICIAL MEASURER OR A NOTARY PUBLIC.)

Date: _____ Signature of Notary or Official Measurer: _____

250 Station Drive
Missoula, MT 59801
(406) 542-1888

BOONE AND CROCKETT CLUB®
OFFICIAL SCORING SYSTEM FOR NORTH AMERICAN BIG GAME TROPHIES

**NON-TYPICAL
AMERICAN ELK (WAPITI)**

MINIMUM SCORES
AWARDS ALL-TIME
385   385

Abnormal Points	
Right Antler	Left Antler
1 2/8	2 4/8
15 6/8	16
5	2 5/8
6 1/8	2 5/8
2 4/8	1 3/8
	3
SUBTOTALS 30 5/8	28 1/8
E. TOTAL 58 6/8	

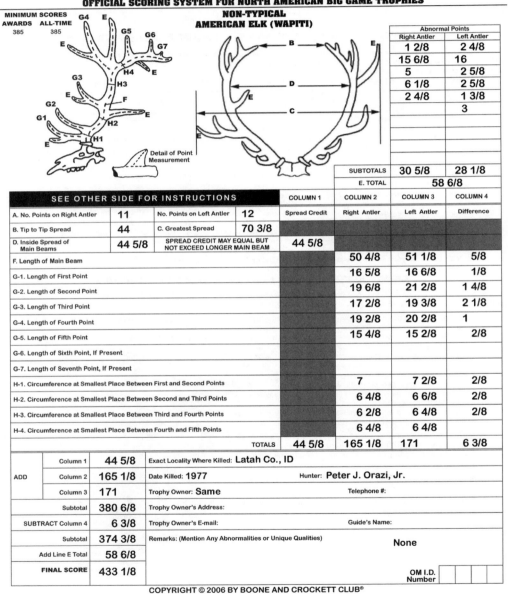

Detail of Point Measurement

SEE OTHER SIDE FOR INSTRUCTIONS			COLUMN 1	COLUMN 2	COLUMN 3	COLUMN 4
			Spread Credit	Right Antler	Left Antler	Difference
A. No. Points on Right Antler	11	No. Points on Left Antler 12				
B. Tip to Tip Spread	44	C. Greatest Spread 70 3/8				
D. Inside Spread of Main Beams	44 5/8	SPREAD CREDIT MAY EQUAL BUT NOT EXCEED LONGER MAIN BEAM	44 5/8			
F. Length of Main Beam				50 4/8	51 1/8	5/8
G-1. Length of First Point				16 5/8	16 6/8	1/8
G-2. Length of Second Point				19 6/8	21 2/8	1 4/8
G-3. Length of Third Point				17 2/8	19 3/8	2 1/8
G-4. Length of Fourth Point				19 2/8	20 2/8	1
G-5. Length of Fifth Point				15 4/8	15 2/8	2/8
G-6. Length of Sixth Point, If Present						
G-7. Length of Seventh Point, If Present						
H-1. Circumference at Smallest Place Between First and Second Points				7	7 2/8	2/8
H-2. Circumference at Smallest Place Between Second and Third Points				6 4/8	6 6/8	2/8
H-3. Circumference at Smallest Place Between Third and Fourth Points				6 2/8	6 4/8	2/8
H-4. Circumference at Smallest Place Between Fourth and Fifth Points				6 4/8	6 4/8	
		TOTALS	44 5/8	165 1/8	171	6 3/8

ADD	Column 1	44 5/8	Exact Locality Where Killed: **Latah Co., ID**
	Column 2	165 1/8	Date Killed: **1977** Hunter: **Peter J. Orazi, Jr.**
	Column 3	171	Trophy Owner: **Same** Telephone #:
	Subtotal	380 6/8	Trophy Owner's Address:
SUBTRACT Column 4		6 3/8	Trophy Owner's E-mail: Guide's Name:
	Subtotal	374 3/8	Remarks: (Mention Any Abnormalities or Unique Qualities) **None**
	Add Line E Total	58 6/8	
	FINAL SCORE	**433 1/8**	OM I.D. Number

I, **Ryan Hatfield** , certify that I have measured this trophy on **5/13/2006**

PRINT NAME   MM/DD/YYYYY

at **Pullman, WA**

STREET ADDRESS   CITY   STATE/PROVINCE

and that these measurements and data are, to the best of my knowledge and belief, made in accordance with the instructions given.

Witness: _____ Signature: _____ I.D. Number

B&C OFFICIAL MEASURER

INSTRUCTIONS FOR MEASURING NON-TYPICAL AMERICAN ELK (WAPITI)

All measurements must be made with a 1/4-inch wide flexible steel tape to the nearest one-eighth of an inch. (Note: A flexible steel cable can be used to measure points and main beams only.) Enter fractional figures in eighths, without reduction. Official measurements cannot be taken until the antlers have air dried for at least 60 days after the animal was killed.

- **A. Number of Points on Each Antler:** To be counted a point, the projection must be at least one inch long, with length exceeding width at one inch or more of length. All points are measured from tip of point to nearest edge of beam as illustrated. Beam tip is counted as a point but not measured as a point. **Point totals do not add into the final score.**
- **B. Tip to Tip Spread** is measured between tips of main beams. **Tip to tip spread does not add into the final score.**
- **C. Greatest Spread** is measured between perpendiculars at a right angle to the center line of the skull at widest part, whether across main beams or points. **Greatest spread does not add into the final score.**
- **D. Inside Spread of Main Beams** is measured at a right angle to the center line of the skull at widest point between main beams. Enter this measurement again as the Spread Credit if it is less than or equal to the length of the longer main beam; if greater, enter longer main beam length for Spread Credit.
- **E. Total of Lengths of all Abnormal Points:** Abnormal Points are those non-typical in location (such as points originating from a point or from bottom or sides of main beam) or pattern (extra points, not generally paired). Measure in usual manner and record in appropriate blanks.
- **F. Length of Main Beam** is measured from the center of the lowest outside edge of burr over the outer side to the most distant point of the main beam. The point of beginning is that point on the burr where the center line along the outer side of the beam intersects the burr, then following generally the line of the illustration.
- **G-1-2-3-4-5-6-7. Length of Normal Points:** Normal points project from the top or front of the main beam in the general pattern illustrated. They are measured from nearest edge of main beam over outer curve to tip. Lay the tape along the outer curve of the beam so that the top edge of the tape coincides with the top edge of the beam on both sides of point to determine the baseline for point measuremen Record point length in appropriate blanks.
- **H-1-2-3-4. ircumf ences** are taken as detailed in illustration for each measurement.

ENTRY AFFIDAVIT FOR ALL HUNTE T KEN TROPHIES

For the pur   of e   y into the Boone and Crockett Club's® records, North Americ n b   game harvested by the use of the following methods o u   following conditions are ineligible:

- I.   Spottin   erding game from the air, followed by landing in its vicinity fo   he   rpos   rsui and shooting;
- II.   Herding   asing with the aid of any motorized equipment;
- III.   Use of ele   nic communication devices to guide hunters to ga   artific   ting, electronic light intensifying devices (night vision opti   sights wi h built-in electronic range-finding capabilities, the   imaging equipment, electronic game calls or cameras/ti   /motio tracking devices that transmit images and other i   mation to the hunter;
- IV.   Confined by   ficial   arriers, including escape-proof fenced enclosures
- V.   Transplanted   purpos of commercial shooting;
- VI.   By the use of tra   r phar aceuticals;
- VII.   While swimming,   ss in eep snow, or helpless in any other natu   r art f ial medium;
- VIII.   On another hunter's
- IX.   Not i   pliance w   ame laws or regulations of the f   ent or of any state, province, territory, or tribal co   ations or ds;

I certify t   on t   taken in   ns listed above. In signing this statement, I understand that if th   h   sented r fraudulent in any respect, it will not be accepted into the Award   ture editions of **Records of North American Big Game** 2) futu

FAIR   e ethical, sportsmanlike and lawful pursuit and taking of any free-ranging wild   does not give the hunter an improper advantage over such game animals.

The   himal that it deems to have been taken in an unethical manner or under cond

Date   TURE MUST BE WITNESSED BY AN OFFICIAL MEASURER OR A NOTARY PUBLIC.)

Date: _____   ary or Official Measurer: _____

Records of
North American
Big Game

250 Station Drive
Missoula, MT 59801
(406) 542-1888

BOONE AND CROCKETT CLUB®
OFFICIAL SCORING SYSTEM FOR NORTH AMERICAN BIG GAME TROPHIES

ROOSEVELT'S AND TULE ELK

MINIMUM SCORES		
	AWARDS	ALL-TIME
Roosevelt's	275	290
Tule	270	285

KIND OF ELK (check one)
☐ Roosevelt's
■ Tule

Crown Points	
Right Antler	Left Antler
13 7/8	17 3/8

I. Crown Points Total	31 2/8

Abnormal Points	
Right Antler	Left Antler

Detail of Point Measurement

TOTAL TO E

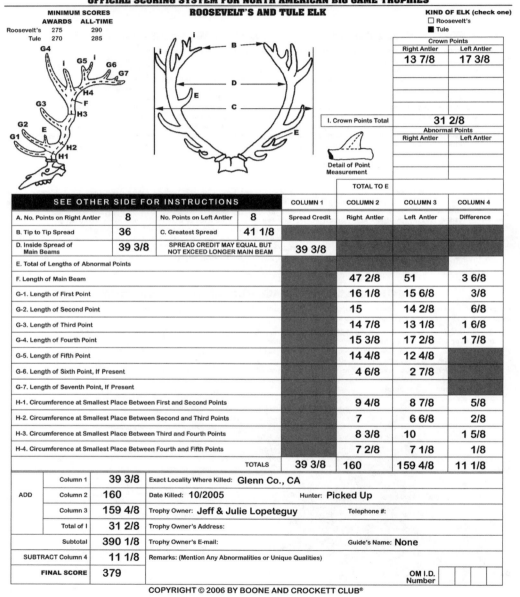

SEE OTHER SIDE FOR INSTRUCTIONS				COLUMN 1	COLUMN 2	COLUMN 3	COLUMN 4
				Spread Credit	Right Antler	Left Antler	Difference
A. No. Points on Right Antler	8	No. Points on Left Antler	8				
B. Tip to Tip Spread	36	C. Greatest Spread	41 1/8				
D. Inside Spread of Main Beams	39 3/8	SPREAD CREDIT MAY EQUAL BUT NOT EXCEED LONGER MAIN BEAM	39 3/8				
E. Total of Lengths of Abnormal Points							
F. Length of Main Beam					47 2/8	51	3 6/8
G-1. Length of First Point					16 1/8	15 6/8	3/8
G-2. Length of Second Point					15	14 2/8	6/8
G-3. Length of Third Point					14 7/8	13 1/8	1 6/8
G-4. Length of Fourth Point					15 3/8	17 2/8	1 7/8
G-5. Length of Fifth Point					14 4/8	12 4/8	
G-6. Length of Sixth Point, If Present					4 6/8	2 7/8	
G-7. Length of Seventh Point, If Present							
H-1. Circumference at Smallest Place Between First and Second Points					9 4/8	8 7/8	5/8
H-2. Circumference at Smallest Place Between Second and Third Points					7	6 6/8	2/8
H-3. Circumference at Smallest Place Between Third and Fourth Points					8 3/8	10	1 5/8
H-4. Circumference at Smallest Place Between Fourth and Fifth Points					7 2/8	7 1/8	1/8
			TOTALS	39 3/8	160	159 4/8	11 1/8

ADD	Column 1	39 3/8	Exact Locality Where Killed: **Glenn Co., CA**
	Column 2	160	Date Killed: **10/2005** — Hunter: **Picked Up**
	Column 3	159 4/8	Trophy Owner: **Jeff & Julie Lopeteguy** — Telephone #:
	Total of I	31 2/8	Trophy Owner's Address:
	Subtotal	390 1/8	Trophy Owner's E-mail: — Guide's Name: **None**
	SUBTRACT Column 4	11 1/8	Remarks: (Mention Any Abnormalities or Unique Qualities)
	FINAL SCORE	379	

OM I.D. Number

COPYRIGHT © 2006 BY BOONE AND CROCKETT CLUB®

I, __Ralph Stayner__ , certify that I have measured this trophy on __4/24/2007__
PRINT NAME   MM/DD/YYYYY

at __Cabela's, Fort Worth, TX__
STREET ADDRESS   CITY   STATE/PROVINCE

and that these measurements and data are, to the best of my knowledge and belief, made in accordance with the instructions given.

Witness: _____ Signature: _____ I.D. Number [ ][ ][ ][ ]
B&C OFFICIAL MEASURER

INSTRUCTIONS FOR MEASURING ROOSEVELT'S AND TULE ELK

All measurements must be made with a 1/4-inch wide flexible steel tape to the nearest one-eighth of an inch. (Note: A flexible steel cable can be used to measure points and main beams only.) Enter fractional figures in eighths, without reduction. Official measurements cannot be taken until the antlers have air dried for at least 60 days after the animal was killed.

A. Number of Points on Each Antler: to be counted a point, the projection must be at least one inch long, with length exceeding width at one inch or more of length. All points are measured from tip of point to nearest edge of beam as illustrated. Beam tip is counted as a point but not measured as a point. **Point totals do not add into the final score.**

B. Tip to Tip Spread is measured between tips of main beams. **Tip to tip spread does not add into the final score.**

C. Greatest Spread is measured between perpendiculars at a right angle to the center line of the skull at widest part, whether across main beams or points. **Greatest spread does not add into the final score.**

D. Inside Spread of Main Beams is measured at a right angle to the center line of the skull at widest point between main beams. Enter this measurement again as the Spread Credit if it is less than or equal to the length of the longer main beam; if greater, enter longer main beam length for Spread Credit.

E. Total of Lengths of all Abnormal Points: Abnormal Points are those non-typical in location or pattern occurring below G-4. Measure in usual manner and record in appropriate blanks. Note: do not confuse with Crown Points that may occur in the vicinity of G-4, G-5, G-6, etc.

F. Length of Main Beam is measured from the center of the lowest outside edge of burr over the outer side to the most distant point of the main beam. The point of beginning is that point on the burr where the center line along the outer side of the beam intersects the burr, then following generally the line of the illustration.

G-1-2-3-4-5-6-7. Length of Normal Points: Normal points project from the top or front of the main beam in the general pattern illustrated. They are measured from nearest edge of main beam over outer curve to tip. Lay the tape along the outer curve of the beam so that the top edge of the tape coincides with the top edge of the beam on both sides of point to determine the baseline for point measurement. Record point length in appropriate blanks.

H-1-2-3-4. Circumferences are taken as detailed in illustration for each measurement.

I. Crown Points: From the well-defined Royal on out to end of beam, all points other than the normal points in their typical locations are Crown Points. This includes points occurring on the Royal, on other normal points, on Crown Points, and on the bottom and sides of main beam after the Royal. Measure and record in appropriate blanks provided and add to score below.

ENTRY AFFIDAVIT FOR ALL HUNTER-TAKEN TROPHIES

To be eligible for entry into the Boone and Crockett Club® records, North American big game harvested by the use of the following methods or under the following conditions are ineligible:

I. Spotting or herding game from the air, followed by landing in its vicinity for the purpose of pursuit and shooting;

II. Herding or chasing with the aid of any motorized equipment;

III. Use of electronic communication devices to guide hunters to game, artificial lighting, electronic light intensifying devices (night vision optics), sights with built-in electronic range-finding capabilities, thermal imaging equipment, electronic game calls or cameras/timers/motion tracking devices that transmit images and other information to the hunter;

IV. Confined by artificial barriers, including escape-proof fenced enclosures;

V. Transplanted for the purpose of commercial shooting;

VI. By the use of traps or pharmaceuticals;

VII. While swimming, helpless in deep snow, or helpless in any other natural or artificial medium;

VIII. On another hunter's license;

IX. Not in full compliance with the game laws or regulations of the federal government or of any state, province, territory, or tribal council on reservations or tribal lands;

I certify that the trophy scored on this chart was not taken in violation of the conditions listed above. In signing this statement, I understand that if the information provided on this entry is found to be misrepresented or fraudulent in any respect, it will not be accepted into the Awards Program and 1) all of my prior entries are subject to deletion from future editions of **Records of North American Big Game** 2) future entries may not be accepted.

FAIR CHASE, as defined by the Boone and Crockett Club®, is the ethical, sportsmanlike and lawful pursuit and taking of any free-ranging wild, native North American big game animal in a manner that does not give the hunter an improper advantage over such game animals.

The Boone and Crockett Club® may exclude the entry of any animal that it deems to have been taken in an unethical manner or under conditions deemed inappropriate by the Club.

Date: _____ Signature: _____
(SIGNATURE MUST BE WITNESSED BY AN OFFICIAL MEASURER OR A NOTARY PUBLIC.)

Date: _____ Signature of Notary or Official Measurer: _____

250 Station Drive
Missoula, MT 59801
(406) 542-1888

BOONE AND CROCKETT CLUB®
OFFICIAL SCORING SYSTEM FOR NORTH AMERICAN BIG GAME TROPHIES

TYPICAL
MULE DEER AND BLACKTAIL DEER

MINIMUM SCORES	AWARDS	ALL-TIME
mule deer	180	190
Columbia blacktail	125	135
Sitka blacktail	100	108

KIND OF DEER (check one)
☐ mule deer
☐ Columbia blacktail
■ Sitka blacktail

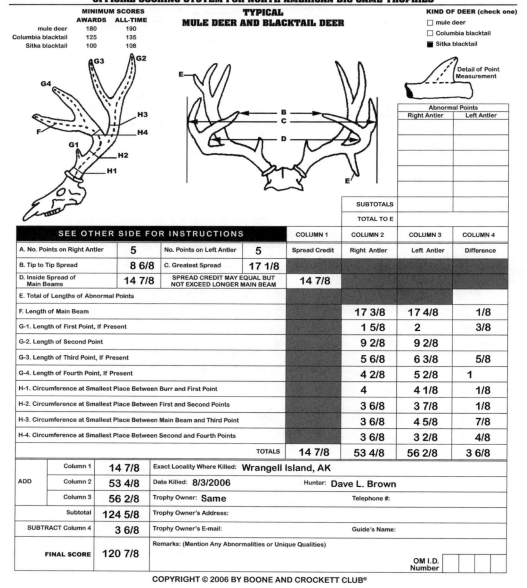

Detail of Point Measurement

Abnormal Points	
Right Antler	Left Antler
SUBTOTALS	
TOTAL TO E	

SEE OTHER SIDE FOR INSTRUCTIONS			COLUMN 1	COLUMN 2	COLUMN 3	COLUMN 4
			Spread Credit	Right Antler	Left Antler	Difference
A. No. Points on Right Antler	5	No. Points on Left Antler — 5				
B. Tip to Tip Spread	8 6/8	C. Greatest Spread — 17 1/8				
D. Inside Spread of Main Beams	14 7/8	SPREAD CREDIT MAY EQUAL BUT NOT EXCEED LONGER MAIN BEAM — 14 7/8				
E. Total of Lengths of Abnormal Points						
F. Length of Main Beam				17 3/8	17 4/8	1/8
G-1. Length of First Point, If Present				1 5/8	2	3/8
G-2. Length of Second Point				9 2/8	9 2/8	
G-3. Length of Third Point, If Present				5 6/8	6 3/8	5/8
G-4. Length of Fourth Point, If Present				4 2/8	5 2/8	1
H-1. Circumference at Smallest Place Between Burr and First Point				4	4 1/8	1/8
H-2. Circumference at Smallest Place Between First and Second Points				3 6/8	3 7/8	1/8
H-3. Circumference at Smallest Place Between Main Beam and Third Point				3 6/8	4 5/8	7/8
H-4. Circumference at Smallest Place Between Second and Fourth Points				3 6/8	3 2/8	4/8
		TOTALS	14 7/8	53 4/8	56 2/8	3 6/8

ADD	Column 1	14 7/8	Exact Locality Where Killed: Wrangell Island, AK
	Column 2	53 4/8	Date Killed: 8/3/2006 — Hunter: Dave L. Brown
	Column 3	56 2/8	Trophy Owner: Same — Telephone #:
	Subtotal	124 5/8	Trophy Owner's Address:
SUBTRACT	Column 4	3 6/8	Trophy Owner's E-mail: — Guide's Name:
FINAL SCORE		120 7/8	Remarks: (Mention Any Abnormalities or Unique Qualities)

OM I.D. Number

COPYRIGHT © 2006 BY BOONE AND CROCKETT CLUB®

I, __James F. Baichtal__ , certify that I have measured this trophy on __11/13/2006__

PRINT NAME   MM/DD/YYYYY

at __Thorne Bay, Alaska__

STREET ADDRESS   CITY   STATE/PROVINCE

and that these measurements and data are, to the best of my knowledge and belief, made in accordance with the instructions given.

Witness: _____ Signature: _____ I.D. Number ☐☐☐☐

B&C OFFICIAL MEASURER

INSTRUCTIONS FOR MEASURING TYPICAL MULE AND BLACKTAIL DEER

All measurements must be made with a 1/4-inch wide flexible steel tape to the nearest one-eighth of an inch. (Note: A flexible steel cable can be used to measure points and main beams only.) Enter fractional figures in eighths, without reduction. Official measurements cannot be taken until the antlers have air dried for at least 60 days after the animal was killed.

- **A. Number of Points on Each Antler:** To be counted a point, the projection must be at least one inch long, with length exceeding width at one inch or more of length. All points are measured from tip of point to nearest edge of beam. Beam tip is counted as a point but not measured as a point. **Point totals do not add into the final score.**
- **B. Tip to Tip Spread** is measured between tips of main beams. **Tip to tip spread does not add into the final score.**
- **C. Greatest Spread** is measured between perpendiculars at a right angle to the center line of the skull at widest part, whether across main beams or points. **Greatest spread does not add into the final score.**
- **D. Inside Spread of Main Beams** is measured at a right angle to the center line of the skull at widest point between main beams. Enter this measurement again as the Spread Credit **if** it is less than or equal to the length of the longer main beam; if greater, enter longer main beam length for Spread Credit.
- **E. Total of Lengths of all Abnormal Points:** Abnormal Points are those non-typical in location such as points originating from a point (exception: G-3 originates from G-2 in perfectly normal fashion) or from bottom or sides of main beam, or any points beyond the normal pattern of five (including beam tip) per antler. Measure each abnormal point in usual manner and enter in appropriate blanks.
- **F. Length of Main Beam** is measured from the center of the lowest outside edge of burr over the outer side to the most distant point of the Main Beam. The point of beginning is that point on the burr where the center line along the outer side of the beam intersects the burr, then following generally the line of the illustration.
- **G-1-2-3-4. Length of Normal Points:** Normal points are the brow tines and the upper and lower forks as shown in the illustration. They are measured from nearest edge of main beam over outer curve to tip. Lay the tape along the outer curve of the beam so that the top edge of the tape coincides with the top edge of the beam on both sides of point to determine the baseline for point measurement. Record point lengths in appropriate blanks.
- **H-1-2-3-4. Circumferences** are taken as detailed in illustration for each measurement. If brow point is missing, take H-1 and H-2 at smallest place between burr and G-2. If G-3 is missing, take H-3 halfway between the base and tip of G-2. If G-4 is missing, take H-4 halfway between G-2 and tip of main beam.

ENTRY AFFIDAVIT FOR ALL HUNTER TAKEN TROPHIES

For the purpose of entry into the Boone and Crockett Club's® records, North America big game harvested by the use of the following methods or under the following conditions are ineligible:

- I. Spotting or herding game from the air, followed by landing in its vicinity for purpose of pursuit and shooting;
- II. Herding or chasing with the aid of any motorized equipment;
- III. Use of electronic communication devices to guide hunters to game, artificial lighting, electronic light intensifying devices (night vision optics), sights with built-in electronic range-finding capabilities, thermal imaging equipment, electronic game calls or cameras/timers/motion tracking devices that transmit images and information to the hunter;
- IV. Confined by artificial barriers, including escape-proof fenced enclosures;
- V. Transplanted for the purpose of commercial shooting;
- VI. By the use of traps or pharmaceuticals;
- VII. While swimming, helpless in deep snow, or helpless in any other natural or artificial medium;
- VIII. On another hunter's license;
- IX. Not in full compliance with the game laws or regulations of the federal government or of any state, province, territory, or tribal council on reservations or tribal lands;

I certify that the trophy scored on this chart was not taken in violation of the conditions listed above. In signing this statement, I understand that if the information provided on this entry is found to be misrepresented or fraudulent in any respect, it will not be accepted into the Awards Program and 1) all of my prior entries are subject to deletion from future editions of Records of North American Big Game 2) future entries may not be accepted.

FAIR CHASE, as defined by the Boone and Crockett Club®, is the ethical, sportsmanlike and lawful pursuit and taking of any free-ranging wild, native North American big game animal in a manner that does not give the hunter an improper advantage over such animals.

The Boone and Crockett Club® may exclude the entry of any animal that it deems to have been taken in an unfair manner or under conditions deemed inappropriate by the Club.

Date: _____ Signature of Hunter: _____

(SIGNATURE MUST BE WITNESSED BY AN OFFICIAL MEASURER OR A NOTARY PUBLIC.)

Date: _____ Signature of Notary or Official Measurer: _____

250 Station Drive
Missoula, MT 59801
(406) 542-1888

BOONE AND CROCKETT CLUB®
OFFICIAL SCORING SYSTEM FOR NORTH AMERICAN BIG GAME TROPHIES

NON-TYPICAL
MULE DEER AND BLACKTAIL DEER

MINIMUM SCORES	AWARDS	ALL-TIME
mule deer	215	230
Columbia blacktail	155	155
Sitka blacktail	118	118

KIND OF DEER (check one)
- ■ mule deer
- ☐ Columbia blacktail
- ☐ Sitka blacktail

Abnormal Points	
Right Antler	Left Antler
1 7/8	2
1 5/8	1 3/8
1 1/8	2 6/8
5 5/8	2 1/8
12	5 5/8
2 3/8	6 2/8
8 5/8	1 2/8
1 2/8	6 7/8
SUBTOTALS 51 3/8	36 1/8
E. TOTAL	87 4/8

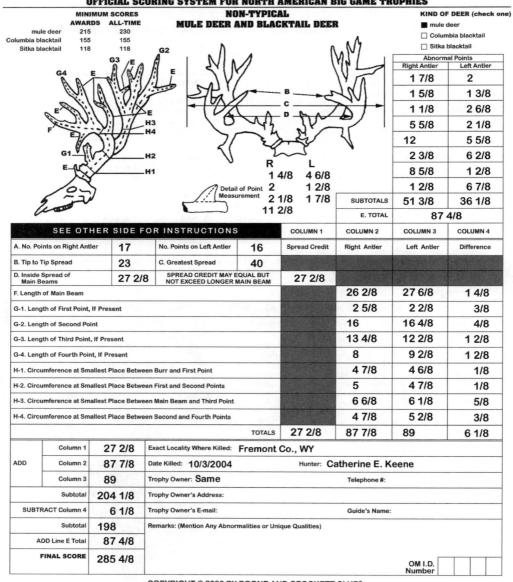

R   L
1 4/8   4 6/8
2   1 2/8
2 1/8   1 7/8
11 2/8

Detail of Point Measurement

SEE OTHER SIDE FOR INSTRUCTIONS			COLUMN 1	COLUMN 2	COLUMN 3	COLUMN 4
A. No. Points on Right Antler	17	No. Points on Left Antler	16	Spread Credit	Right Antler	Left Antler	Difference

	COLUMN 1	COLUMN 2	COLUMN 3	COLUMN 4
A. No. Points on Right Antler **17** No. Points on Left Antler **16**	Spread Credit	Right Antler	Left Antler	Difference
B. Tip to Tip Spread **23** C. Greatest Spread **40**				
D. Inside Spread of Main Beams **27 2/8** SPREAD CREDIT MAY EQUAL BUT NOT EXCEED LONGER MAIN BEAM	27 2/8			
F. Length of Main Beam		26 2/8	27 6/8	1 4/8
G-1. Length of First Point, If Present		2 5/8	2 2/8	3/8
G-2. Length of Second Point		16	16 4/8	4/8
G-3. Length of Third Point, If Present		13 4/8	12 2/8	1 2/8
G-4. Length of Fourth Point, If Present		8	9 2/8	1 2/8
H-1. Circumference at Smallest Place Between Burr and First Point		4 7/8	4 6/8	1/8
H-2. Circumference at Smallest Place Between First and Second Points		5	4 7/8	1/8
H-3. Circumference at Smallest Place Between Main Beam and Third Point		6 6/8	6 1/8	5/8
H-4. Circumference at Smallest Place Between Second and Fourth Points		4 7/8	5 2/8	3/8
TOTALS	27 2/8	87 7/8	89	6 1/8

ADD			
	Column 1	27 2/8	Exact Locality Where Killed: **Fremont Co., WY**
ADD	Column 2	87 7/8	Date Killed: **10/3/2004** Hunter: **Catherine E. Keene**
	Column 3	89	Trophy Owner: **Same** Telephone #:
	Subtotal	204 1/8	Trophy Owner's Address:
SUBTRACT Column 4		6 1/8	Trophy Owner's E-mail: Guide's Name:
	Subtotal	198	Remarks: (Mention Any Abnormalities or Unique Qualities)
ADD Line E Total		87 4/8	
FINAL SCORE		285 4/8	

OM I.D. Number

I, **Ralph Stayner** _____ , certify that I have measured this trophy on **04/23/2007**
PRINT NAME

at **Cabela's**   **Ft Worth, TX** _____   MM/DD/YYYYY
STREET ADDRESS   CITY   STATE/PROVINCE

and that these measurements and data are, to the best of my knowledge and belief, made in accordance with the instructions given.

Witness: _____   Signature: _____   I.D. Number [ ][ ][ ][ ]
                                              B&C OFFICIAL MEASURER

INSTRUCTIONS FOR MEASURING NON-TYPICAL MULE DEER AND BLACKTAIL

All measurements must be made with a 1/4-inch wide flexible steel tape to the nearest one-eighth of an inch. (Note: A flexible steel cable can be used to measure points and main beams only.) Enter fractional figures in eighths, without reduction. Official measurements cannot be taken until the antlers have air dried for at least 60 days after the animal was killed.

A. Number of Points on Each Antler: To be counted a point, the projection must be at least one inch long, with length exceeding width at one inch or more of length. All points are measured from tip of point to nearest edge of beam as illustrated. Beam tip is counted as a point but not measured as a point. **Point totals do not add into the final score.**

B. Tip to Tip Spread is measured between tips of main beams. **Tip to tip spread does not add into the final score.**

C. Greatest Spread is measured between perpendiculars at a right angle to the center line of the skull at widest part, whether across main beams or points. **Greatest spread does not add into the final score.**

D. Inside Spread of Main Beams is measured at a right angle to the center line of the skull at widest point between main beams. Enter this measurement again as the Spread Credit if it is less than or equal to the length of the longer main beam; if greater, enter longer main beam length for Spread Credit.

E. Total of Lengths of all Abnormal Points: Abnormal Points are those non-typical in location such as points originating from a point (exception: G-3 originates from G-2 in perfectly normal fashion) or from bottom or sides of main beam, or any points beyond the normal pattern of five (including beam tip) per antler. Measure each abnormal point in usual manner and enter in appropriate blanks.

F. Length of Main Beam is measured from the center of the lowest outside edge of burr over the outer side to the most distant point of the main beam. The point of beginning is that point on the burr where the center line along the outer side of the beam intersects the burr, then following generally the line of the illustration.

G-1-2-3-4. Length of Normal Points: Normal points are the brow tines and the upper and lower forks as shown in the illustration. They are measured from nearest edge of main beam over outer curve to tip. Lay the tape along the outer curve of the beam so that the top edge of the tape coincides with the top edge of the beam on both sides of point to determine the baseline for point measurement. Record point lengths in appropriate blanks.

H-1-2-3-4. Circumferences are taken as detailed in illustration for each measurement. If brow point is missing, take H-1 and H-2 at smallest place between burr and G-2. If G-3 is missing, take H-3 halfway between the base and tip of G-2. If G-4 is missing, take H-4 halfway between G-2 and tip of main beam.

ENTRY AFFIDAVIT FOR ALL HUNTER-TAKEN TROPHIES

For the purpose of entry into the Boone and Crockett Club's® records, North American big game harvested by the use of the following methods or under the following conditions are ineligible:

   I. Spotting or herding game from the air, followed by landing in its vicinity for the purpose of pursuit and shooting;
   II. Herding or chasing game with the aid of any motorized equipment;
   III. Use of electronic communication devices to guide hunters to game, artificial lighting, electronic light intensifying devices (night vision optics), sights with built-in electronic range-finding capabilities, thermal imaging equipment, electronic game calls or cameras/timers/motion tracking devices that transmit images and other information to the hunter;
   IV. Confined by artificial barriers, including escape-proof fenced enclosures;
   V. Transplanted for the purpose of commercial shooting;
   VI. By the use of traps or pharmaceuticals;
   VII. While swimming, helpless in deep snow, or any other natural or artificial medium;
   VIII. On another hunter's license;
   IX. Not in full compliance with the game laws or regulations of the federal government or of any state, province, territory, or tribal council on reservations or tribal lands;

I certify that the trophy scored on this chart was not taken in violation of the conditions listed above. In signing this statement, I understand that if the information provided on this entry is found to be misrepresented or fraudulent in any respect, it will not be accepted into the Awards Program and 1) all of my prior entries are subject to deletion from future editions of Records of North American Big Game 2) future entries may not be accepted.

FAIR CHASE, as defined by the Boone and Crockett Club®, is the ethical, sportsmanlike pursuit and taking of any free-ranging wild, native North American big game animal in a manner that does not give the hunter an improper advantage over such game animals.

The Boone and Crockett Club® may exclude the entry of any animal that it deems to have been taken in an unethical manner or under conditions deemed inappropriate by the Club.

Date: _____   Signature of Hunter: _____
                         (SIGNATURE MUST BE WITNESSED BY AN OFFICIAL MEASURER OR A NOTARY PUBLIC.)

Date: _____   Signature of Notary or Official Measurer: _____

Records of
North American
Big Game

250 Station Drive
Missoula, MT 59801
(406) 542-1888

BOONE AND CROCKETT CLUB®
OFFICIAL SCORING SYSTEM FOR NORTH AMERICAN BIG GAME TROPHIES

TYPICAL
WHITETAIL AND COUES' DEER

MINIMUM SCORES	AWARDS	ALL-TIME
whitetail	160	170
Coues'	100	110

KIND OF DEER (check one)
■ whitetail
☐ Coues'

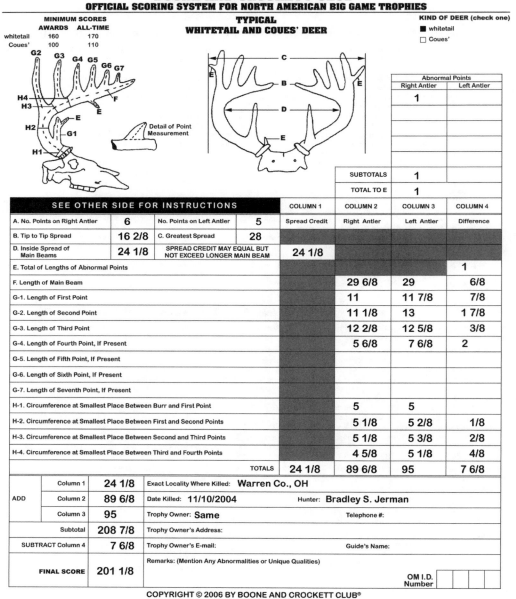

Abnormal Points	
Right Antler	Left Antler
1	

SUBTOTALS	1	
TOTAL TO E	1	

SEE OTHER SIDE FOR INSTRUCTIONS				COLUMN 1	COLUMN 2	COLUMN 3	COLUMN 4
A. No. Points on Right Antler	6	No. Points on Left Antler	5	Spread Credit	Right Antler	Left Antler	Difference
B. Tip to Tip Spread	16 2/8	C. Greatest Spread	28				
D. Inside Spread of Main Beams	24 1/8	SPREAD CREDIT MAY EQUAL BUT NOT EXCEED LONGER MAIN BEAM		24 1/8			
E. Total of Lengths of Abnormal Points							1
F. Length of Main Beam					29 6/8	29	6/8
G-1. Length of First Point					11	11 7/8	7/8
G-2. Length of Second Point					11 1/8	13	1 7/8
G-3. Length of Third Point					12 2/8	12 5/8	3/8
G-4. Length of Fourth Point, If Present					5 6/8	7 6/8	2
G-5. Length of Fifth Point, If Present							
G-6. Length of Sixth Point, If Present							
G-7. Length of Seventh Point, If Present							
H-1. Circumference at Smallest Place Between Burr and First Point					5	5	
H-2. Circumference at Smallest Place Between First and Second Points					5 1/8	5 2/8	1/8
H-3. Circumference at Smallest Place Between Second and Third Points					5 1/8	5 3/8	2/8
H-4. Circumference at Smallest Place Between Third and Fourth Points					4 5/8	5 1/8	4/8
			TOTALS	24 1/8	89 6/8	95	7 6/8

ADD	Column 1	24 1/8
	Column 2	89 6/8
	Column 3	95
	Subtotal	208 7/8
SUBTRACT Column 4		7 6/8
FINAL SCORE		201 1/8

Exact Locality Where Killed: **Warren Co., OH**
Date Killed: **11/10/2004**   Hunter: **Bradley S. Jerman**
Trophy Owner: **Same**   Telephone #:
Trophy Owner's Address:
Trophy Owner's E-mail: Guide's Name:
Remarks: (Mention Any Abnormalities or Unique Qualities)

OM I.D. Number

COPYRIGHT © 2006 BY BOONE AND CROCKETT CLUB®

I, __Gary L. Trent__ , certify that I have measured this trophy on __01/15/2005__
PRINT NAME   MM/DD/YYYY

at __Waynesville, Ohio__
STREET ADDRESS   CITY   STATE/PROVINCE

and that these measurements and data are, to the best of my knowledge and belief, made in accordance with the instructions given.

Witness: _____   Signature: _____   I.D. Number
B&C OFFICIAL MEASURER

INSTRUCTIONS FOR MEASURING TYPICAL WHITETAIL AND COUES' DEER

All measurements must be made with a 1/4-inch wide flexible steel tape to the nearest one-eighth of an inch. (Note: A flexible steel cable can be used to measure points and main beams only.) Enter fractional figures in eighths, without reduction. Official measurements cannot be taken until the antlers have air dried for at least 60 days after the animal was killed.

A. Number of Points on Each Antler: To be counted a point, the projection must be at least one inch long, with the length exceeding width at one inch or more of length. All points are measured from tip of point to nearest edge of beam as illustrated. Beam tip is counted as a point but not measured as a point. **Point totals do not add into the final score.**

B. Tip to Tip Spread is measured between tips of main beams. **Tip to tip spread does not add into the final score.**

C. Greatest Spread is measured between perpendiculars at a right angle to the center line of the skull at widest part, whether across main beams or points. **Greatest spread does not add into the final score.**

D. Inside Spread of Main Beams is measured at a right angle to the center line of the skull at widest point between main beams. Enter this measurement again as the Spread Credit if it is less than or equal to the length of the longer main beam; if greater, enter longer main beam length for Spread Credit.

E. Total of Lengths of all Abnormal Points: Abnormal Points are those non-typical in location (such as points originating from a point or from bottom or sides of main beam) or extra points beyond the normal pattern of points. Measure in usual manner and enter in appropriate blanks.

F. Length of Main Beam is measured from the center of the lowest outside edge of burr over the outer side to the most distant point of the main beam. The point of beginning is that point on the burr where the center line along the outer side of the beam intersects the burr, then following generally the line of the illustration.

G-1-2-3-4-5-6-7. Length of Normal Points: Normal points project from the top of the main beam. They are measured from nearest edge of main beam over outer curve to tip. Lay the tape along the outer curve of the beam so that the top edge of the tape coincides with the top edge of the beam on both sides of the point to determine the baseline for point measurements. Record point lengths in appropriate blanks.

H-1-2-3-4. Circumferences are taken as detailed in illustration for each measurement. If brow point is missing, take H-1 and H-2 at smallest place between burr and G-2. If G-4 is missing, take H-4 halfway between G-3 and tip of main beam.

ENTRY AFFIDAVIT FOR ALL HUNTER-TAKEN TROPHIES

For the purpose of entry into the Boone and Crockett Club's® records, North American big game harvested by the use of the following methods or under the following conditions are ineligible:

   I.   Spotting or herding game from the air, followed by landing in its vicinity for the purpose of pursuit and shooting;

   II.   Herding or chasing with the aid of any motorized equipment;

   III.   Use of electronic communication devices to guide hunters to game, artificial lighting, electronic light intensifying devices (night vision optics), sights with built-in electronic range-finding capabilities, thermal imaging equipment, electronic game calls or cameras/timers/motion tracking devices that transmit images and other information to the hunter;

   IV.   Confined by artificial barriers, including escape-proof fenced enclosures;

   V.   Transplanted for the purpose of commercial shooting;

   VI.   By the use of traps or pharmaceuticals;

   VII.   While swimming, helpless in deep snow, or helpless in any other natural or artificial medium;

   VIII.   On another hunter's license;

   IX.   Not in full compliance with the game laws or regulations of the federal government or of any state, province, territory, or tribal council on reservations or tribal lands;

I certify that the trophy scored on this chart was not taken in violation of the conditions listed above. In signing this statement, I understand that if the information provided on this entry is found to be misrepresented or fraudulent in any respect, it will not be accepted into the Awards Program and 1) all of my prior entries are subject to deletion from future editions of **Records of North American Big Game** 2) future entries may not be accepted.

FAIR CHASE, as defined by the Boone and Crockett Club, is the ethical, sportsmanlike and lawful pursuit and taking of any free-ranging wild, native North American big game animal in a manner that does not give the hunter an improper advantage over such game animals.

The Boone and Crockett Club may exclude the entry of any animal that it deems to have been taken in an unethical manner or under conditions deemed inappropriate by the Club.

Date: _____   Signature of Hunter: _____
(SIGNATURE MUST BE WITNESSED BY AN OFFICIAL MEASURER OR A NOTARY PUBLIC.)

Date: _____   Signature of Notary or Official Measurer: _____

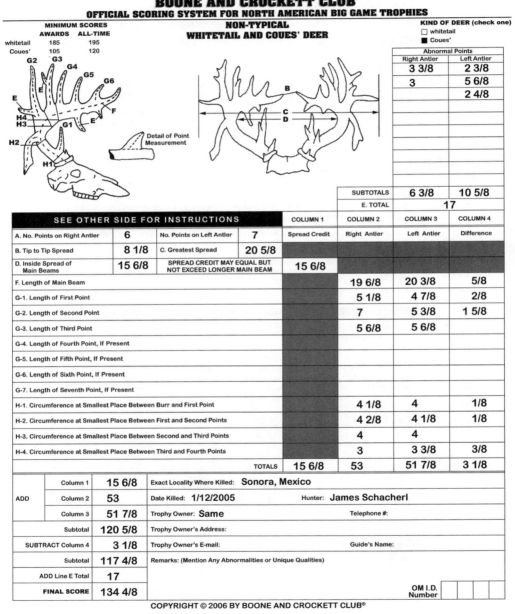

<table>
</table>

Records of North American Big Game

250 Station Drive
Missoula, MT 59801
(406) 542-1888

BOONE AND CROCKETT CLUB®
OFFICIAL SCORING SYSTEM FOR NORTH AMERICAN BIG GAME TROPHIES

NON-TYPICAL
WHITETAIL AND COUES' DEER

MINIMUM SCORES

	AWARDS	ALL-TIME
whitetail	185	195
Coues'	105	120

KIND OF DEER (check one)
☐ whitetail
■ Coues'

Abnormal Points

Right Antler	Left Antler
3 3/8	2 3/8
3	5 6/8
	2 4/8

SUBTOTALS	6 3/8	10 5/8
E. TOTAL	17	

Detail of Point Measurement

SEE OTHER SIDE FOR INSTRUCTIONS

				COLUMN 1	COLUMN 2	COLUMN 3	COLUMN 4
A. No. Points on Right Antler	6	No. Points on Left Antler	7	Spread Credit	Right Antler	Left Antler	Difference
B. Tip to Tip Spread	8 1/8	C. Greatest Spread	20 5/8				
D. Inside Spread of Main Beams	15 6/8	SPREAD CREDIT MAY EQUAL BUT NOT EXCEED LONGER MAIN BEAM		15 6/8			
F. Length of Main Beam					19 6/8	20 3/8	5/8
G-1. Length of First Point					5 1/8	4 7/8	2/8
G-2. Length of Second Point					7	5 3/8	1 5/8
G-3. Length of Third Point					5 6/8	5 6/8	
G-4. Length of Fourth Point, If Present							
G-5. Length of Fifth Point, If Present							
G-6. Length of Sixth Point, If Present							
G-7. Length of Seventh Point, If Present							
H-1. Circumference at Smallest Place Between Burr and First Point					4 1/8	4	1/8
H-2. Circumference at Smallest Place Between First and Second Points					4 2/8	4 1/8	1/8
H-3. Circumference at Smallest Place Between Second and Third Points					4	4	
H-4. Circumference at Smallest Place Between Third and Fourth Points					3	3 3/8	3/8
			TOTALS	15 6/8	53	51 7/8	3 1/8

ADD	Column 1	15 6/8	Exact Locality Where Killed: **Sonora, Mexico**	
	Column 2	53	Date Killed: **1/12/2005**	Hunter: **James Schacherl**
	Column 3	51 7/8	Trophy Owner: **Same**	Telephone #:
	Subtotal	120 5/8	Trophy Owner's Address:	
SUBTRACT Column 4		3 1/8	Trophy Owner's E-mail:	Guide's Name:
	Subtotal	117 4/8	Remarks: (Mention Any Abnormalities or Unique Qualities)	
ADD Line E Total		17		
FINAL SCORE		134 4/8		OM I.D. Number

COPYRIGHT © 2006 BY BOONE AND CROCKETT CLUB®

I, <u>Horace Gore</u>, certify that I have measured this trophy on <u>3/17/2005</u>

PRINT NAME   MM/DD/YYYYY

at <u>American Bank, Gonzales, Texas</u>

STREET ADDRESS   CITY   STATE/PROVINCE

and that these measurements and data are, to the best of my knowledge and belief, made in accordance with the instructions given.

Witness: _____ Signature: _____ I.D. Number

B&C OFFICIAL MEASURER

INSTRUCTIONS FOR MEASURING NON-TYPICAL WHITETAIL AND COUES' DEER

All measurements must be made with a 1/4-inch wide flexible steel tape to the nearest one-eighth of an inch. (Note: A flexible steel cable can be used to measure points and main beams only.) Enter fractional figures in eighths, without reduction. Official measurements cannot be taken until the antlers have air dried for at least 60 days after the animal was killed.

    A. Number of Points on Each Antler: To be counted a point, the projection must be at least one inch long, with the length exceeding width at one inch or more of length. All points are measured from tip of point to nearest edge of beam as illustrated. Beam tip is counted as a point but not measured as a point. **Point totals do not add into the final score.**

    B. Tip to Tip Spread is measured between tips of main beams. **Tip to tip spread does not add into the final score.**

    C. Greatest Spread is measured between perpendiculars at a right angle to the center line of the skull at widest part, whether across main beams or points. **Greatest spread does not add into the final score.**

    D. Inside Spread of Main Beams is measured at a right angle to the center line of the skull at widest point between main beams. Enter this measurement again as the Spread Credit if it is less than or equal to the length of the longer main beam; if greater, enter longer main beam length for Spread Credit.

    E. Total of Lengths of all Abnormal Points: Abnormal Points are those non-typical in location (such as points originating from a point or from bottom or sides of main beam) or extra points beyond the normal pattern of points. Measure in usual manner and enter in appropriate blanks.

    F. Length of Main Beam is measured from the center of the lowest outside edge of burr over the outer side to the most distant point of the main beam. The point of beginning is that point on the burr where the center line along the outer side of the beam intersects the burr, then following generally the line of the illustration.

    G-1-2-3-4-5-6-7. Length of Normal Points: Normal points project from the top of the main beam. They are measured from nearest edge of main beam over outer curve to tip. Lay the tape along the outer curve of the beam so that the top edge of the tape coincides with the top edge of the beam on both sides of the point to determine the baseline for point measurement. Record point lengths in appropriate blanks.

    H-1-2-3-4. Circumferences are taken as detailed in illustration for each measurement. If brow point is missing, take H-1 and H-2 at smallest place between burr and G-2. If G-4 is missing, take H-4 halfway between G-3 and tip of main beam.

ENTRY AFFIDAVIT FOR ALL HUNTER-TAKEN TROPHIES

For the purpose of entry into the Boone and Crockett Club's® records, North American big game harvested by the following methods or under the following conditions are ineligible:

    I.   Spotting or herding game from the air, followed by landing in its vicinity for the purpose of pursuit and shooting;

    II.   Herding or chasing with the aid of any motorized equipment;

    III.   Use of electronic communication devices to guide hunters to game, artificial lighting, electronic light intensifying devices (night vision optics), sights with built-in electronic range-finding capabilities, thermal imaging equipment, electronic game calls or cameras/timers/motion tracking devices that transmit images and other information to the hunter;

    IV.   Confined by artificial barriers, including escape-proof fenced enclosures;

    V.   Transplanted for the purpose of commercial shooting;

    VI.   By the use of traps or pharmaceuticals;

    VII.   While swimming, helpless in deep snow, or helpless in any other natural or artificial medium;

    VIII.   On another hunter's license;

    IX.   Not in full compliance with the game laws or regulations of the federal government or of any state, province, territory, or tribal council on reservations or tribal lands;

I certify that the trophy scored on this chart was not taken in violation of the conditions listed above. In signing this statement, I understand that if the information provided on this entry is found to be misrepresented or fraudulent in any respect, it will not be accepted into the Awards Program and 1) all of my prior entries are subject to deletion from future editions of **Records of North American Big Game** and 2) future entries may not be accepted.

FAIR CHASE, as defined by the Boone and Crockett Club®, is the ethical, sportsmanlike and lawful pursuit and taking of any free-ranging wild, native North American big game animal in a manner that does not give the hunter an improper advantage over such animals.

The Boone and Crockett Club® may exclude the entry of any animal that it deems to have been taken in an unethical manner or under conditions deemed inappropriate by the Club.

Date: _____ Signature of Hunter: _____

(SIGNATURE MUST BE WITNESSED BY AN OFFICIAL MEASURER OR A NOTARY PUBLIC.)

Date: _____ Signature of Notary or Official Measurer: _____

Records of
North American
Big Game

250 Station Drive
Missoula, MT 59801
(406) 542-1888

BOONE AND CROCKETT CLUB®
OFFICIAL SCORING SYSTEM FOR NORTH AMERICAN BIG GAME TROPHIES

MOOSE

MINIMUM SCORES		
	AWARDS	ALL-TIME
Canada	185	195
Alaska-Yukon	210	224
Shiras	140	155

KIND OF MOOSE (check one)
- ■ Canada
- ☐ Alaska-Yukon
- ☐ Shiras

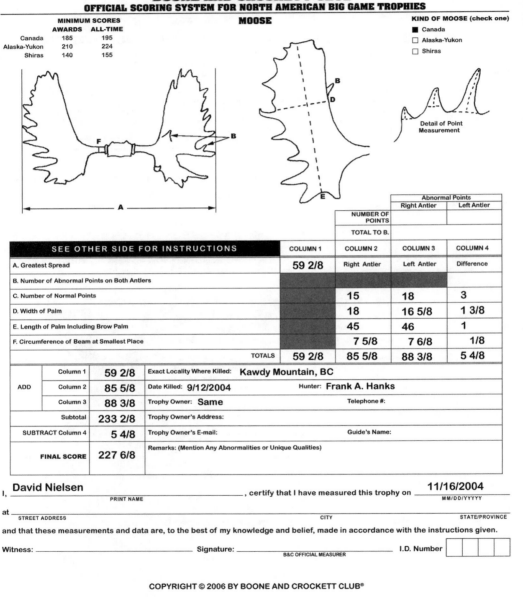

Detail of Point
Measurement

		Abnormal Points	
		Right Antler	Left Antler
NUMBER OF POINTS			
TOTAL TO B.			

SEE OTHER SIDE FOR INSTRUCTIONS	COLUMN 1	COLUMN 2	COLUMN 3	COLUMN 4
A. Greatest Spread	59 2/8	Right Antler	Left Antler	Difference
B. Number of Abnormal Points on Both Antlers				
C. Number of Normal Points		15	18	3
D. Width of Palm		18	16 5/8	1 3/8
E. Length of Palm Including Brow Palm		45	46	1
F. Circumference of Beam at Smallest Place		7 5/8	7 6/8	1/8
TOTALS	59 2/8	85 5/8	88 3/8	5 4/8

ADD	Column 1	59 2/8
	Column 2	85 5/8
	Column 3	88 3/8
	Subtotal	233 2/8
SUBTRACT Column 4		5 4/8
FINAL SCORE		227 6/8

Exact Locality Where Killed: **Kawdy Mountain, BC**

Date Killed: **9/12/2004**   Hunter: **Frank A. Hanks**

Trophy Owner: **Same**   Telephone #:

Trophy Owner's Address:

Trophy Owner's E-mail: Guide's Name:

Remarks: (Mention Any Abnormalities or Unique Qualities)

I, **David Nielsen** _____ , certify that I have measured this trophy on **11/16/2004**
      PRINT NAME   MM/DD/YYYYY

at _____
   STREET ADDRESS   CITY   STATE/PROVINCE

and that these measurements and data are, to the best of my knowledge and belief, made in accordance with the instructions given.

Witness: _____ Signature: _____ I.D. Number [ ][ ][ ][ ]
                                          B&C OFFICIAL MEASURER

INSTRUCTIONS FOR MEASURING MOOSE

Measurements must be made with a 1/4-inch wide flexible steel tape to the nearest one-eighth of an inch. Enter fractional figures in eighths, without reduction. Official measurements cannot be taken until antlers have air dried for at least 60 days after animal was killed.

A. Greatest Spread is measured between perpendiculars in a straight line at a right angle to the center line of the skull.

B. Number of Abnormal Points on Both Antlers: Abnormal points are those projections originating from normal points or from the upper or lower palm surface, or from the inner edge of palm (see illustration). Abnormal points must be at least one inch long, with length exceeding width at one inch or more of length.

C. Number of Normal Points: Normal points originate from the outer edge of palm. To be counted a point, a projection must be at least one inch long, with the length exceeding width at one inch or more of length. Be sure to verify whether or not each projection qualifies as a point.

D. Width of Palm is taken in contact with the undersurface of the palm, at a right angle to the inner edge of the palm. The line of measurement should be taken from the inside edge of the palm to a dip between bumps or points at the widest outside edge of the palm. If there are no bumps or points, the width measurement is taken at the widest part of the palm. The line of measurement should begin at the midpoint of the inner edge of the palm and end at the midpoint of the edge of the palm between points or bumps, which gives credit for the desirable characteristic of palm thickness.

E. Length of Palm, including brow palm, is taken in contact with the undersurface of the palm, parallel to the inner edge, from dips between bumps or points at the top edge of the palm to dips between qualifying points (if present) on the brow palm. If a bay is present, measure across the open bay if the proper line of measurement is parallel to the inner edge and follows this path. The line of measurement should begin and end at the midpoint of the palm edges, which gives credit for the desirable characteristic of palm thickness.

F. Circumference of Beam at Smallest Place is taken as illustrated.

ENTRY AFFIDAVIT FOR ALL HUNTER-TAKEN TROPHIES

For the purpose of entry into the Boone and Crockett Club's® records, North American big game harvested by the use of the following methods or under the following conditions are ineligible:

I. Spotting or herding game from the air, followed by landing in its vicinity for the purpose of pursuit and shooting;
II. Herding or chasing with the aid of any motorized equipment;
III. Use of electronic communication devices to guide hunters to game, artificial lighting, electronic light intensifying devices (night vision optics), sights with built-in electronic range-finding capabilities, thermal imaging equipment, electronic game calls or cameras/timers/motion tracking devices that transmit images and other information to the hunter;
IV. Confined by artificial barriers, including escape-proof fenced enclosures;
V. Transplanted for the purpose of commercial shooting;
VI. By the use of traps or pharmaceuticals;
VII. While swimming, helpless in deep snow, or helpless in any other natural or artificial medium;
VIII. On another hunter's license;
IX. Not in full compliance with the game laws or regulations of the federal government or of any state, province, territory, or tribal council on reservations or t   b   lands;

I certify that the trophy scored on   art was not taken in violation of the conditions listed above. In signing this statement, I underst nd that if the information provided on   ntry is found to be misrepresented or fraudulent in any respect, it will not be accepted into the Awards Program and 1) all of my pr   ies a e subject to deletion from   editions of **Records of North American Big Game** 2) future entries may not be accepted

FAIR CHASE, as defined by the Boone a   lub®, is the et   and lawful pursuit and taking of   g wild, native North American big gai e an   er that d   impro er advan age over su   s.

The Boone and Crockett Club® may ex lud   y a   n tak n in an ethi al conditions deemed inappropriate by th C

Date: _____ Signature

(PUBLIC.)

Date: _____ Signature of Nota

250 Station Drive
Missoula, MT 59801
(406) 542-1888

BOONE AND CROCKETT CLUB®
OFFICIAL SCORING SYSTEM FOR NORTH AMERICAN BIG GAME TROPHIES

CARIBOU

	MINIMUM SCORES	
	AWARDS	ALL-TIME
mountain	360	390
woodland	265	295
barren ground	375	400
Central Canada		
barren ground	345	360
Quebec-Labrador	365	375

KIND OF CARIBOU (check one)
- ☐ mountain
- ☐ woodland
- ☐ barren ground
- ☐ Central Canada
-   barren ground
- ■ Quebec-Labrador

Detail of Point
Measurement

SEE OTHER SIDE FOR INSTRUCTIONS		COLUMN 1	COLUMN 2	COLUMN 3	COLUMN 4
		Spread Credit	Right Antler	Left Antler	Difference
A. Tip to Tip Spread	38 7/8				
B. Greatest Spread	48 7/8				
C. Inside Spread of Main Beams	45 6/8	SPREAD CREDIT MAY EQUAL BUT NOT EXCEED LONGER MAIN BEAM	45 6/8			
D. Number of Points on Each Antler Excluding Brows			18	17	1
Number of Points on Each Brow			6	5	
E. Length of Main Beam			53 4/8	51 4/8	2
F-1. Length of Brow Palm or First Point			18 6/8	17 3/8	
F-2. Length of Bez or Second Point			22	24 4/8	2 4/8
F-3. Length of Rear Point, If Present			6 6/8	5 2/8	1 4/8
F-4. Length of Second Longest Top Point			17 4/8	13 2/8	4 2/8
F-5. Length of Longest Top Point			19 3/8	17 7/8	1 4/8
G-1. Width of Brow Palm			12 3/8	11	
G-2. Width of Top Palm			3 6/8	5 1/8	1 3/8
H-1. Circumference at Smallest Place Between Brow and Bez Point			5 2/8	5 2/8	
H-2. Circumference at Smallest Place Between Bez and Rear Point			5 1/8	5 2/8	1/8
H-3. Circumference at Smallest Place Between Rear Point and First Top Point			5 3/8	5 2/8	1/8
H-4. Circumference at Smallest Place Between Two Longest Top Palm Points			7 7/8	7 6/8	1/8
	TOTALS	45 6/8	201 5/8	191 3/8	14 4/8

ADD	Column 1	45 6/8	Exact Locality Where Killed: **Clearwater Lake, QC**
	Column 2	201 5/8	Date Killed: **10/3/2005** Hunter: **Woody Groves**
	Column 3	191 3/8	Trophy Owner: **Same** Telephone #:
	Subtotal	438 6/8	Trophy Owner's Address:
SUBTRACT Column 4		14 4/8	Trophy Owner's E-mail: Guide's Name:
FINAL SCORE		424 2/8	Remarks: (Mention Any Abnormalities or Unique Qualities)

OM I.D. Number

I, _____ **André Beaudry** _____ , certify that I have measured this trophy on __ **06/11/2006** __
    PRINT NAME   MM/DD/YYYYY

at __ **Granby, Québec, Canada** __
    STREET ADDRESS   CITY   STATE/PROVINCE

and that these measurements and data are, to the best of my knowledge and belief, made in accordance with the instructions given.

Witness: _____ Signature: _____ I.D. Number ☐☐☐
                                               B&C OFFICIAL MEASURER

INSTRUCTIONS FOR MEASURING CARIBOU

All measurements must be made with a 1/4-inch wide flexible steel tape to the nearest one-eighth of an inch. (Note: A flexible steel cable can be used to measure points and main beams only.) Enter fractional figures in eighths, without reduction. Official measurements cannot be taken until the antlers have air dried for at least 60 days after the animal was killed.

A. Tip to Tip Spread is measured between tips of main beams. **Tip to tip spread does not add into the final score.**

B. Greatest Spread is measured between perpendiculars at a right angle to the center line of the skull at widest part, whether across main beams or points. **Greatest spread does not add into the final score.**

C. Inside Spread of Main Beams is measured at a right angle to the center line of the skull at widest point between main beams. Enter this measurement again as the Spread Credit if it is less than or equal to the length of the longer main beam; if greater, enter longer main beam length for Spread Credit.

D. Number of Points on Each Antler: To be counted a point, a projection must be at least one-half inch long, with length exceeding width at one-half inch or more of length. Beam tip is counted as a point but not measured as a point. There are no "abnormal" points in caribou.

E. Length of Main Beam is measured from the center of the lowest outside edge of burr over the outer side to the most distant point of the main beam. The point of beginning is that point on the burr where the center line along the outer side of the beam intersects the burr, then following generally the line of the illustration.

F-1-2-3. Length of Points are measured from nearest edge of beam over outer curve to tip. Lay the tape along the outer curve of the beam so that the top edge of the tape coincides with the top edge of the beam on both sides of point to determine the baseline for point measurement. Record point lengths in appropriate blanks.

F-4. Length of Points are measured from the tip of the point to the top of the beam, then at a right angle to the bottom edge of beam. The second Longest Top Point cannot be a point branch of the Longest Top Point.

G. Width of Brow is measured in a straight line from top edge to lower edge, as illustrated, with measurement line at a right angle to main axis of brow.

H. Top Palm is measured from midpoint of lower edge of main beam to midpoint of a dip between points, at widest part of palm. The line of measurement begins and ends at midpoints of palm edges, which gives credit for palm thickness.

H-1-2-3-4. Circumferences are taken as illustrated for measurements. If brow point is missing, take H-1 at smallest point between burr and bez point. If rear point is missing, take H-2 and H-3 measurements at smallest place between bez and first top point. Do not depress the tape into any dips of the palm or main beam.

ENTRY AFFIDAVIT FOR ALL HUNTER-TAKEN TROPHIES

For the purpose of entry into the Boone and Crockett Club's® records, North American big game harvested by the use of the following methods or under the following conditions are ineligible:

I. Spotting or herding game from the air, followed by landing in its vicinity for the purpose of pursuit and shooting;
II. Herding or chasing with the aid of any motorized equipment;
III. Use of electronic communication devices to guide hunters to game, artificial lighting, electronic light intensifying devices (night vision optics), sights with built-in electronic range-finding capabilities, thermal imaging equipment, electronic game calls or cameras/timers/motion tracking devices that transmit images and other information to the hunter;
IV. Confined by artificial barriers, including escape-proof fenced enclosures;
V. Transplanted for the purpose of commercial shooting;
VI. By the use of traps or pharmaceuticals;
VII. While swimming, helpless in deep snow, or helpless in any other natural or artificial medium;
VIII. On another hunter's license;
IX. Not in full compliance with the game laws or regulations of the federal government or of any state, province, territory, or tribal council on reservations.

I certify that the trophy scored on this chart was not taken in violation of the conditions listed above. In signing this statement, I understand that if the information provided on this entry is found to be misrepresented or fraudulent in any respect, it will not be accepted into the Awards Program and 1) all of my prior entries are subject to deletion from future editions of **Records of North American Big Game** 2) future entries may not be accepted.

FAIR CHASE, as defined by the Boone and Crockett Club, is the ethical, sportsmanlike and lawful pursuit and taking of any free-ranging wild, native North American big game animal in a manner that does not give the hunter an improper advantage over such game animals.

The Boone and Crockett Club may exclude the entry of any animal that it deems to have been taken in an unethical manner or under conditions deemed inappropriate by the Club.

Date: _____ Signature of Hunter: _____
                                      (SIGNATURE MUST BE WITNESSED BY AN OFFICIAL MEASURER OR A NOTARY PUBLIC.)

Date: _____ Signature of Notary or Official Measurer: _____

250 Station Drive
Missoula, MT 59801
(406) 542-1888

BOONE AND CROCKETT CLUB®
OFFICIAL SCORING SYSTEM FOR NORTH AMERICAN BIG GAME TROPHIES

PRONGHORN

MINIMUM SCORES	
AWARDS	ALL-TIME
80	82

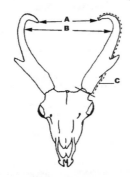

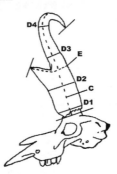

SEE OTHER SIDE FOR INSTRUCTIONS			COLUMN 1	COLUMN 2	COLUMN 3
A. Tip to Tip Spread		6 1/8	Right Horn	Left Horn	Difference
B. Inside Spread of Horns		10 3/8			
C. Length of Horn			15 2/8	15 3/8	1/8
D-1. Circumference of Base			7 3/8	7 3/8	
D-2. Circumference at First Quarter	Location of First Quarter Circumference:	3 27/32	8 2/8	8	2/8
D-3. Circumference at Second Quarter	Location of Second Quarter Circumference:	7 11/16	5	5	
D-4. Circumference at Third Quarter	Location of Third Quarter Circumference:	11 17/32	3 3/8	3 4/8	1/8
E. Length of Prong			6 6/8	6 4/8	2/8
		TOTALS	46	45 6/8	6/8

ADD	Column 1	46	Exact Locality Where Killed: Carbon Co., UT	
	Column 2	45 6/8	Date Killed: 9/1/2003	Hunter: Rick D. Ullery
	Subtotal	91 6/8	Trophy Owner: Same	Telephone #:
	SUBTRACT Column 3	6/8	Trophy Owner's Address:	
FINAL SCORE		91	Trophy Owner's E-mail:	Guide's Name:
			Remarks: (Mention Any Abnormalities or Unique Qualities)	

At the time of official measurement, were the sheaths reattached to the cores by the use of some type of filler or adhesive? ☐ Yes ☐ No

I, __Kirk Kelso__ , certify that I have measured this trophy on __11/28/2003__
PRINT NAME   MM/DD/YYYY

at __Tucson, Arizona__
STREET ADDRESS   CITY   STATE/PROVINCE

and that these measurements and data are, to the best of my knowledge and belief, made in accordance with the instructions given.

Witness: _____ Signature: _____ I.D. Number [ ][ ][ ][ ]
                                            B&C OFFICIAL MEASURER

INSTRUCTIONS FOR MEASURING PRONGHORN

All measurements must be made with a 1/4-inch wide flexible steel tape to the nearest one-eighth of an inch. Enter fractional figures in eighths, without reduction. Official measurements cannot be taken until horns have air dried for at least 60 days after the animal was killed.

- **A. Tip to Tip Spread** is measured between tips of horns. **Tip to tip spread does not add into the final score.**
- **B. Inside Spread of Horns** is measured at a right angle to the center line of the skull, at widest point between horns. **Inside spread does not add into the final score.**
- **C. Length of Horn** is measured on the outside curve on the general line illustrated. The line taken will vary with different heads, depending on the direction of their curvature. Measure along the center of the outer curve from tip of horn to a point in line with the lowest edge of the base, using a straight edge to establish the line end.
- **D-1. Circumference of Base** is measured at a right angle to axis of horn. Do not follow irregular edge of horn; the line of measurement must be entirely on horn material.
- **D-2-3-4. Divide measurement C** of longer horn by four. Starting at base, mark both horns at these quarters (even though the other horn is shorter) and measure circumferences at these marks. If the prong interferes with D-2, move the measurement down to just below the swelling of the prong. If D-3 falls in the swelling of the prong, move the measurement up to just above the prong.
- **E. Length of Prong:** Measure from the tip of the prong along the upper edge of the outer side to the horn; then continue around the horn to a point at the rear of the horn where a straight edge across the back of both horns touches the horn, with the latter part being at a right angle to the long axis of horn.

ENTRY AFFIDAVIT FOR ALL HUNTER-TAKEN TROPHIES

For the purpose of entry into the Boone and Crockett Club's® records, North American big game harvested by the use of the following methods or under the following conditions are ineligible:

- I. Spotting or herding game from the air, followed by landing in its vicinity for the purpose of pursuit and shooting;
- II. Herding or chasing with the aid of any motorized equipment;
- III. Use of electronic communication devices to guide hunters to game, artificial lighting, electronic light intensifying devices (night vision optics), sights with built-in electronic range-finding capabilities, thermal imaging equipment, electronic game calls or cameras/timers/motion tracking devices that transmit images and other information to the hunter;
- IV. Confined by artificial barriers, including escape-proof fenced enclosures;
- V. Transplanted for the purpose of commercial shooting;
- VI. By the use of traps or pharmaceuticals;
- VII. While swimming, helpless in deep snow, or helpless in any other natural or artificial medium;
- VIII. On another hunter's license;
- IX. Not in full compliance with the game laws or regulations of the federal government or of any state, province, territory, or tribal council on reservations or tribal lands;

I certify that the trophy scored on this chart was not taken in violation of the conditions listed above. In signing this statement, I understand that if the information provided on this entry is found to be misrepresented or fraudulent in any respect, it will not be accepted into the Awards Program and 1) all of my prior entries are subject to deletion from future editions of **Records of North American Big Game** 2) future entries may not be accepted.

FAIR CHASE, as defined by the Boone and Crockett Club®, is the ethical, sportsmanlike and lawful pursuit and taking of any free-ranging wild, native North American big game animal in a manner that does not give the hunter an improper advantage over such game animals.

The Boone and Crockett Club® may exclude the entry of any animal that it deems to have been taken in an unethical manner or under conditions deemed inappropriate by the Club.

Date: _____   Signature of Hunter: _____

(SIGNATURE MUST BE WITNESSED BY AN OFFICIAL MEASURER OR A NOTARY PUBLIC)

Date: _____   Signature of Notary or Official Measurer: _____

Records of
North American
Big Game

250 Station Drive
Missoula, MT 59801
(406) 542-1888

BOONE AND CROCKETT CLUB®
OFFICIAL SCORING SYSTEM FOR NORTH AMERICAN BIG GAME TROPHIES
BISON

MINIMUM SCORES
AWARDS   ALL-TIME
115   115

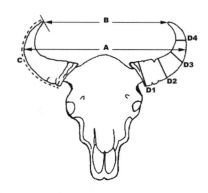

SEE OTHER SIDE FOR INSTRUCTIONS		COLUMN 1	COLUMN 2	COLUMN 3
A. Greatest Spread	33 6/8	Right Horn	Left Horn	Difference
B. Tip to Tip Spread	28 2/8			
C. Length of Horn		20 7/8	21 1/8	2/8
D-1. Circumference of Base		14 7/8	15 2/8	3/8
D-2. Circumference at First Quarter	Location of First Quarter Circumference: 5 9/32	12 4/8	12 2/8	2/8
D-3. Circumference at Second Quarter	Location of Second Quarter Circumference: 10 9/16	10 6/8	10 6/8	
D-4. Circumference at Third Quarter	Location of Third Quarter Circumference: 15 27/32	6 5/8	6 4/8	1/8
	TOTALS	65 5/8	65 7/8	1

ADD	Column 1	65 5/8	Exact Locality Where Killed: **Custer Co., SD**
	Column 2	65 7/8	Date Killed: **01/11/2006** Hunter: **Jeffrey S. Shoaf**
	Subtotal	131 4/8	Trophy Owner: **Same** Telephone #:
	SUBTRACT Column 3	1	Trophy Owner's Address:
	FINAL SCORE	130 4/8	Trophy Owner's E-mail: Guide's Name:
			Remarks: (Mention Any Abnormalities or Unique Qualities)

I, **Lester W. Jass**
PRINT NAME
, certify that I have measured this trophy on **10/03/2006**
MM/DD/YYYYY

at **Rapid City, SD**
STREET ADDRESS   CITY   STATE/PROVINCE

and that these measurements and data are, to the best of my knowledge and belief, made in accordance with the instructions given.

Witness: _____   Signature: _____   I.D. Number
B&C OFFICIAL MEASURER

COPYRIGHT © 2006 BY BOONE AND CROCKETT CLUB®

BOONE AND CROCKETT CLUB'S

INSTRUCTIONS FOR MEASURING BISON

All measurements must be made with a 1/4-inch wide flexible steel tape to the nearest one-eighth of an inch. Wherever it is necessary to change direction of measurement, mark a control point and swing tape at this point. Enter fractional figures in eighths, without reduction. Official measurements cannot be taken until horns have air dried for at least 60 days after the animal was killed.

- **A. Greatest Spread** is measured between perpendiculars at a right angle to the center line of the skull. **Greatest spread does not add into the final score.**
- **B. Tip to Tip Spread** is measured between tips of horns. **Tip to tip spread does not add into the final score.**
- **C. Length of Horn** is measured from the lowest point on underside over outer curve to a point in line with the tip. Use a straight edge, perpendicular to horn axis, to end the measurement.
- **D-1. Circumference of Base** is measured at right angle to axis of horn. Do not follow the irregular edge of horn; the line of measurement must be entirely on horn material.
- **D-2-3-4. Divide measurement C** of longer horn by four. Starting at base, mark both horns at these quarters (even though the other horn is shorter) and measure the circumferences at these marks, with measurements taken at right angles to horn axis.

ENTRY AFFIDAVIT FOR ALL HUNTER-TAKEN TROPHIES

For the purpose of entry into the Boone and Crockett Club's® records, North American big game harvested by the use of the following methods or under the following conditions are ineligible:

- I. Spotting or herding game from the air, followed by landing in its vicinity for the purpose of pursuit and shooting;
- II. Herding or chasing with the aid of any motorized equipment;
- III. Use of electronic communication devices to guide hunters to game, artificial lighting, electronic light intensifying devices (night vision optics), sights with built-in electronic range-finding capabilities, thermal imaging equipment, electronic game calls or cameras/timers/motion tracking devices that transmit images and other information to the hunter;
- IV. Confined by artificial barriers, including escape-proof fenced enclosures;
- V. Transplanted for the purpose of commercial shooting;
- VI. By the use of traps or pharmaceuticals;
- VII. While swimming, helpless in deep snow, or helpless in any other natural or artificial medium;
- VIII. On another hunter's license;
- IX. Not in full compliance with the game laws or regulations of the federal government or of any state, province, territory, or tribal council on reservations or tribal lands;

I certify that the trophy scored on this chart was not taken in violation of the conditions listed above. In signing this statement, I understand that if the information provided on this entry is found to be misrepresented or fraudulent in any respect, it will not be accepted into the Awards Program and 1) all of my prior entries are subject to deletion from future editions of **Records of North American Big Game** 2) future entries may not be accepted.

FAIR CHASE, as defined by the Boone and Crockett Club®, is the ethical, sportsmanlike and lawful pursuit and taking of any free-ranging wild, native North American big game animal in a manner that does not give the hunter an improper advantage over such game animals.

The Boone and Crockett Club® may exclude the entry of any animal that it deems to have been taken in an unethical manner or under conditions deemed inappropriate by the Club.

Date: _____ Signature of Hunter: _____

(SIGNATURE MUST BE WITNESSED BY AN OFFICIAL MEASURER OR A NOTARY PUBLIC.)

Date: _____ Signature of Notary or Official Measurer: _____

Records of
North American
Big Game

250 Station Drive
Missoula, MT 59801
(406) 542-1888

BOONE AND CROCKETT CLUB®
OFFICIAL SCORING SYSTEM FOR NORTH AMERICAN BIG GAME TROPHIES

ROCKY MOUNTAIN GOAT

MINIMUM SCORES	
AWARDS	ALL-TIME
47	50

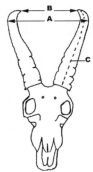 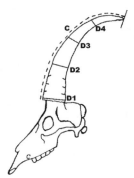

SEE OTHER SIDE FOR INSTRUCTIONS		COLUMN 1	COLUMN 2	COLUMN 3
A. Greatest Spread	9	Right Horn	Left Horn	Difference
B. Tip to Tip Spread	8 3/8			
C. Length of Horn		11 2/8	11 2/8	
D-1. Circumference of Base		5 6/8	5 6/8	
D-2. Circumference at First Quarter	Location of First Quarter Circumference: **2 13/16**	5	5	
D-3. Circumference at Second Quarter	Location of Second Quarter Circumference: **5 5/8**	3 4/8	3 4/8	
D-4. Circumference at Third Quarter	Location of Third Quarter Circumference: **8 7/16**	1 6/8	1 6/8	
	TOTALS	27 2/8	27 2/8	

ADD	Column 1	27 2/8	Exact Locality Where Killed: **Revillagigedo Island, AK**
	Column 2	27 2/8	Date Killed: **8/1/2004** Hunter: **Edward Toribio**
Subtotal		54 4/8	Trophy Owner: **Same** Telephone #:
SUBTRACT Column 3			Trophy Owner's Address:
FINAL SCORE		54 4/8	Trophy Owner's E-mail: Guide's Name:
			Remarks: (Mention Any Abnormalities or Unique Qualities)

I, **Douglas N. Larsen** , certify that I have measured this trophy on **10/11/2004**

PRINT NAME   MM/DD/YYYYY

at **Douglas, AK**

STREET ADDRESS   CITY   STATE/PROVINCE

and that these measurements and data are, to the best of my knowledge and belief, made in accordance with the instructions given.

Witness: _____ Signature: _____ I.D. Number ☐☐☐☐

B&C OFFICIAL MEASURER

COPYRIGHT © 2006 BY BOONE AND CROCKETT CLUB®

INSTRUCTIONS FOR MEASURING ROCKY MOUNTAIN GOAT

All measurements must be made with a 1/4-inch wide flexible steel tape to the nearest one-eighth of an inch. Wherever it is necessary to change direction of measurement, mark a control point and swing tape at this point. Enter fractional figures in eighths, without reduction. Official measurements cannot be taken until horns have air dried for at least 60 days after the animal was killed.

- **A. Greatest Spread** is measured between perpendiculars at a right angle to the center line of the skull. **Greatest spread does not add into the final score.**
- **B. Tip to Tip spread** is measured between tips of the horns. **Tip to tip spread does not add into the final score.**
- **C. Length of Horn** is measured from the lowest point in front over outer curve to a point in line with tip.
- **D-1. Circumference of Base** is measured at a right angle to axis of horn. Do not follow irregular edge of horn; the line of measurement must be entirely on horn material.
- **D-2-3-4. Divide measurement C** of longer horn by four. Starting at base, mark both horns at these quarters (even though the other horn is shorter) and measure circumferences at these marks, with measurements taken at right angles to horn axis.

ENTRY AFFIDAVIT FOR ALL HUNTER-TAKEN TROPHIES

For the purpose of entry into the Boone and Crockett Club's® records, North American big game harvested by the use of the following methods or under the following conditions are ineligible:

- I.   Spotting or herding game from the air, followed by landing in its vicinity for the purpose of pursuit and shooting;
- II. Herding or chasing with the aid of any motorized equipment;
- III. Use of electronic communication devices to guide hunters to game, artificial lighting, electronic light intensifying devices (night vision optics), sights with built-in electronic range-finding capabilities, thermal imaging equipment, electronic game calls or cameras/timers/motion tracking devices that transmit images and other information to the hunter;
- IV. Confined by artificial barriers, including escape-proof fenced enclosures;
- V.   Transplanted for the purpose of commercial shooting;
- VI. By the use of traps or pharmaceuticals;
- VII. While swimming, helpless in deep snow, or helpless in any other natural or artificial medium;
- VIII. On another hunter's license;
- IX. Not in full compliance with the game laws or regulations of the federal government or of any state, province, territory, or tribal council on reservations or tribal lands;

I certify that the trophy scored on this chart was not taken in violation of the conditions listed above. In signing this statement, I understand that if the information provided on this entry is found to be misrepresented or fraudulent in any respect, it will not be accepted into the Awards Program and 1) all of my prior entries are subject to deletion from future editions of **Records of North American Big Game** 2) future entries may not be accepted.

FAIR CHASE, as defined by the Boone and Crockett Club®, is the ethical, sportsmanlike and lawful pursuit and taking of any free-ranging wild, native North American big game animal in a manner that does not give the hunter an improper advantage over such game animals.

The Boone and Crockett Club® may exclude the entry of any animal that it deems to have been taken in an unethical manner or under conditions deemed inappropriate by the Club.

Date: _____   Signature of Hunter: _____
(SIGNATURE MUST BE WITNESSED BY AN OFFICIAL MEASURER OR A NOTARY PUBLIC.)

Date: _____   Signature of Notary or Official Measurer: _____

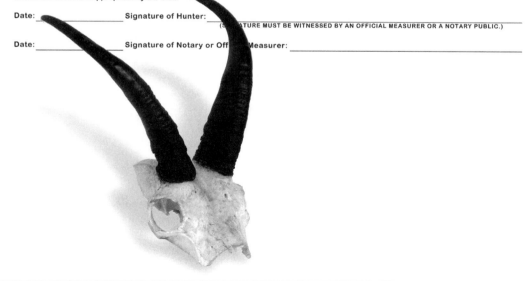

250 Station Drive
Missoula, MT 59801
(406) 542-1888

BOONE AND CROCKETT CLUB®
OFFICIAL SCORING SYSTEM FOR NORTH AMERICAN BIG GAME TROPHIES

MUSK OX

MINIMUM SCORES	
AWARDS	ALL-TIME
105	105

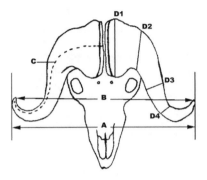

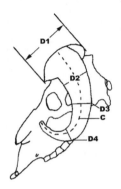

SEE OTHER SIDE FOR INSTRUCTIONS			COLUMN 1	COLUMN 2	COLUMN 3
A. Greatest Spread		31 4/8	Right Horn	Left Horn	Difference
B. Tip to Tip Spread		30 4/8			
C. Length of Horn			28 2/8	28 6/8	4/8
D-1. Width of Boss			12 1/8	11 3/8	6/8
D-2. Width at First Quarter	Location of First Quarter Width:	7 3/16	7 2/8	7 1/8	1/8
D-3. Circumference at Second Quarter	Location of Second Quarter Circumference:	19 3/8	11 7/8	12	1/8
D-4. Circumference at Third Quarter	Location of Third Quarter Circumference:	21 9/16	5 7/8	6 3/8	4/8
		TOTALS	65 3/8	65 5/8	2

ADD	Column 1	65 3/8	Exact Locality Where Killed: **Coppermine River, Nunavut**	
	Column 2	65 5/8	Date Killed: **4/12/2006**	Hunter: **Jim Shockey**
Subtotal		131	Trophy Owner: **Same**	Telephone #:
SUBTRACT Column 3		2	Trophy Owner's Address:	
FINAL SCORE		129	Trophy Owner's E-mail:	Guide's Name:
			Remarks: (Mention Any Abnormalities or Unique Qualities)	

I, **Fred W. Pringle** _____, certify that I have measured this trophy on **6/15/2006**
PRINT NAME   MM/DD/YYYYY

at **Victoria, B.C.** _____
STREET ADDRESS   CITY   STATE/PROVINCE

and that these measurements and data are, to the best of my knowledge and belief, made in accordance with the instructions given.

Witness: _____ Signature: _____ I.D. Number ☐☐☐☐
B&C OFFICIAL MEASURER

INSTRUCTIONS FOR MEASURING MUSK OX

All measurements must be made with a 1/4-inch wide flexible steel tape and adjustable calipers to the nearest one-eighth of an inch. Enter fractional figures in eighths, without reduction. Official measurements cannot be taken until horns have air dried for at least 60 days after the animal was killed.

- **A. Greatest Spread** is measured between perpendiculars at a right angle to the center line of the skull. **Greatest spread does not add into the final score.**
- **B. Tip to Tip Spread** is measured between tips of horns. **Tip to tip spread does not add into the final score.**
- **C. Length of Horn** is measured along center of upper horn surface, staying within curve of horn as illustrated, to a point in line with tip. Attempt to free the connective tissue between the horns at the center of the boss to determine the lowest point of horn material on each side. Hook the tape under the lowest point of the horn and measure the length of horn, with the measurement line maintained in the center of the upper surface of horn following the converging lines to the horn tip. A flexible steel cable may be substituted for the 1/4-inch steel tape for this measurement only.
- **D-1. Width of Boss** is measured with calipers at greatest width of the boss, with measurement line forming a right angle with horn axis. It is often helpful to measure D-1 before C, marking the midpoint of the boss as the correct path of C.
- **D-2-3-4. Divide measurement C** of longer horn by four. Starting at base, mark both horns at these quarters (even though the other horn is shorter). Then, using calipers, measure width of boss at D-2, making sure the measurement is at a right angle to horn axis and in line with the D-2 mark. Circumferences are then measured at D-3 and D-4, with measurements being taken at right angles to horn axis.

ENTRY AFFIDAVIT FOR ALL HUNTER-TAKEN TROPHIES

For the purpose of entry into the Boone and Crockett Club's® records, North American big game harvested by the use of the following methods or under the following conditions are ineligible:

- I. Spotting or herding game from the air, followed by landing in its vicinity for the purpose of pursuit and shooting;
- II. Herding or chasing with the aid of any motorized equipment;
- III. Use of electronic communication devices to guide hunters to game, artificial lighting, electronic light intensifying devices (night vision optics), sights with built-in electronic range-finding capabilities, thermal imaging equipment, electronic game calls or cameras/timers/motion tracking devices that transmit images and other information to the hunter;
- IV. Confined by artificial barriers, including escape-proof fenced enclosures;
- V. Transplanted for the purpose of commercial shooting;
- VI. By the use of traps or pharmaceuticals;
- VII. While swimming, helpless in deep snow, or helpless in any other natural or artificial medium;
- VIII. On another hunter's license;
- IX. Not in full compliance with the game laws or regulations of the federal government or of any state, province, territory, or tribal council on reservations or tribal lands;

I certify that the trophy scored on this chart was not taken in violation of the conditions listed above. In signing this statement, I understand that if the information provided on this entry is found to be misrepresented or fraudulent in any respect, it will not be accepted into the Awards Program and 1) all of my prior entries are subject to deletion from future editions of **Records of North American Big Game** 2) future entries may not be accepted.

FAIR CHASE, as defined by the Boone and Crockett Club®, is the ethical, sportsmanlike and lawful pursuit and taking of any free-ranging wild, native North American big game animal in a manner that does not give the hunter an improper advantage over such game animals.

The Boone and Crockett Club® may exclude the entry of any animal that it deems to have been taken in an unethical manner or under conditions deemed inappropriate by the Club.

Date:_____ Signature of Hunter:_____
(SIGNATURE MUST BE WITNESSED BY AN OFFICIAL MEASURER OR A NOTARY PUBLIC.)

Date:_____ Signature of Notary or Official Measurer:_____

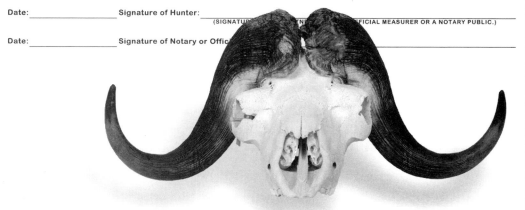

Records of North American Big Game

250 Station Drive
Missoula, MT 59801
(406) 542-1888

BOONE AND CROCKETT CLUB®
OFFICIAL SCORING SYSTEM FOR NORTH AMERICAN BIG GAME TROPHIES

SHEEP

	MINIMUM SCORES	
	AWARDS	ALL-TIME
bighorn	175	180
desert	165	168
Dall's	160	170
Stone's	165	170

KIND OF SHEEP (check one)

☐ bighorn
■ desert
☐ Dall's
☐ Stone's

PLUG NUMBER

_____

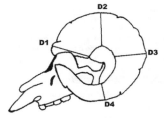

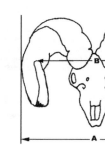

Measure to a Point in Line With Horn Tip

SEE OTHER SIDE FOR INSTRUCTIONS		COLUMN 1	COLUMN 2	COLUMN 3
A. Greatest Spread (Is Often Tip to Tip Spread)	22	Right Horn	Left Horn	Difference
B. Tip to Tip Spread	18 4/8			
C. Length of Horn		37 4/8	38 4/8	
D-1. Circumference of Base		17 1/8	17	1/8
D-2. Circumference at First Quarter	Location of First Quarter Circumference: 9 5/8	16 5/8	16 4/8	1/8
D-3. Circumference at Second Quarter	Location of Second Quarter Circumference: 19 2/8	13 7/8	13 6/8	1/8
D-4. Circumference at Third Quarter	Location of Third Quarter Circumference: 28 7/8	8 7/8	8 7/8	
	TOTALS	94	94 5/8	3/8

ADD	Column 1	94	Exact Locality Where Killed: **Hidalgo Co., NM**
	Column 2	94 5/8	Date Killed: **9/20/2006** Hunter: **Russell A. Young**
	Subtotal	188 5/8	Trophy Owner: **Same** Telephone #:
	SUBTRACT Column 3	3/8	Trophy Owner's Address:
	FINAL SCORE	188 2/8	Trophy Owner's E-mail: Guide's Name:
			Remarks: (Mention Any Abnormalities or Unique Qualities)

I, **Kirk Kelso**
PRINT NAME
, certify that I have measured this trophy on **11/20/2006**
MM/DD/YYYYY

at **Longton, Kansas**
STREET ADDRESS CITY STATE/PROVINCE

and that these measurements and data are, to the best of my knowledge and belief, made in accordance with the instructions given.

Witness: _____ Signature: _____ I.D. Number [ ][ ][ ][ ]
B&C OFFICIAL MEASURER

INSTRUCTIONS FOR MEASURING SHEEP

All measurements must be made with a 1/4-inch wide flexible steel tape to the nearest one-eighth of an inch. Enter fractional figures in eighths, without reduction. Official measurements cannot be taken until horns have air dried for at least 60 days after the animal was killed.

- **A. Greatest Spread** is measured between perpendiculars at a right angle to the center line of the skull. **Greatest spread does not add into the final score.**
- **B. Tip to Tip Spread** is measured between tips of horns. **Tip to tip spread does not add into the final score.**
- **C. Length of Horn** is measured from the lowest point in front on outer curve to a point in line with tip. Do not press tape into depressions. The low point of the outer curve of the horn is considered to be the low point of the frontal portion of the horn, situated above and slightly medial to the eye socket (not the outside edge). Use a straight edge, perpendicular to horn axis, to end measurement on "broomed" horns.
- **D-1. Circumference of Base** is measured at a right angle to axis of horn. Do not follow irregular edge of horn; the line of measurement must be entirely on horn material.
- **D-2-3-4. Divide measurement C** of longer horn by four. Starting at base, mark both horns at these quarters (even though the other horn is shorter) and measure circumferences at these marks, with measurements taken at right angles to horn axis.

ENTRY AFFIDAVIT FOR ALL HUNTER-TAKEN TROPHIES

For the purpose of entry into the Boone and Crockett Club's® records, North American big game harvested by the use of the following methods or under the following conditions are ineligible:

- I. Spotting or herding game from the air, followed by landing in its vicinity for the purpose of pursuit and shooting;
- II. Herding or chasing with the aid of any motorized equipment;
- III. Use of electronic communication devices to guide hunters to game, artificial lighting, electronic light intensifying devices (night vision optics), sights with built-in electronic range-finding capabilities, thermal imaging equipment, electronic game calls or cameras/timers/motion tracking devices that transmit images and other information to the hunter;
- IV. Confined by artificial barriers, including escape-proof fenced enclosures;
- V. Transplanted for the purpose of commercial shooting;
- VI. By the use of traps or pharmaceuticals;

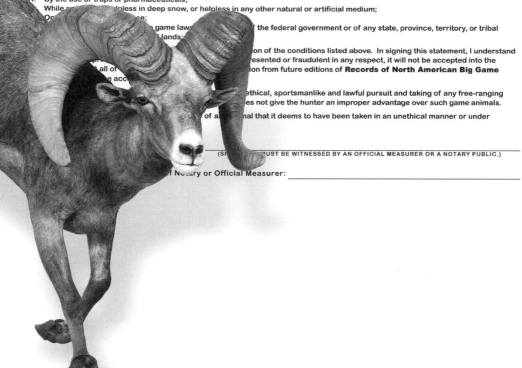

While _____ helpless in deep snow, or helpless in any other natural or artificial medium;

On _____ game laws _____ of the federal government or of any state, province, territory, or tribal _____ lands;

_____ on of the conditions listed above. In signing this statement, I understand _____ all o _____ resented or fraudulent in any respect, it will not be accepted into the _____ e acc _____ ion from future editions of **Records of North American Big Game**

_____ ethical, sportsmanlike and lawful pursuit and taking of any free-ranging _____ es not give the hunter an improper advantage over such game animals.

_____ of a _____ nal that it deems to have been taken in an unethical manner or under

_____ (S _____ UST BE WITNESSED BY AN OFFICIAL MEASURER OR A NOTARY PUBLIC.)

_____ f N _____ ary or Official Measurer: _____

FIELD PHOTOGRAPHS COURTESY OF THE TROPHY OWNERS

TROPHY FIELD PHOTOS FROM THE 26TH BIG GAME AWARDS PROGRAM 2004-2006

26th Big Game Awards Program Sponsors

ABOVE: Dall's sheep — 161 3/8
LOCATION: Talkeetna Mts., AK — 2003
HUNTER: Stanley J. Schmidt
LISTING ON PAGE: 547

TOP LEFT: typical Sitka blacktail deer

SCORE: 111 1/8

LOCATION: Exchange Cove, AK
   – 2004

HUNTER: Wade J. Washke

LISTING ON PAGE: 440

TOP RIGHT: grizzly bear

SCORE: 24 7/16

LOCATION: Ogilvie Mts., YT – 2005

HUNTER: Gordon D. Crawford

LISTING ON PAGE: 398

BOTTOM: mountain caribou

SCORE: 360 6/8

LOCATION: Mackenzie Mts., NT
   – 2006

HUNTER: Carla Pierson

LISTING ON PAGE: 507

TOP LEFT: Dall's sheep

SCORE: 165

LOCATION: Chugach Mts., AK – 2005

HUNTER: L. Victor Clark

LISTING ON PAGE: 546

TOP RIGHT: typical whitetail deer

SCORE: 170 6/8

LOCATION: Fulton Co., IL – 2003

HUNTER: Michael C. Vaka

LISTING ON PAGE: 456

BOTTOM: tule elk

SCORE: 314 1/8

LOCATION: Colusa Co., CA – 2006

HUNTER: Mathew J. Garcia

LISTING ON PAGE: 416

ABOVE: mountain caribou

SCORE: 396 3/8

LOCATION: Little Rancheria River, BC — 2006

HUNTER: Kent D. Petovello

LISTING ON PAGE: 506

TOP LEFT: Canada moose
SCORE: 198 4/8
LOCATION: Telegraph Creek, BC
– 2004
HUNTER: John C. Marsh
LISTING ON PAGE: 497

TOP RIGHT: non-typical mule deer
SCORE: 225 7/8
LOCATION: San Juan Co., UT
– 2004
HUNTER: Lon J. Bess
LISTING ON PAGE: 431

BOTTOM: Alaska brown bear
SCORE: 27 3/16
LOCATION: Wernicke River, AK
– 2004
HUNTER: Ray Aderholt
LISTING ON PAGE: 401

ABOVE: pronghorn
SCORE: 82
LOCATION: Great Sand Hills, SK — 2006
HUNTER: Kelsey M. Seidle
LISTING ON PAGE: 524

ABOVE: Alaska brown bear

SCORE: 26 12/16

LOCATION: Black River, AK— 2005

HUNTER: Jim C. Grisham

LISTING ON PAGE: 401

BOONE AND CROCKETT CLUB'S

TOP LEFT: typical whitetail deer	**TOP RIGHT:** Rocky Mountain goat	**BOTTOM:** Roosevelt's elk
SCORE: 173 3/8	**SCORE:** 51	**SCORE:** 314 3/8
LOCATION: Waupaca Co., WI – 2004	**LOCATION:** Falls River, BC – 2004	**LOCATION:** Coos Co., OR – 2005
HUNTER: Peter L. Radies	**HUNTER:** Joseph R. Russo	**HUNTER:** Kirk E. Winward
LISTING ON PAGE: 451	**LISTING ON PAGE:** 532	**LISTING ON PAGE:** 414

TOP LEFT: typical American elk

SCORE: 380

LOCATION: Lincoln Co., NV – 2005

HUNTER: Kurt W. Jensen

LISTING ON PAGE: 408

TOP RIGHT: desert sheep

SCORE: 173 5/8

LOCATION: Maricopa Co., AZ – 2005

HUNTER: Michael A. Ronning

LISTING ON PAGE: 544

BOTTOM: bison

SCORE: 116 4/8

LOCATION: Custer Co., SD – 2004

HUNTER: Dan S. Muchow

LISTING ON PAGE: 531

BOONE AND CROCKETT CLUB'S

ABOVE: non-typical whitetail deer
SCORE: 222 2/8
LOCATION: Ramsey Co., MN — 2006
HUNTER: Debra J. Luzinski
LISTING ON PAGE: 475

ABOVE: musk ox
SCORE: 106 2/8
LOCATION: Ellice River, NU— 2004
HUNTER: Ronald J. Bartels
LISTING ON PAGE: 537

TOP LEFT: cougar
SCORE: 14 11/16
LOCATION: Rio Blanco Co., CO
  – 2003
HUNTER: Matt E. Vaughn
LISTING ON PAGE: 404

TOP RIGHT: pronghorn
SCORE: 83
LOCATION: Moffat Co., CO – 2005
HUNTER: John C. Vanko
LISTING ON PAGE: 522

BOTTOM: typical Coues' whitetail
SCORE: 103 4/8
LOCATION: Sonora, MX – 2005
HUNTER: Eric D. Stanosheck
LISTING ON PAGE: 493

ABOVE: non-typical mule deer
SCORE: 237 3/8
LOCATION: Yuma Co., CO — 2003
HUNTER: Kerry S. Smith
LISTING ON PAGE: 430

TOP LEFT: Alaska brown bear
SCORE: 27 11/16
LOCATION: Mallard Duck Bay, AK
 – 2006
HUNTER: Mark J. Yost
LISTING ON PAGE: 401

TOP RIGHT: non-typical whitetail
 deer
SCORE: 191 6/8
LOCATION: Hidalgo Co., TX – 2005
HUNTER: Cullen R. Looney
LISTING ON PAGE: 487

BOTTOM: Alaska-Yukon moose
SCORE: 218 6/8
LOCATION: King Salmon River, AK
 – 2002
HUNTER: Glenn R. Koch
LISTING ON PAGE: 501

TOP LEFT: typical Sitka blacktail deer
SCORE: 100 1/8
LOCATION: Deadman Bay, AK – 2005
HUNTER: Larry E. Sides, Jr.
LISTING ON PAGE: 440

TOP RIGHT: pronghorn
SCORE: 82 4/8
LOCATION: Carbon Co., WY – 2005
HUNTER: Jared J. Mason
LISTING ON PAGE: 523

BOTTOM: typical whitetail deer
SCORE: 173 7/8
LOCATION: Delaware Co., OH – 2003
HUNTER: Jeff A. Daily
LISTING ON PAGE: 451

ABOVE: desert sheep

SCORE: 174 5/8

LOCATION: Baja Calif., MX — 2004

HUNTER: Derek A. Burdeny

LISTING ON PAGE: 544

ABOVE: typical American elk
SCORE: 387 3/8
LOCATION: Mohave Co., AZ — 2004
HUNTER: Dorothy J. Harber
LISTING ON PAGE: 406

TOP: desert sheep

SCORE: 168

LOCATION: San Bernardino Co.,
   CA – 2003

HUNTER: James C. Hankla

LISTING ON PAGE: 545

BOTTOM: barren ground caribou

SCORE: 388

LOCATION: Bonnet Plume River,
   YT – 2003

HUNTER: Larry D. Hancock

LISTING ON PAGE: 510

RIGHT: typical Coues' whitetail

SCORE: 124 6/8*

LOCATION: Cochise Co., AZ – 2004

HUNTER: Daniel J. Filleman

LISTING ON PAGE: 493

TOP LEFT: black bear

SCORE: 20

LOCATION: Peel Inlet, BC – 2002

HUNTER: Greg T. Nelson

LISTING ON PAGE: 397

TOP RIGHT: non-typical whitetail deer

SCORE: 207 2/8

LOCATION: Moultrie Co., IL – 2004

HUNTER: Don R. Higgins

LISTING ON PAGE: 479

BOTTOM: pronghorn

SCORE: 82

LOCATION: Catron Co., NM – 2005

HUNTER: Harry R. Martz, Jr.

LISTING ON PAGE: 524

ABOVE: Rocky Mountain goat

SCORE: 47

LOCATION: Lincoln Co., MT — 2005

HUNTER: Mick T. Waletzko

LISTING ON PAGE: 535

ABOVE: non-typical whitetail deer

SCORE: 196 5/8

LOCATION: Lincoln Co., OK — 2005

HUNTER: Waylon L. Johnson

LISTING ON PAGE: 484

TOP LEFT: typical American elk
SCORE: 402 5/8
LOCATION: Athabasca River, AB
  – 2004
HUNTER: William J. Huppertz
LISTING ON PAGE: 406

TOP RIGHT: typical Columbia
  blacktail deer
SCORE: 141 4/8
LOCATION: Mendocino Co., CA
  – 2003
HUNTER: Brett C. Gomes
LISTING ON PAGE: 435

BOTTOM: desert sheep
SCORE: 168
LOCATION: Nye Co., NV – 2004
HUNTER: John V. Zenz
LISTING ON PAGE: 545

ABOVE: Central Canada barren ground caribou

SCORE: 364 2/8

LOCATION: Nejanilini Lake, MB — 2004

HUNTER: Robert Andjelic

LISTING ON PAGE: 512

TOP: typical mule deer

SCORE: 184

LOCATION: Eagle Co., CO – 2005

HUNTER: William J. McEwen

LISTING ON PAGE: 425

BOTTOM: pronghorn

SCORE: 80 4/8

LOCATION: Cibola Co., NM – 2004

HUNTER: Robert M. Aikin

LISTING ON PAGE: 527

RIGHT: black bear

SCORE: 20 12/16

LOCATION: Skowl Arm, AK – 2003

HUNTER: George A. Pickel

LISTING ON PAGE: 391

ABOVE: typical mule deer
SCORE: 199 5/8
LOCATION: Mesa Co., CO — 2005
HUNTER: Timothy R. Viele
LISTING ON PAGE: 418

BOONE AND CROCKETT CLUB'S

TOP LEFT: Canada moose
SCORE: 191 6/8
LOCATION: Williston Lake, BC
  – 2005
HUNTER: Kathy S. Haldorson
LISTING ON PAGE: 498

TOP RIGHT: non-typical whitetail
  deer
SCORE: 207 7/8
LOCATION: Last Mountain Lake,
  SK – 2005
HUNTER: Dana Morrison
LISTING ON PAGE: 478

BOTTOM: Rocky Mountain goat
SCORE: 48 2/8
LOCATION: Tracy Arm, AK – 2005
HUNTER: Bruce S. Ivey
LISTING ON PAGE: 534

ABOVE: pronghorn

SCORE: 80 4/8

LOCATION: Natrona Co., WY — 2004

HUNTER: Gary Nehring

LISTING ON PAGE: 527

TOP LEFT: bighorn sheep

SCORE: 182 2/8

LOCATION: Cadomin, AB – 2005

HUNTER: Jill P. Frederick

LISTING ON PAGE: 540

TOP RIGHT: typical whitetail deer

SCORE: 161

LOCATION: Douglas Co., WI – 2003

HUNTER: Jeffrey D. Waters

LISTING ON PAGE: 470

BOTTOM: bison

SCORE: 120 2/8

LOCATION: Custer Co., SD – 2003

HUNTER: Scott R. Gold

LISTING ON PAGE: 530

TOP LEFT: Central Canada barren ground caribou
SCORE: 363 3/8
LOCATION: Bekere Lake, NT – 2003
HUNTER: Richard W. Gilbert
LISTING ON PAGE: 512

TOP RIGHT: Stone's sheep
SCORE: 168 1/8
LOCATION: Lapie Lake, BC – 2004
HUNTER: Patrick L. Kirsch
LISTING ON PAGE: 548

BOTTOM: cougar
SCORE: 14 13/16
LOCATION: Morgan Co., UT – 2005
HUNTER: Glen O. Hallows
LISTING ON PAGE: 403

ABOVE: typical whitetail deer

SCORE: 170 2/8

LOCATION: Bow River, AB — 2004

HUNTER: Gene Parent

LISTING ON PAGE: 457

ACKNOWLEDGEMENTS
Boone and Crockett Club's
26th Big Game Awards, 2004-2006

Data compiled and book assembled with the able assistance of:

Eldon L. "Buck" Buckner – Chairman, Boone and Crockett Club's Records Committee

Mark B. Steffen – Chairman, Boone and Crockett Club's Publications Committee

Jack Reneau – Director of Big Game Records, Boone and Crockett Club

Ryan Hatfield – Assistant Director of Big Game Records, Boone and Crockett Club

Sandra Poston – Office Manager, Boone and Crockett Club

Julie T. Houk – Director of Publications, Boone and Crockett Club

Keith Balfourd – Director of Marketing, Boone and Crockett Club

Amy Hutchison – Associates Program Manager, Boone and Crockett Club

Jodi Bishop – Development Program Manager, Boone and Crockett Club

Dariusz Janczewski – Assistant Graphic Designer, Boone and Crockett Club

Wendy Nickelson – File Clerk, Boone and Crockett Club

Ina Crist – Receptionist, Boone and Crockett Club

Copy Editing by:

Jack Reneau – Director of Big Game Records, Boone and Crockett Club

Ryan Hatfield – Assistant Director of Big Game Records, Boone and Crockett Club

Mark B. Steffen – Publications Committee Chairman, Boone and Crockett Club

Todd Woodard – Houston, Texas

Mule deer painting on dust jacket by:

Ken Carlson – Kerrville, Texas

Special Trophy Handling:

Ken Witt – B&C Official Measurer – Arlington, Texas

Fred J. King – B&C Professional Member and Official Measurer – Gallatin Gateway, Montana

Dallas Safari Club – Dallas, Texas

Craig A. Cook – B&C Regular Member and Official Measurer – Anchorage, Alaska

Howard P. Monsour – B&C Regular Member and Official Measurer – Bluff Dale, Texas

Danny Sebastian – Cabela's – Fort Worth, TX

Mark Dowse – Cabela's – Sidney, Nebraska

Jeff Montgomery – Cabela's – Sidney, Nebraska

Travis Thomsen – Cabela's – Sidney, Nebraska

Pat Hudak – Cabela's – Sidney, Nebraska

Printed and bound by:

Sheridan Books – Chelsea, Michigan

Limited Editions binding by:

Roswell Book Binding – Phoenix, Arizona